# RACE and ETHNIC RELATIONS in the TWENTY-FIRST CENTURY

## History, Theory, Institutions, and Policy

Edited by
Rashawn Ray

*University of Maryland, College Park*

cognella | ACADEMIC PUBLISHING

Bassim Hamadeh, CEO and Publisher
Kassie Graves, Director of Acquisitions
Jamie Giganti, Senior Managing Editor
Jess Estrella, Senior Graphic Designer
Amy Stone, Field Acquisitions Editor
Kaela Martin, Project Editor
Natalie Lakosil, Licensing Manager
Rachel Singer, Associate Editor

 cognella | ACADEMIC PUBLISHING

# CONTENTS

◻◼◼

# PART 2  THEORETICAL AND CONCEPTUAL PERSPECTIVES

# RACE AND ETHNIC RELATIONS IN THE TWENTY-FIRST CENTURY

*By Rashawn Ray*

R ace continues to be at the center of social life to determine opportunities and shape social interactions. Yet, many Whites and racial/ethnic minorities alike perceive race to be less significant now than in the past. Many believe we are moving into a color-blind society where class matters more (Wilson 1978).[*] Now some may argue that President Obama's recent election is an indication of racial progress. Although this is true in some respects, President Obama's symbolic victory for racial change cannot overshadow the fact that the Voting Rights Act of 1965[†] has to be periodically renewed or that a 2007 Supreme Court decision is viewed by some as reversing the Brown v. Board of Education decision that desegregated schools.[‡] These mandates are important considering that U.S. neighborhoods and schools were more segregated in 2005 than in 1965, further highlighting the relegated and marginalized status placed upon racial/ethnic minority groups (Sewell 2010).

We cannot forget what occurred in the 1960s toward the end of the Civil Rights Movement when public opinion polls showed that Whites had significantly become more tolerant of Blacks in work and school contexts (Bobo 2001). By the late 1960s, Whites' racial attitudes about schools, employment, and neighborhoods had shifted back to mirror those before 1960 (Muhammad 2010). This shift in racial attitudes tells us that it is easy for a society to revert back to previous forms of accepted prejudice. Paraphrasing Harry Belafonte's statement, the glass is half full, but it is also half

---

[*] In *The Declining Significance of Race*, Wilson (1978) contends that race is declining in significance as a major social structural factor in society and instead being supplemented by class inequality.

[†] The Voting Rights Act of 1965 aimed to make the Fifteenth Amendment a reality by outlawing discriminatory voting practices that have disenfranchised Blacks since the founding of the United States.

[‡] The Parents Involved in Community Schools v. Seattle School District No. 1, et al. (Also known as the Louisville, Jefferson County, KY case; 2007) Supreme Court decision ruled 5–4 to prohibit allocating spots solely to racially integrate public schools. The Supreme Court also did not recognize racial diversity in schools as a priority.

empty. Moreover, we have come a long way as a society, but we still have a ways to go for true racial equality.

Race determines whom individuals decide to hire (Bertrand and Mullainathan 2004; Pager 2004), rent an apartment or a house to (Sewell 2010), or treat equally in school (Lewis 2010), work, and neighborhood settings. As a social structural factor, race determines individual-level processes that shape meso-level mechanisms and influence institutional conditions on a macro-level. These mechanisms and conditions structure where individuals live and work, who they interact with and marry, or do not marry, (Ray 2010), and how much money they make and wealth they accumulate (Conley 2000; Oliver and Shapiro 1995). With this in mind, scholars and community activists cannot discuss education, the labor market, health, the criminal justice system, voting, or community involvement without understanding why it is important for individuals to be conscious of how race and ethnic relations continue to structure their lives in the 21st century.

## DEFINING RACE AND ETHNICITY

Race can be defined as ethnoracial, historically rooted distinctions or social constructions (Bobo and Fox 2003). Ethnicity, on the other hand, can be classified as the sharing of a common ancestry, history, and/or culture of a group. Race is systematically rooted in the culture of social life to create, establish, maintain, and enhance group differences (Bonilla-Silva 1997; Omi and Winant 1994). Because race is an organizing principle, it facilitates the development of two social systems that formulate hierarchical patterns at the micro-, meso-, and macro-levels which then dictate status, power, and prestige structures (Bonilla-Silva 1997).

"Racism is a set of institutional conditions of group inequality and an ideology of racial domination, in which the latter is characterized by a set of beliefs holding that the subordinate racial group is biologically or culturally inferior to the dominant racial group" (Bobo and Fox 2003: 319). Moreover, racism is a social system that conveys an ideology of inferiority, which is often affiliated with individual- and group-level prejudice and discrimination. Similar to sexism, racism alters social systems and various institutional arrangements whereby the entire institution becomes racialized. For minority groups, racism leads to a divergence in various outcomes such as lower educational attainment (Lewis 2010), lower occupational prestige (Bertrand and Mullainathan 2004), relatively deprived neighborhoods (Sewell 2010), schools (Kozol 1991, 2005), and hospitals, and worse mental and physical health (Cummings and Jackson 2008; Gilbert 2010).

Furthermore, in the definition of racism, we can see how ancestry, history, and culture all uniquely contribute to racial and ethnic classification. Biological inferiority corresponds to ancestry, cultural inferiority corresponds to culture, and ideology of racial domination corresponds to history. Therefore, race and ethnicity are inextricably linked to each other to convey that there is indeed an embedded, taken-for-granted hierarchy among groups. Throughout history, this hierarchy has hoodwinked and bamboozled individuals into thinking that these outcomes are from circumstances rooted in psychological, genetic, biological, and motivational differences between racial/ethnic groups (Drake 1987; Zuberi 2001).

## RACE AND THE INDIVIDUAL V. STRUCTURAL DILEMMA

Individuals normally exhibit individual- or structural-thinking regarding racial disparities. Individual-thinking entails believing that racial/ethnic groups such as Blacks are in their current socioeconomic condition due to genetic inferiority or a lack of motivation. Structural-thinking, on the other hand, takes into account that racial/ethnic groups face discrimination and racism, which inhibits their upward mobility. This distinction generally falls along racial and policy lines. Blacks and Latinos are more likely than Whites to exhibit structural-thinking and believe race-based policies such as affirmative action are fair and just. Conversely, Whites are more likely to exhibit individual-thinking, believe Blacks are responsible for their current socioeconomic position, and oppose race-based policies (Bobo 1988; Duster 1999; Bobo and Klugel 2003; Hunt 2007).

Hunt (2007) investigates whether Blacks, Latinos/Hispanics, and Whites differ in their explanations of the socioeconomic divide between Blacks and Whites.[*] He asks, why are Blacks in their current state? Using data from the 1977–2004 General Social Surveys, Hunt (2007) finds that Whites' preference for the innate inferiority explanation (i.e., genetic argument) has decreased over time. Instead, Whites' racial attitudes are split among three explanations including a purely motivational explanation, a purely educational explanation, and a combination between these two explanations. On the other hand, Blacks' and Hispanics' preference for structural explanations including

the explanation that Blacks' current socioeconomic status stems from discrimination has decreased over time. In turn, Blacks' and Hispanics' racial attitudes about the Black/White socioeconomic divide have become more similar to that of Whites' racial attitudes over time. Nonetheless, Blacks are more likely to endorse a discrimination-based explanation. While only 31 percent of Whites believe Blacks are in their current state due to discrimination (which has also decreased over the years), 61 percent of Blacks still agree with this explanation.

The problem with the individual- versus structural-thinking dichotomy is that these perspectives are inherently opposed to each other. What mediates these two opposing views is a perseverance perspective. Perseverance affords individuals the flexibility to believe that Blacks and other minority groups face discrimination but also can still persevere to be upwardly mobile. Hunt's (2007) findings capture this. Because structural-thinking takes into account that Blacks are discriminated against in social institutions including education and the labor market, it decreases Whites' probability of perceiving Blacks as competitive threats and as being unmotivated or pathologically deficient. There are, however, potential racial differences regarding the reasoning for the perseverance perspective. Generally, Whites choose either the individual- or structural-thinking perspective. Some Blacks, on the other hand, may choose both perspectives. Although most Blacks incorporate discrimination into their beliefs about the Black/White socioeconomic divide, the discrimination explanation does not preclude them from thinking that Blacks should persevere. And Blacks have a long history of persevering. Despite a continuance of institutional and individual acts of discrimination (Drake 1987; Zuberi 2001), Blacks have overcome (Davis 1981; hooks 1981; Taylor et al. 1990; Billingsley 1992). In fact, in the 1960s, "We shall overcome" became the theme of the

---

[*] It should be noted that the terms Black/African-American, Latino/Hispanic, and White/Caucasian are capitalized and used interchangeably throughout this anthology. Similar to Anderson and Collins ([1992] 2001), this decision is based upon the fact that these terms have political and scientific connotations that deserve the proper names. Although some may state that the terms "Black" and "White" do not need to be capitalized, I contend that these terms are historically linked on census and public documents that did once render a proper connotation. Additionally, just like Latinos, Asians, and Blacks/African-Americans, Whites are a racial group and should come to be recognized as such, instead of the taken-for-granted absence of racialization.

Civil Rights Movement (Morris 1994). This is the essence of the perseverance perspective.

In survey research, this interactive relationship between structural and individual/motivational explanations often surfaces to imply that Blacks have shifted from a structural explanation to an individual explanation. Actually, Blacks seem to exhibit a perseverance perspective that is unable to accurately be captured in the wording of many survey questions in large-scale data sets. Consequently, this current phrasing does not allow for the perseverance perspective to be adequately captured. Therefore, the perseverance perspective must be discussed as an alternative to the individual- versus structural-thinking dichotomy. This allows for us to move past simple group affiliations and the traditional Black/White dichotomy of racial politics. This important perspective is where this anthology is situated.

## GOAL OF THE ANTHOLOGY

*Race and Ethnic Relations in the Twenty-First Century* examines the major theoretical and empirical approaches regarding race/ethnicity. Its goal is to continue to place race and ethnic relations in a contemporary, intersectional, and cross-comparative context and progress the discipline to include groups outside the Black/White dichotomy. This text examines the main assumptions that construct individuals' perceptions of what race is and how it matters. Using various sociological theories, social psychological theories, and subcultural approaches, this book gives students a sociohistorical, theoretical, and institutional frame with which to view race and ethnic relations in the 21st century. It highlights how race/ethnicity continues to act as a boundary that forms meaningful social groupings and divisions. Readers will see how the social construction of race, based on the falsifying of the science of race, is used to justify the exploitation of race for economic gains. By utilizing this anthology, students will be armed with the theoretical, sociohistorical, and empirical tools to progress in their understandings of how race/ethnicity shapes their social interactions, life chances, and the social institutions in which they are embedded.

## ORGANIZATION OF THE ANTHOLOGY

*Race and Ethnic Relations in the Twenty-First Century* is organized in four parts—1) The Sociohistorical Context of Race; 2) Theoretical and Conceptual Perspectives; 3) The Cumulative Pipeline of Persistent Institutional Racism; and 4) Confronting the Pipeline: Social Policy Issues. It is composed of a total of 30 articles, chapters, and original essays. This anthology also includes introductory section essays and a list of supplementary readings and resources for teaching race in the classroom and general usage.[*]

The bookends of the anthology include essays by James Jones and Lawrence Bobo from President Bill Clinton's *One America in the 21st Century: The President's Initiative on Race*. Jones' essay discusses why the United States has not progressed as much as expected since Du Bois' prolific statement in 1903. Du Bois stated, "The problem of the 20th century is the problem of the color-line" (Du Bois 1903). Jones contends that America must engage in a serious, in-depth conversation on race. Other scholars ditto Jones' assertions and argue that Du Bois' statement is just as prolific now as it was then (Feagin 1991; Bonilla-Silva 1997; Zuberi 2001). Despite the significance of Du Bois' statement, and the American Sociological Association's acknowledgement of Du Bois' accomplishments (mostly by naming the

---

[*] Most of the works cited in the introductory essays are also in this anthology. The ones that are not in the anthology will be listed in the supplemental readings and resource list at the end of each introductory essay. The works from this essay are listed in Part I.

Career of Distinguished Scholarship Award the Du Bois Award), a majority of undergraduate and graduate social theory courses do not include Du Bois' theories or a lecture on race. Similarly, most introduction to sociology courses scantly address race. Considering that few individuals have candid conversations about race across racial/ethnic lines, Jones' essay on "the embedded nature of race" is a great way to start a discussion about race in the 21st century. Likewise, Bobo's essay is a great way to conclude this anthology. Bobo discusses the importance of moving from theoretical principles about race to practical solutions for racial problems. Considering students' pessimism about the future outlook of race and ethnic relations, it is important to highlight some positive outcomes from the past 50 years and optimism about the future.

Part I—The Sociohistorical Context of Race—situates race within a sociohistorical context to discuss the origins and central processes of race that shape social outcomes. Since race is real in its consequences (i.e., outcomes), individuals assume that race must be real in its circumstances (i.e., origins) (Zuberi 2001). Therefore, it is important to convey that race is indeed a social construct that has real consequences for individuals (Feagin 2001). Furthermore, it must be made clear that race is an organizing principle that is ingrained in the institutions of society (Bonilla-Silva 1997). Using readings by Tukufu Zuberi, Joe Feagin, and St. Clair Drake, this section highlights how the social construction of race, based on the falsifying of the science of race, is used to justify the exploitation of race for economic gains.

Part II—Theoretical and Conceptual Perspectives—draws attention to the major theories and concepts on race and ethnic relations. This section showcases readings on racial formation, individual and structural racism, prejudice and discrimination,

whiteness, race-gender-sexuality, colorism and lookism, assimilation, immigration, group threat theory, contact theory, ethnic conflict, citizenship, nationalism, and human rights.

Part III—The Cumulative Pipeline of Persistent Institutional Racism—draws attention to how race structures institutional forms of racism. Unlike some edited books on race that focus on a specific racial/ethnic group in different chapters, this section illuminates how structural racism functions similarly through mechanisms and processes in institutions including neighborhoods and communities, education, the labor market, the criminal justice system, and health care to determine outcomes (e.g., constraints and privileges) of all racial/ethnic groups.

Part IV—Confronting the Pipeline: Social Policy Issues—addresses ways to ameliorate race-based inequalities. This section highlights the formation of affirmative action and welfare. This section also focuses on micro-level forms of social change including mentorship and social activism.

In sum, it is my hope that this book will be useful for scholars and students generally interested in a race anthology that provides a much needed social structural perspective to issues of race. It highlights structural mechanisms and institutional conditions that create and maintain inequalities across groups. These mechanisms and conditions not only apply to groups in the U.S. but also extend to the treatment and experiences of racial/ethnic groups in other parts of the world including Somalis in Great Britain (Pettigrew 1998), Asians in New Zealand, Turks in Germany (Koopmans and Statham 1999), and North Africans in Israel (Schwartz et al., 1991). It should be noted that I do not purport to provide an exhaustive review of the literature. Rather, I have selected studies that draw our attention to a sociohistorical, theoretical, institutional, and policy-focused agenda that conceptualizes race as a social structural factor that functions on a micro-, meso-, and macro-level.

## ACKNOWLEDGMENTS

I want to thank the University Readers staff including Bassim Hamadeh, Becky Smith, Al Grisanti, Jessica Knott, Jennifer Bowen, Monica Hui, and Wes Ye. I would also like to thank the contributors who supplied original essays for this anthology including Keon Gilbert, Chikarlo R. Leak, R. L'Heureux Lewis, Alta Mauro, Shiri Noy, Evangeleen Pattison, Victor Ray, Jason Robertson, and Abigail A. Sewell. Thank you for taking time out of your busy schedules. Additionally, I want to recognize Mike Wenger and Johanna Marcelino. It would have been nice to continue our collaboration. Next, I want to acknowledge my mentors and scholars who have supplied me with a broad base of racial knowledge and advice over the years. These scholars include Wanda Rushing, Quincy Stewart, Donna Eder, Pam Jackson, Brian Powell, Khalil Muhammad, Eduardo Bonilla-Silva, Tukufu Zuberi, Aldon Morris, Prudence Carter, and Patricia Hill Collins. I am fortunate to be in your lineage of academic growth and development. Finally, I want to give thanks to my family for their continued support and faith in my efforts toward social change. My wife Cynthia has always displayed unwavering encouragement for my efforts including reading over sections of my work and understanding late night writing binges. As always, I will forever appreciate and love Joslyn, Gladys, and Rosalind. Thank you all.

---

## DEDICATION

This book is dedicated to the students and individuals I encounter who believe that I have something worth sharing with the world.

# The Embedded Nature of 'Race' Requires a Focused Effort to Remove the Obstacles to a Unified America

*By Dr. James M. Jones*

Race has been one of the most enduring divisive social and psychological phenomena since the Founding of this country. As the twentieth century enjoys its last moments, the issue of race continues to reverberate in every facet of our society. W. E. B. Du Bois challenged this century in 1903 when he claimed the problem of the twentieth century was the problem of the color line. From slavery to freedom we have come a long way. But we are not all the way to freedom yet. It is not any one person or faction's fault. Rather, it is the result of the deep and pervasive penetration of race into our collective psyche and social institutions. We struggle for liberty, for equality and have made great strides. But our Founding Fathers also believed that fraternity was a core value for this nation. We have insisted without compromise on liberty for individuals. We have aspired to equality without regard to skin color, and tried to make our laws and our customs reflect that value. But race keeps us from success. We have not worked as hard, or as well toward fraternity, which in the aggregate is community. We have been stymied by our racial differences, because we have not figured out how to get on the same page when everyone has either no book, or a different one. I believe President Clinton's Initiative on Race is a clear acknowledgement that true community cannot be achieved in America unless we bridge the racial divides.

There are two perspectives that have voice in contemporary society. One argues that focusing on race is exactly the wrong approach to national unity. By granting race any significance, this view suggests, we give credence to its divisive and destructive influence. Only by ignoring it, or at least not consciously acknowledging it in any meaningful way, the progress in race relations we have made this century will continue. Focusing on race, this view asserts, hinders this progress. William Bennett once told a group of Black children in Atlanta on the anniversary of the birth of Martin Luther King, that "People of good will disagree about the means [but] I don't think anybody disagrees about the ends … I think the best means to achieve the ends of a colorblind society is to proceed as if we were a colorblind society … I think the best way to treat people is as if their race did not make any difference." (Sawyer, 1986, p. A8)

A second view argues that we must focus on race because not to do so, fails to meet the need for redress created by historic racial biases. The need to focus on race was clearly expressed by the late Supreme Court Justice William Brennan who made the following observation in his opinion on the Bakke case in 1978:

"A race-conscious remedy ... [is necessary to achieve] a fully-integrated society, one in which color of a person's skin will not determine the opportunities available to him or her ... If ways are not found to remedy [under-representation of minorities in the professions]. The country can never achieve ... a society that is not race-conscious ... In order to get beyond racism; we must first take account of race. There is no other way ... In order to treat persons equally, we must treat them differently."

—Justice William Brennan

We are faced with the question of whether the path to a fairer and more unified America can best be achieved by ignoring race, or by staring it in the face and defeating its most sinister and insidious influences on our society and our psyches. It is my belief and there is ample evidence to support it, that race continues to matter in ways that may be more subtle than those who would have us ignore race, understand.

I will share with you today, some of the ways race matters and some of the evidence that illustrates this conclusion. I also acknowledge that by focusing on race, we run the risk of exaggerating the differences we attach to it and perhaps misleading our selves about the degree to which it affects us everyday. But I am persuaded by two of my students who are both white, both young and have experienced race in their everyday life. One student

grew up in a small rural town in Pennsylvania and described how life in his small high school provided daily hassles for the one black student in his school. Worse, it brought daily insults and crude and lewd racial jokes that created an image of black people that perpetuated a stereotype of their hostility, stupidity and laziness. Before he had even seen a Black person, he reported he had the idea that a black guy would stick him up and rob him. He even thought that Black people on TV were just acting, and when they went home, they acted just like the stereotype.

A second student, from Long Island, New York, reported that she had many black and white friends. However, she found herself continually anxious that she would betray some hidden prejudice toward them. She didn't feel any such thing, but was not sure that she was without prejudice. She often felt anxious that some of her white friends, who were perhaps less conscious of race than she, would be more inclined to make that sort of comment. For both of these honest and well-meaning students, race is an issue.

It is a daunting task you face, engaging the nation in a focus on race. In our nation's history, race has always been used as a marker of difference in valued attributes and capacities. Race provides a convenient and simple means to establish who is on top, in the middle and on the bottom, who is deserving and who is not. And having made that distinction, we may then rationalize and explain why citizens of this country are segregated in certain strata, behave in ways that we find unwholesome, and need to be treated differently. Race is a word that has divided and denigrated and now by confronting it, talking about it, we hope to heal, to unite. I applaud the President and I applaud you the Board for taking this on. Community is not something you can create by executive order. It is not something that will happen because we want it to. It can only happen when people find they have common ground and are better off because they cooperate than if they don't. To make that happen across the racial divides that exist in this country, we have to take it on, shine a light on it, bridge the gaps and figure out how to make our institutions operate as supportive, not antagonistic, accomplices to the community we seek.

There are four points I wish to make. I will state them and then develop them in more detail.

- First, race is not so much something that resides in the genes of a group of people, but in the social attitudes and beliefs of society. Race is a social not a biological construct.
- Second, the significance of race rests in its cumulative influence on the psyches and social arrangements of this nation. We cannot isolate and segregate its influence in a given era, a given belief or in a given person.
- Third, race is a term whose use and impact is far more consequential for those who have been the targets of hostile actions than those who have perpetrated them, or been the incidental beneficiaries of their consequences.
- Fourth, social psychological research clearly shows that ignoring race in a race-neutral or 'colorblind' way may do a disservice to the targets of racial bias as well as to those who presume themselves to be free of racial bias.

Let me begin with point number one.

First, race is not so much something that resides in the genes of a group of people, but in the social attitudes and beliefs of society. Race is a social not a biological construct

One of the reasons why race is so divisive is that it is associated with biological differences. Biological differences are thought to be hard wired, immutable and to describe some essential quality of people who are classified by race. The Swedish taxonomist Linneaus described the psychological as well as the physical characteristics on which he classified American Indians, Europeans, Asians and Africans in psychological terms. By his account, Indians are tenacious and ruled by custom. Europeans are haughty and ruled by opinion. Asians are inflexible and ruled by rites. Africans are indulgent and ruled by caprice. These defining characteristics or attributes are not only assumed to be true of members of these racial groups, but take on differential value within the cultural system. Race gives value and takes it away. It inflames a situation because it hearkens to the days when it was widely believed that racial differences were biological, and accounted for superior and inferior human capabilities.

In America, Indians were considered savage, wanting of civilization. Their salvation, in this view, was education, which in the aim of civilizing them, taught them to reject their cultural heritage. Who Indians were as a race was defined by the United States government, and inculcated in Indians schools. In contemporary times, basketball announcer Billy Packer referred to Allen Iverson as a "tough monkey" when he drove the lane lifted his wiry 6' frame up to slam-dunk over much taller players. Almost immediately, calls came in to the Capital Center and to CBS calling for Packer's removal. Why? Because a monkey invokes biology, ape-like, primitive. We Americans are still hypersensitive to any reference to biology when it comes to race. The fact is that there is no biological basis to race that is meaningful. An American Association for the Advancement of Science (AAAS) panel, including Nobel Laureate scientists noted that: ... from a biological viewpoint the term race has become so encumbered with superfluous and contradictory meanings, erroneous concepts, and emotional reactions that it has almost completely lost its utility ... It is hoped that the understanding of the biological nature of populations [their preferred term] will eventually lead to the abandonment of the term race."

An important question for us is why does race persist given its terribly divisive and denigrating nature, and its scientific inutility? It persists because it has a meaningful and prominent place in our cultural history. Race helps us to make sense of who we are, where we have come from, and even where we are going. But the meaning of race is constructed from what we do, say, and think as a society. Just as we have created race by our actions and deeds, we can un-create it. There is a strong push to replace the term 'race' with the term 'ethnicity'. The horror of race is its biological implication, and the association with biological heritability and immutability. The fixed nature of race is countered by the mutable notion of ethnicity, a changing cultural identity, that is more fluid and under greater personal control. There is merit in the notion of ethnicity, but it will take more than a semantic end run to eliminate race from our minds and our hearts. Perhaps the conversation on race could have as its main agenda, the negotiation of the demise of race as a meaningful and acceptable way to think about Americans.

Second, the significance of race rests in its cumulative influence on the psyches and social arrangements of this nation. We cannot isolate and segregate its influence in a given era, a given belief or in a given person.

Our history as a nation is to a significant degree a racialist history. By that I mean that race has been a belief, a symbol that stands for a value-based division of people in America. As early as the framing of our Constitution, the debate over the humanity of slaves of African descent surfaced in the most basic judgment of political representation. Southerners wanted to count their slaves in the enumeration of their state populations because their number would bring them a larger political representation in Congress. The Northerners wanted slaves counted as property so that slaveholders would pay their fair share of property taxes. In federalist paper #54, Alexander Hamilton considered that a slave could not be 100% person AND 100% property. In one of many political compromises that served the political ends of White businessmen and politicians, slaves were divested of two-fifths their humanity. This degradation of persons of African descent endures as the beginning of the systematic dehumanization of that group of people who helped found this nation.

That inhumanity, though, is not just an unfortunate handling of a bad situation, slavery, but was tied to beliefs and attitudes that we have not fully rid ourselves of today. Thomas Jefferson wrote a doctrine of the inalienable rights of man and thus championed perhaps the most singular expression of the American ethos, individual liberties and freedoms. Yet in his heart, this is what he believed:

> In general [Blacks] existence appears to participate more of sensation than reflection … [I]n memory they are equal to whites, in reason much inferior … [and] in imagination they are dull, tasteless, and anomalous … I advance it therefore … that the blacks, whether originally a different race, or made distinct by time and circumstances, are inferior to whites … Will not a lover of natural history, then, … excuse an effort to keep those in the department of Man as distinct as nature has formed them?
>
> (Thomas Jefferson, *Notes on Virginia* 1787)

The belief about blacks, and the proposition that racial segregation is a valid indeed natural consequence of natural law, is as much a part of our cultural history as is the belief in the inalienable rights of man. Addressing the contemporary influences of this historical aspect of our cultural history is part of our education.

It is not a far distance from this viewpoint and belief, to the sale of blacks on Wall Street. What percentage of dehumanization is too much? It seems perhaps not a surprise, given this history, that in 1919 in East St. Louis, a man can be burned to death, while his executioners mug for the camera. And the excitement shown by these men is reversed by the ugliness and disdain, and hatred shown by these young people who were so offended by Ms. Elizabeth Eckford's determination to go to the public high school in Little Rock. And in recent days, we learn of the apology of the young women shown here hurling invective and venom at Ms. Eckford tells another important story; we are substantially influenced by the norms, beliefs and expectations to which we are socialized. Not to excuse her behavior, but race is bigger than individuals who act in the name of race. You have seen this photograph often in recent days as President Clinton and the Little Rock nine and the citizens of Little Rock recalled that time. For some it was celebration of progress. For others, it was a diversion from the real and continuing racial problems that still beset Little Rock.

American Indians were thought to be savage and uncivilized. Commissioner of Indian Affairs, Henry Price expressed this view in 1881: "… savage and civilized life cannot live and prosper on the same ground. One of the two must die … To civilize them [America Indians], which was once only a benevolent fancy, has now become an absolute necessity, if we mean to save them."

Such as there was interest in One America, it was in terms that denigrated the value and culture of people of color. One of the biggest concerns among American Indians today is rethinking what education means. Repeatedly and with a sense of cultural survival, Indian Education begins with the premise that American education for Indian people is genocidal. The following photograph shows Indian students at the Carlisle Indian School. The next slide shows a Q&A from an exam of an Indian student at Hampton Institute in Virginia in 1885 (See Table 1).

**Table 1**

| Questions: | Student Answers: |
| --- | --- |
| 9. To what race do we all belong? | The human race |
| 10. How many classes belong to this race? | There are five large classes belonging to the human race. |
| 11. Which are the first? | The white people are the strongest. |
| 12. Which is the next? | The Mongolians or yellows. |
| 13. The next? | The Ethiopian or blacks. |
| 14. Next? | The Americans or reds. |
| 15. Tell me something of the white people. | The Caucasian is away ahead of all the other races—he thought more than any other race, He thought that somebody, must have made the earth, and if the white people did not find that out, nobody would never know it—it is God who made the world. (Adams, 1988, p. 1756–76.) |

We could claim that we would no longer find such a thing in a classroom. But when do such effects dissipate in the collective minds of Americans? Certainly this civilization-savage distinction was not extinguished by the Western movies of the 1950's and 1960's! Although contemporary disagreements about the nicknames of sports teams have led to many changes, we are long way from an understanding of Indian life that supports a unified America.

The following slide offers another image that persists in our collective psyches. President Franklin Roosevelt signed Executive Order #9066 on February 19, 1942, that gave authority to the Secretary of Defense to exclude all persons, citizens and aliens, from designated areas to provide security against sabotage or espionage. American citizens are rounded up and taken by train to Santa Anita racetrack to be deployed to Internment Camps. And perhaps as symbolic an image of racism as there is, the swastika is hateful and represents the lowest of human ugliness. These are images of America. These are images that must be confronted and incorporated into a unified America. We cannot ignore them, we cannot deny them meaning in contemporary life because they happened a long time ago.

There is a cumulative consequence of race in this society that challenges our fundamental notions of fairness as well as personal responsibility. We are influenced by our past in ways that are not always obvious. It is too much to claim that four centuries of bigotry and bias, institutional deprivation and cultural oppression were eliminated by an act of Congress. We have been on a constant course of improving opportunities, access and possibility across centuries, but we have not by any means undone the legacy of racism.

At the University of Delaware I teach a course on Psychological Perspectives on Black Americans. Students are required to make a class presentation in groups of two. A couple of years ago, a white student asked the only black student in the class to be her partner. The black woman declined, stating that she did not accept the white student's motivation for asking her. The black woman perceived the white student as curious about her. She did not want to enter into a partnership that made her a guinea pig. The white woman was crushed. She might have been offended, but was instead devastated that her sense of fairness, objectivity, and decency was not only challenged but rejected. She burst into tears. This had never happened before and the only thing I could think to tell them was "this is not about the two of you." This divergence of understanding and meaning could be traced to the troubled history of race in America. In a sense, they were playing out the mistrust targets have of racist oppressors. Moreover, they illustrated that simply having good intentions is not enough in a society that is so charged with the distortions that our racial history has created. It is my contention that we all live everyday with this cultural history and we should never assume that we can understand each other fully from the facts of our experience. Our national conversation must try to unravel these influences and reach a common ground that acknowledges the divergence of experience, feelings, beliefs that comes with our divergent racial experiences. An apology for slavery does little to promote this understanding.

Third, race is a term whose use and impact is far more consequential for those who have been the targets of hostile or discriminatory actions than those who have perpetrated them, or been incidentally privileged by them.

In our society, the primary effect of race has been to marginalize people who could be easily defined by racial categories. One result of this marginalization is that one's racial heritage is pitted against an American identity. Consider the following interview of Jesse Jackson by Marvin Kalb on *Meet the Press* in 1984. This was Jackson's first run for the presidential nomination of the Democratic Party, and he was making a respectable showing in the polls.

> Kalb: The question [is] are you a Black man who happens to be an American running for the presidency, or are you an American who happens to be a Black man running for the presidency?
>
> Jackson: Well, I'm both an American and a Black at one and the same time. I'm both of these ...
>
> Kalb: What I'm trying to get at is something that addresses a question no-one seems able to grasp and that is, are your priorities deep inside yourself, to the degree that anyone can look inside himself, those of a Black man who happens to be an American or the reverse?
>
> Jackson: Well I was born Black in America, I was not born American in Black! You are asking a funny kind of Catch-22 question. My interests are national interests.

(Excerpted from Meet the Press, February 13, 1984)

There are two perspectives to note here. From Kalb's view, it seems that Jackson could not be both black and American at the same time and in equal measure. One identity had to be primary and one secondary. We have created a conflict situation for many of our citizens of color by which their well-being is split into two halves. America's image of race has dissected people of color. Ignoring race will not make them whole.

From Jackson's point of view, the challenge to be a wholly integrated person whose racial or cultural heritage is not in opposition to, but a contributing element of, his American identity is one of the difficult and subtle psychological consequences of how race has been employed in America. Jackson's response to Kalb speaks to this desire to be whole, to be one with oneself as well as the rest of society.

But there is a flip side to this conflict. The majority of Americans are advantaged in ways that may not reach their consciousness. It did reach the consciousness of one young White man, Joshua Solomon who had an experience that very few people have. He experienced his whiteness for 20 years, then by taking skin altering medications, became Black. After only one week, young Solomon abandoned his experiment. He reported the following lesson from his experience: "I have been White for 20 years and I always assumed a level of dignity and respect. No matter how much money I had in my pocket, I could go into a store and be treated with respect. However, I realized that when I became a Black man, all that went away. I learned how much White privilege I enjoyed just by being White."

While Whites are generally privileged, or at least given the benefit of the doubt, too often, persons of color are simply doubted! Nat Hentoff described the following encounter of two young Latino men, American citizens, returning to Philadelphia from vacation in Jamaica.

When James Garcia and Evaristo Vazquez returned from Jamaica, they went to claim their luggage at Newark Airport, and were surrounded by customs agents, put into separate rooms and strip searched. These searches revealed nothing illegal and neither did a search of their luggage. Agents decided to x-ray James and Evaristo and took them away to St. Francis hospital in handcuffs to be x-rayed. Shackled at the ankles and handcuffed to the beds, the x-rays were taken. Again, nothing illegal was found. Without so much as an apology, they were returned to the airport and released. James Garcia asked the United States agents why they had been singled out. He was asked in return his nationality and age. He replied, "Hispanic and I'm 24 and my friend is 25." The agent replied, "well, there you go."

Race matters in America. Its meaning has consequences often harmful, and usually troublesome. Research by Carmen Arroyo and Edward Zigler showed that the more adolescents shied away from their racial identity, a concept they call "racelessness," the better they did in school, but the greater risk they had for depression and poor mental health. Embracing your racial or ethnic identity often puts you in conflict with acceptance in broader American society, leading to a win-lose proposition. Our conversation on race must convert such win-lose propositions to win-win scenarios.

There is much discussion of standards that must not be compromised by any use of race in the decision making in our schools or on the job. Research by Claude Steele at Stanford has shown that a psychological state of stereotype vulnerability can explain dramatic decreases in test performance of both African Americans and women. Stereotype vulnerability refers to a disruptive apprehension based on the fear that one will either verify or be judged by a negative stereotype about one's racial group.

Steele & Aronson (1995) tested this idea by having White and Black subjects perform a very difficult test comprised of the most difficult items from the Graduate Record Exam. The test was introduced either as "diagnostic" or "non-diagnostic" of their true ability. Steele and Aronson reasoned that only when the test was thought to be diagnostic would it arouse stereotype vulnerability. The next figure shows the result of performance under these two different conditions for Black and White Stanford University undergraduates. As the figure shows, when the test was thought to be non-diagnostic of their ability, Black students performed just as well as Whites. However, when they thought it might reveal their ability in a domain in which their group is stereotypically not expected to do well, they did more poorly than Whites. What is dramatically important about this study, is that by simply changing the context of the tests, racial parity on performance was obtained. Also indicative of the troubling meaning of race in our society, they found that having participants write down their race prior to taking the non-diagnostic test led Black participants to score lower than Whites. The psychological process that leads to these findings is fairly complex, but it rests on the idea that the negative stereotype of your group may cause a level of apprehension that interferes with performance, even when the person himself has had success in the past. This finding underscores the pernicious and subtle effects race may have in our society. What is perhaps the most important thing for you to consider, is that our assumptions that performances are due solely to the ability or capacity of the performer may be very wrong-headed. We adopt standards based on the assumption that performance is an accurate and reliable indication of a person's true ability. But as this research shows, ones ability may be compromised by the insinuation of race. The more we seek to test the ability of our students, and the less we understand about the racial factors beyond ability that affect their performance, the further we will be from a unified America.

Fourth, social psychological research clearly shows that ignoring race in a race-neutral or 'colorblind' way may do a disservice to the targets of racial bias as well as those who presume themselves to be free of racial bias.

The idea that we must ignore race to get beyond it is a popular view these days. But people are treated differently on account of race. Social psychological research demonstrates in study after study, that race influences our most basic human responses. If we do not acknowledge that, if we do not believe that, we are ignoring a very significant influence in our daily lives. This is not about laws, and government, but about the deep-seated beliefs that affect us in ways silent and often unknown. Our racial expectations influence what we see in others and what we feel inside. Moreover, these perceptions and feelings affect others with whom we interact. Race is a ubiquitous presence in our society. There are numerous scientific studies that illustrate various aspects of these racial effects. I will describe briefly four of them.

### 1. The Self-fulfilling Prophesy: Making an Applicant Unqualified

Carl Word, Mark Zanna and Joel Cooper asked Princeton male undergraduates to interview several black and white high school students and select one for their team. These mixed high school college teams were expected to engage in some competitive academic games. The researchers found that Princeton men interviewed the black students differently from the white students. When interviewing black students they sat further away, on more of an angle, spoke less fluently, and terminated the interview sooner. The authors next trained white Princeton men to interview in a manner that reflected the differential racial patterns detected for White and for Black students in the previous experiment, and then had them interview other white Princeton men for a summer job. The interview style followed either the White or Black pattern. Independent judges who knew nothing of the interview style variation rated the applicants. The results showed that the White applicants, who were interviewed as if they were black, were judged to be less qualified. This self-fulfilling prophecy suggests that we communicate our feelings, anxieties or simple dislike to others and in so doing, we affect their behavior. But failing to realize how our behavior has influenced theirs, we conclude confidently that we can draw objective conclusions

about them. In this manner, we actually create the world that we expect! When it comes to race, we perpetually re-create the cultural notions of race in our everyday interaction and encounters.

### 2. The Chameleon Effect: Hostile Reactions to Race

John Bargh, Mark Chen and Lara Burrows showed that race affects basic expressions of emotions. They suggest that thinking about a behavior can increase the likelihood we will engage in it. Just as trying not to think about something, makes it more difficult to expunge it from our mind, this research suggests that trying not to think about race may have the ironic consequence of making race more salient. Bargh and colleagues suggest that race can prime us to act in ways that derive from our experience not from our intentions. To show this, they had white participants perform a very long and boring task of determining whether an array of many circles on a computer screen consisted of an odd or even number of circles. After about 45 minutes and 130 trials, the computer flashed an error message and noted the data were lost and they would have to begin again. A hidden camera captured their responses and later, judges rated them for hostility. The experimenter came into the room, checked the equipment and told them they would have to start again, and rated their hostility. The critical variable was whether or not the participants had been sub-liminally exposed to a series of photographs of black or white faces. Since the stereotype of blacks has been shown to contain aggressive and hostile traits, the authors assumed that the black faces would make hostility more salient in the participants. Thus relative to those who were exposed to white faces, those who had seen these black faces would react to their frustration in a more hostile way. Slide F shows the results of this experiment and as you can see participants who saw black faces (indicated by the dark bars) reacted with more hostility than those who saw white faces. Race matters and affects us at very personal levels of human response.

### 3. Behavioral Confirmation: Hostile Reactions to Race Makes Others More Hostile

Chen and Bargh's experiments showed that racial reactivity could influence the course of interaction with another person. Participants were again subliminally exposed to Black or White faces then asked to play a game with a partner that required the participant to give clues to the partner who tried to guess what word he was supposed to say. The partner's behavior was videotaped and later rated for hostility. Results showed that the black photos increased the hostility of participants as it had in the previous study. But further, their increased hostility increased the hostility of the partners with whom they interacted. This research suggests a chain of race influences beginning when one person's behavior is affected by a racial event, then expanding to others with whom he or she may interact. We are perceiving and detecting behaviors that have multiple influences. Race is not so much something we see in others, but a reflection of the image we project. We know also that teacher's expectations of children's ability influences somehow, how well the children do in school. Expectations of others are profoundly influenced by race. Again we see that race matters.

### 4. When Insults Matter: Race Affects Aggressive Responses to Insults

In my last research illustrations, Rogers and Prentice-Dunn demonstrated that reactions to a personal insult diverge with the race of the insulter. Participants were asked to use electric shock to train a subject in biofeedback. Learners were either black or white, and half of both races insulted the participant. The degree to which the participants used a higher level of shock and held the shock button down longer indicated their aggression. The next slide shows that when they were not insulted, participants were slightly less aggressive toward black than white learners. But when they had been insulted, their aggression escalated significantly more toward the black than the white learner.

Considering the results of this research, we have to ask what treating people as if their race made no difference means. We clearly know that race has been a central player in the evolution of America. We are a different country because of the way race has affected us than we would have been had there never been slaves, never been Jim Crow, never been the Civil War, never been the 1960s. Race lingers in our minds and hearts. Innocence on race is hard to achieve. I believe that the world looks different from different sides of racial divides. To approach the community of one people in America we must see the world from multiple sides. That is what a dialogue on race must be about. There are plenty of social scientists to tell us how far we have come and the best way to move further on the subject of race. But it seems to me that it is not up to others to tell us what matters and what doesn't, that racism is over or that it lies behind every social policy we promulgate.

I believe that we need to explore the depth of race in our psyche, and try to understand the divergent perceptions, the palpable anxiety and fears, the hopes, dreams and expectations. And we should do this with honesty and humility. Like creating community, you can't create open conversation on race by executive declarations. But there are many people who are already talking and want to talk more. In spite of the fact that race opens wounds, talking about it is an important way to create one America in the 21st century. Not to do so, leaves unchallenged and unexamined the variety of ways in which race insinuates itself in our everyday life.

Let me summarize in the simplest terms, the points my presentation makes:

1. The historical legacy of race influences what we feel and believe.
2. Although race has no biological legitimacy, its demise cannot be asserted but must be negotiated by affected parties.
3. Subtle effects of race influence what we feel, think, believe and how we act.
4. Race effects are complex and ubiquitous. Ignoring them is not an option.

I close with a haiku that I wrote to reflect one of the important reasons why we have to have a conversation on race.

# PART I

## The Sociohistorical Context of Race

# ▢▪▪ THE SCIENCE, SOCIAL CONSTRUCTION, AND EXPLOITATION OF RACE

*By Rashawn Ray*

The Sociohistorical Context of Race—highlights how the social construction of race, based on the falsifying of the science of race, is used to justify the exploitation of race for economic gains. In this section, race is situated within a sociohistorical context to discuss the origins and central outcomes of race. Since race is real in its consequences (i.e., outcomes), individuals assume that race must be real in its circumstances (i.e., origins) (Zuberi 2001). Therefore, it is important to convey that race is indeed a social construct that has real structural consequences for individuals (Feagin 2001). Furthermore, it must be made clear that race is an organizing principle that is ingrained in the institutions of society that marginalizes and exploits minority group members (Drake 1987; Bonilla-Silva 1997).

## THE SCIENCE OF RACE

Race can be conceptualized as ethnoracial, historically rooted distinctions or social constructions. Ethnicity, on the other hand, can be classified as a subgroup that shares a common ancestry, history, and/or culture (Bobo and Fox 2003). While numerous studies show that no biological or genetic differences exist among races that have significant psychological, mental, or physical origins, most individuals profess that there are innate racial differences between groups (Zuberi 2001). These include stereotypes such as Asians being short yet intelligent, Blacks being physically superior yet intellectually inferior, and Whites being the standard and epitome of humanity.

Humans are one species regardless of skin color, dialect, eye shape, and/or hair texture. In fact, individuals show more genetic variation within races than among them. In other words, a Black person and a White person can be genetically more similar to each other than two White people or two Black people. While differences seem to develop through health disparities (Gilbert 2010), IQ tests (Lewis 2010), and physical prowess, most of these differences are rooted in socialization, environmental factors, cultural variation, and perceptions of opportunities. Altogether, the science of race is only skin deep and instead differences between groups are based upon structural consequences.

## THE INVENTION OF RACE

So if race is indeed a social construction, how was race invented, and by whom? As Zuberi (2001) discusses, race was formally posited in the mid 1700s by Carolus (Carl) Linnaeus, a Swedish taxonomist, who asserted that people looked different. Linnaeus argued that because people looked different, there had to be psychological traits associated with these physical differences related to skin color. Accordingly, Linnaeus split humans into four subspecies—americanus, europaeus, asiaticus, and afer—each associated with a major continent. The German naturalist Blumenback introduced five racial categories—American, Caucasoid, Malay, Mongoloid, and Ethiopian—with each race associated with a color (i.e., white, yellow, red, brown, black). It should be noted that Negroid, which means black, later replaced the term Ethiopian. In turn, many of the Biblical associations with Ethiopians were lost. It should also be noted that Whites were the group doing the racial classifying. Some scholars argue this explains why Whites were placed on top of the racial hierarchy and used whiteness as the pure marker of perfection. Subsequently, other groups fall in line based on skin color from lightest to darkest. This was of course about 150 years after American slavery, thus a system of racial groupings already existed before Linnaeus' formal classification.

In *The Origin of Species*, Charles Darwin (1859) developed the theory of evolution, which asserts that through survival of the fittest, the most superior species will evolve and adapt to its environment. This is where the term race is such an intriguing choice of words. By classifying groups as races, it insinuates that groups are indeed competing and racing to be the fittest. Similarly, eugenics, which was developed in 1865 by Sir Francis Galton, a cousin of Charles Darwin, asserts that through a unique combination of nature versus nurture whereby various interventions are constructed, the perfect human can be created to enhance intelligence levels, save society's resources, and decrease human suffering. Some of these interventions include selective breeding, genetic engineering, in vitro fertilization, and forced sterilization. Eugenics movements have been criticized for justifying state-sponsored discrimination and human rights violations. Recently, some researchers have called for a resurgence into the study of eugenics through new forms of technology. Critics of eugenics insinuate that the "perfect human" will leave out the actual racial pluralism that exists in the world.

As a result of these theories and their implications for race, external physical characteristics (e.g., skin color, hair color and texture, eye color) came to be accepted as reflecting psychological and mental abilities that imply racial superiority or inferiority (Ray 2010). These assumptions, however, are refuted by researchers who note that individuals of every racial group have the same characteristics. More importantly, researchers have never found a gene for race. British fraternal twins are a good example. In 2005, a mixed race couple (that most would classify as Black on skin color alone) gave birth to one brown-skinned, brown eyed, and black haired girl and one fair-skinned, blue eyed, and blond haired girl. In other words, a Black couple had a Black *and* White baby at the same time. While these types of births are rare, they are not uncommon. These twins are validation for those who claim that the science of racial separatism is only skin deep. Still, stereotypes regarding physical characteristics persisted through the falsifying of cranium weight and facial angles as determinants for intelligence. Scientists constructed White brains to be larger than Black brains and used this form of pseudoscience to shape public opinion and public policy.

Through the formulation of theories and concepts to describe and categorize humans, race moved from being a rumor to being a social reality and became a means to separate groups. Darwin's theory of evolution and natural selection became the scientific basis for justifying that differences exist among racial groups. Galton's eugenics theory became the scientific basis to carry out preserving so-called racial purity. "Color prejudice thus became fused with beliefs in biological determinants to produce White racism" (Drake 1987). Collectively, these theories spurred Social Darwinism where scientific studies sought to justify the classification of racial groups.

## THE SOCIAL CONSTRUCTION OF RACE

Phenotypic features such as skin color, hair color, hair texture, and eye color that have been purported as classifying racial groups actually change over the life course based on how these genetic features interact with the environment. Ask yourself a few simple questions:

- Has your hair color or eye color changed from birth?
- Does your skin color change with exposure to light?
- Does your hair color or eye color change from season to season depending on the temperature of your environment?

If you answered yes to some or all of these questions, you are not alone. Most individuals' phenotypic features change over the life course. And yet, these features that change within each of us were/ are used as justification for racial classification and exploitation.

We can even think about the simple definitions of White and Black. White is classified as purity, cleanliness, and innocence. It is the color that brides, doctors, and nurses traditionally wear. Altogether, white is the absence of color and the

essence of what is considered good and positive. On the contrary, black is classified as evil, bad, and satanic. Black is the color people wear at funerals and symbolizes death.[*]

Images of Barbie and Aunt Jemima display this White/Black duality. Barbie is traditionally portrayed as pretty, queen-like, and angelic, while Aunt Jemima is frequently portrayed as dark-skinned, overweight, and ugly. In the 1950s and 1960s, Barbie and Aunt Jemima were some of the few caricatures of White and Black women seen by youth across racial lines. Messages that individuals receive about race from social institutions such as the media shape how individuals are socially constructed to view race, currently and historically. We receive unconscious messages on a daily basis in all facets of our lives that reinforce the ideology of race. Thus, the ideology of race shapes attitudes and perceptions and all aspects of social life that have real consequences for individuals' opportunities and social interactions. Even children are continuously subjected to messages and images that racially classify groups.

For example, Drs. Kenneth and Mamie Clarks'[†] doll experiments found that Black children often preferred to play with White dolls compared to

---

[*] If you take a historical perspective on the color Black, it actually symbolized authority, power, and royalty.

[†] Dr. Kenneth Clark was the first Black to obtain a PhD from Columbia University in 1940 with his wife right behind him as the first Black woman to obtain a PhD from Columbia University in 1943. Dr. Kenneth Clark became a full professor in 1942 at City College in New York City and later became the President of the American Psychological Association. Collectively, Drs. Kenneth and Mamie Clark founded the Northside Development Center for Child Development in Harlem. The Clarks were expert witnesses in the Brigg v. Elliot case, which was one of the influential cases that set the tone for the infamous Brown v. Board of Education Supreme Court case.

Black dolls and often classified their own skin color as a lighter shade than it actually was. Additionally, children often viewed White as good and pretty and Black as bad and ugly. The Clarks concluded that racial identity and self-awareness develop as early as 3 years old. Although it would seem as though this form of racial identity among Blacks is a thing of the past, unfortunately it is not. In a 2005 documentary, entitled *A Girl Like Me*, Kiri Davis replicated the Clarks' doll study and found similar results. *A Girl Like Me* is a short, intriguing documentary that captures how stereotypes affect the racial identities of minority group members.

Another documentary that should be of interest to those studying the social construction of race is *A Class Divided,* which is a compelling film about the establishment of ingroups/outgroups and the socialization of internalized prejudices, stereotypes, and discrimination. Third grade teacher Jane Elliott's "Blue Eyes/Brown Eyes" exercise, which was originally conducted following the assassination of Dr. Martin Luther King, Jr. in 1968, places a hierarchical distinction between blue-eyed and brown-eyed students. The documentary shows how quickly prejudice attitudes and discriminatory behavior can commence. Years later the students return as adults to discuss their experiences with the exercise and how it has shaped their beliefs about race and privilege. In part three of the documentary, Elliot conducts the study with adults.

## THE EXPLOITATION OF RACE

The social construction of race based on the falsifying of the science of race lead to the exploitation of race. Three examples are fitting here. First, Nazi Germany's "racial hygiene" programs during the 1930s and 1940s sought to preserve the human race by exterminating all Jews. The Aryan nation, commonly associated with Nazi Germany and Adolf Hitler, categorized themselves as the pure breeds.

While the Nazis could not find consistent recognizable physical characteristics to distinguish Germans from Jews, they resulted to forcing Jews to wear yellow armbands and have only traditional Jewish names. Germans were told to only marry and breed with blue-eyed and blond-haired humans. As part of the sterilization process, over 40,000 individuals including Jews, Gypsies, Jehovah witnesses, Blacks, and homosexuals were sterilized from 1934–1937. The Holocaust formally lasted from 1933–1945 and more than 5.7 million Jews were killed in Germany. Interestingly, Adolf Hitler, the leader of Nazi Germany, had brown hair and dark eyes.

Second, the U.S. Public Health Service conducted an experiment on 399 Black male farmers in Alabama from 1932–1972. Known as the Tuskegee Syphilis Experiment, these men were never told that they had syphilis and instead told that they had "bad blood" so that doctors and researchers could document the effect syphilis has on the human body. In turn, these farmers were denied proper care for the disease. This tragic event did not come to light until after the experiment was over with one doctor stating, "As I see it, we have no further interest in these patients until they die" (Jones 1993).

Third, The Transatlantic Slave Trade lasted formally in the U.S. from 1619–1865 and led to the deaths of over 20 million Africans. While slavery and bondage existed in human history, until the Transatlantic Slave Trade, the racialization of slavery did not exist (Zuberi 2001). Approximately 8 million Africans died during the Middle Passage, which was the transport voyage from Africa to the Americas. On the slave ships, Africans were handcuffed and shackled next to other Africans who did not speak their language so that they would not be able to communicate. Africans would go for days without seeing sunlight. In turn, they were forced to urinate and defecate on themselves and one another. When Africans were brought to the deck of the ship, they had cold, salt ocean water thrown on them and their wounds from whippings and beatings.

Once brought to the Americas, they were publicly sold at an auction like a piece of equipment such as a vehicle or appliance. Africans were then broken down like one would break a horse or a wild animal. Whites would take the African male who they considered to be the strongest mentally and physically and mutilate and murder him in front of the other slaves. White slave owners and caretakers would beat the African male to a pulp instilling fear in the other slaves. After that, they would tie each of his arms and legs to a horse. They would beat the horses in opposite directions until they ripped the African's body in separate pieces. Subsequently, Whites would select the second strongest African slave and beat him to a pulp until he yelled out his newly selected name by the slave owner. This established a precedent that African males had lost their power and would be beaten brutally for exerting any form of agency. Additionally, African women were savagely raped by White slave owners and caretakers. Altogether, if any individuals should be classified as embodying "the survival of the fittest," survivors of atrocities such as the Transatlantic Slave Trade and the Holocaust should be in that category.

In sum, race started out as a rumor, as a myth. This myth of racial difference was transmitted across media outlets, pulpits, classrooms, and stages. In turn, race has become one of the main social structural factors to determine life chances and opportunities. Subsequently, the social construction of race, based on the falsifying of the science of race, is continuously used to justify the exploitation of race for economic gains.

## SUPPLEMENTAL READINGS AND RESOURCES

A Class Divided (Blue Eye/ Brown Eye Experiment). Frontline PBS Documentary.

Anderson, Margaret L. and Patricia Hill Collins. 2001. Race, Class, and Gender; An Anthology, 4th Edition. Belmont, CA: Wadsworth.

Bobo. Lawrence and Cybelle Fox. 2003. "Race, Racism, and Discrimination: Bridging Problems, Methods, and Theory in Social Psychological Research." Social Psychology Quarterly, Special Issue: Race, Racism, and Discrimination 64: 319–332.

Davis, Kiri. 2005. A Girl Like Me. Independent Documentary.

Du Bois, W. E. B. [1899] 1995. The Philadelphia Negro: A Social Study. Philadelphia: University of Pennsylvania Press.

Du Bois, W. E. B. 1903. The Souls of Black Folk. New York: Dover.

Du Bois, W. E. B. 1939. Black Folk, Then and Now: An Essay in the History and Sociology of the Negro Race. New York: Henry Holt.

Havard's Implicit Association Tests. https://implicit.harvard.edu/implicit/demo/

Muhammad, Khalil Gibran. 2010. The Condemnation of Blackness: Race, Crime, and the Making of Modern Urban America. Cambridge: Harvard University Press.

Williams, Juan. 1987. Eyes on the Prize. America's Civil Rights Years (1954–1965). PBS.

Wilson, William Julius. 1978. The Declining Significance of Race: Blacks and Changing American Institutions. Chicago: University of Chicago Press.

# SCIENCE OF RACE

# THE EVOLUTION OF RACIAL CLASSIFICATION

*By Tukufu Zuberi*

The racialization of social and economic stratification required the classification of human beings by their physical characteristics.[1] The physical classification of human populations took on added meaning during the process of racial colonization and slavery. Both racial slavery and colonialism required a dehumanizing discourse. One of the first intellectual articulations of this discourse was the Great Chain of Being. The classical idea of the Great Chain of Being ranked all creation, including the Creator, hierarchically. The Chain of Being classified creation from inanimate objects upward through lowly animals, women, and men, to God. In the European mind, the use of the Chain of Being to support and justify the enslavement of Africans was obvious.[2]

The Chain of Being maintained that humans shared a close affinity with beasts. It followed, therefore, that the lowest human beings were closely related to the highest animals. Given the belief in Europe that the ape was the highest animal, it followed that the lowest group of human beings would be apelike. The economic desire to justify the enslavement of Africans played an important role in shaping the eighteenth-century opinion among some European scholars that Africans were just above the ape on the Great Chain of Being.

The chain ranged from simple to very complex beings. Common descent was not critical to this idea. Stratification within a particular race and among different races was the work of the Creator. With European colonialism came knowledge of the "technologically primitive" populations of the Americas, Africa, Asia, and Oceania. Not only were there inferior races within Europe, but races inferior to those were found among peoples of color.

The idea of a racial hierarchy assumed a class hierarchy. Both colonialism and enslavement are class relationships, and the idea of a racial hierarchy justified the existence of these relationships in the past. The idea of the primitive African was key in discussions of the Great Chain. The Dutch settlers originally referred to the Khoikhoi as Hottentots.[3] The African "Hottentots" became a common reference to the bottom of the human population.[4] Eighteenth- and nineteenth-century intellectuals commonly referred to Hottentots as the lowest of the savage races.

Ideologies and social theories of racial hierarchy supported European colonization.[5] "Race" identified various forms of religious and social differences.

That some people were less advanced technologically or militarily than others was seen as the will of God, the consequence of environment, or the outcome of differences in moral character. Within Europe the idea of the Great Chain of Being led British colonists in seventeenth-century Ulster to attempt to enslave the Irish. This attempt failed, but soon afterward Africans were successfully enslaved in Virginia, the Carolinas, and Georgia.

The racial theories of the seventeenth and eighteenth centuries were grounded in the notion of "divine providence" and justified the enslavement of Africans and the colonization of the Americas, Asia, and Africa. The theories held that God had ordained that Europe should rule the world, and various religious leaders were willing to give decrees to this effect.[6]

Justifying racial stratification was essential for the system of enslavement to exist in the Americas. Enslavement is a form of domination. Domination and its companions exploitation and marginalization refer to social relationships in which one population benefits as the other suffers. The degree of suffering can vary from society to society; however, the degree to which the dominant class depends on the exploited population does not determine the extent to which the exploited are marginalized. The dominant class's partial dependence may entail the destruction of the exploited class. This has been the case in the interaction of several indigenous Caribbean populations with European settler population.[7] Or the dominant class's more general dependence may entail coexistence with the exploited population, as in the case of South Africa and Brazil, for example. This continuum of domination allows us to avoid extremist arguments without sacrificing the force of the idea of domination. The various degrees of dominant-exploited and dominant-marginalized relationships may be placed on a continuum ranging from a point prior to equality to one just the other side of extermination or genocide. Domination needs justification in an age of democracy. As racially stratified societies entered the twentieth century, they needed to justify this domination. Social Darwinism and eugenics provided the first scientific justification of continued racial stratification by "democratic" societies.

The nineteenth-century justifications of racial stratification are rooted in the eighteenth-century development of evolutionary theory in biology and social statistics. The shift from natural history to biology gave new life to old ideas of racial hierarchy. When the Great Chain of Being no longer carried the weight of legitimacy, science came to the rescue, beginning with the theories of evolution. The Swedish natural historian Carolus Linnaeus led the way, formulating the first scientific classification of human populations. His scheme was based on the outward appearance of specimens. In his *Systema Naturae* (1735) human beings made up one of several categories of animals but did not occupy a superior category. Human beings were divided into four subspecies (*americanus, europaeus, asiaticus,* and *afer*) on the basis of appearance and personality. He even suggested that the Hottentot and the European did not derive from the same origin and that the *afer* was black, impassive, and lazy compared with the white, serious, and strong *europaeus*.

Linnaeus's system was thought to be crude and inadequate, and refinements followed in Johann Friedrich Blumenbach's *On the Natural Variety of Mankind* (1795). Linnaeus's system was based on anatomical and cultural characteristics. Using only anatomical (morphological) characteristics, Blumenbach divided human beings into five categories: American, Caucasian, Ethiopian, Malay, and Mongolian. His five races became identified with the skin colors red, white, black, brown, and yellow. He maintained that all human beings belonged to one species and that his categories merely signaled breaks in a continuum. Blumenbach's work both clashed with and complemented the work of many naturalists of the time, but it was singularly important in challenging the legitimacy of the Great Chain of Being.

Linnaeus established the perspective, or more specifically the paradigm, within which scientific research on racial diversity was conducted. This perspective included the idea that the goal of data collection on human differences involved the determination of a small number of fundamental categories into which all human variation could be collapsed. Advances in statistics, craniometry, and genetics added information but did so within this paradigm developed by Linnaeus.

Many other individuals, particularly Jean-Baptiste de Monet de Lamarck, played key roles in the development of European theories of evolution and race.[8] As Charles Darwin himself noted, Lamarck was one of the first naturalists to formulate "the doctrine that all species, including man, are descended from other species."[9] Lamarck argued that evolution occurred through the inheritance of acquired characteristics, not natural ones. In his major work, *Zoological Philosophy* (1809), Lamarck also dismissed the possibility of taxonomic categories and random variation, arguing instead that individual organisms acquired new habits in new environments and that their anatomical structure responded to their habitat in order to survive. Through their responses, lower forms of creation were able to rise up the Great Chain of Being. Lamarck's views would play an important role in the development of social science nearly a century later, as we will see below.

The worldview of the seventeenth century, as envisioned by Thomas Hobbes, presented human existence as *bellum omnium contra omnes,* a war of all against all. In 1798 Thomas R. Malthus applied the Hobbesian worldview in his population perspective, linking the issue of survival to population growth and the competition for natural resources.[10] Malthus was the first to argue scientifically for population control, by showing that populations grew geometrically whereas resources grew only arithmetically. He argued that population growth had to be kept in check lest misery and poverty become the predominant conditions in society. Because the competition for resources was natural, he contended that the poor and the powerless constituted a natural social occurrence. Attempts by society to help the poor would simply add to the problem, by increasing their numbers, and so should be abandoned. Poverty was a fact of nature and a product of God's will.

At the same time Malthus emphasized personal responsibility as the operative factor in the competition for natural resources. The poor were poor because of their individual characteristics, not because of their social position or the society they lived in. Governmental intervention in the natural workings of the economy thus was bound to fail. The distribution of rewards within society reflected individual accomplishment rather than historical and social circumstances; to engineer a change within society by welfare or any type of "wealth transfer" would lead to more misery and would be an act against nature and God.

Malthus was concerned that Europe in general and Britain in particular maintain a naturally strong and healthy people.[11] For Malthus, the issue of civilization versus barbarism was the most important distinction among and within societies. In his view, the population problem was one of moral discipline and probity.

Malthus's ideas had a profound impact on the way people viewed population problems in society. It is too easy, however, to overstate his influence in the formation of the idea of race. The doctrine of colonialism did not wait upon Malthus's arrival, nor was the racism to come simply a result of Malthus's *Essay on the Principle of Population.* In fact, racism was not a result of conflict between the very dissimilar peoples of Europe (whites) and those of the rest of the world (people of color); rather, it was conceived in the class systems of Europe. Without relying on natural selection, post-Malthusian and pre-Darwinian thinkers such as Joseph Arthur de Gobineau provided systematic explanations of why the uncivilized races could never achieve higher levels of civilization. In his landmark work, *Essay on the Inequality of Human Races* (1854–55), Gobineau explained that the principle of equality was misguided because of the superiority of the Aryan race. Gobineau, himself a count, argued that the nobility descended from superior progenitors and were therefore the only ones capable of ruling. The poor came from inferior progenitors and were thus politically incompetent.

Even before Malthus, states in the Americas were firmly grounded in the notions of European racial superiority.[12] The wars with the indigenous American population and the proslavery practices and arguments of politicians and propagandists made the idea of racial inferiority a living fact, one that was supported by the moral order of European people and "God." Europeans declared themselves owners and governors of the lands of nonwhite, "heathen" Others, and when they met with resistance, they were "forced into lawful war" in the name of preserving civilization and upholding righteousness. The colonial and slave practices of the era in which Gobineau lived required this new source of legitimacy.

However, Malthus's ideas were critical in the development of evolutionary thought. Charles Darwin himself observed:

> Fifteen months after I had begun my systematic enquiry, I happened to read for amusement Malthus on *Population*, and being well prepared to appreciate the struggle for existence which everywhere goes on from long-continued observation of the habits of animals and plants, it at once struck me that under these circumstances favorable variations would tend to be preserved and unfavorable ones be destroyed. The result of this would be a new species. Here, then I had at last got a theory by which to work.[13]

It is through Malthus's theoretical connection to Darwin that he had a critical impact on scholarly perspectives of ranking differences such as race. Malthus's perspective was both quantitative and tended toward ranking.

In 1859 Darwin fundamentally challenged Lamarck's argument with the publication of *On the Origin of Species by Means of Natural Selection or the Preservation of Favored Races in the Struggle for Life.* Darwin's reading of Malthus's *Essay on the Principle of Population* alerted him to the struggle for existence that was, in his view, responsible for natural selection through competition. Darwin went a step further than Malthus did by applying the principle of natural selection to every living thing.

Darwin's work was another blow to the religious theories of race based on the Great Chain of Being. The morphological view of species—that they are fixed in form and structure—dovetails with the assumptions of the Great Chain of Being that the Creator designs each form of life. Darwin disagreed with this morphological view. He argued that species formed populations of diverse individuals who adapted to different environments in such a way that their successors' characteristics would change through natural selection. Species did not progress and become better; they became diverse. In addition, unlike earlier evolutionary theorists such as Lamarck, Darwin separated the idea of evolution from the idea of progress, shifting the focus from generational improvement to generational diversity.[14]

At first, social scientists saw Darwin's emphasis on heredity as a limitation to social reform. The idea that nature was continually selecting for fitness suggested that humanitarian attempts to promote equality were of little avail. Though Darwin would become the god of eugenics, European eugenicists persisted in ignoring the nonmorphological implications of Darwin's view regarding race. Some, such as Karl Pearson, would even advocate a morphological view of species. Despite these contradictions, social scientists called evolutionary theories of race Social Darwinism.

Darwin suggested that all animal and plant populations differ from one another; that the potential for natural increase in the population is greater than the resources available to support it, as Malthus argued before him; that as a result natural selection favors the survival of those individuals within the population best suited for the environment in which they live or exist; and that the characteristics of a population gradually evolve over time. A new, secular phase in the study of race began with the attempt to apply in sociology the principles Darwin set out in biology. For a considerable period social scientists took biological precepts as their guidelines, focusing on the definition of different races rather than on the relationships among them.

Darwin's theory of natural selection holds that one species evolves into another. With this revolutionary idea, debates about the human races were radically altered. Writers began to argue that if man evolved from apelike ancestors and there were no "white" apes, then the white race is the most evolved. Thus, the races of color, which Europeans considered culturally and spiritually more primitive, were closer to the nonhuman progenitor (the ape), and the white populations of Europe represented the latest and highest form of evolutionary progress.

Pioneered by the English sociologist Herbert Spencer in the late nineteenth century, Social Darwinism became the dominant theory of sociological thought and played an important role in the prevailing ideology of racism. Like Darwin, Spencer viewed Malthus's population perspective as the principal force in evolution. Unlike Darwin, however, Spencer based his view of evolution on Lamarck.

Social scientists tended to think that Darwin's theory of natural selection mirrored contemporary social processes.[15] The same competitive individualism lay at the root of laissez-faire capitalism and became the key to economic development and progress. According to economist John Maynard Keynes:

> Hume and Paley, Burke and Rousseau, Godwin and Malthus, Cobbett and Huskisson, Bentham and Coleridge, Darwin and Bishop of Oxford, were all, it was discovered, preaching practically the same thing—individualism and *laissez-faire*. This was the Church of England and those her apostles, whilst the company of the economists were there to prove that the least deviation into impiety involved financial ruin.[16]

Darwin viewed species as a population of varying individuals with no fixed type, and contemporary political economists viewed society as individuals with different and divergent interests.

Darwin had maintained that certain biological differences conferred survival advantages on some organisms in the struggle for existence. Spencer interpreted Darwin's findings as demonstrating that the survival of the fittest resulted from the struggle for existence. Then, however, he applied Lamarck's theories, arguing that social evolution developed progressively. Spencer wrote:

> Whether it be in the development of the Earth, in the development of life under its surface, in the development of Society,

of Government, of Manufactures, of Commerce, of Language, Literature, Science, Art, this same evolution of the simple into the complex, through successive differentiations, holds throughout. From the earliest traceable cosmical changes down to the latest results of civilization, we shall find that the transformation of homogenous into the heterogeneous, is that in which progress essentially consists.[17]

Spencer argued that the evolutionary laws applicable in the physical world paralleled those guiding human cultural developments. Civilization moved from the homogeneous to the heterogeneous, from the undifferentiated to the differentiated;[18] racial, social, and cultural differences represented various *stages* of evolution. At the turn of the twentieth century, Social Darwinism was extremely influential, and Spencer was one of the most popular academics in the world.[19]

American Social Darwinists argued that African enslavement gave Africans an unnatural advantage by *increasing* their life expectancy and health. Thus began the debate over the enslaved Africans' quality of life in the Americas. According to several prominent scholars, emancipation produced the conditions that would lead to the ultimate elimination of the African population in the United States, as the struggle for existence would find the free African wanting in the competition with a European-origin population. "Some southerners saw in emancipation nothing but extermination for the Negro Race. The Provisional Governor of Florida became almost tearful over the impending fate of the Negroes and the guilt of the North."[20]

The Social Darwinists' struggle-for-existence theory was supported by the "black disappearance hypothesis."[21] One of its first exponents, Francis Amasa Walker, a former Civil War general, was the census superintendent for the 1870, 1880, and 1890 censuses. Walker argued in 1891 that Africans were a distinct population with a limited ability to survive in a nation like the United States, thus leading to their disappearance.[22] Using census data, Walker suggested that the decline in the proportion of Africans in the United States indicated African inferiority; he connected this inferiority to the African physical appearance and inability to miscegenate with the European-origin population.

Five years later, Frederick L. Hoffman published his exhaustive study, "Race Traits and Tendencies of the American Negro."[23] Based on more than fifty years of data on population dynamics and race, Hoffman's article argued that emancipation was a positive process because of the anticipated devastation it would bring upon Africans in the United States. His study clearly attempted to bolster Walker's justification of racial stratification. Contrary to Hoffman's predictions, it became clear by the early twentieth century that Africans would not become "extinct" in the United States. However, social scientists continued to refer to this hypothesis in their justifications of racial stratification.[24]

Like Social Darwinists, black-disappearance advocates saw African-origin populations as inferior participants in the struggle for existence. But unlike Social Darwinists, black-disappearance advocates were influenced by the empiricism of the German School of History.[23] Walter Wilcox, a chief statistician for the 1890 census, a leading economist and a professor at Cornell University, and Hoffman believed that statistics lent legitimacy to their views on racial stratification, and both employed statistical and demographic analysis in their research. The list of racial statisticians reads like a Who's Who of early social statisticians.

These ideas of the struggle for existence and the black-disappearance hypothesis mark a transition in the theorizing of race and the elevation of racial statistics. The Social Darwinists' ideas assumed that racial differences were natural differences. Most scholars believed race was part of the *natural* world; they viewed racial differences as the natural order of the world. The black-disappearance hypothesis required a quantitative analysis of the racial struggle for existence and superiority.

Social Darwinism had a short life among American social scientists. By the turn of the century social scientists were turning their attentions away from Spencer's theories of evolution. Social Darwinism sought to defend the status quo on the basis of a laissez-faire attitude. Thus, it looked down on the intervention of the state in society. American sociologists tended to reject Social Darwinism and its evolutionary theories as the basis of social behavior and difference.[26] As Hofstadter notes, "The most important change in sociological method was its estrangement from biology, and the tendency to place social studies on a psychological foundation."[27] Lester Ward, the first president of the American Sociological Society in 1906, advocated the need for an evaluation of the psychic factor in civilization. The new social psychology portrayed the individual as being endowed with propensities, interests, and habits, and not simply bounded by pleasure-pain and stimulus-response processes.

Spencer, like Malthus, hoped that social science would provide the evidence that discouraged social reform. However, by the turn of the century the spirit of social reform had grown, and social science was increasingly supportive of this effort. As social theorists increasingly criticized Social Darwinism, the evolutionary perspective was revived in a new guise. The revolution in genetics research and a new statistical theory of evolution had serious consequences for social thought. Unlike Social Darwinism, the new evolutionary theory—eugenics—advocated social reform and suggested the most extreme forms of social engineering. This change was clearly articulated by Cooley:

But why not make selection conscious and intelligent, and thus improve the stock of men somewhat as we do that of animals? There has, in fact, arisen a science of Eugenics, or Race-Improvement, seeking to stimulate the propagation of desirable types of human heredity and prevent that of undesirable types. … Scientific tests should be made of all children to ascertain those that are feeble-minded or otherwise hopelessly below a normal capacity followed by a study of their families to find whether these defects are hereditary.[28]

Like many social scientists, Charles H. Cooley was a Darwinist but not a Social Darwinist. Cooley was clearly a believer in evolution and a follower of Darwin's evolutionary theory.[29] Also, his ideas show the significant influence of eugenics by the beginning of the twentieth century.

## NOTES

1. For a classic description of this, see Winthrop D. Jordan, *White Over Black: American Attitudes Toward the Negro*, 1550–1812 (Chapel Hill: University of North Carolina Press, 1968), 216–28.

2. As Jordan observes, "Though other people, most notably the Indians, were enslaved by Europeans, slavery was typically a Negro-white relationship. This fact in itself inevitably meant that the Negro would not be accorded a high place when Europeans set about arranging the varieties of men on a grand scale. No one thought of the Great Chain of Being as originating in differences in power or social status between human groups; to do so would have been to blaspheme the Creator. However, this did not prevent the idea of the Chain of Being

from being applied to social relationships" (ibid., 227).

3. Leonard Thompson, *A History of South Africa* (New Haven: Yale University Press, 1995), 58; Wesseling *Divide and Rule,* 264.

4. For some examples of how the term *Hottentot* was used in speech and writing, see the quotations in Bernard M. Magubane, *The Making of a Racist State: British Imperialism and the Union of South Africa, 1875–1910* (Trenton, N.J.: Africa World Press, 1996), 13,41–42, 44, 144, 211–12, 330–31, 386; also see Saul Dubow, *Scientific Racism in Modern South Africa* (Cambridge: Cambridge University Press, 1995), 20–22.

5. See St. Clair Drake, *Black Folk Here and There: An Essay in History and Anthropology* (Los Angeles: University of California, Center for Afro-American Studies, 1987), vol. 2, chapters 4, 6, and 7.

6. Eric Williams, *Capitalism and Slavery* (Chapel Hill: University of North Carolina Press, 1944), 3–4; Mahmood Mudimbe, *The Invention of Africa: Gnosis, Philosophy, and the Order of Knowledge* (Bloomington: Indiana University Press, 1988), 20, 51–54; Robin Blackburn, *The Making of New World Slavery: From the Baroque to the Modern, 1492–1800* (London: Verso, 1997), 103.

7. See Clark Spencer Larsen, Christopher B. Ruff, Margaret J. Schoeninger, and Dale L. Hutchinson, "Population Decline and Extinction in La Florida," in *Disease and Demography in the Americas,* ed. John W. Verano and Douglas H. Ubelaker (Washington, D.C.: Smithsonian Institution Press, 1992), 25–39; and Russell Thornton *Holocaust and Survival A Population History Since 1492* (Norman: University of Oklahoma Press, 1987), chapter 3.

8. Some of the others include the Count de Buffon. See Jonathan Marks, *Human Biodiversity: Genes, Race, and History* (New York: Aldine de Gruyter, 1995), chapter 1.

9. Charles Darwin, *On the Origin of Species by Means of Natural Selection, or the Preservation of Favored Races in the Struggle for Life* (1859; reprint, New York: Modern Library, 1995), 3.

10. He did so in the anonymously published *An Essay on the Principle of Population as It Affects the Future Improvement of Society, with Remarks on the Speculations of Mr. Goodwin, M. Condorcet and Other Writers* (London: J. Johnson, 1798). Malthus's work served three related purposes: it elaborated a theory of natural selection; it disputed the radical progressivism of Godwin and Condorcet; and it presented a systematic opposition to legislative changes (then proposed) in the Poor Laws in Great Britain that would make welfare payments proportional to family size. After admitting that he wrote the essay, Malthus responded to his critics by publishing a revised version of it, entitled *An Essay on the Principle of Population; or, a View of Its Past and Present Effects on Human Happiness; with an Inquiry into Our Prospects Respecting the Future Removal or Mitigation of the Evils Which It Occasions,* ed. Donald Winch (1826; Cambridge: Cambridge University Press, 1992). (All quotations come from this revised version.) Malthus went on to publish seven editions of the *Essay on the Principle of Population.* Other writers, such as Antoine-Nicolas de Condorcet and William Godwin, had addressed the issue of the social consequences of population growth. However, Malthus's *Essay* was the most influential book to systematically connect population growth to its social consequences.

11. However, he doubted the efficacy of attempts at selective breeding. For example, Malthus

doubted Condorcet's idea of "organic perfectibility": "The foundations therefore, on which the arguments for the organic perfectibility of man rest, are unusually weak, and can only be considered as mere conjectures. It does not, however, by any means, seem impossible, that by an attention to breed, a certain degree of improvement, similar to that among animals, might take place among men ... As the human race however could not be improved in this way, without condemning all the bad specimens to celibacy, it is not probable that any attention to breed should ever become general ..." (Malthus, *An Essay on the Principle of Population*, 170–71).

12. Jordan, *White over Black*, chapters 1 and 2; and Drake, *Black Folk Here and There*, chapter 7.

13. Charles Darwin, *Autobiography and Selected Letters*, ed. Francis Darwin (1887; reprint, New York: Dover Press, 1958), 42–43.

14. For a more detailed description and contrast among the early evolutionary theorists, see Marks, *Human Biodiversity*, chapter 1.

15. Richard Hofstadter, *Social Darwinism in American Thought* (Boston: Beacon Press, 1944), 143–69. In this important chapter Hofstadter demonstrates how evolutionary theory had a profound impact upon psychology, anthropology, sociology, and ethics. He argues that evolutionary theory was not as successful in economics. However, economists of the time and immediately following the period he observed argued differently.

16. John Maynard Keynes, *The Collected Writings of John Maynard Keynes* (London: Macmillan, 1972), 9:276–77.

17. Herbert Spencer, *Essays: Scientific, Political, and Speculative* (New York: D. Appleton, 1896), 10.

18. Herbert Spencer, *Principles of Sociology* (1885; reprint, New York: D. Appleton, 1901–1907),

1:95, 432–34, 550–56, 614–22, 757, 764; 2:242–43; 3:331.

19. J. S. Haller, *Outcasts from Evolution: Scientific Attitudes of Racial Inferiority, 1859–1900* (Urbana: University of Illinois Press, 1971), 128, 153.

20. W. E. B. Du Bois, *Black Reconstruction in America, 1860–1880* (1935; reprint, New York: Atheneum, 1992), 139.

21. See William Darity Jr., "Many Roads to Extinction: Early AEA Economists and the Black Disappearance Hypothesis," *History of Economics Review* 21 (1994): 47–64.

22. Francis Amasa Walker, "The Colored Race in the United States," *Forum* 11 (1891): 501–9.

23. Hoffman's conclusions spoke to the racial prejudices of Social Darwinists: "Nothing is more clearly shown from this investigation than that the southern black man at the time of emancipation was healthy in body and cheerful in mind. He neither suffered inordinately from disease nor from impaired bodily vigor. His industrial capacities as a laborer were not of a low order, nor was the condition of servitude such as to produce in him morbid conditions favorable to mental disease, suicide, or intemperance. What are the conditions thirty years after? The pages of this work give but one answer, an answer which is a most severe condemnation of modern attempts of superior races to lift inferior races to their own elevated position ... In the plain language of the facts brought together, the colored race is shown to be the downward grade tending toward a condition ... when disease will be more destructive, vital resistance still lower, when the number of births will fall below the deaths, and gradual extinction of the race take place" (Frederick L. Hoffman, "Race Traits and Tendencies of the American Negro," *Publications of the American*

*Economic Association* 11, nos. 1, 2, and 3 (1896): 311–12).

24. For a prominent example, see Charles Horton Cooley, *Social Organization: A Study of the Larger Mind* (1909; reprint, New York: Schocken Books, 1962), 295.

25. Darity, "Many Roads to Extinction."

26. The same could be said about some European social scientists as well. For example, see the Max Weber and Karl Marx quotations above in the introduction.

27. Hofstadter, *Social Darwinism in American Thought*, 157.

28. Charles Horton Cooley, *Human Nature and the Social Order* (1902; reprint, New York: Schocken Books, 1964), 12–13. In his later work Cooley was more critical of eugenic research (see Charles Horton Cooley, *Social Process* (New York: Charles Scribner's Sons, 1918], 206). In *Social Process*, Cooley criticizes the eugenicists for not learning from Darwin.

29. For an example of Cooley's Darwinist research, see Cooley, *Human Nature and Social Order*, 35–80. Cooley's ideas were more consistent with the ideas stressed by John Dewey regarding the social conditioning of an individual's reaction patterns (compare Cooley's work with John Dewey, *Human Nature and Conduct* [New York: Modern Library, 1930], 21–22).

# SOCIAL CONSTRUCTION OF RACE

# RACIST AMERICA

## RACIST IDEOLOGY AS A SOCIAL FORCE

*By Joe R. Feagin*

## CREATING A RACIST IDEOLOGY

The dramatic expansion of Europe from the 1400s to the early 1900s eventually brought colonial exploitation to more than 80 percent of the globe. The resulting savagery, exploitation, and resource inequalities were global, and they stemmed, as W. E. B. Du Bois has noted, from letting a "single tradition of culture suddenly have thrust into its hands the power to bleed the world of its brawn and wealth, and the willingness to do this."[1] However, for the colonizing Europeans it was not enough to bleed the world of its labor and resources. The colonizers were not content to exploit indigenous peoples and view that exploitation simply as "might makes right." Instead, they vigorously justified what they had done for themselves and their descendants. Gradually, a broad racist ideology rationalized the oppression and thereby reduced its apparent moral cost for Europeans.

An ideology is a set of principles and views that embodies the basic interests of a particular social group. Typically, a broad ideology encompasses expressed attitudes and is constantly reflected in the talk and actions of everyday life. One need not know or accept the entire ideology for it to have an impact on thought or action. Thus, each person may participate only in certain fragments of an ideology. Ideologies are usually created by oppressors to cover what they do, and counterideologies are often developed by the oppressed in their struggle against domination. Here we examine a critical aspect of the social reproduction of systemic racism from one generation to the next. The perpetuation of systemic racism requires an intertemporal reproducing not only of racist institutions and structures but also of the ideological apparatus that buttresses them.

The early exploitative relationships that whites developed in regard to African Americans and Native Americans were quickly rationalized, and they became enduring racist relations. From the beginning, racial oppression has been webbed into most arenas of American life, including places of work and residence, and activities as diverse as eating, procreating, and child rearing. Racist practices in these life worlds create, and are in turn shaped by basic racist categories in the language and minds of Americans, especially white Americans. A racist ideology has overarching principles and beliefs that provide an umbrella for more specific racist attitudes, prejudices, and stereotypes.

Major ideological frameworks, including racist frameworks, are typically created, codified, and maintained by those at the top of a society, although this construction takes place in ongoing interaction with the views and practices of ordinary citizens. Those with the greater power have the greater ability to impose their own ideas on others. As Karl Marx and Friedrich Engels long ago pointed out, "the ideas of the ruling class are in every epoch the ruling ideas: i.e. the class, which is the ruling material force of society, is at the same time its ruling intellectual force."[2] Elites have dominated the creation, discussion, and dissemination of system-rationalizing ideas in business, the media, politics, education, churches, and government. While there is indeed much popularly generated racist imagery and discourse, even this is usually codified and embellished by the elites. As with most important ideas, if the elites had been opposed to the development of the racist ideology, they would have actively combated it, and it would likely have declined in importance. Thus, in his detailed analysis of the racist ideas and actions of presidents from George Washington to Bill Clinton, Kenneth O'Reilly has shown that conventional wisdom about presidents following a racist populace is wrongheaded. The historical evidence shows that most of the men who control U.S. political institutions have worked hard "to nurture and support the nation's racism."[3] Racist thought did not come accidentally to the United States. It was, and still is, actively developed and propagated.

## THE EMERGING ANTIBLACK IDEOLOGY: EARLY VIEWS

For several centuries white ministers, business people, political leaders, academics, scientists, and media executives have developed and disseminated to all Americans a complex and variegated racist ideology that defends the theft of land and labor from Americans of color. The antiblack version of this ideology is the most developed; it has included a variety of religious, scientific, and psychosexual rationalizations for oppression. Although the ideology has been elaborated and changed somewhat over time, in all its variations it has operated to rationalize white power and privilege.

From the 1600s to the 1800s English and other European Protestants dominated the religious scene on the Atlantic coast of North America, and their religious views incorporated notions of European superiority and non-European inferiority. The early English Protestants regarded themselves as Christian and civilized, but those they conquered as unchristian and savage. Religious and cultural imperialism accompanied economic imperialism.

Most of the new colonists from Europe saw themselves as Christian people of virtue and civilization. From the first century of American colonization these Europeans frequently portrayed themselves as "virtuous republicans." They did not, or should not, have the instinctual qualities of the "creatures of darkness," the black and red Calibans they saw in their stereotyped images. Europeans were rational, ascetic, self-governing, and sexually controlled, while the African and Native American others were irrational, uncivilized, instinctual, and uncontrolled.[4] The first non-Europeans with whom many European colonists came into contact were Native Americans. Rationalizing the often brutal destruction of Native American societies, European colonists developed early on some negative images of Native Americans. Native Americans were "uncivilized savages" to be killed off or pushed beyond the boundaries of European American society. Moreover, much white thinking about indigenous peoples in the first centuries alternated between great hostility, such as can be seen in the Declaration of Independence's complaint about "merciless Indian savages," and the paternalism seen in the image of a "noble savage" who was independent of the vices of Europeans. Novelists such as James Fenimore Cooper heralded what they saw as the diversity in character of the "native warrior of North America. In war, he is daring, boastful, cunning, ruthless … in peace, just, generous, hospitable, revengeful, superstitious, modest, and commonly chaste."[5]

## EARLY COLOR CODING: THE LINK TO SLAVERY

In the first century of North American slavery the antiblack ideology was becoming ever more developed and comprehensive. The emerging ideology increasingly focused not only on the blackness of the others but also on the whiteness of Europeans. Africans and African Americans were viewed as physically, aesthetically, morally, and mentally inferior to whites—differences that were regarded as more or less permanent. "Whiteness" was created in opposition to "blackness," in comparison to which it was not only different but quite superior. Indeed, from the seventeenth century forward black women, men, and children were "constructed as lazy, ignorant, lascivious, and criminal; Whites as industrious, knowledgeable, virtuous, and law-abiding."[6]

Significantly, the antiblack image was not "out there," but rather in the white mind and emotions. In their thinking and imaging, some whites went so far as to view the dark skin of Africans as a "natural infection" or as "pollution." A leading medical educator of the late 1700s, Dr. Benjamin Rush, thought the dark skin color of African Americans resulted from a type of leprosy that could be cured with medical treatment.[7]

The U.S. Constitution recognized the slave economy and implicitly incorporated an ideology of white supremacy in such provisions as the one that counted an African American as only "three-fifths" of a person. After the new nation was created, the unifying of growing numbers of immigrants from various European countries was done in part through the legal and political doctrines buttressing white privilege and superiority. In the first naturalization law in 1790, the new U.S. Congress made the earliest political statement on citizenship. Naturalization was restricted to "white persons." Whiteness thereby became an official government category; only European immigrants could qualify to become citizens of the new United States. The legal doctrines established by Congress and the courts helped to shape and unify the white consciousness, including that of the nation's leadership.[8]

## EMOTIONAL UNDERPINNINGS

From the seventeenth century to the present the ideology justifying antiblack oppression, while overtly cognitive and legally enshrined, has had a strong emotional base. Antiblack attitudes and actions among whites have long been linked to or supported by such emotions as hate, fear, guilt, and repulsion. W. E. B. Du Bois suggested that color barriers are created not only out of overt maliciousness but also by "unconscious acts and irrational reactions unpierced by reason."[9]

For instance, many whites have been emotionally obsessed with what they term "racial mixing." Strong and irrational emotions are evident in the taboos and laws against interracial sex and marriage, which have long been considered to be extremely "unnatural" and "abominable" by many whites. In 1662 the colony of Virginia established the first law against interracial sex, and in 1691 a law against interracial marriage was enforced by banishment. White Virginians, scholars have noted, were very "disturbed by the racial intermingling, especially white-Negro mixtures, and introduced laws to prevent what they saw as the 'abominable mixture and spurious issue' by penalizing whites who engaged in interracial sex."[10] Mixed-ancestry Americans were viewed not only as inferior but also as degrading what Benjamin Franklin called a "lovely" whiteness. As Franklin argued, white "amalgamation with the other color produces a degradation to which no lover of his country, no lover of excellence in the human character can innocently consent."[11] Like most whites of the eighteenth century, Franklin seems to have developed a deep fear of black Americans. A slaveholder for several decades, then a leading abolitionist later in life, Franklin openly opposed slavery not because of its inhumanity but because of its negative impact on the whiteness of the American population. Ironically and significantly, for most of American history it was white men who were the most likely to cross the color line and force sex on black women.

Strong emotions are evident in the white violence that has long targeted black Americans. While most of the bloodthirsty lynchings of black Americans took place after the Civil War, they were preceded before that war by barbaric beatings, rape, torture, and mutilation of Africans and African Americans on slave ships, farms, and plantations. The early white notion that African Americans were "dangerous savages" and "degenerate beasts" played a role in rationalizing this violence. To deserve such treatment "the black man presumably had to be as vicious as the racists claimed; otherwise many whites would have had to accept an intolerable burden of guilt for perpetrating or tolerating the most horrendous cruelties and injustices."[12] After slavery, the racist ideology legitimated lynchings, whose sadistic character suggests deep and shared white emotions of guilt, hatred, and fear.

Fear is central to the ideology and attitudes woven through the system of antiblack oppression. Significantly, of the three large-scale systems of social oppression—racism, sexism, and classism—only racism involves the dominant group having a deep and often obsessively emotional fear of the subordinate group. This is not generally true

for men, who dominate women in the system of sexism, nor is it true for the capitalists who exploit workers in the class-stratified capitalist system.

## DEVELOPING AN EXPLICIT IDEOLOGY OF "RACE"

The ideology rationalizing exploitation did not develop all at once, but was elaborated as colonialism expanded around the globe. First, as we saw above, the "others" were viewed as religiously and culturally inferior. This brought an early accent on a hierarchy of inferior and superior groups. Later on, those oppressed were seen as distinctive "races" that were inferior in physical, biological, and intellectual terms to Europeans. A clearly delineated concept of "race" as a distinctive pseudobiological category was developed by northern Europeans and European Americans about the time of the American Revolution.

By the late 1700s these hierarchical relations were increasingly explained in overtly bioracial terms. This biological determinism read existing European prejudices back into human biology; then it read that biology as rationalizing social hierarchy. Those at the bottom were less than human; they were alleged to have smaller, and thus inferior, brains. Reflecting on European imperialism in the late nineteenth and early twentieth centuries, Frantz Fanon stressed the point that this colonialism was about much more than labor or resource exploitation, for it involved broad social domination constructed in racist terms. European colonialism created the modern idea of "race" across the globe. "In the colonies the economic substructure is also a superstructure. The cause is the consequence; you are rich because you are white, you are white because you are rich."[13] This new racist ideology had three important elements: (1) an accent on physically and biologically distinctive categories called "races"; (2) an emphasis on "race" as the primary determinant of a group's essential personality and cultural traits; and (3) a hierarchy of superior and inferior racial groups.

America's prominent theorist of liberty, Thomas Jefferson, contended that black Americans were an inferior "race." In *Notes on the State of Virginia*, written in the late eighteenth century, Jefferson articulated what were the first developed arguments by an American intellectual for black inferiority. Blacks are said to be inferior to whites in reasoning, imagination, and beauty. Blacks are alleged to favor white beauty "as uniformly as is the preference of the Oranootan [Orangutan] for the black women over those of his own species." Blacks are alleged to be more adventuresome than whites because they have a "want of forethought," to be unreflective, and—perhaps most amazing—to feel life's pain less than whites. Blacks are alleged to have produced no important thinkers, poets, musicians, or intellectuals. Improvement in black minds comes only when there is a "mixture with whites," which Jefferson argues "proves that their inferiority is not the effect merely of their condition of life."[14]

## SCIENTIFIC RACISM

As early as the 1730s the Swedish botanist and taxonomist, Carolus Linneaus, distinguished four categories of human beings—black, white, red, and yellow. Though he did not explicitly use the idea of "race," he associated skin color with cultural traits— with whites being superior and blacks inferior. Between the 1770s and the 1790s the prominent German anatomist and anthropologist, Johann Blumenbach, worked out a racial classification that became influential. At the top of his list of "races" were what Blumenbach called the "Caucasians" (Europeans), a term he coined because in his judgment the people of the Caucasus were the most beautiful of the European peoples. Lower on the list were the Mongolians (Asians), the Ethiopians (Africans), the Americans (Native Americans), and the Malays (Polynesians). "White" was viewed as the oldest color of mankind, and white had degenerated into the darker skin colors.[15]

The new scientific racism firmly encompassed the notion of a specific number of races with different physical characteristics, a belief that these characteristics were hereditary, and the notion of a natural hierarchy of inferior and superior races. In their broad sweep these racist ideas were not supported by careful scientific observations of all human societies but rather were buttressed with slanted reports gleaned by European missionaries, travelers, and sea captains from their experiences with selected non-European societies. Most scientists of the late eighteenth and early nineteenth centuries, while presenting themselves as objective observers, tried to marshal evidence for human differences that the white imperialists' perspective had already decided were important to highlight.[16]

## CELEBRATING AND EXPANDING THE RACIST IDEOLOGY

In the United States distinguished lawyers, judges, and political leaders promoted scientific racism and its white-supremacist assumptions. In the first half of the nineteenth century whites with an interest in slavery dominated the political and legal system. This influence was conspicuous in the infamous *Dred Scott v. John F. A. Sandford* (1857) decision. Replying to the petition of an enslaved black American, a substantial majority of the U.S. Supreme Court ruled that Scott was not a citizen under the Constitution and had no rights. Chief Justice Roger Taney, a slaveholder, argued that African Americans "had for more than a century before [the U.S. Constitution] been regarded as beings of an inferior order, and altogether unfit to associate with the white race, either in social or political relations; and so far inferior, that they had no rights which the white man was bound to respect; and that the negro might justly and lawfully be reduced to slavery for his benefit. He was bought and sold, and treated as an ordinary article of merchandise and traffic, whenever a profit could be made by it. This opinion was at that time fixed and universal in the civilized portion of the white race."[17] The Dred Scott decision showed that the racist ideology was both elaborate and well established.

Senators and presidents played their role in articulating and spreading this ideology. President James Buchanan, a northerner, urged the nation to support the racist thinking of the *Dred Scott* decision. Moreover, several years before he became president, in his debate with Senator Stephen A. Douglas, Abraham Lincoln argued that the physical difference between the races was insuperable, saying, "I am not nor ever have been in favor of the social and political equality of the white and black races: that I am not nor ever have been in favor of making voters of the free negroes, or jurors, or qualifying them to hold office or having them to marry with white people. ... I as much as any other man am in favor of the superior position being assigned to the white man."[18] Lincoln, soon to be the "Great Emancipator," had made his white supremacist views clear, views later cited by southern officials in the 1960s struggle to protect legal segregation and still quoted by white supremacist groups today.

With the end of Reconstruction in 1877 came comprehensive and coercive racial segregation in the South. Distinguished judges, including those on the Supreme Court, played a key role in solidifying the extensive segregation of black Americans and in unifying white defenses of institutionalized racism. In *Plessy v. Ferguson* (1896) a nearly unanimous Supreme Court legitimated the fiction of "separate but equal" for black and white Americans in a case dealing with racially segregated railroad cars. This separate-but-equal fiction was legal for more than half a century, until the 1954 *Brown v. Board of Education of Topeka*

decision and until broken down further by the civil rights laws of the 1960s. There was widespread agreement in the elites and in the general white population about the desirability of thorough and compulsory segregation for black men, women, and children.

## SOCIAL DARWINISM

In his influential writings Charles Darwin applied his evolutionary idea of natural selection not only to animal development but also to the development of human "races." He saw natural selection at work in the killing of the indigenous peoples of Australia by the British, wrote of blacks as a category between whites and gorillas, and spoke against social programs for the "weak" because they permitted the least desirable people to survive. The "civilized races" would eventually replace the "savage races throughout the world."[19]

During the late 1800s and early 1900s a perspective called "social Darwinism" developed the ideas of Darwin and argued aggressively that certain "inferior races" were less evolved, less human, and more apelike than the "superior races." Prominent social scientists like Herbert Spencer and William Graham Sumner argued that social life was a life-and-death struggle in which the best individuals would win out over inferior individuals. Sumner argued that wealthy Americans, who were almost entirely white at the time, were products of natural selection and essential to the advance of civilization. Black Americans were seen by many of these openly racist analysts as a "degenerate race" whose alleged "immorality" was a racial trait.[20]

By the late 1800s a eugenics movement was spreading among scientists and other intellectuals in Europe and the United States. Eugenicists accented the importance of breeding the "right" types of human groups. Britain's Sir Francis Galton argued for improving the superior race by human intervention. Like Galton, U.S. eugenicists opposed "racial mixing" (or "miscegenation") because it destroyed racial purity. Allowing "unfit races" to survive would destroy the "superior race" of northern Europeans. Those from the lesser races, it was decided, should be sterilized or excluded from the nation. Such views were not on the fringe, but had the weight of established scientists, leading politicians, and major business leaders. Thus, in 1893 Nathaniel S. Shaler, a prominent scientist and dean at Harvard University, argued that black Americans were inferior, uncivilized, and an "alien folk" with no place in the body politic. In social Darwinist fashion, he spoke of their eventual extinction under the processes of natural law.[21]

Scientific racism was used by white members of Congress to support passage of discriminatory congressional legislation, including the openly racist 1924 immigration law excluding most immigrants other than northern Europeans. In this period overtly racist ideas were advocated by all U.S. presidents. Former president Theodore Roosevelt openly favored scientific racism.[22] President Woodrow Wilson was well-known as an advocate of the superiority of European civilization over all others, including those of Africa. As president, Wilson increased the racial segregation of the federal government. Significantly, no less a racist leader than Adolf Hitler would later report having been influenced by Wilson's writings. (In its contemporary sense, the term *racism* first appeared in a 1933 German book by Magnus Hirschfeld, who sought to counter the Nazi and other European racists' notion of a biologically determined hierarchy of races.)[23]

In 1921 President Warren G. Harding, who had once been linked to the Ku Klux Klan, said he rejected any "suggestion of social equality" between blacks and whites, citing a popular racist book as evidence the "race problem" was a global problem. Not long before he became president, Calvin Coolidge wrote in *Good Housekeeping* magazine,

"Biological laws tell us that certain divergent people will not mix or blend. The Nordics propagate themselves successfully. With other races, the outcome shows deterioration on both sides."[24] Ideas of white supremacy and rigid segregation were openly advocated by top political leaders.

## PERPETUATING THE RACIST IDEOLOGY: CONTEMPORARY AMERICA

Periodically, the racist ideology framed in the first two centuries of American development has shifted somewhat in its framing or emphases. Those in charge have dressed it up differently for changing social circumstances, though the underlying framework has remained much the same. Some new ideas have been added to deal with pressures for change from those oppressed, particularly ideas about government policy. After World War II, aspects of the dominant racist ideology were altered somewhat to fit the new circumstances of the 1950s and 1960s, during which black Americans increasingly challenged patterns of compulsory racial segregation.

In recent decades white elites have continued to dominate the transmission of new or refurbished ideas and images designed to buttress the system of racial inequality, and they have used ever more powerful means to accomplish their ends. The mass media now include not only the radio, movies, and print media used in the past, but television, music videos, satellite transmissions, and the Internet.

Today, for the most part, the mass media are still controlled by whites. Just under 90 percent of the news reporters, supervisors, and editors at newspapers and magazines across the United States are white. On television whites are overrepresented in managerial jobs, and as on-air reporters; they are greatly overrepresented as "experts" in the mass media. Americans of color have only a token presence in the choice and shaping of news reports and media entertainment. The concentration of media control in a few corporations has increased dramatically in recent decades. In the early twenty-first century, fewer than two dozen corporations control much of the mass media, and that number is likely to decrease further. In addition, the mass media, especially television, are substantially supported by corporate advertisers, and advertisers have significant command over programming. Thus, information about racial matters is usually filtered and whitewashed through a variety of elite-controlled organizations. This filtering is not a coordinated conspiracy, but reflects the choices of many powerful whites socialized to the dominant framing in regard to racial issues.[25]

Looking for data and stories, reporters and journalists typically seek out established government, business, academic, and think-tank reports and experts. The right wing of the U.S. ruling class, a large segment, has historically been the most committed to the racist ideology and has pressed for repression of protests against oppression. The liberal wing of the white elite is much smaller and often more attuned to popular movements; it has been willing to liberalize the society to some degree and to make some concessions to protesters for the sake of preserving the society. (The center of the elite has waffled between the two poles.) In the late 1960s and 1970s many experts consulted by top executives in government and the mass media came from think tanks usually espousing the views of those in the center or on the left of the ruling elite. Becoming very concerned about this, wealthy conservatives began in the 1970s to lavishly fund right-wing think tanks and to press aggressively conservative views of U.S. society on universities, politicians, and media owners. In recent years the right-wing think tanks—including the American Enterprise Institute, the Manhattan Institute, and the Heritage Foundation—have been very successful in getting their experts into mainstream discussions and debates. Working alongside a large group of other conservative intellectuals, media experts, and activists, these right-wing think tanks continue to be successful in an indoctrination campaign aimed at shaping public views on racial and other social issues.[26]

Most Americans now get their news from commercial television and radio programs. The largest single source is local news programming.[27] Using these local and national media, the white elites have the capability to mobilize mass consensus on elite-generated ideas and views; this consensus often provides an illusion of democracy. These elites encourage collective ignorance by allowing little systematic information critical of the existing social and political system to be circulated through the media to the general population.

With the national racial order firmly in place, most white Americans, from childhood on, come to adopt the views, assumptions, and proclivities of previous generations and established white authorities. In this manner the system of racism is reproduced from one generation of whites to the next.

## INCREASED EQUALITY RHETORIC

From the 1960s onward the rhetoric of racial equality, or at least of an equality of opportunity, grew in volume among members of the white elite, including presidents and members of Congress. The black protests and rebellions of the 1950s and 1960s had an important effect in eradicating not only the system of the legal segregation but also most public defense of racial discrimination by the nation's white leadership. Since the late 1960s most leaders have proclaimed the rhetoric of racial and ethnic equality.

The structural dismantling of a large-scale system of compulsory segregation did require a new equality emphasis in the prevailing racial ideology. However, while the structural position of whites and blacks had changed somewhat, at least officially, most whites—in the elites and the general public—did not seem interested in giving up significant white power or privilege. Thus, the racist ideology was altered in some ways but continued to incorporate many of its old features, and it continued to rationalize white privilege—now under conditions of official desegregation. There had long been some fairness language in the prevailing ideology—for example, most whites thought blacks were treated fairly—but now notions of fairness and equality of opportunity were moved to the forefront. The acceptance by the white elite and public of the principles of equal opportunity and desegregation in regard to schools, jobs, and public accommodations did *not* mean that most whites desired for the federal government to implement large-scale integration of these institutions.

## A MORE CONSERVATIVE ORIENTATION: 1969 TO THE PRESENT

Beginning around 1969, with the arrival of Richard Nixon's presidential administration, the rhetoric of equality was increasingly accompanied by a federal government backing off from its modest commitment to desegregation and enforcement of the new civil rights laws. At the local level, there was increased police repression of aggressive dissent in the black community, such as the illegal attacks on Black Panthers and other militant black groups by local police and FBI agents. The old racist images of dangerous black men and black welfare mothers were dusted off and emphasized by prominent white leaders who often spouted the rhetoric of equality at the same time. Moreover, the liberal wing of the white elite, which had provided some funding for the civil rights movement and other social movements of the 1960s, significantly reduced its support for these movements.[28]

By the mid-1970s the right wing of the ruling elite was accelerating its attack on the liberal

thinking associated with the new civil rights laws. Since the 1970s a growing number of conservative organizations have worked aggressively in pressing Congress, the federal courts, and the private sector to eviscerate or eliminate antidiscrimination programs such as affirmative action efforts, as well as an array of other government social programs. This signaled the increasing influence on national policy of a more conservative Republican Party that represented, almost exclusively, the interests of white Americans. Moreover, even at the top of the Democratic Party there was also some shift to the right, which could be seen in the relatively modest antidiscrimination policies of the Jimmy Carter and Bill Clinton administrations.

The shift away from government action to remedy discrimination was associated with a reinvigoration of notions about inferior black intelligence and culture. In the 1970s, and increasingly in the 1980s and 1990s, numerous white journalists, politicians, and academics were critical of what they saw as too-liberal views in regard to black Americans and remedies for discrimination and defended arguments about black intellectual or cultural inferiority. In public policy discussions, increasingly led by white conservatives, there was a renewed emphasis on the view that only the individual, not the group, is protected from discrimination under U.S. law.

The federal courts provide an important example of this conservative shift. In the decades since the 1970s these courts have often ruled that group-remedy programs against racial discrimination violate the U.S. Constitution, which they assert only recognizes the rights of individuals, not groups. For instance, in 1989 a conservative Supreme Court handed down a major decision, *City of Richmond, Virginia v. J. A. Croson Co.*, which knocked down a local program designed to remedy past discrimination against black and other minority businesses.[29] The high court ruled in favor of a white-run construction company, the plaintiff, which argued that the municipal government had unconstitutionally set aside business for minority companies. The court ruled that the city of Richmond had not made a compelling case for racial discrimination, even though the defendant's statistics showed that in a city whose population was one-half black, *less than 1 percent of the city government's business* went to black-owned firms.

## STILL ARGUING FOR BIOLOGICAL "RACES"

In recent years some social and behavioral scientists have joined with certain physical scientists to continue to press for the idea of biological races and to connect that idea to concerns over government social policies. Since the late 1960s several social scientists at leading universities, including Arthur Jensen and Richard Herrnstein, have continued to argue that racial-group differences in average scores on the so-called IQ tests reveal genetic differences in intelligence between black and white Americans. Their views have been influential, especially on white politicians and the white public. In 1969 the *Harvard Educational Review* lent its prestige to a long article by Jensen, a University of California professor. The arguments presented there and Jensen's later arguments in the next two decades have received much national attention, including major stories in *Time, Newsweek, U.S. News and World Report, Life,* and major newspapers. Jensen has argued that on the average blacks are born with less intelligence than whites, and that the "IQ" test data support this contention. In addition, he has suggested that high birth rates for black Americans could result in a lowering of the nation's overall intelligence level.[30]

Perhaps the most widely read example of biological determinism is a 1990s book, *The Bell Curve,* which sold more than a half million copies. Into the twenty-first century it is still being cited and read. Like Jensen, the authors of *The*

*Bell Curve*—the late Harvard University professor Richard Herrnstein and prominent author Charles Murray—argue that IQ test data show that black (and Latino) Americans are inferior in intelligence to whites. Though the authors have no training in genetics, they suggest that this supposed inferiority in intelligence results substantially from genetic differences. Thus, biological differences account to a substantial degree for racial inequalities. The fact that the book has sold many copies and has been widely debated in the media—in spite of the overwhelming evidence against its arguments—strongly suggests that biologically oriented racist thinking is still espoused by a large number of white Americans, including those who are well-educated. Indeed, Herrnstein and Murray explicitly suggest that their views are *privately shared* by many well-educated whites, including those in the elite, who are unwilling to speak out publicly. This book was launched during a major press conference at the conservative American Enterprise Institute. This publicity insured that the book would get much national attention, while antiracist books have generally gotten far less media play.[31]

Racist arguments about contemporary intelligence levels are grounded in nearly four hundred years of viewing blacks as having an intelligence inferior to that of whites. Today, such views are much more than an academic matter. They have periodically been used by members of Congress and presidential advisors in the White House to argue against antidiscrimination and other government programs that benefit Americans of color. Given this elite activity, it is not surprising to find these views in the white public.

Another aspect of older racist views that can be found in new dress is the idea of what one might call "cultural racism"—the view that blacks have done less well than whites because of their allegedly deficient culture with its weak work ethic and family values. As early as the seventeenth century, black Americans were seen as inferior in civilization and morality to white colonists. These blaming-the-victim views have regularly been resuscitated among the white elites and passed along to ordinary Americans as a way of explaining the difficult socioeconomic conditions faced by black Americans.

Since the 1970s leading magazines have published articles accenting some version of this perspective on what came to be called the black "underclass"; the perspective accents the allegedly deficient morality and lifestyle of many black Americans. Prominent author Ken Auletta wrote an influential set of *New Yorker* articles, later expanded in his book *The Underclass*. He accented the black underclass and its supposed immorality, family disorganization, and substandard work ethic.[32] A later article in the *Chronicle of Higher Education* surveyed the growing research on the underclass, noting that "the lives of the ghetto poor are marked by a dense fabric of what experts call 'social pathologies'—teenage pregnancies, out-of-wedlock births, single-parent families, poor educational achievement, chronic unemployment, welfare dependency, drug abuse, and crime—that, taken separately or together, seem impervious to change."[33] To the present day, similar stories designed to explain black problems in cultural terms regularly appear in the local and national media across the nation.

## A WHITEWASHED WORLDVIEW

This antiblack ideology links in so many ways to so much of white thought and behavior that we might speak of it as a broad worldview. Seen comprehensively, all the mental images, prejudiced attitudes, stereotypes, fictions, racist explanations, and rationalizations that link to systemic racism make up a white racist worldview, one deeply imbedded in the dominant culture and institutions. The U.S. system of racism is not just something that affects black Americans and other Americans of color, for it is central to the lives of white Americans as well. It determines how whites think about themselves, about their ideals, and about their nation.

In the early 1900s European immigrants to the United States came to accept this worldview and its implicit assumption that being "American" means being white. This has not changed much in the intervening years. Today the term "American" still means "white"—at least for the majority of white Americans, and probably for most people across the globe. One can pick up most newspapers or news magazines and find "American" or "Americans" used in a way that clearly accents *white* Americans. Take this sentence from a news writer in a Florida newspaper: "The American Public isn't giving government or police officers the blind trust it once did."[34] Clearly, "American" here means "white American," for the majority of blacks have never blindly trusted the police.

One research analysis examined all the articles in sixty-five major English-language newspapers for a six-month period and estimated that there were thousands of references to "black Americans" or "African Americans" in the articles. However, in the same newspapers there were *only forty-six* mentions of "white Americans."[35] In almost every case these mentions by newspaper writers occurred in connection with "black Americans," "blacks," or "African Americans." (The exceptions were three cases in which "white Americans" was used in connection with "Native Americans" or "Korean Americans.") A similar pattern was found for major magazines. Not once was the term "white Americans" used alone in an article; if used, it was always used in relation to another racial category. The same study examined how congressional candidates were described in news articles in the two weeks prior to the November 1998 elections. In every case white congressional candidates were *not* described as "white," but black congressional candidates were always noted as being "black."[36] In the United States blackness is usually salient and noted, while whiteness generally goes unmentioned, except when reference is specifically made to white connections to other racial groups.

Being "American" still means, in the minds of many people, including editors and writers in the media, being white. This need not be a conscious process. For several centuries most whites have probably not seen the routines of their everyday lives as framed in white. "Race" is often not visible when one is at the top of the social hierarchy. Today, major social institutions, those originally created by whites centuries ago, are still dominated by whites. Yet from the white standpoint they are not white, just normal and customary. They are not seen for what they actually are—whitewashed institutions reflecting in many of their aspects the history, privileges, norms, values, and interests of white Americans. When whites live in these customary arrangements, they need not think in overtly racist terms. Nonetheless, when whites move into settings where they must confront people of color in the United States or elsewhere, they usually foreground their whiteness, whether consciously or unconsciously.

## FEAR OF A MULTIRACIAL, MULTICULTURAL FUTURE

Today, many white analysts still see Western civilization as under threat from groups that are not white or European. Racist thinking is more than rationalizing oppression, for it also represents a defensive response, a fear of losing power to Americans of color. In recent years many advocates of white superiority have directed their attacks at the values or cultures of new immigrants of color coming to the United States, as well as at black Americans. In one recent interview study elite numerous white men openly expressed some fear of the growth of

Americans of color in the United States, seeing Western civilization as under threat.[37]

We observe examples of this fear among U.S. politicians and intellectuals. For example, in several speeches and articles Patrick Buchanan, media pundit and once a candidate for the Republican presidential nomination, has argued that "our Judeo-Christian values are going to be preserved and our Western heritage is going to be handed down to future generations and not dumped on some landfill called multiculturalism."[38] Once again, we see the linkage between religion and a strong sense of European supremacy. We also see a concern for the reproduction of the white-dominated system from current to future generations. In addition, Buchanan told one interviewer that "if we had to take a million immigrants in, say, Zulus next year or Englishmen, and put them in Virginia, what group would be easier to assimilate and would cause less problems for the people of Virginia? There is nothing wrong with us sitting down and arguing that issue that we are a European country, [an] English-speaking country."[39] The Zulus, who are Africans, seem to represent in his mind the specter of strange or savage hordes who would not assimilate well into the nation. Ironically, Africans have been in the nation longer than Buchanan's Irish ancestors, and Virginia has been home to African Americans for nearly four centuries.

## CONCLUSION

The systemic racism that is still part of the base of U.S. society is interwoven with a strong racist ideology that has been partially reframed at various points in U.S. history, but which has remained a well-institutionalized set of beliefs, attitudes, and concepts defending white-on-black oppression. Until the late 1940s commitment to a white supremacist view of the world was proud, openly held, and aggressive. Most whites in the United

States and Europe, led by elites, took pride in forthrightly professing their racist perspectives on other peoples and their racist rationalizations for Western imperialistic adventures. Brutal discrimination and overt exploitation were routinely advocated. Indeed, white domination of the globe was "seen as proof of white racial superiority."[40]

Beginning in the late 1940s, however, the open expression of a white supremacist ideology was made more difficult by a growing American awareness of actions of the racist regime in Nazi Germany. In addition, by the 1950s and 1960s growing black civil rights protests against U.S. racism—with their counterideology of black liberation—and the U.S. struggle with the Soviet Union made the open expression of a white supremacist ideology less acceptable. The dominant racist ideology changed slowly to reflect these new conditions, with a new accent on equality of opportunity and some support for moderate programs to break down the nation's segregated institutions. Still, as we have seen, many aspects of the old racist ideology were dressed up in a new guise, and they persist, with some barnacle-like additions, to the present day. From the beginning, the age-old idea of the superiority of white (Western) culture and institutions has been the most basic idea in the dominant ideology rationalizing oppression.

For some time now, most whites have viewed the last few centuries of societal development in terms of a broad imagery equating "human progress" with Western civilization. We hear or see phrases like "Western civilization is an engine generating great progress for the world" or "Africans have only seen real advancement because of their contacts with Western civilization." Western imperialism's bringing of "civilization" or "democracy" to other peoples is made to appear as an engine of great progress, with mostly good results. However, this equating of "progress" with European civilization conceals the devastating consequences of imperialism and colonialism. The actual reality was—and often still is—brutal, bloody, oppressive, or genocidal in consequence for those colonized. When whites speak of Western civilization as equivalent to great human progress, they are talking about the creation of social systems that do not take into serious consideration the interests and views of the indigenous or enslaved peoples whose resources were ripped from them, whose societies were destroyed, and whose lives were cut short. Images of Western civilization, like the racist ideologies of which they are often part, are too often used to paper over the sordid realities of Western colonialism and imperialism.

## DISCUSSION QUESTIONS

1. What is a racist ideology, and when did it first develop in North America?

2. Are elites or the rank-and-file population most responsible for the growth and importance of the racist ideology?

3. Is the racist ideology still important today? How and where?

4. Have prominent presidents and scientists played an important role in the development of racist ideas and notions? If so, how and when?

5. What is social Darwinism, and is it still important in U.S. society today?

## NOTES

1. W. E. B. Du Bois, *Dusk of Dawn: An Essay Toward an Autobiography of a Race Concept* (New Brunswick, NJ: Transaction Books, 1984 [1940]), p. 144.

2. Karl Marx and Friederich Engels, *The German Ideology,* ed. R. Pascal (New York: International Publishers, 1947), p. 39.

3. Kenneth O'Reilly, *Nixon's Piano: Presidents and Racial Politics from Washington to Clinton* (New York: Free Press, 1995), p. 11.

4. Ronald T. Takaki, *Iron Cages: Race and Culture in 19th Century America* (Oxford: Oxford University Press, 1990), pp. 11–14.

5. James Fenimore Cooper, *The Last of the Mohicans* (1826), as quoted in Emily Morison Beck, ed., *John Bartlett's Familiar Quotations, 15th ed.* (Boston: Little Brown, 1980), p. 463.

6. Tomás Almaguer, *Racial Fault Lines* (Berkeley and Los Angeles: University of California Press, 1994), p. 28.

7. Takaki, *Iron Cages*, pp. 30–34.

8. See Frances Lee Ansley, "Stirring the Ashes: Race, Class and the Future of Civil Rights Scholarship," *Cornell Law Review* 74 (September, 1989): 993.

9. W. E. B. Du Bois, *Dusk of Dawn: An Essay Toward an Autobiography of a Race Concept* (New Brunswick, NJ: Transaction Books, 1984 [1940]), p. 6.

10. A. Leon Higginbotham, Jr., and Barbara K. Kopytoff, "Racial Purity and Interracial Sex in the Law of Colonial and Antebellum Virginia," *Georgetown Law Journal* 77 (August 1989): 1671.

11. Benjamin Franklin, quoted in Takaki, *Iron Cages*, p. 50; Claude-Anne Lopez and Eugenia W. Herbert, *The Private Franklin: The Man and His Family* (New York: Norton, 1975), pp. 194–95.

12. George Frederickson, *The Black Image in the White Mind* (Hanover, NH: Wesleyan University Press, 1971), p. 282.

13. Frantz Fanon, *The Wretched of the Earth* (New York: Grove Press, 1963), p. 32.

14. Thomas Jefferson, *Notes on the State of Virginia*, ed. Frank Shuffelton (New York: Penguin, 1999 [1785]), pp. 145, 147–48.

15. William H. Tucker, *The Science and Politics of Racial Research* (Urbana: University of Illinois Press, 1994), pp. 8–9; Ivan Hannaford, *Race: The History of an Idea in the West* (Baltimore: Johns Hopkins University Press, 1996), pp. 205–207.

16. Audrey Smedley, *Race in North America* (Boulder, CO: Westview Press, 1993), p. 26.

17. *Dred Scott v. John F. A. Sandford*, 60 U.S. 393, 407–408 (1857).

18. Abraham Lincoln, "The Sixth Joint Debate at Quincy, October 13, 1858," in *The Lincoln-Douglas Debates: The First Complete, Unexpurgated Text*, ed. Harold Holzer (New York: HarperCollins, 1993), p. 283.

19. Charles Darwin, quoted in Frederickson, *The Black Image in the White Mind*, p. 230.

20. See Joe R. Feagin, *Subordinating the Poor: Welfare and American Beliefs* (Englewood Cliffs, NJ: Prentice-Hall, 1975), pp. 35–36; and Frederick L. Hoffman, "Vital Statistics of the Negro," *Arena* 5 (April 1892): 542, cited in Frederickson, *The Black Image in the White Mind*, pp. 250–51.

21. John Higham, *Strangers in the Land* (New York: Atheneum, 1963), pp. 96–152; Tucker, *The Science and Politics of Racial Research*, p. 35.

22. Tucker, *The Science and Politics of Racial Research*, p. 93.

23. See Theodore Cross, *Black Power Imperative: Racial Inequality and the Politics of Nonviolence* (New York: Faulkner, 1984), p. 157; Magnus Hirschfeld, *Racism*, trans. and ed. by Eden and Cedar Paul (London: V. Gollancz, 1938). The book was published in German in 1933.

24. Warren G. Harding and Calvin Coolidge, each quoted in Tucker, *The Science and Politics of Racial Research*, p. 93.

25. David K. Shipler, "Blacks in the Newsroom," *Columbia Journalism Review*, May/June 1998, pp. 81, 26–29; Robert M. Entman et al.,

*Mass Media and Reconciliation: A Report to the Advisory Board and Staff, The President's Initiative on Race* (Washington, D.C., 1998); Edward Herman, "The Propaganda Model Revisited," *Monthly Review* 48 (July 1996): 115.

26. Sidney Blumenthal, *The Rise of the Counter-Establishment* (New York: Times Books, 1986), pp. 4–11, 133–70; Peter Steinfels, *The Neoconservatives: The Men Who Are Changing America's Politics* (New York: Touchstone, 1979), pp. 214–77.

27. Franklin D. Gilliam Jr., and Shanto Iyengar, "Prime Suspects: the Effects of Local News on the Viewing Public," University of California at Los Angeles, unpublished paper, n.d.

28. Thomas Ferguson and Joel Rodgers, *Right Turn: The Decline of the Democrats and the Future of American Politics* (New York: Hill and Wang, 1986), pp. 65–66.

29. *City of Richmond, Virginia v. J.A. Croson Co.*, 488 U.S. 469 (1989).

30. Arthur R. Jensen, "How Much Can We Boost IQ and Scholastic Achievement?" *Harvard 99 Educational Review* 39 (1969): 1–123.

31. Jean Stefancic and Richard Delgado, *No Mercy: How Conservative Think Tanks and 100 Foundations Changed America's Social Agenda* (Philadelphia: Temple University Press, 1996), p. 34.

32. Ken Auletta, *The Underclass* (New York: Random House, 1982).

33. Ellen K. Coughlin, "Worsening Plight of the Underclass Catches Attention," *Chronicle of Higher Education,* March 1988, A5.

34. I draw here on Nick Mrozinske, "Derivational Thinking and Racism," unpublished research paper, University of Florida, fall, 1998.

35. The search algorithm did not allow searches for the word "whites" alone, because this picks up the surnames of individuals in the Lexis/Nexis database.

36. Mrozinske, "Derivational Thinking and Racism."

37. Rhonda Levine, "The Souls of Elite White Men: White Racial Identity and the Logic of Thinking on Race," paper presented at annual meeting, Hawaiian Sociological Association, February 14, 1998.

38. Patrick Buchanan, quoted in Clarence Page, "U.S. Media Should Stop Abetting Intolerance," *Toronto Star,* December 27, 1991, A27.

39. Patrick Buchanan, quoted in John Dillin, "Immigration Joins List of '92 Issues," *Christian Science Monitor,* December 17, 1991, 6.

40. Frank Furedi, *The Silent War: Imperialism and the Changing Perception of Race* (New Brunswick, NJ: Rutgers University Press, 1998), p. 1.

## SELECTED BIBLIOGRAPHY

Cross, Theodore. *Black Power Imperative: Racial Inequality and the Politics of Nonviolence* (New York: Faulkner, 1984).

Du Bois, W. E. B. *Dusk of Dawn: An Essay Toward an Autobiography of a Race Concept* (New Brunswick, NJ: Transaction Books, 1984 [1940]).

Furedi, Frank. *The Silent War: Imperialism and the Changing Perception of Race* (New Brunswick, NJ: Rutgers University Press, 1998).

O'Reilly, Kenneth. *Nixon's Piano: Presidents and Racial Politics from Washington to Clinton* (New York: Free Press, 1995).

Smedley, Audrey. *Race in North America* (Boulder, CO: Westview Press, 1993).

Takaki, Ronald T. *Iron Cages: Race and Culture in 19th Century America* (Oxford: Oxford University Press, 1990).

Tucker, William H. *The Science and Politics of Racial Research* (Urbana: University of Illinois Press, 1994).

# EXPLOITATION OF RACE

# □■■ White Racism and the Black Experience

*By St. Clair Drake*

The Black Experience began thousands of years before the phenomenon of White Racism appeared in human history, generated as it was by European economic and political expansion overseas beginning in the fifteenth century A.D. The roots of the Black Experience, as described in chapter 3 of this volume, lie deep in the prehistory and history of the Nile Valley, the Sahara Desert, and the northern savannah lands of Africa. It is a story that involves the extensive dispersion of black people, within the African continent and beyond it, and diverse contacts with other races.

To understand the complexity of the Black Experience in its full temporal and spatial amplitude, it is necessary to distinguish between White Racism and less drastic forms of prejudice through which colored people are sometimes stigmatized. These, although unjust and injurious to group welfare and individual personality development, are less devastating in their effects than White Racism. They are diffused negative prejudices involving stereotypes at the cognitive level and pejorative attitudes at the emotional level, neither of which are sanctioned with a systematic ideology or embodied in institutional structures. This chapter describes the manner in which antiblack, and especially anti-Negro, prejudices of some antiquity were mobilized as one part of the developing phenomenon of racism in Europe. It also describes the ongoing refinement of concepts dealing with racism.

The processes are outlined by which White Racism developed as a special type of nineteenth-century pseudoscientific racism, functionally related to the African slave trade and to colonial imperialism in Africa and Asia. It is noted that at some times and in some places, color prejudice against black people has existed without developing into White Racism. It should be noted that other forms of racism than White Racism exist, in which presumed ancestry rather than skin-color or other physical features is the criterion for invidious distinction.

Finally, this chapter emphasizes the need for distinguishing between prejudice against "blackness" in general and "Negroidness" in particular. Negative esthetic evaluations of "Negroidness," although rarely examined in detail, are here discussed because they persist tenaciously and reinforce negative beliefs about the intelligence and personality traits of black people, and thereby affect the life chances and self-esteem of people so evaluated.

Prejudices of this type have a tendency to linger after racist dogmas have been widely discredited and public and private agencies have come into being to work actively against racial discrimination. They are deeply entrenched, even in some societies where the more blatant forms of institutional racism have never existed.

Some aspects of the Black Experience in eighteenth-century North America are presented as a significant historical baseline for considering ironies and inconsistencies, paradoxes and contradictions, that constitute elements of continuity and change in the expression of white attitudes toward "blackness" and "Negroidness."

## COLOR PREJUDICE THEN AND NOW

In 1782, seven years after he had drafted the Declaration of Independence with a preamble declaring, "We hold these truths to be self-evident, that all men are created equal," Thomas Jefferson, the Virginia planter-scholar, rationalized the continuing enslavement of black people.[1] Of the men and women whom he and other white people owned, he wrote:

> This unfortunate difference of colour, and perhaps of faculty, is a powerful obstacle to the emancipation of these people ... I advance it therefore as a suspicion only, that the blacks, whether originally a distinct race, or made distinct by time and circumstances, are inferior to the whites in the endowments both of body and mind.[2]

After contrasting the slaves of classical antiquity with those in North America, to the disadvantage of the latter, Jefferson invoked a theory of biological inheritance to explain the suspected inferiority: "It is not against experience to suppose, that different species of the same genus, or varieties of the same species, may possess different qualifications."[3] Yet Jefferson believed that there was some hope for Blacks, because "the improvement of blacks in body and mind, in the first instance of their mixture with the whites, has been observed by everyone, and proves that their inferiority is not the effect merely of their condition of life."[4]

But Jefferson opposed further experiments in miscegenation and was sure that his countrymen would erect rigid barriers against intermixture if the slaves were ever emancipated. He proposed the deportation and colonization abroad of any freed Blacks, insisting that to let them remain would imbed an unassimilable mass of people in the nation's heart, about whose fate the "superior" governing race would become embroiled in bitter controversy and perhaps warfare. Black insurrection, too, was a specter that haunted Jefferson, and he was convinced that if the slaves were not eventually freed and colonized in Africa, the Caribbean, or the far western reaches of the continent, their continued presence would "produce convulsions, which [would] probably never end but in the extermination of the one race or the other race."[5]

Jefferson may have had only "suspicions" about the *intellectual* inferiority of Blacks, but he had no doubts about their *esthetic* inferiority.[6] The contrast between the black and white head and face helped to create an unbridgeable gulf.

> The first difference which strikes us is that of colour ... And is this difference of no importance? Is it not the foundation of a greater or less share of beauty in the two races? Are not the fine mixtures of red and white, the expressions of every passion by greater or less suffusions of colour in the one, preferable to that eternal monotony, which reigns in the countenances, that immoveable veil of

black which covers all the emotions, of the other race? Add to these, flowing hair, a more elegant symmetry of form, their own judgment in favour of the whites, declared by their preference of them, as uniformly as is the preference of the Orangotan for the black women over those of his own species.[7]

Nearly thirty years after Jefferson's observations on "blackness" were circulated, a witty, clever, and skeptical reply to the Sage of Monticello was published anonymously. Historians attribute the piece to a fellow planter, George Tucker. The reply was written in the form of a letter from the Virginia planter to a fictitious French friend.

I hasten to answer your question, whether the blacks here are really inferior to the whites by nature as well as by law. I have examined the passage in Jefferson's Notes, to which you direct me, and can assure you, that as far as I have seen, there is no just excuse for his remarks. I am afraid, indeed, that his opinion is but too popular here, as I have heard several masters ready to justify their severity to these poor wretches, by alleging that they are an inferior race, created only to be slaves. What a horrible doctrine, my dear D——, and what a pity that any gentleman of Mr. J.'s reputation for talents, should lend it the countenance of his name.

Jefferson's critic took special delight in responding to the observations imputing ugliness to black people. His comments, quoted below, on Jefferson's panegyric to Caucasian beauty show that even within the Virginia slaveholding planter class it was possible to assert the relativity of esthetic standards and to question the universality of a color symbolism that equated Black with evil. Thus, he continues:

As to our author's remarks, indeed, upon the comparative beauty of the two races, I must certainly agree with him in taste, (tho' I own I was a little surprised at his decision after the stories I have heard of him) … I am not quite so satisfied, however, as he seems to be about making my own judgment the standard of taste for all the world. Their preference of the whites … can hardly be regarded as a concession of the point in our favour … Nor is this supposed preference of theirs by any means universal … In Africa, too, where artificial associations [i.e., slavery] do not influence their natural notions in the same way, the blacks appear to discover no such partiality for the beauty of the whites. On the contrary we are told that, in their rude pictures, they are always sure to paint their angels black and the devil white.[8]

In his letter Tucker referred also to accounts of intelligent travelers to England who reported that "women of the lower order seem to feel no great qualms of taste in associating with wooly-headed husbands."[9] He need not have gone to the Mother Country to find examples of this particular kind of miscegenation. It was frequent enough in Virginia and Maryland, when these colonies were first established, to induce the planters in both states to pass laws severely penalizing free white women who married African slaves, and later making all sexual relations between Blacks and whites illegal.[10] Such laws never inhibited white males of any social level from consorting with the "wooly-headed" women, a custom that persisted long after slavery was abolished in the South. Tucker's reference to stories he had heard about Jefferson concerned the allegation, widely discussed at the time, that Sally Hemings, a slave at Monticello, had borne him five children. Despite doubts expressed by earlier biographers concerned with protecting Jefferson's image, the authenticity of the story is accepted by some recent students of Jefferson's life.[11]

Tucker's remark is relevant to our discussion not only for the hint of this Founding Father's hypocrisy in practicing the miscegenation he loudly denounced, but also because of what it reveals about the contemporary use of the term *black* in referring to Africans and their progeny, pure and mixed. Latin American readers, if Tucker had any, would have considered irrelevant his allusion to Jefferson's inconsistency in deriding Blacks esthetically but having this slave woman as a mistress. Sally was very light in color and would not have been considered "black" by Latin American standards. That Tucker referred to these stories at all in discussing Jefferson's attitude toward "blackness" indicates that the North American custom of calling a person "black" when believed to have any "ascertainable trace" of Negro ancestry was already in existence. Some of the sources refer to Sally Hemings as "Black Sal," although contemporary gossips usually called the high-spirited quadroon "Dashing Sally."

Extending the term *black* to include Afro-Americans with "only a small amount of 'Negro blood'," as Tucker did by inference in the case of Sally Hemings, is a peculiarly North American practice. In Latin American countries, words that mean "Black" or "Negro" usually are confined to the so-called "extreme" or "pronounced" Negroid physical type, what some anthropologists call the "True Negro." This composite consists of several traits of the head and face: very dark skin-color, thick and everted lips, flat nose, frizzled ("kinky") hair, and projection of the lower face, technically known as alveolar prognathism. The tendency to characterize this configuration of traits as "ugly" and even "repulsive" is still prevalent throughout the Americas, as it was in Thomas Jefferson's day. Even many of the descendants of the African slaves have had a tendency to accept the white group's designation of this combination of physical features as "ugly," and to prefer a less Negroid physiognomy for themselves, their spouses, and their progeny. There was no effective challenge to such self-demeaning attitudes toward the Negro body image until the Afro-American youth of the 1960s flung forth a defensively defiant slogan—"Black is Beautiful"—and began wearing their hair "natural" and rejecting the use of skin-lightening preparations. (Marcus Garvey's Universal Negro Improvement Association had raised the issue some forty years previously, but without lasting effect.)[12]

It is important to note that it is "Negroidness," not dark skin-color alone, that has inspired esthetic type, some anthropologists have added refinements that Caucasians find unattractive, such as thin "shanks" of lower limbs and very narrow pelvis, or the opposite—steatopygy—in women. Insofar as their writings are popularized, they focus attention on anatomical differences that most laymen did not know existed, and they often raise disquieting questions about their significance. Occasionally, too, a physical anthropologist will smuggle in his personal esthetic biases. For instance, one well-known American anthropologist, the late Carleton Coon, in an otherwise scholarly and relatively objective book, includes an idiosyncratic judgment of this type. In discussing an East African ethnic group, he praises the women for their beauty but does so with offensive insensitivity for the feelings of black professors and students who might use the book. He writes of the Somali people that they are characterized by "a degree of beauty seldom seen in Europe, with high conical breasts in the women, totally unlike *the pendulous negroid udders* so common among Gallas and Amharas [italics added]."[13]

For an anthropologist to imply that hanging breasts constitute a racial trait distinguishing "Negroes" is unprofessional, to say the least. Furthermore, the author insists that Somalis are not Negroes," although he notes that they carry some Negro genes and are often dark brown in skin-color. There is also a widespread related tendency to refer to some Asian and Oceanic peoples as "handsome," even though their skins are dark brown. In these cases straight hair and so-called refined features, not skin-color, are decisive in making the esthetic judgment.

Jefferson and Tucker expressed their esthetic preference for the Caucasian physical type—skin-color as well as hair type and other features—during a period when there were few literate black people outside the Islamic Arabic-speaking world. Carleton Coon wrote at a time when there were millions of potential black readers and probably hundreds of actual users of his book in colleges and universities. Although negative attitudes toward "Negroidness" still may be widespread in the United States today, they have to a great extent been repressed into the unconscious or remain unstated for reasons of political prudence or courtesy. In any event, few people would insult their Afro-American fellow citizens by publicly expressing a distaste, if they felt it, for "pronounced Negro features." Such sensitivity does not prevail in most of Latin America and the Middle East, or in Europe, for that matter. Derogatory jokes, cartoons, nicknames, epithets, patronizing endearments, and stereotyped roles on the stage and in music halls are prevalent there but would evoke protests from groups monitoring civil rights in the United States. Their disappearance here reflects some profound changes in American life.

A glance at magazine and newspaper display advertising, at athletic heroes and models, television performers and politicians, would suggest that the contemporary American public does not consider all persons with pronounced Negro facial traits to be unattractive. In fact, they never have, but

now, for the first time, there is an open display of willingness to concede attractiveness in some cases. Afro-Americans have always been aware that often the same people who used the stereotype for selfish ends in one situation applied an esthetic norm in their personal relations with black people that distinguished between beautiful and ugly, attractive and unattractive, *within* the same "extreme Negro type" they demeaned.

It is significant that Tucker, in responding to Jefferson's comments about Blacks, made one commonsense judgment that has become the norm for most Americans: *"After all, whether the blacks are uglier or handsomer than the whites can prove nothing as to the inferiority of the endowments of mind* [italics added]."[14] This point of view has come to prevail, even though throughout the latter part of the nineteenth century and the first third of the twentieth century linkage between the esthetic devaluation of Negroes and the idea of intellectual inferiority was reinforced by the pseudosciences of phrenology and anthropometry. High-vaulted foreheads and perpendicular profiles became signs of high intelligence in the popular mind. The fight against Hitlerism between 1933 and 1945 discredited both of these props for a racism that itself became discredited.

Benjamin Franklin of Pennsylvania, a contemporary of Jefferson and Tucker, thought that Negroes were "not deficient in natural understanding." One of his reasons for opposing the slave trade, however, was motivated by a mild form of color prejudice fed by esthetic biases. On one occasion he wrote: "Why increase the sons of Africa by planting them in America where we have so fair an Opportunity, by excluding all Blacks and Tawneys, of increasing the lovely white and Red? But perhaps I am partial to the complexion of my Country for such kind of Partiality is natural to mankind."[15] His objection to "tawneys" extended to some Europeans, for he was disturbed by the fact that the Germans "are generally of what we call a swarthy Complexion." He remarked in despair that "the Number of white People in the world is proportionately very small." Franklin's sensitivity to skin-color was part of his own ancestral social tradition, and he was convinced that the English "make the principal Body of White People on the Face of the Earth." The English of his day and the North American colonists shared a type of prejudice against dark skin-color that included some Europeans, but it was focused most strongly on Negroes, whose bodies were important objects in their mercantile trade and whose labor was essential to the prosperity of their colonies. Some of the same European neighbors whom they considered their inferiors had also exhibited color prejudice against Negroes for centuries, but it was predominantly an esthetic judgment and did not result in social systems that consigned all Negroes to a special caste or to the lowest rungs of a class system, and did not equate "blackness" with slave status. The contrast between this pre-sixteenth-century type of Mediterranean and Middle Eastern color prejudice and that of societies permeated with racism, such as those in the Americas came to be, is as striking as it is significant. Yet some observers would call any manifestations of color prejudice "racism."

## VARIETIES OF RACISM

Historian Philip Curtin, in discussing esthetic prejudices and some forms of ethnocentrism, insists that "any of these views may be labeled 'racism' of some variety but they need to be kept separate from the full-blown pseudo-scientific racism which dominated so much of European thought between the 1840's and the 1940's."[16] The term racism, until extended in recent years to include cultural chauvinism, referred to a form of racial prejudice that was justified by the dogma that some groups of people inherit characteristics—intellectual and temperamental—that make them inferior to others. A belief in biological determinism is at the root of all such racist thinking. Ideology used to justify systems that institutionalize domination of one racial group over another is referred to by many scholars as "racist doctrine," and some speak of "ideological racism" as distinct from more diffuse expressions of racial prejudices.

That American slavery generated racism is undeniable. Thomas Jefferson and his social stratum lived a way of life based upon *racial slavery*, a form of bondage that differed profoundly from systems of slavery prevalent in the Old World. In the new system the slave owner was expected to differ in physical type from the enslaved. The existence of a few exceptional cases of slaveholders who were allowed to rise from the "inferior black race" was considered an anomaly, and no whites could ever *"fall"* into a state of slavery. The system was justified by the deeply felt, and sometimes theologically sanctioned, belief that black people were born to serve white people. Benjamin Franklin's racial prejudices were typical of the North, where ideological racism was unnecessary since slavery was not an integral part of the socioeconomic system.

Anthropologist Ashley Montagu, commenting on the relatively recent emergence of ideological racism in human history, notes that it was not until the latter part of the eighteenth century that "the alleged inborn differences between peoples were erected into the doctrine of racism, … a melange of rationalizations calculated to prove that the Negro was created with articulate speech and hands so that he might be of service to his master the white man."[17] It was not until after the middle of the nineteenth century, however, that a full-blown, systematic racist ideology with "scientific" support took shape.

The concept of a hierarchy of ability based upon biological inheritance is at the root of the theory of ideological racism. It was used during the nineteenth century to interpret European national rivalries and class antagonism, as well as to defend the enslavement of Africans. It was integrated into the Darwinian concepts of "struggle for survival" and "survival of the fittest." So, in addition to races as anthropologists or laymen perceived them, ethnic groups (and even social classes) that could not be recognized by color and physiognomy were thought of as having a "racial" inheritance and were graded according to their presumed level of inborn intelligence and peculiarities of temperament. They were even called "races." In Europe, anthropologists placed "Nordics" at the top, "Alpines" in the middle, and "Mediterraneans" at the bottom in a racial hierarchy that depended mainly upon cranial measurements for distinguishing the groups, although blondness, or lack of it, was a criterion too. When this type of racial thinking—characteristic of some anthropologists and speculative historians—was applied globally, all Europeans were at the top, a superior group of Caucasoid whites with variations among themselves but superior to all "colored" peoples. Linguists, historians, and philosophers elaborated a theory that placed the hypothetical "Aryans" at the top of the list of Caucasian culture bearers.

The most widely read disseminators of these views placed Anglo-Saxon or Teutonic elites at the pinnacle—designating them the "Aryans" who served as the "guardians of civilization," protecting it not only for themselves but also for the benefit of "the lesser breeds without the law, half savage and half child," as Rudyard Kipling called them. Since most of these "lesser breeds" were colored people living in Africa, Asia, and Oceania, as well as Indians and recently freed black slaves in the Americas, the "civilizing mission" was called "The White Man's Burden." *Color prejudice thus became fused with beliefs in biological determinism to produce White Racism.*

The specific referent used to differentiate enslaved Africans and their descendants from their masters in the Americas was the dark color of their skin. Thus,

the kind of racism associated with the systems of slavery prevailing throughout the Americas was one example of *White* Racism. Slavery had existed for millennia before 1492, when European settlement began in the New World. It had existed in various places since remote antiquity without the support of either color prejudice or racist theories. Blacks and whites frequently enslaved their own kind, as well as one another. Yet, until the transatlantic slave trade in black bodies began near the end of the fifteenth century, *racial slavery* did not exist, even though prejudice against the Negro phenotype can be documented as far back as the first century of the Christian Era. Racism, as we define it, came even later. But it is important to remember that *racism can exist without the reinforcement of color prejudice, just as color prejudice can exist apart from racism (and does within many black communities).*

Once racism did appear in history, it was not always in the form of White Racism (that is, racism directed at colored people). The popularizers of racist theory, such as Count de Gobineau and Houston Stewart Chamberlain, graded all Europeans into the Aryan-Alpine-Mediterranean hierarchy. Jews and Gypsies were relegated to pariah status.[18] Even the system of ranking white people was suffused with color prejudice, for the darkness of southern Europeans as compared with northern Europeans symbolized inferiority, and suspected infusions of Negro blood in the past were sometimes inferred. Lothrop Stoddard, the American popularizer of de Gobineau's ideas, in *Racial Realities in Europe*, attributes cultural decline to what German Nazi theorists later called the "negrification" of parts of Europe. Stoddard wrote:

> To conquer and hold Portugal's vast colonial empire required great fleets and armies which took the very cream of the Portuguese stock. At the beginning of their heroic period the Portuguese were

an almost purely Mediterranean stock, energetic, intelligent and with marked literary and artistic qualities. ... And then, in a trifle over a hundred years, it was all over! ... The drain on the Portuguese stock had been frightful and the resulting racial impoverishment was therefore even more lamentable ... Furthermore, upon this racially impoverished people fell a fresh misfortune—the incoming of inferior alien blood. The half-deserted countryside fell into the hands of great landowners who imported gangs of negro slaves drawn from Portugal's African colonies. This was particularly true of Southern Portugal, where a semitropical climate and a fertile soil made negro slavery highly profitable. *In time the population of Southern Portugal became distinctly tinged with negro blood, which produced a depressing and degrading effect upon the national character* [italics added].[19]

This kind of racist thinking reached its apogee under Hitler's National Socialism, culminating in German justifications for World War II and the Holocaust. As one American political scientist summarized the Nazi "race myth" in 1935:

The new Germany envisages world history as a conflict between races. The white or "Aryan" race is the source of all culture, the Negro is an inferior breed, and the Jew, as another representative of *Untermenschentum* or subhumanity, is the source of all corruption. The Germans represent the highest point of Aryan development.[20]

In 1933 a Nazi periodical carried the following recommendations for Nazi youth:

Every Aryan hero should marry only a blonde Aryan woman with blue, wide-open eyes, a long oval face, a pink and white skin, a narrow nose, a small mouth and under all circumstances virginal. A blond, blue-eyed man must marry no brunette, no Mediterranean-type woman with short legs, black hair, hooked nose, full lips, a large mouth, and an inclination to plumpness. A blond, blue-eyed Aryan hero must marry no Negroid type of woman with the well-known Negro head and thinnish body.[21]

Racist ideology usually involves an esthetic appraisal of physical features, a mythology about traits of mind and personality correlated with physical features, and an almost mystical belief in the power of "blood" to elevate or to taint.

## WHITE RACISM AND PSEUDOSCIENCE

### The Unique Onus of "Negroidness"

Racist thinking has victimized various European and Asiatic groups, and White Racism has functioned in the oppression of Asians as well as Africans. But since the sixteenth century black people everywhere have been subjected to the most sustained and severe racist assaults upon their bodies and psyches. The reasons for the extreme animus against "blackness" require an explanation separate from that which accounts for White Racism in general. The epoch of constant, relentless derogation of Africans and peoples of African descent is drawing to a close because of forces convergent since World War II, especially the emergence of a group of independent African nations. But in attacking the color prejudice that remains as a legacy of slavery and colonial imperialism, consideration must be given to the way in which Blacks became the central target of White Racism. The crucial factor, of course, was the traffic in black bodies, which flourished from the sixteenth century through part of the nineteenth century, and the enslavement of black people throughout the Americas. With the end of slavery, colonial imperialism on the continent of Africa shifted the scene of exploitation of African laborers to their home soil and reinforced antiblack ideologies that had emerged during the slavery period.

However, long before racist ideologies were systematized to defend the interests of those who profited from slavery and colonial imperialism, black people were being stereotyped. As mentioned above, derogatory appraisals of "Negroidness" existed in different parts of the world prior to the sixteenth century and were used in discrimination against and coercion of Blacks. By the mid-eighteenth century, intellectuals in Europe and the Americas were categorizing the Negro as an inferior creature in "The Great Chain of Being."[22] This philosophical concept of a universe with God at the apex and everything else in its place below, though not originally intended to function ideologically, was eventually used for justifying economic and political interests.

Racist thinking was also generated unwittingly by the activities of people who were interested in science for its own sake, especially the taxonomic aspects of it. They developed various kinds of hierarchical schemes that placed Africans "close to the ape."[23] At first this practice was based upon the obvious resemblance of certain species of anthropoids to all human beings in facial features. Winthrop Jordan, in a brilliant discussion entitled "Negroes, Apes and Beasts" in his book *White Over Black,* points out the unconscious anxieties that arise from this physical similarity in a culture with a Puritan bias. He felt that Negroes, especially, suffered from unconscious white negative emotions because "it is apparent, however unpalatable the apparency may be, that certain superficial characteristics of the West African Negro sustain (and perhaps helped initiate) the popular connection with the ape." Even Africans, in legends and folklore, speak of these resemblances, although it should be noted that some English writers have also thought they recognized a pronounced simian look in lower-class Irish faces! Darwinism, in its vulgarized forms, accentuated the idea that Negroes were "*closest* to the ape," and this implied inferiority as well as whatever derogatory esthetic appraisals Europeans might make.

Many of the early taxonomists should not be blamed for the use to which the defenders of slavery put their attempts at scientific classification, which in themselves did not imply racial inferiority. Others, however, were outright apologists for slavery and deliberately defamed and caricatured the Africans. Grist for the mills of intellectual speculation was supplied by taxonomists who sometimes accorded desirable attributes to Negroes, although usually in a patronizing manner. Negroes were sometimes said to have a gift for music, to be meek, gentle, forgiving, and long-suffering. Black people sometimes accept these appraisals of their "distinctive" nature.[24]

## The Flourishing of Pseudoscientific Racism

Racist ideology burgeoned during the late nineteenth century when ethnocentric evaluations made by Europeans were merged with theories of biological determinism and anthropometry. Ethnic groups, nations, and tribes about whom judgments of inborn superiority and inferiority were made were now referred to colloquially as "races." Some anthropologists tried without success to restrict the term *race* to groups of human beings characterized by common anthropometric measurements of the cranium and the body and with certain combinations of hair type, skin-color, and eye coloring. However, journalists and politicians insisted upon applying the word *race* to nationalities, referring for instance, to the "British race" or the "French race," neither of which had enough anatomical homogeneity to meet anthropological criteria. The wide variation led to myths about some pure ancestral type that had once existed but had been diluted and sometimes "polluted."

There was a widespread tendency, too, to regard as "races" some ethnic groups that could not be defined by common anatomical traits, the Jewish people being the best-known example. Here the principle was to stress a presumed common heredity that resulted in distinctive behavioral traits and modes of thought and feeling, which were manifested despite the wide range of physical types in the group. Thus, among Jews, the Ashkenazim type from Eastern Europe, the Sephardic type from the Mediterranean, and the Falashas, or Black Jews, from Africa were all considered part of "the Jewish race." During the 1930s, when Hitler's Institute of Racial Biology set out to define Jews as those with at least one Jewish grandparent, it became evident that thousands of these individuals looked like any other Germans. Jews were made identifiable only by being compelled to wear yellow armbands and to use only Jewish names.

The term "race" was also applied to highly variable groups like the Afro-Americans and the Coloreds of South Africa, both products of known types of miscegenation. Some contemporary sociologists use the term social race to refer to any kind of group defined as a race in law or by custom that would not have enough anatomical homogeneity to be defined as a race by anthropometrists. On the whole, however, some degree of physical likeness is assumed or imagined when the word "race" is used to designate a group.

Widespread interest in the classification of plants, animals, and people concentrated attention upon Africans during the eighteenth century. Linnaeus, the great Swedish taxonomist, in his *Systema Naturae* (1735), grouped mankind into four "races" just below the species level: White, Yellow, Red, and Black, each associated with a major continent. The German naturalist Blumenbach introduced the concept of three major races: Caucasian, Mongolian, and Ethiopian. The names represented those geographical areas providing what Blumenbach considered the most esthetically pleasing examples of the races.[25] (It is significant that this principle was eventually abandoned when *Negro* replaced *Ethiopian,* a color designation superseding a geographical one. All of the pleasant associations with which Christendom had invested the highly romanticized Biblical kingdom of Ethiopia were lost when this change was made.)[26] The earliest classifications did not group the races into a hierarchy in which some were considered inferior to others, but this evenhanded treatment did not survive as taxonomy developed.

The American historian Philip Curtin is convinced that the principle of ranking groups used by the eighteenth-century taxonomists was motivated by an unstated ethnocentric assumption. *"All of them began by putting the European variety at the top of the scale. This was natural enough, if only an unthinking reflection of cultural chauvinism* [italics added]." Since these people were white, whiteness took on special characteristics and colored people were classed as inferior. How, then, to rank the others? *"One solution was to concentrate on skin color. If whiteness of skin was the mark of the highest race, than darker races would be inferior in the increasing order of their darkness* [italics added]."[27]

An integral part of racist thought among those who stressed anatomy as a social marker was the belief that external traits of physiognomy reflected inner states of mental ability and personality orientation. There was a deep stratum of popular belief that fostered the easy adoption of what was presented as "scientific" physical anthropology during the early nineteenth century. It was generally believed, for instance, that redheaded people were passionate and fiery, that "coarse" features indicated dull minds, and that "refined" features indicated sharp minds. Negro features were considered *very* coarse. Anthropologists, in classifying the people of Europe, placed a great deal of emphasis upon a single cranial statistic—the cephalic index—which expresses the relation between the length and breadth of the head. What the cephalic index was to the anthropologists, phrenology was to nineteenth-century laymen; thus it was easy to popularize ideas that spoke of dolichocephalic (long-headed) whites as superior to those who were brachycephalic (broad-headed).[28]

Anthropometrists gave a spurious aura of "scientific" authenticity to the process of defining races and assigning racial traits. *During the last decade of the eighteenth century, Peter Campier invented "the facial angle" for calculating the skull's degree of prognathism. This was a so-called diagnostic trait for determining whether a fossil skull or the cranium of a living person was "Negro." A "typical Negro" was supposed to have pronounced prognathism, which, according to Campier, signified the lowest variety of human being.* The French biologist Cuvier became the high priest of the anthropometrists during the early 1800s, and measurements made on the human body were vested with a mystique far out of proportion to their scientific worth.

In his sixteen-volume work entitled *The Animal Kingdom,* published between 1827 and 1835, Cuvier expressed certain unscientific conclusions along with his esthetic preferences. Thus, he wrote:

> The negro *[sic]* race is confined to the South of Mount Atlas. Its characters are black complexion, wooly hair,

> compressed cranium, and flattish nose. In the prominence of the lower part of the face [prognathism], the thickness of the lips, it manifestly approaches to the monkey tribe. The hordes of which this variety is composed have always remained in a state of complete barbarism.

He contrasted the Blacks to the Europeans:

> The Caucasian [race], to which we ourselves belong, is chiefly distinguished by the beautiful form of the head, which approximates to a perfect oval. It is also remarkable for variations in the shade of the complexion, and colour of the hair. From this variety have sprung the most civilized nations, and such as have most generally exercised dominion over the rest of mankind.[29]

Having sung the praises of "The Master Race," Cuvier proceeded to give grudging credit to the "Mongolian variety" for having formed "mighty empires," but noted that "its civilization has long appeared stationary." Curtin notes that only Blumenbach among the biological writers made a serious effort to correct the dominant tendencies of the science of physical anthropology. In some of his later writings, Blumenbach not only moderated his own earlier racial chauvinism but tried to make a reasoned case for Negro equality.[30]

In his early works, however, Blumenbach had contributed to the derogatory stereotype of "*The Negro*" as ugly and repulsive.[31] He wrote that Caucasians had "in general the kind of appearance which *according to our opinion of symmetry* we consider most handsome and becoming [italics added]." Like Tucker, he recognized the relativity of esthetic evaluations. Although Blumenbach had selected the word *Ethiopian* (which had favorable connotations) to represent Africans, his description of the type was unflattering:

> *Colour black ... forehead knotty, uneven, malar bones protruding outward; eyes very prominent; nose thick; mixed up as it were with the wide jaws; alveolar edge narrow, elongated in front; upper primaries obliquely prominent; lips very puffy, chin retreating; many are bandy legged* [italics added].[32]

He later changed the name to "Negro" to fit his unflattering description. Science now had begun to provide "authoritative" details to reinforce an emerging popular caricature of "*The* Negro."

This derogatory stereotype developed during the eighteenth century within a narrow circle of British and continental intellectuals, made up of clergymen, physicians, professors, and philosophers, who lived on salaries from the church or the university or from the largesse of patrons. The group also included a few people whose wealth permitted them to pursue natural history as an unpaid profession or hobby. The physical anthropologists among them contributed measurements made on skeletons and occasional living humans, but before the nineteenth century they, like the other naturalists, had rarely seen an African in their own countries and never in Africa. For details about the distribution of physical types and their customs, all were dependent upon accounts brought out of sub-Saharan Africa by explorers, sailors and soldiers, merchants, and missionaries since the time of classical Greece.

**Propagation of the Negro Stereotype**

Concurrent with the anthropometrists' and intellectuals' "scientific" abstraction, a popular image of "*The* Negro" was elaborated by journalists, dramatists and choreographers, racist orators, cartoonists, book illustrators, and in the theater and cinema.[33] Most of the black people whom white people actually knew had to be continuously explained as exceptions to the stereotypes. Yet this stereotyped image of "*The* Negro" shaped the basic attitudes of fear and contempt directed at Africans and peoples of African descent when they were considered in the abstract or collectively.[34] These stereotypes also became cues for treatment of individual black persons. A caricature of the Negro physique, which distorted reality and overgeneralized certain traits found at one extreme within a very diversified African population, was elaborated. The caricature was then invested with what were assumed to be inherited mental and temperamental qualities.

The stereotype was transmitted to the British and American masses by the popular press, the pulpit, the lecture platform, and the stage. The role of the blackface minstrel show is a case in point. Those in Africa and the Americas who were in continuous contract with black people may sometimes have used the stereotype for propaganda ends, but black individuals were at least recognized in their full range of personality types, daily behaviors, and roles. A wide variety of features and facial expressions was apparent among black people when they were treated as persons, not as abstractions. However, once the stereotype was rooted in the culture, people had an initial tendency to react to their preconceived ideas of what a black person was—or even looked like—rather than to the person in the flesh. Nevertheless, there was nothing about the tendency that absolutely determined the act. Other factors could offset the effect of the stereotype on actual face-to-face behavior.

West Indian planters, anxious to justify the enslavement of Blacks when under attack from humanitarians and religious sectarians in England, used the stereotype continuously, even when their own behavior belied any serious acceptance of it as a guide to conduct. For instance, Edward Long's

*History of Jamaica* (1774) painted an extremely unflattering picture of Africans, and Philip Curtin states that Long was "expressing the common prejudice of the West Indies" when he wrote that Africans were a "brutish, ignorant, idle, crafty, treacherous, bloody, thievish, mistrustful, and superstitious people" with "a covering of wool, like the bestial fleece, instead of hair." According to Long, Blacks were inferior in "faculties of mind" and had a "bestial and fetid smell."[35] Such stereotypes did not inhibit extensive miscegenation or prevent white Jamaicans from becoming dependent upon the food grown and sold by enterprising slaves in their spare time. Derogatory images of this type were not deliberately fostered after the abolition of slavery (between 1834 and 1838) until the churches began to emphasize Christian missionary work in Africa during the latter part of the nineteenth century. Then, as a part of the powerful international missionary movement, West Indian preachers, as well as those in England and the United States, emphasized the "savagery" of the heathen in order to mobilize financial and moral support for their efforts to save souls and to civilize Africa.[36] They added to Long's list of undesirable attributes the idea that cannibalism and human sacrifice were ingrained Negro habits.

It is one of the ironies of the eighteenth and nineteenth centuries that a large proportion of the "friends of the Negro" who fought to abolish both slavery and the slave trade believed in the intellectual inferiority and esthetic repulsiveness of the people whose cause they espoused. Abolitionist Abbé Raynal, who inspired the great black Haitian liberator Toussaint L'Ouverture, wrote that "negro blood is perhaps mingled in all the ferments which transform, corrupt and destroy our people." Voltaire wrote that the whites were "superior to these Negroes, as the Negroes are to the apes, as the apes to the oysters."[37] Thomas Jefferson was thus not alone in his belief that Negroes had the right to

be free but did not have the intellectual potential of other races. Until his experiences with black abolitionists and black soldiers changed his mind during the Civil War, Abraham Lincoln's attitudes were close to those of Jefferson, including the belief that once the slaves were freed they should be deported from the United States.[38]

## THE CHANGING FUNCTIONS OF RACISM AND COLOR PREJUDICE

### Ideology and Institutional Change

The coincidence of humanitarian and religious reform movements with a decline in the profitability of slavery in the Americas led to the abolition of the transatlantic slave trade and slavery. This occurred in British territories between 1834 and 1838, and earlier in much of Latin America. After a four-year Civil War in the United States, the contradiction between the sentiments expressed in the Declaration of Independence and actual practice was eliminated with the emancipation of the slaves in 1865. Brazil and Cuba, in the 1880s, were the last countries to give the quietus to *racial slavery* in the Western Hemisphere.

However, neither color prejudice nor racism disappeared with the end of slavery. In the United States, white workers found both to be useful tools in their attempts to restrict the competition of the exslaves who had become free workers, and employers used both race prejudice and racism in a policy of divide-and-rule toward the American working class. Racial hostility that might have slowly disappeared was now revitalized because of functional utility. Economic interests, racism, and color prejudice reinforced each other. The type of extreme vilification of black people represented by the Jamaican planter Edward Long was very rare in the United States until after slavery was abolished. Then competition between Blacks and poor whites elicited a kind of virulent stereotyping that the planter class had never found necessary in defending its interests in the South of the United States. While black people remained the primary target of White Racism in the United States, Orientals and Latin Americans were victimized too, and white immigrant workers became the objects of racism not reinforced by color. Antiracist countercurrents existed but had little influence. Then a halt in the escalation of racism occurred in the 1930s when the worldwide fight against Hitlerism began and institutional antiracist action emerged.[39]

Overt ideological racism has declined impressively everywhere since World War II except in the Republic of South Africa, and it is now in slow retreat there. More subtle forms of institutional racism have replaced ideological racism and, through policies of "tokenism" and "integration," have made color prejudice a less important force in North America than it was before the Civil Rights Revolution in the South and the Black Power upsurge throughout the country.

## Twentieth-Century Forms of Racism and Color Prejudice

As slavery was disappearing in the Western Hemisphere, the partition of Africa was beginning. By the time of the outbreak of World War I, all of Africa except Ethiopia and Liberia had been divided into colonies or protectorates of some European power (along with one Afro-European condominium). Both color prejudice and racism were fused in these structures of domination to constitute a system of White Racism. At the ideological level, the so-called Hamitic Hypothesis emerged to explain that all advanced cultural development in Africa had derived from lighter-skinned, more Caucasoid, less Negroid people.[40] In French, Portuguese, and Belgian colonies in Africa, the favoring of mulatto progeny born out

of wedlock to the consorts of administrators and settlers generated social strata in which light skin-color became an index of high status. Although World War II began a reversal of many of the processes that have sustained White Racism, that phenomenon has not been fully eliminated. South Africa is the last bastion of White Supremacy on the continent. Furthermore, color prejudice in favor of whiteness has persisted in some social contexts within new African nations, despite the fact that, in the political sphere, Africanization has often tipped the scales in the other direction.

Despite the disappearance of colonial imperialism in the Caribbean during the 1960s, *color* prejudice against blackness has remained strong in some areas and insidiously active in others. This is also true in many parts of Latin America. In some places it is functional only in the private sphere when people are choosing intimate associates and marriage partners. But in other areas there is widespread color discrimination in employment and political preferment.[41] There is reason to believe that in public situations Negroid physiognomy or even mere darkness of complexion can seriously limit individual opportunity throughout Latin America and much of the Muslim world. There is considerable disagreement as to the degree of persistence of color prejudice, especially against Negroid people, in areas where socialist revolutions have taken place and where official opposition to all forms of color prejudice as well as discrimination exists.[42]

## BLACK PERSPECTIVES ON RACISM

### Defining Racism

What came to be called "vindicating the Negro" emerged to counteract White Racism. It involved correcting stereotypes, setting the record straight, and substituting a more accurate picture of reality.

This process, begun by literate white antislavery leaders and unlettered Afro-American preachers using Biblical arguments, was assumed as a duty by literate black ministers during the late eighteenth century. They developed a prepolitical ideology called "Ethiopianism." By the end of the nineteenth century, black historians had developed a Pan-African perspective as an important part of the "vindication movement," and the names of Edward Wilmot Blyden and W. E. B. Du Bois are well known in this regard.[43]

The first generation of black intellectuals who became concerned with the historical and psychological roots of racism utilized the concepts available to social scientists of their time.[44] By the end of World War I, the "vindicationist" focus was on the problem of changing the stereotypes and the conventional social attitudes clustered around them, of trying to alter those "overgeneralized prejudgments" that social psychologist Gordon W. Allport defines as always present in "racial prejudice." He, like others of his profession, stresses the point that "prejudice is not inborn but acquired," and that "throughout childhood and youth there are many opportunities for irreversible and unfavorable belief systems to become set." Prejudices operating as "inflexible, rigid and erroneous generalizations about groups of people" may express themselves in behavior that denies members of some stereotyped group full access to economic, political, and social opportunities. If the group is defined as a "race," such prejudice can give rise to *racial* discrimination. Although racial discrimination "ultimately rests on *prejudice*," the two processes are not identical. Individuals may harbor prejudices without expressing them if the sociocultural situation provides no reward for doing so or actually provides punishments for those who discriminate against another race.[45]

During the 1950s and 1960s Afro-American scholars became more concerned with refining the concept of racism, than with discussing either prejudice or discrimination, because racism is a concept that places emphasis upon underlying cognitive orientations that find expression in attitudes and behavior and affect systems of control. As used throughout the 1930s and 1940s, when Blacks became familiar with the term, *racism* was used almost exclusively to mean a systematic theory of innate and inherited inferiority or superiority of human beings. It was later used to emphasize differential power relationships.

Within the past two decades, the term *racism* has acquired many referents other than the system of ideas that grades people invidiously in a hierarchy. In fact, the term has become a useful propaganda stick with which to beat a variety of enemies. However, continued imprecision of definition will make it less and less useful in achieving black liberation goals. That is why black spokesmen have tended to cling to the restricted cluster of meanings subsumed in a definition proposed by Stokely Carmichael and Charles V. Hamilton in *Black Power* (1967): "*the predication of decisions and policies on considerations of race for purposes of subordinating a racial group* [italics added]."[46] They place emphasis upon the *actions* of one group as it attempts to dominate and control another, the subordinated group being a *racial* group, rather than upon racism as ideology. A few black scholars and leaders in liberation struggles display an interest, as intellectuals, in the constant refinement of concepts used by white scholars as they discuss the plight of black people, but most prefer to work with social science formulations that help them to clarify goals and to devise techniques for changing the status of black people vis-à-vis white power structures.[47]

## Classifying Types of Racism

The Carmichael-Hamilton book drew a distinction between *individual racism* and *institutional racism* that quickly gained wide currency. The term *institutional racism* is now used to describe situations where, although there may not be deliberate intent to act in an unfavorable, discriminatory fashion, the objective result of various actions is reinforcement of subordination and control over a racial group and an inequitable distribution of power and prestige.[48] The term is used even in some cases where discrimination on the basis of race or color within a social system does not require the support of a body of racist theory and may persist in spite of prevailing antiracist ideology. For example, the rules, regulations, and norms for recruitment of personnel into a voluntary association, a bureaucracy, or an educational institution are sometimes set up in such a way that they automatically operate to the disadvantage of some racial group. In such a case, people whom Gordon Allport would classify as "unprejudiced discriminators" often enforce rules that have a racist outcome.[49]

Affirmative action programs are directed at coping with such forms of institutional racism, and this conceptualization has been of great value during a period in U.S. history when it has become unfashionable for whites to admit belief in the inherent inferiority of any racial or ethnic group, when some white people accept the idea that to be racist is to be "sick,"[50] and when the increased economic and political power of nonwhite peoples often makes expressions of overt prejudice counterproductive. In fact, reversal of the antiblack stereotype has actually become advantageous to some business enterprises in a period of consumerism, when display advertising directed at black people as a potential market utilizes attractive black images, and when multinational corporations publicize pictures of their black employees. But racism in more covert forms remains.

A South African Bantu scholar-psychiatrist, Noel Chabani Manganyi, reflecting upon these changes, has called attention to a distinction drawn by Joel Kovel, an American scholar, between *dominative* racism and *metaracism,* and sounded a warning.

> Popular opinion would lead us to believe that the end of the overtly colonial period in certain parts of Africa and elsewhere and the elimination of discriminatory practices against blacks in the Western world marked the end of racism against blacks ... The dominative racist thrived in the United States and in parts of Europe and Africa before independence when manifest social-political institutions existed to support racism and racist behavior. With the disappearance of these structures, the metaracist, sleeker in his ways, made his appearance ... A metaracist may very well continue to be afflicted with unconscious racist fantasies that have survived the changes in manifest social organization. He remains a social risk because, in racially extreme situations, he can always be expected to regress into the dominative mold.

Concerned with the psychological dimensions of "white backlash," with what whites perceive as "reverse discrimination" in the United States, and with changes he foresees someday in his native South Africa, Manganyi continued:

> Institutional changes involving political, social and economic systems represent an essential beginning in the process of social change. To eradicate racism in the institutional life of a society it is not sufficient to demystify the unconscious

ramifications involved in the fantasy social structure underlying such a system. But in clinical experience, patients in psychotherapy desperately resist the possible loss of their neuroses. On the collective level, the difficulties of working through the fantasy social structure supporting racism raises many practical problems which society prefers to ignore.

Manganyi is among those psychologists who are convinced that this "fantasy social structure" arises from a type of white child rearing that equates blackness with the devalued lower parts of the body (genital-anal). Subordinating black people serves certain psychological needs, related to "the alienation of man in industrial society," that have come from "elevating the mechanism of repression into a virtue in the organization of society."[51]

Some writers, among them Eldridge Cleaver in *Soul on Ice* and Frantz Fanon in *Black Skins, White Masks,* emphasize a view similar to Manganyi's neo-Freudian analysis, but most black intellectuals do not rank this kind of explanation very high. Whether Black Nationalists, pragmatic liberals, or Marxists, they usually share the prevalent social-environmental explanations provided by academic sociology and psychology. An extreme form of Black Nationalism rejects psychoanalytical explanations of White Racism but accepts even more deterministic theories, part mystical, part biological. For instance, the Black Muslims once defined all Whites as "Devils" whose inborn nature it was to oppress colored people. Such views have even penetrated Afro-American intellectual circles. For instance, in 1974, the *Black Scholar* published a debate between the Afro-American poet Madhubuti (once known as Don Lee) and Kalamu Ya Salaam, another Afro-American writer, on the issue of whether the white person is "by nature" antiblack. Madhubuti asserted that Blacks have had to bear the burden of inborn white racist propensities. Kalamu Ya Salaam objected, insisting that "what your color means and/or says about you varies directly from society to society, directly dependent on historical and contemporary conditions. The meaning of skin color, just as skin color itself, is also not static, but rather is relative, is dependent on time, place, and circumstances." This view has been elaborated by a number of black scholars engaged in reconciling Marxism with an ideology of black solidarity, and is taken for granted by most black scholars regardless of their politics.[52]

## Racism and Capitalism

Oliver Cromwell Cox, an Afro-Trinidadian sociologist, has suggested that the concept of racism is so time-bound and culture-bound that it has no applicability beyond the past five or six hundred years, and only limited pertinence within that time span. He warns against confusing racism and race prejudice with the more general concept of ethnocentrism. *Cox insists that, unlike color prejudice and slavery, both of which antedated it, racism was uniquely associated with capitalist growth and expansion.* He wrote in 1976:

> Racism, like race prejudice, is a relatively recent human development; it did not always exist ... Racism, as we know it in modern times, is not merely verbal recognition of physical differences, ethnocentric comparisons among peoples, early mythological speculations about various known peoples in the design of creation, or invidious remarks by ancient conquerors about the physical and cultural traits of the vanquished ... Racism ... provides Europeans with a moral rationale for their subjugation and exploitation of "inferior peoples."[53]

In an earlier work, Cox had stated his essentially Marxist view in stronger terms. After defining "racial antagonism" as a phenomenon that "had its rise only in modern times," he proceeded to state the hypothesis that

> racial exploitation and race prejudice developed among Europeans with the rise of capitalism and nationalism, and ... because of the worldwide ramifications of capitalism all racial antagonisms can be traced to the policies and attitudes of the leading capitalist people, the white people of Europe and North America.[54]

Most Marxists would make a more cautious formulation today, stressing the point that while racism as a systematic doctrine and racial prejudice institutionalized in systems of caste, class, and slavery were products of capitalist expansion overseas, this did not apply to *all* racial antagonisms." Yet Marxist scholarship has not seriously addressed itself to the special problem of the origins and functions of racial prejudice directed against Negroes and blackness (nor has non-Marxian scholarship done so, for that matter).

During the Depression years, as several varieties of Marxist thought became prevalent and popular, some historians and social scientists implied that "blackness" became a symbol of low status and undesirability only with the fifteenth-century expansion of Europe overseas, the subsequent rise of the transatlantic slave trade, and the later colonial imperialism in Africa. Derogation of blackness was seen as one aspect of an ideology elaborated to defend the exploitation of Africans and their descendants as well as to "brainwash" them into accepting their subordinate status. Such traditional Marxist analyses did not draw a clear distinction between color prejudice as a variable distinct from both racism and specific types of social systems such as slavery, caste, or class. Third World Marxists have, however, forced recognition of these distinctions. They stress that Africans and people of African descent have had to bear the heavy burden of being black in addition to the class burden of being slaves, peasants, and proletarians. Their insights have brought greater clarity to Marxist analysis.[55]

Color prejudice targeted against black people is only one form of racial prejudice and discrimination, and one aspect of White Racism. It existed long before the emerging capitalist system-shaped—the character of modern racism. Because skin-color prejudice is a specialized subset of attitudes and behaviors about race that affect the fate of all black people, it is the primary concern of this work. Our emphasis in this book is upon searching out the way in which skin-color prejudice against black people originated, describing how it became articulated to modern capitalism. Another, forthcoming book, "Africa and the Black Diaspora," explains where and why it persists in the Western Hemisphere in the form of postslavery systems of caste and class in which skin-color remains a significant factor in social stratification and social mobility.

Color prejudice appears in various forms in some of the socialist societies replacing capitalist economies in various parts of the world, although institutionalized racism is absent. In reacting to White Racism, currents of antiwhite feeling have arisen among colored people, and in some areas these have been incorporated into political movements for political independence or for the establishment of more egalitarian societies. Jean-Paul Sartre used the term *antiracist racism* to describe this phenomenon, but some black leaders refuse to accept the designation *racist* for their political use of antiwhite sentiments. This necessary mobilization of the oppressed around the issue of race has a reactionary potential, nevertheless, that must be resisted.[56]

An understanding of the dynamics of prejudice against "Negroidness" can be furthered by comparing early stages of single societies with later stages (diachronic approach), and by comparing different societies existing at the same time (synchronic approach). Both methods are used in the chapters that follow the discussion of race relations theory in chapter 2.

# PART 2

## THEORETICAL AND CONCEPTUAL PERSPECTIVES

# RACIAL ATTITUDES RESEARCH

## DEBATES, MAJOR ADVANCES, AND FUTURE DIRECTIONS

*By Rashawn Ray*

Most psychological studies document that attitudes rarely change. Sociological studies, on the other hand, highlight the importance of institutional arrangements and social contexts as impacting attitudes and behaviors in spite of certain beliefs.* The racial attitudes literature is an exemplar of the connection between psychological and sociological perspectives (Bobo 1988; Bobo Zubrinsky 1996; Bobo and Fox 2003). Racial attitudes originate from psychological studies on intergroup attitudes to explain prejudice. Theories and explanations used to assess racial attitude trends tend to develop from theoretical and empirical research on race and intergroup relations. Intergroup relations is a disciplinary hybrid between sociology and political science (Brewer and Kramer 1985). Before Schuman and Gruenberg's (1970) and Pettigrew's

(1979) research, the literature in this area focused on cognition, prejudice, and group position (Festinger and Kelley 1951; Allport 1954; Blumer 1958; Pettigrew 1958; Frisbie and Neidert 1977). In the 1980s, racial attitude research began to be investigated by sociologists to formulate theories to explain the trends about race and racism (Jackman and Muha 1984; Jackman and Crane 1986; Schuman, Steeh, and Bobo 1985; Schuman and Bobo 1988; Bobo 1988). This research mostly focused on Black/White patterns. More recently, racial attitudes research has become more multiracial (Bobo and Zubrinsky 1996; Bonilla-Silva 1996; Dixon 2006; Hunt 2007) and cross-comparative (Quillian 1995; 1996; Pettigrew 1998).

While there have been many theoretical and empirical debates that have shaped sociological understanding of the causes and consequences of racial attitudes, I choose to focus on what I consider the most prominent ones. Theoretically, I illuminate major theories on prejudice including theories on group position, racism, and contact. I then offer insights into the theoretical, methodological, and empirical directions that I see the racial attitudes literature progressing in the 21st century.

---

* Eagly and Chaiken (1993) define an attitude as "a psychological tendency that is expressed by evaluating a particular entity with some degree of favor or disfavor" (Eagly and Chaiken 1993: 1). Moreover, attitudes are tendencies, which are not essentially enduring dispositions but can be learned and unlearned and often result in a good or bad evaluation.

## MAJOR THEORETICAL DEBATES

### Prejudice and Group Position

Prejudice can be categorized as the cognitive or emotional/affective component of intergroup perceptions (Brewer and Kramer 1985; Eagly and Chaiken 1993). It is a type of attitude that is generally related to a specific discriminatory behavior. In order to show that prejudice attitudes lead to specific acts of discrimination, there must be other dispositional factors that can speak to this relationship. Blumer's theory of prejudice (1958) argues that "a sense of group position grows out of a history of unequal power relations between groups" (Quillian 1995: 588). This is commonly termed "fraternal deprivation." Contrary to fraternal deprivation, Bobo's (1983) "realistic conflict theory" argues that the subordinate group is a threat to the dominant group's resources and accepted practices (Bobo 1983). Realistic conflict theory illuminates the link between subjective group perceptions and real group interests (Quillian 1995).

Quillian (1995) uses multi-level data to extend Blumer's theory of prejudice (1958), evaluate immigration, and expand past the Black/White dichotomy. Investigating group threat in 12 European countries, Quillian (1995) finds that the proportional representation of the subordinate group and current economic conditions impact collective group threat. He asserts that future research must incorporate individual- and group-level interactions to determine the specific factors that cause racial/ethnic or national group threat. In a subsequent study, Quillian (1996) investigates the impact regional and temporal changes have on attitudes toward African-Americans. Scholars know little about how racial attitudes have changed over time relative to regional and temporal changes. Quillian (1996) finds that the growth in income explains about 25 percent of the total decline in prejudice from the early 1970s to the mid-1980s.

About 50 percent of the traditional prejudice displayed in the South can be accounted for by regional differences in per capita income and racial composition. Due to the proportional representation and lower incomes of Whites living in the South, as compared to Whites from other regions, they may perceive Blacks as more of a competitive threat.

Bobo and Hutchings (1996) aim to expand Blumer's theory of group position to a multiracial social context. Using data from the 1992 Los Angeles County Social Survey that spans Blacks, Whites, Latinos, and Asians, they find that Blumer's theory offers the most compelling theory for including social psychological processes to explain that self-interest, prejudice, stratification beliefs, group threat, and competition are rooted historically in collective and relational contexts. Racial attitudes are contingent upon the race/ethnicity of the group being evaluated and the race/ethnicity of the evaluator. Individuals who perceive their group to face unjust treatment are more likely to report that other groups are competitive threats. Moreover, African-Americans, followed by Latinos, Asians, and Whites, in that order, are most likely to perceive other groups as competitive threats. Bobo and Hutchings (1996) claim that the racial subordination that African-Americans have experienced is the reason for these findings. Structural-thinking decreases Whites' probability of perceiving Blacks as competitive threats. Individual-thinking, on the other hand, leads Whites to perceive Latinos and Asians as competitive threats.

Pettigrew's (1979) "ultimate attribution error" probably represents one of the strongest theoretical debates that have shaped the causes of racial attitudes.[*] The ultimate attribution error states that desirable characteristics exhibited by individuals

---

[*] Pettigrew's theory extended Allport's (1954) cognitive analysis of prejudice.

in the ingroup are attributable to innate dispositions, whereas desirable characteristics exhibited by individuals in the outgroup are attributable to exceptional behavior or social structural and contextual factors. Conversely, undesirable characteristics exhibited by individuals in the outgroup are more likely to be perceived by individuals in the ingroup as innate dispositions. Pettigrew (1958) and Tajfel's work (1970) documents that prejudice attitudes are not innate personality characteristics but rather socialized phenomena. Despite consistent findings that there are no innate differences between racial/ethnic groups, many Whites' racial attitudes about Blacks still center on innate differences.

## Racism

While many theories have been formulated to explain racial attitude trends, there is agreement that race matters and that the current social arrangement of society privileges Whites over minorities (Mcintosh 1988; Wise 2008). Some theories on modern and subtle forms of racism include symbolic racism (Kinder and Sears 1981), aversive racism (Gaertner and Dovidio (1986), ambivalent racism (Katz et al. 1986), and structural racism (Bonilla-Silva 1997). Symbolic racism argues that overt, blatant racism has been supplemented for a new type of covert racism that is difficult to recognize according to the traditional discrimination criteria. Instead, racism is represented by symbolic beliefs about social issues and policies (e.g., affirmative action and housing). In other words, attitudes normally categorized as self-interest, "are actually reflections of residual racial resentments and resistance to racial integration" (Brewer and Kramer 1985: 231).

Bobo's line of work (1983; 1988) challenges this position and argues that group conflict explains Whites' opposition to busing and housing. Similar to Bobo's position, Pettigrew (1985) argues that symbolic racism is not symbolic at all but real in

its consequences. Still, Pettigrew asserts that racism must be placed into a broader context in order to capture the effects of self-interest, stratification beliefs, and cognitive biases. Drawing attention to internal racism, Williams and colleagues (1999) find that after controlling for racial prejudice, Whites who are for equal opportunities believe that certain racial/ethnic groups dominate over others and believe in the innate superiority of Whites. Interestingly, some of these individuals support affirmative action and government help for Blacks.

## Contact Theory

Allport's (1958) contact theory of prejudice asserts that interracial contact must meet five conditions to be affective—1) contact should not occur in a competitive context; 2) contact must be a series of contacts compared to one event; 3) contact must be personal, informal, and one-on-one; 4) contact should be legal; and 5) contact environment or setting must be perceived as equal.* Festinger and Kelley (1951) find that social contact with members of a lower status group increases favorability if members of the higher status group already have favorable perceptions of the lower status group. Comparatively, social contact increases the unfavorability and hostility toward the lower status group if members of the higher status group already have unfavorable perceptions of the lower status group. In other words, social contact enhances preconceived notions individuals have about groups going into the interaction. Festinger terms this the "communication theory of attitude change."

---

* Jackman and Crane (1986) argue that unfortunately few interracial contacts occur in this manner. Dixon (2006) goes into much more detail about contact theory and ethnic conflict in this anthology.

Although this theoretical premise on group dynamics has been tested through the years, recent research on contact theory argues that the communication theory of attitude change established by Festinger varies by race/ethnicity (Dixon 2006). Dixon (2006) finds that group threat and contact theories of prejudice operate differently for African-Americans, Asians, and Latinos interactions with Whites. While contact with Asians and Latinos reduces the group threat perceived by Whites, contact with African-Americans does not. In other words, favorable interactions with an African-American only change the perception Whites have of that individual and not all African-Americans. Comparatively, social contact with Latinos and Asians alters the entire perception of the group and reduces group threat. From the perspective of Whites, Dixon (2006) argues there seems to be a racial/ethnic hierarchy whereby Whites are at the top, followed by Asians, then Latinos, and ending with African-Americans on the bottom.

Jackman and Crane (1986) examine the major assumptions of the contact theory of prejudice. Contrary to some literature that suggests intimacy is key for altering racial attitudes, they find that personal interracial contact is selective. Moreover, intimacy is less important relative to the socioeconomic status of the individual coming in contact with Whites. In other words, Whites' negative attitudes toward Blacks decrease significantly when they have Black friends whose socioeconomic status is higher than their own. This mechanism does not, however, decrease Whites' racial attitudes of neighborhood integration or racial policies. Jackman and Crane (1986) conclude optimistically that the diversity of contacts is more important than the intimacy of contacts. They maintain a positive view that with time prejudice attitudes will diminish as more Whites have contact with higher-status Blacks. McLaren (2003) finds that intimate contact in the form of friendships can reduce anti-immigrant

prejudice in Europe. Similar to Jackman and Crane (1986), however, McLaren (2003) is cautious to translate these findings to the U.S. where Blacks have had a unique experience with racial inequality.

Bobo and Zubrinsky (1996) investigate intergroup attitudes towards racial integration. They assert that in order to understand racial attitudes, causal models must incorporate the attitudes of other racial/ethnic groups to progress past the Black/White dichotomy. Using data from the 1992 Los Angeles County Social Survey, they find that negative group stereotypes are still vast and prominent. For Whites, this translates into opposition toward racial integration. Among Blacks and Latinos, hostile feelings of other groups form opposition toward racial integration. Although cities such as Los Angeles are regarded as more diverse, Bobo and Zubrinsky (1996) find that diversity may actually lead to more racial segregation, prejudice, and discrimination. As a result, they do not see racial segregation ending in the near future. Similar to Dixon (2006), these scholars argue that there is a clear racial hierarchy with Whites at the top and Blacks at the bottom. These scholars' assertions direct attention to Bonilla-Silva's (2004) article on moving toward a tri-racial stratification system in the U.S.

Overall, while scholars agree that contact is important, there is much debate as to what type of contact and how much contact matters. Contact also varies by racial group and is dictated by how many racial groups are in a particular social environment. Still, the racial attitudes literature has come to a consensus on some issues. First, scholars generally agree that sources of racial attitudes derive from prejudice, racism, and group position. Second, innate differences, motivation, and structural racism are the main explanations for the current racial and socioeconomic hierarchy (Bobo and Kluegel 1993; Quillian 1995; Schuman and Krysan 1999; Hunt 2007). Third, education does not always mean more liberal racial attitudes (Jackman and Muha 1984; Steeh and Schuman 1992).[*] Fourth, Whites' racial attitudes do not always align with their attitudes toward race-target policies (Bobo and Kluegel 1993). Finally, proportional representation and region matter (Quillian 1995; 1996; Taylor 1998; Hunt 2007).

## FUTURE DIRECTIONS IN RACIAL ATTITUDE RESEARCH

From a social psychological standpoint, early work in the area of cognitive and group processes usually lacked a distinct empirical focus and mainly limited its gaze on Whites or employed a White-centered perspective for other racial/ethnic groups (Garza 1969; Harrington and Fine 2000). Accordingly, little is known about what minority groups think about Whites, what minority groups think of one another, and what minority groups think of their own group. In other words, scholars do not know much about what racial/ethnic groups think of themselves in relation to other groups, particularly adolescents who will be the next generation of creators and sustainers of cultural, economic, and social capital. Furthermore, we still know very little about minorities' racial attitudes over time.

The racial attitudes literature also needs to become more intersectional in its empirical research. This literature has at times failed to follow the data

and explore intersections among variables such as gender and class that mediate findings on race. Pettigrew, along with a few other scholars including Bobo and Schuman, has argued for years that race cannot be evaluated as a single indicator any longer and must incorporate class effects. While I concur with Pettigrew (1985), it is important to add gender as an intersectional variable.[†] While race is likely to remain at the center of social life, it cannot be evaluated without assessing its relationship with class and gender (Bonilla-Silva 1997; Yancey 2003). Accordingly, attitude research needs to address past experiences, events, and life stressors that possibly trigger sustaining attitudes. Social context also needs to be incorporated (Eagly and Chaiken 1993). Additionally, researchers need to start taking into account situational variables to assess how the social environment and timing of data collection impact racial attitudes (Hill 1981; Maio et al. 2003).

To make these extensions, racial attitude research needs to include a diverse set of methodological procedures. Current survey causal models cannot explain whether policy beliefs are a result of policy changes or policy choices, or assess whether racial attitudes are a direct result of motivation or perseverance explanations. This is a major reason for many of the theoretical debates and empirical

---

[*] Jackman and Muha (1984) integrate literature on intergroup attitudes and educational institutions to argue for a new approach to explain racial attitudes. They assert that dominant social groups typically construct ideologies that legitimate the status quo. In turn, individuals with higher levels of education are usually "sophisticated practitioners" of their group's ideology (Jackman and Muha 1984: 751). These sophisticated practitioners then employ savvy and sophisticated strategies to not seem prejudice.

[†] Johnson and Marini (1998) examine gender differences in racial attitudes. Using a national sample of high school seniors, they find that women express more favorable attitudes than men. White women, compared to White men, express a significantly greater amount of favorability towards Blacks. This attitudinal difference between White men and White women are also captured in Weis' (2004) vivid account of White working class adolescents in rural America. However, Weis also finds that as these women age, they become some of the main sustainers of racial inequality by acting as gatekeepers between their children and classmates of other races.

limitations of this body of work. Survey-based experiments reduce the effects of respondent self-reporting, promote a step by step process to hypotheses generation and testing, allow for more generalizability, and can be incorporated into survey analyses that classify individuals by common social demographics (Schuman and Bobo 1988).

**Theoretical Linkages to Social Psychology**

Although I critique the racial attitudes literature above, it has much to offer social psychological research on social structure and personality (SSP) and theories on group processes. First, Bobo (2000) asserts that a Du Boisian perspective on racial attitudes is warranted. By incorporating Du Bois' (1899, 1903, 1939) theoretical framework into analyses on racial attitudes, research will be in a better position to link macrosocial conditions to microsocial processes and display the interplay between social structure and personality. Second, this research can be related to expectation states theory and exchange theory. Since exchange theory is linked with economics and expectation states theory is linked with social identity theory, they appease part of the racial attitude debate that has resonated in the literature for over 25 years. Given that racial attitudes are interpreted primarily to be individualistic (Jackman and Crane 1986), social identity can place these attitudes more on a group level.

Bobo and Hutchings (1996) suggest that future research needs to incorporate large multiracial samples from a variety of communities and settings, untangle the effects of power resources as they relate to proportional representation, and incorporate skill levels and political organizations, leadership, participation, and relative group economic inequality. I would also add religion to this future research agenda. Religion should be explored to see what

type of effect it has on racial attitudes, particularly with the expansion of multiracial, mega churches.

Overall, the racial attitudes literature needs to become more multi-ethnic, multi-method, and multivariate in its analysis. The literature should incorporate proportional representation, immigration, skin color, and religion as variables of interest. Racial attitude research can also benefit from incorporating social psychological theories including social identity theory, expectation states theory, exchange theory, and the framework of SSP in order to make larger claims to explain some of the causes and consequences of racial inequality. I hope that this section of the anthology that focuses on racial formation, individual and structural racism, prejudice and discrimination, whiteness, race-gender-sexuality, colorism, lookism, assimilation, immigration, group threat theory, contact theory, ethnic conflict, citizenship, nationalism, and human rights continues to move the literature in that direction.

## SUPPLEMENTAL READINGS AND RESOURCES

Allport, Gordon W. 1954. *The Nature of Prejudice.* Reading, MA: Addison-Wesley.

Bobo. Lawrence. 1988. "Attitudes toward the Black Political Movement: Trends, Meaning, and Effects on Racial Policy Preferences." *Social Psychology Quarterly* 51: 287–302.

Bobo. Lawrence and Vincent L. Hutchings. 1996. "Perceptions of Racial Group Competition: Extending Blumer's Theory of Group Position to a Multiracial Social Context." *American Sociological Review* 61: 951–972.

Bobo, Lawrence and James R. Kluegel. 1993. "Opposition to Race-Targeting: Self-Interest, Stratification Ideology, or Racial Attitudes?" *American Sociological Review* 58: 443–464.

Bobo. Lawrence and Camille L. Zubrinsky. 1996. "Attitudes on Residential Integration: Perceived Status Differences, Mere In-Group Preference, or Racial Prejudice?" *Social Forces*, 74: 883-909.

Bonilla-Silva, Eduardo. 1997. "Rethinking Racism: Toward a Structural Interpretation." *American Sociological Review* 62: 465–480.

Bonilla-Silva, Eduardo. 2003. *Racism without Racist: Color-Blind Racism and the Persistence of Racial Inequality in the United States*. Lanham, MD: Rowman and Littlefield.

Brewer, Marilynn B. and Kramer, Roderick M. 1985. "The Psychology of Inter-group Attitudes and Behavior." *Annual Review of Psychology* 36: 219–43.

Cobas, Jose and Joe Feagin. 2008. "Language Oppression and Resistance: The Case of Middle Class Latinos in the United States." *Ethnic and Racial Studies* 31: 390–410.

Du Bois, W. E. B. 1901. "The Relation of the Negroes to the Whites in the South," *Annals of the American Academy of Political and Social Science*, 18: 121–140.

Eagly, A. H. and S. Chaiken. 1993. *The Psychology of Attitudes*. Forth Worth, TX: Harcourt Brace Jovanovich.

Feagin, Joe R. 1991. "The Continuing Significance of Race: Antiblack Discrimination in Public Places," *American Sociological Review* 56: 101–116.

Festinger, Leon and Harold H. Kelley. 1951. *Changing Attitudes through Social Contact*. Ann Arbor, MI: Lithoprinted.

Frankenberg, Ruth. 1993. *White Women, Race Matters: The Social Construction of Whiteness*. University of Minnesota Press.

Frisbie, W. Parker and Lisa Neidert. 1977. "Inequality and the Relative Size of Minority Populations: A Comparative Analysis." *American Journal of Sociology* 82: 1007–1030.

Gaertner, S. L., and Dovidio, J. F. 1986. "The Aversive form of Racism." In J. F. Dovidio and S. L. Gaertner (Eds.). *Prejudice, Discrimination, and Racism*. Orlando, FL: Academic Press.

Garza, Joseph M. 1969. "Race, the Achievement Syndrome, and Perception of Opportunity." *Phylon* 30: 338–354.

Harrington, Brooke, and Fine, Gary. A. 2000 "Opening the 'Black Box:' Small Groups and Twenty-First-Century Sociology." *Social Psychology Quarterly* 63 312–323.

Herring, Cedric. 2003. "Skin Deep and Complexion in the 'Color-Blind Era'" Pps. 1–21 In *Skin Deep: How Race and Complexion Matter in the "Color-Blind Era."* (Eds.) Cedric Herring, Verna M. Keith, and Hayward Derrick Horton. Chicago: University of Illinois Press.

Hunt, Matthew O. 2007. "African-American, Hispanic, and White Beliefs about Black-White Inequality: 1977–2004." *American Sociological Review* 72: 390–415.

Jackman, Mary R. and Marie Crane. 1986. ""Some of My Best Friends Are Black …": Interracial Friendship and Whites' Racial Attitudes." *The Public Opinion Quarterly* 50: 459–486.

Jackman, Mary R. and Michael J. Muha. 1984. "Education and Intergroup Attitudes: Moral Enlightenment, Superficial Democratic Commitment, or Ideological Refinement?" *American Sociological Review* 49: 751–769.

Katz, I., Wackenhut, J., & Hass, R.G. 1986. " Pps. 35–59 In J. F. Dovidio and S. L. Gaertner (Eds.). *Prejudice, Discrimination, and Racism*. Orlando, FL: Academic Press.

Kinder, Donald R., and David 0. Sears. 1981. "Prejudice and Politics: Symbolic Racism versus Racial Threats to the Good Life." *Journal of Personality and Social Psychology* 40: 414–31.

Koopmans, Ruud and Paul Statham. 1999. "Challenging the Liberal Nation-State? Post-nationalism, Multiculturalism and the Collective Claims Making of Migrants and Ethnic Minorities in

Britain and Germany." *The American Journal of Sociology* 105: 652–696.

Li, Qiong and Marilynn B. Brewer. 2004. What Does it Mean to be an American? Patriotism, Nationalism, and American Identity after 9/11. *Political Psychology* 25: 727–739.

Lieberson, Stanley. 1961. "A Societal Theory of Race and Ethnic Relations." *American Review of Sociology* 26: 902–910.

McLaren, Lauren M. 2003. "Anti-Immigrant Prejudice in Europe: Contact, Threat Perception, and Preferences for the Exclusion of Migrants." *Social Forces* 81: 909–936.

Pettigrew, Thomas F. 1958. "Personality and Sociocultural Factors in Intergroup Attitudes: A Cross-National Comparison." *Journal of Conflict Resolution* 2: 29–42.

Pettigrew, Thomas F. 1979. "The Ultimate Attribution Error: Extending Allport's Cognitive Analysis of Prejudice." *Personality and Social Psychology Bulletin* 5: 461–476.

Pettigrew, Thomas F. 1998. "Reactions toward the New Minorities of Western Europe." *Annual Review of Sociology* 24: 77–103.

Quillian, Lincoln. 1995. "Prejudice as a Response to Perceived Group Threat: Population Composition and Anti-Immigrant and Racial Prejudice in Europe." *American Sociological Review* 60: 586–611.

Quillian, Lincoln. 1996. "Group Threat and Regional Change in Attitudes Toward African-Americans." *The American Journal of Sociology* 102: 816–860.

Schuman, Howard and Lawrence Bobo. 1988. "Survey-Based Experiments on White Racial Attitudes Toward Residential Integration." *The American Journal of Sociology*, 94: 273-299.

Schuman, Howard and Barry Gruenberg. 1970. "The Impact of City on Racial Attitudes." *The American Journal of Sociology* 76: 213–261.

Schuman, Howard and Maria Krysan. 1999. "A Historical Note on Whites' Beliefs about Racial Inequality." *American Sociological Review*, 64: 847–855.

Schuman, Howard, Charlotte Steeh, and Lawrence Bobo. 1985. *Racial Attitudes in America: Trends and Interpretations*. Cambridge: Harvard University Press.

Schwartz, S. et al. 1991. "Separating Class and Ethnic Prejudice: A Study of North African and European Jews in Israel." *Social Psychology Quarterly* 54: 287–298.

Takaki, Ronald. "Asian Americans: The Myth of the Model Minority." From *Strangers from a Different Shore: A History of Asian-Americans*, Boston: Little-Brown.

Williams, David R., James S. Jackson, Tony N. Brown, Myriam Torres, Tyrone A. Forman, and Kendrick Brown. 1999. "Traditional and Contemporary Prejudice and Urban Whites' Support for Affirmative Action and Government Help." *Social Problems*, 46: 503–527.

Wise, Tim. 2008. "(Proto)Typical White Denial: Reflections on Racism and Uncomfortable Realities."

# Individual and Structural Racism

# ☐■■ RACIAL FORMATION

## UNDERSTANDING RACE AND RACISM IN THE POST-CIVIL RIGHTS ERA

*By Michael Omi and Howard Winant*

In 1982–83, Susie Guillory Phipps unsuccessfully sued the Louisiana Bureau of Vital Records to change her racial classification from black to white. The descendent of an 18th century white planter and a black slave, Phipps was designated "black" in her birth certificate in accordance with a 1970 state law which declared anyone with at least 1/32nd "Negro blood" to be black.

The Phipps case raised intriguing questions about the concept of race, its meaning in contemporary society, and its use (and abuse) in public policy. Assistant Attorney General Ron Davis defended the law by pointing out that some type of racial classification was necessary to comply with federal record-keeping requirements and to facilitate programs for the prevention of genetic diseases. Phipps's attorney, Brian Begue, argued that the assignment of racial categories on birth certificates was unconstitutional and that the 1/32nd designation was inaccurate. He called on a retired Tulane University professor who cited research indicating that most Louisiana whites have at least 1/20th "Negro" ancestry.

In the end, Phipps lost. The court upheld the state's right to classify and quantify racial identity.[1]

Phipps's problematic racial identity, and her effort to resolve it through state action, is in many ways a parable of America's unsolved racial dilemma. It illustrates the difficulties of defining race and assigning individuals or groups to racial categories. It shows how the racial legacies of the past—slavery and bigotry—continue to shape the present. It reveals both the deep involvement of the state in the organization and interpretation of race, and the inadequacy of state institutions to carry out these functions. It demonstrates how deeply Americans both as individuals and as a civilization are shaped, and indeed haunted, by race.

Having lived her whole life thinking that she was white, Phipps suddenly discovers that by legal definition she is not. In U.S. society, such an event is indeed catastrophic.[2] But if she is not white, of what race is she? The state claims that she is black, based on its rules of classification,[3] and another state agency, the court, upholds this judgment. Despite the classificatory standards that have imposed an either-or logic on racial identity, Phipps will not in fact "change color." Unlike what would have happened during slavery times if one's claim to whiteness was successfully challenged, we can assume that despite the outcome of her legal challenge, Phipps will remain in most of the social relationships she had occupied before the trial. Her socialization, her familial and friendship networks, her cultural orientation, will not change. She will simply have to wrestle with her newly acquired "hybridized" condition. She will have to confront the "other" within.

The designation of racial categories and the assignment of race is no simple task. For centuries, this question has precipitated intense debates and conflicts, particularly in the U.S.—disputes over natural and legal rights, over the distribution of resources, and indeed, over who shall live and who shall die.

A crucial dimension of the Phipps case is that it illustrates the inadequacy of claims that race is a mere matter of variations in human physiognomy, that it is simply a matter of skin "color." But if race cannot be understood in this manner, how can it be understood? We cannot fully hope to address this topic—no less than the meaning of race, its role in society, and the forces that shape it—in one chapter, nor indeed in one book. Our goal in this chapter, however, is far from modest: we wish to offer at least the outlines of a theory of race and racism.

## WHAT IS RACE?

There is a continuous temptation to think of race as an essence, as something fixed, concrete and objective. And there is also an opposite temptation: to imagine race as a mere illusion, a purely ideological construct that some ideal non-racist social order would eliminate. It is necessary to challenge both these positions, to disrupt and reframe the rigid and bipolar manner in which they are posed and debated, and to transcend the presumably irreconcilable relationship between them.

The effort must be made to understand race as an unstable and "decentered" complex of social meanings constantly being transformed by political struggle. With this in mind, let us propose a definition: *race is a concept that signifies and symbolizes social conflicts and interests by referring to different types of human bodies.* Although the concept of race invokes biologically-based human characteristics (so-called "phenotypes"), selection of these particular human features for purposes of racial signification is always and necessarily a social and historical process. In contrast to the other major distinction of this type, that of gender, there is no biological basis for distinguishing among human groups along the lines of race.[4] Indeed, the categories employed to differentiate among human groups along racial lines reveal themselves, upon serious examination, to be at best imprecise, and at worst completely arbitrary.

If the concept of race is so nebulous, can we not dispense with it? Can we not "do without" race, at least in the "enlightened" present? This question has been posed often, and with greater frequency in recent years.[5] An affirmative answer would of course present obvious practical difficulties: it is rather difficult to jettison widely held beliefs, beliefs which moreover are central to everyone's identity and understanding of the social world. So the attempt to banish the concept as an archaism is at best counterintuitive. But a deeper difficulty, we believe, is inherent in the very formulation of this schema, in its way of posing race as a problem, a misconception left over from the past, and suitable now only for the dustbin of history.

A more effective starting point is the recognition that despite its uncertainties and contradictions, the concept of race continues to play a fundamental role in structuring and representing the social world. The task for theory is to explain this situation. It is to avoid both the utopian framework that sees race as an illusion we can somehow "get beyond," and also the essentialist formulation that sees race as something objective and fixed, a biological datum.[6] Thus we should think of race as an element of social structure rather than as an irregularity within it; we should see race as a dimension of human representation rather than an illusion. These perspectives inform the theoretical approach we call racial formation.

## RACIAL FORMATION

We define racial formation as *the sociohistorical process by which racial categories are created, lived out, transformed, and destroyed.* Our attempt to elaborate a theory of racial formation will proceed in two steps. First, we argue that racial formation is a process of historically situated projects in which human bodies and social structures are represented and organized. Next we link racial formation to the evolution of hegemony, the way in which society is organized and ruled. Such an approach, we believe, can facilitate understanding of a whole range of contemporary controversies and dilemmas involving race, including the nature of racism, the relationship of race to other forms of differences, inequalities, and oppression such as sexism and nationalism, and the dilemmas of racial identity today.

From a racial formation perspective, race is a matter of both social structure and cultural representation. Too often, the attempt is made to understand race simply or primarily in terms of only one of these two analytical dimensions.[7] For example, efforts to explain racial inequality as a purely social structural phenomenon are unable to account for the origins, patterning, and transformation of racial difference. Conversely, many examinations of racial difference—understood as a matter of cultural attributes a la ethnicity theory, or as a society-wide signification system, a la some poststructuralist accounts—cannot comprehend such structural phenomena as racial stratification in the labor market or patterns of residential segregation.

An alternative approach is to think of racial formation processes as occurring through a linkage between structure and representation. Racial projects do the ideological "work" of making these links. A racial project is simultaneously an interpretation, representation, or explanation of racial dynamics, and an effort to reorganize and redistribute resources along particular racial lines. Racial projects connect what race means in a particular discursive practice and the ways in which both social structures and everyday experiences are racially organized, based upon that meaning. Let us consider this proposition, first in terms of large-scale or macro-level social processes, and then in terms of other dimensions of the racial formation process.

## RACIAL FORMATION AS A MACRO-LEVEL SOCIAL PROCESS

To interpret the meaning of race is to frame it social structurally. Consider for example, this statement by Charles Murray on welfare reform:

> My proposal for dealing with the racial issue in social welfare is to repeal every bit of legislation and reverse every court decision that in any way requires, recommends, or awards differential treatment according to race, and thereby put us back onto the track that we left in 1965. We may argue about the appropriate limits of government intervention in trying to enforce the ideal, but at least it should be possible to identify the ideal: Race is not a morally admissible reason for treating one person differently from another. Period.[8]

Here there is a partial but significant analysis of the meaning of race: it is not a morally valid basis upon which to treat people "differently from one another." We may notice someone's race, but we cannot act upon that awareness. We must act in a "color-blind" fashion. This analysis of the meaning of race is immediately linked to a specific conception of the role of race in the social structure: it can play no part in government action, save in "the enforcement of the ideal." No state policy can legitimately require, recommend, or award different status according to race. This example can be classified as a particular type of racial project in the present-day U.S.—a "neoconservative" one.

Conversely, to recognize the racial dimension in social structure is to interpret the meaning of race. Consider the following statement by the late Supreme Court Justice Thurgood Marshall on minority "set-aside" programs:

> A profound difference separates governmental actions that themselves are racist, and governmental actions that seek to remedy the effects of prior racism or to prevent neutral government activity from perpetuating the effects of such racism.[9]

Here the focus is on the racial dimensions of social structure—in this case of state activity and policy. The argument is that state actions in the past and present have treated people in very different ways according to their race, and thus the government cannot retreat from its policy responsibilities in this area. It cannot suddenly declare itself "color-blind" without in fact perpetuating the same type of differential, racist treatment.[10] Thus, race continues to signify difference and structure inequality. Here, racialized social structure is immediately linked to an interpretation of the meaning of race. This example too can be classified as a particular type of racial project in the present-day U.S.—a "liberal" one.

These two examples of contemporary racial projects are drawn from mainstream political debate; they may be characterized as center-right and center-left expressions of contemporary racial politics.[11] We can, however, expand the discussion of racial formation processes far beyond these familiar examples. In fact, we can identify racial projects in at least three other analytical dimensions: first, the political spectrum can be broadened to include radical projects, on both the left and right, as well as along other political axes. Second, analysis of racial projects can take place not only at the macro-level of racial policy-making, state activity, and collective action, but also at the level of everyday experience. Third, the concept of racial projects can be applied across historical time, to identify racial formation dynamics in the past. We shall now offer examples of each of these types of racial projects.

## THE POLITICAL SPECTRUM OF RACIAL FORMATION

We have encountered examples of a neoconservative racial project, in which the significance of race is denied, leading to a "color-blind" racial politics and "hands off" policy orientation; and of a "liberal" racial project, in which the significance of race is affirmed, leading to an egalitarian and "activist" state policy. But these by no means exhaust the political possibilities. Other racial projects can be readily identified on the contemporary U.S. scene. For example, "far right" projects, which uphold biologistic and racist views of difference, explicitly argue for white supremacist policies. "New right" projects overtly claim to hold "color-blind" views, but covertly manipulate racial fears in order to achieve political gains.[12] On the left, "radical democratic" projects invoke notions of racial "difference" in combination with egalitarian politics and policy.

Further variations can also be noted. For example, "nationalist" projects, both conservative and radical, stress the incompatibility of racially-defined group identity with the legacy of white supremacy, and therefore advocate a social structural solution of separation, either complete or partial.[13] As we saw in Chapter 3, nationalist currents represent a profound legacy of the centuries of racial absolutism that initially defined the meaning of race in the U.S. Nationalist concerns continue to influence racial debate in the form of Afrocentrism and other expressions of identity politics.

Taking the range of politically organized racial projects as a whole, we can "map" the current pattern of racial formation at the level of the public sphere, the "macro-level" in which public debate and mobilization takes place.[14] But important as this is, the terrain on which racial formation occurs is broader yet.

## RACIAL FORMATION AS EVERYDAY EXPERIENCE

Here too racial projects link signification and structure, not so much as efforts to shape policy or define large-scale meaning, but as the applications of "common sense." To see racial projects operating at the level of everyday life, we have only to examine the many ways in which, often unconsciously, we "notice" race.

One of the first things we notice about people when we meet them (along with their sex) is their race. We utilize race to provide clues about who a person is. This fact is made painfully obvious when we encounter someone whom we cannot conveniently racially categorize—someone who is, for example, racially "mixed" or of an ethnic/racial group we are not familiar with. Such an encounter becomes a source of discomfort and momentarily a crisis of racial meaning.

Our ability to interpret racial meanings depends on preconceived notions of a racialized social structure. Comments such as, "Funny, you don't look black," betray an underlying image of what black should be. We expect people to act out their apparent racial identities; indeed we become disoriented when they do not. The black banker harassed by police while walking in casual clothes through his own well-off neighborhood, the Latino or white kid rapping in perfect Afro patois, the unending faux pas committed by whites who assume that the non-whites they encounter are servants or tradespeople, the belief that nonwhite colleagues are less qualified persons hired to fulfill affirmative action guidelines, indeed the whole gamut of racial stereotypes—that "white men can't jump," that Asians can't dance, etc. etc.—all testify to the way a racialized social structure shapes racial experience and conditions meaning. Analysis of such stereotypes reveals the always present, already active link between our view of the social structure—its demography, its laws, its customs, its threats—and our conception of what race means.

Conversely, our ongoing interpretation of our experience in racial terms shapes our relations to the institutions and organizations through which we are imbedded in social structure. Thus we expect differences in skin color, or other racially coded characteristics, to explain social differences. Temperament, sexuality, intelligence, athletic ability, aesthetic preferences, and so on are presumed to be fixed and discernible from the palpable mark of race. Such diverse questions as our confidence and trust in others (for example, clerks or salespeople, media figures, neighbors), our sexual preferences and romantic images, our tastes in music, films, dance, or sports, and our very ways of talking, walking, eating, and dreaming become racially coded simply because we live in a society where racial awareness is so pervasive. Thus in ways too comprehensive even to monitor consciously, and despite periodic calls—neoconservative and otherwise—for us to ignore race and adopt "color-blind" racial attitudes, skin color "differences" continue to rationalize distinct treatment of racially-identified individuals and groups.

To summarize the argument so far: the theory of racial formation suggests that society is suffused with racial projects, large and small, to which all are subjected. This racial "subjection" is quintessentially ideological. Everybody learns some combination, some version, of the rules of racial classification, and of her own racial identity, often without obvious teaching or conscious inculcation. Thus are we inserted in a comprehensively racialized social structure. Race becomes "common sense"—a way of comprehending, explaining, and acting in the world. A vast web of racial projects mediates between the discursive or representational means in which race is identified and signified on the one hand, and the institutional and organizational forms in which it is routinized and standardized on the other. These projects are the heart of the racial formation process.

Under such circumstances, it is not possible to represent race discursively without simultaneously locating it, explicitly or implicitly, in a social structural (and historical) context. Nor is it possible to organize, maintain, or transform social structures without simultaneously engaging, once more either explicitly or implicitly, in racial signification. Racial formation, therefore, is a kind of synthesis, an outcome, of the interaction of racial projects on a society-wide level. These projects are, of course, vastly different in scope and effect. They include large-scale public action, state activities, and interpretations of racial conditions in artistic, journalistic, or academic fora,[15] as well as the seemingly infinite number of racial judgments and practices we carry out at the level of individual experience.

Since racial formation is always historically situated, our understanding of the significance of race, and of the way race structures society, has changed enormously over time. The processes of racial formation we encounter today, the racial projects large and small which structure U.S. society in so many ways, are merely the present-day outcomes of a complex historical evolution. The contemporary racial order remains transient. By knowing something of how it evolved, we can perhaps better discern where it is heading. We therefore turn next to a historical survey of the racial formation process, and the conflicts and debates it has engendered.

## THE EVOLUTION OF MODERN RACIAL AWARENESS

The identification of distinctive human groups, and their association with differences in physical appearance, goes back to prehistory, and can be found in the earliest documents—in the Bible, for example, or in Herodotus. But the emergence of a modern conception of race does not occur until the rise of Europe and the arrival of Europeans in the Americas. Even the hostility and suspicion with which Christian Europe viewed its two significant non-Christian "others"—the Muslims and the Jews—cannot be viewed as more than a rehearsal for racial formation, since these antagonisms, for all their bloodletting and chauvinism, were always and everywhere religiously interpreted.[16]

It was only when European explorers reached the Western Hemisphere, when the oceanic seal separating the "old" and the "new" worlds was breached, that the distinctions and categorizations fundamental to a racialized social structure, and to a discourse of race, began to appear. The European explorers were the advance guard of merchant capitalism, which sought new openings for trade. What they found exceeded their wildest dreams, for never before and never again in human history has an opportunity for the appropriation of wealth remotely approached that presented by the "discovery."[17]

But the Europeans also "discovered" people, people who looked and acted differently. These "natives" challenged their "discoverers'" preexisting conceptions of the origins and possibilities of the human species.[18] The representation and interpretation of the meaning of the indigenous peoples' existence became a crucial matter, one which would affect the outcome of the enterprise of conquest. For the "discovery" raised disturbing questions as to whether all could be considered part of the same "family of man," and more practically, the extent to which native peoples could be exploited and enslaved. Thus religious debates flared over the attempt to reconcile the various Christian metaphysics with the existence of peoples who were more "different" than any whom Europe had previously known.[19]

In practice, of course, the seizure of territories and goods, the introduction of slavery through the encomienda and other forms of coerced native labor, and then through the organization of the African slave trade—not to mention the practice of outright extermination—all presupposed a worldview which distinguished Europeans, as children of God, full-fledged human beings, etc., from "others." Given the dimensions and the ineluctability of the European onslaught, given the conquerors' determination to appropriate both labor and goods, and given the presence of an axiomatic and unquestioned Christianity among them, the ferocious division of society into Europeans and "others" soon coalesced. This was true despite the famous 16th-century theological and philosophical debates about the identity of indigenous peoples.[20]

Indeed debates about the nature of the "others" reached their practical limits with a certain dispatch. Plainly they would never touch the essential: nothing, after all, would induce the Europeans to pack up and go home. We cannot examine here the early controversies over the status of American souls. We simply wish to emphasize that the "discovery" signaled a break from the previous proto-racial awareness by which Europe contemplated its "others" in a relatively disorganized fashion. In other words, we argue that the "conquest of America" was not simply an epochal historical event—however unparalleled in its importance. It was also the advent of a consolidated social structure of exploitation, appropriation, domination. Its representation, first in religious terms, but soon enough in scientific and political ones, initiated modern racial awareness.

The conquest, therefore, was the first—and given the dramatic nature of the case, perhaps the greatest—racial formation project. Its significance was by no means limited to the Western Hemisphere, for it began the work of constituting Europe as the metropole, the center, of a series of empires which could take, as Marx would later write, "the globe for a theater."[21] It represented this new imperial structure as a struggle between civilization and barbarism, and implicated in this representation all the great European philosophies, literary traditions, and social theories of the modern age.[22] In short, just as the noise of the "big bang" still resonates through the universe, so the overdetermined construction of world "civilization" as a product of the rise of Europe and the subjugation of the rest of us, still defines the race concept.

## FROM RELIGION TO SCIENCE

After the initial depredations of conquest, religious justifications for racial difference gradually gave way to scientific ones. By the time of the Enlightenment, a general awareness of race was pervasive, and most of the great philosophers of Europe, such as Hegel, Kant, Hume, and Locke, had issued virulently racist opinions.

The problem posed by race during the late 18th century was markedly different than it had been in the age of conquest, expropriation, and slaughter. The social structures in which race operated were no longer primarily those of military conquest and plunder, nor of the establishment of thin beachheads of colonization on the edge of what had once seemed a limitless wilderness. Now the issues were much more complicated: nation-building, establishment of national economies in the world trading system, resistance to the arbitrary authority of monarchs, and the assertion of the "natural rights" of "man," including the right of revolution.[23] In such a situation, racially organized exploitation, in the form of slavery, the expansion of colonies, and the continuing expulsion of native peoples, was both necessary and newly difficult to justify.

The invocation of scientific criteria to demonstrate the "natural" basis of racial hierarchy was both a logical consequence of the rise of this form of knowledge, and an attempt to provide a more subtle and nuanced account of human complexity in the new, "enlightened" age. Spurred on by the classificatory scheme of living organisms devised by Linnaeus in *Systema Naturae* (1735), many scholars in the eighteenth and nineteenth centuries dedicated themselves to the identification and ranking of variations in humankind. Race was conceived as a biological concept, a matter of species. Voltaire wrote that "The negro race is a species of men (sic) as different from ours ... as the breed of spaniels is from that of greyhounds," and in a formulation echoing down from his century to our own, declared that "If their understanding is not of a different nature from ours ... it is at least greatly inferior. They are not capable of any great application or association of ideas, and seem formed neither for the advantages nor the abuses of philosophy."[24]

Jefferson, the preeminent exponent of the Enlightenment doctrine of "the rights of man" on North American shores, echoed these sentiments:

> In general their existence appears to participate more of sensation than reflection. ... [I]n memory they are equal to whites, in reason much inferior ... [and] in imagination they are dull, tasteless,

and anomalous. ... I advance it therefore ... that the blacks, whether originally a different race, or made distinct by time and circumstances, are inferior to the whites. ... Will not a lover of natural history, then, one who views the gradations in all the animals with the eye of philosophy, excuse an effort to keep those in the department of Man (sic) as distinct as nature has formed them?[25]

Such claims of species distinctiveness among humans justified the inequitable allocation of political and social rights, while still upholding the doctrine of "the rights of man." The quest to obtain a precise scientific definition of race sustained debates that continue to rage today. Yet despite efforts ranging from Dr. Samuel Morton's studies of cranial capacity[26] to contemporary attempts to base racial classification on shared gene pools,[27] the concept of race has defied biological definition.

In the 19th century, Count Joseph Arthur de Gobineau drew upon the most respected scientific studies of his day to compose his four-volume *Essay on the Inequality of Races* (1853–1855).[28] He not only greatly influenced the racial thinking of the period, but his themes would be echoed in the racist ideologies of the next one hundred years: beliefs that superior races produced superior cultures and that racial intermixtures resulted in the degradation of the superior racial stock. These ideas found expression, for instance, in the eugenics movement launched by Darwin's cousin, Francis Galton, which had an immense impact on scientific and sociopolitical thought in Europe and the United States.[29] In the wake of civil war and emancipation, and with immigration from southern and Eastern Europe as well as East Asia running high, the U.S. was particularly fertile ground for notions such as social darwinism and eugenics.

Attempts to discern the scientific meaning of race continue to the present day. For instance, an essay by Arthur Jensen that argued that hereditary factors shape intelligence not only revived the "nature or nurture" controversy, but also raised highly volatile questions about racial equality itself.[30] All such attempts seek to remove the concept of race from the historical context in which it arose and developed. They employ an essentialist approach that suggests instead that the truth of race is a matter of innate characteristics, of which skin color and other physical attributes provide only the most obvious, and in some respects most superficial, indicators.

## FROM SCIENCE TO POLITICS

It has taken scholars more than a century to reject biologistic notions of race in favor of an approach that regards race as a social concept. This trend has been slow and uneven, and even today remains somewhat embattled, but its overall direction seems clear. At the turn of the century Max Weber discounted biological explanations for racial conflict and instead highlighted the social and political factors that engendered such conflict.[31] W. E. B. Du Bois argued for a sociopolitical definition of race by identifying "the color line" as "the problem of the 20th century."[32] Pioneering cultural anthropologist Franz Boas rejected attempts to link racial identifications and cultural traits, labeling as pseudoscientific any assumption of a continuum of "higher" and "lower" cultural groups.[33] Other early exponents of social, as opposed to biological, views of race included Robert E. Park, founder of the "Chicago school" of sociology, and Alain Leroy Locke, philosopher and theorist of the Harlem renaissance.[34]

Perhaps more important than these and subsequent intellectual efforts, however, were the political struggles of racially defined groups themselves. Waged all around the globe under a variety of banners such as anti-colonialism and civil rights, these battles to challenge various structural and cultural racisms have been a major feature of 20th century politics. The racial horrors of the 20th century—colonial slaughter and apartheid, the genocide of the holocaust, and the massive bloodlettings required to end these evils—have also indelibly marked the theme of race as a political issue par excellence.

As a result of prior efforts and struggles, we have now reached the point of fairly general agreement that race is not a biologically given but rather a socially constructed way of differentiating human beings. While a tremendous achievement, the transcendence of biologistic conceptions of race does not provide any reprieve from the dilemmas of racial injustice and conflict, nor from controversies over the significance of race in the present. Views of race as socially constructed simply recognize the fact that these conflicts and controversies are now more properly framed on the terrain of politics. By privileging politics in the analysis that follows we do not mean to suggest that race has been displaced as a concern of scientific inquiry, or that struggles over cultural representation are no longer important. We do argue, however, that race is now a preeminently political phenomenon. Such an assertion invites examination of the evolving role of racial politics in the U.S. This is the subject to which we now turn.

## DICTATORSHIP, DEMOCRACY, HEGEMONY

For most of its existence both as a European colony and as an independent nation, the U.S. was a racial dictatorship. From 1607 to 1865—258 years—most nonwhites were firmly eliminated from the sphere of politics.[35] After the civil war there was the brief egalitarian experiment of Reconstruction which terminated ignominiously in 1877. In its wake followed almost a century of legally sanctioned segregation and denial of the vote, nearly absolute in the South and much of the Southwest, less effective in the North and far West, but formidable in any case.[36] These barriers fell only in the mid-1960s, a mere quarter-century ago. Nor did the successes of the black movement and its allies mean that all obstacles to their political participation had now been abolished. Patterns of racial inequality have proven, unfortunately, to be quite stubborn and persistent.

It is important, therefore, to recognize that in many respects, racial dictatorship is the norm against which all U.S. politics must be measured. The centuries of racial dictatorship have had three very large consequences: first, they defined "American" identity as white, as the negation of racialized "otherness"—at first largely African and indigenous, later Latin American and Asian as well.[37] This negation took shape in both law and custom, in public institutions and in forms of cultural representation. It became the archetype of hegemonic rule in the U.S. It was the successor to the conquest as the "master" racial project.

Second, racial dictatorship organized (albeit sometimes in an incoherent and contradictory fashion) the "color line," rendering it the fundamental division in U.S. society. The dictatorship elaborated, articulated, and drove racial divisions not only through institutions, but also through psyches, extending up to our own time the racial obsessions of the conquest and slavery periods.

Third, racial dictatorship consolidated the oppositional racial consciousness and organization originally framed by marronage[38] and slave revolts, by indigenous resistance, and by nationalisms of various sorts. Just as the conquest created the "native" where once there had been Pequot, Iroquois, or Tutelo, so too it created the "black" where once there had been Asante or Ovimbundu, Yoruba or Bakongo.

The transition from a racial dictatorship to a racial democracy has been a slow, painful, and contentious one; it remains far from complete. A recognition of the abiding presence of racial dictatorship, we contend, is crucial for the development of a theory of racial formation in the U.S. It is also crucial to the task of relating racial formation to the broader context of political practice, organization, and change.

In this context, a key question arises: In what way is racial formation related to politics as a whole? How, for example, does race articulate with other axes of oppression and difference—most importantly class and gender—along which politics is organized today?

The answer, we believe, lies in the concept of *hegemony*. Antonio Gramsci—the Italian communist who placed this concept at the center of his life's work—understood it as the conditions necessary, in a given society, for the achievement and consolidation of rule. He argued that hegemony was always constituted by a combination of coercion and consent. Although rule can be obtained by force, it cannot be secured and maintained, especially in modern society, without the element of consent. Gramsci conceived of consent as far more than merely the legitimation of authority. In his view, consent extended to the incorporation by the ruling group of many of the key interests of subordinated groups, often to the explicit disadvantage of the rulers themselves.[39] Gramsci's treatment of hegemony went even farther: he argued that in order to consolidate their hegemony, ruling groups must elaborate and maintain a popular system of ideas and practices—through education, the media, religion, folk wisdom, etc.—which he called "common sense." It is through its production and its adherence to this "common sense," this ideology (in the broadest sense of the term), that a society gives its consent to the way in which it is ruled.[40]

These provocative concepts can be extended and applied to an understanding of racial rule. In the Americas, the conquest represented the violent introduction of a new form of rule whose relationship with those it subjugated was almost entirely coercive. In the U.S., the origins of racial division, and of racial signification and identity formation, lie in a system of rule that was extremely dictatorial. The mass murders and expulsions of indigenous people, and the enslavement of Africans, surely evoked and inspired little consent in their founding moments.

Over time, however, the balance of coercion and consent began to change. It is possible to locate the origins of hegemony right within the heart of racial dictatorship, for the effort to possess the oppressor's tools—religion and philosophy in this case—was crucial to emancipation (the effort to possess oneself). As Ralph Ellison reminds us, "The slaves often took the essence of the aristocratic ideal (as they took Christianity) with far more seriousness than their masters."[41] In their language, in their religion with its focus on the Exodus theme and on Jesus's tribulations, in their music with its figuring of suffering, resistance, perseverance, and transcendence, in their interrogation of a political philosophy that sought perpetually to rationalize their bondage in a supposedly "free" society, the slaves incorporated elements of racial rule into their thought and practice, turning them against their original bearers.

Racial rule can be understood as a slow and uneven historical process that has moved from dictatorship to democracy, from domination to hegemony. In this transition, hegemonic forms of racial rule—those based on consent—eventually came to supplant those based on coercion. Of course, before this assertion can be accepted, it must be qualified in important ways. By no means has the U.S. established racial democracy at the end of the century, and by no means is coercion a thing of the past. But the sheer complexity of the racial questions U.S. society confronts today, the welter of competing racial projects and contradictory racial experiences that Americans undergo, suggests that hegemony is a useful and appropriate term with which to characterize contemporary racial rule.

## RACE, RACISM, AND HEGEMONY

Parallel to the debates on the concept of race, recent academic and political controversies about the nature of racism have centered on whether it is primarily an ideological or structural phenomenon. Proponents of the former position argue that racism is first and foremost a matter of beliefs and attitudes, doctrines and discourse, which only then give rise to unequal and unjust practices and structures.[42] Advocates of the latter view see racism as primarily a matter of economic stratification, residential segregation, and other institutionalized forms of inequality that then give rise to ideologies of privilege.[43]

From the standpoint of racial formation, these debates are fundamentally misguided. They discuss the problem of racism in a rigid "either-or" manner. We believe it is crucial to disrupt the fixity of these positions by simultaneously arguing that ideological beliefs have structural consequences, and that social structures give rise to beliefs. Racial ideology and social structure, therefore, mutually shape the nature of racism in a complex, dialectical, and overdetermined manner.

Even those racist projects that at first glance appear chiefly ideological turn out upon closer examination to have significant institutional and social structural dimensions. For example, what we have called "far right" projects appear at first glance to be centrally ideological. They are rooted in biologistic doctrine, after all. The same seems to hold for certain conservative black nationalist projects that have deep commitments to biologism.[44] But the unending stream of racist assaults initiated by the far right, the apparently increasing presence of skinheads in high schools, the proliferation of neo-Nazi websites on the Internet, and the appearance of racist talk shows on cable access channels, all suggest that the organizational manifestations of the far right racial projects exist and will endure.[45]

By contrast, even those racisms that at first glance appear to be chiefly structural upon closer examination reveal a deeply ideological component. For example, since the racial right abandoned its explicit advocacy of segregation, it has not seemed to uphold—in the main—an ideologically racist project, but more primarily a structurally racist one. Yet this very transformation required tremendous efforts of ideological production. It demanded the rearticulation of civil rights doctrines of equality in suitably conservative form, and indeed the defense of continuing large-scale racial inequality as an outcome preferable to (what its advocates have seen as) the threat to democracy that affirmative action, busing, and large-scale "race-specific" social spending would entail.[46] Even more tellingly, this project took shape through a deeply manipulative coding of subtextual appeals to white racism, notably in a series of political campaigns for high office that have occurred over recent decades. The retreat of social policy from any practical commitment to racial justice, and the relentless reproduction and divulgation of this theme at the level of everyday life—where whites are now "fed up" with all the "special treatment" received by nonwhites, etc.—constitutes the hegemonic racial project at this time. It therefore exhibits an unabashed structural racism all the more brazen because on the ideological or signification level it adheres to a principle to "treat everyone alike."

In summary, the racism of today is no longer a virtual monolith, as was the racism of yore. Today, racial hegemony is "messy." The complexity of the present situation is the product of a vast historical legacy of structural inequality and invidious racial representation, which has been confronted during the post-World War II period with an opposition more serious and effective than any it had faced before. The result is a deeply ambiguous and contradictory spectrum of racial projects, unremittingly conflictual racial politics, and confused and ambivalent racial identities of all sorts.

## DISCUSSION QUESTIONS

1. In recent years civil rights advocates have brought suit against companies like CSX railroad and Fleet Bank on the grounds that they profited from African slavery in their early years. For example, the lawsuits alleged that corporate ancestors of CSX used slave labor to lay railroad track and to build railroad facilities; they charged that corporate ancestors of Fleet Bank (which merged with Bank of America in 2004) insured plantation owners' "property" (the slaves themselves) in the antebellum South against the risk of slaves running away.

   In your view what merit do these lawsuits have? Should contemporary corporations be liable for their predecessors' collaboration with slavery? Are the descendents of slaves entitled to compensation because their ancestors' labor was (allegedly) coerced by CSX's antecedents or because their ancestors' bodies were (allegedly) insured by Fleet's corporate founders against loss to their slavemasters? Is the black community as a whole entitled to such compensation?

2. The United States is becoming a lot less white. Projecting current population (and immigration) trends forward to the year 2050, the U.S. Census Bureau predicts that in 2050, the population will be about 25% Latino/Hispanic, 17% black, and 9% Asian American. In many of the largest cities in the U.S., whites are already a minority. The state of California, which was about 75% white in 1975, was only about 42% white in 2007.

   What are the implications of these population trends for racial formation in the United States? How in your view will the country adapt to these patterns? For example, do you foresee a greater acceptance among whites of their minority status? Or do you think there will be greater hostility to members of "other" groups? What racial projects do you expect whites to be carrying out as a result of their declining proportion of the U.S. population?

3. In 2005 white families' average net worth (the monetary value of investments savings, and property belong to these families) was approximately 11x the average net worth of black families. This inequality in wealth distribution had grown significantly over the four decades since the passage of civil rights legislation in the 1960s.

In your view what accounts for the continuing (and in some ways increasing) gap between blacks and whites in the present, supposedly "color-blind" era?

4. In 1997 golf star Tiger Woods referred to himself as "Cablinasian" on the Oprah Winfrey TV program. He said that it bothered him when people referred to him as black, since he is one-fourth black, one-fourth Thai, one-fourth Chinese, one-eighth white and one-eighth American Indian.

Discuss Woods's self-identification as a racial project. In what ways is he situating himself in the U.S. racial mosaic? What are the implications for him (and for other Americans) of his invention of a "Cablinasian" identity?

5. Starting in the 1970s, and more intensively since then, many politicians, academics, and public figures have argued that the United States is becoming a "color-blind" society. (The term actually goes back to Justice Harlan's dissent in the landmark *Plessy v. Ferguson* decision of 1896.) Yet survey results continue to show persistent beliefs in black inferiority, laziness, and criminality.

Is there a discrepancy here, or can these two trends be reconciled? Discuss these views on race as conflicting or overlapping racial projects.

## NOTES

1. *San Francisco Chronicle*, September 14, 1982, May 19, 1983. Ironically, the 1970 Louisiana law was enacted to supersede an old Jim Crow statute which relied on the idea of "common report" in determining an infant's race. Following Phipps' unsuccessful attempt to change her classification and have the law declared unconstitutional, a legislative effort arose which culminated in the repeal of the law. See *San Francisco Chronicle*, June 23, 1983.

2. Compare the Phipps case to Andrew Hacker's well-known "parable" in which a white person is informed by a mysterious official that "the organization he represents has made a mistake" and that "… [a]ccording to their records …, you were to have been born black: to another set of parents, far from where you were raised." How much compensation, Hacker's official asks, would "you" require to undo the damage of this unfortunate error? See Hacker, *Two Nations: Black and White, Separate, Hostile, Unequal* (New York: Charles Scribner's Sons, 1992), pp. 31–32.

3. On the evolution of Louisiana's racial classification system, see Virginia Dominguez, *White By Definition: Social Classification in Creole Louisiana* (New Brunswick: Rutgers University Press, 1986).

4. This is not to suggest that gender is a biological category while race is not. Gender, like race, is a social construct. However, the biological division of humans into sexes—two at least, and possibly intermediate ones as well—is not in dispute. This provides a basis for argument over gender divisions—how natural?" etc.—which does not exist with regard to race. To ground an argument for the "natural" existence of race, one must resort to philosophical anthropology.

5. "The truth is that there are no races; there is nothing in the world that can do all we ask race

to do for us. … The evil that is done is done by the concept, and by easy—yet impossible—assumptions as to its application." (Kwame Anthony Appiah, *In My Father's House: Africa in the Philosophy of Culture* (New York: Oxford University Press, 1992.) Appiah's eloquent and learned book fails, in our view, to dispense with the race concept, despite its anguished attempt to do so; this indeed is the source of its author's anguish. We agree with him as to the non-objective character of race, but fail to see how this recognition justifies its abandonment. This argument is developed below.

6. We understand essentialism as *belief in real, true human essences, existing outside or impervious to social and historical context*. We draw this definition, with some small modifications, from Diana Fuss, *Essentially Speaking: Feminism, Nature, & Difference* (New York: Routledge, 1989), p. xi.

7. Michael Omi and Howard Winant, "On the Theoretical Status of the Concept of Race," in Warren Crichlow and Cameron McCarthy, eds., *Race, Identity, and Representation in Education* (New York: Routledge, 1993).

8. Charles Murray, *Losing Ground: American Social Policy, 1950–1980* (New York: Basic Books, 1984), p. 223.

9. Justice Thurgood Marshall, dissenting in *City of Richmond v. J.A. Croson Co.*, 488 U.S. 469 (1989).

10. See, for example, Derrick Bell, "Remembrances of Racism Past: Getting Past the Civil Rights Decline," in Herbert Hill and James E. Jones, Jr., eds., *Race in America: The Struggle for Equality* (Madison: The University of Wisconsin Press, 1993), pp. 75–76; Gertrude Ezorsky, *Racism and Justice: The Case for Affirmative Action* (Ithaca: Cornell University Press, 1991), pp. 109–111; David Kairys, *With Liberty and Justice for Some: A Critique of the Conservative Supreme Court* (New York: The New Press, 1993), pp. 138–41.

11. Howard Winant has developed a tentative "map" of the system of racial hegemony in the U.S. circa 1990, which focuses on the spectrum of racial projects running from the political right to the political left. See Winant, "Where Culture Meets Structure: Race in the 1990s," in idem, *Racial Conditions: Theories, Politics, Comparisons* (Minneapolis: University of Minnesota Press, 1994).

12. A familiar example is use of racial "code words." Recall George Bush's manipulations of racial fear in the 1988 "Willie Horton" ads, or Jesse Helms's use of the coded term "quota" in his 1990 campaign against Harvey Gantt.

13. From this perspective, far right racial projects can also be interpreted as "nationalist." See Ronald Walters, "White Racial Nationalism in the United States," *Without Prejudice* I, 1 (Fall, 1987).

14. Howard Winant has offered such a "map" in "Race: Theory, Culture, and Politics in the United States Today," in Marcy Darnovsky et al., eds., *Contemporary Social Movements and Cultural Politics* (Philadelphia: Temple University Press, 1994).

15. We are not unaware, for example, that publishing this work is in itself a racial project.

16. Although the Inquisition pioneered racial anti-semitism with its doctrine of "limpieza de sangre" (the claim that Jews could not be accepted as converts because their blood was "unclean"), anti-semitism only began to be seriously racialized in the 18th century, as George L. Mosse shows in *Toward the Final Solution: A History of European Racism* (New York: Howard Fertig, 1978).

17. As Marx put it:

The discovery of gold and silver in America, the extirpation, enslavement, and entombment in mines of the aboriginal population, the beginning of the conquest and looting of the East Indies, the turning of Africa into a warren for the commercial hunting of blackskins, signalized the rosy dawn of the era of capitalist production. These idyllic proceedings are the chief momenta of primitive accumulation. (Karl Marx, *Capital*, Vol. I (New York: International Publishers, 1967), p. 751.)

David E. Stannard argues that the wholesale slaughter perpetrated upon the native peoples of the Western hemisphere is unequalled in history, even in our own bloody century. See his *American Holocaust: Columbus and the Conquest of the New World* (New York: Oxford University Press, 1992).

18. Winthrop Jordan provides a detailed account of the sources of European attitudes about color and race in *White Over Black: American Attitudes Toward the Negro, 1550–1812* (New York: Norton, 1977 [1968]), pp. 3–43.

19. In a famous instance, a 1550 debate in Valladolid pitted the philosopher and translator of Aristotle, Gines de Sepulveda, against the Dominican Bishop of the Mexican state of Chiapas, Bartolome de Las Casas. Discussing the native peoples, Sepulveda argued that

> In wisdom, skill, virtue and humanity, these people are as inferior to the Spaniards as children are to adults and women to men; there is as great a difference between them as there is between savagery and forbearance, between violence and moderation,

almost—I am inclined to say, as between monkeys and men (Sepulveda, "Democrates Alter," quoted in Tsvetan Todorov, *The Conquest of America: The Question of the Other* (New York: Harper and Row, 1984), p. 153).

In contrast, Las Casas defended the humanity and equality of the native peoples, both in terms of their way of life—which he idealized as one of innocence, gentleness, and generosity—and in terms of their readiness for conversion to Catholicism, which for him as for Sepulveda was the true and universal religion (Las Casas, "Letter to the Council of the Indies," quoted ibid, p. 163). William E. Connolly interrogates the linkages proposed by Todorov between early Spanish colonialism and contemporary conceptions of identity and difference in *Identity/Difference: Democratic Negotiations of Political Paradox* (Ithaca: Cornell University Press, 1991), pp. 40–48.

20. In Virginia, for example, it took about two decades after the establishment of European colonies to extirpate the indigenous people of the greater vicinity; 50 years after the establishment of the first colonies, the elaboration of slave codes establishing race as prima facie evidence for enslaved status was well under way. See Jordan, *White Over Black*.

21. *Capital*, p. 751.

22. Edward W. Said, *Culture and Imperialism* (New York: Alfred A. Knopf, 1993).

23. David Brion Davis, *The Problem of Slavery in The Age of Revolution* (Ithaca: Cornell University Press, 1975).

24. Quoted in Thomas F. Gossett, *Race: The History of an Idea in America* (New York: Schocken Books, 1965), p. 45.

25. Thomas Jefferson, "Notes on Virginia" [1787], in Merrill D. Peterson, *Writings of Thomas Jefferson* (New York: The Library of America, 1984), pp. 264–66, 270. Thanks to Prof. Kimberly Benston for drawing our attention to this passage.

26. Proslavery physician Samuel George Morton (1799–1851) compiled a collection of 800 crania from all parts of the world which formed the sample for his studies of race. Assuming that the larger the size of the cranium translated into greater intelligence, Morton established a relationship between race and skull capacity. Gossett reports that "In 1849, one of his studies included the following results: the English skulls in his collection proved to be the largest, with an average cranial capacity of 96 cubic inches. The Americans and Germans were rather poor seconds, both with cranial capacities of 90 cubic inches. At the bottom of the list were the Negroes with 83 cubic inches, the Chinese with 82, and the Indians with 79." Gossett, *Race: The History of an Idea in America*, p. 74. More recently, Steven Jay Gould has reexamined Morton's data, and shown that his research data were deeply, though unconsciously, manipulated to agree with his "a priori conviction about racial ranking." Gould, *The Mismeasure of Man* (New York: W. W. Norton, 1981), pp. 50–69.

27. Definitions of race founded upon a common pool of genes have not held up when confronted by scientific research which suggests that the differences *within* a given human population are every bit as great as those *between* populations. See L. L. Cavalli-Sforza, "The Genetics of Human Populations," *Scientific American*, (September 1974), pp. 81–89.

28. A fascinating summary critique of Gobineau is provided in Tsvetan Todorov, *On Human Diversity: Nationalism, Racism, and Exoticism in French Thought*, trans. Catherine Porter (Cambridge, MA: Harvard University Press, 1993), esp. pp. 129–40.

29. Two good histories of eugenics are Allen Chase, *The Legacy of Malthus* (New York: Knopf, 1977); Daniel J. Kelves, *In the Name of Eugenics: Genetics and the Uses of Human Heredity* (New York: Knopf, 1985).

30. Arthur Jensen, "How Much Can We Boost IQ and Scholastic Achievement?" *Harvard Educational Review*, 39 (1969), pp. 1–123.

31. See Weber, *Economy and Society*, Vol. I (Berkeley: University of California Press, 1978), pp. 385–87; Ernst Moritz Manasse, "Max Weber on Race," *Social Research*, Vol. 14 (1947), pp. 191–221.

32. Du Bois, *The The Souls of Black Folk* (New York: Penguin, 1989 [1903]), p. 13. Du Bois himself wrestled heavily with the conflict between a fully sociohistorical conception of race, and the more essentialized and deterministic vision he encountered as a student in Berlin. In "The Conservation of Races" (1897) we can see his first mature effort to resolve this conflict in a vision which combined racial solidarity and a commitment to social equality. See Du Bois, "The Conservation of Races," in Dan S. Green and Edwin D. Driver, eds., *W. E. B. Du Bois On Sociology and the Black Community* (Chicago: University of Chicago Press, 1978), pp. 238–49; Manning Marable, *W. E. B. Du Bois: Black Radical Democrat* (Boston: Twayne, 1986), pp. 35–38. For a contrary, and we believe incorrect reading, see Appiah, *In My Father's House*, pp. 28–46.

33. A good collection of Boas's work is George W. Stocking, ed., *The Shaping of American Anthropology, 1883–1911: A Franz Boas Reader* (Chicago: University of Chicago Press, 1974).

34. Robert E. Park's *Race and Culture* (Glencoe, IL: Free Press, 1950) can still provide insight;

see also Stanford H. Lyman, *Militarism, Imperialism, and Racial Accommodation: An Analysis and Interpretation of the Early Writings of Robert E. Park* (Fayetteville: University of Arkansas Press, 1992); Locke's views are concisely expressed in Alain Leroy Locke, *Race Contacts and Interracial Relations*, ed. Jeffrey C. Stewart (Washington, D.C.: Howard University Press, 1992), originally a series of lectures given at Howard University.

35. Japanese, for example, could not become naturalized citizens until passage of the 1952 McCarran-Walter Act. It took over 160 years, since the passage of the Naturalization Law of 1790, to allow all "races" to be eligible for naturalization.

36. Especially when we recall that until around 1960, the majority of blacks, the largest racially-defined minority group, lived in the South.

37. The construction of whiteness and its tropes of identity is explored in numerous studies, far too many to cite here. Some outstanding examples are Toni Morrison, *Playing In The Dark*: Whiteness and the Literary Imagination (Cambridge, MA: Harvard University Press, 1992); Michael Paul Rogin, *Fathers and Children: Andrew Jackson and the Subjugation of the American Indian* (New York: Knopf, 1975; Richard Drinnon, *Facing West: The Metaphysics of Indian-hating and Empire-building* (Minneapolis: University of Minnesota Press, 1980).

38. This term refers to the practice, widespread throughout the Americas, whereby runaway slaves formed communities in remote areas, such as swamps, mountains, or forests, often in alliance with dispossessed indigenous peoples.

39. Antonio Gramsci, *Selections from the Prison Notebooks*, edited and translated by Quintin Hoare and Geoffrey Nowell Smith (New York: International Publishers, 1971), p. 182.

40. Anne Showstack Sassoon, *Gramsci's Politics*, 2nd. ed. (London: Hutchinson, 1987); Sue Golding, *Gramsci's Democratic Theory: Contributions to Post-Liberal Democracy* (Toronto: University of Toronto Press, 1992).

41. Ralph Ellison, *Shadow and Act* (New York: New American Library, 1966), p. xiv.

42. See Miles, *Racism*, p. 77. Much of the current debate over the advisability and legality of banning racist hate speech seems to us to adopt the dubious position that racism is primarily an ideological phenomenon. See Mari J. Matsuda et al., *Words That Wound: Critical Race Theory, Assaultive Speech, and the First Amendment* (Boulder, CO: Westview Press, 1993).

43. Or ideologies which mask privilege by falsely claiming that inequality and injustice have been eliminated. See Wellman, *Portraits of White Racism*.

44. Racial teachings of the Nation of Islam, for example, maintain that whites are the product of a failed experiment by a mad scientist.

45. Elinor Langer, "The American Neo-Nazi Movement Today," *The Nation*, July 16/23, 1990.

46. Such arguments can be found in Nathan Glazer, *Affirmative Discrimination*, Charles Murray, *Losing Ground*, and Arthur M. Schlesinger, Jr., *The Disuniting of America*, among others.

# FROM BI-RACIAL TO TRI-RACIAL

## TOWARDS A NEW SYSTEM OF RACIAL STRATIFICATION IN THE U.S.A.

*By Eduardo Bonilla-Silva*

## ABSTRACT

In this article I argue that the bi-racial order (white vs non-white) typical of the United States is undergoing a profound transformation. Because of drastic changes in the demography of the nation as well as changes in the racial structure of the world-system, the United States is developing a complex, Latin America-like racial order. Specifically, I suggest that the new order will have two central features: three loosely organized racial strata (white, honorary white, and the collective black) and a pigmento-cratic logic. I examine some objective, subjective, and social interaction indicators to assess if the Latin Americanization thesis holds some water. Although more refined data are needed to conclusively make my case, the available indicators support my thesis. I conclude this article by outlining some of the potential implications of Latin Americanization for the future of race relations in the United States.

**Keywords:** Tri-racial; pigmentocracy; skin-tone; colour-blind; Latin America; racism.

## INTRODUCTION

For demographic (the relative large size of the black population) and historical reasons (the centrality of blacks to the national economic development from the seventeenth to the middle part of the twentieth century), the United States has had a bi-racial order (white versus the rest) fundamentally anchored on the black-white experience (Feagin 2000).[1] Albeit regions such as the Southwest, states such as California (Almaguer 1994), and sub-areas in some states (the case of 'tri-racial isolates', see Daniels 2002) have had more complex racial dynamics, the larger bi-racial system has always posed the outer limits. This has meant historically that those on the nonwhite side of the divide (blacks, Native Americans, Asians, and Latinos) have shared similar experiences of colonialism, oppression, exploitation, and racialization (Ammott and Matthai 1991). Hence, being nonwhite has meant having restricted access to the multiple 'wages of whiteness' (Roediger 1991) such as good housing, decent jobs, and a good education.

Nevertheless, the post-civil rights era has brought changes in how racial stratification seems to operate. For example, significant gaps in status have emerged between groups that previously shared a common denizen position in the racial order. Asian Americans in particular have almost matched the socio-economic standing of whites and, in some areas (e.g., educational attainment), have surpassed them (but see Note 4). For example, in selective colleges across the nation, Asian Americans are represented at three to ten times their national proportion (US News and World Report 2003). Another example of the changes is the high rate of interracial dating and marriage between Latinos and Whites and Asians and Whites (Qian and Lichter 2000; Moran 2001). These interracial unions, coupled with the collapse of formal segregation, have created the political space for 'multiracial activists'

to force the Census Bureau in 2000 to allow respondents to pick all the races they felt apply to them (Parker and Song 2001; Daniels 2002). Yet another instance of the changes in contemporary America is that few whites endorse segregationist views in surveys. This has been heralded by some as reality as 'the end of racism' (D'Souza 1995) or as 'the declining significance of race' (Wilson 1978). Lastly, blacks have been surpassed by Latinos as the largest minority group (by 2001, the Census noted that Hispanics were 13 per cent of the population and blacks 12 per cent).

I propose that all this reshuffling denotes that the bi-racial order typical of the United States, which was the exception in the world-racial system,[2] is evolving into a complex and loosely organized tri-racial stratification system similar to that of many Latin American and Caribbean nations (Degler

**Figure 1.** *Preliminary map of tri-racial system in the USA*

---

**"Whites"**
Whites
New Whites (Russians, Albanians, etc.)
Assimilated white Latinos
Some multiracials
Assimilated (urban) Native Americans
A few Asian-origin people

---

**"Honorary Whites"**
Light-skinned Latinos
Japanese Americans
Korean Americans
Asian Indians
Chinese Americans
Middle Eastern Americans
Most multiracials
Filipino Americans

---

**"Collective Black"**
Vietnamese Americans
Hmong Americans
Laotian Americans
Dark-skinned Latinos
Blacks
New West Indian and African immigrants
Reservation-bound Native Americans

---

1986; Wade 1997). Specifically, I argue the emerging tri-racial system will be comprised of 'whites' at the top, an intermediary group of 'honorary whites' similar to the coloureds in South Africa during formal apartheid (Fredrickson 1981), and a non-white group or the 'collective black' at the bottom. In Figure 1, I sketch what these three groups may look like.[3] I hypothesize that the white group will include 'traditional' whites, new 'white' immigrants and, in the near future, totally assimilated white Latinos (e.g., former Secretary of Education Lauro Cabazos, the football coach of The University of Wisconsin Barry Alvarez, and actors such as Martin Sheen), lighter-skinned multiracials (Rockquemore and Brunsma 2002), and other sub-groups; the intermediate racial group or honorary whites will comprise most light-skinned Latinos (e.g., most Cubans and segments of the Mexican and Puerto Rican communities), Japanese Americans, Korean Americans, Asian Indians, Chinese Americans, Filipinos, and most Middle Eastern Americans; and, finally, that the collective black group will include blacks, dark-skinned Latinos, Vietnamese, Cambodians and Laotians.

As a tri-racial system (or Latin- or Caribbean-like racial order), race conflict will be buffered by the intermediate group, much like class conflict is when the class structure includes a large middle class (Bottomore 1968). Furthermore, colour gradations, which have always been important matters of within-group differentiation, will become more salient factors of stratification. Lastly, Americans, like people in complex racial stratification orders, will begin making nationalists' appeals ('We are all Americans'), decry their racial past, and claim they are 'beyond race' (Martinez-Echazabal 1998). (For a full discussion of the major racial patterns in Latin American societies, see Bonilla-Silva and Glover forthcoming).

I recognize that my thesis is broad (attempting to classify where everyone will fit in the racial order),

bold (making a prediction about the future of race relations), and hard to verify empirically with the available data (there is no data set that includes systematic data on the skin tone of all Americans). Hence, my goals in this article are somewhat more modest. First, I explain why I contend a tri-racial system is emerging. Second, I examine if the available objective (e.g., data on income and education), subjective (e.g., racial attitudes and racial self-classification), and social interactional indicators (intermarriage and residential choices) point in the direction of a tri-racial order. Lastly, I discuss what may be the political implications of this new order for the racial politics of the future.

## WHY WOULD A TRI-RACIAL SYSTEM BE EMERGING IN THE USA NOW?

Why would race relations in the United States be moving towards a tri-racial regime at this point in history? The reasons are multiple. First, the demography of the nation is changing. Racial minorities are up to 30 per cent of the population and, as population projections suggest, may become a numeric majority in the year 2050 (US Bureau of the Census 1996). And these projections may be slightly off downward as early releases from the 2000 Census suggest that the Latino population was about 12.5 per cent of the population, almost one percentage point higher than the highest projection and the proportion of the white population (77.1 per cent white or in combination) was slightly lower than originally expected (Grieco and Cassidy 2001).

The rapid darkening of America is creating a situation similar to that of many Latin American and Caribbean nations where the white elites realized their countries were becoming 'black' or 'Indian' and devised a number of strategies to whiten their population and maintain white power (Helg 1990). Although whitening the population through immigration or classifying many newcomers as white

(Warren and Twine 1997; Gans 1999) is a possible solution to the new American demography, a more plausible accommodation to the new racial reality, and one that would still help maintain 'white supremacy' (Mills 1997), is to (1) create an intermediate racial group to buffer racial conflict, (2) allow some newcomers into the white racial strata, and (3) incorporate most immigrants into the collective black strata.

Second, as part of the tremendous reorganization that transpired in America in the post-civil rights era, a new kinder and gentler white supremacy emerged which Bonilla-Silva has labelled elsewhere as the 'new racism' (Smith 1995; Bonilla-Silva 2001). In post-civil rights America the maintenance of systemic white privilege is accomplished socially, economically, and politically through institutional, covert, and apparently nonracial practices. Whether in banks or universities, in stores or housing markets, 'smiling discrimination' tends to be the order of the day. This kinder and gentler form of white supremacy has produced an accompanying ideology: the ideology of colour-blind racism. This ideology denies the salience of race, scorns those who talk about race, and increasingly proclaims that 'We are all Americans' (for a detailed analysis of colour-blind racism, see Bonilla-Silva 2003).

Third, race relations have become globalized (Lusane 1997). The once almost all-white Western nations have now 'interiorized the other' (Miles 1993). The new world-systemic need for capital accumulation has led to the incorporation of 'dark' foreigners as 'guest workers' and even as permanent workers (Schoenbaum and Pond 1996). Thus, today European nations have racial minorities in their midst who are progressively becoming an underclass (Castles and Miller 1993; Cohen 1997), have developed an internal 'racial structure'

(Bonilla-Silva 1997) to maintain white power, and have a curious racial ideology that combines ethnonationalism with a race-blind ideology similar to the colour-blind racism of the United States today (for more on this, see Bonilla-Silva 2000).

This new global racial reality will reinforce the trend towards tri-racialism in the United States as versions of colour-blind racism will become prevalent in most Western nations (Winant 2001). Furthermore, as many formerly almost-all white Western countries (e.g., Germany, France, England, etc.) become more and more racially diverse, tri-racial divisions may surface in these societies too.

Fourth, the convergence of the political and ideological actions of the Republican Party, conservative commentators and activists, and the so-called 'multi-racial' movement (Rockquemore and Brunsma 2002), has created the space for the radical transformation of the way we gather racial data in America. One possible outcome of the Census Bureau categorical back-and-forth on racial and ethnic classifications is either the dilution of racial data or the elimination of race as an official category (Nobles 2000).

Lastly, the attack on affirmative action, which is part of what Stephen Steinberg (1995) has labelled as the 'racial retreat', is the clarion call signalling the end of race-based social policy in the United States. Although it is still possible to save a watered-down version of this programme, at this point, this seems doubtful. Again, this trend reinforces my thesis because the elimination of race-based social policy is, among other things, predicated on the notion that race no longer affects minorities' status. Hence, as in many countries of the world, the United States may eliminate race by decree and maintain—or even increase—the level of racial inequality (for recent data on Brazil, see Lovell and Wood 1998).

## A LOOK AT THE DATA

### A) Objective indicators of standing of the three racial strata

If the racial order in the United States is becoming tri-racial, significant gaps in socio-economic status between whites, honorary whites, and the collective black should be developing. The available data suggest this is the case. In terms of income, as Table 1 shows, Latino groups that are mostly white (Argentines, Chileans, Costa Ricans, and Cubans) have per capita incomes that are 40–100 per cent higher that those of Latino groups that are predominantly comprised of dark-skinned people (Mexicans, Puerto Ricans, Dominicans). The exceptions in Table 1 (Bolivians and Panamanians) are examples of self-selected immigrants. For example, four of the largest ten concentrations of Bolivians are in the state of Virginia, a state with just 7.2 per cent Latinos.[4] Table 1 also reveals a similar pattern for Asians: a severe income gap is emerging among honorary white Asians (Japanese,

Koreans, Filipinos, and Chinese) and those I classify as belonging to the collective black (Vietnamese, Cambodian, Hmong, and Laotians). (Data on educational standing and poverty rates analysed elsewhere (Bonilla-Silva and Glover forthcoming) exhibit the same pattern.)

Substantial group differences are also evident in the occupational status of the groups (based on data from 1990 PUMS not shown in table form). White Latinos, although far from whites, are between 50–100 per cent more likely to be represented in the 'Managerial and Professional' and 'Technical' categories than dark-skinned Latinos (for example, whereas 32 per cent of Costa Ricans are in such categories, only 17 per cent of Mexicans are). Along the same lines, elite Asians are even more likely to be well-represented in the higher prestige occupational categories than underclass Asians (for example, 45 per cent of Asian Indians are in 'Professional' and 'Technical' jobs, but only 5 per cent of Hmong, 9 per cent of Laotians, 10 per cent of Cambodians, and 23 per cent of Vietnamese.[5]

**Table 1.** *Mean Per Capita Income\* (\$) of Different Ethnic Groups, 1990*

| Latinos | Mean income | Asian Americans | Mean income |
|---|---|---|---|
| Mexican Americans | 6,470.05 | Chinese | 12,695.05 |
| Puerto Ricans | 7,250.20 | Japanese | 15,801.93 |
| Cubans | 11,727.21 | Koreans | 10,177.38 |
| Guatemalans | 7,103.94 | Asian Indians | 15,857.61 |
| Salvadorans | 6,745.21 | Filipinos | 12,313.99 |
| Costa Ricans | 10,615.79 | Taiwanese | 13,310.58 |
| Panamanians | 10,701.25 | Hmong | 1,191.89 |
| Argentines | 15,506.40 | Vietnamese | 7,930.65 |
| Chileans | 12,727.60 | Cambodians | 3,759.82 |
| Bolivians | 10,661.95 | Laotians | 4,520.04 |
| Whites | 12,159.18 | Whites | 12,159.18 |
| Blacks | 7,210.56 | Blacks | 7,210.56 |

*Source*: 1990 PUMS 5% sample.

\* I use per capita income as family income distort the status of some groups (particularly Asians and Whites) as some groups have more people than others contributing toward the family income.

## B) Subjective indicators of 'consciousness' of three racial strata

Social psychologists have amply demonstrated that it takes very little for groups to form, develop a common view, and adjudicate status positions to nominal characteristics (Tajfel 1970; Ridgeway 1991). Thus, it should not be surprising if objective gaps in income, occupational status, and education between these various groups is contributing to group formation. That is, honorary whites may be classifying themselves as 'white' or believing they are better than the 'collective black'. If this is happening, this group should also be in the process of developing white-like racial attitudes befitting their new social position and differentiating (distancing) themselves from the 'collective black'. In line with my thesis, I also expect whites to be making distinctions between honorary whites and the collective black, specifically, exhibiting a more positive outlook towards the former than towards the latter. Finally, if a tri-racial order is emerging, I speculate the 'collective black' will begin to exhibit a diffused and contradictory racial consciousness as blacks and Indians tend to do throughout Latin America and the Caribbean (Hanchard 1994; Wade 1997). I examine data for the first corollary and will mention general findings on the latter two in the final section.

### 1) Latinos' self-reports on race:

Historically, most Latinos have classified themselves as 'white', but the proportion who do so varies tremendously by group. Hence, as Table 2 shows, whereas 60 per cent or more of the members of the Latino groups I regard as honorary white classify themselves as white, 50 per cent or less of the members of the groups I regard as belonging to the collective black do so. As a case in point, whereas Mexicans, Puerto Ricans, and Central Americans are very likely to report 'Other' as their preferred 'racial' classification, most Costa Ricans, Cubans, Chileans, and Argentines choose the 'white' descriptor. This Census 1990 data mirrors the results of the 1988 Latino National Political Survey (de la Garza et al. 1992).

**Table 2.** *Racial self-classification by selected Hispanic-origin groups, 1990*

|  | White | Black | Other | Native American | Asian |
|---|---|---|---|---|---|
| Dominicans | 29.34 | 24.61 | 44.79 | 0.78 | 0.49 |
| Salvadorans | 38.96 | 0.89 | 59.19 | 0.33 | 0.63 |
| Guatemalans | 41.55 | 1.41 | 54.97 | 0.54 | 1.54 |
| Hondurans | 47.80 | 8.17 | 43.48 | 0.36 | 0.19 |
| Puerto Ricans | 46.42 | 4.90 | 47.46 | 0.25 | 0.98 |
| Mexicans | 50.63 | 0.72 | 47.37 | 0.79 | 0.49 |
| Costa Ricans | 59.38 | 6.51 | 32.99 | 0.54 | 0.58 |
| Colombians | 64.07 | 0.25 | 33.55 | 0.32 | 0.49 |
| Bolivians | 68.08 | 0.35 | 30.99 | 0.06 | 0.53 |
| Venezuelans | 73.45 | 3.42 | 22.16 | 0.49 | 0.49 |
| Chileans | 74.61 | 0.25 | 24.17 | 0.44 | 0.54 |
| Cubans | 84.76 | 3.13 | 11.75 | 0.08 | 0.29 |
| Argentines | 85.06 | 0.23 | 14.33 | 0.02 | 0.36 |

*Source*: 1990 PUMS 5% sample.

## 2) 'Racial' distinctions among Asians:

While Asians tend to vote panethnically on political issues (Espiritu 1992), distinctions between native-born and foreign-born (e.g., American-born Chinese and foreign-born Chinese) and between economically successful and unsuccessful Asians, are developing. In fact, according to various analysts, given the tremendous diversity of experiences among Asian Americans, 'all talk of Asian panethnicity should now be abandoned as useless speculation' (San Juan 2000, p. 10). Leland Saito (1998), in his *Race and Politics*, points out that many Asians have reacted to the 'Asian flack' they are experiencing with the rise in Asian immigration by fleeing the cities of immigration, disidentifying from new Asians, and invoking the image of the 'good immigrant'. In some communities, this has led to older, assimilated segments of a community to dissociate from recent migrants. For example, a Nisei returning to his community after years of overseas military service, told his dad the following about the city's new demography: 'Goddamn dad, where the hell did all these Chinese come from? Shit, this isn't even our town anymore (Ibid., p. 59)'.

To be clear, my point is not that Asian Americans have not engaged in coalition politics and, in various locations, engaged in concerted efforts to elect Asian American candidates (Saito 1998). My point is that the group labelled 'Asian Americans' is profoundly divided along many axes and to forecast that many of those already existing divisions will be racialized by whites (e.g., sexploitation of Asian women by lonely white men in the 'Oriental bride' market) (Kitano and Daniels 1995) as well as by Asian Americans themselves (e.g., intra-Asian preferences seem to follow a racialized hierarchy of desire) (see data on this in Tuan 1998 and Moran 2001).

## 3) Latinos' and Asians' racial attitudes:

The incorporation of the *majority* of Latinos as 'colonial subjects' (Puerto Ricans), refugees from wars (Central Americans), or illegal migrant workers (Mexicans) has foreshadowed subsequent patterns of integration into the American racial order. Nevertheless, the incorporation of a minority of Latinos as 'political refugees' (Cubans, Chileans, and Argentines) or as 'neutral' immigrants trying to better their economic situation (Costa Rica, Colombia) has allowed them a more comfortable ride in America's racial boat (Pedraza 1985). Therefore, whereas the incorporation of most Latinos has meant becoming 'nonwhite', for a few it has meant becoming almost white.

The identification of most Latinos as 'racial others' has led them to be more likely to be pro-black than pro-white. For example, the proportion of Mexicans and Puerto Ricans who indicate feeling very warm towards blacks is much higher (about 12 percentage points for Mexicans and 14 percentage points for Puerto Ricans) than towards Asians (the readings in the 'thermometer' range from 0 to 100 and the higher the 'temperature', the more positive are the feelings towards the group in question). In contrast, the proportion of Cubans who feel very warm towards blacks is 10 to 14 percentage points *lower* than Mexicans and Puerto Ricans. Cubans are also more likely to feel very warm towards Asians than towards blacks. More fitting of my thesis, as Table 3 shows, is that although Latinos who identify as 'white' express similar empathy towards blacks and Asians, those who identify as 'black' express the most positive feelings towards blacks (about 20 degrees warmer towards blacks than towards Asians).

Various studies have documented that Asians tend to hold anti-black and anti-Latino attitudes. For instance, Bobo, Zubrinsky, Johnson, and Oliver (1995) found that Chinese residents of Los Angeles expressed negative racial attitudes toward blacks. One Chinese resident stated, 'Blacks in

**Table 3.** *Latinos' affect toward Blacks and Asians by Latino ethnicity and racial self-classification*

|  | Blacks | Asians |
|---|---|---|
| **Latino ethnicity** | | |
| Mexicans | 60.07 | 52.88 |
| Puerto Ricans | 60.24 | 50.81 |
| Cubans | 56.36 | 56.99 |
| **Racial self-classification** | | |
| White | 57.71 | 53.49 |
| Black | 69.62 | 48.83 |
| Latino self-referent | 61.01 | 53.10 |

*Source*: Forman, Martinez, and Bonilla-Silva "Latinos' Perceptions of Blacks and Asians: Testing the Immigrant Hypothesis" (Unpublished Manuscript).

general seem to be overly lazy' and another asserted, 'Blacks have a definite attitude problem' (Bobo, Zubrinsky, Johnson, and Oliver 1995, p. 78; for a more thorough analysis, see Bobo and Johnson 2000). Studies on Korean shopkeepers in various locales have found that over 70 per cent of them hold anti-black attitudes (Min 1996; Weitzer 1997; Yoon 1997).

### C) Social interaction among members of the three racial strata

If a tri-racial system is emerging, one would expect more social (e.g., friendship, associations as neighbours, etc.) and intimate (e.g., marriage) contact between whites and honorary whites than between whites and members of the collective black. A cursory analysis of the interracial marriage and segregation data suggests this seems to be the case.

### 1) Interracial marriage:
Although most marriages in America are still intra-racial, the rates vary substantially by group. Whereas 93 per cent of whites and blacks marry within-group, 70 per cent of Latinos and Asians do so and only 33 per cent Native Americans marry Native Americans (Moran 2001, p. 103). More

significantly, when one disentangles the generic terms Asians' and 'Latinos', the data fit even more closely my thesis. For example, among 'Latinos', Cubans, Mexicans, Central Americans, and South Americans have higher rates of outmarriage than Puerto Ricans and Dominicans (Gilbertson, Fitzpatrick, and Yang 1996). Although interpreting the Asian American outmarriage patterns is very complex (groups such as Filipinos and Vietnamese have higher than expected rates partly due to the Vietnam War and the military bases in the Philippines), it is worth pointing out that the highest rate belongs to Japanese Americans and Chinese Americans (Kitano and Daniels 1995) and the lowest to Southeast Asians.

Furthermore, racial assimilation through marriage ('whitening') is significantly more likely for the children of Asian-white and Latino-white unions than for those of black-white unions. Hence, whereas only 22 per cent of the children of black fathers and white mothers are classified as white, the children of similar unions among Asians are twice as likely to be classified as white (Waters 1999). For Latinos, the data fit my thesis even closer as Latinos of Cuban, Mexican, and South American origin have high rates of exogamy compared to Puerto Ricans and Dominicans (Gilbertson, Fitzpatrick, and Yang 1996). I concur with Moran's (2001) speculation that this may reflect the fact that because Puerto Ricans and Dominicans are generally more dark-skinned, they have restricted chances for outmarriage to whites in a highly racialized marriage market.

2) *Residential segregation of Latinos and Asians*:
An imperfect measure of interracial interaction is the level of neighbourhood 'integration'. Researchers have shown that Latinos are less segregated from and are more exposed to whites than blacks (Massey and Denton 1987). Yet, they have also documented that dark-skinned Latinos (Dominicans and Puerto Ricans) experience rates of residential segregation which are similar to blacks. Thus, not surprisingly, in cities with a significant (10 per cent or higher) Latino presence, such as San Antonio, Chicago, New York, Long Beach, the index of residential dissimilarity[6] in 2000 is 60, 62, 67 and 63 per cent respectively (Lewis Mumford Center 2001).

Asians are generally less segregated from whites than blacks and Latinos. However, they have experienced an increase in residential segregation in recent years (White, Biddlecom and Guo 1993; Frey and Farley 1996). Part of the increase may be the result of the arrival of newer immigrants from Southeast Asia (Vietnam, Cambodia, and Laos) over the last two decades (Frey and Farley 1996). The relatively large Asian population in the San Francisco area, which accounts for about 21 per cent of the area's total population, has a dissimilarity index of .501, near the Latino index of .500, but less than the index for blacks at .640 (Logan 2001). Most metropolitan areas in the United States, however, do not have as large a population of Asians, and thus may not have reached the racial 'tipping point' that brings on residential segregation.

## CONCLUDING REMARKS: TRI-RACIAL ORDER, RACIAL POLITICS, AND THE FUTURE OF WHITE SUPREMACY IN AMERICA

I have presented a broad thesis about the future of race relations in the United States.[7] I argued that a new racial matrix, similar to that existing in Latin American and Caribbean societies, is developing and will eventually replace the old bi-racial one. In the emerging Amerikkka, 'blacks', 'Latinos', and 'Asians' can be found in any of the three loose racial strata. Therefore, as many members of minority groups experience 'racial redistricting' (Gallagher 2003), doing research on these groups will be more complex. Analysts will have to come to terms with the fact that many of the racial and ethnic categories we have used in the past are losing empirical purchase (how useful is the Latino category to comprehend the dissimilar experiences of Argentineans and Puerto Ricans?) as well as of the reality that members within some of these groups have vastly different experiences (is the category Cuban sufficient to understand the life trajectories of black and white 'Cubans'?).[8]

However, at this early stage of the analysis, and given the limitations of the available data on 'Latinos' and Asians' (most of the data is not parcelled out by subgroups and there is limited information by skin-tone), it is hard to make a conclusive case for Latin Americanization. Nevertheless, almost all the objective, subjective, and social interaction indicators I reviewed point in the direction one would expect if a tri-racial system is emerging. 'Honorary whites', the crucial group in my thesis, do better than members of the 'collective black', and have developed a racial attitudinal profile that is closer to that of whites, and prefer to associate with whites (a preference pattern that is reciprocated) than with members of the 'collective black'.[9]

Before I proceed to discuss the larger implications of Latin Americanization, I must clarify a number of points to avoid confusion. First, the three groups I describe will be *loosely organized* and need not act collectively or be conscious of their groupness to share a common social location. Borrowing from Marx's discussions on class, some of these racial strata will be 'race *in* itself rather than 'race *for* itself'. Second, I expect higher levels of collective action and consciousness among the poles of the racial order (i.e., among whites and the collective black much as in Latin America and the Caribbean). Third, the honorary white strata, which will be the most unstable group in this new order, is the product of the socio-political needs of whites to maintain white supremacy given local and international changes but, at the same time, actors in this group will develop their own agency.[10] Regardless of the reasons for its existence, members of this strata will defend their status vis-à-vis those below and try to achieve racial mobility through whitening as intermediate racial groups have done in the Caribbean and Latin America (Nettleford 1973; Wade 1997; Alleyne 2002).

If my prediction is right, what may be the consequences for race relations in the United States? First, racial politics will change dramatically. The 'us' versus 'them' racial dynamic will lessen as 'honorary whites' grow in size and social importance. This group is likely to buffer racial conflict—or derail it—as intermediate groups do in many Latin American countries. Two incidents reported by Norman Matloft in an Op-Ed piece in the *San Francisco Chronicle* (1997) are examples of things to come:

> In the newsletter of the Oakland chapter of the Organization of Chinese Americans, editor Peter Eng opined: "Chinese-Americans will need to separate and distance ourselves from other ethnic immigrant groups" and suggested

that Latino immigration was a burden to society.

> Elaine Kim, a Korean-American UC Berkeley professor, has written that a major Latino organization suggested to her [actually to Korean community activist Bong Huan Kim-NM] that Asians and Latinos work together against blacks in an Oakland redistricting proposal. And an Asian/Latino coalition is suing Oakland, claiming it awards too many city contracts to black-owned firms.

Second, the ideology of colour-blind racism (Bonilla-Silva 2001, 2003) will become even more salient among whites and honorary whites and will also impact members of the collective black. This ideology will help to glue the new social system and further buffer racial conflict.

Third, if the state decides to stop gathering racial statistics, the struggle to document the impact of race in a variety of social venues will become monumental. More significantly, because state actions always impact upon civil society, if the state decides to erase race from above, the *social* recognition of 'races' in the polity may become harder. Americans may develop a Latin American- or Caribbean-like 'disgust' for even mentioning anything that is race-related.

Fourth, the deep history of black-white divisions in the United States has been such that the centrality of the black identity will not dissipate. Research on the 'black elite', for instance, shows they exhibit racial attitudes in line with their racial rather than class group (Dawson 1994). That identity may be taken up by dark-skinned Latinos as it is being rapidly taken up by most West Indians (Kasinitz, Battle, and Miyares 2001) and some Latinos (Rodriguez 2000). For example, Al, a fifty-three-year-old Jamaican engineer interviewed by Milton Vickerman (1999), stated:

> I have nothing against Haitians; I have nothing against black Americans ... If you're a nigger, you're a nigger, regardless of whether you are from Timbuktu ... There isn't the unity that one would like to see ... Blacks have to appreciate blacks, no matter where they are from. Just look at it the way I look at it: That you're the same.

However, even among blacks, I predict some important changes. Their racial consciousness will become more diffused. For example, blacks are already developing a more disarticulated and blunted oppositional consciousness than ever before in American history (see Chapter 7 in Bonilla-Silva 2003). Furthermore, the external pressure of 'multiracials' in white contexts (Rockquemore and Brusma 2002) and the internal pressure of 'ethnic' blacks may change the notion of 'blackness' and even the position of some 'blacks' in the system. Colourism may become an even more important factor as a way of making social distinctions among 'blacks' (Keith and Herring 1991).

Fifth, the new order will force a reshuffling of *all* racial identities. Certain 'racial' and 'ethnic' claims may dissipate (or, in some cases, decline in significance) as mobility will increasingly be seen as based on (1) whiteness or near-whiteness and (2) intermarriage with whites (this seems to be the case among many Japanese Americans, particularly those who have intermarried). For example, the biracial project can be seen as a rejection of blackness hoping to achieve entrance into or, at least, nearness to whiteness (Minkalani 2003). This dissipation of ethnicity will not be limited to 'honorary whites' as members of the 'collective black' strata strive to position themselves higher in the new racial totem pole based on degrees of proximity or closeness to whiteness. Will Vietnamese, Hmongs, Laoatians and other members of the Asian underclass coalesce with blacks and dark-skinned Latinos or will they try to distance themselves from them and struggle to emphasize their 'Americanness'?

Lastly, the new racial stratification system will be more effective in maintaining 'white supremacy' (Mills 1997). Whites will still be at the top of the social structure but will face fewer race-based challenges, and racial inequality will remain and may even widen as is the case throughout Latin America and the Caribbean (Nascimento and Nascimento 2001). And, to avoid confusion about my claim regarding 'honorary whites', let me clarify that their standing and status will be dependent upon whites' wishes and practices. 'Honorary' means they will remain secondary, will still face discrimination, and will not receive equal treatment in society. For example, although Arab Americans will be regarded as 'honorary whites', their treatment in the post-11 September era suggests their status as 'white' and American' is tenuous at best.[11] Likewise, albeit substantial segments of the Asian American community may become 'honorary white', they will also continue to suffer from discrimination and be regarded in many quarters as 'perpetual foreigners'.

Therein lie some weaknesses of the emerging tri-racial order and the possibilities for challenging it. Members of the 'collective black' must be the backbone of the movement challenging the new order, as they are the ones who will remain literally 'at the bottom of the well'. However, if they want to be successful, they must wage, in coalition with progressive Asian and Latino organizations, a concerted effort to politicize the segments I label 'honorary whites' and make them aware of the *honorary* character of their status. This is the way out of the impending new racial quandary. We need to short-circuit the belief in near-whiteness as the solution to status differences and create a coalition of all 'people of colour' and their white allies. If the tri-racial, Latin American- or Caribbean-like model of race prevails and 'pigmentocracy' crystallizes, most Americans will scramble for the meagre wages that near-whiteness will provide to those willing to play the 'we are all American' game.

## ACKNOWLEDGEMENTS

This article could not have come into existence had it not been for an invitation by Professors Tyrone A. Forman and Amanda E. Lewis, from the University of Illinois at Chicago, to present at a conference in 2001. The paper benefited from discussions with my partner, Mary Hovsepian, a Palestinian sociologist at Texas A&M University. I also wish to acknowledge the two anonymous reviewers of *ERS* as well as the Guest Editor of this special issue, Miri Song, for their valuable feedback. Last but not least, I thank David G. Embrick, a graduate student of sociology at Texas A&M University, for assisting me with the final editing of this article.

## NOTES

1. This does not mean that blacks and whites have been the *only* racial actors in the United States's history or that more complex race relations have not existed before in some areas of the country. It just means that the macro-level racial dynamics in the United States, unlike those in many other parts of the world, have been bifurcated and that the black-white foundation has served as the yardstick to treat all other groups since the creation of the United States in 1776 (see Chapter 7 in Feagin 2000).

2. For a discussion on the racialization of the world-system, see Etienne Balibar and Immanuel Wallerstein, *Race, Nation, and Class: Ambiguous Identities* (London: Verso, 1991).

3. Figure 1 is heuristic rather than definitive and, thus, the main purpose of this map is to sketch how these three racial strata might look. Therefore, a few of racial or ethnic groups I place in these loosely structured groups may be out of place and not all the ethnic groups that comprise the United States are included.

4. An important matter to disentangle empirically in the future is if the immigrant groups we label 'honorary whites' come with the racial, class, or race/class capital before they achieve honorary white status, that is, are they allowed to fit this intermediate position because of their class or because of their racial or because of a combination of race and class status? The case of West Indians—who come to the Unites States with class advantages (e.g., educational and otherwise) and yet 'fade to black' in a few generations (that is, become 'black') suggest that the 'racial' status of the group has an independent effect in this process (Kasinitz, Battle, and Miyares 2001). Similarly, Filipinos come to the United States highly educated and acculturated yet, because they experience severe racial discrimination, second-and third-generation Filipinos' self-identify as Filipino-American (Le Espiritu and Wolf 2001. For a similar finding on Vietnamese, see Zhou 2001).

5. It is important to point out that occupational representation in a category does not mean equality. Chan (1991) shows that many Asians are pushed into self-employment after suffering occupational sedimentation in professional jobs. See also Ronald Takaki, *A Different Mirror: A History of Multicultural America* (Boston: Little, Brown & Co., 1993).

6. The index of residential dissimilarity expresses the percentage of a minority population that would have to move to result in a perfectly even distribution of the population across census

tracts. This index runs from 0 (no segregation) to 100 (total segregation) and its symmetrical (not affected by population size).

7. I am not alone in making this kind of prediction. Arthur K. Spears (1999), Suzanne Oboler (2000), Gary Okihiro (1994), Mari Matsueda (1996) have made similar claims recently.

8. This separation within the Cuban ethnic group may already be happening. See Mirta Ojito (2001) 'Best of Friends, Worlds Apart', in *How Race is Lived in America,* Correspondents of the *New York Times,* pp. 23–39 (New York: Henry Holt and Company).

9. I recognize there are alternative interpretations to these findings. One could claim that what is happening is that class is becoming more salient than race (but see Note 3), or that education and nativity are becoming better predictors of mobility. Unfortunately, no data set includes all these elements as well as the ones I suggest are becoming central to control for all these variables. In the mean time, the fact that indicators in three different areas line up in the expected direction gives me confidence that my thesis is likely.

10. For an excellent collection analysing, among other things, the instability of intermediate mulatto and *mestizo* groups in Latin America and, at the same time, their agency in articulating a stake in whiteness, see *Race & Nation in Modern Latin America,* edited by Nancy P. Appelbaum *et al.* (Chapel Hill and London: University of North Carolina Press, 2003).

11. However, I still contend that most Arab Americans will be part of this intermediate strata. First, although recent immigrants remain loyal to their ethnic communities, older, well-established Arab Americans put their emphasis 'not on their ethnicity but on their Americanism' (Suleiman 1994). Second, even though recent immigrants experience some economic hardships, the Census data indicate that Arab Americans have levels of education, income, and occupational standing similar to the majority community (Schopmeyer 2000). Lastly, although I acknowledge the vulnerability of Arab Americans in post-11 September America, there are two things to note. First, this has not led Arab Americans to develop a political programme of identification and cooperation with racial minorities. Second, we must not forget that other groups, such as Japanese Americans, suffered equal indignities in the past (in the 1940s, they were interned in concentration camps, and in the 1990s they were treated as traitors during the 50th anniversary of Pearl Harbor) and yet did not become a racial underclass or change their racial attitudes and political behaviour towards the racial groups at the bottom of America's racial barrel.

## REFERENCES

ALMAGUER, TOMÁS 1994 *Racial Fault Lines: The Historical Origins of White Supremacy in California*, Berkeley, Los Angeles, and London: The University of California Press

ALLEYNE, MERVYN C. 2002 *The Construction and Representation of Race and Ethnicity in the Caribbean and the World*, Mona and Kingston: University of the West Indies Press

AMOTT, TERESA and MATTHEAI, LESLIE 1991 *Race, Gender, and Work: A Multicultural History of Women in the United States*, Boston, MA: South End Press

APPLEBAUM, NANCY P., MACPHERSON, ANNE S. and ROSEMBLATT, KARIN ALEJANDRA (eds) 2003 *Race & Nation in Modern Latin America*, Chapel Hill and London: University of North Carolina Press

BALIBAR, ETIENNE and WALLERSTEIN, IMMANUEL 1991 *Race, Nation, and Class: Ambiguous Identities*, London: Verso

BOBO, LAWRENCE and JOHNSON, DEVON 2000 'Racial attitudes in a prismatic metropolis: mapping identity, stereotypes, competition, and views on affirmative action', in Lawrence Bobo, Melvin Oliver, James Johnson and Abel Valenzuela (eds), *Prismatic Metropolis,* New York: Russell Sage Foundation, pp. 81–166

BOBO, LAWRENCE, ZUBRINSKY, CAMILLE, JOHNSON, JAMES JR, and OLIVER, MELVIN 1995 'Work orientation, job discrimination, and ethnicity', *Research in the Sociology of Work,* vol. 5, pp. 45–85

BONILLA-SILVA, EDUARDO and GLOVER, KAREN S. forthcoming 'We are all Americans! The Latin Americanization of race relations in the USA, in Amanda E. Lewis and Maria Kry san (eds), *The Changing Terrain of Race and Ethnicity: Theory, Methods and Public Policy,* New York: Russell Sage Foundation

BONILLA-SILVA, EDUARDO 2003 *Racism Without Racists: Color Blind Racism and the Persistence of Racial Inequality,* Boulder, CO: Rowman and Littlefield

——2001 *White Supremacy and Racism in the Post-Civil Rights Era,* Boulder, CO: Lynne Rienner Publishers

——2000 'This is a white country': The racial ideology of the Western nations of the world-system', *Sociological Inquiry,* vol. 70, no. 3, pp. 188–214

——1997 'Rethinking racism: towards a structural interpretation', *American Sociological Review,* vol. 62, no. 3, pp. 465–80

BOTTOMORE, THOMAS B. 1968 *Classes in Modern Society,* New York: Vintage Books

CASTLES, STEPHEN and MILLER, MARK 1993 *The Age of Migration: International Population Movements in the Modern World,* Hong Kong: Macmillan

CHAN, SUCHENG 1991 *Asian Americans: An Interpretive History*, Boston, MA: Twayne Publishers

COHEN, ROBIN 1997 *Global Diasporas: An Introduction*, Seattle, WA: University of Washington Press

DANIELS, REGINALD 2002 *More Than Black? Multiracial Identity and the New Racial Order*, Philadelphia, PA: Temple University Press

DAWSON, MICHAEL C. 1994 *Behind the Mule: Race and Class in African American Politics*, Princeton, NJ: Princeton University Press

DEGLER, CARL N. 1986 *Neither Black nor White: Slavery and Race Relations in Brazil and the United States*, Madison, WI: The University of Wisconsin Press

DE LA GARZA, RODOLFO O., DESIPIO, LOUIS, GARCIA, CHRIS, GARCIA, JOHN and FALCON, ANGELO (eds) 1993 *Latino Voices: Mexican, Puerto Rican, & Cuban Perspectives on American Politics*, Boulder, San Francisco, and Oxford: Westview Press

D'SOUZA, DINESH 1995 *The End of Racism: Principles for a Multiracial Society*, New York: Free Press

ESPIRITU, YEN LE 1992 *Asian American Panethnicity: Bridging Institutions and Identities*, Philadelphia, PA: Temple University Press

ESPIRITU, YEN LE and WOLF, DIANE 2001 'The paradox of assimilation: Children of Filipino immigrants in San Diego', in Ruben Rumbaut and Alejandro Portes (eds), *Ethnicities: Children of Immigrants in America,* Berkeley and New York: University of California Press and Russell Sage Foundation

FEAGIN, JOE R. 2000 *Racist America: Roots, Current Realities, and Future Reparations*, London and New York: Routledge

FREDRICKSON, GEORGE M 1981 *White Supremacy*, Oxford, New York, Toronto, and Melbourne: Oxford University Press

FREY, WILLIAM H. and REYNOLDS, FARLEY 1996 'Latino, Asian, and Black segregation in U.S.

metropolitan areas: are multi-ethnic metros different?', *Demography*, vol. 33, no. 1, pp. 35–50

GALLAGHER, CHARLES A. 2003 'Racial redistricting: expanding the boundaries of whiteness', in Heather Dalmage (ed.), *The Multiracial Movement: The Politics of Color*, New York: SUNY Press, pp. XX

GANS, HERBERT J. 1999 *The Possibility of a New Racial Hierarchy in the Twenty-First Century United States*, Chicago, IL: The University of Chicago Press

GILBERTSON, GRETA A., FITZPATRICK, JOSEPH P. and LIJUN, YANG 1996 'Hispanic outmarriage in New York City-new evidence from 1991', *International Immigration Review*, vol. 30

GRIECO, ELIZABETH M. and CASSIDY, RACHEL C. 2001 *Overview of Race and Hispanic Origin 2000*, Washington: U.S. Government Printing Office

HANCHARD, MICHAEL 1994 *Orpheus and Power: The Movimiento Negro of Rio de Janeiro and Sao Paulo, Brazil, 1945–1988*, Princeton, NJ: Princeton University Press

HELG, ALINE 1990 'Race in Argentina and Cuba, 1880–1930: Theory, policies, and popular reaction', in Richard Graham (ed.), *The Idea of Race in Latin America, 1870–1940*, Austin: University of Texas Press, pp. 37–69

KASINITZ, PHILIP, BATTLE, JUAN and MIYARES, INES 2001 'Fade to black? The children of West Indian immigrants in southern Florida', in Ruben G Rumbaut and Alejandro Portes (eds), *Ethnicities: Children of Immigrants in America*, Berkeley, CA: University of California Press, pp. 267–300

KEITH, VERNA M. and HERRING, CEDRIC 1991 'Skin tone and stratification in the Black community', *American Journal of Sociology*, vol. 97, no. 3, pp. 760–78

KITANO, HARRY H. L. and DANIELS, ROGERS 1995 *Asian Americans: Emerging Minorities*, 2nd edn, Englewood Cliffs, NJ: Prentice Hall

LEWIS MUMFORD CENTER 2001 *Racial and Ethnic Population Totals, Dissimilarity Indices and Exposure for Metropolitan Areas, 1990–2000*

LOGAN, JOHN R. 2001 *From Many Shores: Asians in Census 2000*, in Report by the Lewis Mumford Center for Comparative Urban and Regional Research, Albany: University of Albany

LOVELL, PEGGY A. and WOOD, CHARLES H. 1998 'Skin color, racial identity, and life chances in Brazil', *Latin American Perspectives*, vol. 25, no. 3, pp. 90–109

LUSANE, CLARENCE 1997 *Race in the Global Era: African Americans at the Millennium*, Boston, MA: South End Press

MARTINEZ-ECHAZABEL, LOURDES 1998 'Mestizaje and the discourse of national/cultural identity in Latin America, 1845–1959', *Latin American Perspectives*, vol. 25, no. 3, pp. 21–42

MASSEY, DOUGLAS S. and DENTON, NANCY A. 1987 'Trends in the residential segregation of Blacks, Hispanics, and Asians: 1970–1980', *American Sociological Review*, vol. 52, no. 6, pp. 802–825

MATLOFF, NORMAN 1997 'Asians, Blacks, and intolerance', *San Francisco Chronicle*, 20 May

MATSUEDA, MARI J. 1996 *Where is Your Body? And Other Essays on Race, Gender and the Law*, Boston, MA: Beacon Press

MILES, ROBERT 1993 *Racism After 'Race Relations'*, London: Routledge

MILLS, CHARLES W 1997 *The Racial Contract*, Ithaca and London: Cornell University Press

MIN, PYONG GAP 1996 *Caught in the Middle: Korean Communities in New York and Los Angeles*, Berkeley, CA: University of California Press

MINKALANI, MINKAH 2003 'Rejecting Blackness and claiming Whiteness: antiblack Whiteness in the biracial project', in Ashley Doane and Eduardo

Bonilla-Silva (eds), *White Out: The Continuing Significance of Racism*, New York and London: Routledge, pp. 81–94

MORAN, RACHEL 2001 *Interracial Intimacy: The Regulation of Race and Romance*, Chicago and London: The University of Chicago Press

NASCIMENTO, ABDIAS and NASCIMENTO, ELISA LARKIN 2001 'Dance of deception: a reading of race relations in Brazil', in Charles Hamilton *et al.* (eds), *Beyond Racism*, Boulder and London: Lynne Rienner Publishers, pp. 105–56

NETTLEFORD, REX 1973 'National identity and attitudes toward race in Jamaica', in David Lowenthal and Lambros Comitas (eds), *Consequences of Class and Color: West Indian Perspectives*, New York: Doubleday, pp. 35–55

NOBLES, MELISSA 2000 *Shades of Citizenship: Race and the Census in Modern Politics*, Stanford, CA: Stanford University Press

OKIHIRO, GARY 1994 *Margins and Mainstreams: Asians in American History and Culture*, Seattle, WA: University of Washington Press

OBOLER, SUZANNE 2000 'It must be a fake!' racial ideologies, identities, and the question of rights in Hispanics/Latinos', in Jorge J. E. Gracia and Pablo De Greiff (eds), *The United States: Ethnicity, Race, and Rights*, New York: Routledge, pp. 125–44

OJITO, MIRTA 2001 'Best of friends, worlds apart', in Correspondents of the *New York Times* (eds), *How Race is Lived in America*, New York: Henry Holt and Company, pp. 23–39

PARKER, DAVID and SONG, MIRI 2001 *Rethinking 'Mixed Race*, London: Pluto Press

PEDRAZA, SILVIA 1985 *Political and Economic Migrants in America: Cubans and Mexicans*, Austin, TX: University of Texas Press

QIAN, ZHENCHAO and LICHTER, DANIEL T. 2000 'Measuring marital assimilation: intermarriage among natives and immigrants', *Social Science Research*, vol. 30, pp. 289–312

RIDGEWAY, CECILIA L. 1991 'The social construction of status value: Gender and other nominal characteristics', *Social Forces*, vol. 70, no. 2, pp. 367–86

ROCKQUEMORE, KERRY ANN and BRUNSMA, DAVID L. 2002 *Beyond Black: Biracial Identity in America*, Thousand Oaks, CA: Sage Publications

RODRIGUEZ, CLARA E. 2000 *Changing Race: Latinos, the Census, and the History of Ethnicity in the United States*, New York: New York University Press

ROEDIGER, DAVID 1991 *The Wages of Whiteness: Race and the Making of the American Working Class*, New York: Verso

SAITO, LELAND T. 1998 *Race and Politics: Asian Americans, Latinos, and Whites in a Los Angeles Suburb*, Urbana: University of Illinois Press

SAN JUAN, E. JR. 2000 'The limits of ethnicity and the horizon of historical materialism', in Esther Mikyung Ghymn (ed.) *Asian American Studies: Identity, Images, Issues Past and Present*, New York: Peter Lang, pp. 9–34

SCHOENBAUM, DAVID and POND, ELIZABETH 1996 *The German Question and Other German Questions*, New York: St. Martin's Press

SCHOPMEYER, KIM 2000 A demographic portrait of Arab detroit'. in Nabeel Abraham and Andrew Shyrock (eds), *Arab Detroit: From Margin to Mainstream*, Detroit: Wayne State University Press, pp. 61–94

SMITH, ROBERT C. 1995 *Racism in the Post-Civil Rights Era: Now You See It, Now You Don't*, Albany: State University of New York Press

SPEARS, ARTHUR K. 1999 *Race and Ideology: Language, Symbolism, and Popular Culture*, Detroit: Wayne State University Press

STEINBERG, STEPHEN 1995 *Turning Back: The Retreat from Racial Justice in American Thought and Policy*, Boston, MA: Beacon Press

SULEIMAN, MICHAEL W 1994 Arab Americans and the political process', in Ernest McCarus (ed.),

*The Development of Arab-American Identity*, Ann Arbor, MI: The University of Michigan Press, pp. 37–60

TAKAKI, RONALD 1993 *A Different Mirror: A History of Multicultural America*, Boston, MA: Little, Brown & Co

TAJFEL, H. 1970 'Experiments in intergroup discrimination', *Scientific American*, vol. 223, pp. 96–102

TUAN, MIA 1998 *Forever Foreigners or Honorary Whites? The Asian Ethnic Experience Today*, New Brunswick: Rutgers University Press

US BUREAU OF THE CENSUS 1996 *Population Projections of the United States by Age, Sex, Race, and Hispanic Origin: 1995 to 2050*, Washington D.C.: US Government Printing Office

US NEWS AND WORLD REPORT 2003 *America's Best Colleges*, Washington, D.C.: US News and World Report

VICKERMAN, MILTON 1999 *Crosscurrents: West Indian Immigrants and Race*, New York: Oxford University Press

WADE, PETER 1997 *Race and Ethnicity in Latin America*, London: Pluto Press

WARREN, JONATHAN W and TWINE, FRANCE WINDDANCE 1997 'White Americans, the new minority?: Non-Blacks and the ever-expanding boundaries of Whiteness', *Journal of Black Studies*, vol. 28, no. 2, pp. 200–18

WATERS, MARY C. 1999 *Black Identities: West Indian Immigrant Dreams and American Reality*, Cambridge, MA: Harvard University Press

WEITZER, RONALD 1997 'Racial prejudice among Korean merchants in African American Neighborhoods', *Sociological Quarterly*, vol. 38, no. 4, pp. 587–606

WHITE, MICHAEL J, BIDDLECOM, ANN E. and GUO, SHENYAND 1993 'Immigration, naturalization, and residential assimilation among Asian Americans in 1980', *Social Forces*, vol. 72, no. 1, pp. 93–117

WILSON, WILLIAM J. 1978 *The Declining Significance of Race*, Chicago, IL: The University of Chicago Press

WINANT, HOWARD 2001 *The World is a Ghetto: Race and Democracy Since World War II*, New York: Basic Books

YOON, IN-JIN 1997 *On My Own: Korean Businesses and Race Relations in America*, Chicago, IL: University of Chicago Press

ZHOU, MIN 2001 'Straddling different worlds: The acculturation of Vietnamese refugee children', in Ruben G. Rumbaut and Alejandro Portes (eds), *Ethnicities: Children of Immigrants in America*, Berkeley, CA: University of California Press, pp. 187–227

**EDUARDO BONILLA-SILVA** is an Associate Professor in the Department of Sociology, Texas A&M University, College Station. ADDRESS: Department of Sociology, 4351 TAMU, College Station, TX 77843, USA. Email: bonilla@tamu.edu

# The Social Psychology of Prejudice and Perceived Discrimination

# RACE PREJUDICE AS A SENSE OF GROUP POSITION[*]

*By Herbert Blumer*

In this paper I am proposing an approach to the study of race prejudice different from that which dominates contemporary scholarly thought on this topic. My thesis is that race prejudice exists basically in a sense of group position rather than in a set of feelings which members of one racial group have toward the members of another racial group. This different way of viewing race prejudice shifts study and analysis from a preoccupation with feelings as lodged in individuals to a concern with the relationship of racial groups. It also shifts scholarly treatment away from individual lines of experience and focuses interest on the collective process by which a racial group comes to define and redefine another racial group. Such shifts, I believe, will yield a more realistic and penetrating understanding of race prejudice.

There can be little question that the rather vast literature on race prejudice is dominated by the idea that such prejudice exists fundamentally as a feeling or set of feelings lodged in the individual. It is usually depicted as consisting of feelings such as antipathy, hostility, hatred, intolerance, and aggressiveness. Accordingly, the task of scientific inquiry becomes two-fold. On one hand, there is a need to identify the feelings which make up race prejudice—to see how they fit together and how they are supported by other psychological elements, such as mythical beliefs. On the other hand, there is need of showing how the feeling complex has come into being. Thus, some scholars trace the complex feelings back chiefly to innate dispositions; some trace it to personality composition, such as authoritarian personality; and others regard the feelings of prejudice as being formed through social experience. However different may be the contentions regarding the make-up of racial prejudice and the way in which it may come into existence, these contentions are alike in locating prejudice in the realm of individual feeling. This is clearly true of the work of psychologists, psychiatrists, and social psychologists, and tends to be predominantly the case in the work of sociologists.

Unfortunately, this customary way of viewing race prejudice overlooks and obscures the fact that race prejudice is fundamentally a matter of relationship between racial groups. A little reflective thought should make this very clear. Race prejudice presupposes, necessarily, that racially prejudiced

---

[*] Read at the dedication of the Robert E. Park Building, Fisk University, March, 1956.

Herbert Blumer, "Race Prejudice as a Sense of Group Position," *Pacific Sociological Review*, vol. 1, no. 1, pp. 3-7. Copyright © 1958 by SAGE Publications. Reprinted with permission.

individuals think of themselves as belonging to a given racial group. It means, also, that they assign to other racial groups those against whom they are prejudiced. Thus, logically and actually, a scheme of racial identification is necessary as a framework for racial prejudice. Moreover, such identification involves the formation of an image or a conception of one's own racial group and of another racial group, inevitably in terms of the relationship of such groups. To fail to see that racial prejudice is a matter (a) of the racial identification made of oneself and of others, and (b) of the way in which the identified groups are conceived in relation to each other, is to miss what is logically and actually basic. One should keep clearly in mind that people necessarily come to identify themselves as belonging to a racial group; such identification is not spontaneous or inevitable but a result of experience. Further, one must realize that the kind of picture which a racial group forms of itself and the kind of picture which it may form of others are similarly products of experience. Hence, such pictures are variable, just as the lines of experience which produce them are variable.

The body of feelings which scholars, today, are so inclined to regard as constituting the substance of race prejudice is actually a resultant of the way in which given racial groups conceive of themselves and of others. A basic understanding of race prejudice must be sought in the process by which racial groups form images of themselves and of others. This process, as I hope to show, is fundamentally *a collective process*. It operates chiefly through the public media in which individuals who are accepted as the spokesmen of a racial group characterize publicly another racial group. To characterize another racial group is, by opposition, to define one's own group. This is equivalent to placing the two groups in relation to each other, or defining their positions *vis-à-vis* each other. It is the *sense of social position* emerging from this collective process

of characterization which provides the basis of race prejudice. The following discussion will consider important facets of this matter.

I would like to begin by discussing several of the important feelings that enter into race prejudice. This discussion will reveal how fundamentally racial feelings point to and depend on a positional arrangement of the racial groups. In this discussion I will confine myself to such feelings in the case of a dominant racial group.

There are four basic types of feeling that seem to be always present in race prejudice in the dominant group. They are (1) a feeling of superiority, (2) a feeling that the subordinate race is intrinsically different and alien, (3) a feeling of proprietary claim to certain areas of privilege and advantage, and (4) a fear and suspicion that the subordinate race harbors designs on the prerogatives of the dominant race. A few words about each of these four feelings will suffice.

In race prejudice there is a self-assured feeling on the part of the dominant racial group of being naturally superior or better. This is commonly shown in a disparagement of the qualities of the subordinate racial group. Condemnatory or debasing traits, such as laziness, dishonesty, greediness, unreliability, stupidity, deceit and immorality, are usually imputed to it. The second feeling, that the subordinate race is an alien and fundamentally different stock, is likewise always present. "They are not of our kind" is a common way in which this is likely to be expressed. It is this feeling that reflects, justifies, and promotes the social exclusion of the subordinate racial group. The combination of these two feelings of superiority and of distinctiveness can easily give rise to feelings of aversion and even antipathy. But in themselves they do not form prejudice. We have to introduce the third and fourth types of feeling.

The third feeling, the sense of proprietary claim, is of crucial importance. It is the feeling on the part of the dominant group of being entitled to either exclusive or prior rights in many important areas of life. The range of such exclusive or prior claims may be wide, covering the ownership of property such as choice lands and sites; the right to certain jobs, occupations or professions; the claim to certain kinds of industry or lines of business; the claim to certain positions of control and decision-making as in government and law; the right to exclusive membership in given institutions such as schools, churches and recreational institutions; the claim to certain positions of social prestige and to the display of the symbols and accoutrements of these positions; and the claim to certain areas of intimacy and privacy. The feeling of such proprietary claims is exceedingly strong in race prejudice. Again, however, this feeling even in combination with the feeling of superiority and the feeling of distinctiveness does not explain race prejudice. These three feelings are present frequently in societies showing no prejudice, as in certain forms of feudalism, in caste relations, in societies of chiefs and commoners, and under many settled relations of conquerors and conquered. Where claims are solidified into a structure which is accepted or respected by all, there seems to be no group prejudice.

The remaining feeling essential to race prejudice is a fear or apprehension that the subordinate racial group is threatening, or will threaten, the position of the dominant group. Thus, acts or suspected acts that are interpreted as an attack on the natural superiority of the dominant group, or an intrusion into their sphere of group exclusiveness, or an encroachment on their area of proprietary claim are crucial in arousing and fashioning race prejudice. These acts mean "getting out of place."

It should be clear that these four basic feelings of race prejudice definitely refer to a positional arrangement of the racial groups. The feeling of superiority places the subordinate people *below*; the feeling of alienation places them *beyond*; the

feeling of proprietary claim excludes them from the prerogatives of position; and the fear of encroachment is an emotional recoil from the endangering of group position. As these features suggest, the positional relation of the two racial groups is crucial in race prejudice. The dominant group is not concerned with the subordinate group as such but it is deeply concerned with its position *vis-à-vis* the subordinate group. This is epitomized in the key and universal expression that a given race is all right in "its place." The sense of group position is the very heart of the relation of the dominant to the subordinate group. It supplies the dominant group with its framework of perception, its standard of judgment, its patterns of sensitivity, and its emotional proclivities.

It is important to recognize that this sense of group position transcends the feelings of the individual members of the dominant group, giving such members a common orientation that is not otherwise to be found in separate feelings and views. There is likely to be considerable difference between the ways in which the individual members of the dominant group think and feel about the subordinate group. Some may feel bitter and hostile, with strong antipathies, with an exalted sense of superiority and with a lot of spite; others may have charitable and protective feelings, marked by a sense of piety and tinctured by benevolence; others may be condescending and reflect mild contempt; and others may be disposed to politeness and considerateness with no feelings of truculence. These are only a few of many different patterns of feeling to be found among members of the dominant racial group. What gives a common dimension to them is a sense of the social position of their group. Whether the members be humane or callous, cultured or unlettered, liberal or reactionary, powerful or impotent, arrogant or humble, rich or poor, honorable or dishonorable—all are led, by virtue of sharing the sense of group position, to similar individual positions.

The sense of group position is a general kind of orientation. It is a general feeling without being reducible to specific feelings like hatred, hostility or antipathy. It is also a general understanding without being composed of any set of specific beliefs. On the social psychological side it cannot be equated to a sense of social status as ordinarily conceived, for it refers not merely to vertical positioning but to many other lines of position independent of the vertical dimension. Sociologically it is not a mere reflection of the objective relations between racial groups. Rather, it stands for "what ought to be" rather than for "what is." It is a sense of where the two racial groups *belong*.

In its own way, the sense of group position is a norm and imperative—indeed a very powerful one. It guides, incites, cows, and coerces. It should be borne in mind that this sense of group position stands for and involves a fundamental kind of group affiliation for the members of the dominant racial group. To the extent they recognize or feel themselves as belonging to that group they will automatically come under the influence of the sense of position held by that group. Thus, even though given individual members may have personal views and feelings different from the sense of group position, they will have to conjure with the sense of group position held by their racial group. If the sense of position is strong, to act contrary to it is to risk a feeling of self-alienation and to face the possibility of ostracism. I am trying to suggest, accordingly, that the locus of race prejudice is not in the area of individual feeling but in the definition of the respective positions of the racial groups.

The source of race prejudice lies in a felt challenge to this sense of group position. The challenge, one must recognize, may come in many different ways. It may be in the form of an affront to feelings of group superiority; it may be in the form of

attempts at familiarity or transgressing the boundary line of group exclusiveness; it may be in the form of encroachment at countless points of proprietary claim; it may be a challenge to power and privilege; it may take the form of economic competition. Race prejudice is a defensive reaction to such challenging of the sense of group position. It consists of the disturbed feelings, usually of marked hostility, that are thereby aroused. As such, race prejudice is a protective device. It functions, however shortsightedly, to preserve the integrity and the position of the dominant group.

It is crucially important to recognize that the sense of group position is not a mere summation of the feelings of position such as might be developed independently by separate individuals as they come to compare themselves with given individuals of the subordinate race. The sense of group position refers to the position of group to group, not to that of individual to individual. Thus, *vis-à-vis* the subordinate racial group the unlettered individual with low status in the dominant racial group has a sense of group position common to that of the elite of his group. By virtue of sharing this sense of position such an individual, despite his low status, feels that members of the subordinate group, however distinguished and accomplished, are somehow inferior, alien, and properly restricted in the area of claims. He forms his conception as a representative of the dominant group; he treats individual members of the subordinate group as representative of that group.

An analysis of how the sense of group position is formed should start with a clear recognition that it is an historical product. It is set originally by conditions of initial contact. Prestige, power, possession of skill, numbers, original self-conceptions, aims, designs and opportunities are a few of the factors that may fashion the original sense of group position. Subsequent experience in the relation of the two racial groups, especially in the area of claims, opportunities and advantages, may mould the sense of group position in many diverse ways. Further, the sense of group position may be intensified or weakened, brought to sharp focus or dulled. It may be deeply entrenched and tenaciously resist change for long periods of time. Or it may never take root. It may undergo quick growth and vigorous expansion, or it may dwindle away through slow-moving erosion. It may be firm or soft, acute or dull, continuous or intermittent. In short, viewed comparatively, the sense of group position is very variable.

However variable its particular career, the sense of group position is clearly formed by a running process in which the dominant racial group is led to define and redefine the subordinate racial group and the relations between them. There are two important aspects of this process of definition that I wish to single out for consideration.

First, the process of definition occurs obviously through complex interaction and communication between the members of the dominant group. Leaders, prestige bearers, officials, group agents, dominant individuals and ordinary laymen present to one another characterizations of the subordinate group and express their feelings and ideas on the relations. Through talk, tales, stories, gossip, anecdotes, messages, pronouncements, news accounts, orations, sermons, preachments and the like definitions are presented and feelings are expressed. In this usually vast and complex interaction separate views run against one another, influence one another, modify each other, incite one another and fuse together in new forms. Correspondingly, feelings which are expressed meet, stimulate each other, feed on each other, intensify each other and emerge in new patterns. Currents of view and currents of feeling come into being; sweeping along to positions of dominance and serving as polar points for the organization of thought and sentiment. If the interaction becomes increasingly circular and

reinforcing, devoid of serious inner opposition, such currents grow, fuse and become strengthened. It is through such a process that a collective image of the subordinate group is formed and a sense of group position is set. The evidence of such a process is glaring when one reviews the history of any racial arrangement marked by prejudice.

Such a complex process of mutual interaction with its different lines and degrees of formation gives the lie to the many schemes which would lodge the cause of race prejudice in the make-up of the individual—whether in the form of innate disposition, constitutional make-up, personality structure, or direct personal experience with members of the other race. The collective image and feelings in race prejudice are forged out of a complicated social process in which the individual is himself shaped and organized. The scheme, so popular today, which would trace race prejudice to a so-called authoritarian personality shows a grievous misunderstanding of the simple essentials of the collective process that leads to a sense of group position.

The second important aspect of the process of group definition is that it is necessarily concerned with *an abstract image* of the subordinate racial group. The subordinate racial group is defined as if it were an entity or whole. This entity or whole—like the Negro race, or the Japanese, or the Jews—is necessarily an abstraction, never coming within the perception of any of the senses. While actual encounters are with individuals, the picture formed of the racial group is necessarily of a vast entity which spreads out far beyond such individuals and transcends experience with such individuals. The implications of the fact that the collective image is of an abstract group are of crucial significance. I would like to note four of these implications.

First, the building of the image of the abstract group takes place in the area of the remote and not of the near. It is not the experience with concrete individuals in daily association that gives rise to the definitions of the extended, abstract group. Such immediate experience is usually regulated and orderly. Even where such immediate experience is disrupted the new definitions which are formed are limited to the individuals involved. The collective image of the abstract group grows up not by generalizing from experiences gained in close, first-hand contacts but through the transcending characterizations that are made of the group as an entity. Thus, one must seek the central stream of definition in those areas where the dominant group as such is characterizing the subordinate group as such. This occurs in the "public arena" wherein the spokesmen appear as representatives and agents of the dominant group. The extended public arena is constituted by such things as legislatives assemblies, public meetings, conventions, the press, and the printed word. What goes on in this public arena attracts the attention of large numbers of the dominant group and is felt as the voice and action of the group as such.

Second, the definitions that are forged in the public arena center, obviously, about matters that are felt to be of major importance. Thus, we are led to recognize the crucial role of the "big event" in developing a conception of the subordinate racial group. The happening that seems momentous, that touches deep sentiments, that seems to raise fundamental questions about relations, and that awakens strong feelings of identification with one's racial group is the kind of event that is central in the formation of the racial image. Here, again, we note the relative unimportance of the huge bulk of experiences coming from daily contact with individuals of the subordinate group. It is the events seemingly loaded with great collective significance that are the focal points of the public discussion. The definition of these events is chiefly responsible for the development of a racial image and of the sense of group position. When this public discussion takes the form of a denunciation of the subordinate racial group, signifying that it is unfit and a threat, the discussion becomes particularly potent in shaping the sense of social position.

Third, the major influence in public discussion is exercised by individuals and groups who have the public ear and who are felt to have standing, prestige, authority and power. Intellectual and social elites, public figures of prominence, and leaders of powerful organizations are likely to be the key figures in the formation of the sense of group position and in the characterization of the subordinate group. It is well to note this in view of the not infrequent tendency of students to regard race prejudice as growing out of the multiplicity of experiences and attitudes of the bulk of the people.

Fourth, we also need to perceive the appreciable opportunity that is given to strong interest groups in directing the lines of discussion and setting the interpretations that arise in such discussion. Their self-interests may dictate the kind of position they wish the dominant racial group to enjoy. It may be a position which enables them to retain certain advantages, or even more to gain still greater advantages. Hence, they may be vigorous in seeking to manufacture events to attract public attention and to set lines of issue in such a way as to predetermine interpretations favorable to their interests. The role of strongly organized groups seeking to further special interest is usually central in the formation of collective images of abstract groups. Historical records of major instances of race relations, as in our South, or in South Africa, or in Europe in the case of the Jew, or on the West Coast in the case of the Japanese show the formidable part played by interest groups in defining the subordinate racial group.

I conclude this highly condensed paper with two further observations that may throw additional light on the relation of the sense of group position to race prejudice. Race prejudice becomes entrenched and tenacious to the extent the prevailing social order is rooted in the sense of social position. This has been true of the historic South in our country. In such a social order race prejudice tends to become chronic and impermeable to change. In other places the social order may be affected only to a limited extent by the sense of group position held by the dominant racial group. This I think has been true usually in the case of anti-Semitism in Europe and this country. Under these conditions the sense of group position tends to be weaker and more vulnerable. In turn, race prejudice has a much more variable and intermittent career, usually becoming pronounced only as a consequence of grave disorganizing events that allow for the formation of a scapegoat.

This leads me to my final observation which in a measure is an indirect summary. The sense of group position dissolves and race prejudice declines when the process of running definition does not keep abreast of major shifts in the social order. When events touching on relations are not treated as "big events" and hence do not set crucial issues in the arena of public discussion; or when the elite leaders or spokesmen do not define such big events vehemently or adversely; or where they define them in the direction of racial harmony; or when there is a paucity of strong interest groups seeking to build up a strong adverse image for special advantage—under such conditions the sense of group position recedes and race prejudice declines.

The clear implication of my discussion is that the proper and the fruitful area in which race prejudice should be studied is the collective process through which a sense of group position is formed. To seek, instead, to understand it or to handle it in the arena of individual feeling and of individual experience seems to me to be clearly misdirected.

# REACTIONS TOWARD THE NEW MINORITIES OF WESTERN EUROPE

By Thomas F. Pettigrew

## ABSTRACT

Millions of ex-colonials, "guest workers," refugees, and other immigrants have settled in western Europe during recent decades. Extensive research on this phenomenon broadens sociology's understanding of intergroup relations in industrial societies. Unlike African Americans, these new Europeans are often viewed as not "belonging," and gaining citizenship can be difficult. The chapter discusses four major reactions to the new minorities: prejudice, discrimination, political opposition, and violence. Both blatant and subtle forms of prejudice predict anti-immigrant attitudes. And between 1988 and 1991, a hardening took place in these attitudes. Similarly, direct and indirect discrimination against the new minorities is pervasive. Moreover, anti-discrimination efforts have been largely ineffective. Far-right, anti-immigration political parties have formed to exploit this situation. These openly racist parties have succeeded in shifting the political spectrum on the issue to the right. In addition, violence against third-world immigrants has increased in recent years, especially in nations such as Britain and Germany where far-right parties are weakest. The chapter concludes that these phenomena are remarkably consistent across western Europe. Furthermore, the European research on these topics supports and extends North American research in intergroup relations.

**Key words:** new minorities, blatant prejudice, subtle prejudice

## INTRODUCTION

The world is experiencing two major intergroup trends—massive migration and increased group conflict. An estimated 80 million migrants, almost 2% of the world's population, live permanently or for long periods of time outside their countries of origin (Castles 1993, p. 18). And headlines of intergroup strife fill our newspapers.

These trends are especially evident in western Europe (Solomos & Wrench 1993, Thraenhardt

Thomas F. Pettigrew, "Reactions Toward the New Minorities of Western Europe," *Annual Review of Sociology*, vol. 24, pp. 77-103. Copyright © 1998 by Annual Reviews. Reprinted with permission.

1992a). Somalis in London's East End (Griffiths 1997) and Cypriot entrepreneurs in the city's garment industry (Panayiotopoulos 1996), Russian Jews in Berlin (Doomernik 1997), Peruvian house servants in Barcelona (Escriva 1997), Senegalese street vendors in Italian cities (Campani 1993)—every western European city reveals the arrival of immigrants over recent decades. And every western European nation has seen harsh, often violent, reactions to these new minorities.

An extensive research literature has developed on these groups. This chapter outlines this work with an eye toward enlarging the sociological understanding of intergroup processes. Such a comparison is important for American sociology. The discipline has focused on black-white relations in the United States. This situation is atypical of the world's intergroup situations on many dimensions. African Americans endured two centuries of slavery and another of legal segregation. They still face intense racial barriers. They remain the most residentially segregated and have the lowest intermarriage rates with whites of any American minority (Pettigrew 1988). Nonetheless, African Americans "belong" in the United States (Landes 1955). Not even racists question their citizenship. Moreover, they share a language, religion, and a national culture with other Americans. Indeed, they are major contributors to the most distinctive elements of American culture.

In short, the position of African Americans is vastly different from that of Europe's new minorities. Yet it is the American black-white situation upon which much of sociology's study of intergroup dynamics rests. Hence, current scholarship on the unfolding scene of majority-minority relations in western Europe offers a welcome opportunity to broaden our perspective. Though only a ninth of the chapter's citations are from non-English literatures, works in English by leading European scholars help to compensate.

## THE NEW MINORITIES

### A Rich Variety of Groups and Contexts

The variety of new minorities within contrasting national contexts enhances the comparative value of intergroup phenomena in western Europe. The new Europeans come from Africa, Asia, the Caribbean, the Middle East, and South America. And they typically have cultural backgrounds sharply different from those of their host nations. Seven million, for instance, are Muslims (Peach & Glebe 1995).

This is not an entirely novel experience for the continent. There were mass movements of people after World War I and following the Russian Revolution (Kulischer 1948). And western Europe has long had indigenous minorities—such as the Frisians of the Netherlands and Germany, the Bretons and Corsicans of France, the Scots and Welsh of Great Britain, and the Basques and Catalans of Spain (Foster 1980). But the new minorities offer a more culturally diverse intergroup situation than the traditionally emigrating continent has experienced.

### *FOUR DECADES OF IMMIGRATION*

Driven by both economic opportunities and the decline of European empires, colonial minorities began arriving during the 1950s. Before independence of their native lands, French colonials were French citizens and began coming in growing numbers to France for greater opportunities. In Great Britain, London transport and other employers recruited West Indians for low-wage jobs. While only 2,000 immigrated from the islands in 1952, 26,441 came in 1956. By late 1959, Britain's West Indian population numbered 126,000 (Rich 1990, pp. 181, 188).

An especially troubled group were the South Moluccans. Prized soldiers of the Dutch East Indian Army, they had fought to maintain Dutch colonization. When Indonesia won independence in 1948, many of these soldiers and their families migrated to the Netherlands. But, upon arrival, the Dutch decommissioned them. Stripped of their specialty, many Moluccans became unemployed and remain today dependent on welfare. Their dream of returning to a sovereign South Molucca heightens their plight. Their island is now firmly in Indonesia's grip, and their dream has retarded their adjustment to Dutch society.

The 1960s saw the arrival of contract workers who were not colonials. Many of these misnamed "guest workers" were Europeans. Spanish and Portuguese came to France; Italians to France, Germany, and Belgium; Yugoslavs and Greeks to Germany; and Turks to the Netherlands and Germany. North Africans came soon after to France and the low countries. There were economic and other push factors as well as economic pull factors. Portuguese men, for example, avoided induction into their nation's colonial armies fighting to maintain African colonies.

Rapid industrial expansion in western Europe in the 1960s fueled the worker recruitment. West Germany, undergoing its "economic miracle," desperately needed more workers. It made recruitment treaties with Italy (1955), Spain (1960), Turkey (1961–1964), Morocco (1963), Portugal (1964), Greece (1965), Tunisia (1965), Yugoslavia (1968), and even South Korea (1968) (Thraenhardt 1992b, p. 25). Almost 35,000 North Africans entered France each year during this decade (Creamean 1996, p. 51). Indeed, most western European countries took part in such recruitment efforts in this period.

The boom years ended with rising oil prices in the 1970s and consequent unemployment. Labor recruitment abruptly stopped, and governments developed schemes to encourage the "guest workers" to leave. Yet their numbers fell only slightly. By the 1980s, the new minorities were again growing

in size from three sources: family reunion, the high birth and low death rates of their young populations, and increasing numbers of refugees. By 1995, resident foreign populations ranged from 3.6% in the United Kingdom to 18.9% in Switzerland. More than half of these foreigners are from non-European Union countries (Waldrauch & Hofinger 1997, p. 274).

### DIFFERENT STATUSES

Today the new minorities hold an array of statuses. We distinguish seven types. (For a detailed scheme, see Husbands 1991a.)

1. The most favored are the national migrants—those considered citizens who are seen as returning "home." The special case of the "Saxons" from Romania illustrates the extremes this social construction can assume. Though separated by eight centuries from Germany, these Aussiedler "return" with full citizenship automatically granted them (Me Arthur 1976, Verdery 1985, Wilpert 1993).

2. Citizens of European Union (EU) countries living in other EU countries also are a favored class. Though "foreigners," they have full rights under EU agreements. Of 13 million foreign residents in western Europe in 1993, six million were western Europeans (Muenz 1996, p. 211). Hence, they often constitute a large segment of a nation's foreign residents—such as the Portuguese in France and Italians in Belgium (Martiniello 1992a, 1993; Vranken & Martiniello 1992). Today, however, only rural Portuguese are still migrating in large numbers. Many EU migrants return to their native lands. Among those who remain, many are second- and third-generation residents.

3. Ex-colonial peoples form a large contingent. These groups usually arrived familiar with the host country's culture and language. They include Indians, Pakistanis, and West Indians in the United Kingdom, North Africans and Southeast Asians in France, Eritreans and Somalis in Italy, and Surinamers in the Netherlands. Distinctions are often made among these groups. In Britain, "new commonwealth peoples" is the euphemism for ex-colonials of color (Miles & Phizacklea 1984, Miles & Cleary 1992, p. 131).

4. Recruited workers from such noncolonial countries as Turkey form a fourth group. Germany patterned the "guest worker" (Gastarbeiter) system after the Swiss treatment of Italian workers. The intention was for the recruits to rotate before planting family roots. But the Swiss plan involved mostly service workers. Skilled work required training, and companies were unwilling to rotate their "guests" and lose their human capital investment.

5. Soon families joined the workers, and migratory chains formed. The guests had come to stay (Thraenhardt 1992b).

6. Refugees and asylum seekers are an increasingly large cluster among the new minorities. About 15 million people throughout the world claim this status, though most go from one third-world country to another. While only 5% are in western Europe (Santel 1992, p. 107), their arrivals in EU countries rose rapidly during the 1980s—from 65,000 in 1983 to 289,000 in 1989 (Castles 1993, p. 18). It reached a peak in 1992 with 700,000 applications but, with tightened regulations, declined to 300,000 in 1994 (Koser1996, p. 153).

7. Accepted illegal immigrants are those who, while not legal, are known to authorities and

tolerated as long as they are economically useful. Polish construction workers in Germany and African harvest workers in Italy are two examples. These groups are vulnerable to the whims of officials and the economy, and they receive no social welfare benefits. In contrast, such prosperous illegals as the English in Portugal do not register so as to avoid taxes (Miles 1993).

8. Rejected illegal immigrants are the true illegals. Since there is no perceived economic need for them, authorities often deport them. Organized criminal groups from eastern Europe and Russia are often in this group. Many generalize justifiable opposition to such groups into opposition to all immigrants.

The fuzzy boundaries of these types overlap. Asylum seekers are a highly diverse group and constitute an especially slippery social construction (Castles 1993, p. 19, Joly 1996, Koser 1996, Santel 1992). The 1951 Geneva Convention of the United Nations defined a "political refugee" narrowly: persons with a "well-founded fear" of persecution in their native lands because of their race, religion, nationality, or political opinions. This definition excludes victims of generalized oppression, civil wars, or natural disasters as well as economic refugees. With rapid population and slow economic growth in much of the world, more asylum seekers try to escape poverty—not persecution as the United Nations defines it.

In the 1990s, the European Parliament enunciated its "safe country of origin principle." Designed to harmonize EU policies toward asylum seekers, the Parliament returned to the narrow UN definition to exclude many "unfounded applications" (European Parliament 1997). The policy has had a chilling effect. In the Netherlands, for instance, the number of asylum seekers declined from 53,000 in 1994 to about 21,000 in 1996 (Muus 1996/7).

## Belongingness and Citizenship

The new minorities often find citizenship to be a major barrier. Without the New World's immigration traditions, Europeans lack a "melting pot" metaphor and a sense that immigration is "normal." Nationality often carries biological connotations—"British stock," as Margaret Thatcher phrased it (Thraenhardt 1992b, p. 16). Thus, many view the new minorities as not belonging—even the growing numbers of the second- and third-generation who have lived only in the host nation.

This sense of not belonging interacts with citizenship. Here the nations vary widely (Thraenhardt 1992b). Sweden and the Netherlands are "the most welcoming for immigrants" (Waldrauch & Hofinger 1997, p. 278). They boast the highest rates of naturalization relative to their populations, and they allow voting in local elections for immigrants before citizenship (Hammar 1993). Although becoming more selective (Alund & Schierup 1993), Sweden provides courses in its language and culture, and naturalization for immigrants after five years.

Britain and France, though increasingly restrictive, have allowed extensive naturalization for ex-colonial peoples. And most of the second generation born in the United Kingdom or France receive citizenship. Three nations without former colonial subjects—Germany, Austria, and Switzerland—are by far the most restrictive (Waldrauch & Hofinger 1997). Turks provide a revealing example. By the mid-1990s, less than 5% of resident Turks had gained citizenship in Germany compared to more than a fifth in the Netherlands. In 1995, the Netherlands granted the largest number of naturalizations in its history—71,000, twice that of 1992 (Muus 1996/7).

## A Time of Threat and Change

Western Europe has experienced dramatic economic changes during the final decades of this century. The oil shocks of the 1970s reminded Europeans of the vulnerability of their economies. As in the United States, European governments began to give deficit reduction and global competitiveness priority over social and distributive justice (Stasiulis 1997). "Downsizing" the workforce took hold, and unemployment mounted. Guest-worker programs ended, but the foreigners did not leave. Indeed, more immigrants arrived as families reunited, and the entry of refugees increased. Thus, the urban concentrations of the new minorities expanded. As unemployment intensified from the economic restructuring in the 1980s, it became easy to blame the foreigners.

These economic phenomena took place in a context of equally sweeping political alterations. The power of nation-states began to erode as European unity advanced, while regional claims for autonomy grew. The Communist regimes in the East imploded, the Berlin Wall fell, Yugoslavia broke up into contending ethnic enclaves, and German unification came suddenly. Societal disequilibria swept central and eastern Europe.

Many worried that a "flood" of eastern Europeans would "pour" in. Germany introduced a new Gastarbeiter policy in 1990 involving eastern European governments (Rudolph 1996). Germany now has about a million East European nationals within its borders, most of whom are Polish or from the former Yugoslavia (Carter et al. 1993, p. 492). Overlooked in the public debate is that every western European nation's natural increase (births over deaths) has declined since 1960 while its economy has expanded—making immigration essential for continued prosperity (Munz 1996, Thraenhardt 1996).

Nevertheless, such events create threat. They set the scene for scapegoating the culturally different "others" in their midst. Quillian (1995) shows that group threat is important. Defined as the interaction of high non-EU minority percentage and low gross national product, it accounts for 70% of the variance in anti-immigrant attitude means across the 12 EU nations (also see Fuchs et al. 1993).

## MAJORITY PREJUDICE AGAINST THE NEW MINORITIES

We can assess attitudes toward the new minorities with a rich data source. In 1988, the Eurobarometer Survey 30 asked seven probability samples a range of prejudice measures about a variety of minorities (Reif & Melich 1991). In West Germany, the survey asked 985 majority respondents about Turks. In France, it asked 455 about North Africans and 475 about southeastern Asians. In the Netherlands, it asked 462 about Surinamers and 476 about Turks. And in Great Britain, it asked 471 about West Indians and 482 about Pakistanis and Indians (Pettigrew et al. 1998, Zick 1997).

### Blatant and Subtle Prejudice

Two key measures distinguish between blatant and subtle types of prejudice (Pettigrew & Meertens 1995). Blatant prejudice is the traditional form; it is hot, close, and direct. The ten items that tap it involve open rejection of minorities based on presumed biological differences. Subtle prejudice is the modern form; it is cool, distant, and indirect. The ten items that measure it are not readily recognized as indicators of prejudice. They tap the perceived threat of the minority to traditional values, the exaggeration of cultural differences with the minority, and the absence of positive feelings toward them. American researchers have studied similar distinctions (Pettigrew 1989, Sears 1988). And, as various writers had proposed (Barker 1982, Bergmann & Erb 1986, Essed 1990), it proved equally useful in Europe.

Figure 1 shows the *blatant* and *subtle* scale means for the seven samples. Four major findings emerge. 1. The *subtle* means are consistently higher than those of the *blatant* scale, because the *subtle* items are covert and more socially acceptable

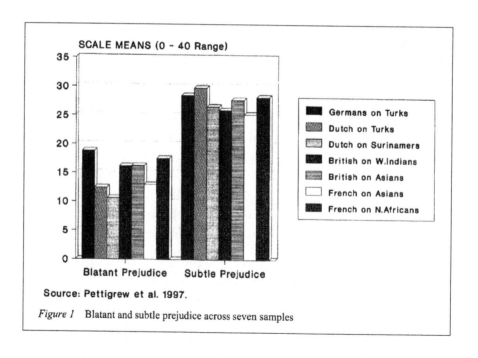

Source: Pettigrew et al. 1997.

*Figure 1* Blatant and subtle prejudice across seven samples

(Pettigrew & Meertens 1995, 1996). 2. The means for *blatant* prejudice are conspicuously higher for German attitudes toward Turks and French attitudes toward North Africans. This result suggests that norms against the open expression of prejudice are weakest in these two instances. The means for *subtle* prejudice, however, reveal less variability. 3. Target differences exist in two nations—less French prejudice against Asians than North Africans, and less Dutch prejudice against Surinamers than Turks. Note these preferences place greater weight on cultural than racial similarities. 4. Observe, too, the distinctive data of the Dutch. They are significantly lower on *blatant* prejudice, but not on *subtle* prejudice. The contrast is striking when we compare similar target groups. The Dutch *blatant* mean for Turks is significantly lower than that of the Germans for Turks. And the Dutch *blatant* mean for Surinamers is significantly lower than that of the British for West Indians. Yet the Dutch *subtle* means are higher than these comparisons. In normative terms, this unique pattern outlines the famed "tolerance" of the Netherlands. There exists a stern Dutch norm against *blatant* prejudice. But *subtle* prejudice slips in under the norm, unrecognized as prejudice (Pettigrew & Meertens 1996).

Across the seven samples, the *blatant* and *subtle* prejudice scales correlate between +.48 and +.70. The two measures share the same correlates in all samples (Meertens & Pettigrew 1997). Both the blatantly and subtly prejudiced are less educated and older. They report less interest in politics but more pride in their nationality. They less often think of themselves as "Europeans" (Pettigrew 1998). They are more politically conservative; but subtle prejudice is not, as some claim, simply a reflection of conservatism (Meertens & Pettigrew 1997). The prejudiced also are more likely to have only ingroup friends (Pettigrew 1997). Finally, they reveal a strong sense of group, but not individual, relative deprivation. Thus, the prejudiced sense a group threat to "people like themselves" from minorities, but not a sense of personal threat. These correlates replicate findings of American research. Since these extensive data involve seven independent samples, four nations, and six target minorities, this replication is of theoretical significance.

## Attitudes Toward Immigration

Do the blatant and subtle prejudice measures predict attitudes toward the salient issue of immigration? Consider the differences among three types of respondents. Equalitarians are those who score below the central point (not the mean) of both the blatant and subtle scales. Bigots score above the central points of both scales. The subtles are the most interesting; they score low on blatant but high on subtle prejudice. They reject crude expressions of prejudice. Still, they view the new minorities as "a people apart" who violate traditional values and for whom they feel little sympathy or admiration. (A fourth logical type, those high on blatant but low on subtle prejudice, occurs in less than 3% of the sample.)

Figures 2 and 3 show the results for all 3800 majority respondents, and these results replicate in all seven samples. In Figure 2, most Bigots wish to restrict immigrants' rights further. Most Equalitarians favor extending immigrants' rights. By contrast, many Subtles simply wish to leave the issue as it is. When asked if government should make citizenship easier for immigrants, the three types line up as expected. While most Equalitarians think naturalization procedures should be easier, most Subtles and Bigots disagree.

The surveys also included a scale of immigration positions that allowed multiple responses. "... The government should ... (1) send all Asians, even those born in France, back to their own country. (2) Send only those Asians who were not born in France back ... (3) Send only those Asians back who are not contributing to the economic livelihood of France. (4) Send only those Asians who have committed severe criminal offenses back ... (5) Send only those Asians who have no immigration documents back ... (6) The government should not send back to their own country any of the Asians now living in France."

In Figure 3, differences between the types also appear on this measure. Many Bigots want to send all immigrants home. Equalitarians often favor not sending back any immigrants. Subtles typically support sending immigrants home only when there is an ostensibly nonprejudicial reason for doing so—if they have committed crimes or do not have

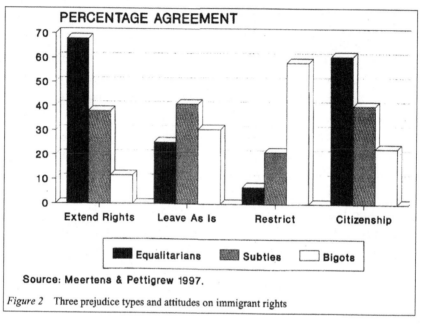

Source: Meertens & Pettigrew 1997.

*Figure 2*  Three prejudice types and attitudes on immigrant rights

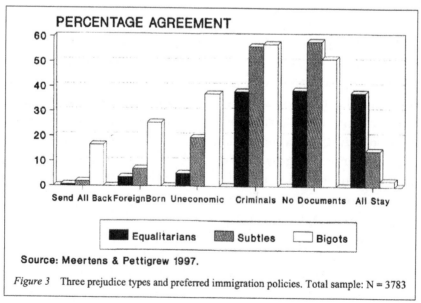

Source: Meertens & Pettigrew 1997.

*Figure 3*  Three prejudice types and preferred immigration policies. Total sample: N = 3783

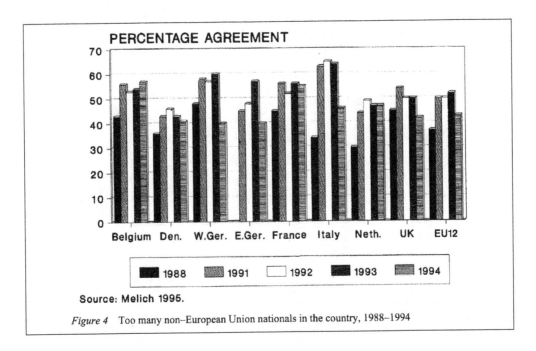

PERCENTAGE AGREEMENT

Legend: 1988, 1991, 1992, 1993, 1994

Source: Melich 1995.

*Figure 4*   Too many non–European Union nationals in the country, 1988–1994

their documents. These differences among the types are statistically significant in all samples.

## Are Attitudes Toward Foreigners Becoming More Negative?

Unfortunately, the Eurobarometer surveys have not repeated the extensive 1988 measures of prejudice. They have, however, repeatedly asked several relevant questions (Melich 1995). Figure 4 shows the rising percentage of Europeans who believe there are "too many" non-EU foreigners in their country. For each national sample shown and the 12 EU nations (EU12) combined, the sharpest increase occurs between 1988 and 1991. (Preunification 1988 data for East Germany were not attainable.) Clear majorities in Belgium, West Germany, France, and Italy agreed during the early 1990s that the number of foreigners is excessive. There was, however, less of this feeling by 1994, especially in Germany and Italy. The decline in Germany may well reflect changes in the constitution that made it difficult for asylum seekers to gain entry.

Figure 5 tells a similar story. Abrupt increases in the numbers of those who wish to restrict the rights of non-EU nationals again occur between 1988 and 1991. Yet not all indicators show this effect. The percentage of respondents who find the presence of non-EU nationals "disturbing" does not rise much over these years. Hence, western European opinion toward foreigners did harden during the years when the issue took center stage and political leaders defined immigration as a serious problem. Yet the increases in negative attitudes are not so large as to explain the rise in political and violent actions against immigrants.

## DISCRIMINATION AGAINST THE NEW MINORITIES

### Direct and Indirect Discrimination

Discrimination against the new minorities is pervasive throughout western Europe (Castles 1984, MacEwen 1995, World Council of Churches Migration Secretariat 1980). But, save for the

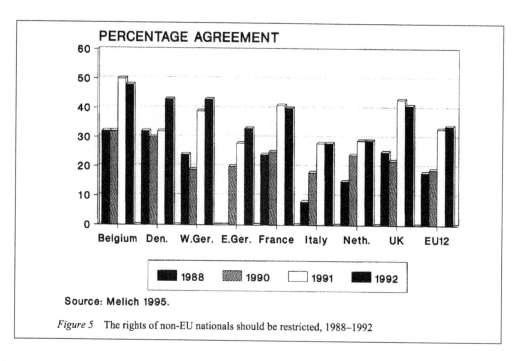

PERCENTAGE AGREEMENT

Source: Melich 1995.

*Figure 5*  The rights of non-EU nationals should be restricted, 1988–1992

United Kingdom and the Netherlands, the problem has received far less attention than that of violence.

Both direct and indirect discrimination are involved (Pettigrew & Taylor 1991). Direct discrimination, like blatant prejudice, is straightforward. It occurs at points where inequality is generated, often intentionally. Indirect discrimination, like subtle prejudice, is less obvious. It involves the perpetuation or magnification of the original injury. It occurs when the inequitable results of direct discrimination are used as a basis for later decisions ("past-in-present discrimination") or decisions in related institutions ("side-effect discrimination"; Feagin & Feagin 1986). Indirect discrimination, a result of systemic patterns, is largely unrecognized in Europe.

Investigators have repeatedly uncovered direct discrimination in England (Amin et al. 1988, Daniel 1968, Gordon & Klug 1984, Smith 1976). Controlled tests reveal the full litany of discriminatory forms involving employment, public accommodations, housing, the courts, insurance, banks, even car rentals. One study sent identical letters for 103 advertised, nonmanual jobs from native white, West Indian, and Asian applicants. The letters contained multiple cues of ethnicity. Firms refused the white an interview only six times when they granted one to a minority candidate. But on 49 occasions, they called the white for an interview and refused to interview the minority candidates (Hubbuck & Carter 1980).

In Germany, a reporter dyed his moustache black, dressed in guest-worker style, and tried to get a drink in bars and cafes throughout Frankfurt. Repeatedly, he was refused service and thrown out (Castles 1984, p. 191). Better-controlled field studies by social scientists reveal differential, face-to-face treatment of the new minorities in Britain, Germany, and the Netherlands (Den Uyl et al. 1986, Klink & Wagner 1998, Sissons 1981). Their results closely resemble those of similar field studies of discriminatory acts in the United States (Crosby et al. 1980).

Employment discrimination poses the most serious problem. In every western European nation, foreigners have far higher unemployment rates than do natives. In 1990 in the Netherlands, Moroccans and Turks had unemployment rates above 40%, and the Surinamese 27% compared with the native Dutch rate of 13% (Pettigrew & Meertens 1996). During the 1974–1977 recession, West German manufacturing reduced its labor force by 765,000—42% of whom were foreign workers (Castles 1984, p. 148).

There are many reasons in addition to discrimination for this situation. The "last-in, first-out" principle selectively affects the younger foreign workers. Being typically less skilled, they are more affected by job upgrading. Foreigners also are more likely to be in older, declining industries in such areas as the Ruhr Valley. Indeed, planners put Gastarbeiter into these industries for cheaper labor precisely because of their decline. Some emphasize these factors to deny any role for discrimination. Yet these factors offer insufficient explanations for the greater unemployment of foreigners. Veenman & Roelandt (1990) tested how much education, age, sex, region, and employment level account for the large group discrepancies in Dutch unemployment rates. They found that these factors explained only a small portion of the differential rates.

Indirect discrimination operates when the inability to obtain citizenship restricts the opportunities of non-EU minorities in most institutions. It restricts their ability to get suitable housing, employment, and schooling for children. A visa is required for travel to other EU countries. In short, the lives of noncitizens are severely circumscribed (Wilpert 1993).

Castles (1984) contends that the guest-worker system was itself a state-controlled system of institutional discrimination. It established the newcomers as a problematic and stigmatized outgroup, suitable for low-status jobs but not for citizenship. For initial victims of such direct discrimination, indirect discrimination in all areas of life was inevitable.

Wilpert goes further. She asserts that Germany's institutions are based on "a dominant ideology which distributes rights according to ethnic origins …" (Wilpert 1993, p. 70). The revealing comparison is between the almost two million Aussiedler and the Gastarbeiter. Officials regard the former as kin often on the thinnest of evidence, though since 1996 a language test must be taken. Aussiedler readily become citizens and receive favorable government treatment. Yet even third-generation Turks, who are at least as culturally "German" as the Aussiedler, are largely denied citizenship and given unfavorable treatment.

## Anti-Discrimination Remediation

Basic rights in Germany are guaranteed only to citizens. So, the disadvantages of noncitizenship include limited means to combat discrimination (Layton-Henry & Wilpert 1994). Extensive German legislation combats anti-Semitism and Nazi ideology, but these laws have proved difficult to apply to noncitizens.

The German constitution explicitly forbids discrimination on the basis of origin, race, language, beliefs, or religion—but not citizenship. Indeed, the Federal Constitutional Court (Bundesverfassungsgericht) has ruled that differential treatment based on citizenship is constitutional if there is a reasonable basis for it, and if it is not wholly arbitrary. In practice, this has meant a court has upheld charging foreign bar owners higher taxes than German bar owners. And restaurants can refuse service to Turks and others on the grounds that their entry might lead to intergroup disturbances. According to the German legal specialist Dan Leskien, Germany needs anti-discrimination legislation with broad enforcement powers and an effective monitoring system (Layton-Henry & Wilpert 1994, pp. 19–22).

Few means of combating discrimination are available in France either. Commentators often view discrimination as "natural," as something universally triggered when a "threshold of tolerance" (*seuil de tolerance*) is surpassed (MacMaster 1991). Without supporting evidence, this rationalization supports quotas and dispersal policies that limit minority access to suitable housing.

The Netherlands, United Kingdom, and Sweden have enacted antidiscrimination legislature that specifically applies to the new minorities. Not coincidentally, these countries make citizenship much easier to obtain than Germany. Yet this legislation has been largely ineffective for two interrelated reasons. First, European legal systems do not allow class action suits—a forceful North American weapon to combat discrimination. Second, European efforts rely heavily on individual complaints rather than systemic remediation. Britain's 1976 Act gave the Commission for Racial Equality power to cast a broad net, but individual complaints remain the chief tool (MacEwen 1993, 1995).

It is a sociological truism that individual efforts are unlikely to alter such systemic phenomena as discrimination. Mayhew (1968) showed how individual suits and complaints are largely nonstrategic. Minorities bring few charges against the worst discriminators, because they avoid applying to them. Complaints about job promotion are common, but they are made against employers who hire minorities. Thus, effective anti-discrimination laws must provide broad powers to an enforcement agency to initiate strategic, institutionwide actions that uproot the structural foundations of discrimination.

## POLITICAL RESPONSES

### The Rise of Far-Right Anti-Immigration Parties

By the 1980s, the new Europeans elicited an increasingly hostile reaction from sectors of the native populations that felt especially threatened. Throughout western Europe, extreme right-wing groups seized on the threat as their central issue. In each election for the European Parliament, the average vote for these anti-immigration parties has risen—3.4% in 1979, 4.9% in 1984 to 5.1% in 1989. By 1994, with an average of 11.1% unemployment in the European Union, the far-right parties garnered 6.9% of the vote and 25 seats (3 from Belgium, 11 each from France and Italy). Indeed, a close relationship is found across countries between the extreme right's share of the European Parliament votes and unemployment (Baimbridge et al. 1994, 1995).

It is a mistake to view the new European right as simply Nazi revivals. To be sure, they share the classic authoritarian personality orientation—calls for a strong leader and law and order, beliefs in conspiracy theories, and an exclusionary view of citizenship. But, as Kitschelt (1995) makes clear, times have changed and so has the radical right. He distinguishes four types of far right. Two have only tiny constituencies—traditional fascists and "welfare chauvinists." Two other types, however, have attracted strong followings—the new radical right and "populist anti-statists." Unlike the first two varieties, these right-wing movements heartily endorse free market capitalism. They are political, not economic, populists. And the anti-statists gain ground in Italy and Austria, where patronage is based on the traditional party system. Yet one central theme runs through all four types—nativism and stern opposition to immigration.

### *Austria*

Begun after World War II under a former member of the Nazi SS, Austria's Freedom Party (FPO) met with only modest success until Joerg Haider became its leader in 1986. A multimillionaire with a populist flair,

Haider fashioned the FPO into the strongest far-right party in western Europe and a major party of Austria. He gained international notoriety when, as governor of Carinthia province, he praised Nazi labor practices as a good way to reduce the welfare rolls (Feen 1996, Wise 1995). Not surprisingly, Haider and his party vigorously oppose immigration, bilingual education, and immigrants' rights.

In 1994, Haider's Freedom Party won 42 of 183 parliamentary seats with more than 22% of the vote. In 1996, the party won 29 seats in Vienna's city council with the anti-immigration slogan, "Vienna must not become like Chicago" (Shanker 1996). Despite Haider's ambiguous remarks about Nazis, he claims the party is leaving its Nazi roots. Indeed, the FPO has strong free market and anti-statist positions (Betz 1994, Kitschelt 1995, Parkinson 1989). It offers a classic case of Kitschelt's (1995) anti-statist type. Nonetheless, violent groups in Austria, such as the one that desecrated a new Jewish cemetery in November 1992, use Nazi symbols and proclaim support for Haider and his party (Husbands 1993, p. 113).

## BELGIUM

Until 1979, the Volksunie was the only nationalist party of Flanders. Then dissidents formed the Vlaams Blok (VB)—a prime example of Kitschelt's "new radical right" type. This party stands for a separate Flanders that would someday join the Netherlands, and it opposes non-European residents. It would set up a fund for their repatriation, expel them after three months of unemployment, prohibit family reunion, and levy a tax on their employers. With this program, the VB has increased its vote in every general election since 1981. Centered in Antwerp, it now attracts about one eighth of Belgium's Flemish voters (Govaert 1995).

## FRANCE

The best known of Europe's far-right parties is Jean-Marie Le Pen's Front National (FN)—another example of "the new radical right." Formed in 1972, the FN suffered repeated electoral reverses until the 1980s. It gained respectability in 1983 when conservatives joined them in a second ballot in the small city of Dreux. From 1984 to the present, the party has consistently attracted between 9% and 16% of the vote in a variety of national elections (Singer 1991; Husbands 1991b, Table 3). In 1995, for example, Le Pen received more than four million votes for president—more than 15% of the total. The FN is a nationalist and populist party that has carved out a stable slot in French politics (Birenbaum 1992, Fysh & Wolfreys 1992, Husbands 1991a, Marcus 1995, Mayer & Perrineau 1992, Shields 1989, Tezenas du Montcel 1995). It is especially strong in cities of the Southeast and Northeast—areas hit hardest by industrial decline and "the exhaustion of the working-class movement" (Wieviorka 1993, p. 64). Yet it also has secured a modest hold throughout the country.

It has a broad policy program, but its key position is anti-immigration. Its leader, Le Pen, expresses blatant bigotry against a range of immigrants and minorities—from Jews to the Harkis who fought with the French against Algerian independence. "Two million unemployed" he asserts, "that's two million immigrants too many" (Gunn 1989, p. 23). Increasingly, the French understand Le Pen's position. National surveys show 53% in 1996, compared with 43% in 1990, "understand the Le Pen vote" considering "the behavior of certain immigrants" (Commission Nationale Consultative des Droits de l'Homme 1997, p. 371).

Given its broad base, the FN's voters do not differ from the general French electorate as much as some writers suggest (Husbands 1991b). There are, however, consistent findings in the many studies of the phenomenon. Like supporters of other radical right parties, FN voters are typically males (women are more attracted to European Green parties; Betz 1994, p. 143). And they are particularly numerous among small businessmen and craftsmen as well as white ex-colonials. Since 1984, the FN has attracted an increasing percentage of manual workers. Yet most of their gains are at the expense of other right-wing parties, not the declining French Communists, as some claim. And those French who live in communities with more than 10% foreign populations are less prejudiced and more accepting of immigrants than are other French (Commission Nationale Consultative des Droits de l'Homme 1997, p. 388). There also is a vigorous anti-FN countermovement (Mayer 1995), fueled by students (Husbands 1991b).

## GERMANY

Le Pen's success inspired the German right. In the 1986 Bavarian state elections, the Christian Social Union (CSU) began a furious campaign against third-world refugees. Their electoral success put the issue on center stage.

This event also saw a new far-right party split from the CSU. With anti-immigration its chief issue, the Republikaners under their leader, Franz Schoenhuber—a former SS member—offered a populist-nationalist alternative similar to that of the Front National. While centered in Bavaria, the Republikaners enjoyed success in elections elsewhere from 1989 to 1993. In 1989, they won 90,000 votes and 11 parliament seats in West Berlin. And they garnered more than two million votes and six seats in a European Parliament election. They also did well in state elections in Baden Wuerttemberg in 1992 and Hessen in 1993. However, the Kohl government's partial adoption of their program blunted their appeal (Atkinson 1993, Thraenhardt 1992b, Wilpert 1993). By the 1994 European Parliament election, their strength had dissipated.

## GREAT BRITAIN

From the 1950s till the late 1960s, a policy consensus on immigration existed between the Labor and Conservative parties. It depoliticized race, allowed limited nonwhite immigration, but did little to improve the status of immigrants (Messina 1989, Rich 1990). The crowning achievement of this era—the 1968 Race Relations Act—lacked the necessary enforcement powers to be effective. North American specialists (including the writer) had warned the act's drafters of the need for structural teeth, but their advice was ignored.

Ending this cozy arrangement, Enoch Powell began an anti-minority campaign in 1968 (Schoen 1977). A maverick Conservative member of Parliament, Powell predicted "rivers of blood" if nonwhites continued to come to Britain. He opposed anti-discrimination legislation and called for immigration restrictions and nonwhite repatriation. His message struck a popular chord in British opinion. So popular, in fact, it broke the consensus and molded the Conservatives into an anti-immigration party. "Almost single-handedly," writes Messina (1989, p. 105), "Powell prepared the intellectual groundwork for the emergence of Margaret Thatcher as Conservative party leader in 1975."

In 1967, England's National Front mobilized far-right opposition to the new minorities. It had minor success, especially in the 1977 elections of the Greater London Council. Yet, as in Germany, the government assumed much of the Front's position. Thatcher won election in 1979, aided by her anti-immigration stand. She slashed the budget of the Commission for Racial Equality and pushed through revisions of the immigration rules designed to end primary nonwhite entry.

## THE NETHERLANDS

Unlike Britain, the major Dutch parties have maintained an enlightened consensus throughout this period. The focus of this consensus, however, has shifted. In the 1980s, it emphasized the collective integration of minorities. Now it stresses the integration of minority individuals into the labor market (Fermin 1997). Still, a misnamed Centrum Party formed in 1980 to exploit the immigration issue. Two years later, it secured one seat in the lower house of parliament (Tweede Kamer). In 1986, the party split into two—the Centrum Party 86 and the Centrum Democrats. Only the latter has secured seats in the Tweede Kamer—one in 1989, three in 1994. Some members sit on municipal councils (van Donselaar 1993). Yet, with only modest strength in a few urban pockets, the Dutch far-right has failed to crack the dominant consensus on the new minorities.

## SWITZERLAND

Economic insecurity is a facilitating factor in far-right opposition to immigration. Yet prosperous Switzerland shows that it is not a necessary factor. An extremist alliance, National Action Against the Swamping of the People and Homeland, came forward with a radical initiative in 1970. It proposed to cut the foreign population almost in half, and the initiative won the support of 46% of Swiss voters. The alliance later split into two small parties, both with parliamentary representation. They have kept immigration controversial, and gained power in Geneva as vigilants (Thraenhardt 1992b, pp. 42–44).

## SOUTHERN EUROPE

For Greece, Italy, Portugal, and Spain, large-scale immigration is a new phenomenon. Long accustomed to emigration, these nations have been slow to adjust to their new situation. Italy has attracted the most immigrants, many of them illegals. Under EU pressure, Italy belatedly began to formulate immigration policies in 1986 (Campani 1993, Martiniello 1992b). Its mishandling of Albanian refugees in 1991, however, revealed how Italy remains unprepared to be an immigrant receiving country (Vasta 1993).

Figures 4 and 5 record the pointed rise in Italian concern over immigration after 1988. This suggests that a sudden increase in foreigners, rather than the actual proportion of foreigners, is key to predicting change in European attitudes toward immigration. In Italy, both national and regional political parties have exploited the public's changing attitudes. At the national level, a neo-fascist party (Movimento Sociale Italiano) and the Partito Repubblicano Italiano have taken anti-immigration positions. And so have regional secessionist parties, especially the Leagues of Tuscany and Lombardy (Martiniello 1992b, Vasta 1993). Indeed, a blatantly racist platform helped the Lega Lombarda gain success in the local elections of May 1990. More recently, the Lega Nord and the Alleanza Nazionale have added to anti-immigration agitation.

## The Thraenhardt Thesis

Thraenhardt (1995) contends that these political phenomena are similar across France, Germany, and the United Kingdom. While far-right efforts have gained only minimal power directly, they have shifted the entire political spectrum to the right on immigration. Left-wing and center politicians have equivocated, sometimes even collaborated. Conservative politicians have exploited the situation for two reasons. First and foremost, they see an opportunity to obscure economic issues and seize a share of the left's labor vote. And, second, they fear the loss of supporters to the far right. Thraenhardt

(1992b, p. 49) credits racist appeals as vital to conservative victories in all three nations.

Conservative governments have made repeated concessions to anti-minority sentiments. They have "played an important role in promoting xenophobia and putting it on the public agenda" (Thraenhardt 1995, p. 337). Former Prime Ministers Thatcher and Major in the United Kingdom, Chancellor Kohl in Germany, and President Chirac in France have all espoused restrictions on immigration and citizenship that partly meet the far right's demands. Note these similarities across the three nations emerged despite sharp differences in their immigrant populations. Note also the policy inconsistency: Conservative parties actively pursued immigration to provide cheap labor for industry; now they stigmatize and scapegoat the foreigners who they earlier had invited.

The Thraenhardt thesis applies beyond Europe. Recall 1968 in the United States when Alabama Governor George Wallace helped to create a climate that moved President Nixon to the right on civil rights. The Republican Party has played "the race card" ever since, and converted the white South into its major base of support (Carmines & Stimson 1989, Kinder & Sanders 1996). Similarly in Australia, the rise of a far-right, populist politician, Pauline Hanson, has pushed Prime Minister John Howard's Liberal Government further to the right on racial and immigration issues.

## VIOLENCE AGAINST THE NEW MINORITIES

### Increasing Anti-Immigrant Violence

Playing "the race card" heightens intergroup tensions and risks violence. Indeed, Europe's political shift to the right accompanied a rise in anti-minority violence (Bjorgo & Witte 1993, Koopmans 1995, Witte 1995). In 1990, violent attacks against African street vendors in Florence, Italy, and the desecration of Jewish graves in Carpentras, France, made headlines.

The most publicized attacks occurred in Germany (Atkinson 1993, Heit-meyer 1993). In September 1991, a mob attacked and besieged a residence of asylum seekers in Hoyerswerda. Soon imitative acts of brutality erupted, the worst being riots and murders in Rostock, Moelln, Solingen, and Magdeburg. Passive onlookers and ineffective police characterized these horrendous events. Initially, Asian and African refugees were the primary targets. Later, Turks also became victims (Wagner & Zick 1997). Moreover, the intensity of the political debates on the constitutional rights of asylum seekers closely paralleled these acts of extreme-right violence (Gerhard 1992, Koopmans 1995, p. 27, Zick & Wagner 1993).

Germany was not alone. Britain (Gordon 1993), France (Lloyd 1993), the Netherlands (van Donselaar 1993), Scandinavia (Bjorgo 1993, Loow 1993), and the rest of Europe have all experienced patterned, anti-minority violence. Differences in record keeping and definitions of violence preclude precise cross-national comparisons (Koopmans 1995, Witte 1995). Nonetheless, sharp differences in racist violence exist. Per million inhabitants over the 1988–1993 period, England and Wales have had as many or even more racist acts as Germany. France, Norway, and Denmark have far lower rates. Switzerland has a high rate of deaths due to racist and extreme-right violence (Koopmans 1995, pp. 9–14). Save for Switzerland, however, the lethality of this European violence has not rivaled that of sectarian violence in Northern Ireland or of the Ku Klux Klan in the late nineteenth century in the southern United States.

The far-right does not commit all the racist violence. Some youthful perpetrators evince little or no right-wing ideology (Willems 1995). Their violence often involves the affect-arousing context of sports (Holland 1995). And not all right-wing targets are minorities. Still, in Germany and the Netherlands in the early 1990s, low-status minorities were the targets of roughly three fourths of far-right violence (Buijs & van Donselaar 1994, pp. 69–70). Significantly, other immigrants—from the EU, Japan, or North America—were rarely victims (Witte 1995, p. 494).

## The Koopmans Thesis

Using social movement theory, Koopmans (1995) offers a two-part explanation for the sharp differences in racist violence among European nations. Following from Thraenhardt's thesis, he first emphasizes the significance of political elites who legitimize the far-right's view of foreigners as unbearable burdens. Thus, respected leaders convert the new minorities into problems. Such legitimization, Koopmans (1995, p. 34) argues, furthers far-right mobilization "… with high mass media resonance and favorable chances of substantive success."

This mobilization, however, need not invoke violence. It also can activate far-right political parties, as shown by the Vlaams Blok and Front National. Hence, Koopmans' second point highlights the importance of such parties. He shows that countries with influential racist parties, such as France, Denmark, and Norway, have experienced relatively low levels of racist violence. By contrast, countries with weak racist parties, such as Germany and the United Kingdom, have had high levels. Even the Netherlands and Sweden, with low levels of general violence and without strong racist parties, have endured mid-levels of such racist attacks.

This second part of Koopmans' thesis is problematic. Aggregate data from only a few nations provide the quantitative support. And Europe's experience between the world wars contradicts the argument. Fascist parties and political violence developed together during those turbulent years. Two divergent theories of human aggression are at issue.

Koopmans is following Freud's (1930) steam-boiler model of a finite amount of aggression. If it can be channeled into political action, then right-wing aggression against minorities should decline. Allport's (1954) feedback model of aggression predicts precisely the opposite. Have the far-right mobilize anti-immigrant feelings, and aggression will increase and spill over into more violence against the new minorities.

Americans can readily apply the first part of Koopmans' thesis. The regressive 1980s and 1990s have seen the erosion in the United States of the sense of inevitability of continued racial progress. Repeated attacks by leading public officials on civil rights, affirmative action, and immigration have produced an intergroup climate comparable to that shaped by Thatcher, Kohl, and Chirac in Europe (Kinder & Sanders 1996). And violence against minorities, especially on college campuses, appears to have risen over these years (US Commission on Civil Rights 1990). Koopman's emphasis on the role of political leaders in violence is also consistent with recent time-series analyses by Green and his colleagues (Green et al. 1997) of ethnic hate crimes in New York City. They find little relationship between these crimes and such macroeconomic conditions as unemployment rates.

## CONCLUSIONS

This chapter emphasizes the negative reactions to western Europe's new minorities. There also is a positive side to the picture. Native populations are slowly adjusting to the new cultures. Parisians have developed a taste for hummus, Berliners for kabab; the Indonesian rijsttafel is a basic of Dutch cuisine.

More importantly, western Europe now boasts anti-racist movements. When the wave of atrocities against foreigners swept Germany in 1992, hundreds of thousands of Germans protested. With torchlight vigils and candlelight demonstrations, they countered "hatred and violence" in Berlin, Hamburg, Munich, and other cities and towns. When the French government tried to discontinue the naturalization of French-born children of foreign parents, students protested with the slogan, "Don't touch my buddy."

Still, increased prejudice, direct and indirect discrimination, political opposition, and extensive violence are major European reactions to the new minorities. These responses represent serious social problems worthy of study for practical, policy reasons. In addition, attention to these problems broadens our understanding of intergroup conflict in industrial societies.

The research to date reveals remarkable agreement across societies. Despite sharp differences in national histories, political systems, and minorities, this new work reveals considerable consistency across the nations of western Europe. It also largely replicates and extends, rather than rebuts, the North American literature.

This chapter has noted many such convergencies. Blatant and subtle prejudice measures scale in nearly identical ways across four nations and diverse minority targets. The scales also share the same correlates across the seven samples, and these correlates replicate North American research. Both types of prejudice also predict attitudes toward immigration in all samples. And throughout the EU, attitudes toward immigrants hardened during the tense 1989–1992 period.

Moreover, a host of established social psychological processes, such as intergroup contact and group relative deprivation, operate in comparable ways in Europe. They typically act as proximal causes of prejudice, serving as mediators for the distal effects of cultural and structural factors (Pettigrew et al. 1998).

The comparabilities extend to discrimination. Examples of both direct and indirect forms abound throughout western Europe. And efforts to combat discrimination have been weak across the continent. In those countries that resist granting citizenship to their new minorities, efficacious remediation of discrimination is extremely difficult. In those countries that have legislated against discrimination, the reliance upon individual complaints limits their effectiveness—again comparable to the North American experience.

Western European nations have seen the rise of far-right political opposition to immigration and the new minorities. While none of these parties has risen to power, this right-wing surge has succeeded in moving the entire political spectrum to the right on the issue. The process closely resembles that of the Wallace movement in the United States and the current Hanson movement in Australia.

Finally, similar patterns of racist violence have swept western Europe. While there is variability across nations in the number of reported incidents, the timing of this violence is similar. In particular, the elite framing of the immigration discourse, especially defining the new minorities as unbearable burdens, relates closely to the violence patterns.

The new European research supports and broadens earlier North American research in intergroup relations. It also extends our understanding in important ways. The chapter has described two of these extensions: the Thraenhardt thesis on the political exploitation of xenophobia and the Koopmans thesis on the mobilization of racist violence.

## ACKNOWLEDGMENTS

I wish to thank James Jackson and Myriam Torres of the University of Michigan, Roel W. Meertens of the University of Amsterdam, Ulrich Wagner of the Philipps University of Marburg, and Andreas Zick of the University of Wuppertal for their invaluable help with data and bibliography. I also greatly appreciate the helpful comments on earlier drafts of this chapter by William Dom-hoff, Roel Meertens,

Amelie Mummendey, Ann Pettigrew, Bernd Simon, Dietrich Thraenhardt, and Ulrich Wagner.

## LITERATURE CITED

Allport GW. 1954. *The Nature of Prejudice.* Reading, MA: Addison-Wesley. pp. 537

Alund A, Schierup CU. 1993. The thorny road to Europe: Swedish immigrant policy in transition. See Solomos & Wrench 1993, pp. 99–114

Amin K, Fernandes M, Gordon P. 1988. *Racism and Discrimination in Britain: A Select Bibliography, 1984–87.* London: Runnymede Trust. pp. 98

Atkinson G. 1993. Germany: nationalism, Nazism and violence. See Bjorgo & Witte 1993, pp. 154–66

Baimbridge M, Burkitt B, Macey M. 1994. The Maastricht Treaty: exacerbating racism in Europe? *Ethn. Racial Stud.* 17: pp. 420–41

Baimbridge M, Burkitt B, Macey M. 1995. The European Parliamentary election of 1994 and racism in Europe. *Ethn. Racial Stud.* 18: pp. 128–30

Barker M. 1982. *The New Racism: Conservatives and the Ideology of the Tribe.* Frederick, MD: Aletheia. pp. 183

Bergmann W, Erb R. 1986. Kommunika-tionslatenz, moral und offentliche mein-ung. *Koln. Zeitschr. Soziol. Sozialpsychol.* 38: pp. 223–46

Betz HG. 1994. *Radical Right-Wing Populism in Western Europe.* New York: St. Martin's Press. 226 pp.

Birenbaum G. 1992. *Le Front National en Politique.* Paris: Balland. pp. 358

Bjorgo T. 1993. Terrorist violence against immigrants and refugees in Scandinavia: patterns and motives. See Bjorgo & Witte 1993, pp. 29–45

Bjorgo T, Witte R, eds. 1993. *Racist Violence in Europe.* New York: St. Martin's Press. pp. 261

Buijs FJ, van Donselaar J. 1994. *Extreem-Rechts: Aanhang, Gewald en Onderzoek.* Leiden: LISWO. pp. 67

Campani G. 1993. Immigration and racism in southern Europe: the Italian case. *Ethn. Racial Stud.* 16: pp. 507–35

Carmines EG, Stimson JA. 1989. *Issue Evolution: Race and the Transformation of American Politics.* Princeton, NJ: Princeton Univ. Press. pp. 217

Carter FW, French RA, Salt J. 1993. International migration between East and West Europe. *Ethn. Racial Stud.* 16: pp. 467–91

Castles S. 1984. *Here for Good: Western Europe's New Ethnic Minorities.* London: Pluto. pp. 259

Castles S. 1993. Migrations and minorities in Europe. Perspectives for the 1990s: eleven hypotheses. See Solomos & Wrench 1993, pp. 17–34

Commission Nationale Consultative des Droits de l'Homme. 1997. *Rapport de la Commission Nationale Consultative des Droits de I 'Homme.* Paris: La Documentation francaise. pp. 442

Creamean L. 1996. Membership of foreigners: Algerians in France. *Arab Stud. Q.* 18: pp. 49–67

Crosby F, Bromley S, Saxe L. 1980. Recent unobtrusive studies of black and white discrimination and prejudice: a literature review. *Psychol. Bull.* 87: pp. 546–63

Daniel WW. 1968. *Racial Discrimination in England.* Harmondsworth, UK: Penguin. pp. 272

Den Uyl R, Choenni CE, Bovenkerk F. 1986. *Mag het ook een Buitenlander Wezen? Discriminatie bij Uitzendburo's.* Utrecht, The Netherlands: Natl. Bur. Against Racism. pp. 45

Doomernik J. 1997. Adaptation strategies among Soviet Jewish immigrants in Berlin. *New Community* 23: pp. 59–73

Escriva A. 1997. Control, composition and character of new migration to south-west Europe: the case of Peruvian women in Barcelona. *New Community* 23: pp. 43–57

Essed P. 1990. *Everyday Racism: Reports from Women of Two Cultures.* Claremont, CA: Hunter House. pp. 288

European Parliament. 1997. *Asylum in the European Union: The "Safe Country of Origin Principle."*. Strasbourg, France: Eur. Parliament. pp. 41

Feagin JR, Feagin CB. 1986. *Discrimination American Style: Institutional Racism and Sexism*. Malabar, FL: Krieger. pp. 246 2nd ed.

Feen RH. 1996. Thunder on the right: Austria's Jorg Haider and Freedom Party. *Migration World Mag.* 24(1–2) pp. 49–50

Fermin A. 1997. Dutch political parties on minority policy, 1977–1995. *Merger* 4(2): pp. 14–15

Foster CR, ed. 1980. *Nations Without a State: Ethnic Minorities in Western Europe*. New York: Praeger. pp. 215

Freud S. 1930. *Civilization and Its Discontents*. Transl. J Riviere. New York: Cape & Smith. pp. 144

Fuchs D, Gerhards J, Roller E. 1993. Wir und die Anderen. Ethnozentrismus in der zwoelf Landeren der europaeischen Ge-meinshaft. *Koln. Zeitschr. Soziol. Sozialpsychol.* 45: pp. 238–53

Fysh P, Wolfreys J. 1992. Le Pen, the National Front and the extreme-right in France. *Parliam. Aff. 45:* pp. 309–26

Gerhard U. 1992. Wenn Fluchtlinge und Ein-wan-derer zu 'Asylantenfluten' wer-den—zum Anteil des Mediendiskurses an rassistischen Pogromen. *Osnabrucker Be-itr. Sprachtheor.* 46: pp. 163–78

Gordon P. 1993. The police and racist violence in Britain. See Bjorgo & Witte 1993, pp. 167–78

Gordon P, Klug F. 1984. *Racism and Discrimination in Britain: A Select Bibliography, 1970–83*. London: Runnymede Trust. pp. 143

Govaert S. 1995. Flander's radical nationalism: how and why the Vlaams Blok ascended. *New Community* 4: pp. 537–49

Green DP, Strolovitch DZ, Wong JS. 1997. Defended neighborhoods, integration, and hate crime. Unpublished ms. Yale Univ. Inst. for Social and Policy Stud., New Haven, CT

Griffiths D. 1997. Somali refugees in Tower Hamlets: clanship and new identities. *New Community* 23: pp. 5–24

Gunn S. 1989. *Revolution of the Right: Europe's New Conservatives*. London: Pluto. pp. 135

Hammer T. 1993. Political participation and civil rights in Scandinavia. See Solomos & Wrench 1993, pp. 115–28

Heitmeyer W. 1993. Hostility and violence towards foreigners in Germany. See Bjorgo & Witte 1993, pp. 17–28

Holland B. 1995. Kicking racism out of football: an assessment of racial harassment in and around football grounds. *New Community* 21: pp. 567–86

Hubbuck J, Carter S. 1980. *Haifa Chance? A Report on Job Discrimination Against Young Blacks in Nottingham*. London: Comm. Racial Equal. pp. 63

Husbands CT. 1991a. The mainstream right and the politics of immigration in France: developments in the 1980s. *Ethn. Racial Stud.* 14: pp. 170–98

Husbands CT. 1991b. The support for the Front National: analyses and findings. *Ethn. Racial Stud.* 14: pp. 382–116

Husbands CT. 1993. Racism and racist violence: some theories and policy perspectives. See Bjorgo & Witte 1993, pp. 113–27

Joly D. 1996. *Haven or Hell? Asylum Policies and Refugees in Europe*. New York: St. Martin's Press. pp. 215

Kinder DR, Sanders LM. 1996. *Divided by Color: Racial Politics and Democratic Ideals*. Chicago: Univ. Chicago Press. pp. 391

Kitschelt H. 1995. *The Radical Right in Western Europe: A Comparative Analysis*. Ann Arbor, MI: Univ. Mich. Press. pp. 332

Klink A, Wagner U. 1998. Discrimination against ethnic minorities in Germany: going back to the field. *J. Appl. Soc. Psychol.* In press.

Koopmans R. 1995. *A Burning Question: Explaining the Rise of Racist and Extreme Right Violence in Western Europe.* Berlin: Wiss.zent. Berlin Soz. forsch. pp. 38

Koser K. 1996. European migration report: recent asylum migration in Europe. *New Community* 22: pp. 151–58

Kulischer E. 1948. *Europe on the Move: War and Population Changes, 1917–47.* New York: Columbia Univ. Press. pp. 377 pp.

Landes R. 1955. Biracialism in American society: a comparative view. *Am. Anthropol.* 57: pp. 1253–63

Layton-Henry Z, Wilpert C. 1994. *Discrimination, Racism and Citizenship: Inclusion and Exclusion in Britain and Germany.* London: Anglo-German Found. Study In-dust. Soc. pp. 30

Lloyd C. 1993. Racist violence and anti-racist reactions: a view of France. See Bjorgo & Witte 1993, pp. 207–20

Loow H. 1993. The cult of violence: the Swedish racist counterculture. See Bjorgo & Witte 1993, pp. 62–79

MacEwen M. 1993. *Enforcing anti-discrimination law in Britain: Here they be monsters.* Presented at Discrim., Racism and Citizenship Conf., Anglo-German Found. Study Indust. Soc, Berlin, Ger.

MacEwen M. 1995. *Tackling Racism in Europe: An Examination of Anti-Discrimination Law in Practice.* Washington, D.C.: Berg. pp. 223

MacMaster N. 1991. The "seuil de tolerance": the uses of a "scientific" racist concept. In *Race, Discourse and Power in France,* ed. M Silverman, pp. 14–28. Aldershot, UK: Avebury. pp. 129

Marcus J. 1995. *The National Front and French Politics: The Resistible Rise of Jean-Marie Le Pen.* London: Macmillan. pp. 212

Martiniello M. 1992a. *Leadership et Pouvoir dans les Communautes d'Origine Immi-gree.* Paris: CIEMI/ L'Harmattan. pp. 317

Martiniello M. 1992b. Italy—the late discovery of immigration. See Thraenhardt 1992a, pp. 195–218

Martiniello M. 1993. Ethnic leadership, ethnic communities' political powerlessness and the state in Belgium. *Ethn. Racial Stud.* 16: pp. 237–55

Mayer N. 1995. The dynamics of Anti-Front National countermovement. *French Polit. Soc.* 13(4): pp. 12–32

Mayer N, Perrineau P. 1992. Why do they vote for Le Pen? *Eur. J. Polit. Res.* 22: pp. 123–41

Mayhew LH. 1968. *Law and Equal Opportunity: A Study of the Massachusetts Commission Against Discrimination.* Cambridge, MA: Harvard Univ. Press. pp. 313

McArthur M. 1976. The "Saxon" Germans: political fate of an ethnic identity. *Dialect. Anthropol.* 1: pp. 349–64

Meertens RW, Pettigrew TF. 1997. Is subtle prejudice really prejudice? *Public Opin. Q.* 61: pp. 54–71

MelichA. 1995. *Comparative European trend survey data on racism and xenophobia.* Presented at Workshop Racist Parties Eur., Inst. d'Etudes Polit. de Bordeaux, France

Messina AM. 1989. *Race and Party Competition in Britain.* New York: Oxford Univ. Press. pp. 200

Miles R. 1993. Introduction—Europe 1993: the significance of changing patterns of migration. *Ethn. Racial Stud.* 16: pp. 459–66

Miles R, Cleary P. 1992. Britain: post-colonial migration in context. See Thraenhardt 1992a, pp. 121–44

Miles R, Phizacklea A. 1984. *White Man's Country: Racism in British Politics.* London: Pluto. 184 pp.

Munz R. 1996. A continent of migration: European mass migration in the 20th century. *New Community* 22: pp. 201–26

MuusP. 1996/1997. International migration to the Netherlands. *Merger* 4(1): pp. 4

Panayiotopoulos PI. 1996. Challenging orthodoxies: Cypriot entrepreneurs in the London garment industry. *New Community* 22: pp. 437–60

Parkinson F, ed. 1989. *Conquering the Past: Austrian Nazism Yesterday and Today.* Detroit, MI: Wayne State Univ. Press. pp. 345

Peach C, Glebe G. 1995. Muslim minorities in western Europe. *Ethn. Racial Stud.* 18: pp. 26–5

Pettigrew TF. 1988. Integration and pluralism. In *Eliminating Racism: Profiles in Controversy,* ed. PA Katz, D Taylor, pp. 19–30. New York: Plenum. 380 pp.

Pettigrew TF. 1989. The nature of modern racism in the United States. *Rev. Int. Psy-chol.Soc.* 2:291–303

Pettigrew TF. 1997. Generalized intergroup contact effects on prejudice. *Pers. Soc. Psychol. Bull.* 23: pp. 173–85

Pettigrew TF. 1998. *Systematizing the predictors of prejudice: an empirical approach.* Univ. Calif, Santa Cruz. Unpubl. ms

Pettigrew TF, Jackson J, Ben Brika J, Lemain G, Meertens RW, et al. 1998. Outgroup prejudice in western Europe. *Eur. Rev. Soc. Psychol.* In press

Pettigrew TF, Meertens RW. 1995. Subtle and blatant prejudice in western Europe. *Eur. J. Soc. Psychol.* 25: pp. 57–75

Pettigrew TF, Meertens RW. 1996. The verzuiling puzzle: understanding Dutch intergroup relations. *Curr. Psychol.* 15: pp. 3–13

Pettigrew TF, Taylor MC. 1991. Discrimination. In *The Encyclopedia of Sociology,* ed. EF Borgatta, ML Borgatta, 1: pp. 498–503. New York: Macmillan. 519 pp.

Quillian L. 1995. Prejudice as a response to perceived group threat: population composition and anti-immigrant and racial prejudice in Europe. *Am. Sociol. Rev.* 60: pp. 586–611

Reif K, Melich A. 1991. *Euro-Barometer 30: Immigrants and Out-Groups in Western Europe, October-November 1988.* Ann Arbor, MI: Inter-Univ. Consort. Polit. Soc. Res. pp. 78

Rich PB. 1990. *Race and Empire in British Politics.* New York: Cambridge Univ. Press. pp. 274 2nd ed.

Rudolph H. 1996. The new gastarbeiter system in Germany. *New Community* 22: pp. 287–300

Santel B. 1992. European community and asylum seekers: the harmonization of asylum policies. See Thraenhardt 1992a, pp. 103–16

Schoen DE. 1977. *Enoch Powell and the Powellites.* New York: St. Martin's Press. pp. 317

Sears DD. 1988. Symbolic racism. In *Eliminating Racism: Profiles in Controversy,* ed. PA Katz, DA Taylor, pp. 53–84. New York: Plenum. pp. 380

Shanker T. 1996. City hell. *New Republic* 215(22): pp. 14–15

Shields JG. 1989. Campaigning on the fringe: Jean-Marie Le Pen. In *The French Presidential Elections of 1988: Ideology and Leadership in Contemporary France,* ed. J Gaffney, pp. 140–57. Aldershot, UK: Dartmouth. pp. 241

Singer D. 1991. The resistible rise of Jean-Marie Le Pen. *Ethn. Racial Stud.* 14: pp. 368–81

Sissons M. 1981. Race, sex and helping behavior. *Br. J. Soc. Psychol.* 20: pp. 285–92

Smith DJ. 1976. *The Facts of Racial Disadvantage: A National Survey.* London: PEP. pp. 257

Solomos J, Wrench J, eds. 1993. *Racism and Migration in Western Europe.* Oxford, UK: Berg. pp. 293

Stasiulis DK. 1997. International migration, rights, and the decline of "actually existing liberal democracy." *New Community* 23: pp. 197–214

Tezenas du Montcel A. 1995. Le Pen: la strategie de la fourmi. *Le Nouvel Econ.* 24: pp. 56–60

Thraenhardt D, ed. 1992a. *Europe: A New Immigration Continent.* Muenster, Ger: Lit. pp. 252

Thraenhardt D. 1992b. Europe—a new immigration continent: policies and politics since 1945 in comparative perspective. See Thraenhardt 1992a, pp. 15–74

Thraenhardt D. 1995. The political uses of xenophobia in England, France and Germany. *Party Polit.* 1: pp. 323–45

Thraenhardt D. 1996. European migration from East to West: present patterns and future directions. *New Community* 22: pp. 227–42

US Commission on Civil Rights. 1990. *Bigotry and Violence on American College Campuses.* Washington, D.C.: US Comm. Civil Rights. pp. 80

van Donselaar J. 1993. The extreme right and racist violence in the Netherlands. See Bjorgo & Witte 1993, pp. 46–61

Vasta E. 1993. Rights and racism in a new country of immigration: the Italian case. See Solomos & Wrench 1993, pp. 83–98

Veenman J, Roelandt T. 1990. Allochtonen: achterstand en achterstelling. In *Arbeids-markt en Maatschappelijke Ongelijkheid*, ed. JJ Schippers, pp. 88–114. Groningen, The Netherlands: Wolters-Noordhoff. pp. 281

Verdery K. 1985. The unmaking of an ethnic collectivity: Transylvania's Germans. *Am. Ethnol.* 12: pp. 62–83

Vranken J, Martiniello M. 1992. Migrants, guest workers and ethnic minorities. Historical patterns, recent trends and social implications of migration in Belgium. See Thraenhardt 1992a, pp. 219–51

Wagner U, Zick A. 1997. Auslander-feindlichkeit, Vorurteile und diskriminier-endes Verhalten. In *Aggression und Ge-walt*, ed. HW Bierhoff, U Wagner, pp. 145–64. Stuttgart: Kohlhammer. pp. 268

Waldrauch H, Hofinger C. 1997. An index to measure the legal obstacles to the integration of immigrants. *New Community* 23: pp. 271–85

Wieviorka M. 1993. Tendencies to racism in Europe: Does France represent a unique case, or is it representative of a trend? See Solomos & Wrench 1993, pp. 55–65

Willems H. 1995. Right-wing extremism, racism or youth violence? Explaining violence against foreigners in Germany. *New Community* 21: pp. 501–23

Wilpert C. 1993. Ideological and institutional foundations of racism in the Federal Republic of Germany. See Solomos & Wrench 1993, pp. 67–81

Wise MZ. 1995. Spandau spandex: Meet Austria's latest fascist. *New Republic* 213(26): pp. 16–17

Witte R. 1995. Racist violence in western Europe. *New Community* 21: pp. 489–500

World Council of Churches Migration Secretariat, ed. 1980. *Migrant Workers and Racism in Europe.* Geneva: World Counc. Churches. pp. 158

Zick A. 1997. *Vorurteile undRassismus: Eine Sozialpsychologische Analyse.* Muenster, Germ: Waxmann. pp. 494

Zick A, Wagner U. 1993. Den Turken geht es besser als uns. Wie Fremde zu Feinden werden. *Psychol. Heute* 20: pp. 48–53

# RACIAL ATTITUDES AND PUBLIC DISCOURSES

# RACIAL ATTITUDES AND RELATIONS AT THE CLOSE OF THE TWENTIETH CENTURY

*By Lawrence D. Bobo*

> The color-line is not static; it bends and buckles and sometimes breaks.
>
> (Drake and Cayton, 1945:101)

Throughout the 1990s, assessments of racial and ethnic relations in the United States suggested that we have become increasingly racially polarized. Essayist and political scientist Andrew Hacker declared that, "a huge racial chasm remains, and there are few signs that the coming century will see it closed" (1992:219). Civil rights activist and legal scholar Derrick Bell offered the bleak analysis that, "racism is an integral, permanent, and indestructible component of this society" (1992:ix). These statements, it seemed, only set the stage for even more dramatic declarations from both Hispanics (Delgado, 1996) and other Blacks (Rowan, 1996). Reaction against such pessimistic analyses seemed inevitable.

In 1997, conservative analysts Stephan and Abigail Thernstrom argued that, "the foundation of progress for many Blacks is no longer fragile. Progress is real and solid" (Thernstrom and Thernstrom, 1997:535). This sentiment was echoed by the eminent historical sociologist Orlando Patterson, who maintained that "being Afro-American is no longer a significant obstacle to participation in the public life of the nation. What is more, Afro-Americans have also become full members of what may be called the nation's moral community and cultural life" (1997:17). Indeed, journalist Jim Sleeper goes so far as to deride the analyses offered by Hacker, Bell, Rowan, Delgado, and others as so much "liberal racism" (1997).

The empirical social science literature examining racial attitudes and relations is no less divided. Sociologist Joe Feagin (1997) recently argued that, "the basic racial problem in the United States is White racism. White racism is a social disease that afflicts the minds, emotions, behaviors, and institutions of Whites. White racism pervades every nook and cranny of U.S. society" (p. 29). Political psychologist David Sears developed a densely argued and analytically detailed critique of the claim that race-neutral political values, as opposed to anti-Black animus, lay at the base of many Whites' discontent with social policies developed on the basis of race. After examining data from three national surveys and one Los Angeles-based survey, Sears and his colleagues concluded:

The strength of the findings here will lay to rest the notion that White opposition to racially targeted policies is primarily motivated by nonracial considerations, or that any racially based motivation is limited to a few poorly educated ethnocentrics or believers in White supremacy. Racism is considerably more widespread in American society than that, it cannot be reduced to the older forms of prejudice familiar in the pre-civil rights era, and it continues to have quite pervasive effects. It is not a pleasant aspect of our society, but it is not one that should be swept under the carpet, either (Sears et al., 1997:49).

Yet, other students of public opinion vehemently disagree. Sears and colleagues' conclusion is directly antithetical to that reached by Sniderman and Carmines (1997). On the basis of a series of experiments embedded in large-scale surveys examining Whites' views about affirmative action, they argued that, "it is simply wrong to suppose that racial prejudice is a primary source of opposition to affirmative action ... racism turns out to be just one of a string of explanations offered for opposition to affirmative action that don't cash out" (Sniderman and Carmines, 1997:144). Likewise, some analysts of trend data have also ventured broad generalizations about a decline in racism. According to public-opinion researchers Niemi et al., "without ignoring real signs of enduring racism, it is still fair to conclude that America has been successfully struggling to resolve its Dilemma and that equality has been gaining in ascendancy over racism" (1989:168).

And so the battle is joined. This great debate, whether waged at the level of public intellectuals or between empirical social scientists, raises serious questions about racial attitudes and relations, as

well as about the success and health of American democracy, as we enter a new century.

## DEVELOPING THE EMPIRICAL ASSESSMENT

The paramount question is whether America is moving toward becoming a genuinely "color-blind" society or stagnating as a society deeply polarized by race. As is by now obvious, studies of racial attitudes in the United States present a difficult dilemma. On the one hand, several recent studies emphasize steadily improving racial attitudes of Whites, especially in terms of their attitudes toward Blacks. These attitudinal trends are reinforced by many more tangible indicators, most notably the size, relative security, and potentially growing influence of the Black middle class. On the other hand, there is evidence of persistent negative stereotyping of racial minorities, evidence of widely divergent views of the extent and importance of racial discrimination to modern race relations, and evidence of deepening feelings of alienation among Blacks (and possibly among members of other minority groups as well). These more pessimistic attitudinal trends are reinforced by such tangible indicators as the persistent problem of racial segregation of neighborhoods and schools, discrimination in access to housing and employment, innumerable everyday acts of racial bias, and numerous signs of the gulf in perception that often separates Blacks and Whites.

Empirical assessment here focuses on five aspects of the research: (1) the predominant trend toward positive change concerning the goals of integration and equal treatment; (2) the evident difficulty of moving from these goals to concrete support for change in social policy and individual living conditions; (3) the problem of persistent stereotyping; (4) the differing views of racial discrimination; and (5) the possible deepening of Black alienation. Wherever possible, trends are emphasized. It is essential to have a sense of whether and how much things have changed if we are to make sense of where we stand today or might head in the future. Although this analysis will emphasize what is known about the views of Whites toward Blacks, at several important points a multiracial perspective will be incorporated.

By way of foreshadowing what is to come, it is important to note that we now have a deeply rooted national consensus on the ideals of racial equality and integration. These high ideals founder, however, on racial differences in preferred levels of integration, they founder on sharp racial differences in beliefs about racial discrimination, they founder on the persistence of negative racial stereotypes, and they result in policy stagnation and mutual misunderstanding. Although America has turned away from Jim Crow racism, it heads into an uncertain future. With specific regard to the Black-White divide, journalist David Shipler comes as close as anyone has to understanding the special character of this cleavage:

> [T]he fountainhead of injustice has been located between Blacks and Whites, and that legacy remains the country's most potent symbol of shame. Nothing tests the nation, or takes the measure of its decency, quite like the rift between Black and White. … I have sought and found common denominators at a level of attitude that transcends boundaries of place. Everywhere I have looked, I have seen a country where Blacks and Whites are strangers to each other (1997:x).

Before proceeding, it seems prudent to provide some anchorage for the terms "race" and "ethnicity," "attitude," "prejudice," and "racism." There is no settled consensus on how to define and use race and ethnicity (Petersen, 1982; Alba, 1992).

Common usage tends to associate "race" with biologically based differences between human groups, differences typically observable in skin color, hair texture, eye shape, and other physical attributes. "Ethnicity" tends to be associated with culture, pertaining to such factors as language, religion, and nationality. There may be quite real differences in physical features that come to be understood as indicia for racial group membership. Yet, it is widely agreed by social scientists that both race and ethnicity are, fundamentally, social constructions (Jones, 1972; Omi and Winant, 1986; Stone, 1985; See and Wilson, 1989).

Some have argued vigorously for discontinuing use of the term "race." Early forceful proponents of this position were Ashley Montagu (1964) and Gordon Allport (1954). More recent advocates are Thernstrom and Thernstrom (1997) and Patterson (1997). "Race" is retained here for two reasons. (1) It still comports with prevailing social usage and understanding. The core mission here is to convey the state of public opinion on these matters; therefore, to introduce new vocabulary inconsistent with what much of the public readily comprehends introduces a distraction. (2) As Petersen eloquently explained, "Whether the removal of a word would also eradicate group antipathies is doubtful; one suspects that with another classification Jews and Gypsies would have been murdered just as beastially. In any case, deleting the term does not remove the need for some designation" (1982:7).

Although perceived racial distinctions often result in sharper and more persistent barriers than ethnic distinctions, this is not invariably the case, and both terms share elements of presumed common descent or ascriptive inheritance. The broad census categories of Asian and Pacific Islander, Hispanic, Black, and White conceal important subgroup differences defined along lines of nativity, national origin, class, gender, and other dimensions.

Social psychologists have long understood "attitudes" to involve "a favorable or unfavorable evaluation of an object" (Schuman, 1995:68). In this case, the objects of attitude are racial and ethnic groups and their attributes, aspects of relations between groups, public policies relevant to race, contact between those groups, and assessments of the character of intergroup relations.[*] Attitudes are, therefore, important guides to likely patterns of social behavior. Racial attitudes, however, are not automatically indicative of racial prejudice or of racism. Both prejudice and racism are themselves complex, internally differentiated concepts. Therefore, it would be inappropriate to interpret patterns revealed by any single racial attitude question, even in relation to a major conceptual grouping, as indicating a fundamental or global change in the level of either prejudice or racism. Such generalizations and interpretations should be made with great caution because social phenomena may remain powerfully "racialized" even as one way of understanding prejudice or racism is undergoing major change (Bonilla-Silva, 1996).

Social psychologist Thomas Pettigrew suggested that prejudice involved "irrationally based negative attitudes against certain ethnic groups and their members" (1981:2). Prejudice thus involved an "antipathy accompanied by a faculty generalization" (Pettigrew, 1981:3). Sociologists Katherine O'Sullivan See and William Julius Wilson suggest that the term "prejudice" be reserved for the "attitudinal dimension of intergroup relations, to the processes of stereotyping and aversion that may persist even in the face of countervailing evidence" (See and Wilson, 1989:227). Prejudice is thus distinct from racism. See and Wilson suggested that

> [R]acism is a more complex belief system that prescribes and legitimates a minority group's or an out-group's subordination by claiming that the group is either biogenetically or culturally inferior. ... There are two components to racism that are not present in prejudice: an ideology that justifies social avoidance and domination by reference to the 'unalterable' characteristics of particular groups and a set of norms that prescribe differential treatment for these groups (See and Wilson, 1989:227).

Many analysts recognize forms of racism that exist at the level of individual attitudes and beliefs (Pettigrew, 1981; Gaertner and Dovidio, 1986; Jones, 1988; Sears, 1988), but there are also good reasons why distinction between the two should be maintained. (1) There is value in clearly differentiating individual and societal levels of analysis. Using the term "prejudice" to speak to the individual level and "racism" to speak to the cultural and societal levels helps to maintain greater conceptual clarity. (2) In a larger social context, where the term "racism" has become heavily loaded with potential to alienate as well as to stigmatize, and given that it has often been used carelessly, there is some value to insisting on delimited and careful use of the term.

---

[*] Thus, we rely on a multidimensional conception of attitudes about race and ethnicity (Jackman, 1977; Bobo, 1983). Although some social scientists still defend the usefulness of thinking of racial attitudes in terms of points along a single prejudice-to-tolerance continuum (Kleinpenning and Hagendoorn, 1993), most analysts acknowledge the usefulness of perceiving racial attitudes as having several broad conceptual types. To be sure, some critics argue that examinations of racial attitudes are intrinsically static and destined simply to show declining prejudice (Bonilla-Silva, 1996; Steinberg, 1998); this view is easily refuted, however, once one adopts a multidimensional framework and devotes even the most cursory attention to empirical studies of change over time (Schuman et al., 1997).

## MAJOR PATTERNS IN RACIAL ATTITUDES AND BELIEFS

### New Principles of Equality and Integration

The single clearest trend shown in studies of racial attitudes has involved a steady and sweeping movement toward general endorsement of the principles of racial equality and integration. The data charted in Figures 9-1, 9-2, and 9-3 show much of this trend. When major national assessments of racial attitudes were first conducted in the early 1940s, 68 percent of Whites expressed the view that Black and White school children should go to separate schools, 54 percent felt that public transportation should be segregated, and 54 percent felt that Whites should receive preference over Blacks in access to jobs. By the early 1960s, percentages of Whites advocating segregation and discrimination had decreased substantially, so much so that the questions on public transportation and access to jobs were dropped from national surveys in the early 1970s (Figure 9-3). By then, virtually all Whites endorsed the idea that transportation should be integrated and that access to jobs should be equal without regard to

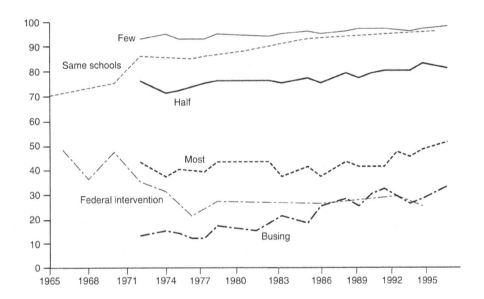

**FIGURE 9-1 Trends in Whites' attitudes about school integration.**

SOURCE: Adapted from Schuman et al. (1997). **Few:** Would you have any objection to sending your children to a school where a few of the children are Blacks? **Half.** [If "no" or don't know to *FEW*] Where half of the children are Blacks? **Most:** [If "no" or don't know to *HALF*]: Where more than half of the children are Blacks? **Same Schools:** Do you think White students and Black students should go to the same schools or to separate schools? **Federal Intervention:** Do you think the federal government should see to it that White and Black children go to the same schools, or should federal officials stay out of this area, as it is not their business? **Busing:** In general, do you favor or oppose the busing of Black and White school children from one school district to another?

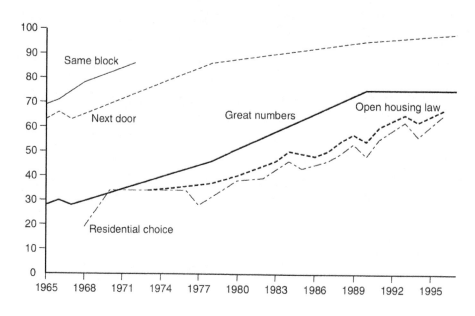

**FIGURE 9-2 Trends in Whites' attitudes about residential choice.**

SOURCE: Adapted from Schuman et al. (1997). ***Same Block:*** If a Black family with the same income and education as you have moved into your block, would it make any difference to you? ***Next Door:*** If Blacks came to live next door, would you move? ***Great Numbers:*** Would you move if Blacks came to live in great numbers in your neighborhood? ***Open Housing Law:*** Suppose there is a community-wide vote on the general housing issue. One law says that a homeowner can decide for himself who to sell his house to, even if he prefers not to sell to Blacks. The second law says that a homeowner cannot refuse to sell to someone because of their race or color. Which law would you vote for? ***Residential Choice:*** Do you agree with this statement? White people have a right to keep Blacks out of their neighborhoods if they want to, and Blacks should respect that right.

race. The issue of integrated schools remained more divided; however, the trend was equally steady. By 1995, fully 96 percent of Whites expressed the view that White and Black school children should go to the same schools (Figure 9-1). Three points about this transformation of basic principles or norms that should guide race relations bear noting.

First, there is some variation in the degree of endorsement of the principle of racial equality and integration. In general, the more public and impersonal the arena, the greater the evidence of movement toward endorsing ideals of integration and equality. Thus, support for unconstrained access

to housing for Blacks has undergone tremendous positive change, but still lags behind endorsement of access to schools and jobs. More telling, racially mixed marriage still encounters some resistance, with one in five Whites as recently as 1990 supporting laws that would ban such marriages, and an even higher percentage expressing personal disapproval of them (Figure 9-4).

Second, Blacks have long rejected segregation. Although the available data for tracing long-term attitudinal trends among Blacks are much more limited than for Whites, it is clear that Blacks have overwhelmingly favored integrated schools and

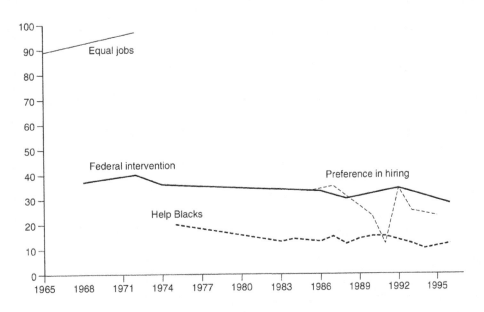

**FIGURE 9-3 Trends in Whites' attitudes about race and employment.**

SOURCE: Adapted from Schuman et al. (1997). ***Equal Jobs:*** Do you think Blacks should have as good a chance as White people to get any kind of job, or do you think White people should have the first chance at any kind of job? ***Federal Intervention:*** Should the federal government see to it that Black people get fair treatment in jobs, or should the federal government leave these matters to the states and local communities? ***Preference in Hiring:*** Are you for or against preferential hiring and promotion of Blacks? [If For] Do you favor preference in hiring and promotion strongly or not strongly [If Against] Do you oppose preference in hiring and promotion strongly or not strongly? ***Help Blacks:*** Some people think that Blacks have been discriminated against for so long that the government has a special obligation to help improve their living standards. Others believe that the government should not be giving special treatment to Blacks. Where would you place yourself on this scale [1. I strongly agree the government is obligated to help Blacks. 3. I agree with both answers. 5. I strongly agree that government shouldn't give special treatment], or haven't you made up your mind on this?

neighborhoods and desired equal access to employment opportunities. And Blacks have long been less likely than Whites to object to racially mixed marriages, presumably because such strictures were viewed as one element in a system of race-based oppression.

Third, the positive trend among Whites on these principles across the domains of schools, public transportation, jobs, housing, politics, and even intermarriage is steady and unabated. Despite intense discussion of a possible "racial backlash" in the 1960s in response to Black protests, or in the 1970s in response to school busing efforts and the implementation of affirmative action, or even in the 1990s in the wake of events such as the riots in Los Angeles, support for principles of racial equality and integration has been sweeping and robust. So much so, that it is reasonable to describe it as a change in fundamental norms with regard to race.

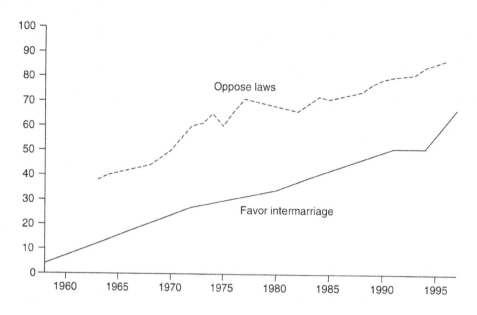

**FIGURE 9-4 Trends in Whites' attitudes about racial intermarriage.**

SOURCE: Adapted from Schuman et al. (1997). ***Oppose Laws:*** Do you think there should be laws against marriages between Blacks and Whites? ***Favor Intermarriage:*** Do you approve or disapprove of marriage between Whites and non-Whites?

## Complexity of Changing How We Live and What We Want Government to Do

Unfortunately, it is not possible to infer from the positive change in attitudes toward principles of equality and integration that either public policy or the texture of day-to-day life for most Americans would quickly come to mirror this apparent consensus on ideals. Consider first the issue of integrating neighborhoods and schools. It is clear that numbers matter (see Figures 9-1 and 9-2). When Whites were asked about living in integrated areas or sending their children to integrated schools, their willingness to do so decreased as the percentage of Blacks rose (compare trends for Few, Half, and Most in Figure 9-1).

Also, the meaning of integration differs for Blacks and Whites. It is clear that most Whites prefer to live in overwhelmingly White neighborhoods even though they are open to living with a small number of Blacks. Blacks prefer to live in integrated neighborhoods, but also prefer to be present in substantial numbers—numbers high enough, however, to generate discomfort for most Whites.

With respect to public policy issues, there have been long-running debates about equal opportunity policies and affirmative action, and the trend data suggest that there is a significant substantive division in opinion. Programs that are compensatory in nature—that aim to equip minorities to be more effective competitors or that engage in special outreach and recruitment efforts—are reasonably popular. Policies that call for explicit racial preferences have long been unpopular, with the use of quotas rejected by Whites and Blacks alike (Lipset and Schneider, 1978; Kluegel and Smith, 1986; Bobo and Kluegel, 1993; Steeh and Krysan, 1996).

There is, however, some divergence of opinion about affirmative-action policies by race. Blacks and

Hispanics tend to support affirmative-action type policies, whether aimed at improving training and competitive resources of minority group members or calling for preferences in hiring and promotion. A majority of Whites support the more compensatory policies, but fewer support preferential policies (Figures 9-5 and 9-6).

## Persistent Negative Stereotyping

A major factor influencing limits to integration and social policy with respect to race lies in the problem of antiminority, especially anti-Black, stereotyping. There is evidence that negative racial stereotypes of minority groups, especially of Blacks and Hispanics, remain common among Whites. As Sniderman and

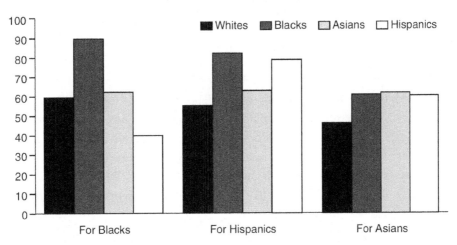

**FIGURE 9-5 Support for race-based job training and education assistance programs, by race.**

SOURCE: Los Angeles Survey of Urban Inequality (1994).

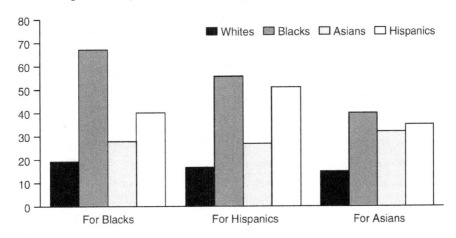

**FIGURE 9-6 Support for race-based preferences in hiring and promotion, by race.**

SOURCE: Los Angeles Survey of Urban Inequality (1994).

Carmines (1997) put it, "it is simply wrong to suppose that there is a shortage of White Americans willing to say, publicly, something overtly negative about Black Americans" (p. 63). There is evidence that minority groups may also stereotype one another, though the story here is a good deal more complicated.

It is important to clarify what is meant by "stereotype." A stereotype is "a set of beliefs about the personal attributes of members of a particular social category" or "a set of cognitions that specify the personal qualities, especially personality traits, of members of an ethnic group" (Ashmore and Del Boca, 1981:13). As Hamilton and Trolier put it, stereotypes are "cognitive structures that contain the perceiver's knowledge, beliefs, and expectations about human groups" (1986:133). Thus, racial stereotyping involves projecting assumptions or expectations about the likely capacities and behaviors of members of a racial or ethnic group onto members of that group. Thus, stereotyping has a strong potential to influence other perceptions about, behavior toward, and patterns of interaction with members of the stereotyped group.

Historically, racial stereotyping denoted beliefs that were categorical or extreme, negative in valence, rigidly held, and as a consequence of these features, inherently bad (Ashmore and Del Boca, 1981; Jackman, 1994). Modern social scientists, however, limit the meaning of the stereotyping concept to the ideas or perceptions about groups, without assuming these ideas are necessarily categorical, negative, rigid, or even bad (Ashmore and Del Boca, 1981; Stephan, 1985). As a matter of definition, it is better to think of stereotypes much like any other cognition. Whether these assumed characteristics exist is thus a matter for empirical assessment. Indeed, some stereotypes may have a kernel of truth in them, such as disproportionate Black dependence on welfare or involvement in crime. Such perceptions become problematic, and more akin to prejudice, to the extent they resist modification when presented with new information, are applied categorically to individuals, or both.

Social psychologists commonly distinguish between cultural stereotypes and personal stereotypes, or personal beliefs. Cultural stereotypes refer to widely shared ideas about members of particular racial or ethnic groups (Devine, 1989; Devine and Elliot, 1995). Any particular individual, while almost certainly aware of the broad cultural stereotype about a salient racial or ethnic group, need not personally accept or adhere to that stereotype. Hence, it is of both analytical and (as we shall argue) practical importance to recognize the distinction.

The impetus to accept or adhere to prevailing stereotypes has several sources or origins (Pettigrew, 1981; Duckitt, 1992; Brown, 1995). Individuals may come to accept stereotypes through

- *social learning:* socialization into a particular culture or other direct contact with members of particular racial or ethnic groups, or vicarious learning experiences such as through the media;
- *motivation:* rationalization of some externality or instrumental consideration—e.g., it is easier to exploit and deny rights to those one perceives as inferior—or of a personality attribute—e.g., ethnocentric, *intolerant*, authoritarian people require others to feel superior to, and so choose to believe more negative stereotypes of others, often minority group members;
- *cognitive biases:* rare or infrequently occurring phenomena, especially if given a strongly negative evaluation, can assume unwarranted prominence in memory, such as a perception of minority group members as prone to crime and violence. In addition, once categorization has occurred, it is common to exaggerate between-group differences and to underestimate within-group variation.

After a long period of inattention, survey researchers began in the 1980s to focus on racial stereotypes, following the work of Mary Jackman. Beginning with Jackman and Senter (1980, 1983) and Jackman (1994), several major social surveys have shown that negative stereotyping of racial and ethnic minorities, especially involving Whites' views of Blacks, remain widespread (Smith, 1990; Sniderman and Piazza, 1993; Sniderman and Carmines, 1997; Bobo and Kluegel, 1993, 1997). In part, this resurgence of interest reflected a move to different ways of measuring stereotypes; bipolar trait rating or other means of expressing relative judgments replaced previous reliance on categorical agree-or-disagree statements. In part, this resurgence of interest reflected a perception that racial stereotypes had, in fact, changed in form of expression to a more qualified nature, which the methodological innovation allowed researchers to tap.

Gauging the exact level of negative stereotyping is not an easy task. One relatively conservative estimate is offered by Sniderman and Piazza (1993) who maintain that:

> Notwithstanding the cliché that Whites will not openly endorse negative racial stereotypes for fear of appearing to be racist, large numbers of them—rarely less than one in every five and sometimes as many as one out of every two—agree with frankly negative characterizations of Blacks, particularly characterizations of Blacks as irresponsible and as failing to work hard and to make a genuine effort to deal with their problems on their own (p. 12).

This accounting is a bit complicated, on two scores. First, many Whites were found also to hold positive-trait perceptions of Blacks, not merely negative ones. Second, only a minority of Whites were found to hold uniformly negative views of Blacks—roughly 22 percent of Sniderman and Carmines' (1997) national sample. In some absolute sense, that almost one quarter of Whites hold consistently negative stereotypical views of Blacks is not a large number; however, given that almost all Whites express some negative stereotypes of Blacks, and nearly one quarter hold firmly negative views, the potential for anti-Black bias in many settings is actually quite large even with these conservative estimates.

It is important to note that the observed spread of negative stereotyping depends on both the exact trait examined and the method of assessment. As regards the method of assessment, absolute ratings of Blacks, for example, tend to reveal less prevalent negative stereotypes than do relative or difference-score ratings comparing images of Whites and of Blacks. For example, Jackman's 1975 survey found that 25 percent of Whites gave absolute negative ratings of Blacks' intelligence, 30 percent gave absolute negative ratings of Blacks' dependability, and 36 percent gave absolute negative ratings of Blacks' industriousness—i.e., believe Blacks are lazy. In contrast to how these White respondents rated Whites as a group, the degree of stereotyping against Blacks was higher; 57 percent gave a more negative relative rating to Blacks concerning intelligence, 56 percent did so concerning dependability, and 37 percent did so concerning laziness.

A similar pattern of nontrivial absolute negative ratings and of even more broadly negative relative ratings of Blacks is obtained from 1990 General Social Survey (GSS) data. Bobo and Kluegel (1997:100–101) show that 31 percent of Whites gave Blacks a low absolute rating in terms of intelligence, 47 percent did so in terms of laziness, 54 percent did so concerning proclivity to violence, and 59 percent did so concerning preference to live off of welfare. The relative ratings are higher in each instance, sometimes substantially so. Thus, the figures are 54 percent rating Blacks as less intelligent compared to the rating for Whites, 62 percent rating Blacks as lazier, 56 percent rating Blacks as more prone to violence, and fully 78 percent rating Blacks as preferring to live off of welfare as compared to Whites.

Jackman and others (Jaynes and Williams, 1989; Bobo, 1997; Bobo and Kluegel, 1997) make the important point that racial stereotypes are now more qualified in character. The perceived differences between Blacks and Whites are expressed, if not also understood, as more a matter of degree than a matter of categorical distinction. But also, the differences appear to be understood or interpreted in more cultural and volitional terms. To the extent there are differences, comparatively few Whites appear to believe they are inherent or biological in origin. These negative stereotypes often also apply in terms of Whites' views of Hispanics (Smith, 1990). Although Whites' views of Asians and Pacific Islanders are seldom as negative as those regarding Blacks and Hispanics, even Asians and Pacific Islanders typically receive unfavorable

relative ratings. The 1990 GSS reported that considerably more than 50 percent of Whites rated Blacks and Hispanics as less intelligent. A similar percentage rated Blacks and Hispanics as prone to violence. Considerably more than two-thirds of Whites rated Blacks and Hispanics as actually preferring to live off welfare.

One example of such patterns is shown in Figure 9-7. Substantial percentages of Whites rated Blacks and Hispanics as less intelligent, preferring to live off welfare, and hard to get along with socially. Research suggests that these stereotypes differ in several important ways from stereotypes that were prevalent in the past. First, they are much more likely to be understood as the product of environmental and group cultural traditions, whereas, in the past, they were unequivocally taken as the product of natural endowment. Second, there is growing evidence that many Whites are aware of traditional negative stereotypes of Blacks, as anyone immersed in American culture would be, but personally reject the negative stereotype and its implications (Devine and Elliot, 1995). The problem is that in many face-to-face interactions, the traditional stereotype

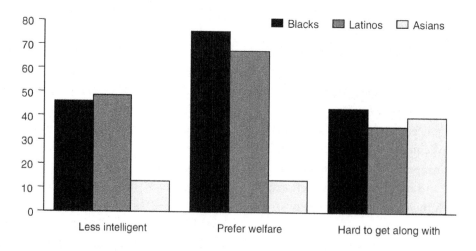

**FIGURE 9-7 Percentage of Whites rating racial minorities as inferior to Whites.**

SOURCE: Los Angeles Survey of Urban Inequality (1994).

controls perception and behavior (Devine, 1989). The end result is bias and discrimination against minorities.

In terms of the social consequences of these stereotypes, research suggests that stereotyping likely influences interpersonal interactions (Anderson, 1990; Feagin and Sikes, 1994), processes of racial residential segregation (Farley et al., 1994; Bobo and Zubrinsky, 1996), and the larger political environment (Bobo and Kluegel, 1993; Hurwitz and Peffley, 1997; Peffley et al., 1997). Research indicating Whites' fearfulness of a Black stranger is indicative. Based on a survey involving the use of sophisticated experimental vignettes, St. John and Heald-Moore (1995) found that Whites were more fearful of a Black stranger than of a White stranger. This was true irrespective of other situational factors such as time of day or neighborhood characteristics. The degree of fear was strongly conditioned by only two factors: age and gender of the Black person (young Black males were feared more than others) and age of the White person (feelings of fear and vulnerability were greatest among older Whites). In subsequent work, St. John and Heald-Moore (1996) found a strong interaction between race of the stranger, level of fear, and level of racial prejudice among Whites.

> We found that for Whites, encounters with Black strangers in public settings evoke more fear of victimization than encounters with White strangers. We also found that the effect of the race of strangers encountered is conditioned by racial prejudice. That is, encounters with Black strangers evoke greater levels of fear in Whites who have high levels of prejudice than in Whites who have lower levels. However, even Whites who gave the least prejudiced response to all the items of the prejudice scale were more

fearful of encounters with Black than with White strangers (1996:281).

This work implies that the interaction between Blacks and Whites in many public settings is rife with the potential for missteps, misunderstanding, and insult. Precisely this sort of dynamic is suggested by events and experiences recounted in qualitative interviews with middle-class Blacks (Feagin, 1991; Cose, 1993; Feagin and Sikes, 1994).

Negative stereotyping appears to play a role in reproducing larger structural patterns of racial residential segregation (Massey and Denton, 1993). Based on data from the 1992 Detroit Area Study (DAS), Farley and colleagues (1994) found that negative stereotyping of Blacks strongly predicted Whites' willingness to share integrated neighborhood space with Blacks. In subsequent work, involving data from the Los Angeles County Social Survey (LACSS), Bobo and Zubrinsky (1996) found that this effect was not restricted to Whites' reactions to Blacks. The effect of negative stereotyping on openness to residential integration also applied when Whites were reacting to the prospect of Hispanic or Asian neighbors. It is important to note that both of these surveys showed that the effect of negative stereotyping on attitudes on residential integration was independent of perceptions about the average class status of Blacks (for 1992 DAS) and of perceptions of the average class status of Blacks, Hispanics, and Asians (for 1992 LACSS). That is, distinctly racial stereotyping influenced Whites' willingness to live in integrated communities.

Stereotyping also appears to play an important role in modern politics, especially with regard to some types of race-targeted social policies (Bobo and Kluegel, 1993) as well as to some issues with a more implicit racial component such as crime (Hurwitz and Peffley, 1997) and welfare-related policy issues (Gilens, 1995, 1996a; Peffley et al., 1997). Research in this area makes clear the general importance of racial attitudes, but also often high-lights the complex and conditional nature of the effects of negative racial stereotyping. For example, using survey-based experimental data from a 1994 survey in Lexington, Kentucky, Hurwitz and Peffley (1997) found that the impact of negative stereotyping of Blacks on Whites' views of crime, criminals, and crime policy issues hinged on other contextual information. Aspects of the nature of the crime, the criminal, and the policy all mattered. To the extent these contextual features were consistent with the broad cultural stereotypes of Blacks—as part of a violent, self-perpetuating, ghetto-inhabiting, poor underclass—the more pronounced the effect of negative stereotyping on the judgments made. For example, stereotypes about Blacks strongly influenced the degree of hostile reactions to a Black car-jacking suspect but not to a Black corporate embezzler. The alleged car-jacker had all the trappings consistent with the cultural-stereotype "street thug" and elicited a powerful resonance with underlying stereotypes about Blacks. The corporate embezzler is a business executive—i.e., did not fit the cultural stereotype of Blacks—and, thus, even though described as Black, did not generate reactions strongly related to underlying stereotypes of Blacks. Hurwitz and Peffley (1997) also found that negative stereotyping encouraged support for punitive responses to crime, but had no impact on views of crime-prevention policies. Thus, stereotyping of Blacks was not uniformly of political relevance, but if other contextual information was stereotype-consistent, a strong reverberation with the underlying stereotype emerged.

## Disagreement About the Prevalence of Racial Discrimination

In many ways, the centerpiece of the modern racial divide comes in the evidence of sharply divergent beliefs about the current level, effect, and nature of discrimination. Blacks and Hispanics, and many Asians as well, feel it and perceive it in most domains of life. Many Whites acknowledge that some discrimination remains, but they tend to downplay its contemporary importance. A comparatively small percentage of Whites, but a comparatively high percentage of Blacks and Hispanics, express the view that there is "a lot" of discrimination against, respectively, Blacks, Hispanics, and Asians seeking "good-paying jobs" (Figure 9-8). It is interesting to note that Blacks and Hispanics have lower, but still substantial, percentages acknowledging belief of such discrimination against the other. Neither Whites, Blacks, Hispanics, nor Asians themselves tend to see "a lot" of discrimination against Asians in obtaining better-paying jobs.

Views of police and the criminal justice system constitute an arena of often-acute racial group differences in opinion. For example, Schuman et al. (1997:265) report that in 1995, approximately 88 percent of Blacks in an ABC News/*Washington Post* poll felt that the police treat Blacks unfairly as compared to only 47 percent of Whites. Their analysis showed that the gap between Blacks' and Whites' views on police treatment actually grew larger between the late 1980s and mid-1990s. This pattern may reflect a number of prominent and dramatic incidents of police abuse during the 1990s such as the Rodney King beating, the Abner Louima beating, and, in 1999, the murder of Amadou Diallo by New York City police. Tuch and Weitzer's (1997) trend analyses showed that Blacks' views of the police tend to exhibit more dramatically adverse reactions in the wake of highly publicized police brutality cases than is true among Whites, and that the adverse impact on views of the police tends to be longer lasting for Blacks as well. Nowhere was the magnitude and palpable tension of this divide more in evidence than along the sharp polarization of views between Blacks and Whites in the wake of the criminal trial of O.J. Simpson for the murder of

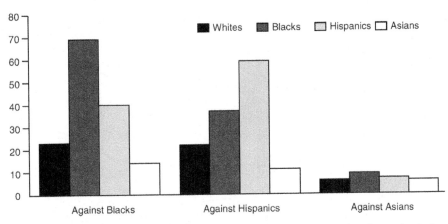

**FIGURE 9-8 Percentage of Whites, Blacks, Hispanics, and Asian/Pacific Islanders who believe there is "a lot" of discrimination in getting good-paying jobs, by race.**

SOURCE: Los Angeles Survey of Urban Inequality (1994).

his ex-wife Nicole Brown Simpson and her friend Ronald Goldman.

Minorities not only perceive more discrimination, they also see it as more "institutional" in character. Many Whites tend to think of discrimination as either mainly a historical legacy of the past or as the idiosyncratic behavior of the isolated bigot. In short, to Whites, the officers who tortured Abner Louima constitute a few bad apples. To Blacks, these officers represent only the tip of the iceberg. To Whites, the Texaco tapes are shocking. To Blacks, the tapes merely reflect that in this one instance the guilty were caught.

But differences in perception cut deeper than this. For Blacks and Hispanics—and, to a lesser extent, Asians—modern racial bias and discrimination are central factors in the problem of minority disadvantage. Although many Whites recognize that discrimination plays some part in higher rates of unemployment, poverty, and a range of hardships in life that minorities often face, the central cause is usually understood to be the level of effort and cultural patterns of the minority group members themselves (Schuman, 1971; Apostle et al., 1983; Kluegel and Smith, 1986; Schuman et al., 1997).

For minorities, especially Blacks, it is understood that the persistence of race problems has something to do with how our institutions operate. For many Whites, larger patterns of inequality are understood as mainly something about minorities themselves.

At issue here is not only how extensive one believes discrimination to be in any particular domain, but also whether one sees individual or social structural factors as key sources of persistent racial economic inequality (Kluegel and Smith, 1982; Kluegel, 1990). Figure 9-9 charts national survey data to show Whites' perceptions and beliefs about, respectively, the individualistic (Figure 9-9a) and the structural (Figure 9-9b) bases of Black-White economic inequality. Two immediate contrasts distinguish the figures. First, endorsement of the various "individualistic" statements is usually higher than that for any "structural" statement. Thus, among the four structural items, only the conceptually ambiguous "no chance for an education" item (Kluegel, 1990) is endorsed by more than 50 percent of Whites, whereas several of the individualistic items exceed 60 percent White agreement. Furthermore, this comparatively weak structural attribution shows a downward trend

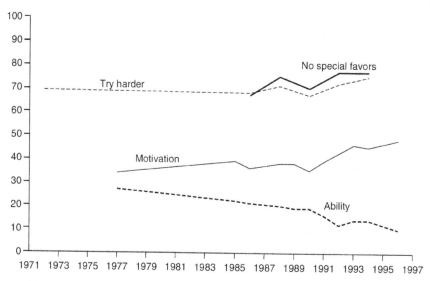

**FIGURE 9-9a Trends in Whites' beliefs about individualistic bases of Black/White economic inequality.**

SOURCE: Adapted from Schuman et al. (1997). *Try Harder*. We asked people why they think White people seem to get more of the good things in life in America—such as better jobs and more money—than Black people do. Do you agree or disagree with each reason as to why White people seem to get more of the good things in life? It's really a matter of some people not trying hard enough; if Blacks would only try harder they would be just as well off as Whites. *No Special Favors*: Irish, Italians, Jewish, and many other minorities overcame prejudice and worked their way up. Blacks should do the same without any special favors. *Motivation*: On the average Blacks have worse jobs, income, and housing than White people. Do you think these differences are mainly due to discrimination? Do you think these differences are because most Blacks just don't have the motivation or will power to pull themselves up out of poverty? *Ability*: (Same introduction as Motivation above) Do you think these differences are … because most Blacks have less inborn ability to learn?

over time. To be sure, the individualistic account of Black-White inequality with the most immediately racist import—a belief in innate differences in ability—has steadily declined and is now endorsed by only a small percentage of Whites. Yet, the most popular view holds that Blacks should "try harder," should get ahead "without special favors," and fall behind because they "lack motivation." Second, several of the individualistic items show small, but noteworthy, trends toward growing acceptance. Thus, these patterns confirm Kluegel's (1990)

speculation that Whites show decreased acceptance of most of the structural bases of racial inequality.

The results of two surveys highlight a crucial distinction between idiosyncratic and episodic, and between institutional and structural, views of discrimination. Local and national surveys showed that high percentages of both Blacks and Whites disapproved of the 1992 Simi Valley jury verdict that exonerated the White Los Angeles police officers who beat Black motorist Rodney King (Bobo et al., 1994). However, in a Los Angeles survey conducted immediately after the verdict

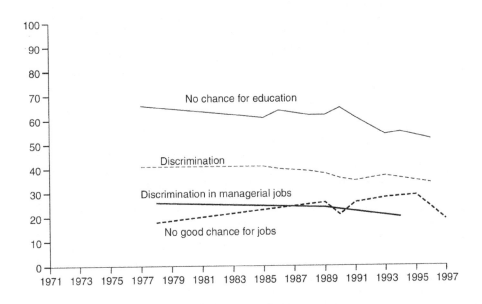

**FIGURE 9-9b Trends in Whites' structural beliefs about Black/White economic inequality.**

SOURCE: Adapted from Schuman et al. (1997). ***Discrimination:*** On the average Blacks have worse jobs, income, and housing than White people. Do you think these differences are … mainly due to discrimination? ***No Chance for Education:*** (Same introduction as Discrimination above) Do you think these differences are … because most Blacks just don't have the chance for education that it takes to rise out of poverty? ***No Chance for Jobs:*** In general, do you think Blacks have as good a chance as White people in your community to get any kind of job for which they are qualified, or don't you think they have as good a chance? ***Discrimination in Managerial Jobs:*** In your area, would you say Blacks generally are discriminated against or not in getting managerial jobs?

and subsequent social upheaval, Blacks and Whites disagreed sharply about whether the courts and criminal justice system were generally unfair to Blacks. Approximately 80 percent of Blacks in Los Angeles agreed that Blacks usually do not get fair treatment in the courts and criminal justice system, compared with only 39 percent of Whites (Bobo et al., 1994:111). Similarly, the DAS survey found that approximately 82 percent of Whites felt that Blacks "very often" or "sometimes" missed out on good housing because individual White owners would not sell or rent to them; 85 percent of Blacks expressed such views (Farley et al., 1993:19). When asked about discrimination by such institutional actors as "real estate agents" and "banks and lenders," however, the Black-White gap in views increased to 22 percent and 34 percent, respectively. Indeed, Blacks saw discrimination as slightly more prevalent by "banks and lenders" than by individual White homeowners.

It is difficult to overestimate the importance of the sharp divide over the understanding and experience of racial discrimination to the present-day racial impasse in America (Sigelman and Welch, 1989). Sustained and constructive discourse about matters of race will surely remain difficult insofar as Blacks are (1) more likely than Whites to see discrimination in particular domains and situations; (2) more likely to see discrimination as institutional rather than episodic; (3) more likely to see discrimination as a central factor in larger patterns of racial inequality; and (4) more likely to regard racial discrimination as personally important and emotionally involving.

### Deepening Pessimism and Alienation

In many corners, there is a feeling of pessimism about the state of race relations. A 1997 survey conducted by the Joint Center for Political and Economic Research found that only 40 percent of Blacks rated race relations in their community as "excellent" or "good" and more than 20 percent rated community race relations as "poor." In contrast, 59 percent of Whites rated local race relations as "excellent" or "good," though better than 10 percent rated them as "poor." The results of a recent Gallup survey are, in some respects, more pessimistic; roughly 33 percent of Blacks and Whites described race relations as having gotten worse in the past year. What is more, 58 percent of Blacks

and 54 percent of Whites expressed the view that "relations between Blacks and Whites will always be a problem for the United States."

This problem takes the form of particularly acute cynicism and alienation among Blacks, though there are signs of frustration among Hispanics and some APIs as well. Among Blacks, University of Chicago political scientist Michael Dawson's National Black Politics Survey, conducted in 1993 (Dawson, 1995), found that 86 percent of Blacks agreed with the statement that "American society just hasn't dealt fairly with Black people." Fifty-seven percent of Blacks rejected the idea that "American society has provided Black people a fair opportunity to get ahead in life," and 81 percent agreed with the idea that "American society owes Black people a better chance in life than we currently have."

A major survey of Los Angeles county residents (the Los Angeles County Social Survey, conducted by this author in 1992) shows that although Blacks expressed the highest and most consistently alienated views, an important percentage of the Hispanic and Asian population did so as well. Thus, for

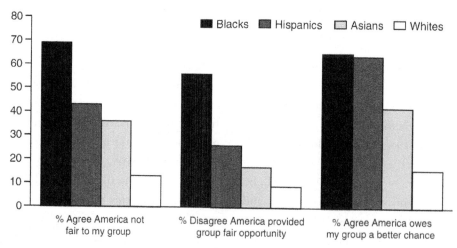

FIGURE 9-10 Percentage of Blacks, Hispanics, Asian/Pacific Islanders, and Whites agreeing or disagreeing with fairness statements regarding ethnic group deprivation.

SOURCE: Los Angeles County Social Survey (1992).

example, 64 percent of Hispanics and 42 percent of Asians agreed with the idea that their groups were owed a better chance in life (Figure 9-10). This places these two groups in between the high sense of deprivation observed among Blacks and the essentially nonexistent feeling of deprivation observed among Whites.

The concern about Black cynicism, however, is acute for two reasons. First, there are signs that the feelings of alienation and deprivation are greatest in an unexpected place: among the Black middle class, especially so among well-educated and high-earning Blacks. Second, there is a concern that these feelings of alienation and deprivation may be contributing to a weakening commitment to the goal of racial integration. Among the potentially discouraging signs in this regard is a recent significant rise in the number of Blacks who think it is time to form a separate national political party (Figure 9-11). The 1993 National Black Politics Survey showed that this figure was at 50 percent, up substantially from about 30 percent in 1984. In addition, Blacks continue to feel a strong connection between the fate of the group as a whole and that of the individual Black. Thus, the 1993 National Black Politics Study shows a slow but steady rise in the percentage of Blacks expressing the view that there was a strong connection between their fate as an individual and the fate of the group as a whole. This tendency is especially pronounced among highly educated Blacks.

In her wide-ranging assessment of data on Black public opinion, political scientist Jennifer Hochschild identifies Black disaffection, particularly among the middle class, as one of the most disturbing trends for the future of American democracy. This disaffection, she finds, expresses itself not merely as "Black rage," grievance, and alienation, but it also involves a deep questioning of the American dream and prospects for the future. On one level, this reflects the uncertainties of racial minority status, especially for the middle class, in a society that has not yet overcome racism (Hochschild, 1995):

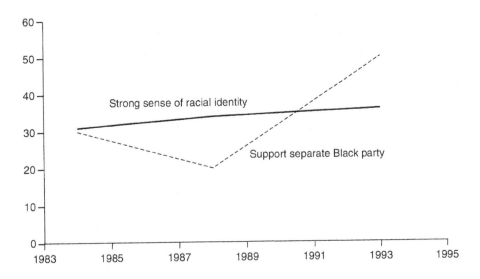

**FIGURE 9-11 Importance of race to Blacks.**

SOURCE: Adapted from Dawson (1994), Tate (1993), and Dawson (1995).

... middle-class Blacks find their lives much more problematic than do middle-class Whites, so the comfort that a broader education, better job, and more money usually bring to Whites is denied to similarly situated Blacks. Thus the paradox of succeeding more and enjoying it less ... (p. 93).

This paradox has quite wide-ranging social implications. Hochschild writes:

Black and White increasingly diverge in their evaluations of whether the American dream encompasses African Americans ... middle-class Blacks are increasingly disillusioned with the very ideology of the dream itself, and poor Blacks may not be far behind.

The ideology of the dream has always relied on previously poor Americans not only achieving upward mobility, but also recognizing that they had done so, feeling gratified, and consequently deepening their commitment to the dream and the nation behind it. That, very roughly speaking, has been the experience of most immigrants. But middle-class Blacks are not following the prescribed pattern. They recognize their own mobility, they are pleased by it, but their commitment to the American dream is declining, not rising. That is an unprecedented risk to an ideology that depends so heavily on faith in its ultimate fairness and benevolence (pp. 86–87).

The sense of alienation among many Blacks then includes a profound critique of American institutions and culture. As Cornell West put it, "The accumulated effect of the Black wounds and scars suffered in a White-dominated society is a deep-seated anger, a boiling sense of rage, and a passionate pessimism regarding America's will to justice" (West, 1993:18).

In an earlier era, these sorts of ideas would have been associated with activist Malcolm X, the "prophet of Black rage," according to Cornell West. The connection between the insight and rhetoric of Malcolm X and the dilemma of the modern Black middle class is not hard to unearth. As West put it, "One rarely encounters a picture of Malcolm X (as one does of Martin Luther King, Jr.) in the office of a Black professional, but there is no doubt that Malcolm X dangles as the skeleton in the closet lodged in the racial memory of most Black professionals" (1993:97).

The survey data, and summaries of them, however, cannot convey the full depth and range of Black responses, and some Black writers have recently given voice to this sense of discontent. In his recent autobiography, journalist Sam Fulwood describes coming to consciousness as a "blue chip Black"—a Black person slated for success in the mainstream White economy. A teacher explains to him that, unlike his friends, he will be attending the traditionally White junior high school, because, as the teacher expressed it to Fulwood, "I am absolutely certain that you can hold your own with the best" White students. This became a defining moment for the young Fulwood, hopeful that a bright future, free of racial bias, would be his. His adult life experiences proved sharply disillusioning, however (Fulwood, 1996):

I evolved that day into a race child. I believed I would, in due time, illuminate the magnificent social changes wrought by racial progress. Overt racial barriers were falling and I, son of a minister and a schoolteacher, fully credentialed members of Charlotte's Black middle class, thought my future would be free of racism and free of oppression. I believed I was standing at the entrance to the Promised Land. Now, as the twentieth century exhausts itself, I am awakening from my blind belief in that American dream. I am angrier than I've ever been (p. 2).

The depth of his sense of rage grew when he returned to the United States from a trip in South Africa:

I returned from South Africa with a new definition of American-style racism and classism, and how they acted like a pair of invisible hands molding the contours of my life. I wasn't in control of my destiny in the United States; I was living in Alice's Wonderland. The rules of life were always defined by someone White who decided whether what I did was acceptable, legal behavior. I knew more of the rules, so I played the game better than poorer Blacks, who didn't know or didn't care to play the game at all. But I was still only a pawn in the White man's match (p. 164).

One acute source of Fulwood's frustration sprang from the inability of Whites to see or even admit the contemporary potency of racism.

Over the course of my life, I realized, so much had changed in me, but so little had changed in the outside world. Racism surrounded me. I could perceive it, but I was powerless to prove conclusively to anyone who was not Black how corrosive it could be (p. 208). ... I have

a boulder of racial attitudes on my back, and at work I must toil among White people and pretend that the dead weight is not there (p. 213).

In the end, Fulwood decides to live in an affluent Black suburb and, more important, to assure that his daughter is raised with a more acute sense of race identity and of the challenge posed by enduring racism than was he. "My daughter," he declares in the opening pages of the book, "will not be a second-generation blue-chip Black, laboring under the mistaken belief that race will one day be coincidental, unimportant or ignored in her life" (1996:5).

Journalist Jill Nelson writes with a deeper sense of bitterness and despair. For her, much of the dilemma of Black middle-class success comes in having to suppress feelings of rage against a society and a world of work still massively insensitive to the historic and modern weight of racism, in order to maintain a precarious middle-class livelihood (Nelson, 1993):

I've also been doing the standard Negro balancing act when it comes to dealing with White folks, which involves sufficiently blurring the edges of my being so that they don't feel intimidated, while simultaneously holding on to my integrity. There is a thin line between Uncle Tomming and Mau-Mauing. To fall off that line can mean disaster. On the one side lies employment and self-hatred: on the other, the equally dubious honor of unemployment with integrity. Walking that line as if it were a tightrope results in something like employment with honor, although I'm not sure exactly how that works (p. 10).

Like Fulwood, the eminent religion scholar C. Eric Lincoln writes of both the permeating quality of the racial divide and the pain of being rendered socially invisible by virtue of race (Lincoln, 1996):

> In America, race is the touchstone of all value, the prism through which all else of significance must be refracted before relationships can be defined or relevance ascertained. There is no order of reality large enough to transcend its pervasiveness, small enough to escape its intrusiveness, or independent enough to avoid its imprimatur (pp. 45–46). … Every Black American knows firsthand the slander of invisibility. Anonymity. It comes in a thousand ways: a word, a gesture, a conversation that moves over and around him as though he or she were not present. Invisibility is most painful when it is preclusive—jobs not offered, invitations not issued, opportunities denied. It is a lifelong incubus from which few if any African Americans ever escape completely, no matter what their achievements. Racial anonymity derives from the presumption of inconsequence—the inconsequence of Black persons and of their achievements, actual or potential (p. 94).

Even mainstream political figures such as Kweisi Mfume, while never succumbing completely to a sense of Black alienation, nonetheless share many of these same sentiments. Mfume describes coming to consciousness in explaining when, during his college days, he changed his name from Frizzell Gray to Kweisi Mfume (Mfume, 1996):

> Anyone who spent more than a moment with me knew that I believed that a terrible hoax was being played on Black people in this country. I believed that most of us were going to live and die without ever having experienced anything near what was promised in the Declaration of Independence about life, liberty, and the pursuit of happiness. We weren't at all protected under the laws of the land—Black people were citizens in name only. We were a people chronically and institutionally disenfranchised, feeding off the scraps of the educational system, the job market, and any other channels leading to a life of dignity. … Yet, Black people were expected to believe in the American Dream as much as White people did. Why should we? The very notion was obscenely cynical, and any Black man or woman who thought differently was living in a fool's paradise. My disdain for the system was evident as a new wave of militancy engulfed my persona. I didn't just *wear* a bush, I *was* a bush that burned with revolutionary fervor, from the wildfires of racism and prejudice that smoldered around me (p. 189, emphasis in original).

These represent a few of the numerous other memoirs that express similar sentiments—bell hooks, Marcus Mabry, Rosemary Bray, or Nathan McCall, to name a few.

## THEORETICAL INTERPRETATIONS OF RACIAL ATTITUDES

To interpret the set of patterns described above is no simple task. To capture their full complexity, four broad schools of thought have been implemented: symbolic racism theory, political ideology and value commitment theory, aversive racism theory, and notions of group position and laissez-faire racism theory. Each theoretical tradition has identified important features of the dynamics of modern racial attitudes and relations. Three of these accounts point to a change or reconfiguration in the nature of racism; the other suggests that more and more matters—beyond race and racism—are important to the discourse about race.

Aversive racism should be distinguished from dominative racism. Dominative racism involves open/overt derogation and oppression of a racial minority group. Aversive racism has been defined by social psychologists Samuel Gaertner and John Dovidio as involving racism among the well intentioned (1986). Accordingly, in the post-Civil Rights era, most Whites hold many racially egalitarian outlooks (as summarized above). Indeed, it is likely racial egalitarianism is an important aspect of self-conception. At the same time, most Whites are exposed to a history, culture, and current set of social forces that encourage negative feelings toward and beliefs about Blacks. This creates, on a level not necessarily open to conscious awareness or manipulation, a deep ambivalence toward Blacks. The practical result, as Gaertner and Dovidio have shown in a convincing program of field and laboratory experimental research, is that whenever the norm of racial egalitarianism is rendered ambiguous, differential and negative treatment of Blacks by Whites tends to occur.

This research is impressive not merely for its experimental basis, but also for focusing on observable behaviors, not merely attitudinal expression. Furthermore, it resonates powerfully with sociological findings, whether ethnographic (Anderson, 1990), in-depth interview material (Feagin and Sikes, 1994), or survey responses (Sigelman and Welch, 1989; Bobo and Suh, 2000; Forman et al., 1997), which point to the subtlety and complex character of much modern racial discrimination. The lesson for the broader argument is that Whites'

attitudes are often ambivalent and that, under certain conditions, that ambivalence can result in substantial and repeated behavioral discrimination against Blacks.

Symbolic racism is a theory of modern prejudice proposed by David Sears and his colleagues (Kinder and Sears, 1981; Sears, 1988). It maintains that a new form of politically potent anti-Black prejudice emerged after the Civil Rights era. The waning of "old-fashioned racism," or more appropriately "Jim Crow racism," which involved overt derogation of Blacks as inferior to Whites and explicit insistence on racial segregation, opened the door to newer, more subtle anti-Black sentiments. These new sentiments fused deeply rooted anti-Black feelings, typically learned early in life, with other long-standing American values such as the Protestant work ethic. Thus, when Blacks demand integration or such policies as affirmative action, according to this theory, many Whites react with opposition based on this attitude. The symbolic racist resents Blacks' demands and views them as unfair impositions on a just and good society. According to Kinder and Sanders (1996) this new type of racial resentment crystallized during the mid- to late 1960s as Whites watched social protest and rising Black militancy pose an increasing challenge to their social order. Although the theory of symbolic racism began as an effort to understand the dynamics of Black-White relations, especially in the political realm, it has been extended to include how Whites respond to Hispanics and to such issues as bilingual education and immigration policies (Huddy and Sears, 1995).

Empirically, research on symbolic racism has sought to establish that narrow, objective self-interest has little bearing on why Black candidates for political office become controversial (Kinder and Sears, 1981; Citrin et al., 1990), or why Whites mobilize against school busing (Sears et al., 1979; McConahay, 1982), or may oppose affirmative action (Sears, 1988). Thus, for example, having children in the public schools or living in an area where busing is used for desegregation does not affect attitudes on school busing.

In addition, symbolic racism research has set out to establish that measures of traditional, old-fashioned racism do not predict issue positions or candidate preferences as strongly as do measures of symbolic racism. Symbolic racism has been measured in a variety of ways, with some recent consensus that it involves resentment of minority demands, resentment of special treatment or consideration of minorities, and a tendency to deny the potency of racial discrimination (Sears, 1988; Kinder and Sanders, 1996). The theory has been the subject of wide controversy and critical assessment (see, e.g., Bobo, 1983, 1988; Schuman et al., 1985; Weigel and Howes, 1985; Sniderman and Tetlock, 1986; Sidanius et al., 1992; Tetlock, 1994; Wood, 1994). Despite the number and findings of these many critical assessments, symbolic-racism researchers have effectively substantiated an important aspect of the issue: racial attitudes have changed in important ways; yet, negative views of Blacks remain both all too common and all too often of tangible political consequence.

One way to understand this change has recently been theorized as a shift from a dominant ideology of "Jim Crow racism" to a dominant ideology of "laissez-faire racism" (Bobo et al., 1997; Bobo and Smith, 1998). Accordingly, we have witnessed the virtual disappearance of overt bigotry, demands for strict segregation, advocacy of governmentally enforced discrimination, and adherence to the belief that Blacks are categorically the intellectual inferiors of Whites. Yet, overt racism has evidently not been supplanted by an embracing and democratic vision of the common humanity, worth, dignity, and equal membership in the polity for Blacks. Instead, the tenacious institutionalized disadvantages and inequalities created by the long slavery and Jim Crow eras are now popularly accepted and condoned

under a modern free-market or laissez-faire racist ideology. This new ideology incorporates negative stereotypes of Blacks; a preference for individualistic, and rejection of structural, accounts of racial inequality; and an unwillingness to see government actively work to dismantle racial inequality. This new pattern of belief is more subtle and covert than its predecessor, making it more difficult to directly confront; it is also more amenable to the more fluid and permeable set of racial divisions in the social order.

Much of the broad empirical basis for the laissez-faire racism argument has been reviewed above. Using data from the 1990 GSS, Bobo and Kluegel (1997) examined four hypotheses derived from the theory of laissez-faire racism and found that (1) contemporary racial stereotyping and negation of social responsibility for Black conditions constitute distinct attitudinal dimensions; (2) traditional, overt racist outlooks were more strongly rooted in region of residence (South versus non-south), age, and level of education than were the elements of laissez-faire racism (stereotyping and social responsibility beliefs), which is consistent with Jim Crow-style racism being older and more regionally specific and laissez-faire racism being a more contemporary, nationally shared outlook; and (3) beliefs about reasons for general, socioeconomic (not race-specific) inequality play a larger role in laissez-faire racism than they did in Jim Crow racism. Bobo and Kluegel (1997) suggest that, "If Jim Crow racism is no longer seen to serve the defense of economic privilege, then there is no reason to expect that beliefs that justify the stratification order in general will affect it. If elements of laissez-faire racism are seen as defending White economic privilege, then justifications of economic inequality in general should motivate stereotyping and the denial of social responsibility for Blacks' conditions" (pp. 96–97). Fourth, they found that although both Jim Crow and laissez-faire racism affect Whites' support for race-targeted social policies, the elements of laissez-faire racism were stronger influences.

Of course, it is possible to doubt the need to invoke racism at all as a central element of the modern racial divide. At least at the level of politics and political debate, this precise point has been the message offered by Paul Sniderman and colleagues (Sniderman and Piazza, 1993; Sniderman and Carmines, 1997). They developed a four-part argument. First, they assert that racism is not an important part of the modern politics of race, especially in terms of the debate over affirmative action. Second, they assert that if many Whites object to affirmative action or other race-targeted policies, it has more to do with broad American values about fairness, justice, individualism, and traditional conservatism than with racism or prejudice. In short, there are principled foundations to the politics of race, deriving from political values and ideology. Accordingly, they feel, those advancing the symbolic-racism argument have seriously misunderstood the current political divide over affirmative action. Third, to the extent prejudice now matters in politics, it is generally most pronounced among the least politically sophisticated segments of the public (Sniderman and Piazza, 1993) and poses the greatest political challenge among liberals (Sniderman and Carmines, 1997). Fourth, there are distinct types of issue agendas in political discourse about race: a social-welfare agenda focusing on the economic circumstances of Blacks; an equal-treatment agenda concerned with banning discrimination; and a race-conscious agenda focusing on preferential treatment of Blacks. In each domain, a different mix of attitudes, values, and beliefs is said to influence political thinking.

Spanning nearly a decade now, Sniderman and colleagues' program of research is innovative, vigorously pursued, and has identified a number of intriguing empirical patterns. By drawing on survey-based experiments, as Schuman and Bobo (1988) proposed, Sniderman and colleagues combined the power of controlled experiments with the representativeness of national surveys: the certainty of casual inference and ability to generalize results are thus greater. Two contributions loom large in this work. First, political ideology is an element in how many Whites think about race-related issues such as affirmative action. There is much debate, as yet unresolved, over how large a role pure ideology plays in race politics (Sidanius et al., 1996). But Sniderman and colleagues have rightly cautioned against a monolithic view that prejudice and racism are the whole story. Second, a number of their experimental results suggest that prejudice against Blacks does more to account for views among liberal Whites than it does among conservative Whites (see, especially, Sniderman and Carmines, 1997). If so, it may be the case that prejudice has less of a role in unifying the right than it does in dividing the left.

## CONCLUSIONS AND IMPLICATIONS

The glass is half-full or the glass is half-empty, depending on what one chooses to emphasize. If one compared the racial attitudes prevalent in the 1940s with those commonly observed today, it is easy to be optimistic. A nation once comfortable as a deliberately segregationist and racially discriminatory society has not only abandoned that view, but now overtly, positively endorses the goals of racial integration and equal treatment. There is no sign whatsoever of retreat from this ideal, despite events that many thought would call it into question. The magnitude, steadiness, and breadth of this change should be lost on no one.

The death of Jim Crow racism has left us in an uncomfortable place, however; a state of laissez-faire racism. We have high ideals, but cannot agree on the depth of the remaining problem—we are open to integration, but in very limited terms and only in specific areas. There is political stagnation over some types of affirmative action, and persistent negative stereotyping of racial minorities; and a wide gulf in perceptions regarding the importance of racial discrimination remains. The level of misunderstanding and miscommunication is, thus, easy to comprehend.

The positive patterns in attitude and belief have important parallels in more concrete social trends. Two examples—demographic data showing modest declines in racial residential segregation in most metropolitan areas, and the growing suburbanization of Blacks, Hispanics, and Asians—match the broad shift in attitudes on the principle of residential integration and openness to at least small amounts of real racial mixing in neighborhoods. In addition, the greater tolerance for interracial marriages, including Black-White marriages, is mirrored in the significant rise in the actual number of such unions, although Black-White intermarriages are the least common form of racial intermarriage for Whites.

We should always bear in mind that attitudes are but one important input to behavior. Most centrally, situational constraints—such as those intended to be addressed by equal opportunity mandates and antidiscrimination laws—or the expectations of significant others in our lives, affect whether, and when, there is a correspondence among attitude, beliefs, and behavior.

Is it possible to change attitudes? The record of change I have reviewed makes it plain that attitudes can change and in important ways. Education and information can help. The better educated, especially those who have gone to college, are typically found to express more positive racial attitudes. It is also clear that many Americans hold inaccurate beliefs about the size of racial minority groups and about such social conditions as group differences in the level of welfare dependency. However, education and information campaigns alone are unlikely to do the job that remains ahead of us if we are

to genuinely become one society in the twenty-first century. Attitudes are most likely to change when the broad social conditions that create and reinforce certain types of outlooks change and when the push to make such change comes from a united national leadership that speaks with moral conviction of purpose. That is, it is essential to speak to joblessness and poverty in the inner city, to failing schools, and to a myriad of forms of racial bias and discrimination that people of color often experience, which has not yet effectively been communicated to all American citizens.

To pose the question directly: Are we moving toward a color-blind society or toward deepening racial polarization? America is not a color-blind society. We stand uncomfortably at a point of defeating Jim Crow racism, but unsure whether, through benign neglect, to allow the current inequalities and polarization to take deeper root, or to face directly and proactively the challenges of bias, miscommunication, and racism that remain.

As a people, we feel quite powerfully the tug, indeed the exhortation, of Dr. King's dream to become a nation that embodies the ideals of racial equality and integration. It is important to seize on the steady commitment to these ideals of racial equality and integration. The risk of failing to do so, is that a new, free-market ideology of racism—laissez-faire racism—may take hold, potentially worsening an already serious racial divide.

## REFERENCES

Alba, R.
  1992 Ethnicity. Pp. 575–584 in *Encyclopedia of Sociology*, E. Borgatta and M. Borgatta, eds. New York: MacMillan.
Allport, G.
  1954 *The Nature of Prejudice*. Reading, Mass.: Addison-Wesley.
Anderson, E.

1990    *Streetwise: Race, Class, and Change in an Urban Community.* Chicago: University of Chicago Press.

Apostle, R., C. Glock, T. Piazza, and M. Suelzle

1983    *The Anatomy of Racial Attitudes.* Berkeley, Calif.: University of California Press.

Ashmore, R., and F. Del Boca

1981    Conceptual approaches to stereotypes and stereotyping. Pp. 1–35 in *Cognitive Processes in Stereotyping and Intergroup Behavior,* D. Hamilton, ed. Hillsdale, N.J.: Erlbaum.

Bell, D.

1992    *Faces at the Bottom of the Well: The Permanence of Racism.* New York: Basic Books. Bobo, L.

1983    Whites opposition to busing: symbolic racism or realistic group conflict? *Journal of Personality and Social Psychology* 45:1196–1210.

1988    Group conflict, prejudice, and the paradox of contemporary racial attitudes. Pp. 85–114 in *Eliminating Racism: Profiles in Controversy,* P. Katz and D. Taylor, eds. New York: Plenum.

1997    The color line, the dilemma, and the dream: Racial attitudes and relations in America at the close of the twentieth century. Pp. 31–55 in *Civil Rights and Social Wrongs: Black-White Relations Since World War II,* J. Higham, ed. University Park: Pennsylvania State University Press.

Bobo, L., and J. Kluegel

1993    Opposition to race-targeting: Self-interest, stratification ideology, or racial attitudes? *American Sociological Review* 58:443–464.

1997    Status, ideology, and dimensions of Whites' racial beliefs and attitudes: Progress and stagnation. Pp. 93–120 in *Racial Attitudes in the 1990s: Continuity and Change,* S. Tuch, and J. Martin, eds. Westport, Conn.: Praeger.

Bobo, L., J. Kluegel, and R. Smith

1997    Laissez-faire racism: The crystallization of a kinder, gentler, anti-Black ideology. Pp. 15–42 in *Racial Attitudes in the 1990s; Continuity and Change,* S. Tuch and J. Martin, eds. Westport, Conn.: Praeger.

Bobo, L., and R. Smith

1998    From Jim Crow racism to laissez faire racism: The transformation of racial attitudes. Pp. 182–220 in *Beyond Pluralism: Essays on the Conception of Groups and Group Identities in America,* W. Katkin, N. Landsman, and A. Tyree, eds. Urbana, 111.: University of Illinois Press.

Bobo, L., and S. Suh

2000    Surveying racial discrimination: Analyses from a multiethnic labor market. Pp. 527–564 in *Prismatic Metropolis: Inequality in Los Angeles,* L. Bobo, M. Oliver, J. Johnson, and A. Valenzuela, Jr., eds. New York: Russell Sage Foundation.

Bobo, L., and C. Zubrinsky

1996    Attitudes on residential integration: Perceived status differences, mere in-group preference, or racial prejudice? *Social Forces* 74:883–909.

Bobo, L., C. Zubrinsky, J. Johnson, and M. Oliver

1994    Public opinion before and after a spring of discontent. Pp. 103–133 in *The Los Angeles Riots: Lessons for the Urban Future,* M. Baldassare, ed. Boulder, Colo.: Westview Press.

Bonilla-Silva, E.

1996    Rethinking racism: Toward a structural interpretation. *American Sociological Review* 62:465–480.

Brown, R.

1995 *Prejudice: Its Social Psychology.* Cambridge, U.K.: Blackwell.

Citrin, J., D. Green, and D. Sears

1990 White reactions to Black candidates: When does race matter? *Public Opinion Quarterly* 54:74–96.

Cose, E.

1993 *The Rage of a Privileged Class.* New York: Harper Collins.

Dawson, M.

1994 *Behind the Mule: Race and Class in African American Politics.* Princeton: Princeton University Press.

1995 Structure and ideology: The shaping of Black public opinion. Unpublished manuscript, Department of Political Science, University of Chicago.

Delgado, R.

1996 *The Coming Race War? And Other Apocalyptic Tales of America After Affirmative Action and Welfare.* New York: New York University Press.

Devine, P.

1989 Stereotypes and prejudice: Their automatic and controlled components. *Journal of Personality and Social Psychology* 56:5–18.

Devine, P., and A. Elliot

1995 Are racial stereotypes really fading? The Princeton trilogy revisited. *Personality and Social Psychology Bulletin* 21:1139–1150.

Drake, St. C, and H. Cayton

1945 *Black Metropolis; A Study of Negro Life in a Northern City.* Chicago: University of Chicago Press.

Duckitt, J.

1992 *The Social Psychology of Prejudice.* New York: Praeger.

Farley, R., C. Steeh, T. Jackson, M. Krysan, and K. Reeves

1993 Continued racial residential segregation in Detroit: 'Chocolate city, vanilla suburbs' revisited. *Journal of Housing Research* 4:1–38.

1994 Stereotypes and segregation: Neighborhoods in the Detroit area. *American Journal of Sociology* 100:750–780.

Feagin, J.

1991 The continuing significance of race: Anti-Black discrimination in public places. *American Sociological Review* 56:101–16.

1997 Fighting White racism: The future of equal rights in the United States. Pp. 29–45 in *Civil Rights and Race Relations in the Reagan-Bush Era,* S. Myers, ed. New York: Praeger.

Feagin, J., and M. Sikes

1994 *Living With Racism: The Black Middle Class Experience.* Boston: Beacon.

Forman, T., D. Williams, and J. Jackson

1997 Race, place and discrimination. *Perspectives on Social Problems* 9:231–261.

Fulwood, S., III

1996 *Waking from the Dream: My Life in the Black Middle Class.* New York: Anchor.

Gaertner, S., and J. Dovidio

1986 The aversive form of racism. Pp. 61–90 in *Prejudice, Discrimination, and Racism,* J. Dovidio and S. Gaertner, eds. New York: Academic Press.

Gilens, M.

1995 Racial attitudes and opposition to welfare. *Journal of Politics* 57:994–1014.

1996a Race coding and White opposition to welfare. *American Political Science Review* 90:593–604.

1996b Race and poverty in America: Public misperceptions and the American news media. *Public Opinion Quarterly* 60:515–541.

Hacker, A.
1992 *Two Nations: Black and White, Separate, Hostile, Unequal.* New York: Scribners.

Hamilton, D., and T. Trolier
1986 Stereotypes and stereotyping: An overview of the cognitive approach. Pp. 127–164 in *Prejudice, Discrimination, and Racism,* J. Dovidio and S. Gaertner, eds. New York: Academic Press.

Hochschild, J.
1995 *Facing up to the American Dream: Race, Class, and the Soul of the Nation.* Princeton: Princeton University Press.

Huddy, L., and D. Sears
1995 Opposition to bilingual education: Prejudice or the defense of realistic interests? *Social Psychology Quarterly* 58:133–143.

Hurwitz, J., and M. Peffley
1997 Public perceptions of race and crime: The role of racial stereotypes. *American Journal of Political Science* 41:375–401.

Jackman, M.
1977 Prejudice, tolerance, and attitudes toward ethnic groups. *Social Science Research* 6:145–169.
1994 *The Velvet Glove: Paternalism and Conflict in Gender, Class, and Race Relations.* Berkeley: University of California Press.

Jackman, M., and M. Senter
1980 Images of social groups: Categorical or qualified? *Public Opinion Quarterly* 44:341–361.

1983 Different, therefore unequal: Beliefs about trait differences between groups of unequal status. *Research in Social Stratification and Mobility* 2:309–335.

Jaynes, G., and R. Williams, Jr.
1989 *A Common Destiny: Blacks and American Society.* Washington, D.C.: National Academy Press.

Jones, J.
1972 *Prejudice and Racism.* New York: McGraw Hill.
1986 Racism: A cultural analysis of the problem. Pp. 279–314 in *Prejudice, Discrimination, and Racism,* J. Dovidio and S. Gaertner, eds. New York: Academic Press.
1988 Racism in Black and White: A bicultural model of reaction and evolution. Pp. 117–136 in *Eliminating Racism: Profiles in Controversy,* P. Katz and D. Taylor, eds. New York: Plenum.

Kinder, D., and L. Sanders
1996 *Divided by Color: Racial Politics and Democratic Ideals.* Chicago: University of Chi cago Press.

Kinder, D., and D. Sears
1981 Prejudice and politics: Symbolic racism versus racial threats to the good life. *Journal of personality and Social Psychology* 40:414–431

Kleinpenning, G., and L. Hagendoorn
1993 Forms of racism and the cumulative dimension of ethnic attitudes. *Social Psychology Quarterly* 56:21–36.

Kluegel, J.
1990 Trends in Whites' explanations of the gap in Black-White socioeconomic status, 1977–1989. *American Sociological Review* 55:512–525.

Kluegel, J., and E. Smith

1982 Whites' beliefs about Blacks' opportunity. *American Sociological Review* 47:518–532. 1986 *Beliefs about Inequality: Americans' Views of What is and What Ought to Be.* New York: Aldine de Gruyter.

Lincoln, C.
1996 *Coming Through the Fire: Surviving Race and Place in America.* Durham, N.C.: Duke University Press.

Lipset, S., and W. Schneider
1978 The Bakke Case: How would it be decided at the Bar of Public Opinion?" *Public Opinion* 1:38–44.

Massey, D., and N. Denton
1993 *American Apartheid: Segregation and the Making of the Underclass.* Cambridge, Mass.: Harvard University Press.

McConahay, J.
1982 Self-interest versus racial attitudes as correlates of anti-busing attitudes in Louisville: Is it the buses or the blacks? *Journal of Politics* 44:692–720.

Mfume, K.
1996 *No Free Ride: From the Mean Streets to the Mainstream.* New York: Ballantine. Montagu, A.
1964 *The Concept of Race.* New York: Collier-Macmillan.

Nelson, J.
1993 *Volunteer Slavery: My Authentic Negro Experience.* Chicago: Noble Press.

Niemi, R., J. Mueller, and T. Smith
1989 *Trends in Public Opinion: A Compendium of Survey Data.* New York: Greenwood.

Omi, M., and H. Winant
1986 *Racial Formation in the United States: From the 1960s to the 1980s.* Routledge & Kegan Paul.

Patterson, O.
1997 *The Ordeal of Integration: Progress and Resentment in America's "Racial" Crisis.* New York: Civitas.

Peffley, M., J. Hurwitz, and P. Sniderman
1997 Racial stereotypes and Whites' political views of Blacks in the context of welfare and crime. *American Journal of Political Science* 41:30–60.

Petersen, W.
1982 Concepts of ethnicity. Pp. 1–26 in *Concepts of Ethnicity: Dimensions of Ethnicity,* S. Thernstrom, A. Orlov, and O. Handlin, eds. Cambridge: Harvard University Press.

Pettigrew, T.
1981 Extending the stereotype concept. Pp. 303–332 in *Cognitive Processes in Stereotyping and Intergroup Behavior,* D. Hamilton, ed. Hillsdale, N.J.: Earlbaum.

Rowan, C.
1996 *The Coming Race War in America: A Wake-Up Call.* New York: Little, Brown.

St. John, C, and T. Heald-Moore
1995 Fear of Black strangers. *Social Science Research* 24:262–280.
1996 Racial prejudice and fear of criminal victimization by strangers in public settings. *Sociological Inquiry* 66:267–284.

Schuman, H.
1971 Free will and determinism in beliefs about race. Pp. 375–380 in *Majority and Minority: The Dynamics of Racial and Ethnic Relations,* N. Yetman and C. Steele, eds. Boston, Mass.: Allyn & Bacon.
1995 Attitudes, beliefs, and behavior. Pp. 68–89 in *Sociological Perspectives on*

*Social Psychology,* K. Cook, G. Fine, and J. House, eds. Boston: Allyn & Bacon.

Schuman, H., and L. Bobo

1988 Survey-based experiments on White racial attitudes toward residential integration. *American Journal of Sociology* 94: 273–299.

Schuman, H., C. Steeh, and L. Bobo

1985 *Racial Attitudes in America: Trends and Interpretations.* Cambridge, Mass.: Harvard University Press.

Schuman, H., C. Steeh, L. Bobo, and M. Krysan

1997 *Racial Attitudes in America: Trends and Interpretations.* Revised edition. Cambridge: Harvard University Press.

Sears, D.

1988 Symbolic racism. Pp. 53–84 in *Eliminating Racism: Profiles in Controversy,* P. Katz and D. Taylor, eds. New York: Plenum.

Sears, D., C. Hensler, and L. Speer

1979 Whites' opposition to busing: Self-interest or symbolic politics? *American Political Science Review* 73:369–384.

Sears, D., C. van Laar, M. Carrillo, and R. Kosterman

1997 Is it really racism? The origins of White Americans' opposition to race-targeted policies. *Public Opinion Quarterly* 61:16–53.

See, K., and W. Wilson

1989 Race and ethnicity. Pp. 223–242 in *Handbook of Sociology,* N.J. Smelser, ed. Beverly Hills, Calif.: Sage.

Shipler, D.

1997 *A Country of Strangers: Blacks and Whites in America.* New York: Knopf.

Sidanius, J., E. Devereux, and F. Pratto

1992 A comparison of symbolic racism theory and social dominance theory as explanations for racial policy attitudes. *Journal of Social Psychology* 132:377–395.

Sidanius, J., F. Pratto, and L. Bobo

1996 Racism, conservatism, affirmative action, and intellectual sophistication: A matter of principled conservatism or group dominance? *Journal of Personality and Social Psychology* 70:476–490.

Sigelman, L., and S. Welch

1989 *Black Americans' Views of Racial Inequality: The Dream Deferred.* New York: Cambridge University Press.

Sleeper, J.

1997 *Liberal Racism.* New York: Viking.

Smith, T.

1990 Ethnic images. General Social Survey Technical Report, No. 19. National Opinion Research Center. University of Chicago.

Sniderman, P., and E. Carmines

1997 *Reaching Beyond Race.* Cambridge: Harvard University Press.

Sniderman, P., and T. Piazza

1993 *The Scar of Race.* Cambridge: Harvard University Press.

Sniderman, P., and P. Tetlock

1986 Symbolic racism: Problems of political motive attribution. *Journal of Social Issues* 42:129–150.

Steeh, C, and M. Krysan

1996 The polls-trends: Affirmative action and the public. *Public Opinion Quarterly* 60:128–158.

Steinberg, S.

1998 Social science and the legitimation of racial hierarchy. *Race and Society* 1:5–14.

Stephan, W.

1985    Intergroup relations. Pp. 599–658 in *Handbook of Social Psychology,* Volume 2, 3rd edition, G. Lindzey and E. Aronson, eds. New York: Random House.

Stone, J.

1985    *Racial Conflict in Contemporary Society.* Cambridge, Mass.: Harvard University Press.

Tate, K.

1993    *From Protest to Politics: The New Black Voters in American Elections.* New York: Russell Sage.

Tetlock, P.

1994    Political psychology or politicized psychology: Is the road to scientific hell paved with good moral intentions? *Political Psychology* 15:509–529.

Thernstrom, S., and A. Thernstrom

1997    *America in Black and White: One Nation Indivisible.* New York: Simon and Schuster.

Tuch, S., and R. Weitzer

1997    The polls-trends: Racial differences in attitudes toward the police. *Public Opinion Quarterly* 61:642–663.

Weigel, R., and P. Howes

1985    Conceptions of racial prejudice: Symbolic racism reconsidered. *Journal of Social Issues* 41:117–138.

West, C.

1993    *Race Matters.* Boston: Beacon.

Wood, J.

1994    Is 'symbolic racism' racism? A review informed by intergroup behavior. *Political Psychology* 15:673–686.

# RACE, GENDER, AND SEXUALITY

# GETTING OFF AND GETTING INTIMATE

## HOW NORMATIVE INSTITUTIONAL ARRANGEMENTS STRUCTURE BLACK AND WHITE FRATERNITY MEN'S APPROACHES TOWARD WOMEN

*By Rashawn Ray and Jason A. Rosow*

## ABSTRACT

Social scientists implicate high-status men as sexually objectifying women. Yet, few have investigated these men's perceptions and accounts of their own experiences. Racial variation in gender relations in college has also received little scholarly attention. Analyzing 30 in-depth, individual interviews and surveys and two focus group interviews from Black and White men at a large university, we find racial differences in approaches toward women. More specifically, Black men exhibit more romantic approaches, whereas White men exhibit more sexual approaches. However, these differences are not solely related to race. Instead, "normative institutional arrangements" (e.g., community size and living arrangements) structure these approaches. We discuss the broader theoretical mechanisms regarding masculine performances, gender attitudes and behaviors, and race. In doing so, this study highlights the importance of "normative institutional arrangements" for understanding how the performances of masculinities are legitimized across racial- and status-group categories of men.

**Keywords:** hegemonic masculinity; sexuality; gender inequality; race; status; normative institutional arrangements; college; fraternity

Despite the proliferation of research on collegiate gender and sexual relations (Martin and Hummer 1989; Boswell and Spade 1996; Armstrong, Hamilton, and Sweeney 2006), we know little about one of the key groups within this institutional arrangement—fraternity men. Meanwhile, we know even less about differences and similarities in Black and White high-status men's relations with women (Brandes 2007; Peralta 2007; Flood 2008). Because fraternity men typically are situated on top of the peer culture hierarchy, a comprehensive understanding of the organization of collegiate social life must take into account how these specific enclaves of men understand and perceive gender relations and sexuality, and whether these understandings and perceptions vary by race.

Scholars have offered three competing explanations regarding racial differences in men's approaches toward women: (a) Black and White men objectify women similarly; (b) Black men objectify women more than White men; (c) White men objectify women more than Black men. The first possibility contends that most men, irregardless of status or race, sexually objectify women in the same manner. Thus, Black and White men's performances in masculinities are expected to be similar. In patriarchal societies, men control sexual and romantic environments by promoting sexually aggressive behavior among men (Clark and Hatfield 1989; Hatfield et al. 1998; Flood 2008). Through the emphasis of the importance of sexual prowess, cultural mandates concerning gender encourage men to "sexually objectify" women and appear "sexual." However, such mandates encourage women to stress relationship viability and appear "romantic" (Hatfield et al. 1998). Hence, men are often authorized to express

themselves sexually, while women who act this way are shunned. This possibility suggests that gender trumps race and status concerning men's interactions with women.

A second possibility is that Black men exhibit more sexually objectifying approaches toward women than do White men. This explanation is most in line with scholarship on Black men's relations with women. More specifically, cultural motifs like the "cool pose" (Majors and Billson 1992) portray Black men as culprits of sexual violence (Majors and Billson 1992; Anderson 1999). However, this perspective, which is echoed with public discourses and much scholarly research, gives the impression that all Black men are part of the same cultural spaces, thereby neglecting the fact that Black men may be part of different sociocultural[1] spaces that yield distinctly different structural consequences for their treatment of women. It should also be noted that the stereotypical nature of Black men as the Mandingo—overly aggressive, sexually promiscuous, physically superior yet intellectually inferior—has long been purported in mainstream discourses (Hunter and Davis 1992; Collins 2004). Race scholars assert this is a problematized, dramatized, and monolithic perception of Black men that is often exacerbated in the media (Staples 1982; Hoberman 1997).

Finally, the third possibility asserts that White men are more sexually objectifying than Black men. By virtue of their presumed greater status and esteem, White men are more likely to control social environments and accept, and even normalize, sexual objectifications of women (Connell 1987; Kimmel and Messner 1989; Kimmel 2006). This perspective echoes the sentiments of women who claim sexual harassment in high-status institutions such as law, academia, and corporate America where White men are typically the controllers of social environments (Kanter 1977). In contrast to the aforementioned "cool pose" some extant literature

* **Authors' Note:** The authors thank the Kinsey Institute, the Center for the Study of the College Fraternity, the Graduate and Professional Student Organization, Student Affairs, and the Vice President's Office of Institutional Development at Indiana University for financial support. We also thank Elizabeth Armstrong, Brian Powell, Rob Robinson, Tim Hallett, Donna Eder, Abigail Sewell, Keon Gilbert, Christi Smith, Judson Everitt, Ann McCranie, the Gender, Race, and Class Research Workshop, and the Social Stratification Writing Workshop. We also thank the anonymous reviewers at *Men and Masculinities* for their helpful and constructive comments. This article is the winner of the 2007 Association of Black Sociologists and 2008 Society for the Study of Social Problems Graduate Student Paper Competitions. Please address correspondence to Rashawn Ray, Department of Sociology, Indiana University, Ballantine Hall 744, 1020 E. Kirkwood Ave. Bloomington, IN 47405; e-mail: rajray@indiana.edu.

finds that Black men's gender attitudes, compared to their White counterparts, are more supportive of gender equality because of a shared oppression and subordination with women (Millham and Smith 1986; Konrad and Harris 2002).

In this article, we assess these three predictions by analyzing 30 in-depth, individual interviews and surveys and two focus group interviews with Black and White high-status fraternity men. We find evidence that White men are more sexually objectifying than their Black counterparts, in support of the third prediction. However, we also find that the reasons behind this pattern go beyond the explanations typically asserted by this prediction and the first two predictions. Collectively, the three explanations noted above neglect the extent to which cultural and social norms are embedded within and shaped by the structure of institutions, and in turn, how structure shapes men's approaches toward women and the performances of masculinities. Accordingly, we contend that "normative institutional arrangements" are one of the key factors that underlie racial differences regarding how men interact with women romantically and sexually on college campuses.

## NORMATIVE INSTITUTIONAL ARRANGEMENTS IN HIGHER EDUCATION

Normative institutional arrangements are boundaries that shape social interactions and establish control over social environments (Gerson and Peiss 1985; Hays 1994; Britton 2003), and one structural mechanism that should be of importance to scholars interested in intersectionality research. Normative institutional arrangements identify social contexts (e.g., social environments in fraternity houses), whereby certain behaviors are more or less acceptable and certain structures hold individuals more or less accountable for their treatment of others. Such arrangements represent taken-for-granted assumptions that are external and exist outside of individuals, "social, durable, and layered" (Hays 1994), and constraining and enabling. Normative institutional arrangements focus on the accepted arrangement of relationships within social institutions. In this article, normative institutional arrangements draw attention to the ways in which performances of masculinities are legitimized across different sociocultural categories of men, and the role structure plays in men's approaches toward women. Here, we showcase the implications of the intersecting forces of race and status by examining two normative institutional arrangements that are common themes in Black and White men's understandings and perceptions of gender and sexual relations: (a) small Black student and Greek communities; (b) living arrangements including a lack of on-campus fraternity houses.

The Black student community at most Predominately White Institutions (PWIs) is small and insular. There is also a limited amount of social interaction between Black and White fraternities and between Black and White students overall (Allen 1992; Massey et al. 2003). Similar to patterns at the societal level, interracial dating is infrequent (Joyner and Kao 2005). As a result, even high-status Black fraternity men are mostly invisible in White social arenas.

In contrast, the relatively small number of Black students and limited interactions with Whites indicate that Black fraternity men are much more visible in the Black community. In fact, this group of Black men aligns with the ideals of what Du Bois (1903, 1939) conceptualized as the "Talented Tenth." Such members of the Black elite are expected to sacrifice personal interests and endeavors to provide leadership and guidance to the Black community (Battle and Wright II 2002). However, being part of the Talented Tenth signifies the monitoring of this group's behavior, particularly actions that are inconsistent with a greater good for the Black community. This monitoring by others on Black fraternity men is intensified in a structural setting with a small community size, and in turn, increases the likelihood that their treatment of women will be publicized and scrutinized by members of their own social community and the broader college and off-campus communities. Although White fraternity men may also be visible, the sheer number of White students leads to them being held less accountable, and consequently, able to perform masculinity in a manner that Black fraternity men cannot.

Not only is the Black community relatively small but Black Greeks have very different on-campus living arrangements than White Greeks. There is a historical legacy of racial discrimination, both within and external to the university, that has traditionally precluded Black fraternities and sororities from gaining equal access to economic resources such as Greek houses and large alumni endowments (Kimbrough and Hutcheson 1998). To date, most Black Greek Letter Organizations (BGLOs) do not have fraternity or sorority houses on university property (Harper, Byars, and Jelke 2005). If they do, these houses normally are not the same size or stature of those of their White counterparts. To the extent that the structure of living arrangements facilitates a certain treatment of women, racial differences in access to housing on-campus may have implications in potential racial differences in approaches toward women.

In sum, the claims by masculinities, sexualities, and race scholars suggest that culture provides a portal whereby men view women as physical objects. However, research in this area suffers from three important shortcomings. First, the structural mechanisms by which normative institutional arrangements promote women's subordination have been underemphasized. Most recently, scholars have called for a resurgence of such research and have pointed to the exploration of contextual and structural factors to uncover these mechanisms (Reskin 2003; Epstein 2007). Second, the perspectives of high-status men remain absent in the literature. Hence, this study seeks to understand how elite men decipher their worlds and how privileged statuses influence the processes underlying gender dynamics. Third, research largely has not explored the potential for racial differences in men's gender relations. Consequently, gender and sexuality research has portrayed men as homogenous proponents of gender inequality, irregardless of race and/or social context.

Our work offers an opportunity to address these gaps in the literature by reporting on interviews with Black and White high-status men. Some high-status Black men (e.g., Black fraternity men) may have attitudes and beliefs that are similar to their White male counterparts. However, due in part to a hyper level of visibility and accountability, Black men may be unable to perform hegemonic masculinity similar to their White male counterparts.[2] Actually, because of a relative lack of accountability and visibility afforded to high-status White fraternity men in this structural setting,[3] it is White men's performances of masculinities that may be closer to that of the "cool pose." Therefore, we hypothesize that Black men will exhibit less sexually objectifying approaches toward women than their White counterparts.

Accordingly, we pose two essential questions (a) Regarding high-status fraternity men's relations with women, are there racial differences in romantic versus sexually objectifying approaches? (b) How do "normative institutional arrangements" structure men's approaches toward women? Because there has been limited empirical research on elite men, we privilege their accounts and voices to gain an insider's perspective into the intersections of masculinities, status, sexuality, and race.

## SETTING AND METHOD

We conducted 30 in-depth individual interviews and surveys, along with two focus group interviews, from 15 Black and 15 White fraternity men at a PWI that we call Greek University (GU). Enrolling approximately 30,000 undergraduates, GU is ideal for this study because of its strong academic reputation, vibrant social life, and party scene. GU's emphasis on Greek life facilitates the examination of gender relations among high-status men. About 20% of GU undergraduates are members of Greek letter organizations, which is larger than similar universities.[4] For members, the Greek system normally offers a home away from home, friendships, and social and philanthropic activities. There are approximately 25 White fraternities with memberships around 100, some with on-campus and some with off-campus status, and five Black fraternities with memberships around 10 and all hold off-campus status.[5] Although approximately 25% of White students are members of Greek organizations, less than 10% of Black students are members of Greek organizations.[6] Black and White fraternities are operated by two different governing bodies, the National Pan-Hellenic Council (NPHC)[7] and the Interfraternity Council (IFC), respectively. Although none of these fraternities appear to explicitly discriminate on the basis of race, there is virtually no overlap in race among members of these organizations.

### Data Collection

To select our sample, we used a reputational approach (Boswell and Spade 1996) to identify high-status fraternities. Relying on rankings of fraternities by members of sororities and fraternities, students in sociology classes, informants in Greek Affairs, and the Assistant Dean of Students that rank fraternities based on popularity, academic and philanthropic events, and athletic prowess, three White fraternities consistently ranked high on all lists. We include all three in our study. Because only five historically Black fraternities are recognized by the NPHC, membership in any of these fraternities normally conveys a certain high-status, particularly at GU because the Black population is only about 4% (1,524). We interviewed members from four of the five Black fraternities. We attempted to interview all five and were gained entry to four. The sampling strategy enables us to check for commonalities and differences within and between race. Participants were recruited by emailing the fraternity presidents to see if the investigators could attend a chapter meeting to make an announcement about the study, invite members to participate, and leave detailed study flyers.

As a Black and White team of male researchers, we note that gender may elicit certain responses with participants de-emphasizing romanticism. We also conducted interviews with the authors matched with participants by race to elicit candid responses about the other racial group. Based on the data presented throughout this article, we are confident that we limited methodological biases. For example, one White respondent states, "Blacks will fuck anything." Another says, "Yeah, my friends at home are Black. They like to put it in girls' asses." Based on our experiences interacting with these respondents, we believe they would not have made these comments if they were being interviewed by a Black interviewer. See the quotation on page 17 for a Black quotation about Whites. These quotations show that respondents did not hesitate to make derogatory statements about the other group.

All the men in our study report being family-oriented and having lofty career goals. Most participants are active on campus and have higher GPAs than non-Greeks. However, a substantial class difference exists between Blacks and Whites. The Black men's self-reported family household income is lower middle class, whereas the White men's self-reported family household income is upper-middle class. Many of the Black fraternity men have scholarships, student loans, and/or jobs to pay for tuition and housing costs, whereas most of the White fraternity men have scholarships and/or their parents pay a substantial portion of their tuition and living expenses. All respondents self-identify as heterosexual (see Table 1).

## Interview Procedure

Most of the data presented come from the individual interviews. In-depth interviews are useful for developing a broad understanding of students' experiences in various aspects of college life and for exploring the meanings students attach to these experiences (Denzin and Lincoln 1994). Similar to Armstrong, Hamilton, and Sweeney (2006), we used an 8-page, semistructured interview guide to ask participants about many topics including the Greek system, race relations, partying, hooking-up, dating, sexual attitudes and experiences, and their goals for the future. With interviews averaging 2 hours, we aimed to obtain a holistic perspective of these men's collegiate lives. All interviews were digitally recorded and transcribed using pseudonyms to ensure personal and organizational anonymity. Following the interviews, we recorded ethnographic field notes to capture aspects of the interview interactions that might not be evident in the transcripts (Emerson, Fretz, and Shaw 1995). At the end of each interview, we asked respondents to complete a paper-and-pencil survey. Data from this survey on sociodemographics, family background,

**Table 1 Descriptive Statistics of Sample by Race**

| Variable | Range | Variable Description | White = 15 | Black = 15 | Total = 30 |
|---|---|---|---|---|---|
| Age | 18–24 | Years | 20.11 | 21.27 | 20.69 |
| Classification | 1–4 | 1 = Freshman, 2 = Sophomore, 3 = Junior, 4 = Senior | 2.22 | 3.73 | 2.98 |
| G.P.A | 0–4 | Cumulative Grade Point Average | 3.31 | 2.92 | 3.12 |
| Living Situation | 0–1 | 0 = Lives off-campus, 1 = Lives in a Fraternity House | 0.87 | 0.00 | 0.45 |
| Years in Fraternity | 1–5 | Years respondent has been a fraternity member | 1.94 | 2.00 | 1.97 |
| Religiosity | 1–4 | 1 = Not at all, 2 = Slightly, 3 = Moderately, 4 = Very | 2.00 | 3.07 | 2.54 |
| Family's Social Class | 1–6 | 1 = Poor, 2 = Working, 3 = Lower-middle, 4 = Middle, 5 = Upper-middle, 6 = Upper | 4.56 | 3.87 | 4.22 |
| Relationship Status | 0–1 | 0 = Single or dating, 1 = Committed relationship | 0.33 | 0.67 | 0.50 |

sexual attitudes and experiences, and relationship history provide contextual information about each respondent.

The focus groups were conducted after the individual interviews were completed to support the individual interviews. Most focus group respondents were part of the 30 individual interviews. The focus groups were used to triangulate the data and focused on themes that evolved from the individual interviews. They also allowed us to interrogate emerging propositions. Because shared discourses are documented to occur in peer groups, the unique environment generated in focus groups was well suited to this project (Morgan 1997; Hollander 2004). Although focus groups have been criticized for their lack of ability to elicit truthful views about gender and sexuality from young men, the interviewers had preexisting knowledge of the men and could question specific accounts and perspectives.

### Analytical Strategy

We use deductive and inductive reasoning as analytic approaches to "double fit" the data with emergent theory and literature (Ragin 1994). We initially allowed analytical categories to emerge as we searched for similarities and differences in how Black and White fraternity men interact with women. Guided by these themes and patterns, we then used deductive reasoning to look for evidence and theories to make sense of the data. We used ATLAS.ti, a qualitative data analysis software package, to connect memos, notes, and transcriptions. After establishing patterns in the coding, we searched the interviews thoroughly again looking for examples that both confirmed and contradicted emerging patterns. Our emerging propositions were then refined or eliminated to explain these negative cases (Rizzo, Corsaro, and Bates 1992).

## RACIALIZING GENDER RELATIONS ON CAMPUS

The interviews suggest that Black fraternity men exhibit more romantic approaches than White fraternity men. Although both groups sexually objectify women, Black men emphasize romanticism more than their White counterparts. They indicate that women are physical objects of enjoyment but should also be respected. White fraternity men make few romantic references and primarily view women as sexual objects.

The following quotations exemplify sexually objectifying approaches. This participant suggests that romance is unnecessary in the quest for gratification.

> Pretty much you do not need to do all that wine and dine them and all that. You can skip all that and just bring them back to the house and do what's important to you. (White)

In two different parts of the interview, a participant explains which factors affect how far he will go with a woman.

> R: If they [women] were decent or just okay, I'll just mess around with them … Get head.
> I: When she gives you head, do you go down on her?
> R: Honestly, I don't like that … I do it every once in a while. Honestly depends how hot the girl is. If I'm drunk and into the girl, I probably would. But other girls, I just make out with them for a little bit.
> R: We were talking for about a week and we started messing around. She starts giving me head, and when I took her shirt off, I put my hand on her

stomach and this girl had abs. I think that's the most disgusting thing. Like, girls with abs, it's like … too masculine. So that like turned me off and I couldn't get off and I never called her again. (White)

Nine of the 15 White participants report engaging in sexual behavior that they do not prefer including performing oral sex because of a woman's desirable physical characteristics. They also rarely describe "hot girls" in terms of social competence and popularity. Reports from Black men also contain sexually objectifying approaches. While describing what he desires in a woman, a participant compares women to cars as he explains why his standards for sexual encounters are lower than for relationships.

I: Are your standards lower for a hookup than a committed relationship?

R: I use this analogy. Some people say it's corny, but whatever. When you have the title of a car, you want it to be nice, but you'll jump in your friend's car. You'll ride, you'll ride anything because it's not your title. But if I'm going to have the title to you, you've got to be nice because you represent me! But now I'll ride in a pinto, but I just won't buy one. (Black)

Although both groups exhibit sexually objectifying approaches, romantic approaches in quality and content are far more prevalent among Black men. They respond when asked to "describe ways you or your friends respect women on campus."

I definitely think my fraternity brothers do a lot of stuff that make them [women] feel appreciated like getting them flowers; whether write them a poem, whether it's just tell them they look beautiful. (Black)

I think you have to treat women with respect. I think because of how society is I think a lot of males have been misshapen to be like the world leader; the dominant figure in the relationship. They wear the pants in the relationship. I feel like I would treat a woman the way that I would want to be treated. (Black)

Conversely, many White men describe a very different notion of respecting women.

We respect women. We won't take advantage of them if they're wasted. If she's puking in our bathroom, one of the pledges will get her a ride home. (White)

One way that I respect women? A lot of ways. I'll never ask if she needs a ride home after we hookup. I'll let her bring it up or let her spend the night. You respect a girl more if you let her stay. (White)

Black and White differences are also evident in responses to "what do you consider a serious relationship?" White men understand a serious relationship primarily in terms of physical monogamy, whereas Black men define serious relationships in terms of socioemotional exchanges.

R: If you're in a serious relationship, you shouldn't be making out … that's wrong.

I: So serious relationships are when you don't cheat on a girl.

R: No. You shouldn't be making out in front of people. If you have a girlfriend you can't be like all over girls at parties. (White)

Serious relationship is pretty much a basic understanding that two people are together. You have somebody to talk to; somebody who is going to be there on the other end of the phone call. When you leave that message they're calling back. Maybe at night you got somebody to cuddle with. Somebody that could possibly cook for you. Somebody that might be taking you out, picking you up. Somebody that is worrying about what you're doing. (Black)

Twelve of the 15 Black fraternity men explain that having someone to "share" and do "special" things with is the best thing about being in a serious relationship.

I'd say you get the companionship, the love. You've got somebody there in daytime hours, not just in nighttime hours. The nine to five hours they're going to be there to go out with you. They might send you out with some stuff, take you out to eat, go see a movie, and like it's that constant companionship. (Black)

Comparatively, only 7 of the 15 White fraternity men mention that this is a benefit of a committed relationship. Instead, 12 of them explain that having a "regular hookup" is the best thing about being in a relationship.

Lots of sex. You can have it everyday without having to go out and get it. It's a lot easier, but you do have to put up with shit occasionally. (White)

The best thing is you don't have to use a condom. It feels better and you can go right to it. And you got someone to call that you know what they want and knows what you like. (White)

In contrast, only 3 of the 15 Black men mention sexual convenience as a benefit of being in a committed relationship.

Perhaps most revealing are the responses to "describe a romantic evening." Black men volunteer specific details without hesitation and reveal intimate knowledge of their partners, thoughtful planning, and intricate execution.

I try to do romantic things on occasion, not just on occasions. On her birthday I surprised her. I told her we were going out to dinner. There is a whole day of events. I left a dozen roses in front of her door. I have a key to her apartment just because she likes to have that kind of security just in case I need to go over there and do something for her. When she came home I had prepared a dinner for her. I cooked her favorite dinner which was spaghetti and she was really surprised. It was a candlelight dinner, lights were off, food all served, salad, and spaghetti. She really liked that and I gave her some more gifts, but the last thing I got her was a ring that she loves. (Black)

Of course, "romantic" does not necessarily imply equitable gender relations. "Romantic" can also have negative connotations for gender relations (e.g., women need to be taken care of, pampered, put on a pedestal). Comparatively, most White men's narratives imply less thought and planning. Only three of them could describe a romantic evening, two of which were descriptions encompassing "dinner and a movie," preferably an "expensive establishment."

I clean up, shave, put on a nice shirt with a nice pair of pants, you come out of the car, you wait for her, open the door for her. Nice expensive restaurant; something with a good reputation. Maybe somewhere someone's parents would take them, because that lets them know you're dropping some cheddar, you know, you're dropping some money. Have some easy conversation, then come back have a few more drinks, and then, you know. {laughs}. (White)

Another White participant says, "Well, on her birthday I got her an ipod. She loved it. I took her out to dinner, an expensive dinner."

Finally, the language used by White fraternity men to describe women in gender interactions suggests sexually objectifying approaches, whereas the language exhibited most frequently by Black fraternity men implies more romantic approaches. White men commonly refer to women as "chicks," "girls," and other belittling terms. Conversely, Black men generally use more "respectful" terms like "women," "ladies," and "females" or refer to individuals by name.[8] As seen in many quotations throughout the article, the examples below illustrate the role of language regarding gender relations.

I know this one time I was real drunk, a little too flirtatious with a female who was actually a friend of mine. I did—I was not trying to hook up with her. Actually, she was trying to hook up with me. And when the alcohol mixed with the flirtatious lady, mixing with me not driving having to be at her house that night. I did regret it when I woke up the next morning {laughs}. (Black)

When the booze settles in you can make mistakes and you'll screw up with a "frat rat" or something. (White)

Collectively, Black excerpts normally acknowledge women's agency, whereas the White accounts typically display the use of the passive voice, whereby a woman is always acted on and never acting. Black men emphasize more romanticism in their accounts regarding experiences with and attitudes about women. However, these differences are not solely related to race.

## NORMATIVE INSTITUTIONAL ARRANGEMENTS STRUCTURE APPROACHES TOWARD WOMEN

We find that differences in men's approaches toward women are structured by normative institutional arrangements centering on community size and living arrangements. Participant accounts suggest that the size of their respective racial communities on campus and the presence or absence of a fraternity house underlie racial differences in romantic versus sexually objectifying approaches toward women.

### Greek and Racially Based Communities

Fraternity men are concerned about their individual and group reputations when making gender relation choices. Thus, they aim to steer clear of certain social scenes to preserve their status as elite men. In the following accounts, participants indicate that to maintain their reputations they normally will not "hookup" with low-status women. We asked, "Are there any women you wouldn't hook up with?"

Fat girls. I stay away from them. Sluts too. They're disgusting. I don't need to hookup with that, that's not *our* [his fraternity] style. (White)

Everyone has the one, two, or three girls that they're like what the hell was I doing? But you don't want to have too many. I mean it's good to hookup, but you don't want to do it with a girl that's easy. If it's a girl that every guy wants and you bring her back it's like, "Wow! You hooked up with that girl? That's impressive!" It feels good. If you hookup with an ugly girl, your friends will give you shit for it. (White)

Yes. They're not attractive. [laughs] That might sound mean, but that's what they are. Not attractive girls. I don't think there's no woman here that's higher than what we think we can reach. And then lower, yes there is a group of people that you should just not touch. I hear a lot of guys in other fraternities say, "Man I wish I could get a girl like that." Instead, we just get the girl like that. (Black)

White fraternity men indicate that the "word" gets around easily within the Greek community regarding gender interactions. They normally engage in a variety of unspoken rules to preserve their reputations. The following White participant describes the "card" rule.

R: You got one card to play. You can hookup with two girls in the same house [sorority organization] and you might be alright. As long as you don't piss off the first one. If you do, you're done. You won't have a chance with any other girls in that house. But you can't play the card unless some time has passed.
I: How much time do you need?

R: It can't be the same weekend for sure. Probably after a week or so you should be okay. (White)

The Greek community seems to hold White fraternity men accountable to sorority women. As the quotation above alludes, it is only for reasons of saving face that will allow them access to other women in the same sorority. Another White participant describes how cheating could result in a bad reputation if he got caught.

I: What would happen if you got caught cheating?
R: The way I could see it [cheating] affecting something is if it's a sorority girl you fuck over.
I: You can't screw with a sorority sister?
R: You could, but you could get the name, you're an asshole, you're a player, or something like that. I mean it might. It could spread around the [her sorority] house. Then you're Blacklisted. (White)

Although repercussions exist with sorority women, there are an abundance of non-Greek women with no reputational constraints. The large number and high percentage of White students give White fraternity men an ample pool of women not connected to the Greek community. When relating with non-Greek women or GDIs,[9] White fraternity men do not have to worry about "the word" getting around. Moreover, White fraternity men can disassociate from the fraternity, blend into the crowd, and interact as they please.

R: GDIs come here and it's like sensory overload. They are like in awe. If you're in awe, it's like so easy. {laughs}

You can say anything to a GDI. Adam makes girls cry.

I: He wouldn't do that to a sorority girl?

R: You make a sorority girl cry she's going to tell all her friends. "I was at XYZ [fraternity] and this guy made me cry and he's such an asshole." If you say it to a GDI, she's going home and you're probably never going to see her again and she's not going to tell all of XYZ [sorority] that you said this and you're not going to have a whole sorority that hates you. (White)

Black fraternity men face a different organizational structure. These men feel that they cannot "do things like other guys."

Because there's only seven [Black Greek] organizations on campus, we have a huge impact on the Black race here. Where there's like 750 different [White] organizations, their impact is not as severe. It's not as deep, especially cause they have more people than our race. (Black)

It's kind a like being on the basketball team or being on a football team. You know what I'm saying? It's kinda like "Eta" [his fraternity name] puts you on the next level. Like you're Black Greek but you are like the … you are supposed to be representing the Black Greek. It's kinda hard to get that out, but when we do something we are suppose to be setting the bar for everybody else. It's like a known thing that we suppose to be setting a bar. You know what I mean? (Black)

Black fraternity men, and many Black students, cannot overcome the reputational constraints of the small Black population. Black men report being very conscious of their behavior when interacting with women. Although White fraternity men can generally be anonymous and "get off" safely, Black fraternity men perceive themselves to be constantly visible and therefore continuously held accountable for their treatment of women.

### The Fraternity House

The organizational structure of "the house" facilitates sex, discourages intimacy, and is used as a resource, which affords White fraternity men control of sexual environments. For instance, these men report that women normally engage in relationships to be associated with a particular fraternity and to have access to fraternity functions and/or alcohol.

I know I'm Jack "B" ["B" represents his fraternity's name], and there's probably a Jack "C," but I don't care. I know she just wants to come to our parties and know someone there. (White)

College-aged women younger than 21 years old seem to rely on fraternities for basic ingredients of the mainstream version of the college experience—big parties and alcohol. In fact, an interview with a White participant was interrupted twice because of orders for alcohol placed by an ex-girlfriend and another woman from the dorm.

"The house" also facilitates a convenient means of engaging sexual behavior. A participant discusses the difference between living in "the house" and living off-campus.

You meet a lot more girls in the house. The frat [house] is easier, a lot easier too in that sense cause coming back from the bars, it's not necessarily like "let's go back to my place." Instead it's like, "Let's go back to the frat [house] and have a couple more drinks." It's like you don't sound like you're trying to hook up with them. "Let's go back to my house and just … get it on" … [laughs] … It's easier. (White)

"The house" also constrains men's gender relations. Although the fraternity houses at GU are impressive mansion-like structures, they are chaotic, nonprivate spaces that promote nonromantic activities. Most White fraternities require a "live-in" period. In the first year, members sleep in cold dorms, which are rooms composed of dozens of bunk beds.

It's like fifty of us sleep together. But you put your beds together and have all these sheets and stuff. It's like a bungalow. But sometimes you can hear other people having sex. (White)

If members earn enough "house points" for representing the fraternity well through activities like philanthropy or sports, they then typically live with three roommates in a tiny bunk-style room.

White fraternity men indicate that they could never "get away" with having romantic time. A White participant says, "There's so many people running around that house, someone's bound to see or hear something." The public nature of fraternity living arrangements is also confirmed in our field notes. While entering a fraternity room to do an interview, the interviewee and interviewer interrupted a roommate who was masturbating. The interviewer reported surprise that the masturbator seemed only slightly uncomfortable with the interruption. This suggests that interruptions like these are commonplace.

Although privacy would intuitively be linked to more sexually objectifying approaches, in the context of Greek social life, a lack of privacy facilitates these approaches by preventing intimacy. While having other people as witnesses should reduce the degree of exploitation, Greek social life is a normative institutional arrangement structured by hegemonic masculinity with sexual prowess as one of its essential ideals. Thus, men who engage in public displays of sexual objectification are applauded. A participant describes one evening in the cold dorm.

Lunch on Fridays are the best. It's like all the stories from Thursday night. It's pretty funny. It's a good time. For instance, Tom came into the cold dorm and he was with his girlfriend and they were really drunk. And he's like, "We're having sex." I was like, "You should have heard him. He punished her."[10] (White)

Romantic displays, because they are not in concert with hegemonic ideals, are sanctioned. For example, participants indicate that men who make romantic displays like saying "I love you" or opting for alone time with a woman over "hanging with the guys" will quickly be referred to as "pussy-whipped."

You don't want to be known as pussy-whipped. Guys that are pussy-whipped are wimps. They just let their girl tell them what to do. You can't count on them. They'll tell you one thing, but if the girl says something different, they're doing what she says. (White)

Another White participant characterizes how public displays of romanticism are considered to be uncool by the general Greek community.

I don't know how romantic it gets. Am I like going to set up a table in my frat room and light a candle? It'd be cool, if I had the balls to do it. (White)

When asked directly "why don't you and your friends have romantic evenings," a White participant explains.

Frat houses aren't the place for that [romantic behavior]. Have you looked around? The place is filthy and you have no privacy. None. I shower with five guys; people always coming in and out. You're never alone. I used to feel weird about it [sex], but now I don't. Like I used to try to be quiet, but I'm having sex less than four feet from my roommate, who's having sex with his girlfriend. You're going to hear something. So you don't worry about it. (White)

Conversely, Black fraternity men's off-campus status offers private space for romantic relations. Most members are scattered across two- to four-person apartments and rental houses. Interviews conducted in bedrooms at Black residencies were devoid of interruptions, whereas interviews with Whites had three to four interruptions, on average. Field notes document that Black men's rooms are frequently decorated with expressions of personal achievement and style, whereas White men's rooms are often decorated with mainstream posters and sexually objectifying appeals. Consider the following field notes.

We conducted the interview in E3's room. He had mafia posters around his room from the movies *Godfather* and *Scarface*. He also had a Dr. Seuss book and a pimp poster in his room as well. E3 is a martial arts champion and has

several of his large trophies in his room and around the house. (Black)

The room was filthy. It felt dirty like it hadn't been disinfected in a while. There were many posters and artifacts on the walls of beer or liquor companies and one wall decoration was of some Dr. Dre records. The coffee table had three Playboy magazines laid out in a fan-like shape and the windows had two suction cup Playboy Bunnies hanging off of them. (White)

A Black participant comments on his interactions with the decoration styles of White men.

I go through some of these [White] male's rooms and that's all they got—they got posters. I mean I just can't have no posters of naked women just *all* around my room. Like when you walk in you see nothing but nude! (Black)

In sum, normative institutional arrangements—the presence or absence of a fraternity "house" and the size of the Greek and racially based community in the larger student population—afford Blacks and Whites different opportunity structures for romantic and sexual relations. The small, highly visible and insular Black communities normally force Black fraternity men to be conscious about their positions as leaders and role models, thus affecting their experiences with and treatment of women. This consciousness often leads Black fraternity men to conveying more romantic approaches toward women. Because of the size of the White student population, White fraternity men often find relief from reputational constraints. "The house" facilitates White fraternity men's relations with women by putting them in control of sexual environments. At the same time, however, the "public" nature of fraternity houses constrains gender relations by providing only nonprivate and unromantic spaces, thereby promoting more sexually objectifying approaches.

## Culture Mediating Normative Institutional Arrangements

Although we have emphasized the importance of structure in approaches toward women, some may assert that maturation or relationship status may be factors. Black fraternity men are one year older and further along in college. Because of different recruitment practices between Black and White fraternities, most Blacks do not become members until their sophomore or junior years, whereas Whites primarily "rush" during their freshman year. Hence, the number of years Blacks and Whites have been fraternity members is roughly the same. So this 1 year age difference should not be overstressed. More importantly, we compared the responses of older White fraternity men with those of their younger counterparts. We find their approaches toward women to be similar. Because Black men tend to be in more committed relationships, it could be argued that higher relationship rates result in more romantic approaches. Our data do not offer much support for this argument. White men in committed relationships still report more sexually objectifying approaches than Black men. Comparatively, Black men who are not in committed relationships report similar romantic approaches to Black men in committed relationships.

Religiosity, however, seems to play a factor in approaches toward women, albeit mediating normative institutional arrangements. A White participant explains why he is still a virgin. He says, "Well, because I'm a Christian. I'm waiting to share that with my wife. It's a faith thing." While explaining how he manages to be a virgin, he explains that "they [women] just have to understand. I don't

do that [intercourse]. It's been tough because girls say "are you serious?" He continues to explain his frustrations with the Greek community's emphasis on sexuality.

> I'm sure you're not going to find too many twenty-two year old virgins around. It's kind of funny too, because it is almost frowned upon around here. It's almost like you're the Black sheep of the crew, because it's socially acceptable to have sex and stuff like that. You see me, nobody ever believes it. But it's almost like a stigma that you're kind of labeled with people that know. Always when people find out it's a surprise to them. (White)

Another participant explains why he does not hookup as often as his fraternity brothers.

> Not as much as some of the guys in this house. I'm not that way. It's a conscious decision. I need to really like the girl and feel comfortable. My parents have been together forever. You don't just do that kind of stuff with just anybody. (White)

Although the two negative cases highlighted above demonstrate the significance of cultural values, they also stress the importance of normative institutional arrangements for approaches toward women. These men feel uncomfortable and are frequently ridiculed and scrutinized by their fraternity brothers and women for not adhering to the hegemonic ideals reinforced by the normative institutional arrangements of Greek social life. Moreover, they are the exceptions that prove the rule.

As an added point of emphasis, focus group and ethnographic field note exerts highlight participants own awareness of the importance of normative institutional arrangements. When Black men were asked in a focus group if things would be different if GU was not a PWI, and instead a Historically Black College or University (HBCU), they unanimously responded, "Yes." If Black men had a house, they think their behavior would be similar to their White counterparts. They perceive "the house" as a place to socialize in large groups that is free from police contact and potentially hostile strangers. If they were the "majority," they perceive being free from the incessant scrutiny of the general campus community. Black men explain how "nice it would be" to not have to represent "every Black man on the planet." An ethnographic field note is fitting here.

> While attending Eta's step practice, the members began discussing their Spring Break plans. They planned to go "road tripping" to Panama City Beach. I asked why Panama City? They replied that it was cheap and a place where they could go and meet new women who do not go to GU. I asked why this was so important. They replied because the new women cannot come back to school and tell everyone else what they did and who they were with. One member replied, "We can just wild out!" (Black)

When White men were asked in a focus group to imagine life without "the house," they replied, "It would be like being a GDI." They further explained that "the house" is "like a face" which enables them to "meet girls." White men also mirror issues of safety indicated by Black men. For instance, they are concerned that if they lose "the house," they would have to go to bars, small house-parties, or third-party vendors and would then have to worry about drinking and driving, public intoxication, and police breaking up parties. In other words,

White fraternity men perceive that losing "the house" would make them "just like everybody else."

## DISCUSSION AND CONCLUSION

We have explored whether there are racial differences in men's approaches toward women. By characterizing elite Black and White fraternity men's understandings of their sexual and romantic relationships, this research fills three critical empirical gaps. First, we explore the perspectives and insights of a group that is often implicated in mainstream discourses in romantic and sexual relations on college campuses—high-status fraternity men. Second, we explicitly compare Black and White men. Third, we examine how the normative institutional arrangements of institutions shape the performances of masculinities.

Our findings suggest that both Black and White fraternity men sexually objectify women; however, Black fraternity men exhibit more romantic approaches in their perceptions of their relations with women. Black college social scenes, particularly Black Greek scenes, are often more gender egalitarian. Although the small size of the Black community and the organizational structure of the Black Greek system generally force Black men to be more conscious about their treatment of women, the organizational structure of the White Greek community facilitates sexually objectifying approaches toward women. White fraternity men also have a larger pool of non-Greek women to engage; therefore, they are held less accountable for their relations with women because of a hyper level of anonymity. Although the presence of a fraternity house enables White fraternity men to be in control of sexual environments, it also constrains gender relations by offering nonprivate and nonintimate spaces.

Unlike the lower class men in studies by Majors and Billson (1992) and Anderson (1999), Black men in this study are more affiliated with Du Bois (1903, 1939) Talented Tenth and double-consciousness concepts.[11] For Black men who identify as or with this elite group, the racialization of high-status institutions holds them more accountable for their treatment of women and constrains their approaches. As a result, some may assert these Black men's attitudes and values about the treatment of women are different from other Black men and their White fraternity male counterparts. Although there is support for this perspective, particularly because Black fraternity men stress more holistic qualities of women and tend to perceive more aspects of romanticism to be masculine, we argue the influential effects normative institutional arrangements have on shaping racial and status differences in men's gender scripts surfaces in the behavior or at the performance level of these men. To save face and status, Black fraternity men have to be more concerned about how their interactions with women are perceived by others. This leads to a unique set of reputational boundaries and constraints for Black fraternity men not exhibited by White fraternity men.

Our emphasis on normative institutional arrangements does not deny the presence of other factors that may be implicated in racial differences. For example, Black men in this study report being more religious than White men. Therefore, we would still expect for them to have cultural values that buffer sexually objectifying approaches. Less religious Black men, however, still exhibit more romantic approaches than the White men in the sample. Thus, we contend these patterns are an artifact of the racialized level of accountability and visibility within the normative institutional arrangements of campus social life. Our research confirms that when normative institutional arrangements are in concert with mainstream hegemonic ideals, sexual objectifications are more likely to occur.

Our findings offer an interesting parallel to Armstrong, Hamilton, and Sweeney's (2006) ethnographic examination of women who reside on a women's floor in a "party dorm." They find that female college students, especially those in their first year and under the legal drinking age, rely on fraternities for parties and alcohol, and consequently, relinquish power and control of social and sexual environments to these men. They conclude that individual, organizational, and institutional practices (e.g., prohibiting alcohol in dormitories) contribute to higher levels of sexual assault.

Our research further argues that structural settings shape how actors perceive others (e.g., as sexual, romantic, and/or holistic others) and reflect the racial and gender dynamics of college campuses including racial segregation and skewed gender ratios. Along these lines, hegemonic masculinity is about much more than gender beliefs and masculine performances. Hegemonic masculinity is also about normative accountability structures and the preservation of normative personal, social, and institutional resources. Privileges across gender, race, and status divides afford White fraternity men less accountability when performing a hegemonic masculine self during interactions with women. As shown here, under certain institutional arrangements, racial disadvantage, as with Black fraternity men, can decrease gender inequality and reduce a traditional hegemonic style of engagement toward women. However, race and/or class advantage, as with White fraternity men, and disadvantage, as with the Black men in Majors and Billson's (1992) and Anderson's (1999) studies, can increase gender inequality and propel a hegemonic presentation of self such as the "cool pose."

Now that we have a greater understanding of the importance of not just being a racial/ethnic minority but also being a numerical minority or majority and how these normative institutional arrangements structure the gender relations of high-status men on campus, future research should investigate how common these patterns are among individuals across a range of institutional settings. Specifically, our research has implications for masculinities and its relationships with White men at small colleges, or where they are the minority group, and men of other racial/ethnic groups in institutional settings where they are the majority group. Although these propositions cannot be sufficiently answered in this study, it does provide a blueprint for how scholars should approach research in this area.

Particularly useful in extrapolating the findings presented here is DeLamater's (1987) recreational-centered approach,[12] whereby approaches toward others are facilitated by contextual and structural factors. Applied here, the recreational approach assumes that actors can exhibit both romantic and sexually objectifying approaches based on the dynamics of the structural setting. Men and women do not fit into monolithic groups. Although the literature has traditionally established a gender dichotomy whereby men exhibit sexual prowess and women cling to romantic ideals, we find men exhibit both sexually objectifying and romantic approaches. By integrating the recreational approach into the discourse on romantic and sexual relations, scholars will be better equipped to extrapolate the interconnections between masculinities, sexualities, gender inequality, and race.

Taken together, our findings suggest that efforts to increase gender equality on college campuses should center on increasing the perceived accountability of men by offering social spaces that enable communicative and intimate gender relations. For example, Boswell and Spade (1996) find that fraternity houses and commercial bars that are low-risk for sexual assault encourage men and women to get acquainted. Although the data implicate the presence of a fraternity house in unequal gender relations, they do not necessarily suggest that the elimination of fraternity houses is required to

accomplish gender equality. Many sorority houses do not seem to have these problems because they have strict guidelines regarding gender ratios, parties, alcohol, and overnight guests (Armstrong, Hamilton, and Sweeney 2006). Thus, the normative institutional arrangements that afford men—in this context White fraternity men—a lack of accountability to exploit hegemonic prowess must be restructured to alter the level of accountability that encourages gender inequality. Our study concludes with an optimistic suggestion: by promoting normative institutional arrangements that facilitate accountability structures and romantic and equitable approaches, improvements toward gender equality are possible.

## NOTES

1. Allport (1954) uses "sociocultural" to refer to the intersection between class (status) and caste (race).

2. Previous research has suggested that Black men's performances of masculinities are constrained by their marginalized status within the racial paradigm (Connell 1987, 1995; Kimmel 1987, 2006; Kimmel and Messner 1989; Hearn 2004). We advance this thesis by focusing on the intersections of race and status within a specific institutional structure (e.g., fraternity house).

3. Edwards (2008) states, "White structural advantage is Whites' disproportionate control or influence over nearly every social institution in this country. This affords Whites the ability to structure social life so that it privileges them. White normativity is the normalization of Whites' cultural practices ... their dominant social location over other racial groups as accepted as just how things are. White normativity also privileges Whites because they, unlike

nonwhites, do not need to justify their way of being."

4. The statistics concerning GU come from Student Activities and Greek Affairs.

5. On-campus status means the fraternity has a fraternity house on university property, whereas off-campus status means the fraternity does not.

6. Since the founding of Phi Beta Kappa (now an honor society), Greek organizations have been an integral part of colleges and universities for more than 200 years (Brown, Parks, and Phillips 2005). Fraternities are national organizations composed of college students that are men, usually designated by Greek letters. Most fraternities were founded on principles such as scholarship, community service, sound learning, and leadership and are distinguished by highly symbolic and secretive rituals. Greek fraternities and sororities are normally high-status organizations on collegiate campuses. Members of Greek fraternities and sororities are often members of student government and honor societies, are frequently some of the most recognizable student leaders on campus, and have higher grades and graduation rates than other students (Kimbrough and Hutcheson 1998).

7. Some of the most influential and celebrated African American leaders—Martin Luther King, W. E. B. Du Bois, Thurgood Marshall, and Maya Angelou—became members of nationally recognized African American fraternities and sororities. Having such a distinguished lineage of past members often makes members of African American fraternities and sororities feel that they must uphold an esteemed legacy (Kimbrough and Hutcheson 1998).

8. Throughout the duration of the project, women were categorized as many sexually objectifying and derogatory terms by Black and White fraternity men including "bitch," "hoe" (whore), "skank," "freak," and "tramp." Most of these names are given to fraternity groupies or women who are perceived to be sexually promiscuous.

9. "GDI" is an acronym for "God Damn Independent," which is a derogatory term used to describe non-Greeks.

10. In this context, the statement "punish her" implies that "Tom" was making his girlfriend moan and that the bed was rocking because of sexual movements.

11. The comparison between this study and the ones by Majors and Billson (1992) and Anderson (1999) should not be overstated. Although the men in all three studies are Black men, they are embedded within different normative institutional arrangements. As asserted in the literature review, minority men exhibit intragroup differences in the performances of masculinities and should be evaluated outside the tradition monolithic box they are often placed within.

12. Although DeLamater (1987) at times interchanges the sexual objectifying approach (which he calls body-centered) with the recreational-centered approach, we choose to distinguish these two approaches. As we have discussed throughout the article, normative institutional arrangements propel more or less sexual objectification and romanticism. The recreational approach allows the researcher the ability to assess complex decisions actors make based on structural settings.

## REFERENCES

Allen, Walter R. 1992. The color of success: African-American college student outcomes at predominantly white and historically black public colleges and universities. *Harvard Educational Review* 62:26–44.

Allport, Gordon W. 1954. *The Nature of Prejudice.* Reading, MA: Addison-Wesley.

Anderson, Elijah. 1999. *Code of the street: Decency, violence, and the moral life of the inner city.* New York, NY: W.W. Norton & Company.

Armstrong, Elizabeth, Laura Hamilton, and Brian Sweeney. 2006. Sexual assault on campus: A multilevel explanation of party rape. *Social Problems* 53:483–99.

Battle, Juan and Earl Wright II. 2002. W. E. B. Du Bois's talented tenth: A quantitative assessment. *Journal of Black Studies* 32:654–72.

Boswell, A. A., and J. Z. Spade. 1996. Fraternities and collegiate rape culture: Why are some fraternities more dangerous places for women? *Gender & Society* 10:133–47.

Brandes, Holger. 2007. Hegemonic Masculinities in East and West Germany (German Democratic Republic and Federal Republic of Germany). *Men and Masculinities*, 10:178–196.

Britton, Dana. M. 2003. *At work in the iron cage: The prison as gendered organization.* New York, NY: New York University Press.

Brown, T. L., G. L. Parks, and C. M. Phillips, eds. 2005. *African American fraternities and sororities: The history and the vision.* Lexington, KY: University Press of Kentucky.

Clark, R. D., and E. Hatfield. 1989. Gender differences in receptivity to sexual offers. *Journal of Psychology and Human Sexuality* 2:39–55.

Collins, Patricia Hill. 2004. *Black sexual politics: African Americans, gender, and the new racism.* New York, NY: Routledge.

Connell, R. W. 1987. *Gender and power.* Stanford, CA: Stanford University Press.

———. 1995. *Masculinities.* Second Ed. Berkeley: University of California Press.

DeLamater, J. 1987. Gender differences in sexual scenarios. In *Females, males, and sexuality: Theories and research,* ed. K. Kelley. Albany, NY: SUNY Press.

Denzin, Norman K., and Yvonna S. Lincoln, eds. 1994. *Handbook of qualitative research.* Thousand Oaks, CA: Sage.

Du Bois, W. E. B. 1903. *The souls of black folk.* New York, NY: Dover.

———. 1939. *Black folk, then and now: An essay in the history and sociology of the Negro race.* New York: Henry Holt.

Edwards, Korie. 2008. Bringing race to the center: The importance of race in racially diverse religious organizations. *Journal for the Scientific Study of Religion* 47:5–9.

Emerson, Richard, Rachel Fretz, and Linda Shaw. 1995. *Writing ethnographic fieldnotes.* Chicago, IL: University of Chicago Press.

Epstein, Cynthia Fuchs. 2007. Women's subordination in global context. *American Sociological Review* 72:1–22.

Flood, Michael. 2008. How bonds between men shape their sexual relations with women. *Men and Masculinities* 10:339–59.

Gerson, Judith M., and Kathy Peiss. 1985. Boundaries, negotiation, consciousness: Reconceptualizing gender relations. *Social Problems* 32:317–31.

Harper, Shaun R., Byars, L. F., and Jelke, T. B. 2005. How Black Greek-Letter Organization Membership Affects Adjustment and Undergraduate Outcomes. In *African American fraternities and sororities: The legacy and the vision,* ed. T. L. Brown, G. S. Parks, and C. M. Phillips, 393–416. Lexington, KY: University Press of Kentucky.

Hatfield, E., S. Sprecher, J. T. Pillemer, D. Greenberger, and P. Wexler. 1998. Gender differences in what is desired in the sexual relationship. *Journal of Psychology and Human Sexuality* 1:39–52.

Hays, Sharon. 1994. Structure and agency and the sticky problem of culture. *Sociological Theory* 12:57–72.

Hearn, Jeff. 2004. From hegemonic masculinity to the hegemony of men. *Feminist Theory* 5:49–72. Hoberman, John. 1997. *Darwin's athletes*. New York, NY: Houghton.

Hollander, Jocelyn A. 2004. The social contexts of focus groups. *Journal of Contemporary Ethnography* 33:605–37.

Hunter, Andrea G., and James E. Davis. 1992. Constructing gender: An exploration of Afro-American men's conceptualization of manhood. *Gender and Society* 6:464–79.

Joyner, Kara, and Grace Kao. 2005. Interracial relationships and the transition to adulthood. *American Sociological Review* 70:563–81.

Kanter, Rosenbath Moss. 1977. Some effects of proportions of group life: Skewed sex ratios and responses to token women. *American Journal of Sociology* 5:965–90.

Kimbrough, Walter M., and Philo A. Hutcheson. 1998. The impact of membership in black Greek-letter organizations on black students' involvement in collegiate activities and their development of leadership skills. *The Journal of Negro Education* 67:96–105.

Kimmel, Michael S., ed. 1987. *Changing men: New directions in research on men and masculinity*. Newbury Park, CA. Sage.

———. 2006. Racism as adolescent male rite of passage: Ex-nazis in scandinavia. *Journal of Contemporary Ethnography* 36:202–18.

Kimmel, Michael S., and Michael A. Messner, eds. 1989. *Men's lives*. New York, NY: Macmillan.

Konrad, A. M., and C. Harris. 2002. Desirability of the Bem sex-role inventory items for women and men: A comparison between African-Americans and European Americans. *Sex Roles* 47:259–72.

Majors, Richard G., and Janet Billson. 1992. *Cool pose: The dilemmas of black manhood in America*. New York, NY: Lexington Books.

Martin, P. Yancey, and R. A. Hummer. 1989. Fraternities and rape on campus. *Gender and Society* 3: 457–73.

Massey, Douglas S., Camille Z. Charles, Garvey F. Lundy, and Mary L. Fischer. 2003. *The source of the river: The social origins of freshman at America's selective colleges and universities*. Princeton, NJ: Princeton University Press.

Millham J., and L. E. Smith. 1986. Sex Role Differential among Black and White Americans: A Comparative Study. *The Journal of Black Psychology* 7:77–90.

Morgan, David L. 1997. *Focus groups and qualitative research*. Thousand Oaks, CA: Sage.

Peralta, Robert L. 2007. College Alcohol Use and the Embodiment of Hegemonic Masculinity among European American Men. *Sex Roles* 56:741–756.

Ragin, Charles C. 1994. Constructing social research: The unity and diversity of method. Thousand Oaks, CA: Sage.

Reskin, Barbara F. 2003. Including mechanisms in our models of ascriptive inequality: 2002 presidential address. *American Sociological Review* 68:1–21.

Rizzo, Thomas A., William A. Corsaro, and John E. Bates. 1992. Ethnographic methods and interpretive analysis: Expanding the methodological options of psychologists. *Developmental Review* 12:101–23.

Staples, R. 1982. *Black masculinity: The black males' role in American society*. San Francisco, CA: Black Scholar.

## ABOUT THE AUTHORS

**Rashawn Ray** is a PhD Candidate in the Department of Sociology at Indiana University-Bloomington. His research interests are social psychology, race, class, and gender, sociology of family, and research methodology. He is currently working on projects focusing on how fraternity men perceive race, status, and gender and how class identities varies by race, gender, and marital status. He is primarily concerned with the impact race/ethnicity, gender, and class have on occupational and educational aspirations and expectations. In 2004, he was awarded two national fellowships—the National Science Foundation Pre-doctoral Fellowship and the National Institute of Mental Health, American Sociological Association Minority Fellowship.

**Jason A. Rosow's** research interests are situated at the nexus of sociology of culture, social psychology, and self and identity. He has spent time in the field conducting interviews and observations with Wilson Palacios on his study of the "club/party" culture of Southwest Florida. He obtained his MA in sociology at Indiana University in 2005 and he is currently working in the private sector.

# COLORISM, LOOKISM, AND TOKENISM

# "One-Drop" to Rule them All?

## Colorism and the Spectrum of Racial Stratification in the Twenty-First Century

*By Victor Ray*

The vast majority of empirical studies of racial stratification in sociology conceptualize different races as if they are internally undifferentiated social categories. In this mode of analysis, scholars use "race" as a categorical variable in a regression equation or as a qualitative unit of analysis. This implies that "race" has a similar inferred causal status for all members in a given racial classification (Zuberi 2001).[*] This style of sociological research tends to assume that races are distinct, "mutually exclusive" social categories, and usually shows that there are substantive and often profound differences in the life chances of Whites and people of color, mostly to the disadvantage of the latter. Much of this work has added greatly to our understanding of racialized social systems and how they divvy up the material and psychological benefits accruing to Whiteness (Mills 1997). However, an exclusive focus on differences *between* races may obscure how racism structures relations *within* minority communities (Collins 2005). As we progress into the 21st century, a central question is: in racialized social systems, do psychological and material benefits also accrue to lightness?

Race scholars have long pointed out that the internal differentiations among people of color may have effects just as profound as those between races. For instance, in his classic *Black Bourgeoisie* (1957), E. Franklin Frazier claimed that lighter-skinned Blacks formed the basis of the post-emancipation Black middle class, as they capitalized on privileges afforded them under slavery. Similarly, nearly all of W. E. B. Du Bois' famous "talented tenth" (1903) were of mixed race, a signal some scholars (not un-problematically)[†] have taken to mean they were

---

[*] This logic is what allows researchers to claim that the "effect" of race has increased or declined in significance (Wilson 1978).

[†] The use of mixed-race status as a proxy for light skin may be of some value, but it can also provide misleading results as it provides *no direct measure of skin tone*. This variation in method may explain recent findings that are at odds with each other. For instance, Gullickson (2005) finds that the effects of colorism have decreased using mixed-race designation as a proxy for color. In addition to this, a reanalysis of the same data showed that Gullickson's findings are most likely driven by significant attrition as the final wave of data included less than 15 light-skinned blacks (Goldsmith et. al. 2006). Finally, scholars who use a direct measure of skin tone, such as Goldsmith (Goldsmith et. al

lighter skinned (Russell et. al. 1993). This process of social differentiation based on skin tone is known as colorism. Colorism operates *both* within and across races.* Colorism can also serve to clarify theories of racism. While racism is often erroneously perceived as an individual attribute of some Whites (Allport 1954), other scholars argue that racism is structural, implicating us all (Omi and Winant 1994). Colorism offers an alternative theoretical approach to describe how an oppressed minority can become complicit in the hegemony of Whiteness. Further, it confirms the theoretical postulate that most actors in a racialized social system contribute to the maintenance of that system (Bonilla-Silva 2006).

Despite recent claims that racism has ended or that we have somehow "transcended" race in the age of Obama, current research indicates that colorism processes have had some historical continuity, as lighter-skinned Blacks continue to have higher socioeconomic status. While the bulk of this essay will discuss the effects of colorism on Blacks, I will also incorporate some evidence illustrating how the virus of colorism has infected other minority communities, leading to patterns of internal differentiation for Asians and Latino/as. I argue that colorism will continue to internally fracture communities of color in the coming century, and that its effects on stratification may even increase. Further, methodological approaches to the study of race that omit measures of colorism are only telling a small part of the racial story. After a brief overview of the historical and current empirical patterns of

colorism in minority communities, I will show how dominant sociological approaches have endorsed a methodological one-drop rule. In conclusion, I will discuss the changing terrain of racial formation (Omi and Winant 1994) and explain why colorism may become a more important factor in understanding the coming racial order.

## THE WAGES OF LIGHTNESS

In his magisterial *Black Reconstruction in America* (1935), Du Bois claimed Whites received psychological gains beyond the obvious material benefits of racial domination. According to Du Bois these White benefits came in the form of greater public amenities and the ability to define themselves against Blacks (Roediger 1991). While Blacks, due to the one-drop rule, did not have the ability to define themselves racially, it seems that internal differentiation led to a "wages of lightness," through which certain Blacks received social benefits through their proximity to White phenotypic norms. Under slavery, Blacks who were partially descended from Whites (often through rape) were more likely to be manumitted, and had greater educational opportunities (Russell et. al. 1993). Further, while the one-drop rule characterized much of the United States, categorizing anyone with the slightest bit of African ancestry as Black (Davis 1991), there was some regional variation in classification schemes. This variable application of the "one-drop rule," in addition to producing some logical absurdities, such as being racially reclassified upon crossing state lines (Browning 1951), also had effects for colorism. According to Cedric Herring's (2004) account of the historical course of colorism, the social holes in the application of hypo-descent allowed some mixed-race Blacks to benefit "from the socioeconomic status of their White fathers" (2004: 4). These benefits were particularly clear in Louisiana, where "more than 80% of the free

---

2007), find that color gradations do indeed matter. More on this below.

* It is important to note that factors other than skin tone, such as education level, hair texture, eye color, and facial features, are also often used to make assessments under colorism. This has prompted some scholars to lament the use of the term "colorism" (Bonilla-Silva 2009) as too narrow to encompass the racial calculus that creates stratification.

population was of mixed ancestry" (2004, 4). Following abolition, these wages of lightness placed lighter-skinned Blacks in a position to compound these advantages; a number of historical studies have shown that light skin tone was related to better socioeconomic outcomes. Herring's (2004) work also claims that the relationship between light complexion and social advantage that held through the Civil Rights Movement continues to produce a number of social outcomes today.

Similar to Du Bois' (1935) description of Whiteness providing a "public and psychological wage," the wages of lightness are not limited to economic outcomes. Colorism has also historically had effects on beauty norms and personal psychology. Drawing on and extending the insights of Bourdieu (1994), Desmond and Emirbayer (2009) call this internalization of White beauty norms a form of "symbolic violence." This "symbolic violence" involves "the process of people of color unknowingly accepting and supporting the terms of their own domination, thereby acting as agents who collude in the conditions from which they suffer" (2009, 347). Using the example of skin-lightening creams and hair relaxers that have been known to cause severe injury, Desmond and Emirbayer (2009) argue that Blacks who subscribe to White beauty norms are responding to imposed social structural conditions in ways that reinforce the very structure devaluing them. In her essay *Whiteness as Property*, legal scholar Harris (1995) provides a particularly chilling account of how the wages of lightness may also have psychological costs. Harris (1995) claims that the symbolic violence of "passing" as White in order to find work and provide resources for her family haunted her grandmother. This passing put her in daily contact with overtly racist Whites who, unaware of the Black woman in their midst, were candid about their racism. Perfectly aware that the racialized social structure made passing "a logical [economic] choice" in her later life, Harris'

grandmother was still enraged that she lived in a society that "made her complicit in her own oppression" and furthered the logic of White supremacy.

This brief historical sketch helps to establish how colorism became instantiated in the Black community, as well as some of the early stratifying processes and psychological costs attributable to skin tone differentiation. More recent research establishes that colorism still stratifies communities. For instance, in an intersectional analysis, several researchers have found that skin color is related to ratings of attractiveness for women (Hill 2002b, Hunter 2004) with light-skinned Black women considered more attractive. Hill (2002a) avoids the "a historical fallacy" (Desmond and Emirbayer 2009) of assuming that the Civil Rights Movement moved us beyond intra-racial stratification by making a direct theoretical connection between the gendered demonization of Black physiology under slavery and current ratings of attractiveness. A number of scholars have found that lighter-skinned Black women are consistently rated as more attractive (Hill 2002b). In this reading, colorism confers a gendered form of social capital (Hunter 2004), as light skin's correlation with socially constructed notions of attractiveness provides advantages for women in dating and marriage markets. Not only are dark-skinned women less likely to be married (Edwards, Carter-Tellison and Herring 2004), but this phenotypic social capital "translates into real material advantages where light-skinned women have access to higher status spouses with more education and presumably higher incomes" (Hunter 2004). Following racial patterns first laid out under slavery, racist patterns of attraction based on notions of colorism continue to affect Black sexuality.

There is also a psychological cost to these patterns of colorism. According to Hunter (2002), light-skinned Mexican-American women and African-American women are subject to questions of ethnic authenticity. That is, because skin tone is seen as a primary signifier of race, light-skinned members of racial groups are often deemed not "Black" or "Mexican" enough. Further, Hunter (2004) cites evidence that light-skinned Blacks are less likely to be concerned with discrimination and Black pride than are their darker-skinned brothers and sisters. However, as with every sociological assertion, context matters. For instance, Verna Keith (2009) presents data showing that the self-esteem of Black women didn't just vary according to skin tone but also according to whether they are in predominantly White or Black environments. She finds that for Black women at historically Black colleges and universities, darker skin is associated with higher levels of self-esteem, whereas in predominantly White environments, skin tone is unrelated to self-esteem. Keith follows Harvey and colleagues (2005) in explaining this disparity by claiming that in predominantly White environments, Whites are primarily focused on Black-White differences, and treat all Blacks the same (2009). The effects of this similar treatment in all-White environments is perhaps best captured in Hochschild and Weaver's (2007) assertion that colorism does not affect the political attitudes of Blacks across the color spectrum. Despite the vast differences in skin tone within the Black community, these scholars claim that internal cohesion is largely a function of Blacks' continued need to present a united front in the fight against White racism.

Colorism also produces stratification that cuts across gender. Although some scholars claim that the significance of skin color has decreased or disappeared for economic outcomes (Gullickson 2005), or that the effects are exaggerated (Hersch 2005) in the post-Civil Rights era, the bulk of the evidence favors the conclusion that colorism continues to internally stratify minority communities. Some scholars claim that the effect of colorism is more predictive of stratification outcomes than *parental socioeconomic status* (Keith and Herring 1991), a

variable classically considered one of the most important for intergenerational stratification (Blau and Duncan 1967). Focusing solely on the economic outcomes of men, Hughes and Hertel (1990) show that colorism creates intra-racial wage differences that are as great as those found between Whites and Blacks when one uses measures that do not include skin tone. Updating this strand of research and advancing a "preference for Whiteness" theory of colorism, Goldsmith and colleagues (Goldsmith et. al. 2007) found "significant evidence of a skin-shade wage gradient where wages fall as skin shade darkens" (2007, 729). For men, colorism has also been shown to influence perceptions of criminality and even the length of criminal sentences (Blair et. al. 2004). In an innovative research design in which raters coded photos of actual Black male murderers according to how stereotypically Black they looked, Eberhart and colleagues (Eberhardt et. al. 2006) found that Blacks who fell into the stereotypical half of the distribution were more than twice as likely to receive the death sentence. Rather than decreasing in significance, convincing evidence suggests that colorism remains a matter of life and death.

Despite the compelling finding that colorism continues to shape the life chances of people of color, the majority of mainstream sociology has largely adopted a methodological one-drop rule (Goldsmith et. al. 2007). This is unfortunate because aggregating across race while ignoring intra-racial variation may obscure substantively important findings and over (or under) estimate racial stratification. However, when adopting colorism measures, scholars should be wary. Researchers have shown that over the life course within a single longitudinal data set, racial categorization can change as people gain or lose social class markers (Saperstein and Penner 2008). Further, Hill (2002a) has shown that simple inclusion of reports of skin tone may not solve this problem, as these also vary by race, with Whites and Blacks having very different conceptions of what constitutes light or dark skin tone.

Clearly, colorism stratifies society across a spectrum, paying material and psychological wages according to phenotypical approximations of Whiteness. Evelyn Nakano Glenn's (2009) excellent recent anthology *Shades of Difference* shows that that colorism has gone global. In contrast to Ronald Takaki's (1989) discussion of a pan-ethnic Asian solidarity being born through the murder of the Chinese-American Vincent Chin, Glenn's (2009) anthology shows that Asian Americans are internally differentiated by colorism. For instance, in an analysis of Asian Indian matrimonial ads in the U.S., Vaid (2009) finds that mention of fair skin in the ads has markedly increased since the 1980's. Similarly, in an analysis of the global trade in skin whitening, Glenn (2009) finds that the consumption of skin whitening products among women from South Africa, India, Latin America, and South East and East Asia, is on the rise. This is despite the severely dangerous nature of skin lightening creams and soaps, which may contain mercury or melanin suppressors. These toxic products can lead to disfiguration and Cushing's syndrome, along with mercury poisoning (Glenn 2009; Thomas 2009).

As a subsystem of White supremacy, colorism has internally stratified communities of color in the U.S. since slavery. Through symbolic violence, communities of color have often participated in their own oppression, valorizing Whiteness by adopting standards of beauty that were intentionally devised to debase them. Colorism has conferred wages of lightness on some people of color while extracting an at times severe psychological cost. However, communities of color have also actively resisted colorism, most notably during the "Black is Beautiful" era of the Civil Rights Movement in the 1960s which embraced Afro-centric styles and undermined White beauty norms. Unfortunately,

there is evidence that colorism may become an even more important stratifying factor in the United States, as we are currently undergoing an unprecedented racial transformation.

## A LIGHTER SHADE OF HATE?: THE FUTURE OF U.S. COLORISM AND THE EMERGENCE OF A TRI-RACIAL ORDER

Recently, a number of scholars have contended that in the coming century, the U.S. will experience a fundamental shift in its racial order (Gans 1999, Bonilla-Silva 2006). Similarly, scholars in the assimilation tradition have contended that racial boundaries are increasingly crossed, blurred, and shifted (Alba and Nee 2003). Citing massive immigration from Latin America and Asia coupled with rising intermarriage rates as signs of racial progress, assimilation scholars have adopted a relatively teleological view of race relations. This view sees America in the coming century awakening from its long racial nightmare. For instance, Lee and Bean (2004) argue that rising rates of intermarriage and the growing multiracial population may indicate that boundaries are weakening overall, providing evidence of the declining significance of race for all groups (2004, 203). In contrast, racial pessimists such as Herbert Gans (1999) see a relatively stable structure shifting in the direction of a primarily "Black/non Black" dichotomy. Citing evidence from tri-racial isolates like the Mississippi Chinese (Loewen 1988) or the historic role of the Creoles in New Orleans, Gans argues that this new racial order will be shaped by social class factors, "deserving" and "undeserving," in his terminology.

Perhaps the most promising model of the future of racial stratification is that of Eduardo Bonilla-Silva (See Bonilla-Silva 2004 in this volume). Bonilla-Silva creates a model that synthesizes the findings of the "new racism" (Bobo 2001, Sears and Henrey 2003, Dovidio 2001) school of post-Civil

Rights scholarship (which claims that racism in the post-Civil Rights era has become less overt and harder to detect) with demographic changes to argue that the United States is moving towards a "Latin America like" system of race. Whereas the U.S., for much of its history, has been governed by the "one-drop" racial classification system, Bonilla-Silva contends that Latin-American systems of race function along a continuum, have high levels of racial mixture and an ideology that ties racial mixture to the state (*Mestizaje*), practice Whitening, and are stratified by colorism or "pigmentocracy" (2006, 182). He characterizes this order as "Tri-Racial," composed of Whites at the top, honorary Whites in the middle (serving a buffer function very similar to the middle class in orthodox Marxism), and a collective Black group at the bottom. Like Gans' model, social class factors play a role in which social actors end up in the various racial strata. Bonilla-Silva's model ultimately predicts a racial order that more cunningly hides its abuses.

Despite early, qualified, empirical support for elements of Bonilla-Silva's model (Forman et. al. 2004), it is not without its detractors. In a recent exchange in *Ethnic and Racial Studies,* Christina Sue (2009) criticized the Latin Americanization Thesis (LAT) for placing a strong emphasis on colorism, for a lack of specificity about the relative strength of boundaries between racial groups, and for homogenizing racial systems in Latin America. Sue, however, did agree that Latin American racial orders tend to use nationalist rhetoric as a cover for racial exploitation (for an excellent example of this in Brazil, see Twine 1998). Bonilla-Silva's reply covers several major points; however, for this review, two main points are perhaps most important for assessing how colorism will affect the coming U.S. racial stratification order. First, Bonilla-Silva (2009) argues that in Latin America the practice of "Whitening" as a social policy and ideological project did indeed allow for a more fluid system of

racial classification that was simultaneously harder to see, as the official ideology denied any internal differentiation. Second, building on his work (Bonilla-Silva and Ray 2009), Bonilla-Silva offers a critique of the Obama phenomenon and the use of "deracialization" in his political career, arguing that Obama's post-racial appeal, his downplaying of his Blackness, his "accommodationist stance on race," and his unwillingness to advocate race-based policies "will exacerbate the existing color-class divide within the Black community" (Bonilla-Silva 2009). Recent social psychological evidence does indeed point to the idea that colorism was a factor in supporting Obama, as his supporters were more likely to claim digitally lightened photographs were more representative of the candidate, while his detractors thought darkened photographs were more representative (Caruso et. al. 2009). In the Obama era, it seems colorism may already be having effects on the socio-political order that "one-drop" methodological procedures are unable to uncover.

In conclusion, colorism has had a sordid history in the United States. Despite the longstanding recognition of scholars of color that beyond race, skin tone provides a wage of lightness, the analysis of colorism has not become a standard practice in sociological analyses of race. Recently, several excellent anthologies (Herring et. al. 2004; Glenn 2009) have begun to fill this hole in the literature. As the U.S. moves towards a more plural racial system, analyses that refuse to incorporate measures of colorism may miss the racial boat by aggregating across racial categories that are shifting under our feet.

## ABOUT THE AUTHOR

Victor Ray is an advanced Graduate Student in Sociology at Duke University and a Ford Foundation Diversity Fellow. His research interests include race and ethnicity, stratification, social psychology, and experimental and qualitative methods. His dissertation is focused on racial and gender differences in mental health, labor market, and family outcomes for veterans returning from Iraq and Afghanistan.

## WORKS CITED

Alba, Richard and Victor Nee. 2003. *Remaking the American Mainstream.* Cambridge: Harvard University Press.

Allport, Gordon W. 1954. *The Nature of Prejudice.* Cambridge: Addison-Wesley.

Blair, Irene V., Charles M. Judd, and Kristine M. Chapleau. 2004. "The Influence of Afrocentric Facial Features in Criminal Sentencing." *Psychological Science* 15(10): 674–679.

Blau, Peter and O.D. Duncan. 1967. *The American Occupational Structure.* New York: Wiley.

Bobo, Lawrence. 2001. "Racial Attitudes and Relations at the Close of the Twentieth Century." In Smelser, Neil J., William Julius Wilson, and Faith Mitchell (Eds). 2001. *America Becoming: Racial Trends and Their Consequences.* Washington, D.C.: National Academy Press.

Bonilla-Silva, Eduardo. 2006. *Racism Without Racists: 2nd Edition.* Oxford: Rowman and Littlefield.

Bonilla-Silva, Eduardo. 2009. "Are the Americas 'sick with racism' or is it a problem at the poles? A reply to Christina A. Sue." *Ethnic and Racial Studies* 32 (6): 1071–1082.

Bonilla-Silva, Eduardo and Victor Ray. 2009. "When Whites Love a Black Leader: Race Matters in Obamerica." *Journal of African American Studies* 13(2): 176–183.

Bourdieu, Pierre. 1994. "Social Space and Symbolic Space." In Calhoun, Craig., Joseph Gerteis, James Moody, Steven Pfaff, and Indermohan Virk (Eds). 2007. *Contemporary Sociological Theory: 2nd Ed.* Malden, Maine: Blackwell Publishing.

Browning, James R. 1951. "Anti-Miscegenation Laws in the United States." *Duke Bar Journal* 1: 27–29.

Caruso, Eugene M., Nicole L. Mead, and Emily Balcetis. 2009. "Political Partisanship Influences Perception of Biracial Candidates' Skin Tone." *Proceeding of the National Academy of Science* 106(48): 20168–20173.

Collins, Patricia Hill. 2005. *Black Sexual Politics: African Americans, Gender, and the New Racism.* New York and London: Routledge.

Davis, James F. 1991. *Who is Black:? One Nation's Definition.* University Park: Penn State University Press.

Desmond, Matthew and Mustafa Emirbayer. 2009. "What is Racial Domination?" *Du Bois Review* 6(2): 335–355.

Dovidio, John F. 2001. "On the Nature of Contemporary Prejudice: The Third Wave." *Journal of Social Issues* 57: 829.

Du Bois. "The Talented Tenth." In Washington, Booker T., (ed.) 1903. *The Negro Problem: a Series of Articles by Representative Negroes of Today.* New York: James Pott and Co.

———. 1935. *Black Reconstruction in America, 1860–1880.* New York: The Free Press.

Eberhardt, J. L., V.J. Purdie-Vaughns, P.G. Davies, & S.L. Johnson. 2006. "Looking Deathworthy: Perceived Stereotypicality of Black Defendants Predicts Capital-sentencing Outcomes." *Psychological Science* 17(5): 383–386.

Edwards, Korie, Katrina Carter-Tellison, and Cedric Herring. "For Richer, For Poorer, Whether Dark or Light: Skin Tone, Marital Status, and Spouse's Earnings." In Herring, Cedric, Verna Keith, and Hayward Derrick Horton (Eds). 2004. *Skin Deep: How Race and Complexion Matter in the "Color-Blind" Era.* Urbana and Chicago: University of Illinois Press.

Forman, Tyrone A., Carla Goar, and Amanda Lewis. 2004. "Neither Black nor White? An Empirical Test of the Latin Americanization Thesis." *Race and Society* 5: 65–84.

Frazier, Franklin. E. 1957. *Black Bourgeoisie*. New York: The Free Press.

Gans, Herbert. "The Possibility of a New Racial Hierarchy in the Twenty-First-Century United States." In Lamont, Michele (Ed). 1999. *The Cultural Territories of Race: Black and White Boundaries*. Chicago and London: The University of Chicago Press and the Russell Sage Foundation.

Glenn, Evelyn Nakano. "Consuming Lightness: Segmented Markets and Global Capital in the Skin Whitening Trade." In Glenn, Evelyn Nakano (Ed). 2009. *Shades of Difference: Why Skin Color Matters*. Stanford: Stanford University Press.

Goldsmith, Arthur., Hamilton, Darrick., and Darity, William. 2006. "Shades of Discrimination: Skin Tone and Wages." *The American Economic Review* 96(2) 242–245.

Goldsmith, Arthur, Darrick Hamilton, and William Darity. 2007. "From Dark to Light: Skin Color and Wages Among African Americans." *Journal of Human Resources* XLII (4): 701–738.

Gullickson, Aaron. 2005. "The Significance of Skin Tone Declines: A Re-Analysis of Skin Tone Differentials in Post-Civil Rights America." *Social Forces* 84(1): 157–180.

Harris, Cheryl. "Whitness as Property." In Crenshaw, K., N. Gotanda, G. Peller, and K. Thomas (Eds). 1995. *Critical Race Theory: Key Writings that Formed the Movement*. New York: The New Press.

Harvey, Richard D., Nicole LaBeach, Ellie Pridgen, and Tammy M. Gocial. 2005. "The Intragroup Stigmatization of Skin Tone Among Black Americans." *Journal of Black Psychology* 31(3): 237–253.

Herring, Cedrick. 2004. *Skin Deep: How Race and Complexion Matter in the "Color-Blind" Era*. Urbana and Chicago: University of Illinois Press.

Hersch, Joni. 2005. "Skin-Tone Effects Among African Americans: Perceptions and Reality." *American Economic Review* 96(2): 251–255.

Hill, Mark. 2002a. "Race of the Interviewer and Perception of Skin Color: Evidence from the Multi-City Study of Urban Inequality." *American Sociological Review* 67: 99–108.

——. 2002b. "Skin Color and the Perception of Attractiveness Among African Americans: Does Gender Make a Difference?" *Social Psychology Quarterly* 65(1): 77–91.

Hochschild, Jennifer L., & Vesla Weaver. 2007. "The Skin Color Paradox and the American Racial Order." *Social Forces* 86: 3–28.

Hughes, Michael, and Bradley Hertel. 1990. "The Significance of Color Remains: A Study of Life Chances, Mate Selection, and Ethnic Consciousness Among Black Americans." *Social Forces* 68(4): 1105–20.

Hunter, Margaret. 2002. "'If You're Light You're Alright': Light Skin Color as Social Capital for Women of Color." *Gender and Society* 16(2): 175–193.

——. "Light, Bright, and Almost White: The Advantages and Disadvantages of Light Skin." In Herring, Cedric., Verna Keith, and Hayward Derrick Horton (Eds). 2004. *Skin Deep: How Race and Complexion Matter in the "Color-Blind" Era*. Urbana and Chicago: University of Illinois Press.

Keith, Verna M., and Cedric Herring. 1991. "Skin Tone and Stratification in the Black Community." *American Journal of Sociology* 97(3): 760–78.

Keith, Verna M. "A Colorstruck World: Skin Tone, Achievement, and Self Esteem Among African American Women." In Glenn, Evelyn Nakano (Ed). 2009. *Shades of Difference: Why Skin Color Matters*. Stanford: Stanford University Press.

Lee, Jennifer and Frank D. Bean. 2004. "America's Changing Color Lines: Immigration, Race/Ethnicity, and Multiracial Identification." *Annual Review of Sociology* 30: 221–242.

Loewen, James. 1988. *The Mississippi Chinese: Between Black and White (2nd Edition)*. Cambridge: Harvard University Press.

Mills, Charles M. 1997. *The Racial Contract*. Ithaca: Cornell University Press.

Omi, Michael and Howard Winant. 1994. *Racial Formation in the United States: From the 1960s to the 1990s*. New York: Routledge.

Penner, Andrew and Saperstein, Aliya. 2008. "How Social Status Shapes Race." *Proceedings of the National Academy of Science* 105 (50): 19628–19630.

Roediger, David. 1991. *The Wages of Whiteness: Race and the Making of the Working Class*. New York: Verso.

Russell, Kathy, Midge Wilson, and Ronald Hall. 1993. *The Color Complex: The Politics of Skin Color Among African Americans*. New York: Doubleday.

Sears, David and P. J. Henry. 2003. "The Origins of Symbolic Racism." *Journal of Personality and Social Psychology* 85: 259–75.

Sue, Christina. 2009. "An Assessment of the Latin Americanization Thesis." *Ethnic and Racial Studies* 32(6): 1058–1070.

Takaki, Ronald. 1989. *Strangers from a Different Shore: A History of Asian-Americans*. Boston: Little, Brown and Company.

Thomas, Lynn M. "Skin Lighteners in South Africa: Transnational Entanglements and Technologies of the Self." In Glenn, Evelyn Nakano (Ed). 2009. *Shades of Difference: Why Skin Color Matters*. Stanford: Stanford University Press.

Twine, France Winddance. 1998. *Racism in a Racial Democracy: The Maintenance of White Supremacy in Brazil*. New Brunswick: Rutgers University Press.

Vaid, Jyotsna. 2009. "Fair Enough?: Color and the Commodification of Self in Indian Matrimonials." In Glenn, Evelyn Nakano (Ed). 2009. *Shades of Difference: Why Skin Color Matters*. Stanford: Stanford University Press.

Wilson, William Julius. 1978. *The Declining Significance of Race: Blacks and Changing American Institutions*. Chicago: The University of Chicago Press.

Zuberi, Tukufu. 2001. *Thicker Than Blood: How Racial Statistics Lie*. Minneapolis: University of Minnesota Press.

# CITIZENSHIP, NATIONALISM, AND HUMAN RIGHTS

# CITIZENSHIP, NATIONALISM, AND HUMAN RIGHTS

*By Shiri Noy*

G iven the impact of globalization, interest in nationalism has seen a recent resurgence in the social sciences. Sociologists too have turned their sights toward understanding the way in which people understand and live their national identity. Though the concept of collective identity appears in classic sociological works (Durkheim's "collective conscience," Marx's "class consciousness" and Weber's interpretive sociology) identity formation as part of a group has been "essentialized" (Cerulo 1997: 386). It is only recently that the core sociological concepts of race, class and gender have been problematized in the context of identity formation (Deaux and Martin 2006; Yuki 2003). As a result of this, researchers have become interested in identity at the group level. This speaks to the importance of examining how identity is negotiated at different levels and in different situations, rather than simply ascribing characteristic (essentialist) identities to individuals.

## NATIONALISM AND IDENTITY THEORY

Social identity theory emphasizes group memberships and the importance of context, positions and roles for identity formation and development and differentiates between identities born of interaction and those owing to structural position (Deaux and Martin 2006; Hogg and White 1995; Hogg and Ridgeway 2003; Yuki 2003). A group, according to Stryker (1980) requires interaction between members, whereas a category requires only cognition of commonality or membership (usually based on a shared trait: gender, ethnicity, etc.). This distinction mirrors the difference between social psychologists and macro-sociologists who usually study, respectively, group and category.

Tajfel's (1978) conception of the differentiation between group and category is also distinguished by interaction though he also discusses the role of what may be described as ideology. The reason for social categorization has been debated: people are "cognitive misers," people are sequential (or even simultaneous) "information processors" and cannot take it all in, people wish to "minimize uncertainty," "maximize pleasure and minimize pain" or categorize themselves in order to enhance self-esteem or decrease low self-esteem. For a *group*, on the other hand, all of these motivations are preceded by or concurrent with interaction among individuals. A group of people may have no characteristics or traits in common but may constitute a group through interaction; That is, they have an interactional situation in common (i.e. they take a class together). A *category* of people, however, most often share a trait or characteristic (which may be differentially salient to various members) (i.e., we are women, we are sociologists), the trait, however, may be environmental/spatial (i.e. we are American citizens). Therefore, much like race, ideas of nationalism have a categorical component when aggregated at the level of individual identification.

## PATRIOTISM AND NATIONALISM

While nationalism has its potentially negative and positive effects, some distinguish these by referring the positive as patriotism and the negative as nationalism. Patriotism is positive love of one's own country. It usually entails pride in achievements and culture, desire to preserve the nation's character and the basis of culture, and identification with other members of the nation. By contrast, nationalism is often related to strong ingroup identification via intergroup differentiation, including the view that one's own country is superior to others and thus should be dominant. Because nationalism and patriotism share the feature of positive ingroup evaluation and pride, they are positively correlated both conceptually and empirically. However, patriotism is correlated with internationalism, while nationalism is negatively correlated with internationalism and positively correlated with militarism. Patriotism may also be related to liberalism and tolerance for diversity, but nationalism is more likely to be associated with authoritarian values and intolerance. Still, patriotism and nationalism are often inextricably linked. Generally, as nationalism increases, prejudice attitudes toward immigration also increases. Conversely, as patriotism increases, prejudice attitudes toward immigration decreases (see Li and Brewer 2004).

## CITIZENSHIP AND NATIONALISM

Unlike nationalism, however, citizenship and race have particular political, social and economic repercussions that are often standardized: citizenship is contingent on particular legal norms and similarly, race and ethnicity, in the U.S. and many other countries can and do have legal ramifications manifested in differential rights and opportunities.

Social scientists have long debating not only the meaning of national identity but also its consequences. On the one hand, nationalism creates solidarity among nationals who feel a sense of kinship and responsibility for the national good. On the other hand, like all attachments to group identification, national attachment is often associated with a maligning and derogation of other nations and their citizens (Li and Brewer 2004).

Smith (1991: 9–11) has further parsed out nationalism as being either ethnic and civic, whereby nationalism can be ascribed (ethnic nationalism, with a focus on "a community of birth and native culture … a community of common descent") and civic (a legal and political community with shared institutions—"a predominantly spatial or territorial conception"). In more ethnically homogenous societies we may expect higher levels of nationalism, though in more ethnically heterogeneous societies it is unclear whether we might expect more subnational and/or supra-national identification given this understanding of nationalism.

## NATIONALISM AND ETHNICITY

State-building is a modern enterprise tied inextricably to the development of capitalism and large-scale markets. There is debate, however, as to which came first: nations or nationalism. If nationalism is the result of states, then nationalism is likely to disappear as globalization occurs and states become a less important social entity. Tilly (1997) proposes distinguishing "national state" from "nation-state," where a nation-state consists of people who share a strong identity, language or religion. National states would be those that attempt to integrate populations through direct rule.

Much of our understanding of the research on ethnic conflict is due to the salience of these issues in the global arena after the collapse of communism. More recent claims to nationalism involve groups both within and across nation-states (e.g., Arab and African nationalism, separatism from Canada by Quebec). As Calhoun (1993) notes, the discourse on nationalism is inherently international: an appeal to the established system of states in claims-makings. Interestingly then, the debate about nationalism consists on the one hand of claims that countries have coalesced and moved beyond ethnicity and others, almost diametrically opposed, that the source of countries and their nationalisms are in ancient ethnicities. Thus, ethnicity is used both as an explanation for nationalism and a challenge to it.

## RACE AND CITIZENSHIP IN THE UNITED STATES

In the United States, there is a long history of debate around race and qualifications for citizenship. Disputes in the U.S. have been particularly intense because of the rights accompanying citizenship (Glenn 2003). Since the American Revolution, Native Americans have been considered parts of other "nations," and hence the rights of citizenship did not extend to them for many decades, and in fact, still, are differentially extended to them (Fredrickson 2003). Slavery, an institution that has shaped so much of social relations in the U.S. to this day, treated African slaves as non-persons, in fact, as property (see Zuberi 2001; Drake 1987 in this anthology).

The constitution declares that, "all men are created equal that they are endowed by their Creator with certain inalienable rights; that among these are life, liberty, and the pursuit of happiness." These statements imply equality of all people, regardless of personal attributes, and indeed, citizenship. However, for purposes of representation and taxation, each slave was to be counted as three-fifths of a free person. As Erickson (2003) describes the extension of male suffrage in the 1820s and 1830s was uneven and racist: in some states Blacks with property who had previously possessed the right to vote were disenfranchised at the same time that all White males were made eligible to vote.

In the U.S. though citizenship was not inextricably tied to voting and suffrage, the extension of voting rights to all but Black men was a clear signal that they were lesser than full citizens. The Supreme Court's Dred Scott decision of 1857 declared that free Blacks could not be citizens of the United States. During the civil war, the Dred Scott decision, was overturned along with the abolition of slavery and the enlistment of Blacks, including freed slaves, in the army that was fighting against the Southern secessionists. While military service qualified people for citizenship, emancipation did not, as is evidenced by the status of antebellum "free Negroes." The classical definition of citizenship in a republic was closely associated with militarism. This idea is interestingly related to Benedict Anderson's (2006 [1983]) discussions of nationalism where nation is an "imagined community" aiming to understand an identity that was so important to a person, so ingrained, that they were willing to die for it.

It was only in 1868 with the ratification of the Fourteenth Amendment to the Constitution that national citizenship was clearly broached:

> "All persons born or naturalized in the United States, and subject to the jurisdiction thereof, are citizens of the United States. No State shall make or enforce

any law which shall abridge the privileges and immunities of citizens of the United States; nor shall any State deprive any person of life, liberty and property, without due process of law; nor deny to any person within its jurisdiction the equal protection of the laws."

This amendment was meant to apply only to emancipated slaves, and not to Native Americans, who were parts of different nations outlined under tribe-negotiated treaties. However, this amendment did not seemingly apply to migrants, and was amended in 1870 when Congress altered the immigration laws by extending the right to become naturalized citizens to immigrants of African descent in addition to the previously stipulated "free White persons." As Fredrickson (2003) notes, this addition of Blacks excluded Asians during a time of high Chinese immigration to California during the 1849 Gold Rush. The discrimination and abuse they encountered on the West Coast did not arouse much sympathy in other regions, and consonant with the racialized understandings of the mid-to-late nineteenth century, both Blacks and Chinese were viewed as inferior races as compared to Whites (Lieberson 1980). Fredrickson (2003: 4) notes that the situation of Asians and Blacks, however, were viewed as different "because of their usefulness to the union cause in the Civil War and to the Republican Party during Reconstruction, Blacks were granted a dispensation—a temporary immunity—to state-sponsored prejudice and discrimination. The Chinese could make no such claims on influential segments of White opinion."

Of course despite citizenship being extended to now African Americans, racism continued and was rampant, with Southern states implementing segregation in the 1890s under the guise of "separate but equal." It is important to note that despite ideas of citizens being equal under law, there have been many historical instances in which citizens have been systematically, that is institutionally and legally, treated differently based on race and ethnicity.

Various forces conspired to improve the conditions of Blacks: on the one hand migration of Southern Blacks to the North restored their right to vote and thereby improved their political standing, in addition, World War II and Nazism prompted a shift in academic understandings of race. The Civil rights movement in the 1950s and 1960s was also influenced by the international arena (Williams 1987; Morris 1994): in the context of the Cold War it was important for the U.S. to promote an image which would ensure the support of newly independent colonies in Africa and Asia, for whose support the Soviet Union was also competing (Fredrickson 2003). The Civil Rights act ensured the legal and political rights of citizenship, although many forms of institutional in addition to personal racism remain (Lewis and Pattison 2010 in this anthology). Fredrickson (2003) notes that: "the growth of ethnic consciousness among Blacks and the desire of Latino and Asian immigrants to preserve aspects of their culture have made "multiculturalism," rather than simple integrationism or assimilationism, the dominant anti-racist ideology in the United States today."

## GLOBALIZATION AND NATIONALISM

While much of the discussion around ethnicity and nationalism centers around whether claiming an ethnic identity is a challenge or a reinforcement of nationalism (with evidence that it can act as both) the relationship between globalization and nationalism also implicates ethnicity. Koopmans and Statham (1999) summarize the idea that nation-states are in decline, citing two main causes for this: 1) social organization at the level of the nation-state is being challenged by globalization, namely the transnational and supranational levels; 2) modern societies are increasingly pluralistic, and this pluralism challenges the state's legitimacy and cohesiveness. Groups of people (sometimes citing ethnicity as their unifying favor) are lobbying and claiming for different rights. In addition to the important new forms of organization, of international organizations and other supra-national entities (for example, the European Union), immigration is seen as contributing to the pluralism which is challenging the nation-state. These sets of challenges have prompted theorists to describe the current era as "postnational."

In this line of thinking, international conventions and discourse about human rights and particularly, rights to one's culture and heritage have created and enhanced opportunities for ethnic minorities and migrants to rally for recognition of their rights by the state in which they reside, whether citizens or not. In addition, ethnic communities are increasingly pursuing transnational ties between diasporic communities, which are in turn cultivating strong ties of their home lands (Koopmans and Statham 1999). Postnationalists argue that rights, which are increasingly granted to noncitizens, are a result of migrants successfully making claims for the universal rights of "personhood" and appealing to human rights. In the postnationalist reality, therefore, rights are decoupled from legal identity, which is the main premise of the citizenship.

Migrant and ethnic rights vary cross-nationally, and what it means to be a migrant or part of an ethnic minority group varies vastly across contexts. Indeed, as you have read about in this reader (Drake 1987; Ray 2010), the legal definition of personhood and the accompanying rights and privileges it entails has been widely historically contested. Koopmans and Statham (1999) show how national identity processes are an explanation for assimilation perspectives. They identify three theoretical perspectives on the making of migrants and use

Germany (ethnocultural exclusionist), France (civic assimilationist), and Great Britain (multicultural pluralist) as empirical examples of each perspective. Germany embodies an ethnocultural exclusionist perspective. Thousands of individuals born in Germany are still classified as "foreigners" (Azlslander). Most of these individuals are without full political rights. These practices make it extremely difficult for these individuals to integrate into society. France, on the other hand, represents the civic assimilationist perspective. This perspective generally offers migrants full rights to become citizens. Countries such as France, however, typically encourage a majority-conformity assimilation position by disavowing cultural pluralism. Lastly, Great Britain has a multicultural pluralist regime. Countries that employ this perspective on migrant making offer easy access to citizenship and support for cultural pluralism.

Citizenship, therefore, has been differentially socially constructed (much like race, gender, etc.) differently across national contexts. What it means to be a citizen, and whether and how this is contingent on racial, ethnic and migrant status, varies widely both cross-nationally and historically. In addition, citizenship has an affective dimension, related more to identity than to legal definitions. Nationalism has the potential to act both as a positive and negative affective attachment: on the one hand increasing in-group solidarity and on the other creating animosity towards non-members. Globalization too is changing the ways in which states and people negotiate definitions of personhood, with increased focus on the rights of people by virtue of their humanity rather than citizenship. Overall, much like all other areas of social life, race and ethnic identity systematically pattern who is what (citizenship and nationalism) which in turn affects who gets what (the rights and privileges associated with citizenship). However, these are not unchanging categories and as the discussions of cross-national differences in Europe on the one hand and changing definitions of citizenship in the U.S. on the other demonstrate, they are variable both geographically (across countries) and historically (over time).

## ABOUT THE AUTHOR

Shiri Noy is a doctoral candidate at the department of Sociology at Indiana University, Bloomington. She received her MA in from the IU Sociology department in 2007. Her research interests center around development, social policy and welfare states in Latin America.

**This essay draws heavily from the following recommended readings:**

Anderson, Benedict. 2006 [1983]. *Imagined Communities*. Verso: New York.

Calhoun, Craig. 1993. "Nationalism and Ethnicity." *Annual Review of Sociology* 19: 211–239.

Cerulo, Karen A. 1997. "Identity Construction: New Issues, New Directions." *Annual Review of Sociology* 23: 385–409.

Deaux, Kay and Daniela Martin. 2003. "Interpersonal Networks and Social Categories: Specifying Levels of Context in Identity Processes." *Social Psychology Quarterly* 66: 101–117.

Fredrickson, George M. 2003. "The Historical Construction of Race and Citizenship in the United States." United Nations Research Institute for Social Development (UNRISD). Available at: http://www.unrisd.org/unrisd/website/document.nsf/0/8A0AE7EACD11F278C1256DD6004860EA?OpenDocument

Glenn, Evelyn Nakano. 2000. "Citizenship and Inequality: Historical and Global Perspectives." *Social Problems* 47:1–20.

Hogg, Michael and Cecilia Ridgeway. 2003. "Social Identity: Sociological and Social Psychological Perspectives." *Social Psychology Quarterly* 66:97–100.

Hogg, M.A., D. J. Terry, and K.M. White. 1995. "A Tale of Two Theories: A Critical Comparison of Identity Theory with Social Identity Theory." *Social Psychology Quarterly*, 58: 255–269.

Koopmans, Ruud and Paul Statham. 1999. "Challenging the Liberal Nation-State? Post-nationalism, Multiculturalism and the Collective Claims Making of Migrants and Ethnic Minorities in Britain and Germany." *The American Journal of Sociology* 105: 652–696.

Li, Qiong and Marilynn B. Brewer. 2004. "What Does it Mean to be an American? Patriotism, Nationalism, and American Identity after 9/11." *Political Psychology* 25: 727–739.

Lieberson, Stanley. 1980. *A Piece of the Pie: Blacks and White Immigrants, 1880–1930*. Berkeley and Los Angeles: University of California Press.

Morris, Aldon D. 1994. *The Origins of the Civil Rights Movement: Black Communities Organizing for Change*. New York, NY: Free Press.

Stryker, Sheldon. 1980. *Symbolic Interactionism: A Social Structural Version*. Menlo Park: Benjamin/Cummings.

Tilly, Charles. 1997. "A Primer On Citizenship?" *Theory and Society* 26: 599–602.

Williams, Juan. 1987. *Eyes on the Prize: America's Civil Rights Years, 1954–1965*. New York. Penguin.

Yuki, Masaki. 2003. "Intergroup Comparison versus Intragroup Relationships: A Cross-Cultural Examination of Social Identity Theory in North American and East Asian Cultural Contexts." *Social Psychology Quarterly* 66: 166–183.

# PART 3

THE CUMULATIVE PIPELINE OF PERSISTENT INSTITUTIONAL RACISM

# THE CUMULATIVE PIPELINE OF PERSISTENT INSTITUTIONAL RACISM

*By Rashawn Ray*

Melvin Kohn declares that "a truly sociological social psychology can settle for no less than systematic effort towards understanding the processes by which the major social institutions of any society affect members of that society" (1989: 32). This section of the anthology focuses on how race functions on an institutional level. Neighborhoods, schools, and the labor market are where we spend most of our time. As social institutions, these macro-level structures collectively operate to determine our attitudes, perceptions, and interactions. Below I briefly discuss how institutional conditions shape attitudes and perceptions and determine interactions. Then, I highlight some key empirical findings on neighborhoods and communities, education, and the labor market. Finally, I focus on media as an institution that will continue to grow in importance as Generations X and Y progress through the life course.

## INSTITUTIONAL RACISM, SOCIAL STRUCTURES, AND NORMATIVE INSTITUTIONAL ARRANGEMENTS

As discussed throughout this anthology, racism is a social system that conveys an ideology of inferiority, which is often affiliated with individual- and group-level prejudice and discrimination. Similar to sexism, racism alters social systems and various normative institutional arrangements whereby the entire institution become racialized. This leads to a divergence in various outcomes such as lower educational outcomes (Lewis 2010), lower occupational prestige (Oliver and Shapiro 1995; Bertrand and Mullainathan. 2004), relatively deprived neighborhoods (Sewell 2010), schools, and hospitals, and worse mental and physical health outcomes (Gilbert and Leak 2010). Hunt and colleagues (2000) make a convincing argument that we should not assume that factors operate similarly across racial groups in work, neighborhood, family, and education contexts.

As indicative of the works in this anthology, race functions on three main levels—1) Micro-level through individual, face-to-face interaction; 2) Meso-level through processes, mechanisms, and normative institutional arrangements; and 3) Macro-level through institutions such as education, the criminal justice system, and the health care system. The social structure refers to aspects of the larger social system that are bounded or determinative patterns of social relationships. Social structures and social processes are organized by institutions such as government, communities, and media which are situated in particular mainstream discourses (Becker and McCall 1990). Discourses become apparent via normalized and accepted institutional practices. These discourses are constantly up for discussion and challenged by various groups and normative institutional arrangements.

Normative institutional arrangements are situated in between the micro- and macro-level of analysis and focus on the accepted arrangement of relationships within social institutions. Furthermore, they are boundaries that shape social interactions and establish control over social environments (Ray and Rosow 2009 in this anthology), and one structural mechanism that should be of importance to scholars interested in race and intersectionality research. Normative institutional arrangements identify social contexts whereby certain behaviors are more or less acceptable, certain structures hold individuals more or less accountable for their treatment of others, and attitudes and perceptions may be altered. Such arrangements represent taken-for-granted assumptions that are external, exist outside of individuals, constraining, and enabling.

Here is an example of the influence of normative institutional arrangements. Hagan, Shedd, and Payne (2005) investigate the impact the size of racial groups in educational settings has on youth's perceptions of police contact. They find that there are breach points or cleavages wherein Blacks and Latinos perceive more police contact when the White population at their school is 15–30 percent. These effects start to diminish when the White population is 0 to 15 percent and 30–45 percent. Collectively, these findings highlight the importance of normative institutional arrangements on perceptions. Below I discuss specific institutions and some key dimensions that make them social entities.

## SOCIAL INSTITUTIONS AND IMPORTANT DIMENSIONS OF SOCIAL LIFE

### Neighborhoods and Communities

A neighborhood is a geographically localized community within a city, town or suburb. A community is defined as a group of individuals living in the same locality and under the same government or power structure. Suburbs are generally located on the outskirts of cities. Urban is typically associated with city life or culture such as Washington D.C, Tokyo, Japan, Frankfurt, Germany, or Durban, South Africa. Rural is generally associated with country life or culture. Although Whites live in cities and minorities live in rural areas, these two terms often have racial undertones where urban means minority and rural means White.

Since most countries have different definitions for what classifies as urban or rural, comparisons on a global scale can become convoluted. In the United States, an incorporated city is legally defined as a government entity with powers delegated by the state and county and created and approved by the voters of the city. A neighborhood, on the other hand, is typically an unincorporated community with no governmental powers. In Sweden and Denmark, a village of 200 people is counted as an urban population, but it takes a city of 30,000 to be considered urban in Japan. Most other countries fall somewhere in between. Australia and Canada use a population of 1,000, Israel and France use 2,000 and the United States and Mexico call an area of 2,500 residents urban.

In Sewell's (2010)—"A Different Menu: Racial Residential Segregation and the Persistence of Racial Inequality"—she candidly discusses how a majority of the neighborhoods in the United States and around the world are actually ghettos and a result of institutional forms of apartheid. Apartheid is the policy or practice of political, legal, economic, and/or social discrimination against individuals of a particular group. Apartheid is mostly associated with South Africa. However, Massey and Denton (1993) argue that we are encountering an American Apartheid right here in the United States with ghettos as the central physical marking. Generally, a ghetto is a section of a city occupied by a minority group who live there because of legal and institutional discrimination and/or social and economic pressure. Ghettos are normally formed in three ways: 1) when members of a particularly group voluntarily choose to live with their own group; 2) when the majority group uses compulsory violence, hostility, or legal barriers to force minority group members into particular areas; or 3) when majority group members are willing and/or able to pay more than minority group members to live with their own group and exclude minority group members.

What is so intriguing about the term "ghetto" is just how racialized it has become. "Ghetto" has now transcended its literary definition to be used figuratively to describe how individuals act (e.g., urban, thug-like, hard, Black) or to strictly label the poor geographic areas that have a large proportion of a particular group such as Black or Latino housing projects. Ghettos are often categorized as drug infested, downtrodden, poor, crime-riddled, and Black. The word ghetto was originally used to refer to Venetian neighborhoods in Italy where Jews were forced to live. The term came into widespread use during World War II and primarily referenced Nazi ghettos. In addition to Black and Jewish ghettos, there are "rural ghettos" that refer to Indian reservations as well as mobile home parks and farm housing tracks that are mostly inhabited by Whites. Interestingly, based on the actual definition of ghetto, suburbs that are predominately one race can also be considered ghettos.

According to Massey and Denton (1993), however, only one group has historically and continuously experienced ghettoization—Blacks. Despite what many individuals think, most Blacks did not choose or develop ghettos. Instead as Sewell (2010) highlights, coordinated institutional acts of discrimination and uncoordinated individual acts of discrimination were utilized to facilitate that certain housing markets would be denied to Blacks in order to create spatial segregation. Neighborhood associations were formed to prevent Blacks from moving into certain neighborhoods. These neighborhood associations continuously lobbied law makers to implement zoning restrictions to exclude Blacks. Restrictive covenants were formed that established no entry into certain neighborhoods for Blacks. Restrictive covenants were contractual agreements signed by neighborhood tenants who agree not to sell, rent, lease, or allow certain groups (i.e., Blacks) to occupy property in a particular neighborhood.[*]

Since Blacks were excluded from certain neighborhoods, they were relegated to others. Contrary to ghettos current arrangement, ghettos limited to Blacks had excessively high renter prices. Thus, White real estate companies and agents had an invested interest to create more of these urban ghettos. White real estate agents would go door to door warning Whites of the "Black invasion" so that they could increase prices and rent to needy Blacks (Massey and Denton 1993). This is called

---

[*] The U.S. Supreme Court finally outlawed restrictive covenants in 1948. Still, residential segregation continued around the country on a local level.

redlining. Redlining is the practice of denying or increasing the costs of essential services such as banking, insurance, health care, grocery stores, and public transportation. The term redlining derives from Chicago in the 1960s where banks actually utilized a red line to mark on a map where they would not give out loans to residents or invest in the community.

On the other side of the ghettoization of Blacks, many Whites flocked to the suburbs. This is commonly termed "White flight." White flight is the departure of Whites from places perceived to be populated by minority group members because of the fear that crime will increase, education quality will decrease, and property values will decrease.* Now, gentrification is commencing in many urban areas across the country including Memphis, Los Angeles, Detroit, Philadelphia, and New Orleans. Gentrification is a process in which low-cost, physically deteriorated neighborhoods experience physical renovation and an increase in property values, along with an influx of wealthier residents who typically displace the prior residents.

Patillo (2007) provides a fascinating empirical examination of middle class Blacks who are often situated in neighborhoods and public spaces between working class and poor Black neighborhoods and middle and upper class White neighborhoods. Patillo finds that middle class Blacks act as middlemen between their lower class Black counterparts and the White power structure in Chicago. Unlike a majority of their middle class predecessors, Patillo contends that many middle class Blacks have the ability to influence power structures to direct resources toward under-funded areas. Considering that sociological research frequently classifies Blacks as a monolithic group, Patillo's research is

important in that it highlights mechanisms that draw attention to the heterogeneity of Blacks.

### Education

As Lewis and Pattison (2010) discuss, education has always been viewed as the "great equalizer." People think that education can solve most of the issues related to racial inequality. This is because most people actually believe that schools are equal and that students are "good" and "bad" instead of schools being "good" and "bad."

Kozol (1991) shows that there are actually "bad" schools, a fact that continues to go under-emphasized. He masterfully documents the woes of inner-city schools in East St. Louis, Missouri, Chicago, Illinois, New York City, New York, Camden, New Jersey, Washington, D.C. and San Antonio, Texas. Kozol paints a portrait of inner-city life as dilapidated, under-funded, under-staffed, under-resourced, overcrowded, and unsanitary. On the other hand, suburban and/or county schools typically have an abundance of resources including a low teacher-student ratio, computers, media stations, and up-to-date science equipment. These schools typically have at least twice as much funding as the schools described in Kozol's study. Due to significant inequalities that result from an unequal distribution of funds for school, which are collected primarily from property taxes, Kozol (2005) argues that schools are placed on unequal grounds that generally fall along racial lines. Kozol (2005) argues that school funding is the primary reason for racial differences in academic achievement. In addition to what I discuss above, Lewis and Pattison (2010) draw attention to the implications racial inequality has for the Black/White achievement gap and perceptions of reasons for this gap historically and currently.

---

* *Why Can't We Live Together* is a good documentary illuminating White flight and its implications and consequences.

## The Labor Market,
## Socioeconomic Status, and Wealth

Scholars in the 1970s predicted that Blacks would finally flourish and begin to assimilate into the middle class (Wilson 1978). However, many of these predictions became null and void in the 1980s. Some scholars argue the influx of crack cocaine and the culture of poverty are reasons why Blacks seem to be lagging behind educationally and economically. Conversely, Oliver and Shapiro (1995) document how President Reagan's policy agenda increased inequality in the 1980s. Similar policies in the George W. Bush administration reduced Clinton's strides of the 1990s and have widened the economic gap among young adults in America. Oliver and Shapiro display that wealth is primarily located in the intergenerational transmission of family wealth and investments. This accumulation of wealth, however, is highly structured by race. Since homes in predominately Black neighborhoods are often under-appreciated and deemed a lower standard than homes in predominately White communities, most Blacks do not have wealth comparable to their White counterparts. As a result, Black families and Black communities have incurred a significant loss of wealth over time.

So why is wealth more important than income for determining racial inequality? Wealth highlights patterns of inequality that go unnoticed by income (Conley 2000). Blacks and Whites face different structures of investment opportunities that have historical and contemporary implications for the intersections of race and class (Massey and Denton 1993; Oliver and Shapiro 1995; Sewell 2010). Through the Sociology of Wealth, Oliver and Shapiro display how social interactions and life outcomes establish a unique set of social circumstances that structure racial inequality.

The Sociology of Wealth includes three main concepts including the "racialization of state policy," "economic detour," and the "sedimentation of racial inequality." The "racialization of state policy" refers to how state policies impair the ability for many Blacks to accumulate wealth. Oliver and Shapiro argue that this racialization can be traced from slavery up to the present and reportedly cost the current generation of Blacks an estimated $82 Billion. The next generation of Blacks is estimated to be behind Whites by $93 Billion in wealth accumulation. Second, "economic detour" highlights the law restrictions that prevented Blacks from navigating the economic open market. This resulted in less business ownership among Blacks. Third, the "sedimentation of racial inequality" highlights the cumulative effects Blacks have faced in social institutions including lower wages in the labor market, poorer schools (Lewis and Pattison 2010), and neighborhood segregation (Sewell 2010). Over time, this sedimentation becomes ingrained in the social structure. Oliver and Shapiro contend that a racial wage tax has accumulated and established two different worlds among middle class Whites and middle class Blacks.

Below, I present statistics to further illuminate the inequalities in the labor market, socioeconomic status, and wealth. A White applicant in the lowest income bracket was more likely to get a mortgage loan than a Black applicant in the highest income bracket. Blacks in the highest income bracket, compared to Whites in the highest income bracket, were denied mortgage loans three times as often. Under-qualified White women are three times more likely than over-qualified Black women to get a job. For every dollar owned by the White middle class, the Black middle class only owns 15 cents. Put another way, for every $100 owned by Whites, Blacks only own $8-$19 (see Oliver and Shapiro 1995). As Bertrand and Mullainathan (2004) show in this anthology, individuals with Black sounding names are 50 percent less likely than those with White sounding names to get a job. As a final note, Pager's (2004) study in this anthology is always a compelling case. Using interactive field experiments, Pager (2003) explores discrimination against minorities and ex-offenders in a low-wage market. She finds that a racial advantage is given to White applicants with a criminal record over Black applicants without a criminal record. Not only do Whites without a criminal record get hired more than Blacks, but Whites with a criminal record get hired more than Blacks without a criminal record.

## Mass Media

Due to the influx of the internet and its entities such as YouTube, Facebook, MySpace, and Twitter, most individuals believe that they actually have good interpretations of social life and various racial groups. Stein (1983: 285) refers to media as "a variety of modes by which senders can record information and/or experiences and transmit them to a large audience fairly rapidly." Forms of media include film, TV, internet, radio, newspapers, magazines, and books. Much of the media, however, is simply a competing curriculum for reality. Professional communicators are frequently overshadowed by amateur communicators on YouTube, blogs, and the like. In the virtual world, the media market can be so saturated that the professional communicators whose main goal is surveillance and reporting go unnoticed. In this regard, I believe that scholars and educators have the ability to show the distinctions between professional and amateur communicators and inform students about how to seek accurate portraits of social life.

There needs to be more research on the implications that modes of mass media have on attitudes and perceptions. Future research can focus on how blogs translate into racial attitudes and have consequences for prejudice and discriminatory behavior. On the other hand, the internet may have under-emphasized qualities that can decrease forms of prejudice.

## SUPPLEMENTAL READINGS AND RESOURCES

Becker, Howard and Michael McCall. 1990. *Symbolic Interaction and Cultural Studies*. Chicago: University of Chicago Press.

Bobo, Lawrence D. and Victor Thompson. 2006. "Unfair by Design: The War on Drugs, Race, and the Legitimacy of the Criminal Justice System." *Social Research* 73: 445–472.

Bowser, Rene. 2001. "Racial Profiling in Health Care: an Institutional Analysis of Medical Treatment Disparities." *Michigan Journal of Race and Law* 7: 79–133.

Browne-Marshall, Gloria. 2007. *Race, Law, and American Society: 1607 to Present*. Routledge.

Conley, Dalton. 2000. "40 Acres and a Mule: The Black-White Wealth Gap in America." *National Forum* 80: 21–24.

Cummings, Jason L and Pamela Braboy Jackson. 2007. "Race, Gender, and SES Disparities in Self-Assessed Health, 1974–2004." *Research on Aging* 30: 137–168.

Engel, Kathleen C. and Patricia A. McCoy. 2008. "From Credit Denial to Predatory Lending: The Challenge of Sustaining Minority Home Ownership." In *Segregation: The Rising Costs for America* (Eds.). James H. Carr, Nandinee K. Kutty. Routledge.

Farley, John E. and Gregory D. Squires. 2005. "Fences and Neighbors: Segregation in 21st Century America." *Contexts* 4: 33-39.

Feagin, Joe R. and Bernice McNair Barnett. 2004. "Success and Failure: How Systematic Racism Trumped the Brown v. Board of Education Decision." *University of Illinois Law Review*. 1099–1130.

Feagin, Joe R. and Karyn D. McKinney. 2003. "The Physical Health Consequences of Racism." Pps. 65–93 in *The Many Costs of White Racism*. Oxford: Rowman and Littlefield Publishers.

Hagan, John, Carla Shedd, and Monique R. Payne. 2005. "Race, Ethnicity, and Youth Perceptions of Criminal Injustice." *American Sociological Review* 70: 381–407.

Hoberman, John. 1997. *Darwin's Athletes: How Sport has Damaged Black America and Preserved the Myth of Race.* New York: Houghton Mifflin.

Jackson, Pamela Braboy and Jason L. Cummings. 2009. "The Health of the Black Middle Class." In *The Handbook of the Sociology of Health, Illness, & Healing: Blueprint for the 21st Century.* (Eds.). Bernice Pescosolido, Jack Martin, Jane McLeod, and Anne Rogers. NewYork: Springer Publishers.

Kozol, Jonathon. 1991. *Savage Inequalities.* New York: HarperCollins.

Kozol, Jonathan. 2005. "Still Separate, Still Unequal: America's Educational Apartheid." *Harper's Magazine.*

Massey, Douglas and Nancy Denton. 1993. *American Apartheid: Segregation and the Making of the Underclass.* Harvard University Press.

McCall, Leslie. 2001. "Sources of Racial Wage Inequality in Metropolitan Labor Markets: Racial, Ethnic, and Gender Differences," *American Sociological Review* 66: 520–541.

Orfield, Gary and Chungmei Lee. 2004. "Brown At 50: King's Dream Or Plessy's Nightmare?" *The Civil Rights Project: Harvard University.*

Stein, Gloria. 1983. "The Effective Use of Mass Media in Sociology Education: Confronting the Competing Curriculum." *Teaching Sociology.*

Tashiro, Cathy. 2005. "The Meaning of Race in Health Care and Research." *Pediatric Nursing* 31, 3/4: 208–210, 305–308.

Tatum, Beverly. 2003. *Why Are All the Black Kids Sitting Together in the Cafeteria*

# INDIVIDUAL AND STRUCTURAL RACISM

# ◻◼◼ A DIFFERENT MENU

## RACIAL RESIDENTIAL SEGREGATION AND THE PERSISTENCE OF RACIAL INEQUALITY

*By Abigail A. Sewell*

"A racially segregated society cannot be a race-blind society ..."
—Douglas S. Massey and Nancy A. Denton

In *American Apartheid*, Massey and Denton (1993) highlight the fundamental role that racial residential segregation plays in curtailing the individual and familial well-being of Blacks in the U.S. Residential segregation refers to the spatial differentiation and composition of two or more population groups (as determined by race/ethnicity, social class, sex, or age classifications) across neighborhoods of a metropolitan area (Acevedo-Garcia, Lochner, Osypuk, and Subramanian 2003). Five geographical patterns characterize residential segregation—*dissimilarity* (the evenness of groups across neighborhoods of an urban area), *isolation* (the probability of exposure/contact of one group to another within neighborhoods), *clustering* (the extent to which neighborhoods dominated by one group are contiguous to each other, or "ghettoized"), *centralization* (the proximity of one group to the central city of an urban area), and *concentration* (the population density of one group in an urban area relative to the population density of other groups) (Massey and Denton 1988).

Racial residential segregation circumscribes the life chances and opportunities of large groups of people sharing a specific location in the racial hierarchy (Massey and Denton 1993). As such, racial residential segregation represents a source of racial inequality that is not strictly rooted within the individual. By isolating people of color from Whites, residential segregation creates geographically-bounded collectivities of disadvantaged people and places based solely on the ascribed social status of race. To understand how neighborhood and community resources and processes create and reinforce racial inequality, the role of racial residential segregation in shaping individual outcomes must be considered.

Metaphorically, racial residential segregation ensures that members of each race will have different menus of life options. Of course, some options may overlap. Yet, the menus provided to different racial groups contrast not only in the type of options available, but also in the quantity of options available; the price of select options; the amount of detail provided about each menu option; and, even more important, whether options are *a la* carte—completely chosen by the guest—or *table d'hôte*—already pre-packaged by the restaurant. Likewise, racial residential segregation creates and perpetuates racial inequality by dictating not only the life chances and opportunities of socially-constructed racial groups, but also the *sheer variety* of those life chances and opportunities, the *personal sacrifices* racial group members must make to capitalize on the opportunities available to them, the *information available* to racial group members about navigating specific life options, and the *flexibility* racial group members have in selecting specific opportunity structures.

Using the U.S. as an example, this chapter will explore the ways that racial residential segregation creates and perpetuates racial inequality. First, an overview of the historical construction of racially segregated neighborhoods will be provided by attending to the system level structures and processes that produce neighborhoods of disadvantage. Second, a critical examination of the social forces accompanying the decline in racial residential segregation will be outlined. The chapter will conclude by considering the implications of racial residential segregation for persistent racial inequalities in developmental outcomes.

## THE RISE OF RACIAL RESIDENTIAL SEGREGATION IN THE U.S.

The spatial isolation of Blacks from Whites in American cities, particularly central cities, represents the most extensive and persistent form of racial residential segregation in the United States (Massey and Denton 1993; Iceland, Weinberg, and Steinmetz 2002). The remainder of this section will focus on the historical processes undergirding the rise of Black-White residential segregation through the 1970s. Although racial stratification is sewn into the fiber of American social life and American social institutions, Blacks and Whites have not always lived isolated from each other. From the first U.S. census in 1790 to the census of 1910, approximately ninety percent of Blacks lived in southern states (U.S. Bureau of the Census 1918). After the Civil War, movement out of the South was slow for Blacks and driven primarily by the economic opportunities presented by Northern employers seeking to break strikes and maintain low wages (Farley 1970). Although the regional clustering of Blacks could be conceived as a sort of racial residential segregation, Whites and Blacks within the southern states and elsewhere in urban areas lived in close proximity to each other (Farley and Allen 1987).

Black urbanization, however, increased rapidly after the Civil War. As a symbolic application of their newfound freedom, Blacks left plantations for southern cities and gravitated toward Union Army camps and areas with Freedman Bureau's (Farley 1970). In the North and West, Blacks comprised more than 3 of 5 urban residents at least as early as 1890. Yet, in the South, only one of five urban residents were Black at the start of World War I. Black enclaves of both regions, however, did not resemble modern urban slums; instead, they covered only a small physical area and were surrounded completely by residences occupied by Whites (Bracey, Meier, and Rudwick 1971). Aside from those Black domestics who lived in the houses of wealthy Whites, Blacks dwelled in poorer quality housing structures situated in the least desirable areas (e.g., predominately White working-class neighborhoods).

Residential intermingling decreased steadily after the Civil War. By the close of the nineteenth century, southern cities began to take on a form of racial residential segregation familiar to that of the twentieth century (Bracey, Meier, and Rudwick 1971). Developers created "darktowns" for Blacks in bad drainage areas; the physical areas concentrated with Blacks grew in size; and the environmental barriers provided by such physical features as railroad tracks, graveyards, and streaming water curtailed Black settlers from venturing into White neighborhoods. In the North, racial residential segregation of the kind observed by Du Bois (1899) in Philadelphia's Seventh Ward also became increasingly familiar

Yet, it was the heavy outmigration of Blacks from the rural South to the cities of the South, North, and West that formally set in motion the ghettoization of blacks witnessed today. Stimulated by the devastating impact of boll weevil infestation on the South's cotton industry and the increased demand for labor in the North's steel, railroad, and manufacturing industries that was unmet by European immigration, over 1.4 million Blacks left the South between 1910 and 1930 during The First Great Migration. As the need for Black labor in the southern agricultural economy decreased after World War II,[*] Black migrants entered urban cities in even more dramatic numbers during the Second Great Migration (Fligstein 1981). In each of the three decades after the onset of World War II, the South lost well over a tenth of its Black population—that is, nearly 5 million southern Blacks migrated to other regions of the U.S. (Farley and Allen 1987).

In urban areas, the isolation of recently-immigrated European ethnics from American Whites steadily declined after 1910, while the isolation of Blacks from Whites increased (Lieberson 1980). As nearly 5 million Blacks entered the urban cities of the North, South, and West, diverse tactics were deployed to confine Blacks to specific areas of the city. For instance, local governments sanctioned restrictive covenants legally prescribing White residents and real estate organizations to not sell or rent to Black settlers (Long and Johnson 1947). In the private realm, real estate agents employed "block busting" to turnover White neighborhoods at the periphery of Black slums while making a substantial profit (Yinger 1995). The block busting process consisted of two symbiotic parts. By stoking fears of neighborhood decline should Blacks settle into White neighborhoods, real estate agents first created panic among White homeowners who were then eagerly willing to sell their homes. Agents would then buy these homes at cheap prices from White families and sell them at competitive prices to Black families willing to pay top price for neighborhoods they perceived were safer than the slums from which they moved.

As the number of Blacks increased in urban areas of the North, tactics were also deployed to deter Blacks from making a meaningful wage. Many labor unions disallowed Blacks from becoming members; and tacit agreements by managers and workers created employment ghettos for Blacks in domestic service and other highly-stigmatized occupations (Farley and Allen 1987). Race riots and racially-motivated "hate strikes" broke out as Blacks struggled to take advantage of the residential and employment opportunities of the newly-settled urban areas and Whites struggled to maintain exclusive access to desirable neighborhoods and jobs (Chicago Commission on Race Relations 1922; Norwood 1997; Roediger 1994; Pattillo 2007; Shogan and Craig 1964). Race riots were also more likely to occur in cities where Blacks did not comprise a substantial portion of the police force and in

[*]   For instance, the number of Black farmers peaked in 1920—when approximately half of American Blacks resided on farms (Farley and Allen 1987). Fifty years later only 4 percent of American Blacks resided on farms. Both economic and institutional factors served to reduce the need for Black farmers. The price of cotton, sugar, and tobacco fell sharply during the late 1920s and early 1930s, and the federal price support provided by the New Deal's Agricultural Adjustment Act benefited the mostly White landowners, but not the mostly Black sharecroppers, tenant farmers, or farm laborers.

cities were city councilmen were less responsive to their constituents (Lieberson and Silverman 1965).

In multiple ways, federal policy also contributed to increasing racial residential segregation through the 60s. First, the boom in suburban residential construction after World War II was funded primarily by subsidies for building single-family tract homes and tax breaks to businesses relocating to the suburbs (Oliver and Shapiro [1995] 2006). The construction of the freeway, federal subsidization of readily-available fuel, and the mass production of automobiles led to a loss of easily-accessible jobs in central cities and virtually ensured the outmigration of Whites to wealth-accumulating suburban tract homes.

Second, the evaluation of racially-mixed and predominately Black communities as unsafe investments for banks originated in the standardization procedures of two institutional components of the federal government (Jackson 1985; Massey and Denton 1993). The Home Owners Loan Corporation (HOLC), created by the Home Owners Loan Act of 1933, systematically included the current or potential racial composition of a community as a factor in the evaluated security risk of properties (Crossney and Bartelt 2005). The Federal Housing Authority, created by the National Housing Act of 1934, employed underwriting manuals in the late 30s that explicitly disfavored the racial integration of neighborhoods and schools (Squires 1994).

Third, the federally-funded and locally-instituted Public Housing Program led to the development of high-density apartment buildings with income limitations that catered to the very poor—buildings disproportionately located in predominately Black neighborhoods and away from the employment opportunities of the suburbs (Schill and Wachter 1995). The inefficient maintenance and management of public housing by local authorities eventually led to vandalism, systemic vacancies, and falling property values in surrounding communities. Together, the aforementioned federal policies and institutions contributed to widespread increases in racial residential segregation into the 70s and a deepened economic divide between Blacks and Whites (Massey and Denton 1993; Oliver and Shapiro [1995] 2006; Wilson 1996).

## THE DECLINE OF RACIAL RESIDENTIAL SEGREGATION IN THE U.S.

Since the 70s, levels of Black-White residential segregation have declined steadily although incrementally (Cutler, Glaeser, and Vigdor 1999). At the onset of the twenty first century, the segregation of Blacks from nonblacks was the lowest it has been since the World War I era (Glaeser and Vigdor 2001). However, not all American cities are experiencing steady declines: Cities of the West and South are more integrated than those of the North and Midwest and the largest metropolitan areas have experienced slower rates of decline or no decline at all over the last 40 years. Further, the residential desegregation of Blacks and Whites during the 90s was most likely to occur in cities experiencing heavy population growth and in cities with changing Black populations (either declining or increasing). Thus, Black-White segregation declined in areas where Black populations previously had been small rather than in areas with medium-to-large Black populations and previously high levels of segregation (Logan, Stults, and Farley 2004).

These patterns suggest that the claws of the aforementioned early twentieth century segregation processes may be weakening; however, at least four concerns remain. First, the decline of Black-White segregation is primarily the result of the mobility patterns of Blacks moving into entirely White tracts, rather than the mobility patterns of Whites moving into racially-mixed or predominately Black tracts (Glaeser and Vigdor 2001). Studies show that while Blacks on average prefer to live in neighborhoods that are 50 percent Black, Whites on average prefer to live in neighborhoods that are 0 to 30 percent Black (Farley and Squires 2005). While Blacks' residential preferences may play some role in persistent racial residential segregation, Whites' residential preferences for largely White neighborhoods *and* their ability to avoid Black neighbors (but less so Asian or Hispanic neighbors) curtails the impact of public policies motivating integration (Quillian 2004).

Second, studies show that Black interregional movers are most likely to be young, highly educated, and female (Hunt, Hunt, and Faulk 2008). However, the poor, unskilled, inner-city residents of hypersegregated urban epicenters remain isolated from quality schools, gainful employment, and healthy environments essential for mobility and self-sufficiency in a postindustrial economy (Wilson 1987, 1996). Despite overall decreases in Black-White residential segregation and minimal population growth for Blacks or Whites since the 70s, the absolute number of Black children and Black households living in poverty increased; the proportion of Blacks living in neighborhoods of concentrated poverty increased; and the number of urban census tracts concentrated with poverty increased (Jargowsky 1994, 1997; Jargowsky and Bane 1990). Over this period, other forms of disadvantage, such as high percentages of single-parent families with children, homicide rates, and joblessness, increasingly clustered into areas that were disproportionately poor and Black (Gephart 1997). Further, income does not necessarily enable Blacks to move out of Black ghettos—middle class and affluent Blacks live in closer proximity to disadvantage than comparable Whites (Jargowsky and Bane 1990; Pattillo 1999).

Third, the clustering of economic and social forms of disadvantage is fostered by the decline of institutional development in racially segregated neighborhoods. The most important source of institutional decline has been the loss of gainful employment opportunities. Since the 70s, joblessness in segregated poor Black neighborhoods has increased profoundly—two of three adults in such areas in Chicago did not hold a job in a typical week of the year (Wilson 1996). No one culprit is responsible for this pattern. The movement of mass production industries to the suburbs, the decline of employment opportunities and occupational mobility for low-skilled workers in the U.S. economy, the reduction of U.S. exports to other parts of the globe, the weakening of the labor movement, and the rising necessity and costs of education and training have contributed to lower wages and less job security for the working poor and fewer jobs and more spells of unemployment for low-skilled workers.

A second source of institutional decline has been public and private economic disinvestment in predominately Black and predominately poor communities. As local municipalities redirected resources from the most impoverished and racially segregated areas and zoning policies and planning commissions targeted poor and Black communities as appropriate locations for waste-disposal sites, urban infrastructures deteriorated (Bullard 1993). Disinvestment in poor, Black, and poor Black communities has led to a decline in the quality of the inner city's housing stock, public buildings, recreational areas and facilities, water supply and waste removal systems.

Stereotyping Blacks as un-creditworthy and Black neighborhoods as unsafe investments ensures that banks resist providing loans not only to Blacks wishing to become homeowners and business owners, but also to persons wishing to start businesses and renovate building structures in predominately Black or racially-mixed neighborhoods (Massey and Denton 1993). Audit studies indicate that Blacks and Hispanics seeking rentals and homes to own face discriminatory real estate agents and landlords approximately half of the time and that acts of discrimination are subtle, continue to steer Blacks from White neighborhoods, and have not declined in frequency across time (Galster 1992; Yinger 1995). Upon obtaining loans, Whites are offered more flexibility in choosing a loan product, higher loan limits, and more affordable insurance policies than are Blacks (Farley and Squires 2005). Even among equally qualified mortgage applicants, Blacks are more likely to have their loan rejected than are Whites.

Fourth and last, the segregation levels of other racial/ethnic groups from Whites, while moderate compared to those of Blacks, has increased since the 70s. Asians, Pacific Islanders, and Hispanics are less evenly distributed across cities than Whites and are more clustered within large contiguous ethnic enclaves than Whites (Iceland, Weinberg, and Steinmetz 2002). Yet, within neighborhoods, they are increasingly more likely to have contact with white neighbors (Charles 2003). In part, these patterns result from changes in immigration policies during the 60s that have facilitated an influx of immigrants from Asia and Latin America (Frey and Farley 1996; Massey and Denton 1987). For example, Hispanic immigrants, particularly Mexican immigrants, experience less success integrating into White neighborhoods than do Hispanic natives (South, Crowder, and Pais 2008)—a pattern that may reinforce future Hispanic-White residential segregation levels as immigration levels increase. Scholars suggest that the rise in immigrant-native segregation during the last half of the twentieth century is bolstered by the racial, economic, and linguistic distinctiveness of recent immigrants, the suburbanization of second and higher generation Americans, and the rise of the automobile as the primary mode of U.S. transportation (Cutler, Glaeser, and Vigdor 2008).

## IMPLICATIONS OF RACIAL RESIDENTIAL SEGREGATION

Racial residential segregation undermines the familial and individual well-being of racially marginalized populations. First, segregation diminishes the potential for and benefits of home ownership—the major source of most Americans' wealth (Charles 2003). Blacks and Hispanics are less likely to own their place of residence and buy homes at higher prices, with less equity, and in poorer quality than similar Whites. Due to their lessened ability to accumulate mortgage equity and occupational wealth, Blacks are also less likely to maintain their class status and transfer wealth to younger generations (Oliver and Shapiro [1995] 2006).

Second, racial residential segregation presents members of different racial groups with different opportunity structures. Opportunity structures (Cloward and Ohlin 1960) are comprised of institutions, social processes, and built environments that shape the character of neighborhood processes—that is, the formal opportunities and constraints, dangers, informal networks, and strains available to residents within a geographical area (Brooks-Gunn, Duncan, and Aber 1997). Neighborhood processes, in turn, influence the responses of individuals, families, and communities to neighborhood conditions created by institutional, social, and environmental opportunity structures.

Third, racial residential segregation weakens the ability of income to protect Black and Hispanic families from the developmental consequences of concentrated disadvantage, violence, physical dilapidation, institutional deficits, and poor quality schools (Charles 2003; Massey and Denton 1993). Blacks, regardless of income, face longer, more morbid lives, poorer educational outcomes, and less occupational mobility than even the most disadvantaged Whites (Blau 2002; Oliver and Shapiro [1995] 2006; Williams and Collins 2000). The spatial expansion of concentrated disadvantage ensures that middle class and affluent Blacks and Hispanics will continue to experience the spillover effect of poor slums and hypersegregated ghettos (Morenoff and Sampson 1997; Pattillo 1999).

Within the U.S., residential segregation does not only characterize the lives of Blacks: Native Americans, Latino/as, Asians, and Pacific Islanders also experience substantial residential isolation from Whites due to forced resettlement policies and contemporary immigration trends. Also, the presence of racial residential segregation is not unique to the American context. Instead, the partitioning of people by race and other aspects of racial stratification, such as ethnicity, skin color, and concentrated disadvantage, has been well-documented across the globe.* Further, urban sprawl, gentrification, and the decline of the manufacturing industry has ushered the spread of slums and ethnic ghettos from central cities into rural and suburban areas.

Academic and policy discussions of racial inequality cannot accurately assess the role of race in contemporary America without fully understanding the historic and contemporary processes undergirding and accompanying racial residential segregation. Neighborhoods comprise a basic setting by which one comes to understand the norms and complexities of society, as neighborhoods structure and constrain the content and availability of one's networks. Due to high levels of segregation in neighborhoods, schools, work, and interpersonal relationships, most Americans do not establish close relationships or engage in regular face-to-face interaction with persons of other races. Racial inequality remains a pernicious force in America precisely because we do not *see* and *engage* people of other races. As an invisible and perceivably blameless background force, racial residential segregation plays a substantial role in maintaining both social distance among members of different racial groups and extensive inequality between races occupying the American social hierarchy.

## ABOUT THE AUTHOR

Abigail A. Sewell is a doctoral candidate in the Department of Sociology at Indiana University. She is also a NSF Graduate Research Fellow, a Ford Foundation Predoctoral Fellow, and a Ronald E. McNair Scholar. Her areas of interest include medical sociology, social psychology, race, and quantitative research methods. Her past projects have examined the role of race in the experience and expression of anger, the development of distrust in medicine and physicians, and the health of black male youth. Research from these projects has been published in the *Journal of Undergraduate Research* and the *Journal of Negro Education* and has received multiple paper awards. Her current projects focus on the health consequences of institutional discrimination in the health care system and changes over time in Blacks' and Whites' attitudes toward the morality and tolerance of homosexuality.

## BIBLIOGRAPHY

Acevedo-Garcia, Dolores, Kimberly A. Lochner, Theresa L. Osypuk, and S. V. Subramanian. 2003. "Future Directions in Residential Segregation and Health Research: A Multilevel Approach." *Am J Public Health* 93: 215–221.

Beinart, William and Saul Dubow. 1995. *Segregation and Apartheid in Twentieth-Century South Africa.* London; New York: Routledge.

Blau, Judith R. 2003. *Race in the Schools: Perpetuating White Dominance?* Boulder, Colo.: Lynne Rienner Publishers.

---

* See research on the residential segregation of racial and ethnic minorities in Brazil (Telles 1992), South Africa (Beinart and Dubow 1995; Christopher 1994), and the U.K. (Phillips 1998; Small 1994).

Bracey, John H., August Meier, and Elliott M. Rudwick. 1971. *The Rise of the Ghetto*. Belmont, Calif.,: Wadsworth Pub. Co.

Brooks-Gunn, Jeanne, Greg J. Duncan, and J. Lawrence Aber. 1997. *Neighborhood Poverty: Contexts and Consequences for Children*, Vol. 1. New York: Russell Sage Foundation.

Bullard, Robert D. 1993. *Confronting Environmental Racism: Voices from the Grassroots*. Boston, Mass.: South End Press.

Charles, Camille Zubrinsky. 2003. "The Dynamics of Racial Residential Segregation." *Annual Review of Sociology* 29:167–207.

Chicago Commission on Race Relations. 1922. *The Negro in Chicago: A Study of Race Relations and a Race Riot*. Chicago, Ill.,: The University of Chicago Press.

Christopher, A. J. 1994. *The Atlas of Apartheid*. New York: London; Johannesburg: South Africa: Routledge; Witwatersrand University Press.

Cloward, Richard A. and Lloyd E. Ohlin. 1960. *Delinquency and Opportunity: A Theory of Delinquent Gangs*. Glencoe, Ill.,: Free Press.

Crossney, KB and DW Bartelt. 2005. "The Legacy of the Home Owners' Loan Corporation." *Housing Policy Debate* 16: 547–574.

Cutler, David M., Edward L. Glaeser, and Jacob L. Vigdor. 1999. "The Rise and Decline of the American Ghetto." *Journal of Political Economy* 107: 455–506.

Cutler, David M., Edward L. Glaeser, and Jacob L. Vigdor. 2008. "Is the Melting Pot Still Hot? Explaining the Resurgence of Immigrant Segregation." *Review of Economics and Statistics* 90: 478–497.

Du Bois, W. E. B. and Isabel Eaton. 1899. *The Philadelphia Negro: A Social Study*. Philadelphia, PA: University of Pennsylvania.

Farley, John E. and Gregory D. Squires. 2005. "Fences and Neighbors: Segregation in 21st-Century America." *Contexts* 4:33-39.

Farley, Reynolds. 1970. *Growth of the Black Ppopulation: A Study of Demographic Trends*. Chicago, IL: Markham Pub. Co.

Farley, Reynolds and Walter R. Allen. 1987. *The Color Line and the Quality of Life in America*. New York: Russell Sage Foundation.

Fligstein, Neil. 1981. *Going North, Migration of Blacks and Whites from the South, 1900-1950*. New York: Academic Press.

Fong, Eric. 1996. "A Comparative Perspective on Racial Residential Segregation: American and Canadian Experiences." *The Sociological Quarterly* 37: 199–226.

Frey, William H. and Reynolds Farley. 1996. "Latino, Asian, and Black Segregation in US Metropolitan Areas: Are Multiethnic Metros Different?" *Demography* 33: 35–50.

Galster, GC. 1992. "Research on Discrimination in Housing and Mortgage Markets: Assessment and Future Directions." *Housing Policy Debate* 3:639-683.

Gephart, Martha A. 1997. "Neighborhoods and Communities as Contexts for Development." Pp. 1–43 in *Neighborhood Poverty: Contexts and Consequences for Children*, vol. 1, edited by J. Brooks-Gunn, G. J. Duncan, and J. L. Aber. New York: Russell Sage Foundation.

Glaeser, EL and JL Vigdor. 2001. "Racial Segregation in the 2000 census: Promising News." *Center on Urban and Metropolitan Policy,* The Brookings Institution, Wahsington, D.C. (available at http://www. brook. edu/es/urban/census/glaeser. pdf accessed on March 7, 2007).

Hunt, Larry L., Matthew O. Hunt, and William W. Falk. 2008. "Who is Headed South? U.S. Migration Trends in Black and White, 1970-2000." *Social Forces* 87: 95–119.

Iceland, John, Daniel H. Weinberg, Erika Steinmetz, and Series CENSR-3 U.S. Census Bureau. 2002. *Racial and Ethnic Residential Segregation in the*

*United States 1980-2000*. Washington, D.C.: U.S. Government Printing Office.

Jackson, Kenneth T. 1985. *Crabgrass Frontier: The Suburbanization of the United States*. New York: Oxford University Press.

Jargowsky, Paul A. 1994. "Ghetto Poverty among Blacks in the 1980s." *Journal of Policy Analysis and Management* 13: 288–310.

—. 1997. *Poverty and Place: Ghettos, Barrios, and the American city*. New York: Russell Sage Foundation.

Jargowsky, Paul A. and Mary J. Bane. 1990. "Ghetto Poverty: Basic Questions." Pp. 16–67 in *Inner-city poverty in the United States*, edited by J. Laurence E. Lynn and M. T. McGeary. Washington, D.C.: National Academy of Sciences Press

Lieberson, Stanley. 1980. *A Piece of the Pie: Blacks and White Immigrants Since 1880*. Berkeley: University of California Press.

Lieberson, Stanley and Arnold R. Silverman. 1965. "The Precipitants and Underlying Conditions of Race Riots." *American Sociological Review* 30: 887–898.

Logan, John R., Brian J. Stults, and Reynolds Farley. 2004. "Segregation of Minorities in the Metropolis: Two Decades of Change." *Demography* 41: 1–22.

Long, Herman H. and Charles Spurgeon Johnson. 1947. *People vs. Property: Race Restrictive Covenants in Housing*. Nashville,: Fisk Univ. Press.

Massey, Douglas S. and Nancy A. Denton. 1987. "Trends in the Residential Segregation of Blacks, Hispanics, and Asians: 1970-1980." *American Sociological Review* 52: 802–825.

—. 1988. "The Dimensions of Residential Segregation." *Social Forces* 67: 281–315.

—. 1993. *American Apartheid: Segregation and the Making of the Underclass*. Cambridge, Mass.: Harvard University Press.

Morenoff, Jeffrey D. and Robert J. Sampson. 1997. "Violent Crime and the Spatial Dynamics of Neighborhood Transition: Chicago, 1970-1990." *Social Forces* 76: 31–64.

Norwood, Stephen H. 1997. "Bogalusa Burning: The War Against Biracial Unionism in the Deep South, 1919." *The Journal of Southern History* 63: 591–628.

Oliver, Melvin L. and Thomas M. Shapiro. [1995] 2006. *Black Wealth/White Wealth: A New Perspective on Racial Inequality, 2nd Ed*. New York, NY: Routledge.

Pattillo, Mary E. 1999. *Black Picket Fences: Privilege and Peril among the Black Middle Class*. Chicago: University of Chicago Press.

—. 2007. *Black on the Block: The Politics of Race and Class in the City*. Chicago: University of Chicago Press.

Phillips, Deborah. 1998. "Black Minority Ethnic Concentration, Segregation and Dispersal in Britain." *Urban Stud* 35:1681-1702.

Quillian, Lincoln. 2002. "Why Is Black-White Residential Segregation So Persistent?: Evidence on Three Theories from Migration Data." *Social Science Research* 31: 197–229.

Roediger, David R. 1994. *Towards the Abolition of Whiteness: Essays on Race, Politics, and Working Class History*. London; New York: Verso.

Schill, Michael H. and Susan M. Wachter. 1995. "The Spatial Bias of Federal Housing Law and Policy: Concentrated Poverty in Urban America." *University of Pennsylvania Law Review* 143: 1285–1342.

Shogan, Robert and Tom Craig. 1964. *The Detroit Race Riot: A Study in Violence*. Philadelphia, PA: Chilton Books.

Small, Stephen. 1994. *Racialised Barriers: The Black experience in the United States and England in the 1980's*. London ; New York: Routledge.

South, Scott J., Kyle Crowder, and Jeremy Pais. 2008. "Inter-neighborhood Migration and Spatial Assimilation in a Multi-ethnic World: Comparing Latinos, Blacks and Anglos." *Social Forces* 87: 415---------443.

Squires, Gregory D. 1994. *Capital and Communities in Black and White: The Intersections of Race, Class, and Uneven Development*. Albany: State University of New York Press.

Telles, Edward E. 1992. "Residential Segregation by Skin Color in Brazil." *American Sociological Review* 57: 186–197.

U.S. Bureau of the Census. 1918. *Negro Population in the United States: 1790–1915*. Washington, D.C.: Government Printing Office. Retrieved January 8, 2010, from http://www.wisconsinhistory.org/turningpoints/search.asp?id=1239.

Williams, D. R. and C. Collins. 2001. "Racial Residential Segregation: A Fundamental Cause of Racial Disparities in Health." *Public Health Rep* 116: 404–16.

Wilson, William J. 1987. *The Truly Disadvantaged: The Inner City, the Underclass, and Public Policy*. Chicago: University of Chicago Press.

—. 1996. *When Work Disappears: The World of the New Urban Poor*. New York: Knopf : Distributed by Random House, Inc.

Yinger, John. 1995. *Closed Doors, Opportunities Lost: The Continuing Costs of Housing Discrimination*. New York: Russell Sage Foundation.

# EDUCATION

# CRACKING THE EDUCATIONAL ACHIEVEMENT GAP(S)

*By R. L'Heureux Lewis and Evangeleen Pattison*

"Education is the civil rights issue of the
21st century."
—United States Secretary of Education
Arne Duncan

Secretary Duncan's statement about education as the civil rights issue of the 21st century is meant to parallel the prognosis of W. E. B. Du Bois in 1903, that "the problem of the 20th century is the problem of the color line." When Du Bois spoke those prophetic words his goal was to set the stage for a critical examination of race relations of the past, present and future with an eye towards the ways that government and everyday people determined opportunity. Duncan's call, whether intentional or not, can be thought of in a similar fashion. There is a long-standing fascination with questions of race, ethnicity and education in the United States because schools are often discussed as the great equalizer (Zhang & Thomas, 2005). In this chapter, we will explore the ways that race has been dealt with in United States public schools and argue that the current discussion of the achievement gap as well as the constellation of policy tools in use are insufficient for addressing the demands of a diversifying and still unequal American society. We argue this is due to a misspecification of the achievement gap as a monolithic social problem and a reductionist examination of the multiple factors affecting student performance and schooling experiences. We articulate this argument through a brief discussion of landmark decisions surrounding race and education, the achievement gap, the role of culture, structural barriers, policy responses and new directions for research on educational inequality.

## UNEQUAL SCHOOLS

The question of race and equal educational opportunity was thrust onto the national landscape with the 1954 Brown v. Topeka, Kansas Board of Education decision. The suit overturned the Plessy v. Ferguson (1896) doctrine which allowed for the legal segregation of public facilities by race. Justice Warren's (1954) statement, "Separate educational facilities are inherently unequal," set in motion regional, state and federal policies designed to address the already deeply rooted inequality in schooling between racial and ethnic groups.

Throughout the 1960s and 1970s the desegregation of public schools was hindered due to large amounts of race-related backlash (Orfield, Eaton, & Harvard Project on School Desegregation, 1996). Protests and stalled legislation allowed many public schools to remain segregated. Another compounding issue that abated desegregation efforts at this time was increasing suburbanization, which ushered many middle and upper income White families into the suburbs. Soon after, middle and upper income Blacks followed, moving out of the core of the city. The flight of middle and upper income Blacks and Whites brought with it the deindustrialization of urban areas resulting in high rates of joblessness and concentrated poverty among the Black and Latino residents left behind (Wilson, 1996). The Civil Rights Project argues that the out-migration of residents, resistance to desegregation plans, and residential choice left contemporary schools more racially segregated than they were during the Jim Crow South (Frankenburg, Lee, & Orfield, 2003). The recent decisions of Parents v. Seattle and Meredith v. Jefferson in 2006 served to severely curb voluntary desegregation and racial balance plans. As a result, schools remain racially and economically segregated with limited policy tools for achieving more equitable facilities.

Schools in urban communities became increasingly dilapidated; in contrast, suburban schools boasted greater resources and educational opportunity. The unbalanced allocation of resources led policy analysts to warn about the unequal school system which was set to leave "a nation at risk" by setting the stage for national failure (National Commission on Teaching and America's Future, 2003). The increasing racial and economic segregation of neighborhoods, which led to the overrepresentation of Black and Latino children in decaying urban schools (Kozol, 1991), has resulted in discussions of urban education becoming synonymous with discussions of Black, Latino, and poor youth in schools.

## THE ACHIEVEMENT GAP

The collection of the National Assessment of Educational Progress (NAEP) in 1972 marked the first systematic study of educational inequality between groups and allowed for comparisons of test score gaps at multiple grade levels. These gaps in average academic performance provide national estimates in the skills-gap among United States school children. The achievement gap between Black-White and Hispanic-White have narrowed over the past 35 years, but this narrowing has been inconsistent (Ferguson, 1998; Grissmer, Flanagan, & Williamson, 1998; Lee, 2002). In addition to the NAEP, gaps are measured using state-standards based tests, which occasionally show reductions in race/ethnicity gaps while the NAEP does not (Turnbull, Grissmer, & Ross, 2000). Sometimes the gains on states-standards tests are used as evidence of improvement in educational inequality, when in reality it may be an artifact of the state-based tests. The most recent estimations of the NAEP demonstrate little progress in reducing the Black-White and Hispanic-White test score gap. This data suggests that the levers of change for educational inequality are not always easily located and executed.

**Table 1. *NAEP Average Scale Score Trend Data***

| Race/Ethnicity | Average scale score | | | |
|---|---|---|---|---|
| | 2003 | 2005 | 2007 | 2009 |
| White | 243 | 246 | 248 | 248 |
| Black | 216 | 220 | 222 | 222 |
| Hispanic | 221 | 225 | 227 | 227 |

While the racial achievement gap has gotten large scaled attention in the past 8 years, this attention is in part misguided because it glosses over the heterogeneity of experiences for Black, White and Latino youth. While gap measurements traditionally draw two racial/ethnic groups into contrast, there is the necessity for further exploration of the intersections of race, gender, class, and nativity on achievement inequality. 50 percent of Black boys who begin high school in the inner-city will not finish with their classmates (The Schott Foundation for Public Education, 2008). Among Latinos, a group that has been plagued with a dropout dilemma, native born Latinos dropout rate in 2007 was 11.2 percent, while immigrant Latinos dropped out at a rate of 21.4 percent (National Center for Education Statistics, 2009). A large portion of immigrant Latino dropouts relates to language barriers and cultural mismatch in schools (Fry, 2003). These two brief examples demonstrate that intersectional analyses are needed to understand variation within reported gaps. Without such levels of specificity, these divergences within larger social groups are missed. Additionally, research must look carefully at the variety of ways that issues such as urbanicity and region play into sociological and policy analysis of schooling. It is not difficult to imagine the experiences of Mexican-American children in Detroit, Michigan are markedly different than the experiences of Cuban-American children in suburban Miami. These types of variations which fall under region, city and nativity, to name a few, are seldom considered in the bulk of large scaled educational policy analysis. These large-scaled analyses provide a broad picture, due to their statistical power, but they eliminate nuance necessary for addressing the ways that race/ethnicity are lived and become meaningful within schools.

## CONSTRUCTED CULTURE

The development of social construction theory in race, gender and social class has emphasized the ways that these categories, once thought to be fixed, are actually fluid and socially defined to be meaningful (Omi & Winant, 1994; Thorne,

1993). These scholars have emphasized that everyday actions create the meanings for these categories and that membership in these groups is iteratively constructed through the actions of individuals, groups and larger social projects.

In the 1980s, Fordham and Ogbu (1986) argued African-American students held an oppositional culture toward schooling. They argued that Black students disengaged from academics because they feared being labeled "White." This theory became a widely popular explanation for achievement disparities between Black and White students despite being rebuffed extensively (Downey & Ainsworth-Darnell, 2002; Harris, 2006). Carter (2005) challenged Fordham and Ogbu and found that youth, both Black and Latino, drew on their own cultural backgrounds and cultural capitals to negotiate the terrain of school and the social world. This suggests that racial and ethnic background can not only be viewed as a deficit on academic achievement but can also be viewed as an asset.

Lareau (2003) argued that a better explanation of observed educational and social inequalities were differences in class-based rearing strategies. She argued that middle class parents utilized concerted cultivation through scheduling their children in structured interactions with adults, for example team sports. In contrast, lower class parents utilized natural growth which led to fewer structured interactions with adults and more peer play. She argued the differences in these strategies served to impair the ability of lower income children to interact with institutions such as schools. While Lareau's analysis resurrected the importance of class in debates about education inequality, the sample of respondents she used makes it difficult to draw accurate claims about the intersecting role of race (Lewis, 2008). Taken together, these social construction theories have advanced understanding of how inequality is woven into the fabric of our school system and provide fruitful areas for larger scaled research on disparities.

## STRUCTURED OPPORTUNITIES

More structural explanations of the gap have concentrated on enduring racial and economic segregation within and outside of schools, inequality between the schools that Whites and minorities attend, as well as segregation within schools (Kozol, 1991; Oakes, 1985; R. J. Skiba, Michael, Nardo, & Peterson, 2002). In popular discourse, these structural differentials have been referred to as structural racism or discrimination. This language however is seldom employed in policy analysis. Policy definitions of discrimination are aligned closely with legal definitions of discrimination (Blank et al., 2004), making support for claims of discrimination difficult to achieve (Pollock, 2008). Instead disproportionality is used to describe observed differences in rates of placement in categories such as tracking, suspension, and special education (R. J. Skiba et al., 2002).

Tracking has been present in American public schooling for nearly a century, but the most recent incarnations of this phenomenon are particularly troubling for racial equality. Jeannie Oakes (1985) found differences in course offerings, levels of academic press, material coverage, as well as quality of instruction in schools where tracking was practiced. This unequal distribution of opportunity to learn serves to accelerate learning for students slotted for the most advanced tracks and lock students in the lower tracks into lower quality education and provide a lesser chance for upward mobility.

In addition to the tracking of African-American and Latino students, rates of suspension and expulsion negatively impact the amount of time spent in the classroom and increase ties to the criminal justice system. The expansion of "zero tolerance" policies throughout the United States is linked to increased out-of-school referrals for minority youth, yet has not resulted in increased safety for children in schools. Additionally, the increased ties between school disciplinary action and local criminal justice systems have enforced what policy analysts and advocates call a schoolhouse to jailhouse pipeline (Advancement Project, 2005).

Disproportionate referral in special education is an expanding area of interest along racial and ethnic lines. There is both over and under referral to special education. In some cases, students in need of referral to special education may not be provided with appropriate resources. Alternatively, in other cases students not in need of special educational resources may be referred. The bulk of attention in this debate goes towards the expansion of classification of soft disorders in which students of color are disproportionately represented (R. Skiba et al., 2008). On the opposite end of the spectrum, Black and Latino students are disproportionately absent from gifted classes. Placement in special education tracks has long term impacts on educational attainment.

Of particular concern for US public schools has been the question of instruction for English Language Learners (ELL). The United States continues to rapidly diversify. As a result, schools have responded by taking a number of paths to address the language and development needs of children whose first language is not English. Maintenance and transitional are two dominant systems that have been used to instruct children who are ELL. Maintenance program are designed to have the ELL develop English skills while maintaining their native language skills. Transitional programs are designed to transition ELL students to English proficiency without maintenance of their native language. While there is evidence of success with transitional programs, the losses of culture and dual language ability remain troubling to many advocates of bilingual education (Moses, 2002).

Although federal policy is not very specific on the path that schools must take to educate ELL, this will continue to serve as a zone of "educational triage" where students receive differential resources, instruction, and opportunity.

## NO CHILD LEFT BEHIND

The No Child Left Behind Act's (2001) introduction by President George Bush drew national attention to the matter of educational inequality along racial lines. NCLB, which was a reauthorization of the Elementary and Secondary Education Act (ESEA) of 1965 was the first national policy which emphasized measurable achievement gains, mandated state standardized tests, and consequences for not making progress towards equal student performance. The passing of NCLB, while lauded by many as advantageous for schools that chronically failed students, was met with considerable resistance due to its emphasis on ratcheting up standards, limiting resources, and provided a limited time horizon for improving schools. This being said, the NCLB act did catapult the achievement gap into the public vocabulary thus making race and ethnicity an area of public interest and concern.

Under the NCLB, schools that fail to make adequate yearly progress for multiple years, are subject to reconstitution or closing. The closing of public schools remains a major issue in urban areas where the majority of Black and Latino students attend school (Popham, 2005). The NCLB was conceived, in part, with the intention of developing a market-based approach to public education where families were provided with a choice between traditional public schools, charter schools, or in the proposed act's original incarnation, voucher supported private education. In theory, this increased choice would serve to increase the performance of failing public schools, given the rising competition. While ideal in concept, the "market" has remained

under-developed with evidence being mixed on the success of charter and voucher programs as well as little discernable influence on traditional public schools' performance (Merrifield, 2009).

Charter schools have continued to expand in urban areas as an alternative source of education for families often locked in poverty. While charter schools are not subject to the same standards nationally, they are often supported, in part, by public school dollars but contain a greater degree of autonomy than traditional public schools. The bulk of evidence on the effectiveness of charter schools has also been mixed, highlighting the wide range of schools which fall under the label "charter" and the diversity in approach to education and results (Bifulco & Ladd, 2006).

## FUTURE DIRECTIONS

There is an increasing need and attempt to tie sociological understanding with the dilemmas of schooling. While many think of school-based reforms as a direct route to educational improvement, lessons from the 1970s, 80s, and 90s in reducing achievement disparities, suggest that gaps will only be reduced in concert with larger social changes (Rothstein, 2004). Because youth are nested in families, networks of peers, and neighborhoods, a synthesis of individual and social factors must be considered if we are to improve educational opportunity (Dornbusch et al., 1991). Currently, the most comprehensive and publicly hailed school and community intervention is the Harlem Children's Zone (HCZ) (Dobbie & Fryer, 2009). The HCZ provides a variety of developmental activities, which serve ages ranging from pre-natal through adulthood with the goal of improving the predominantly Black and Latino neighborhood of Harlem. The HCZ model is currently being extrapolated via federal dollars to a number of urban areas under the recommendation of President Barack Obama.

A significant upcoming frontier beyond traditional urban education will be the study of racial and ethnic inequality in non-high poverty settings. While urban education has become synonymous with the plights of Black and Latino students, both Blacks and Latinos are increasingly suburbanizing populations (R. Alba D., Logan, & Stults, 2000; R. Alba & Logan, 1991). This increased access to better resourced spaces however has not meant greater equity in educational provision and performance. The work of groups such as The Minority Student Achievement Network (MSAN) document the need for new and innovative research and solutions that examine racially and economically heterogeneous settings.

Recent work by Pollack (2004) and R. Lewis (In Press) suggests that race operates in these settings in complex ways that weave unique forms of inequality. Because these districts are characterized by higher amounts of resources they are often characterized as idyllic. However, closer examination reveals continued segregation within these schools, lower access to provided resources, and race-related tensions among children and staff. Because so much emphasis has been placed on urban poverty driving achievement inequalities, spaces like these represent a new frontier for studying race, ethnicity and education.

Lastly, the increasing racial and ethnic diversity of the United States will create new dilemmas and opportunities for educational researcher and practitioners. The Census estimates that by 2030 Black and Hispanic youth will compose approximately 43 percent of the school age population and approximately 48 percent by 2050. This rapid increase will mean that what were once considered "minority issues" will become majority issues and serve to impact the ways that culture is understood and utilized in education.

The achievement gap has become the *lingua franca* of discussions on race, ethnicity and schooling, but as this chapter demonstrates this can be misleading. Further work in the area must move beyond large scaled, non-intersectional analyses and utilize sociological insight to crack the gap. There are as many achievement gaps as there are experiences shaped by race and ethnicity in U.S. schools. The statement of Secretary Duncan suggests that national efforts on issues of race and schooling are just beginning. The dogmatic rigor with which the study of and interventions to racial and ethnic inequality occurred in the 20th century must be replicated and expanded in order for all children to experience a quality education.

## ABOUT THE AUTHORS

R. L'Heureux Lewis is an Assistant Professor of Sociology, Black Studies, and Public Policy at the City College of New York of the City University of New York. His research centers on the examination of racial and class inequality in education, mental health functioning and youth culture. He is currently finishing a book length manuscript on dilemmas of educational inequality in economically and racially diverse settings. He is a former Ford Foundation Fellow and American Sociological Association Fellow.

Evangeleen Pattison is an undergraduate student at the City College of New York of the City University of New York pursuing a B.A. in sociology. She is a recipient of the City College and Weston fellowships and has plans to pursue a Ph.D. in sociology after her graduation in May 2010. Her research centers on the intersection between education, race/ethnicity, stratification and mobility.

# REFERENCES

Advancement Project. (2005). *Education On Lockdown: The Schoolhouse to Jailhouse Track*. The Advancement project.

Alba, R., D., Logan, J. R., & Stults, B. J. (2000). How segregated are middle-class African Americans? *Social Problems, 47*(4), 543–558.

Alba, R., & Logan, J. (1991). Variations on two themes: Racial and ethnic patterns in the attainment of suburban residence. *Demography, 28*(3), 431–453.

Bifulco, R., & Ladd, H. (2006). The impact of charter schools on student achievement: Evidence from North Carolina. *American Education Finance Association, 1*(1), 50–90.

Blank, R., Dabady, M., Citro, C., & National Research Council. Panelon Methods for Assessing Discrimination. (2004). *Measuring racial discrimination*. Washington, D.C.: National Academies Press.

Carter, P. (2005). *Keepin' it real: School success beyond Black and White*. Oxford; New York: Oxford University Press.

Dobbie, W., & Fryer, R., Jr. (2009). Are high quality schools enough to close the achievement gap? Evidence from a social experiment in Harlem. *The National Bureau of Economic Research,*

Dornbusch, S., Mont-Reynaud, R., Ritter, P., Chen, Z., Steinberg, L., Colten, M., et al. (1991). Adolescent stress: Causes and consequences. *Social Institutions and Social Change,* 111–130.

Downey, D., & Ainsworth-Darnell, J. (2002). The search for oppositional culture among Black students. *American Sociological Review, 67*(1), 148.

Ferguson, R. (1998). Can schools narrow the Black-White test score gap? In C. Jencks, & M. Phillips (Eds.), *Black-White test score gap* (pp. 318–374). Washington, D.C.: Brookings Institution Press.

Fordham, S., & Ogbu, J. (1986). Black students' school success: Coping with the 'Burden of acting White'. *The Urban Review, 18,* 176–206.

Frankenburg, E., Lee, C., & Orfield, G. (2003). *A multiracial society with segregated schools: Are we losing the dream?*. Cambridge, MA: Harvard Civil Rights Project.

Fry, R. (2003). *Hispanic youth dropping out of U.S. schools: Measuring the challenge* Pew Hispanic Center.

Grissmer, D., Flanagan, A., & Williamson, S. (1998). Why did the Black-White test score gap narrow in the 1970s and 1980s? In C. Jencks, & M. Phillips (Eds.), *The Black-White test score gap* (pp. 182–226). Washington, D.C.: Brookings Insitution Press.

Harris, A. (2006). I (don't) hate school: Revisiting 'oppositional culture' theory of Blacks' resistance to schooling. *Social Forces, 85*(2), 797–834.

Kozol, J. (1991). *Savage inequalities: Children in America's schools*. New York: Crown Pub.

Lareau, A. (2003). *Unequal childhoods: Class, race, and family life*. Berkeley: University of California Press.

Lee, J. (2002). Racial and ethnic achievement gap trends: Reversing the progress toward equity? *Educational Researcher, 31*(1), 3–12.

Lewis, R. L. (2008). Educational inequality in an affluent setting: An exploration of resources and opportunity. University of Michigan—Ann Arbor).

Lewis, R. L. (in press). "Speaking the Unspeakable: Youth's Perspectives on Racial Importance." *Sociological Studies of Children and Youth.*

Merrifield, J. (2009). Imagined evidence and false imperatives. *Journal of School Choice, 3*(1), 55–78.

Moses, M. S. (2002). *Embracing race: Why we need race-conscious education policy* Teachers College Press.

National Center for Education Statistics. (2009). *The Nation's report card: Trial urban district assessment mathematics 2009 (NCES 2010–452)*. Washington, D.C.: Institute of Education Sciences, U.S. Department of Education.

National Commission on Teaching and America's Future. (2003). *No Dream Denied: A pledge to*

*America's children.* Washington, D.C.: National Commission on Teaching and America's Future.

Oakes, J. (1985). *Keeping track: How schools structure inequality.* New Haven: Yale University Press.

Omi, M., & Winant, H. (1994). *Racial formation in the united states: From the 1960s to the 1990s* (2nd ed.). New York: Routledge.

Orfield, G., Eaton, S., & Harvard Project on School Desegregation. (1996). *Dismantling desegregation: The quiet reversal of brown v. board of education.* New York: New Press: Distributed by W.W. Norton & Company.

Popham, W. J. (2005). *America's "failing" schools: How parents and teachers can cope with no child left behind* (Paperback ed.). New York: Routledge.

Rothstein, R. (2004). *Class and schools: Using social, economic, and educational reform to close the Black-White achievement gap.* New York, N.Y.: Teachers College, Columbia University; Washington, D.C.: Economic Policy Institute.

Skiba, R. J., Michael, R., Nardo, A., & Peterson, R. (2002). The color of discipline: Sources of racial and gender disproportionality in school punishment. *The Urban Review, 34*(4), 317–342.

Skiba, R., Simmons, A., Ritter, S., Gibb, A., Rausch, M. K., Cuadrado, J., et al. (2008). Achieving equity in special education: History, status, and current challenges. *Exceptional Children, 74*(3), 264–288.

The Schott Foundation for Public Education. (2008). Given half a chance: The schott foundation 50 state report on public education and Black males.

Thorne, B. (1993). *Gender play: Girls and boys in school* (Sixth ed.). New Jersey: Rutgers University Press.

Turnbull, B., Grissmer, D., & Ross, M. (2000). Improving research and data collection on student achievement. In D. Grissmer, & J. M. Ross (Eds.), *Analytic issues in the assessment of student achievement* (pp. 299–315). Washington, D.C.: U.S. Department of Education. National Center for Education Statistics.

Wilson, W. (1996). *When work disappears: The world of the new urban poor.* New York: Knopf: Distributed by Random House, Inc.

Zhang, L., & Thomas, S. (2005). Investments in human capital: Sources of variation in the return to college quality. In J. C. Smart (Ed.), *Higher education: Handbook of theory and research, vol. XX* (pp. 241–306). Great Britain: Springer.

# The Labor Market, Socioeconomic Status, and Wealth

# ARE EMILY AND GREG MORE EMPLOYABLE THAN LAKISHA AND JAMAL?

## A FIELD EXPERIMENT ON LABOR MARKET DISCRIMINATION

*By Marianne Bertrand and Sendhil Mullainathan\**

*We study race in the labor market by sending fictitious résumés to help-wanted ads in Boston and Chicago newspapers. To manipulate perceived race, résumés are randomly assigned African-American- or White-sounding names. White names receive 50 percent more callbacks for interviews. Callbacks are also more responsive to résumé quality for White names than for African-American ones. The racial gap is uniform across occupation, industry, and employer size. We also find little evidence that employers are inferring social class from the names. Differential treatment by race still appears to still be prominent in the U.S. labor market. (JEL J71, J64).*

Every measure of economic success reveals significant racial inequality in the U.S. labor market. Compared to Whites, African-Americans are twice as likely to be unemployed and earn nearly 25 percent less when they are employed (Council of Economic Advisers, 1998). This inequality has sparked a debate as to whether employers treat members of different races differentially. When faced with observably similar African-American and White applicants, do they favor the White one? Some argue yes, citing either employer prejudice or employer perception that race signals lower productivity. Others argue that differential treatment by race is a relic of the past, eliminated by some combination of employer enlightenment, affirmative action programs and the profit-maximization motive. In fact, many in this latter camp even feel that stringent enforcement of affirmative action programs has produced an environment of reverse discrimination. They would argue that faced with identical candidates,

\* Bertrand: Graduate School of Business, University of Chicago, 1101 E. 58th Street, R0 229D, Chicago, IL 60637, NBER, and CEPR (e-mail: marianne.bertrand@gsb.uchicago.edu); Mullainathan: Department of Economics, Massachusetts Institute of Technology, 50 Memorial Drive, E52-380a, Cambridge, MA 02142, and NBER (e-mail: mullain@mit.edu). David Abrams, Victoria Bede, Simone Berkowitz, Hong Chung, Almudena Fernandez, Mary Anne Guediguian, Christine Jaw, Richa Maheswari, Beverley

Martis, Alison Tisza, Grant Whitehorn, and Christine Yee provided excellent research assistance. We are also grateful to numerous colleagues and seminar participants for very helpful comments.

employers might favor the African-American one.[*] Data limitations make it difficult to empirically test these views. Since researchers possess far less data than employers do, White and African-American workers that appear similar to researchers may look very different to employers. So any racial difference in labor market outcomes could just as easily be attributed to differences that are observable to employers but unobservable to researchers.

To circumvent this difficulty, we conduct a field experiment that builds on the correspondence testing methodology that has been primarily used in the past to study minority outcomes in the United Kingdom.[†] We send résumés in response to help-wanted ads in Chicago and Boston newspapers and measure callback for interview for each sent résumé. We experimentally manipulate perception of race via the name of the fictitious job applicant. We randomly assign very White-sounding names (such as Emily Walsh or Greg Baker) to half the résumés and very African-American-sounding names (such as Lakisha Washington or Jamal Jones) to the other half. Because we are also interested in how credentials affect the racial gap in callback, we experimentally vary the quality of the résumés used in response to a given ad. Higher-quality applicants have on average a little more labor market experience and fewer holes in their employment history; they are also more likely to have an e-mail address, have completed some certification degree, possess foreign language skills, or have been awarded some honors.[‡] In practice, we typically send four résumés in response to each ad: two higher-quality and two lower-quality ones. We randomly assign to one of the higher- and one of the lower-quality résumés an African-American-sounding name. In total, we respond to over 1,300 employment ads in the sales, administrative support, clerical, and customer services job categories and send nearly 5,000 résumés. The ads we respond to cover a large spectrum of job quality, from cashier work at retail establishments and clerical work in a mail room, to office and sales management positions.

We find large racial differences in callback rates.[§] Applicants with White names need to send about 10 résumés to get one callback whereas applicants with African-American names need to send about 15 résumés. This 50-percent gap in callback is statistically significant. A White name yields as many more callbacks as an additional eight years of experience on a résumé. Since applicants' names are randomly assigned, this gap can only be attributed to the name manipulation.

---

[*] This camp often explains the poor performance of African-Americans in terms of supply factors. If African-Americans lack many basic skills entering the labor market, then they will perform worse, even with parity or favoritism in hiring.

[†] See Roger Jowell and Patricia Prescott-Clarke (1970), Jim Hubbuck and Simon Carter (1980), Colin Brown and Pat Gay (1985), and Peter A. Riach and Judith Rich (1991). One caveat is that some of these studies fail to fully match skills between minority and nonminority résumés. For example some impose differential education background by racial origin. Doris Weichselbaumer (2003, 2004) studies the impact of sex-stereotypes and sexual orientation. Richard E. Nisbett and Dov Cohen (1996) perform a related field experiment to study how employers' response to a criminal past varies between the North and the South in the United States.

[‡] In creating the higher-quality résumés, we deliberately make small changes in credentials so as to minimize the risk of overqualification.

[§] For ease of exposition, we refer to the effects uncovered in this experiment as racial differences. Technically, however, these effects are about the racial soundingness of names. We briefly discuss below the potential confounds between name and race. A more extensive discussion is offered in Section IV, subsection B.

Race also affects the reward to having a better résumé. Whites with higher-quality résumés receive nearly 30-percent more callbacks than Whites with lower-quality résumés. On the other hand, having a higher-quality résumé has a smaller effect for African-Americans. In other words, the gap between Whites and African-Americans widens with résumé quality. While one may have expected improved credentials to alleviate employers' fear that African-American applicants are deficient in some unobservable skills, this is not the case in our data.[*]

The experiment also reveals several other aspects of the differential treatment by race. First, since we randomly assign applicants' postal addresses to the résumés, we can study the effect of neighborhood of residence on the likelihood of callback. We find that living in a wealthier (or more educated or Whiter) neighborhood increases callback rates. But, interestingly, African-Americans are not helped more than Whites by living in a "better" neighborhood. Second, the racial gap we measure in different industries does not appear correlated to Census-based measures of the racial gap in wages. The same is true for the racial gap we measure in different occupations. In fact, we find that the racial gaps in callback are statistically indistinguishable across all the occupation and industry categories covered in the experiment. Federal contractors, who are thought to be more severely constrained by affirmative action laws, do not treat the African-American résumés more preferentially; neither do larger employers or employers who explicitly state that they are "Equal Opportunity Employers." In

Chicago, we find a slightly smaller racial gap when employers are located in more African-American neighborhoods.

The rest of the paper is organized as follows. Section I compares this experiment to earlier work on racial discrimination, and most notably to the labor market audit studies. We describe the experimental design in Section II and present the results in Section III, subsection A. In Section IV, we discuss possible interpretations of our results, focusing especially on two issues. First, we examine whether the race-specific names we have chosen might also proxy for social class above and beyond the race of the applicant. Using birth certificate data on mother's education for the different first names used in our sample, we find little relationship between social background and the name-specific callback rates.[†] Second, we discuss how our results map back to the different models of discrimination proposed in the economics literature. In doing so, we focus on two important results: the lower returns to credentials for African-Americans and the relative homogeneity of the racial gap across occupations and industries. We conclude that existing models do a poor job of explaining the full set of findings. Section V concludes.

## I. PREVIOUS RESEARCH

With conventional labor force and household surveys, it is difficult to study whether differential treatment occurs in the labor market.[‡] Armed only

---

[*] These results contrast with the view, mostly based on nonexperimental evidence, that African-Americans receive higher returns to skills. For example, estimating earnings regressions on several decades of Census data, James J. Heckman et al. (2001) show that African-Americans experience higher returns to a high school degree than Whites do.

[†] We also argue that a social class interpretation would find it hard to explain some of our findings, such as why living in a better neighborhood does not increase callback rates more for African-American names than for White names.

[‡] See Joseph G. Altonji and Rebecca M. Blank (1999) for a detailed review of the existing literature on racial discrimination in the labor market.

with survey data, researchers usually measure differential treatment by comparing the labor market performance of Whites and African-Americans (or men and women) for which they observe similar sets of skills. But such comparisons can be quite misleading. Standard labor force surveys do not contain all the characteristics that employers observe when hiring, promoting, or setting wages. So one can never be sure that the minority and non-minority workers being compared are truly similar from the employers' perspective. As a consequence, any measured differences in outcomes could be attributed to these unobserved (to the researcher) factors.

This difficulty with conventional data has led some authors to instead rely on pseudo-experiments.[*] Claudia Goldin and Cecilia Rouse (2000), for example, examine the effect of blind auditioning on the hiring process of orchestras. By observing the treatment of female candidates before and after the introduction of blind auditions, they try to measure the amount of sex discrimination. When such pseudo-experiments can be found, the resulting study can be very informative; but finding such experiments has proven to be extremely challenging.

A different set of studies, known as audit studies, attempts to place comparable minority and White actors into actual social and economic settings and measure how each group fares in these settings.[†] Labor market audit studies send comparable minority (African-American or Hispanic) and White

auditors in for interviews and measure whether one is more likely to get the job than the other.[‡] While the results vary somewhat across studies, minority auditors tend to perform worse on average: they are less likely to get called back for a second interview and, conditional on getting called back, less likely to get hired.

These audit studies provide some of the cleanest nonlaboratory evidence of differential treatment by race. But they also have weaknesses, most of which have been highlighted in Heckman and Siegelman (1992) and Heckman (1998). First, these studies require that both members of the auditor pair are identical in all dimensions that might affect productivity in employers' eyes, except for race. To accomplish this, researchers typically match auditors on several characteristics (height, weight, age, dialect, dressing style, hairdo) and train them for several days to coordinate interviewing styles. Yet, critics note that this is unlikely to erase the numerous differences that exist between the auditors in a pair.

Another weakness of the audit studies is that they are not double-blind. Auditors know the purpose of the study. As Turner et al. (1991) note: "The first day of training also included an introduction to employment discrimination, equal employment opportunity, and a review of project design and methodology." This may generate conscious or subconscious motives among auditors to generate data consistent or inconsistent with their beliefs about race issues in America. As psychologists know very

---

[*] William A. Darity, Jr. and Patrick L. Mason (1998) describe an interesting nonexperimental study. Prior to the Civil Rights Act of 1964, employment ads would explicitly state racial biases, providing a direct measure of differential treatment. Of course, as Arrow (1998) mentions, discrimination was at that time "a fact too evident for detection."

[†] Michael Fix and Marjery A. Turner (1998) provide a survey of many such audit studies.

[‡] Earlier hiring audit studies include Jerry M. Newman (1978) and Shelby J. McIntyre et al. (1980). Three more recent studies are Harry Cross et al. (1990), Franklin James and Steve W. DelCastillo (1991), and Turner et al. (1991). Heckman and Peter Siegelman (1992), Heckman (1998), and Altonji and Blank (1999) summarize these studies. See also David Neumark (1996) for a labor market audit study on gender discrimination.

well, these demand effects can be quite strong. It is very difficult to insure that auditors will not want to do "a good job." Since they know the goal of the experiment, they can alter their behavior in front of employers to express (indirectly) their own views. Even a small belief by auditors that employers treat minorities differently can result in measured differences in treatment. This effect is further magnified by the fact that auditors are not in fact seeking jobs and are therefore more free to let their beliefs affect the interview process.

Finally, audit studies are extremely expensive, making it difficult to generate large enough samples to understand nuances and possible mitigating factors. Also, these budgetary constraints worsen the problem of mismatched auditor pairs. Cost considerations force the use of a limited number of pairs of auditors, meaning that any one mismatched pair can easily drive the results. In fact, these studies generally tend to find significant differences in outcomes across pairs.

Our study circumvents these problems. First, because we only rely on résumés and not people, we can be sure to generate comparability across race. In fact, since race is randomly assigned to each résumé, the same résumé will sometimes be associated with an African-American name and sometimes with a White name. This guarantees that any differences we find are caused solely by the race manipulation. Second, the use of paper résumés insulates us from demand effects. While the research assistants know the purpose of the study, our protocol allows little room for conscious or subconscious deviations from the set procedures. Moreover, we can objectively measure whether the randomization occurred as expected. This kind of objective measurement is impossible in the case of the previous audit studies. Finally, because of relatively low marginal cost, we can send out a large number of résumés. Besides giving us more precise estimates, this larger sample

size also allows us to examine the nature of the differential treatment from many more angles.

## II. EXPERIMENTAL DESIGN

### A. Creating a Bank of Résumés

The first step of the experimental design is to generate templates for the résumés to be sent. The challenge is to produce a set of realistic and representative résumés without using résumés that belong to actual job seekers. To achieve this goal, we start with résumés of actual job searchers but alter them sufficiently to create distinct résumés. The alterations maintain the structure and realism of the initial résumés without compromising their owners.

We begin with résumés posted on two job search Web sites as the basis for our artificial résumés.[*] While the résumés posted on these Web sites may not be completely representative of the average job seeker, they provide a practical approximation.[†] We restrict ourselves to people seeking employment in our experimental cities (Boston and Chicago). We also restrict ourselves to four occupational categories: sales, administrative support, clerical services, and customer services. Finally, we further restrict ourselves to résumés posted more than six months prior to the start of the experiment. We purge the selected résumés of the person's name and contact information.

During this process, we classify the résumés within each detailed occupational category into two groups: high and low quality. In judging résumé quality, we use criteria such as labor market experience, career profile, existence of gaps in employment,

---

[*] The sites are www.careerbuilder.com and www.americasjobbank.com.

[†] In practice, we found large variation in skill levels among people posting their résumés on these sites.

and skills listed. Such a classification is admittedly subjective but it is made independently of any race assignment on the résumés (which occurs later in the experimental design). To further reinforce the quality gap between the two sets of résumés, we add to each high-quality résumé a subset of the following features: summer or while-at-school employment experience, volunteering experience, extra computer skills, certification degrees, foreign language skills, honors, or some military experience. This résumé quality manipulation needs to be somewhat subtle to avoid making a higher-quality job applicant overqualified for a given job. We try to avoid this problem by making sure that the features listed above are not all added at once to a given résumé. This leaves us with a high-quality and a low-quality pool of résumés.[*]

To minimize similarity to actual job seekers, we use résumés from Boston job seekers to form templates for the résumés to be sent out in Chicago and use résumés from Chicago job seekers to form templates for the résumés to be sent out in Boston. To implement this migration, we alter the names of the schools and previous employers on the résumés. More specifically, for each Boston résumé, we use the Chicago résumés to replace a Boston school with a Chicago school.[†] We also use the Chicago résumés to replace a Boston employer with a Chicago employer in the same industry. We use a similar procedure to migrate Chicago résumés to Boston.[‡] This produces distinct but realistic looking résumés,

similar in their education and career profiles to this subpopulation of job searchers.[§]

## B. Identities of Fictitious Applicants

The next step is to generate identities for the fictitious job applicants: names, telephone numbers, postal addresses, and (possibly) e-mail addresses. The choice of names is crucial to our experiment.[¶] To decide on which names are uniquely African-American and which are uniquely White, we use name frequency data calculated from birth certificates of all babies born in Massachusetts between 1974 and 1979. We tabulate these data by race to determine which names are distinctively White and which are distinctively African-American. Distinctive names are those that have the highest ratio of frequency in one racial group to frequency in the other racial group.

As a check of distinctiveness, we conducted a survey in various public areas in Chicago. Each respondent was asked to assess features of a person with a particular name, one of which is race. For each name, 30 respondents were asked to identify the name as either "White," "African-American," "Other," or "Cannot Tell." In general, the names led respondents to readily attribute the expected race for the person but there were a few exceptions and these names were disregarded.[**]

The final list of first names used for this study is shown in Appendix Table Al. The table reports

---

[*]  In Section III, subsection B, and Table 3, we provide a detailed summary of résumé characteristics by quality level.

[†]  We try as much as possible to match high schools and colleges on quality and demographic characteristics.

[‡]  Note that for applicants with schooling or work experience outside of the Boston or Chicago areas, we leave the school or employer name unchanged.

[§]  We also generate a set of different fonts, layouts, and cover letters to further differentiate the résumés. These are applied at the time the résumés are sent out.

[¶]  We chose name over other potential manipulations of race, such as affiliation with a minority group, because we felt such affiliations may especially convey more than race.

[**]  For example, Maurice and Jerome are distinctively African-American names in a frequency sense yet are not perceived as such by many people.

the relative likelihood of the names for the Whites and African-Americans in the Massachusetts birth certificates data as well as the recognition rate in the field survey.[*] As Appendix Table A1 indicates, the African-American first names used in the experiment are quite common in the population. This suggests that by using these names as an indicator of race, we are actually covering a rather large segment of the African-American population.[†]

Applicants in each race/sex/city/résumé quality cell are allocated the same phone number. This guarantees that we can precisely track employer callbacks in each of these cells. The phone lines we use are virtual ones with only a voice mailbox attached to them. A similar outgoing message is recorded on each of the voice mailboxes but each message is recorded by someone of the appropriate race and gender. Since we allocate the same phone number for applicants with different names, we cannot use a person name in the outgoing message.

While we do not expect positive feedback from an employer to take place via postal mail, résumés still need postal addresses. We therefore construct fictitious addresses based on real streets in Boston and Chicago using the White Pages. We select up to three addresses in each 5-digit zip code in Boston and Chicago. Within cities, we randomly assign addresses across all résumés. We also create eight e-mail addresses, four for Chicago and four for Boston.[‡] These e-mail addresses are neutral with respect to both race and sex. Not all applicants are given an e-mail address. The e-mail addresses are used almost exclusively for the higher-quality résumés. This procedure leaves us with a bank of names, phone numbers, addresses, and e-mail addresses that we can assign to the template résumés when responding to the employment ads.

## C. Responding to Ads

The experiment was carried out between July 2001 and January 2002 in Boston and between July 2001 and May 2002 in Chicago.[§] Over that period, we surveyed all employment ads in the Sunday editions of *The Boston Globe* and *The Chicago Tribune* in the sales, administrative support, and clerical and customer services sections. We eliminate any ad where applicants were asked to call or appear in person. In fact, most of the ads we surveyed in these job categories ask for applicants to fax in or (more rarely) mail in their résumé. We log the name (when available) and contact information for each employer, along with any information on the position advertised and specific requirements (such as education, experience, or computer skills). We also record whether or not the ad explicitly states that the employer is an equal opportunity employer.

For each ad, we use the bank of résumés to sample four résumés (two high-quality and two low-quality) that fit the job description and

---

[*] So many of names show a likelihood ratio of ∞ because there is censoring of the data at five births. If there are fewer than five babies in any race/name cell, it is censored (and we do not know whether a cell has zero or was censored). This is primarily a problem for the computation of how many African-American babies have "White" names.

[†] We also tried to use more White-sounding last names for White applicants and more African-American-sounding last names for African-American applicants. The last names used for White applicants are: Baker, Kelly, McCarthy, Murphy, Murray, O'Brien, Ryan, Sullivan, and Walsh. The last names used for African-American applicants are: Jackson, Jones, Robinson, Washington, and Williams.

[‡] The e-mail addresses are registered on Yahoo.com, Angelfire.com, or Hotmail.com.

[§] This period spans tighter and slacker labor markets. In our data, this is apparent as callback rates (and number of new ads) dropped after September 11, 2001. Interestingly, however, the racial gap we measure is the same across these two periods.

TABLE 1—MEAN CALLBACK RATES BY RACIAL SOUNDINGNESS OF NAMES

| | Percent callback for White names | Percent callback for African-American names | Ratio | Percent difference (*p*-value) |
|---|---|---|---|---|
| Sample: | | | | |
| All sent resumes | 9.65 | 6.45 | 1.50 | 3.20 |
| | [2,435] | [2,435] | | (0.0000) |
| Chicago | 8.06 | 5.40 | 1.49 | 2.66 |
| | [1,352] | [1,352] | | (0.0057) |
| Boston | 11.63 | 7.76 | 1.50 | 4.05 |
| | [1,083] | [1,083] | | (0.0023) |
| Females | 9.89 | 6.63 | 1.49 | 3.26 |
| | [1,860] | [1,886] | | (0.0003) |
| Females in administrative jobs | 10.46 | 6.55 | 1.60 | 3.91 |
| | [1,358] | [1,359] | | (0.0003) |
| Females in sales jobs | 8.37 | 6.83 | 1.22 | 1.54 |
| | [502] | [527] | | (0.3523) |
| Males | 8.87 | 5.83 | 1.52 | 3.04 |
| | [575] | [549] | | (0.0513) |

*Notes:* The table reports, for the entire sample and different subsamples of sent resumes, the callback rates for applicants with a White-sounding name (column 1) an an African-American-sounding name (column 2), as well as the ratio (column 3) and difference (column 4) of these callback rates. In brackets in each cell is the number of resumes sent in that cell. Column 4 also reports the *p*-value for a test of proportion testing the null hypothesis that the callback rates are equal across racial groups.

requirements as closely as possible.* In some cases, we slightly alter the résumés to improve the quality of the match, such as by adding the knowledge of a specific software program.

One of the high- and one of the low-quality résumés selected are then drawn at random to receive African-American names, the other high- and low-quality résumés receive White names.[†] We use male and female names for sales jobs, whereas we use nearly exclusively female names for administrative and clerical jobs to increase callback rates.[‡] Based on sex, race, city, and résumé quality, we assign a résumé the appropriate phone number. We also select at random a postal address. Finally, e-mail addresses

are added to most of the high-quality résumés.[§] The final résumés are formatted, with fonts, layout, and cover letter style chosen at random. The résumés are then faxed (or in a few cases mailed) to the employer. All in all, we respond to more than 1,300 employment ads over the entire sample period and send close to 5,000 résumés.

### D. Measuring Responses

We measure whether a given résumé elicits a callback or e-mail back for an interview. For each phone or e-mail response, we use the content of the message left by the employer (name of the applicant, company name, telephone number for contact) to match the response to the corresponding résumé-ad pair.[¶] Any attempt by employers to contact applicants via postal mail cannot be measured in

---

* In some instances, our résumé bank does not have four résumés that are appropriate matches for a given ad. In such instances, we send only two résumés.

† Though the same names are repeatedly used in our experiment, we guarantee that no given ad receives multiple résumés with the same name.

‡ Male names were used for a few administrative jobs in the first month of the experiment.

§ In the first month of the experiment, a few high-quality résumés were sent without e-mail addresses and a few low-quality résumés were given e-mail addresses. See Table 3 for details.

¶ Very few employers used e-mail to contact an applicant back.

our experiment since the addresses are fictitious. Several human resource managers confirmed to us that employers rarely, if ever, contact applicants via postal mail to set up interviews.

### E. Weaknesses of the Experiment

We have already highlighted the strengths of this experiment relative to previous audit studies. We now discuss its weaknesses. First, our outcome measure is crude, even relative to the previous audit studies. Ultimately, one cares about whether an applicant gets the job and about the wage offered conditional on getting the job. Our procedure, however, simply measures callbacks for interviews. To the extent that the search process has even moderate frictions, one would expect that reduced interview rates would translate into reduced job offers. However, we are not able to translate our results into gaps in hiring rates or gaps in earnings.

Another weakness is that the résumés do not directly report race but instead suggest race through personal names. This leads to various sources of concern. First, while the names are chosen to make race salient, some employers may simply not notice the names or not recognize their racial content. On a related note, because we are not assigning race but only race-specific names, our results are not representative of the average African-American (who may not have such a racially distinct name).[*] We return to this issue in Section IV, subsection B.

Finally, and this is an issue pervasive in both our study and the pair-matching audit studies, newspaper ads represent only one channel for job search. As is well known from previous work, social networks are another common means through which people find jobs and one that clearly cannot

be studied here. This omission could qualitatively affect our results if African-Americans use social networks more or if employers who rely more on networks differentiate less by race.[†]

## III. RESULTS

### A. Is There a Racial Gap in Callback?

Table 1 tabulates average callback rates by racial soundingness of names. Included in brackets under each rate is the number of résumés sent in that cell. Row 1 presents our results for the full data set. Résumés with White names have a 9.65 percent chance of receiving a callback. Equivalent résumés with African-American names have a 6.45 percent chance of being called back. This represents a difference in callback rates of 3.20 percentage points, or 50 percent, that can solely be attributed to the name manipulation. Column 4 shows that this difference is statistically significant.[‡] Put in other words, these results imply that a White applicant should expect on average one callback for every 10 ads she or he applies to; on the other hand, an African-American applicant would need to apply to about 15 different ads to achieve the same result.[§]

How large are these effects? While the cost of sending additional résumés might not be large per se, this 50-percent gap could be quite substantial when compared to the rate of arrival of new job

---

[*] As Appendix Table A1 indicates, the African-American names we use are, however, quite common among African-Americans, making this less of a concern.

[†] In fact, there is some evidence that African-Americans may rely less on social networks for their job search (Harry J. Holzer, 1987).

[‡] These statistical tests assume independence of callbacks. We have, however, verified that the results stay significant when we assume that the callbacks are correlated either at the employer or first-name level.

[§] This obviously assumes that African-American applicants cannot assess a priori which firms are more likely to treat them more or less favorably.

openings. In our own study, the biggest constraining factor in sending more résumés was the limited number of new job openings each week. Another way to benchmark the measured return to a White name is to compare it to the returns to other résumé characteristics. For example, in Table 5, we will show that, at the average number of years of experience in our sample, an extra year of experience increases the likelihood of a callback by a 0.4 percentage point. Based on this point estimate, the return to a White name is equivalent to about eight additional years of experience.

Rows 2 and 3 break down the full sample of sent résumés into the Boston and Chicago markets. About 20 percent more résumés were sent in Chicago than in Boston. The average callback rate (across races) is lower in Chicago than in Boston. This might reflect differences in labor market conditions across the two cities over the experimental period or maybe differences in the ability of the MIT and Chicago teams of research assistants in selecting résumés that were good matches for a given help-wanted ad. The percentage difference in callback rates is, however, strikingly similar across both cities. White applicants are 49 percent more likely than African-American applicants to receive a callback in Chicago and 50 percent more likely in Boston. These racial differences are statistically significant in both cities.

Finally, rows 4 to 7 break down the full sample into female and male applicants. Row 4 displays the average results for all female names while rows 5 and 6 break the female sample into administrative (row 5) and sales jobs (row 6); row 7 displays the average results for all male names. As noted earlier, female names were used in both sales and administrative job openings whereas male names were used close to exclusively for sales openings.[*]

_____

[*] Only about 6 percent of all male résumés were sent in response to an administrative job opening.

Looking across occupations, we find a significant racial gap in callbacks for both males (52 percent) and females (49 percent). Comparing males to females in sales occupations, we find a larger racial gap among males (52 percent versus 22 percent). Interestingly, females in sales jobs appear to receive more callbacks than males; however, this (reverse) gender gap is statistically insignificant and economically much smaller than any of the racial gaps discussed above.

Rather than studying the distribution of callbacks at the applicant level, one can also tabulate the distribution of callbacks at the employment-ad level. In Table 2, we compute the fraction of employers that treat White and African-American applicants equally, the fraction of employers that favor White applicants and the fraction of employers that favor African-American applicants. Because we send up to four résumés in response to each sampled ad, the three categories above can each take three different forms. Equal treatment occurs when either no applicant gets called back, one White and one African-American get called back or two Whites and two African-Americans get called back. Whites are favored when either only one White gets called back, two Whites and no African-American get called back or two Whites and one African-American get called back. African-Americans are favored in all other cases.

As Table 2 indicates, equal treatment occurs for about 88 percent of the help-wanted ads. As expected, the major source of equal treatment comes from the high fraction of ads for which no callbacks are recorded (83 percent of the ads). Whites are favored by nearly 8.4 percent of the employers, with a majority of these employers contacting exactly one White applicant. African-Americans, on the other hand, are favored by only about 3.5 percent of employers. We formally test whether there is symmetry in the favoring of Whites over African-Americans and African-Americans over Whites.

TABLE 2—DISTRIBUTION OF CALLBACKS BY EMPLOYMENT AD

| Equal Treatment: | No Callback | 1W + 1B | 2W + 2B |
|---|---|---|---|
| 88.13 percent | 83.37 | 3.48 | 1.28 |
| [1,166] | [1,103] | [46] | [17] |
| Whites Favored (WF): | 1W + 0B | 2W + 0B | 2W + 1B |
| 8.39 percent | 5.59 | 1.44 | 1.36 |
| [111] | [74] | [19] | [18] |
| African-Americans Favored (BF): | 1B + 0W | 2B + 0W | 2B + 1W |
| 3.48 percent | 2.49 | 0.45 | 0.53 |
| [46] | [33] | [6] | [7] |
| $Ho$: WF = BF | | | |
| $p = 0.0000$ | | | |

*Notes:* This table documents the distribution of callbacks at the employment-ad level. "No Callback" is the percent of ads for which none of the fictitious applicants received a callback. "1W + 1B" is the percent of ads for which exactly one White and one African-American applicant received a callback. "2W + 2B" is the percent of ads for which exactly two White applicants and two African-American applicants received a callback. "Equal Treatment" is defined as the sum of "No Callback," "1W + 1B," and "2W + 2B." "1W + 0B" is the percent of ads for which exactly one White applicant and no African-American applicant received a call back. "2W + 0B" is the percent of ads for which excatly two White applicants and no African-American applicant received a callback. "2W + 1B" is the percent of ads for which exactly two White applicants and one African-American applicant received a callback. "Whites Favored" is defined as the sum of "1W + 0B," "2W + 0B," and "2W + 1B." "1B + 0W" is the percent of ads for which exactly one African-American applicant and no White applicant received a callback. "2B + 0W" is the percent of ads for which exactly two African-American applicants and no White applicant received a callback. "2B + 1W" is the percent of ads for which exactly two African-American applicants and one White applicant received a callback. "African-Americans Favored" is defined as the sum of "1B + 0W," "2B + 0W," and "2B + 1W." In brackets in each cell is the number of employment ads in that cell. "*Ho*: WF = WB" reports the *p*-value for a test of symmetry between the proportion of employers that favor White names and the proportion of employers that favor African-American names.

We find that the difference between the fraction of employers favoring Whites and the fraction of employers favoring African-Americans is statistically very significant ($p = 0.0000$).

## B. Do African-Americans Receive Different Returns to Résumé Quality?

Our results so far demonstrate a substantial gap in callback based on applicants' names. Next, we would like to learn more about the factors that may influence this gap. More specifically, we ask how employers respond to improvements in African-American applicants' credentials. To answer this question, we examine how the racial gap in callback varies by résumé quality.

As we explained in Section II, for most of the employment ads we respond to, we send four different résumés: two higher-quality and two lower-quality ones. Table 3 gives a better sense of which factors enter into this subjective classification. Table 3 displays means and standard deviations of

the most relevant résumé characteristics for the full sample (column 1), as well as broken down by race (columns 2 and 3) and résumé quality (columns 4 and 5). Since applicants' names are randomized, there is no difference in résumé characteristics by race. Columns 4 and 5 document the objective differences between résumés subjectively classified as high and low quality. Higher-quality applicants have on average close to an extra year of labor market experience, fewer employment holes (where an employment hole is denned as a period of at least six months without a reported job), are more likely to have worked while at school, and to report some military experience. Also, higher-quality applicants are more likely to have an e-mail address, to have received some honors, and to list some computer skills and other special skills (such as a certification degree or foreign language skills) on their résumé. Note that the higher- and lower-quality résumés do not differ on average with regard to applicants' education level. This reflects the fact that all sent résumés, whether high or low quality, are chosen to

TABLE 3—RESUME CHARACTERISTICS: SUMMARY STATISTICS

| Sample: | All resumes | White names | African-American | Higher quality | Lower quality |
|---|---|---|---|---|---|
| Characteristic: | | | | | |
| College degree | 0.72 | 0.72 | 0.72 | 0.72 | 0.71 |
| $(Y = 1)$ | (0.45) | (0.45) | (0.45) | (0.45) | (0.45) |
| Years of experience | 7.84 | 7.86 | 7.83 | 8.29 | 7.39 |
| | (5.04) | (5.07) | (5.01) | (5.29) | (4.75) |
| Volunteering experience? | 0.41 | 0.41 | 0.41 | 0.79 | 0.03 |
| $(Y = 1)$ | (0.49) | (0.49) | (0.49) | (0.41) | (0.16) |
| Military experience? | 0.10 | 0.09 | 0.10 | 0.19 | 0.00 |
| $(Y = 1)$ | (0.30) | (0.29) | (0.30) | (0.39) | (0.06) |
| E-mail address? | 0.48 | 0.48 | 0.48 | 0.92 | 0.03 |
| $(Y = 1)$ | (0.50) | (0.50) | (0.50) | (0.27) | (0.17) |
| Employment holes? | 0.45 | 0.45 | 0.45 | 0.34 | 0.56 |
| $(Y = 1)$ | (0.50) | (0.50) | (0.50) | (0.47) | (0.50) |
| Work in school? | 0.56 | 0.56 | 0.56 | 0.72 | 0.40 |
| $(Y = 1)$ | (0.50) | (0.50) | (0.50) | (0.45) | (0.49) |
| Honors? | 0.05 | 0.05 | 0.05 | 0.07 | 0.03 |
| $(Y = 1)$ | (0.22) | (0.23) | (0.22) | (0.25) | (0.18) |
| Computer skills? | 0.82 | 0.81 | 0.83 | 0.91 | 0.73 |
| $(Y = 1)$ | (0.38) | (0.39) | (0.37) | (0.29) | (0.44) |
| Special skills? | 0.33 | 0.33 | 0.33 | 0.36 | 0.30 |
| $(Y = 1)$ | (0.47) | (0.47) | (0.47) | (0.48) | (0.46) |
| Fraction high school dropouts in applicant's zip code | 0.19 | 0.19 | 0.19 | 0.19 | 0.18 |
| | (0.08) | (0.08) | (0.08) | (0.08) | (0.08) |
| Fraction college or more in applicant's zip code | 0.21 | 0.21 | 0.21 | 0.21 | 0.22 |
| | (0.17) | (0.17) | (0.17) | (0.17) | (0.17) |
| Fraction Whites in applicant's zip code | 0.54 | 0.55 | 0.54 | 0.53 | 0.55 |
| | (0.33) | (0.33) | (0.33) | (0.33) | (0.33) |
| Fraction African-Americans in applicant's zip code | 0.31 | 0.31 | 0.31 | 0.32 | 0.31 |
| | (0.33) | (0.33) | (0.33) | (0.33) | (0.33) |
| Log(median per capital income) in applicant's zip code | 9.55 | 9.55 | 9.55 | 9.54 | 9.56 |
| | (0.56) | (0.56) | (0.55) | (0.54) | (0.57) |
| Sample size | 4,870 | 2,435 | 2,435 | 2,446 | 2,424 |

*Notes:* The table reports means and standard deviations for the resume characteristics as listed on the left. Column 1 refers to all resumes sent; column 2 refers to resumes with White names; column 3 refers to resumes with African-American names; column 4 refers to higher-quality resumes; column 5 refers to lower-quality resumes. See text for details.

be good matches for a given job opening. About 70 percent of the sent résumés report a college degree.[*]

The last five rows of Table 3 show summary characteristics of the applicants' zip code address. Using 1990 Census data, we compute the fraction of high school dropouts, fraction of college educated or more, fraction of Whites, fraction of African-Americans and log(median per capital income) for each zip code used in the experiment. Since addresses are randomized within cities, these

neighborhood quality measures are uncorrelated with race or résumé quality.

The differences in callback rates between high- and low-quality résumés are presented in Panel A of Table 4. The first thing to note is that the résumé quality manipulation works: higher-quality résumés receive more callbacks. As row 1 indicates, we record a callback rate of close to 11 percent for White applicants with a higher-quality résumé, compared to 8.5 percent for White applicants with lower-quality résumés. This is a statistically significant difference of 2.29 percentage points, or 27 percent ($p = 0.0557$). Most strikingly, African-Americans experience much less of an increase in callback rate for similar improvements in their credentials.

---

[*] This varies from about 50 percent for the clerical and administrative support positions to more than 80 percent for the executive, managerial, and sales representatives positions.

| | Panel A: Subjective Measure of Quality (Percent Callback) | | | |
| --- | --- | --- | --- | --- |
| | Low | High | Ratio | Difference (*p*-value) |
| White names | 8.50 | 10.79 | 1.27 | 2.29 |
| | [1,212] | [1,223] | | (0.0557) |
| African-American names | 6.19 | 6.70 | 1.08 | 0.51 |
| | [1,212] | [1,223] | | (0.6084) |
| | Panel B: Predicted Measure of Quality (Percent Callback) | | | |
| | Low | High | Ratio | Difference (*p*- value) |
| White names | 7.18 | 13.60 | 1.89 | 6.42 |
| | [822] | [816] | | (0.0000) |
| African-American names | 5.37 | 8.60 | 1.60 | 3.23 |
| | [819] | [814] | | (0.0104) |

*Notes:* Panel A reports the mean callback percents for applicant with a White name (row 1) and African-American name (row 2) depending on whether the resume was subjectively qualified as a lower quality or higher quality. In brackets is the number of resumes sent for each race/quality group. The last column reports the *p*-value of a test of proportion testing the null hypothesis that the callback rates are equal across quality groups within each racial group. For Panel B, we use a third of the sample to estimate a probit regression of the callback dummy on the set of resume characteristics as displayed in Table 3. We further control for a sex dummy, a city dummy, six occupation dummies, and a vector of dummy variables for job requirements as listed in the employment ad (see Section III, subsection D, for details). We then use the estimated coefficients on the set of resume characteristics to estimate a predicted callback for the remaining resumes (two-thirds of the sample). We call "high-quality" resumes the resumes that rank above the median predicted callback and "low-quality" resumes the resumes that rank below the median predicted callback. In brackets is the number of resumes sent for each race/quality group. The last column reports the *p*-value of a test of proportion testing the null hypothesis that the callback percents are equal across quality groups within each racial group.

African-Americans with higher-quality résumés receive a callback 6.7 percent of the time, compared to 6.2 percent for African-Americans with lower quality résumés. This is only a 0.51-percentage-point, or 8-percent, difference and this difference is not statistically significant (*p* = 0.6084).

Instead of relying on the subjective quality classification, Panel B directly uses résumé characteristics to classify the résumés. More specifically, we use a random subsample of one-third of the résumés to estimate a probit regression of the callback dummy on the résumé characteristics listed in Table 3. We further control for a sex dummy, a city dummy, six occupation dummies, and a vector of job requirements as listed in the employment ads.* We then use the estimated coefficients on the résumé characteristics to rank the remaining two-thirds of the résumés by predicted callback. In Panel B, we classify as "high" those résumés that have above-median-predicted callback; similarly,

we classify as "low" those résumés that have below-median-predicted callback. As one can see from Panel B, qualitatively similar results emerge from this analysis. While African-Americans do appear to significantly benefit from higher-quality résumés under this alternative classification, they benefit less than Whites. The ratio of callback rates for high- versus low-quality résumés is 1.60 for African Americans, compared to 1.89 for Whites.

In Table 5, we directly report the results of race-specific probit regressions of the callback dummy on résumé characteristics. We, however, start in column 1 with results for the full sample of sent résumés. As one can see, many of the résumé characteristics have the expected effect on the likelihood of a callback. The addition of an e-mail address, honors, and special skills all have a positive and significant effect on the likelihood of a callback.[†] Also, more experienced applicants are more likely

_____

* See Section III, subsection D, for more details on these occupation categories and job requirements.

_____

† Note that the e-mail address dummy, because it is close to perfectly correlated with the subjective résumé-quality variable, may in part capture some other unmeasured ré-

TABLE 5—Effect of Resume Characteristics on Likelihood of Callback

| Dependent Variable: Callback Dummy Sample: | All resumes | White names | African-American names |
|---|---|---|---|
| Years of experience (*10) | 0.07 | 0.13 | 0.02 |
| | (0.03) | (0.04) | (0.03) |
| Years of experience$^2$ (*100) | −0.02 | −0.04 | −0.00 |
| | (0.01) | (0.01) | (0.01) |
| Volunteering? (Y = 1) | −0.01 | −0.01 | 0.01 |
| | (0.01) | (0.01) | (0.01) |
| Military experience? (Y = 1) | −0.00 | 0.02 | −0.01 |
| | (0.01) | (0.03) | (0.02) |
| E-mail? (Y = 1) | 0.02 | 0.03 | −0.00 |
| | (0.01) | (0.01) | (0.01) |
| Employment holes? (Y = 1) | 0.02 | 0.03 | 0.01 |
| | (0.01) | (0.02) | (0.01) |
| Work in school? (Y = 1) | 0.01 | 0.02 | −0.00 |
| | (0.01) | (0.01) | (0.01) |
| Honors? (Y = 1) | 0.05 | 0.06 | 0.03 |
| | (0.02) | (0.03) | (0.02) |
| Computer skills? (Y = 1) | −0.02 | −0.04 | −0.00 |
| | (0.01) | (0.02) | (0.01) |
| Special skills? (Y = 1) | 0.05 | 0.06 | 0.04 |
| | (0.01) | (0.02) | (0.01) |
| *Ho:* Resume characteristics effects are all zero (*p*-value) | 54.50 | 57.59 | 23.85 |
| | (0.0000) | (0.0000) | (0.0080) |
| Standard deviation of predicted callback | 0.047 | 0.062 | 0.037 |
| Sample size | 4,870 | 2,435 | 2,435 |

*Notes:* Each column gives the results of a probit regression where the dependent variable is the callback dummy. Reported in the table are estimated marginal changes in probability for the continuous variables and estimated discrete changes for the dummy variables. Also included in each regression are a city dummy, a sex dummy, six occupation dummies, and a vector of dummy variables for job requirements as listed in the employment ad (see Section III, subsection D, for details). Sample in column 1 is the entire set of sent resumes; sample in column 2 is the set of resumes with White names; sample in column 3 is the set of resumes with African-American names. Standard errors are corrected for clustering of the observations at the employment-ad level. Reported in the second to last row are the *p*-values for a $\chi^2$ testing that the effects on the resume characteristics are all zero. Reported in the second to last row is the standard deviation of the predicted callback rate.

to get called back: at the average number of years of experience in our sample (eight years), each extra year of experience increases the likelihood of a callback by about a 0.4 percentage point. The most counterintuitive effects come from computer skills, which appear to negatively predict callback, and employment holes, which appear to positively predict callback.

The same qualitative patterns hold in column 2 where we focus on White applicants. More importantly, the estimated returns to an e-mail address, additional work experience, honors, and special skills appear economically stronger for that

sumé characteristics that may have led us to categorize a given résumé as higher quality.

racial group. For example, at the average number of years of experience in our sample, each extra year of experience increases the likelihood of a callback by about 0.7 percentage point.

As might have been expected from the two previous columns, we find that the estimated returns on these résumé characteristics are all economically and statistically weaker for African-American applicants (column 3). In fact, all the estimated effects for African-Americans are statistically insignificant, except for the return to special skills. Résumé characteristics thus appear less predictive of callback rates for African-Americans than they are for Whites. To illustrate this more saliently, we predict callback rates using either regression estimates in column 2 or regression estimates in column 3. The standard

TABLE 6—EFFECT OF APPLICANT'S ADDRESS ON LIKELIHOOD OF CALLBACK

Dependent Variable: Callback Dummy

| Zip code characteristic: | Fraction Whites | | Fraction college or more | | Log(per capital income) | |
|---|---|---|---|---|---|---|
| Zip code characteristic | 0.020 | 0.020 | 0.054 | 0.053 | 0.018 | 0.014 |
| | (0.012) | (0.016) | (0.022) | (0.031) | (0.007) | (0.010) |
| Zip code characteristic* African-American name | — | −0.000 | — | −0.002 | — | 0.008 |
| | | (0.024) | | (0.048) | | (0.015) |
| African-American name | — | −0.031 | — | −0.031 | — | −0.112 |
| | | (0.015) | | (0.013) | | (0.152) |

*Notes:* Each column gives the results of a probit regression where the dependent variable is the callback dummy. Reported in the table is the estimated marginal change in probability. Also included in columns 1, 3, and 5 is a city dummy; also included in columns 2, 4, and 6 is a city dummy and a city dummy interacted with a race dummy. Standard errors are corrected for clustering of the observations at the employment-ad level.

deviation of the predicted callback from column 2 is 0.062, whereas it is only 0.037 from column 3. In summary, employers simply seem to pay less attention or discount more the characteristics listed on the résumés with African-American-sounding names. Taken at face value, these results suggest that African-Americans may face relatively lower individual incentives to invest in higher skills.[*]

## C. Applicants' Address

An incidental feature of our experimental design is the random assignment of addresses to the résumés. This allows us to examine whether and how an applicant's residential address, all else equal, affects the likelihood of a callback. In addition, and most importantly for our purpose, we can also ask whether African-American applicants are helped relatively more by residing in more affluent neighborhoods.

We perform this analysis in Table 6. We start (columns 1, 3, and 5) by discussing the effect of neighborhood of residence across all applicants. Each of these columns reports the results of a probit regression of the callback dummy on a specific zip code characteristic and a city dummy. Standard errors are corrected for clustering of the observations

at the employment-ad level. We find a positive and significant effect of neighborhood quality on the likelihood of a callback. Applicants living in Whiter (column 1), more educated (column 3), or higher-income (column 5) neighborhoods have a higher probability of receiving a callback. For example, a 10-percentage-point increase in the fraction of college-educated in zip code of residence increases the likelihood of a callback by a 0.54 percentage point (column 3).

In columns 2, 4, and 6, we further interact the zip code characteristic with a dummy variable for whether the applicant is African-American or not. Each of the probit regressions in these columns also includes an African-American dummy, a city dummy, and an interaction of the city dummy with the African-American dummy. There is no evidence that African-Americans benefit any more than Whites from living in a Whiter, more educated zip code. The estimated interactions between fraction White and fraction college educated with the African-American dummy are economically very small and statistically insignificant. We do find an economically more meaningful effect of zip code median income level on the racial gap in callback; this effect, however, is statistically insignificant.

In summary, while neighborhood quality affects callbacks, African-Americans do not benefit more than Whites from living in better neighborhoods. If ghettos and bad neighborhoods are particularly

---

[*] This of course assumes that the changes in job and wage offers associated with higher skills are the same across races, or at least not systematically larger for African-Americans.

stigmatizing for African-Americans, one might have expected African-Americans to be helped more by having a "better" address. Our results do not support this hypothesis.

## D. Job and Employer Characteristics

Table 7 studies how various job requirements (as listed in the employment ads) and employer characteristics correlate with the racial gap in callback.

Each row of Table 7 focuses on a specific job or employer characteristic, with summary statistics in column 2. Column 3 shows the results of various probit regressions. Each entry in this column is the marginal effect of the specific characteristic listed in that row on the racial gap in callback. More specifically, each entry is from a separate probit regression of a callback dummy on an African-American dummy, the characteristic listed in that row and the interaction of that characteristic with

TABLE 7—EFFECT OF JOB REQUIREMENT AND EMPLOYER CHARACTERISTICS ON RACIAL DIFFERENCES IN CALLBACKS

| Job requirement: | Sample mean (standard deviation) | Marginal effect on callbacks for African-American names |
|---|---|---|
| Any requirement? (Y = 1) | 0.79 | 0.023 |
| | (0.41) | (0.015) |
| Experience? (Y = 1) | 0.44 | 0.011 |
| | (0.49) | (0.013) |
| Computer skills? (Y = 1) | 0.44 | 0.000 |
| | (0.50) | (0.013) |
| Communication skills? (Y = 1) | 0.12 | −0.000 |
| | (0.33) | (0.015) |
| Organization skills? (Y = 1) | 0.07 | 0.028 |
| | (0.26) | (0.029) |
| Education? (Y = 1) | 0.11 | −0.031 |
| | (0.31) | (0.017) |
| Total number of requirements | 1.18 | 0.002 |
| | (0.93) | (0.006) |

| Employer characteristic: | Sample mean (standard deviation) | Marginal effect on callbacks for African-American names |
|---|---|---|
| Equal opportunity employer? (Y = 1) | 0.29 | −0.013 |
| | (0.45) | (0.012) |
| Federal contractor? (Y = 1) | 0.11 | −0.035 |
| (N = 3,102) | (0.32) | (0.016) |
| Log(employment) | 5.74 | −0.001 |
| (N = 1,690) | (1.74) | (0.005) |
| Ownership status: | | |
| (N = 2,878) | | |
| Privately held | 0.74 | 0.011 |
| | | (0.019) |
| Publicly traded | 0.15 | −0.025 |
| | | (0.015) |
| Not-for-profit | 0.11 | 0.025 |
| | | (0.042) |
| Fraction African-Americans in employer's zip code | 0.08 | 0.117 |
| (N = 1,918) | (0.15) | (0.062) |

*Notes:* Sample is all sent resumes (N = 4,870) unless otherwise specified in column 1. Column 2 reports means and standard deviations (in parentheses) for the job requirement or employer characteristic. For ads listing an experience requirement, 50.1 percent listed "some," 24.0 percent listed "two years or less," and 25.9 percent listed "three years or more." For ads listing an education requirement, 8.8 percent listed a high school degree, 48.5 percent listed some college, and 42.7 percent listed at least a four-year college degree. Column 3 reports the marginal effect of the job requirement or employer characteristic listed in that row on differential treatment. Specifically, each cell in column 3 corresponds to a different probit regression of the callback dummy on an African-American name dummy, a dummy for the requirement or characteristic listed in that row and the interaction of the requirement or characteristic dummy with the African-American name dummy. Reported in each cell is the estimated change in probability for the interaction term. Standard errors are corrected for clustering of the observations at the employment-ad level.

the African-American dummy. The reported coefficient is that on the interaction term.

We start with job requirements. About 80 percent of the ads state some form of requirement. About 44 percent of the ads require some minimum experience, of which roughly 50 percent simply ask for "some experience," 24 percent less than two years, and 26 percent at least three years of experience. About 44 percent of ads mention some computer knowledge requirement, which can range from Excel or Word to more esoteric software programs. Good communication skills are explicitly required in about 12 percent of the ads. Organization skills are mentioned 7 percent of the time. Finally, only about 11 percent of the ads list an explicit education requirement. Of these, 8.8 percent require a high school degree, 48.5 percent some college (such as an associate degree), and the rest at least a four-year college degree.[*]

Despite this variability, we find little systematic relationship between any of the requirements and the racial gap in callback. The point estimates in column 3 show no consistent economic pattern and are all statistically weak. Measures of job quality, such as experience or computer skills requirements, do not predict the extent of the racial gap. Communication or other interpersonal skill requirements have no effect on the racial gap either.[†]

We also study employer characteristics. Collecting such information is a more difficult task since it is not readily available from the employment ads we respond to. The only piece of employer information we can directly collect from the employment ad is whether or not the employer explicitly states being an "Equal Opportunity Employer." In several cases, the name of the employer is not even mentioned in the ad and the only piece of information we can rely on is the fax number which applications must be submitted to. We therefore have to turn to supplemental data sources. For employment ads that do not list a specific employer, we first use the fax number to try to identify the company name via Web reverse-lookup services. Based on company names, we use three different data sources (*Onesource Business Browser, Thomas Register,* and *Dun and Bradstreet Million Dollar Directory, 2001*) to track company information such as total employment, industry, and ownership status. Using this same set of data sources, we also try to identify the specific zip code of the company (or company branch) that résumés are to be sent to. Finally, we use the Federal Procurement and Data Center Web site to find a list of companies that have federal contracts.[‡] The racial difference in callback rates for the subsamples where employer characteristics could be determined is very similar in magnitude to that in the full sample.

Employer characteristics differ significantly across ads. Twenty-nine percent of all employers explicitly state that they are "Equal Opportunity Employers." Eleven percent are federal contractors and, therefore, might face greater scrutiny under affirmative action laws. The average company size is around 2,000 employees but there is a lot of variation across firms. Finally, 74 percent of the firms are privately held, 15 percent are publicly traded, and 11 percent are not-for-profit organizations.

Neither "Equal Opportunity Employers" nor federal contractors appear to treat African-Americans

---

[*] Other requirements sometimes mentioned include typing skills for secretaries (with specific words-per-minute minimum thresholds), and, more rarely, foreign language skills.

[†] Other ways of estimating these effects produce a similar nonresult. Among other things, we considered including a city dummy or estimating the effects separately by city; we also estimated one single probit regression including all requirements at once.

[‡] This Web site (www.fpdc.gov) is accurate up to and including March 21, 2000.

more favorably. In fact, each of these employer characteristics is associated with a larger racial gap in callback (and this effect is marginally significant for federal contractors). Differential treatment does not vary with employer size.* Point estimates indicate less differential treatment in the not-for-profit sector; however, this effect is very noisily estimated.†

In an unpublished Appendix (available from the authors upon request), we also study how the racial gap in callback varies by occupation and industry. Based on the employment ad listings, we classify the job openings into six occupation categories: executives and managers; administrative supervisors; sales representatives; sales workers; secretaries and legal assistants; clerical workers. We also, when possible, classify employers into six industry categories: manufacturing; transportation and communication; wholesale and retail trade; finance, insurance, and real estate; business and personal services; health, educational, and social services. We then compute occupation and industry-specific racial gaps in callback and relate these gaps to 1990 Census-based measures of occupation and industry earnings, as well as Census-based measures of the White/African-American wage gap in these occupations and industries.

We find a positive White/African-American gap in callbacks in all occupation and industry categories (except for transportation and communication).

While average earnings vary a lot across the occupations covered in the experiment, we find no systematic relationship between occupation earnings and the racial gap in callback. Similarly, the industry-specific gaps in callback do not relate well to a measure of inter-industry wage differentials. In fact, while the racial gap in callback rates varies somewhat across occupations and industries, we cannot reject the null hypothesis that the gap is the same across all these categories.

The last row of Table 7 focuses on the marginal effect of employer location on the racial gap in callback.‡ We use as a measure of employer location the zip code of the company (or company branch) résumés were to be sent to. More specifically, we ask whether differential treatment by race varies with the fraction of African-Americans in the employer's zip code. We find a marginally significant positive effect of employer location on African-American callbacks but this effect is extremely small. In regressions not reported here (but available from the authors upon request), we reestimate this effect separately by city. While the point estimates are positive for both cities, the effect is only statistically significant for Chicago.

## IV. INTERPRETATION

Three main sets of questions arise when interpreting the results above. First, does a higher callback rate for White applicants imply that employers are discriminating against African-Americans? Second, does our design only isolate the effect of race or is the name manipulation conveying some other factors than race? Third, how do our results relate to different models of racial discrimination?

---

* Similar results hold when we measure employer size using a total sales measure rather than an employment measure.

† Our measurement of the racial gap by firm or employer type may not be a good indicator of the fraction of African-Americans actually employed in these firms. For example, "Equal Opportunity Employers" may receive a higher fraction of African-American résumés. Their actual hiring may therefore look different from that of non "Equal Opportunity Employers" when one considers the full set of résumés they receive.

‡ For previous work on the effect of employer location on labor market discrimination, see, for example, Steven Raphael et al. (2000).

## A. Interpreting Callback Rates

Our results indicate that for two identical individuals engaging in an identical job search, the one with an African-American name would receive fewer interviews. Does differential treatment within our experiment imply that employers are discriminating against African-Americans (whether it is rational, prejudice-based, or an other form of discrimination)? In other words, could the lower callback rate we record for African-American résumés *within our experiment* be consistent with a racially neutral review of the *entire pool* of résumés the surveyed employers receive?

In a racially neutral review process, employers would rank order résumés based on their quality and call back all applicants that are above a certain threshold. Because names are randomized, the White and African-American résumés we send should rank similarly on average. So, irrespective of the skill and racial composition of the applicant pool, a race-blind selection rule would generate equal treatment of Whites and African-Americans. So our results must imply that employers use race as a factor when reviewing résumés, which matches the legal definition of discrimination.

But even rules where employers are not trying to interview as few African-American applicants as possible may generate observed differential treatment in our experiment. One such hiring rule would be employers trying to interview a target level of African-American candidates. For example, perhaps the average firm in our experiment aims to produce an interview pool that matches the population base rate. This rule could produce the observed differential treatment if the average firm receives a higher proportion of African-American résumés than the population base rate because

African-Americans disproportionately apply to the jobs and industries in our sample.[*]

Some of our other findings may be consistent with such a rule. For example, the fact that "Equal Opportunity Employers" or federal contractors do not appear to discriminate any less may reflect the fact that such employers receive more applications from African-Americans. On the other hand, other key findings run counter to this rule. As we discuss above, we find no systematic difference in the racial gap in callback across occupational or industry categories, despite the large variation in the fraction

---

[*] Another variant of this argument is that the (up to) two African-American résumés we sent are enough to significantly distort the racial composition of the entire applicant pool. This is unlikely for two reasons. First, anecdotal evidence and the empirically low callback rates we record suggest that firms typically receive many hundreds of résumés in response to each ad they post. Hence, the (up to) four résumés we send out are unlikely to influence the racial composition of the pool. Second, the similar racial gap in callback we observe across the two cities goes counter to this interpretation since the racial composition base rates differ quite a lot across these two cities. Another variant of this argument is that, for some reason, the average firm in our sample receives a lot of high-quality résumés from African-American applicants and much fewer high-quality résumés from White applicants. Hypothetically, this might occur if high-quality African-Americans are much more likely to use help-wanted ads rather than other job search channels. If employers perform within-race comparisons and again want to target a certain racial mix in their interviewing and hiring, our African-American résumés may naturally receive lower callbacks as they are competing with many more high-quality applicants. This specific argument would be especially relevant in a case where the average sampled employer is "known" to be good to African-Americans. But our selection procedure for the employment ads did not allow for such screening: we simply responded to as many ads as possible in the targeted occupational categories.

of African-Americans looking for work in those categories. African-Americans are underrepresented in managerial occupations, for example. If employers matched base rates in the population, the few African-Americans who apply to these jobs should receive a higher callback rate than Whites. Yet, we find that the racial gap in managerial occupations is the same as in all the other job categories. This rule also runs counter to our findings on returns to skill. Suppose firms are struggling to find White applicants but overwhelmed with African-American ones. Then they should be less sensitive to the quality of White applicants (as they are trying to fill in their hiring quota for Whites) and much more sensitive to the quality of Black applicants (when they have so many to pick from). Thus, it is unlikely that the differential treatment we observe is generated by hiring rules such as these.

## B. Potential Confounds

While the names we have used in this experiment strongly signal racial origin, they may also signal some other personal trait. More specifically, one might be concerned that employers are inferring social background from the personal name. When employers read a name like "Tyrone" or "Latoya," they may assume that the person comes from a disadvantaged background.[*] In the extreme form of this social background interpretation, employers do not care at all about race but are discriminating only against the social background conveyed by the names we have chosen.[†]

---

[*] Roland Fryer and Steven Levitt (2003) provide a recent analysis of social background and naming conventions amongst African-Americans.

[†] African-Americans as a whole come from more disadvantaged backgrounds than Whites. For this social class effect to be something of independent interest, one must assert that African-Americans with the African-American

While plausible, we feel that some of our earlier results are hard to reconcile with this interpretation. For example, in Table 6, we found that while employers value "better" addresses, African-Americans are not helped more than Whites by living in Whiter or more educated neighborhoods. If the African-American names we have chosen mainly signal negative social background, one might have expected the estimated name gap to be lower for better addresses. Also, if the names mainly signal social background, one might have expected the name gap to be higher for jobs that rely more on soft skills or require more interpersonal interactions. We found no such evidence in Table 7.

We, however, directly address this alternative interpretation by examining the average social background of babies born with the names used in the experiment. We were able to obtain birth certificate data on mother's education (less than high school, high school or more) for babies born in Massachusetts between 1970 and 1986.[‡] For each

---

names we have selected are from a lower social background than the average African-American and/or that Whites with the White names we have selected are from a higher social background than the average White. We come back to this point below.

[‡] This longer time span (compared to that used to assess name frequencies) was imposed on us for confidentiality reasons. When fewer than 10 births with education data available are recorded in a particular education-name cell, the exact number of births in that cell is not reported and we impute five births. Our results are not sensitive to this imputation. One African-American female name (Latonya) and two male names (Rasheed and Hakim) were imputed in this way. One African-American male name (Tremayne) had too few births with available education data and was therefore dropped from this analysis. Our results are qualitatively similar when we use a larger data set of California births for the years 1989 to 2000 (kindly provided to us by Steven Levitt).

---

TABLE 8—CALLBACK RATE AND MOTHER'S EDUCATION BY FIRST NAME

| White female | | | African-American female | | |
|---|---|---|---|---|---|
| Name | Percent callback | Mother education | Name | Percent callback | Mother education |
| Emily | 7.9 | 96.6 | Aisha | 2.2 | 77.2 |
| Anne | 8.3 | 93.1 | Keisha | 3.8 | 68.8 |
| Jill | 8.4 | 92.3 | Tamika | 5.5 | 61.5 |
| Allison | 9.5 | 95.7 | Lakisha | 5.5 | 55.6 |
| Laurie | 9.7 | 93.4 | Tanisha | 5.8 | 64.0 |
| Sarah | 9.8 | 97.9 | Latoya | 8.4 | 55.5 |
| Meredith | 10.2 | 81.8 | Kenya | 8.7 | 70.2 |
| Carrie | 13.1 | 80.7 | Latonya | 9.1 | 31.3 |
| Kristen | 13.1 | 93.4 | Ebony | 9.6 | 65.6 |
| Average | | 91.7 | Average | | 61.0 |
| Overall | | 83.9 | Overall | | 70.2 |
| Correlation | −0.318 | (p = 0.404) | Correlation | −0.383 | (p = 0.309) |

| White male | | | African-American male | | |
|---|---|---|---|---|---|
| Name | Percent callback | Mother education | Name | Percent callback | Mother education |
| Todd | 5.9 | 87.7 | Rasheed | 3.0 | 77.3 |
| Neil | 6.6 | 85.7 | Tremayne | 4.3 | — |
| Geoffrey | 6.8 | 96.0 | Kareem | 4.7 | 67.4 |
| Brett | 6.8 | 93.9 | Darnell | 4.8 | 66.1 |
| Brendan | 7.7 | 96.7 | Tyrone | 5.3 | 64.0 |
| Greg | 7.8 | 88.3 | Hakim | 5.5 | 73.7 |
| Matthew | 9.0 | 93.1 | Jamal | 6.6 | 73.9 |
| Jay | 13.4 | 85.4 | Leroy | 9.4 | 53.3 |
| Brad | 15.9 | 90.5 | Jermaine | 9.6 | 57.5 |
| Average | | 91.7 | Average | | 66.7 |
| Overall | | 83.5 | Overall | | 68.9 |
| Correlation | −0.0251 | (p = 0.949) | Correlation | −0.595 | (p = 0.120) |

*Notes:* This table reports, for each first name used in the experiment, callback rate and average mother education. Mother education for a given first name is defined as the percent of babies born with that name in Massachusetts between 1970 and 1986 whose mother had at least completed a high school degree (see text for details). Within each sex/race group, first names are ranked by increasing callback rate. "Average" reports, within each race-gender group, the average mother education for all the babies born with one of the names used in the experiment. "Overall" reports, within each race-gender group, average mother education for all babies born in Massachusetts between 1970 and 1986 in that race-gender group. "Correlation" reports the Spearman rank order correlation between callback rate and mother education *within* each race-gender group as well as the *p*-value for the test of independence.

first name in our experiment, we compute the fraction of babies with that name and, in that gender-race cell, whose mothers have at least completed a high school degree.

In Table 8, we display the average callback rate for each first name along with this proxy for social background. Within each race-gender group, the names are ranked by increasing callback rate. Interestingly, there is significant variation in callback rates by name. Of course, chance alone could produce such variation because of the rather small

number of observations in each cell (about 200 for the female names and 70 for the male names).*

---

* We formally tested whether this variation was significant by estimating a probit regression of the callback dummy on all the personal first names, allowing for clustering of the observations at the employment-ad level. For all but African-American females, we cannot reject the null hypothesis that all the first name effects in the same race-gender group are the same. Of course, a lack of a rejection does not mean there is no underlying pattern in the

The row labeled "Average" reports the average fraction of mothers that have at least completed high school for the set of names listed in that gender-race group. The row labeled "Overall" reports the average fraction of mothers that have at least completed high school for the full sample of births in that gender-race group. For example, 83.9 percent of White female babies born between 1970 and 1986 have mothers with at least a high school degree; 91.7 percent of the White female babies with one of the names used in the experiment have mothers with at least a high school degree.

Consistent with a social background interpretation, the African-American names we have chosen fall below the African-American average. For African-American male names, however, the gap between the experimental names and the population average is negligible. For White names, both the male and female names are above the population average.

But, more interestingly to us, there is substantial between-name heterogeneity in social background. African-American babies named Kenya or Jamal are affiliated with much higher mothers' education than African-American babies named Latonya or Leroy. Conversely, White babies named Carrie or Neil have lower social background than those named Emily or Geoffrey. This allows for a direct test of the social background hypothesis within our sample: are names associated with a worse social background discriminated against more? In the last row in each gender-race group, we report the rank-order correlation between callback rates and mother's education. The social background hypothesis predicts a positive correlation. Yet, for all four categories, we find the exact opposite. The $p$-values indicate that we cannot reject independence at standard significance levels except in the case of

African-American males where we can almost reject it at the 10-percent level ($p = 0.120$). In summary, this test suggests little evidence that social background drives the measured race gap.

Names might also influence our results through familiarity. One could argue that the African-American names used in the experiment simply appear odd to human resource managers and that any odd name is discriminated against. But as noted earlier, the names we have selected are not particularly uncommon among African-Americans (see Appendix Table A1). We have also performed a similar exercise to that of Table 8 and measured the rank-order correlation between name-specific callback rates and name frequency within each gender-race group. We found no systematic positive correlation.

There is one final potential confound to our results. Perhaps what appears as a bias against African-Americans is actually the result of *reverse discrimination*. If qualified African-Americans are thought to be in high demand, then employers with average quality jobs might feel that an equally talented African-American would never accept an offer from them and thereby never call her or him in for an interview. Such an argument might also explain why African-Americans do not receive as strong a return as Whites to better résumés, since higher qualification only strengthens this argument. But this interpretation would suggest that among the better jobs, we ought to see evidence of reverse discrimination, or at least a smaller racial gap. However, as we discussed in Section III, subsection D, we do not find any such evidence. The racial gap does not vary across jobs with different skill requirements, nor does it vary across occupation categories. Even among the better jobs in our

---

between-name variation in callbacks that might have been detectable with larger sample sizes.

sample, we find that employers significantly favor applicants with White names.[*]

## C. Relation to Existing Theories

What do these results imply for existing models of discrimination? Economic theories of discrimination can be classified into two main categories: taste-based and statistical discrimination models.[†] Both sets of models can obviously "explain" our average racial gap in callbacks. But can these models explain our other findings? More specifically, we discuss the relevance of these models with a focus on two of the facts that have been uncovered in this paper: (i) the lower returns to credentials for African-Americans; (ii) the relative uniformity of the race gap across occupations, job requirements and, to a lesser extent, employer characteristics and industries.

Taste-based models (Gary S. Becker, 1961) differ in whose prejudiced "tastes" they emphasize: customers, coworkers, or employers. Customer and co-worker discrimination models seem at odds with the lack of significant variation of the racial gap by occupation and industry categories, as the amount of customer contact and the fraction of White employees vary quite a lot across these categories. We do not find a larger racial gap among jobs that explicitly require "communication skills" and jobs for which we expect either customer or coworker contacts to be higher (retail sales for example).

Because we do not know what drives employer tastes, employer discrimination models could be consistent with the lack of occupation and industry variation. Employer discrimination also matches the finding that employers located in more African-American neighborhoods appear to discriminate somewhat less. However, employer discrimination models would struggle to explain why African-Americans get relatively lower returns to their credentials. Indeed, the cost of indulging the discrimination taste should increase as the minority applicants' credentials increase.[‡]

Statistical discrimination models are the prominent alternative to the taste-based models in the economics literature. In one class of statistical discrimination models, employers use (observable) race to proxy for *unobservable* skills (e.g., Edmund S. Phelps, 1972; Kenneth J. Arrow, 1973). This class of models struggle to explain the credentials effect as well. Indeed, the added credentials should lead to a larger update for African-Americans and hence greater returns to skills for that group.

A second class of statistical discrimination models "emphasize the precision of the information that employers have about individual productivity" (Altonji and Blank, 1999). Specifically, in these models, employers believe that the same observable signal is more precise for Whites than for African-Americans (Dennis J. Aigner and Glenn G. Cain, 1977; Shelly J. Lundberg and Richard Startz, 1983; Bradford Cornell and Ivo Welch, 1996). Under such models, African-Americans receive lower returns to observable skills because employers place less weight on these skills. However, how

---

[*] One might argue that employers who reverse-discriminate hire through less formal channels than help-wanted ads. But this would imply that African-Americans are less likely to find jobs through formal channels. The evidence on exit out of unemployment does not paint a clear picture in this direction (Holzer, 1987).

[†] Darity and Mason (1998) provide a more thorough review of a variety of economic theories of discrimination.

[‡] One could, however, assume that employer tastes differ not just by race but also by race and skill, so that employers have greater prejudice against minority workers with better credentials. But the opposite preferences, employers having a particular distaste for low-skilled African-Americans, also seem reasonable.

reasonable is this interpretation for our experiment? First, it is important to note that we are using the same set of résumé characteristics for both racial groups. So the lower precision of information for African-Americans cannot be that, for example, an employer does not know what a high school degree from a very African-American neighborhood means (as in Aigner and Cain, 1977). Second, many of the credentials on the résumés are in fact externally and easily verifiable, such as a certification for a specific software.

An alternative version of these models would rely on bias in the observable signal rather than differential variance or noise of these signals by race. Perhaps the skills of African-Americans are discounted because affirmative action makes it easier for African-Americans to get these skills. While this is plausible for credentials such as an employee-of-the-month honor, it is unclear why this would apply to more verifiable and harder skills. It is equally unclear why work experience would be less rewarded since our study suggests that getting a job is more, not less, difficult for African-Americans.

The uniformity of the racial gap across occupations is also troubling for a statistical discrimination interpretation. Numerous factors that should affect the level of statistical discrimination, such as the importance of unobservable skills, the observability of qualifications, the precision of observable skills and the ease of performance measurement, may vary quite a lot across occupations.

This discussion suggests that perhaps other models may do a better job at explaining our findings. One simple alternative model is lexicographic search by employers. Employers receive so many résumés that they may use quick heuristics in reading these résumés. One such heuristic could be to simply read no further when they see an African-American name. Thus they may never see the skills of African-American candidates and this could explain why these skills are not rewarded. This might

also to some extent explain the uniformity of the race gap since the screening process (i.e., looking through a large set of résumés) may be quite similar across the variety of jobs we study.[*]

## V. CONCLUSION

This paper suggests that African-Americans face differential treatment when searching for jobs and this may still be a factor in why they do poorly in the labor market. Job applicants with African-American names get far fewer callbacks for each résumé they send out. Equally importantly, applicants with African-American names find it hard to overcome this hurdle in callbacks by improving their observable skills or credentials.

Taken at face value, our results on differential returns to skill have possibly important policy implications. They suggest that training programs alone may not be enough to alleviate the racial gap in labor market outcomes. For training to work, some general-equilibrium force outside the context of our experiment would have to be at play. In fact, if African-Americans recognize how employers reward their skills, they may rationally be less willing than Whites to even participate in these programs.

---

[*]   Another explanation could be based on employer stereotyping or categorizing. If employers have coarser stereotypes for African-Americans, many of our results would follow. See Melinda Jones (2002) for the relevant psychology and Mullainathan (2003) for a formalization of the categorization concept.

| White female Name | L(W)/L(B) | Perception White | African-American female Name | L(B)/L(W) | Perception Black |
|---|---|---|---|---|---|
| Allison | ∞ | 0.926 | Aisha | 209 | 0.97 |
| Anne | ∞ | 0.962 | Ebony | ∞ | 0.9 |
| Carrie | ∞ | 0.923 | Keisha | 116 | 0.93 |
| Emily | ∞ | 0.925 | Kenya | ∞ | 0.967 |
| Jill | ∞ | 0.889 | Lakisha | ∞ | 0.967 |
| Laurie | ∞ | 0.963 | Latonya | ∞ | 1 |
| Kristen | ∞ | 0.963 | Latoya | ∞ | 1 |
| Meredith | ∞ | 0.926 | Tamika | 284 | 1 |
| Sarah | ∞ | 0.852 | Tanisha | ∞ | 1 |
| Fraction of all births: | | | Fraction of all births: | | |
| 3.8 percent | | | 7.1 percent | | |

| White male Name | L(W)/L(B) | Perception White | African-American male Name | L(B)/L(W) | Perception Black |
|---|---|---|---|---|---|
| Brad | ∞ | 1 | Darnell | ∞ | 0.967 |
| Brendan | ∞ | 0.667 | Hakim | | 0.933 |
| Geoffrey | ∞ | 0.731 | Jamal | 257 | 0.967 |
| Greg | ∞ | 1 | Jermaine | 90.5 | 1 |
| Brett | ∞ | 0.923 | Kareem | ∞ | 0.967 |
| Jay | ∞ | 0.926 | Leroy | 44.5 | 0.933 |
| Matthew | ∞ | 0.888 | Rasheed | ∞ | 0.931 |
| Neil | ∞ | 0.654 | Tremayne | ∞ | 0.897 |
| Todd | ∞ | 0.926 | Tyrone | 62.5 | 0.900 |
| Fraction of all births: | | | Fraction of all births: | | |
| 1.7 percent | | | 3.1 percent | | |

*Notes:* This table tabulates the different first names used in the experiment and their identifiability. The first column reports the likelihood that a baby born with that name (in Massachusetts between 1974 and 1979) is White (or African-American) relative to the likelihood that it is African-American (White). The second column reports the probability that the name was picked as White (or African-American) in an independent field survey of people. The last row for each group of names shows the proportion of all births in that race group that these names account for.

# REFERENCES

**Aigner, Dennis J. and Cain. Glenn G.** "Statistical Theories of Discrimination in Labor Markets." *Industrial and Labor Relations Review,* January 1977, *30*(1), pp. 175–87.

**Altonji, Joseph G. and Blank, Rebecca M.** "Race and Gender in the Labor Markey," in Orley Ashenfelter and David Card, eds., *Handbook of labor economics,* Vol. 30. Amsterdam: North-Holland, 1999, pp. 3143–259.

**Arrow, Kenneth, J.** "The Theory of Discrimination," in Orley Ashenfelter and Albert Rees, eds., *Discrimination in labor markets.* Princeton, NJ: Princeton University Press, 1973, pp. 3–33.

—— "What Has Economics to Say about Racial Discrimination?" *Journal of Economic Perspectives,* Spring 1998, *72*(2), pp. 91–100.

**Becker, Gary S.** *The economics of discrimination,* 2nd Ed. Chicago: University of Chicago Press, 1961.

**Brown, Colin and Gay, Pat.** *Racial discrimination 17 years after the act.* London: Policy Studies Institute, 1985.

**Cornell, Bradford and Welch, Ivo.** "Culture, Information, and Screening Discrimination." *Journal of Political Economy,* June 1996, *104*(3), pp. 542–71.

**Council of Economic Advisers.** *Changing America: Indicators of social and economic well-being by race and Hispanic origin.* September 1998, http://w3.access.gpo.gov/eop/ca/pdfs/ca.pdf.

**Cross, Harry; Kenney, Genevieve; Mell, Jane and Zimmerman, Wendy.** *Employer hiring practices: Differential treatment of Hispanic and Anglo job applicants.* Washington, D.C.: Urban Institute Press, 1990.

Darity, William A., Jr. and Mason, Patrick L. "Evidence on Discrimination in Employment: Codes of Color, Codes of Gender." *Journal of Economic Perspectives,* Spring 1998, *72*(2), pp. 63–90.

Fix, Michael and Turner, Margery A., eds. *A national report card on discrimination in America: The role of testing.* Washington, D.C.: Urban Institute Press, 1998.

Fryer, Roland and Levitt, Steven. "The Causes and Consequences of Distinctively Black Names." Mimeo, University of Chicago, 2003.

Goldin, Claudia and Rouse, Cecilia. "Orchestrating Impartiality: The Impact of Blind Auditions on Female Musicians." *American Economic Review,* September 2000, *90*(4), pp. 715–41.

Heckman, James J. "Detecting Discrimination." *Journal of Economic Perspectives,* Spring 1998, *72*(2), pp. 101–16.

Heckman, James J.; Lochner, Lance J., and Todd, Petra E. "Fifty Years of Mincer Earnings Regressions." Mimeo, University of Chicago, 2001.

Heckman, James J. and Siegelman, Peter. "The Urban Institute Audit Studies: Their Methods and Findings," in Michael Fix and Raymond J. Struyk, eds., *Clear and convincing evidence: Measurement of discrimination in America.* Lanham, MD: Urban Institute Press, 1992, pp. 187–258.

Holzer, Harry J. "Informal Job Search and Black Youth Unemployment." *American Economic Review,* June 1987, *77*(3), pp. 446–52.

Hubbuck, Jim and Carter, Simon. *Half a chance? A report on job discrimination against young blacks in Nottingham.* London: Commission for Racial Equality, 1980.

James, Franklin and DelCastillo, Steve W. "Measuring Job Discrimination by Private Employers Against Young Black and Hispanic Seeking Entry Level Work in the Denver Metropolitan Area." Mimeo, University of Colorado-Denver, 1991.

Jones, Melinda. *Social psychology of prejudice.* Saddle River, NJ: Pearson Education, 2002.

Jowell, Roger and Prescott-Clark, Patricia. "Racial Discrimination and White-Collar Workers in Britain." *Race,* November 1970, *77*(4), pp. 397–417.

Lundberg, Shelly J. and Starz, Richard. "Private Discrimination and Social Intervention in Competitive Labor Market." *American Economic Review,* June 1983, *75*(3), pp. 340–47.

McIntyre, Shelby J.; Moberg, Dennis J. and Posner, Barry Z. "Discrimination in Recruitment: An Empirical Analysis: Comment." *Industrial and Labor Relations Review,* July 1980, *55*(4), pp. 543–47.

Mullainathan, Sendhil. "Thinking Through Categories." Mimeo, Massachusetts Institute of Technology, 2003.

Neumark, David. "Sex Discrimination in Restaurant Hiring: An Audit Study." *Quarterly Journal of Economics,* August 1996, *777*(3), pp. 915–42.

Newman, Jerry M. "Discrimination in Recruitment: An Empirical Analysis." *Industrial and Labor Relations Review,* October 1978, *52*(1), pp. 15–23.

Nisbett, Richard E. and Cohen, Dov. *The culture of honor: The psychology of violence in the South.* Boulder, CO: Westview Press, 1996.

Phelps, Edmund S. "The Statistical Theory of Racism and Sexism." *American Economic Review,* September 1972, *62*(4), pp. 659–61.

Raphael, Steven; Stoll, Michael A. and Holzer, Harry J. "Are Suburban Firms More Likely to Discriminate against African Americans?" *Journal of Urban Economics,* November 2000, *48*(3), pp. 485–508.

Riach, Peter A. and Rich, Judity. "Testing for Racial Discrimination in the Labour Market." *Cambridge Journal of Economics,* September 1991, *75*(3), pp. 239–56.

Turner, Margery A.; Fix, Michael and Struyk, Raymond J. *Opportunities denied, opportunities diminished: Racial discrimination in hiring.* Washington, D.C.: Urban Institute Press, 1991.

Weichselbaumer, Doris. "Sexual Orientation Discrimination in Hiring." *Labour Economics,* December 2003, *70*(6), pp. 629–42.

—— "Is it Sex or Personality? The Impact of Sex-Stereotypes on Discrimination in Applicant Selection." *Eastern Economic Journal,* Spring 2004, *50*(2), pp. 159–86.

# Black Wealth / White Wealth

## Wealth Inequality Trends

*By Melvin L. Oliver and Thomas M. Shapiro*

The growth and dispersion of wealth continues a trend anchored in the economic prosperity of post-World War II America. Between 1995 and 2001, the median net worth of all American families increased 39 percent, and median net financial assets grew by 60 percent. The growth of pension accounts (IRAs, Keogh plans, 401(k) plans, the accumulated value of defined contribution pension plans, and other retirement accounts) and stock holdings seems to account for much of this wealth accumulation.

While wealth grew and spread to many American families, there was little action at the bottom of the wealth spectrum as the percent of families with zero or negative net worth only dropped from 18.5 to 17.6, and those with no financial assets fell from 28.7 to 25.5.

Wealth remains highly concentrated, especially financial wealth, which excludes home equity. In 2001, the richest 5 percent of American households controlled over 67 percent of the country's financial wealth; the bottom 60 percent had 8.8 percent; and the bottom 40 percent just 1 percent.[1]

The context of wealth growth and inequality in the last decade situates our concern about racial inequality and the progress of American families, as indeed, the rich have gotten richer. The number of families with net worth of $10 million or more in 2001 quadrupled since 1980. A *New York Times* article even bemoaned how the super rich are leaving the mere rich far behind.[2] These 338,400 hyper-rich families emerged as the biggest winners in the new global economy, as new technologies spurred by tax incentives evolved, as the stock market soared, and as top executives in the corporate world received astronomical pay.

The wealthy were the biggest beneficiaries of tax policy during President George W. Bush's first term. In fact, the bulk of the 2001 tax cuts—53 percent—will go to the top 10 percent of taxpayers.[3] The tax cut share of the top 0.1 percent will amount to a 15 percent slice of the total value of the tax cut pie. Another reason that the wealthiest fare much better is that the tax cuts over the past decade have sharply lowered tax rates on income from investments, such as capital gains, interest, and dividends. While there are many reasons for the continuing wealth inequality trend, government policy has clearly abetted, encouraged, and privileged the property, capital, and income of America's wealthiest families.

## WHAT FACTS HAVE CHANGED?

In 1995 when *Black Wealth/White Wealth* was published, we presented data that were in many respects a new way of gauging the economic progress of black Americans vis-à-vis white Americans. Most commentators and analysts were familiar and comfortable with income comparisons that provided a window on whether there was growing or declining racial economic inequality. But the focus on wealth, "the net value of assets (e.g., ownership of stocks, money in the bank, real estate, business ownership, etc.) less debts," created a different gestalt or perspective on racial inequality.

This gestalt had two dimensions.[4] The first is the conceptual distinction between income and assets. While income represents the flow of resources earned in a particular period, say a week, month, or year, assets are a stock of resources that are saved or invested. Income is mainly used for day-to-day necessities, while assets are special monies not normally used for food or clothing but are rather a "surplus resource available for improving life chances, providing further opportunities, securing prestige, passing status along to one's family," and securing economic security for present and future generations.[5] The second dimension is the quantitative; to what extent is there parity between blacks and whites on assets? Do blacks have access to resources that they can use to plan for their future, to enable their children to obtain a quality education, to provide for the next generation's head start, and to secure their place in the political community? For these reasons, we focused on inequality in wealth as the sine qua non indicator of material well-being. Without sufficient assets, it is difficult to lay claim to economic security in American society.

The baseline indicator of racial wealth inequality is the black-white ratio of median net worth. To what degree are blacks approaching parity with whites in terms of net worth? The change in gestalt is amply demonstrated in comparisons of black-white median income ratios to black-white median net worth ratios. For example, the 1988 data reported on in *Black Wealth/White Wealth* showed that black families earned sixty-two cents for every dollar of median income that white families earned. However, when the comparisons shift to wealth, the figure showed a remarkably deeper and disturbing level of racial inequality. For every dollar of median net worth that whites controlled, African Americans controlled only eight cents![6]

How has this landmark indicator of racial inequality changed since then? Using the most recent data available, it appears, not unsurprisingly, that the level of racial wealth inequality has not changed but has shown a stubborn persistence that makes the data presented in 1995 more relevant than ever because the pattern we discerned suggests a firmly embedded racial stratification. The most optimistic analyses suggest that the black-white median net worth ratio is 0.10, that is, blacks have control of ten cents for every dollar of net worth that whites possess.[7] However, the most pessimistic estimate indicates that the ratio is closer to seven cents on the dollar.[8] This slim range demonstrates that the level of wealth inequality has not changed appreciably since the publication of *Black Wealth/White Wealth*.[9] However, the story is far more complex.

Using 1988 data, we tabulated the racial wealth gap at $60,980.[10] By 2002 the racial wealth gap increased to $82,663, meaning the wealth of the average African American family fell further behind whites by more than $20,000 over this period. Isolating the period and dynamics of the past decade a little more closely, the racial wealth gap grew by $14,316 between 1996 and 2002. In the decade since *Black Wealth/White Wealth*, then, white wealth grew and then leveled off; black wealth grew and then declined. As a result, the overall racial wealth gap ratio persists at a dime on the dollar, and the dollar amount of the racial wealth gap grew.

Some contradictory facts and new dimensions of financial life in America have affected the persistence of the black-white racial wealth gap. They include a strong economy of the 1990s that enabled greater savings, especially in employer-based savings programs, but which has petered out recently; a stock market bust that punished some of the newest entrants into the market most severely; increasing credit card debt; a growing trend of black home ownership complemented by growing sub-prime and predatory lending directed at minority communities; and growth in the working poor due to the influx of the Temporary Assistance for Needy Families program population into the labor market. This mix of factors weaves the mosaic underlying the story of the continuing racial wealth gap in the first decade of the twenty-first century.

## THE STORY OF THE PERSISTENCE OF THE RACIAL WEALTH GAP

Traditionally, economists assume that wealth accumulation is the consequence of a "combination of inheritance, earnings, and savings and is enhanced by prudent consumption and investment patterns over a person's life course."[11] How these individual variables interact with the human capital attributes of family members, their education, their occupation, and their ability to begin asset accumulation at an early stage in their life course (the earlier one begins to accumulate assets, the more wealth one can accrue) moves us forward in explaining how differential accumulation occurs. But these individual factors are not the whole story.

As *Black Wealth/White Wealth* convincingly demonstrated, wealth accumulation occurs in a context where these individual attributes unfold to produce varying levels of wealth for different families and social groupings. It has been the different "opportunity structure" for savings and investment that African Americans have faced when compared with whites that has helped to structure racial inequality in wealth holding.

We developed a sociology of wealth and racial inequality in *Black Wealth/White Wealth*, which situated the study of wealth among concerns with race, class, and social inequality. This theoretical framework elucidated the social context in which wealth generation occurs and demonstrated the unique and diverse social circumstances that blacks and whites face. Three concepts we developed provided a sociologically grounded approach to understand the racial wealth gap and highlighted how the opportunity structure disadvantages blacks and contributes to massive wealth inequalities between the races. The first concept, racialization of state policy, explores how state policy has impaired the ability of most black Americans to accumulate wealth from slavery throughout American history to contemporary institutional discrimination. The "economic detour" helps us understand the relatively low level of entrepreneurship among the small scale and segmentally niched businesses of black Americans, leading to an emphasis on consumer spending as the route to economic assimilation. The third concept—the sedimentation of racial inequality—explores how the cumulative effects of the past have seemingly cemented blacks to the bottom of America's economic hierarchy in regards to wealth.

These concepts do much to show how this differential opportunity structure developed and worked to produce black wealth disadvantages. It also builds a strong case that layering wealth deprivation generation after generation has been central in not only blacks' lack of wealth but also whites' privileged position in accumulating wealth. As we noted:

> What is often not acknowledged is that the accumulation of wealth for some whites is intimately tied to the poverty

of wealth for most blacks. Just as blacks have had "cumulative disadvantages," whites have had "cumulative advantages." Practically every circumstance of bias and discrimination against blacks has produced a circumstance and opportunity of positive gain for whites.[12]

The past opportunity structure that denied blacks access or full participation in wealth-building activities serves as a powerful deterrent to current black ambitions for wealth. Without an inheritance that is built on generations of steady economic success, blacks, even when they have similar human capital and class position, lag far behind their white counterparts in their quest to accumulate a healthy nest egg of assets. In *Black Wealth/White Wealth* we examined those current institutional and structural constraints that African Americans faced in the 1980s and early 1990s that curtailed and limited the ability of many African Americans to build assets. One area we focused upon was housing, the largest single element of most American's portfolio of assets, and a major part of the wealth in most African American's asset portfolio. We identified a number of institutional constraints ranging from differential access to mortgages, higher costs of mortgages, and differential levels of equity accumulation in homes owing to persistent residential segregation.

We want to extend this mode of theorizing and analysis to the period of the 1990s and into the first decade of the twenty-first century. We attempt to formulate a compelling picture of why African Americans continue to lag so far behind whites in asset holding. Here we focus on the social context of the labor market, the stock and housing market, and growing debt.

## THE RISE AND DECLINE OF A TIGHT LABOR MARKET AND A BULL STOCK MARKET

*Black Wealth/White Wealth* documented wealth data that reflected a period in the American economy characterized by relatively high unemployment rates and a stagnant economy. However, this period was followed by one of the largest and longest economic expansions in the history of the United States. From its beginning in March 1991 to its ending in November 2001, the United States endured a record expansion. Positive economic indicators that were in sharp contrast to the previous period characterized this expansion. For example, family incomes went from stagnation during the 1979 to 1993 period, where they grew only 0.7 percent over the entire time frame to an increase of 17 percent, or more than $7,000 per family, from 1993 to 2000. In terms of job growth, during the 1992 to 2000 period, the nation created more jobs than at any similar period in American history: 22.6 million, 92 percent of which were in the private sector. Moreover, in contrast to the previous period, where 1.9 million manufacturing jobs were lost, the 1992 to 2000 period saw manufacturing job growth increase by 303,000. Finally, the unemployment rate fell by 42 percent, reaching below 5 percent from July 1997 through January 2001. The 4 percent unemployment rate in 2000—the lowest in over 30 years—stands in striking contrast to an average unemployment rate of 7.1 percent for the 1980 to 1992 period.[13]

For African Americans this was a period of tight labor markets that led to greater levels of labor force participation owing to the existence of greater demand for their participation in the economy. Employers made "extra efforts ... to overcome the barriers created by skill and spatial mismatch" to reach out to African American workers to fill their growing labor needs.[14] Moreover, "employers may find discrimination more costly when the economy is strong and their usually preferred type of job candidate is fully employed elsewhere."[15] In the throes of a heated and tight labor market, *Business Week* proclaimed, "With the economy continuing to expand and unemployment at its lowest point in 30 years, companies are snapping up minorities, women, seniors, and anyone else willing to work for a day's pay."[16]

African Americans, however, did not wholly benefit from this extraordinary period in American history. Black joblessness continued to be a problem. The historical ratio of two-to-one black-to-white unemployment rates persisted with black men averaging 7.1 percent compared with 3 percent for white men, while black women averaged 6.8 compared with 3.2 percent for white women in the latter half of 1999.[17] Nevertheless, those African Americans who were employed during this period saw real wage gains that could be translated into savings, investments, and an increase in net worth.

Another aspect of the expansion of the economy during the 1990s was the rapid rise in the stock market. Fueled by technology stocks and the growth of key stocks like Microsoft, Sun, Yahoo, and other new stock offerings in the technology sector, the stock market started to attract investments not only from high-income and high-wealth individuals, but also from an increasing number of middle-class families and even working-class families. This investment was facilitated by growing participation in employer-sponsored savings programs that enabled employees to make tax-deferred and/or matched contributions through payroll deductions. The ease of the transaction and the constant media and public interest in the high-flying stock market encouraged mass participation. The market rose steadily and rapidly. Beginning from a monthly average in 1992 in the low 400s, the Standard and Poor's 500 tripled in size by 1999.[18] If one were lucky enough to purchase Microsoft or Yahoo early then his or her gains would have been astronomical.

For example, when Yahoo was first available as a public offering shares were sold for $1.24. By December 1999 Yahoo listed for $108.17.[19] It was the desire for these kinds of returns that fueled an overheated market and led to the description of "irrational exuberance" concerning the frenzy for the "market."[20]

African Americans, while constrained by resources, also entered into this frenzy. The decade of the 1990s was the breakthrough era for African American involvement in the stock market. Facilitated by employer savings plans and, for the first time, sought after by stock and brokerage firms, African Americans invested readily into the market. In 1996 blacks had a median value of $4,626 invested in stocks and mutual funds. At the height of the market, that value had almost doubled to $8,669. During this period African American stock market investors had closed the black-white ratio of stock market value from twenty-eight cents on the dollar to forty cents on the dollar. However, the market's plunge after 1999 sent African American portfolio values down to a median average of $3,050. This brought the black-white ratio of stock market value back in line with the 1996 level, eroding all the gains that the bull market had bestowed.[21]

African Americans did better in 401(k) and thrift savings plans, which were more likely to be diversified holdings. In 1996 African American investors held a median average of $6,939 in these instruments. With the market surging and regular savings deposits facilitated by payroll deductions, African Americans increased their value in savings or thrift plans to a median average of $10,166 in 2002. The comparison to whites is quite interesting in regard to thrift plans. Between 1996 and 2002 African Americans closed the black-white ratio slightly from 0.43 to 0.50. This is in striking contrast to the data on stock ownership.[22]

## HOME OWNERSHIP, NEW MORTGAGE, AND CREDIT MARKETS

Over the past several years more families than ever across the United States have been able to buy homes. Home ownership rates reached 69 percent in 2004, a historic high. The main reasons for the high level of home ownership include the new mortgage market, where capital is readily available to both families and economic sectors where home ownership was always part of the American Dream—but in dream only. With home ownership comes the opportunity to accumulate wealth because the value of homes appreciates over time. Indeed, approximately two-thirds of all the wealth of America's middle class families is not in stocks, bonds, investments, or savings accounts but in the form of home equity.

Home equity is the most important wealth component for average American families, and even though home ownership rates are lower, it is even more prominent in the wealth profiles of African American families. Although housing appreciation is very sensitive to many characteristics relating to a community's demographics and profile (which realtors euphemistically call "location, location, location"), overall home ownership has been a prime source of wealth accumulation for black families. For example, for the average black home owner, homes created $6,000 more wealth between 1996 and 2002.[23] However, fundamentally racialized dynamics create and distribute housing wealth unevenly. The Federal Reserve Board kept interest rates at historically low levels for much of this period, and this fueled both demand and hastened converting home equity wealth into cash.

*Black Wealth/White Wealth* demonstrated the color coding of home equity, and Shapiro's 2004 book, *The Hidden Cost of Being African American*, updates the data and extends our understanding of how residential segregation affects home equity. The typical home owned by white families increased in value by $28,000 more than homes owned by blacks. Persistent residential segregation, especially in cities where most blacks live, explains this equity difference as a compelling index of bias that costs blacks dearly. This data point corroborates other recent research demonstrating that rising housing wealth depends upon a community's demographic characteristics, especially racial composition. One study concludes that homes lost at least 16 percent of their value when located in neighborhoods that are more than 10 percent black. Thus, a "segregation tax" visits black home owners by depressing home values and reducing home equity in highly segregated neighborhoods.[24] Shapiro summarizes the case: "The only prudent conclusion from these studies is that residential segregation costs African American home owners enormous amounts of money by suppressing their home equity in comparison to that of white home owners. The inescapable corollary is that residential segregation benefits white home owners with greater home equity wealth accumulation."[25] Furthermore, most African American families rent housing and thus are not positioned to accumulate housing wealth, mainly because of affordability, credit, and access issues.

The home mortgage marketplace has evolved considerably since 1990, when mortgage packages were offered at a unitary price reflecting the terms of the loan, targeting prospective home owners who met stringent credit history rules and financial criteria. As housing wealth grew and the United States mortgage market became integrated into the global market system, mortgage products proliferated and thus have changed the way American families buy homes. Underwriting standards have become more relaxed, both as financial institutions ease rules to compete in this evolving market and as federal regulations and oversight have become less stringent.[26]

Minorities are making significant inroads into all segments of the housing market. Indeed, important components feeding the general trends of increasing rates of new home construction and home value appreciation include the demographic push from new immigrants, the accomplishments of second-generation immigrants, and the success of a segment of African American families. In 2004, home ownership reached historic highs as 69 percent of American families live in a home they own. In 1995, 42.2 percent of African American families owned homes, increasing to a historic high, 49.5 percent, in 2004. This 17.3 percent increase in African American home ownership is quite remarkable, indicating striving, accomplishment, and success. The black-white home ownership gap in 1995 stood at 28.5 percent and narrowed to 26.2 percent in 2004.[27] We might expect the home ownership gap to continue closing as black home ownership starts from a considerably lower base while the higher white rate may be close to exhausting the potential of those who want to become home owners.

In 1995, access to credit for minorities was a major issue. Financial institutions responded both to criticisms regarding credit discrimination and to the newly discovered buying capacity of minorities. Increasing numbers of African American and Hispanic families gained access to credit cards throughout the 1990s: 45 percent of African American and 43 percent of Hispanic families held credit cards in 1992 and by 2001 nearly 60 percent of African American and 53 percent of Hispanic families held credit cards.[28] The irony here is that as access to credit broadened under terms highly favorable to lenders, debt became rampant and millions of families became ensnared in a debt vice.

Credit card debt nearly tripled from $238 billion in 1989 to $692 billion in 2001.[29] These figures represent family reliance on financing consumption through debt, especially expensive credit in the form of credit cards and department store charge cards. During the 1990s, the average American family experienced a 53 percent increase in credit card debt—the average family's card debt rising from $2,697 to $4,126. Credit card debt among low-income families increased 184 percent. Even high-income families became more dependent on credit cards: There was 28 percent more debt in 2001 than in 1989. The main sources of credit card debt include spiraling health care costs, lower employer coverage of health insurance, and rising housing costs amid stagnating or declining wages after 2000 and increasingly unsteady employment for many. This suggests strongly that the increasing debt is not the result of frivolous or conspicuous spending or lack of budgetary discipline; instead, deferring payment to make ends meet is becoming the American way for many to finance daily life in the new economy.

Given that a period of rising income did not lift the African American standard of living, and given the context of overall rising family debt, an examination of the racial component of credit card debt furthers our understanding of the contemporary processes associated with the continuation of the economic detour and the further sedimentation of inequality. The average credit card debt of African Americans increased 22 percent between 1992 and 2001, when it reached an average of nearly $3,000.[30] Hispanic credit card debt mirrored blacks by rising 20 percent in the same period to $3,691. As we know, the average white credit card debt was higher, reaching $4,381 in 2001. One of the most salient facts involves the magnitude and depth of African American reliance on debt. Among those holding credit cards with balances, nearly one in five African Americans earning less than $50,000 spend at least 40 percent of their income paying debt service. In other words, in every 8-hour working day these families labor 3.2 hours to pay off consumer debt. Even though black families carry smaller monthly balances, a higher percentage of their financial resources goes toward servicing debt.

The median net worth of African American families at the end of 2002 was $5,988, essentially the same as it was in 1988.[31] Again, it is not as if nothing happened since we wrote *Black Wealth/White Wealth*; indeed, African American fortunes expanded with good times and contracted with recessions and the bursting of the stock market bubble. In the last decade, the high point of African American (and Hispanic) wealth accumulation was 1999, when it registered $8,774, just before the bursting of the stock market bubble in early 2000. Between 1999 and 2002, African American wealth declined from $8,774 to $5,988, wiping out more than a decade's worth of financial gains.

Median wealth and racial wealth gap data tell us about absolute wealth accumulation and the relative positioning of African American families. Another sense of the dynamics of the last ten years concerns the dispersion of assets among African American families. In 1996, 31.9 percent of African American families owned zero net worth or—worse still—had bottom lines that put them in the red. By 1999, this figure declined to 28.2 percent but deteriorated again after the stock market burst and the beginning of the recession, by increasing to 32.3 percent in 2002. This has left more African American families in absolute asset poverty than at the time of the book's initial publication.

## NEW DYNAMICS OF MARKETS AND INSTITUTIONS

As we have indicated, the decade between 1995 and 2006 really is marked off by two distinct periods: African American family wealth accumulates considerably and more families move into positive wealth positions until early 2000. From 2000 through 2005, however, the financial wealth of African American families made a U-turn, both losing actual wealth and increasing the number of families with zero or negative wealth once more.

Throughout the entire period, home ownership and home equity continued to rise for all segments of American families, including African Americans. An important narrative, then, involves this great expansion of financial wealth, home ownership, and housing wealth; understanding what happened to this wealth; examining the opportunities this new wealth created, especially for financial institutions looking for new markets; and importantly, the impact of these developments and new dynamics on African Americans.

## HOUSING WEALTH AND ITS USES

Households cashed out $407 billion worth of equity from homes in just three years, 2002 through 2004, in the refinancing boom that began in 2001. Although such data have not been collected for very long, American families were refinancing homes at record levels, three times higher than any other period.[32] Nearly half of all mortgage debt was refinanced between 2002 and 2003, averaging $27,000 in equity per home in the early stages of the refinancing wave.[33]

As mortgage interest rates fell to record low levels during the refinance boom, and as housing continued to appreciate and result in wealth accumulation, many Americans cashed out home equity to pay down debt and finance living expenses, trading off wealth to pay off past consumption and fund new purchases.

Refinancing at lower interest rates and hence lower monthly payments is certainly a good deal for families paying off mortgages because it leaves more money in the family budget for living expenses, discretionary purchases, or savings. We need to ask the important question of how families used this bonanza. Investing in human capital through continued education or career retooling, investing in other financial instruments, building a business, home improvements, and similar choices expand opportunities, improve living standards, and may launch further social mobility. On the other hand, paying down high-interest debt may slow down temporarily the debt-driven consumption treadmill but most likely does not improve the long-term standard of living or life chances of a family, and certainly does not improve the future wealth accumulation picture. Slightly over one-half used housing wealth to cover living expenses and to pay down store and credit cards. Another 25 percent used funds for consumer expenditures such as vehicle purchases and medical expenses. Thus it appears that a majority of households used these new home equity loans to convert credit card debt and current living expenses into long-term mortgage debt.

One result is that between 1973 and 2004, home owners' equity actually fell—from 68.3 percent to 55 percent so that Americans own less of their homes today than they did in the 1970s and early 1980s. And, it is worth remembering that home equity is by far the largest source of wealth for the vast majority of American families. The intersection of wealth and race illustrates the magnified importance of home equity for African Americans and Hispanics. Among whites, home equity represented 38.5 percent of their entire wealth portfolio in 2002. In sharp contrast, home equity accounted for 63 percent of wealth among African Americans and 61 percent for Hispanics.[34]

## THE DARK SIDE OF HOME OWNERSHIP

Subprime lending is targeted to prospective home-buyers with blemished credit histories or with high levels of debt who otherwise would not qualify for conventional mortgage loans. A legitimate niche for these kinds of loans brings home ownership within the grasp of millions of families. These loan products are essential in expanding home ownership rates. In return for these riskier investments, financial institutions charge borrowers higher interest rates, often requiring higher processing and closing fees, and often containing special loan conditions like prepayment penalties, balloon payments, and adjustable interest rates.

The subprime market expanded greatly in the last decade as part of new, aggressive marketing strategies among financial institutions hungrily eyeing rising home ownership and seeing promising new markets. Moreover, the mortgage finance system in the United States became well integrated into global capital markets, which offer an ever-growing array of financial products, including subprime loans. Subprime loan originations grew fifteen-fold, from $35 billion to $530 billion between 1994 and 2004. Reflecting the increasing importance of subprime loans to the financial industry, the subprime share of mortgage loans has seen a parallel meteoric rise from less than 4 percent in 1995 to representing about 17 percent of mortgage loans in 2004.[35]

Loan terms like prepayment penalties and balloon payments increase the risk of mortgage foreclosure in subprime home loans, even after controlling for the borrower's credit score, loan terms, and varying economic conditions.[36] One study from the Center for Community Capitalism demonstrates that subprime prepayment penalties and balloon payments place Americans at substantially greater risk of losing their homes.

Delinquency (falling behind in mortgage payments) and losing one's home through foreclosure are hitting vulnerable neighborhoods hardest. Concentrated foreclosures can negatively affect the surrounding neighborhoods, threatening to undo community building and revitalization efforts achieved through decades of collaborative public-private partnerships, community organizing, and local policy efforts.

Los Angeles is a case in point.[37] In a short three-year period, 2001 to 2004, over 14,000 Los Angeles families lost their homes through foreclosure. The foreclosure rate is highest in the most vulnerable neighborhoods. In predominately minority neighborhoods (80 percent or more minority) of Los Angeles County the foreclosure rate is almost four times the rate that it is in neighborhoods where minorities are less than 20 percent of the population. In the City of Los Angeles, foreclosures occur nearly twelve times more often in predominately minority communities compared with areas that have fewer than 20 percent minorities. Los Angeles is not alone; data from Atlanta, Baltimore, Boston, Chicago, and others show that Los Angeles is part of the larger, national pattern.

A study examining pricing disparities in the mortgage market provides more context, placing the Los Angeles story in a broader pattern. Of all conventional loans to blacks, nearly 30 percent were subprime compared with only 10 percent for whites.[38] These ratios would be in closer alignment in lending markets operating with maximum efficiency and equity. Creditworthy criteria, like debt-to-income ratios, do not explain the greater propensity for African Americans to receive subprime loans. The report also discovered that subprime loans in minority communities increased with levels of racial segregation. This finding suggests an alarming new form of modern redlining that targets minority neighborhoods for subprime loans.

Using a testing methodology adapted from those that explored job discrimination, the National Community Reinvestment Coalition was able to explore how pricing disparities resulting from intensified subprime lending in minority areas occurred. Essentially, white and black testers with similar credit records and qualifications applied for preapproval for mortgages. Given similar scripts and profiles (with African Americans actually presenting better qualifications), the testing uncovered a 45 percent rate of disparate treatment based on race. The testing revealed practices that may have destructive effects on African American families and communities. These include: differences in interest rates quoted; differences in information about fees, rates, loan programs, and loan terms; and whites more often referred up to the lender's prime lending division. In *Black Wealth/White Wealth* we wrote that differences in loan rejection rates and interest rates did not result from discriminatory lending practices but from blacks bringing fewer financial assets to the mortgage table; as a result, they paid higher loan terms. Racial pricing disparities and the targeted spread of subprime lending to minority communities, however, now persuades us that minority America is experiencing a new form of redlining organized by race and geographic space.

*Black Wealth/White Wealth* demonstrated the power of policy, government, institutions, and history to order and maintain racial inequality. The previous sections show further the significance of financial institutions in granting access to credit and the terms of credit, and the increasing dependence on credit and debt. The basis for excluding African Americans from opportunities and creating different rules in the competition for success is no longer just who is a capable worker. Now we must add who is a worthy credit risk and on what terms. Job discrimination against individual blacks based on perceived characteristics is not the only major arena in the struggle against inequality; exclusion in terms of creditworthiness is as well.

## DISCUSSION QUESTIONS

1. What are the three sociological concepts that help us understand the racial wealth gap and highlight how opportunity structure disadvantages blacks and contributes to massive wealth inequalities between the races?

2. African Americans continue to lag behind whites in asset holdings. Discuss the effects of the social context of the labor market, the stock and housing market, and growing debt.

3. To what degree are blacks approaching parity with whites in terms of net worth?

4. How did the subprime mortgage crisis affect minority communities differently than non-minority communities? Looking ahead, discuss what long-term impact this may have on wealth accumulation among African Americans.

## NOTES

1. Wolff, 2004.
2. Johnson, 2005.
3. Johnson, 2005.
4. Oliver and Shapiro, p. 30
5. Oliver and Shapiro, p. 32.
6. Oliver and Shapiro, pp. 85–86.
7. Shapiro, 2004a.
8. Kochhar.
9. Federation of Consumer Services data yield a more narrowed ratio. These data are inconsistent with virtually all other data measuring wealth inequality. We are not confident with its methodology or operational definitions of wealth. See Consumer Federation of America and BET.com, 2003.
10. We adjusted the 1988 figure originally reported in the book to reflect 2002 dollars.
11. Oliver and Shapiro, p. 36.
12. Oliver and Shapiro, p. 51.
13. The National Bureau of Economic Research's Business Cycle Committee keeps track of business expansions and recessions; see http://www.nber.org/cycles/recessions.html. For a general overview of the Clinton expansion's impact on the poor, see Blank and Ellwood.
14. Bradbury, p. 14, and Holzer, Raphael, and Stoll.
15. Bradbury, p. 14.
16. Bradbury, p. 15.
17. Bradbury, p. 4.
18. Shiller. Also see http://www.irrationalexuberance.com/index.htm for historical data on the stock market.
19. See quarterly stock prices for Yahoo at http://finance.yahoo.com/q/hp?s=Y HOO&a=03&b=12&c=1996&d=07&e=14&f=2005&g=m&z=66&y=66.
20. The origin of the descriptor "irrational exuberance" is found in a speech by Federal Reserve Board Chairman Alan Greenspan, 1996.
21. These data are from a survey of high-income blacks (yearly incomes of $50,000 or more) sponsored by Ariel Mutual Funds/Charles Schwab & Co., Inc. This very valuable survey examines the financial behavior, asset value, and composition of this group of African Americans. See Black Investor Survey.
22. Black Investor Survey.
23. Kochhar, p. 18.
24. Rusk.
25. Shapiro, 2004a.
26. The exemplar for "easing" regulatory oversight and financial institution accountability was the repeal of the Glass-Steagall Act of 1933. This act was designed to protect the public from between commercial banks, insurance companies, and brokerage firms, which contributed to the stock market crash of 1929. The Financial Services Modernization Act of 1999 does away with restrictions on the integration of banking, insurance, and stock trading, which has encouraged a rash of mergers leading to greater concentration in the financial sector. As a result, banks were looking for new markets and were anxious to provide new products. As part of the 1999 Act, regular oversight opportunities provided to community organizations through the Community Reinvestment Act were relaxed considerably. Consequently, the frequency of CRA examinations was limited. See Berton and Futterman.

27. Joint Center for Housing Studies, 2005.
28. Silva and Epstein.
29. Draut and Silva.
30. Silva and Epstein.
31. This section uses SIPP data from 2002 as reported in the Pew Hispanic Center report.
32. Joint Center for Housing Studies, 2004.
33. Silva.
34. These are based on distribution of mean worth, so the figure for whites, in particular, because of the skewed distribution, looks low and vastly understates the importance of home equity in the wealth portfolios of middle-class white families (Kochhar).
35. Joint Center for Housing Studies, 2005.
36. Quercia, Stegman, and Davis.
37. Duda and Apgar.
38. National Community Reinvestment Coalition; Adams.

## REFERENCES

Adams, John. 1988. "Growth of U.S. Cities and Recent Trends in Urban Real Estate Values." In *Cities and Their Vital Systems*, ed., J. H. Ausubel and R. Herman. Washington, D.C.: National Academy Press. 108–45.

Berton, Brad, and Susan Futterman. 2003. "Community Groups see Continuing Chill on CRA, Affordable Housing Finance." http://www.housingfinance.com/ahf/articles/2002/02OctCommunityLeanding/BET.com.

Black Investor Survey. "Saving and Investing Among Higher Income African-American and White Americans," July 2005. http://www.arielmutuafunds.com//funds/2004-survey/2004%20AAIS%20FULL%20EXTERNAL.ppt.

Blank, Rebecca, and David T. Ellwood. 2002. "The Clinton Legacy for America's Poor." in *American Economic Policy in the 1990s*, Jeffrey A. Frankel and Peter A. Orszag. Cambridge, MA: MIT Press.

Bradbury, Katharine L. 2000. "Rising Tide in the Labor Market: To What Degree do Expansions Benefit the Disadvantaged?" *New England Economic Review* 4 (May/June): 3–33.

Consumer Federation of America. 2003. "More African-Americans Save and Begin to Close Wealth Gap." http://www.consumerfed.org/102903blackamsaves.pdf.

Duda, Mark, and William Apgar. 2004. Mortgage Foreclosure Trends in Los Angeles: Patterns and Policy Issues. A report prepared for the Los Angeles Neighborhood Housing Services.

Greenspan, Alan. 1996. The Challenge of Central Banking in a Democratic Society. Address to the American Enterprise Institute at the Washington Hilton Hotel, December 5, 1996.

Holzer, Harry, Steven Raphael, and Michael A. Stoll. 2003. "Employers in the Boom: How Did the hiring of Unskilled Workers Change During the 1990s?" http://www.urban.org/UploadedPDF/410780_BoomPaper.pdf.

Johnson, David Cay. 2005. "Richest are Leaving Even the Rich Far Behind," *New York Times*, June 5.

Joint Center for Housing Studies of Harvard University. 2004. The State of the Nation's Housing. Cambridge, MA.

Joint Center for Housing Studies of Harvard University. 2005. The State of the Nation's Housing. Cambridge, MA.

Kochhar, Rakesh. 2004. *The Wealth of Hispanic Households: 1996 to 2002*. Washington, D.C.: Pew Hispanic Center.

National Community Reinvestment Coalition. 2005. Preapprovals and Pricing Disparities in the Mortgage Marketplace, June 2005. http://ncrc.org/pressandpubs/press_releases/documents/Preapproval_Report_June05.pdf.

Oliver, Melvin L., and Thomas M. Shapiro. 1995. *Black Wealth/White Wealth: A New Perspective* on *Racial Inequality*. New York and London: Routledge.

Quercia, Roberto G., Michael A. Stegman, and Walter R. Davis. 2005. "The Impact of Predatory Loan Terms on Subprime Foreclosures." Center for Community Capitalism. http://www.kenan-flagler.unc.edu/assets/documents/foreclosurepaper.pdf.

Rusk, David. 2001. *The 'Segregation Tax': The Cost of Racial Segregation of Black Homeowners*. Washington, D.C.: Brookings Institution Center on Urban and Metropolitan Policy.

Shapiro, Thomas M. 2004a. *The Hidden Cost of Being African American: How Wealth Perpetuates Inequality*. New York: Oxford University Press.

Shiller, Robert J. 2005. *Irrational Exuberance*. Princeton, NJ: Princeton University Press.

Silva, Javier. 2005. *A House of Cards: Financing the American Dream*. New York: Demos.

Silva, Javier, and Rebecca Epstein. 2005. *Costly Credit: African Americans and Latinos in Debt*. New York: Demos.

Wolff, Edward N. 2004. "Changes in Household Wealth in the 1980s and 1990s." In the U.S. Economics Working Paper Archive, Number 47. Annandale-on-Hudson, NY: The Levy Economics Institute.

# THE MARK OF A CRIMINAL RECORD

*By Devah Pager[*]*

Among those recently released from prison, nearly two-thirds will be charged with new crimes and 40 percent will return to prison within three years. Those who are not reincarcerated have poorer employment and incomes than those without criminal records. But there is strong disagreement over the reasons that ex-offenders do so poorly after release. Does incarceration itself actually lead to lower employment and income? Or do the poor outcomes of ex-offenders merely arise from the environmental and personal histories that sent them to prison in the first place—the broken families, the poor neighborhoods, the lack of education and absence of legitimate opportunities, the individual tendencies toward violence or addiction?[1]

Survey research has consistently shown that incarceration is linked to lower employment and income. Many hypotheses have been proposed for this relationship: the labeling effects of criminal stigma, the disruption of social and family networks, the loss of human capital, institutional trauma, and legal barriers to employment. It is, however, difficult, using survey data, to determine which of these mechanisms is at work and whether, for any given mechanism, the results are due to the effect of imprisonment or to preexisting characteristics of people who are convicted. A further issue, given racial disparities in imprisonment rates, is whether the effect of a criminal record is more severe for African American than it is for white ex-offenders.

In the research reported here I sought to answer three primary questions about the mechanisms driving the relationship between imprisonment and employment.[2] First, to what extent do employers use information about criminal histories to make hiring decisions? Second, does race, by itself, remain a major barrier to employment? Its continued significance has been questioned in recent policy debates.[3] Third, does the effect of a criminal record differ for black and white applicants? Given that many Americans hold strong and persistent views associating race and crime, does a criminal record trigger a more negative response for African American than for white applicants?

---

[*]   Devah Pager is Assistant Professor of Sociology at Princeton University.

## THE EMPLOYMENT AUDIT

Just as a college degree may serve as a positive credential for those seeking employment, a prison term attaches a "negative credential" to individuals, certifying them in ways that may qualify them for discrimination or social exclusion. Using an experimental audit design, I have been able to isolate that institutional effect, holding constant many background and personal characteristics that otherwise make it very difficult to disentangle cause and effect.[4]

In an employment audit, matched pairs of individuals ("testers") apply for real job openings to see whether employers respond differently to applicants on the basis of selected characteristics. The methodology combines experimental methods with real-life contexts. It is particularly valuable for those with an interest in discrimination, and has primarily been used to study characteristics such as race, gender, and age that are protected under the Civil Rights Act.

Several states, including Wisconsin, have expanded fair employment legislation to protect individuals with criminal records from discrimination by employers, because of their concern about the consequences of the rapid expansion and the skewed racial and ethnic composition of the ex-offender population over the last three decades. Under this legislation, employers are warned that past crimes may be taken into account only if they closely relate to the specific duties required by the job—as, for example, if a convicted embezzler applies for a bookkeeping position, or a sex offender for a job at a day care center. Because of the Wisconsin legislation barring discrimination on the basis of a criminal record, we might expect circumstances to be, if anything, more favorable to the employment of ex-offenders than in states without legal protections.

This audit was conducted between June and December, 2001, in Milwaukee, Wisconsin, which in population, size, racial composition, and employment rate is typical of many major American cities. At the time, the local economy was moderately strong and unemployment rates ranged between 4 and 5.2 percent.[5]

I used two audit teams of 23-year-old male college students, one consisting of two African Americans and the other of two whites. All were bright and articulate, with appealing styles of self-presentation. Characteristics that were not already identical, such as education and work experience, were made to appear identical for the purposes of the audit. Within each team, one auditor was randomly assigned a "criminal record" for the first week; then week by week auditors took turns playing the ex-offender role. The "criminal record" consisted of a nonviolent, felony drug conviction (possession of cocaine with intent to distribute). If the employment application did not request information about previous convictions, ways were found to include that information—for example, by reporting work experience in the correctional facility and citing a parole officer as a reference.

The audit teams applied to separate sets of jobs drawn from the Sunday classified section of the city's major daily newspaper, the *Milwaukee Journal Sentinel,* and from Jobnet, a state-sponsored Web site for employment listings. Since nearly 90 percent of state prisoners have no more than a high school diploma, the job openings chosen were for entry-level positions requiring no previous experience and no education beyond high school (see Figure 1). All openings were within 25 miles of downtown Milwaukee; a majority were in the suburbs or surrounding counties.[6] The survey audited 350 employers, 150 by the white audit team and 200 by the black team.

The audit study focused only on the first stage in the employment process—the stage most likely to be affected by the barrier of a criminal record. Auditors visited the employers, filled out applications, and

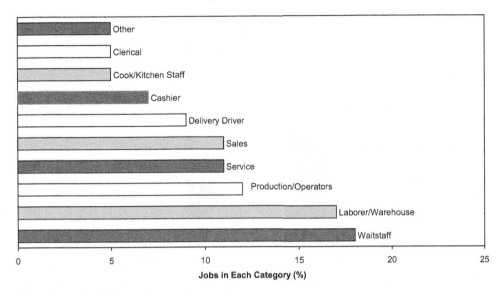

Figure 1. *The jobs in the Milwaukee audit sample.*

went as far as they could during that first interview. They did not return for a second visit. Thus our critical variable of interest was the proportion of cases in which employers called the applicant after the first visit. Reference checks were included as an outcome, in the belief that it would be important to have a former employer or parole officer vouch for applicants with criminal records. As it turned out, employers paid virtually no attention to references; only 4 out of 350 actually checked.

Even though employers are not allowed to use criminal background information to make hiring decisions, about three-quarters of employers in this sample explicitly asked if the applicant had ever been convicted of a crime and, if so, for details. A much smaller proportion, just over a quarter, indicated that they would perform a background check (employers are not required to say if they intend to, and this doubtless represents a lower-bound estimate). The use of background checks by employers has been increasing steadily, however, because of greater ease of access to criminal history information and growing concerns over security.

To what extent are applicants with criminal backgrounds dropped at the beginning of the process? For answers, we turn to the results of the audit.

## THE EFFECTS OF A CRIMINAL RECORD AND RACE ON EMPLOYMENT

Given that all testers presented nearly identical credentials, the different responses they encountered can be attributed fully to the effects of race and criminal background.

The results in Figure 2 suggest that a criminal record has severe effects. Among whites, applicants with criminal records were only half as likely to be called back as equally qualified applicants with no criminal record.

The second question involved the significance of race, by itself, in shaping black men's employment prospects, and here too the audit offered an unequivocal answer (Figure 2). The effect of race was very large, equal to or greater than the effect of a criminal record. Only 14 percent of black men without criminal records were called back,

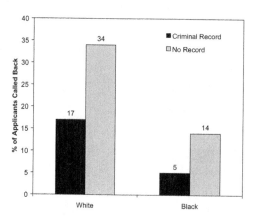

**Figure 2.** *The effect of a criminal record in the Milwaukee audit sample.*

a proportion equal to or less than even than the number of whites *with* a criminal background. The magnitude of the race effect found here corresponds very closely to effects found in previous audit studies directly measuring racial discrimination.[7] Since 1994, when the last major audit was reported, very little has changed in the reaction of employers to minority applicants, at least in Milwaukee.

In addition to the strong independent effects of race and criminal record, evidence suggests that the combination of the two may intensify the negative effects: black ex-offenders are one-third as likely to be called as black applicants without a criminal record. It seems that employers, already reluctant to hire blacks, are even more wary of those with proven criminal involvement. None of our white testers was asked about a criminal record before submitting his application, yet on three occasions black testers were questioned. Our testers were bright, articulate young men, yet the cursory review that entry-level applicants receive leaves little room for these qualities to be noticed.

In some cases, testers reported that employers' levels of responsiveness changed dramatically once they had glanced down at the criminal record questions. Employers seemed to use the information as a screening mechanism, without probing further into the context or complexities of the applicant's situation. But in a few circumstances employers expressed a preference for workers who had recently been released from prison because (in one case) "they tend to be more motivated and are more likely to be hard workers" and (in the case of a janitorial job) the job "involved a great deal of dirty work." Despite these cases, the vast majority of employers were reluctant to take a chance on applicants with a criminal record.

The evidence from this audit suggests that the criminal justice system is not a peripheral institution in the lives of young disadvantaged men. It has become a dominant presence, playing a key role in sorting and stratifying labor market opportunities for such men. And employment is only one of the domains affected by incarceration. Further research is needed to understand its effects on housing, family formation, and political participation, among others, before we can more fully understand its collateral consequences for social and economic inequality.

# NOTES

1. For discussions of the effect of incarceration, see, e.g., J. Grogger, "The Effect of Arrests on the Employment and Earnings of Young Men," *Quarterly Journal of Economics* 110 (1995): 51–72; B. Western, "The Impact of Incarceration on Wage Mobility and Inequality," *American Sociological Review* 67, no. 4 (2002): 526–46.

2. This research is reported in D. Pager, "The Mark of a Criminal Record," *American Journal of Sociology* 108, no. 5 (2003): 937–75. IRP thanks the University of Chicago Press for permission to summarize the article.

3. See, for example, D. Neal and W. Johnson, "The Role of Premarket Factors in Black-White Wage Differences," *Journal of Political Economy* 104, no. 5 (1996): 869–95; S. Steele, *The Content of Our Character: A New Vision of Race in America* (New York: Harper Perennial, 1991).

4. The method of audit studies was pioneered in the 1970s with a series of housing audits conducted by the Department of Housing and Urban Development, and was modified and applied to employment by researchers at the Urban Institute in the early 1990s. M. Turner, M. Fix, and R. Struyk, *Opportunities Denied, Opportunities Diminished: Racial Discrimination in Hiring* (Washington, D.C.: Urban Institute Press, 1991).

5. Bureau of Labor Statistics, Local Area Unemployment Statistics. Last accessed March 2003. <http://www.bls.gov/lau/home.htm>

6. Over 90 percent of recent, entry-level job openings in Milwaukee were located in the outlying counties and suburbs, and only 4 percent in the central city. J. Pawasarat and L. Quinn, "Survey of Job Openings in the Milwaukee Metropolitan Area: Week of May 15, 2000," Employment and Training Institute Report, University of Wisconsin-Milwaukee, 2000.

7. M. Bendick, Jr., C. Jackson, and V. Reinoso, "Measuring Employment Discrimination through Controlled Experiments," *Review of Black Political Economy* 23 (1994): 25–48.

# THE CRIMINAL JUSTICE SYSTEM

# ▢▪▪ Toward a Theory of Race, Crime, and Urban Inequality

By Robert J. Sampson and William Julius Wilson

Our purpose in this chapter is to address one of the central yet difficult issues facing criminology—race and violent crime. The centrality of the issue is seen on several fronts: the leading cause of death among young black males is homicide (Fingerhut and Kleinman 1990, 3292), and the lifetime risk of being murdered is as high as 1 in 21 for black males, compared with only 1 in 131 for white males (U.S. Department of Justice 1985). Although rates of violence have been higher for blacks than whites at least since the 1950s (Jencks 1991), record increases in homicide since the mid-1980s in cities such as New York, Chicago, and Philadelphia also appear racially selective (Hinds 1990; James 1991; Recktenwald and Morrison 1990). For example, while white rates remained stable, the rate of death from firearms among young black males more than doubled from 1984 to 1988 alone (Fingerhut et al. 1991). These differentials help explain recent estimates that a resident of rural Bangladesh has a greater chance of surviving to age 40 than does a black male in Harlem (McCord and Freeman 1990). Moreover, the so-called drug war and the resulting surge in prison populations in the past decade have taken their toll disproportionately on the minority community (Mauer 1990). Overall, the evidence is clear that African-Americans face dismal and worsening odds when it comes to crime in the streets and the risk of incarceration.

Despite these facts, the discussion of race and crime is mired in an unproductive mix of controversy and silence. At the same time that articles on age and gender abound, criminologists are loath to speak openly on race and crime for fear of being misunderstood or labeled racist. This situation is not unique, for until recently scholars of urban poverty also consciously avoided discussion of race and social dislocations in the inner city lest they be accused of blaming the victim (see W. J. Wilson 1987). And when the topic is broached, criminologists have reduced the race–crime debate to simplistic arguments about culture versus social structure. On the one side, structuralists argue for the primacy of "relative deprivation" to understand black crime (e.g., Blau and Blau 1982), even though the evidence on social class and crime is weak at best. On the other side, cultural theorists tend to focus on an indigenous culture of violence in black ghettos (e.g., Wolfgang and Ferracuti 1967), even though the evidence there is weak too.

Still others engage in subterfuge, denying race-related differentials in violence and focusing instead on police bias and the alleged invalidity of official crime statistics (e.g., Stark 1990). This in spite of evidence not only from death records but also from survey reports showing that blacks are disproportionately victimized by, and involved in, criminal violence (Hindelang 1976, 1978). Hence, much like the silence on race and inner-city social dislocations engendered by the vociferous attacks on the Moynihan Report in the 1960s, criminologists have, with few exceptions (e.g., Hawkins 1986; Hindelang 1978; Katz 1988), abdicated serious scholarly debate on race and crime.

In an attempt to break this stalemate we advance in this chapter a theoretical strategy that incorporates both structural and cultural arguments regarding race, crime, and inequality in American cities. In contrast to psychologically based relative deprivation theories and the subculture of violence, we view the race and crime linkage from contextual lenses that highlight the very different ecological contexts that blacks and whites reside in—regardless of individual characteristics. The basic thesis is that macrosocial patterns of residential inequality give rise to the social isolation and ecological concentration of the truly disadvantaged, which in turn leads to structural barriers and cultural adaptations that undermine social organization and hence the control of crime. This thesis is grounded in what is actually an old idea in criminology that has been overlooked in the race and crime debate—the importance of communities.

## THE COMMUNITY STRUCTURE OF RACE AND CRIME

Unlike the dominant tradition in criminology that seeks to distinguish offenders from nonoffenders, the macrosocial or community level of explanation asks what it is about community structures and cultures that produce differential rates of crime (Bursik 1988; Byrne and Sampson 1986; Short 1985). As such, the goal of macrolevel research is not to explain individual involvement in criminal behavior but to isolate characteristics of communities, cities, or even societies that lead to high rates of criminality (Byrne and Sampson 1986; Short 1985). From this viewpoint the "ecological fallacy"—inferring individual-level relations based on aggregate data—is not at issue because the unit of explanation and analysis is the community.

The Chicago School research of Clifford Shaw and Henry McKay spearheaded the community-level approach of modern American studies of ecology and crime. In their classic work *Juvenile Delinquency and Urban Areas*, Shaw and McKay (1942) argued that three structural factors—low economic status, ethnic heterogeneity, and residential mobility—led to the disruption of local community social organization, which in turn accounted for variations in crime and delinquency rates (for more details see Kornhauser 1978).

Arguably the most significant aspect of Shaw and McKay's research, however, was their demonstration that high rates of delinquency persisted in certain areas over many years, regardless of population turnover. More than any other, this finding led them to reject individualistic explanations of delinquency and focus instead on the processes by which delinquent and criminal patterns of behavior were transmitted across generations in areas of social disorganization and weak social controls (1942; 1969, 320). This community-level orientation led them to an explicit contextual interpretation of correlations between race/ethnicity and delinquency rates. Their logic was set forth in a rejoinder to a critique in 1949 by Jonassen, who had argued that ethnicity had direct effects on delinquency. Shaw and McKay countered:

The important fact about rates of delinquency for Negro boys is that they, too, vary by type of area. They are higher than the rates for white boys, but it cannot be said that they are higher than rates for white boys in comparable areas, since it is impossible to reproduce in white communities the circumstances under which Negro children live. Even if it were possible to parallel the low economic status and the inadequacy of institutions in the white community, it would not be possible to reproduce the effects of segregation and the barriers to upward mobility (1949, 614).

Shaw and McKay's insight almost a half century ago raises two interesting questions still relevant today. First, to what extent do black rates of crime vary by type of ecological area? Second, is it possible to reproduce in white communities the structural circumstances in which many blacks live? The first question is crucial, for it signals that blacks are not a homogeneous group any more than whites are. Indeed, it is racial stereotyping that assigns to blacks a distinct or homogeneous character, allowing simplistic comparisons of black-white group differences in crime. As Shaw and McKay recognized, the key point is that there is heterogeneity among blacks in crime rates that correspond to community context. To the extent that the causes of black crime are not unique, its rate should thus vary with specific ecological conditions in the same way that the white crime rate does. As we shall now see, recent evidence weighs in Shaw and McKay's favor.

### Are the Causes of Black Crime Unique?

Disentangling the contextual basis for race and crime requires racial disaggregation of both the crime rate and the explanatory variables of theoretical interest.

This approach was used in recent research that examined racially disaggregated rates of homicide and robbery by juveniles and adults in over 150 U.S. cities in 1980 (Sampson 1987). Substantively, the theory explored the effects of black male joblessness and economic deprivation on violent crime as mediated by black family disruption. The results supported the main hypothesis and showed that the scarcity of employed black males relative to black females was directly related to the prevalence of families headed by women in black communities (W. J. Wilson 1987). In turn, black family disruption was substantially related to rates of black murder and robbery, especially by juveniles (see also Messner and Sampson 1991). These effects were independent of income, region, density, city size, and welfare benefits.

The finding that family disruption had stronger effects on juvenile violence than on adult violence, in conjunction with the inconsistent findings of previous research on individual-level delinquency and broken homes, supports the idea that the effects of family structure are related to macro-level patterns of social control and guardianship, especially for youth and their peers (Sampson and Groves 1989). Moreover, the results suggest why unemployment and economic deprivation have had weak or inconsistent direct effects on violence rates in past research—joblessness and poverty appear to exert much of their influence indirectly through family disruption.

Despite a tremendous difference in mean levels of family disruption among black and white communities, the percentage of white families headed by a female also had a large positive effect on white juvenile and white adult violence. In fact, the predictors of white robbery were shown to be in large part identical in sign and magnitude to those for blacks. Therefore, the effect of black family disruption on black crime was independent of commonly cited alternative explanations (e.g., region, density, age composition) and could not be attributed to unique cultural factors within the black community given the similar effect of white family disruption on white crime.

To be clear, we are not dismissing the relevance of culture. As discussed more below, our argument is that if cultural influences exist, they vary systematically with structural features of the urban environment. How else can we make sense of the systematic variations within race—for example, if a uniform subculture of violence explains black crime, are we to assume that this subculture is three times as potent in, say, New York as in Chicago (where black homicide differs by a factor of three)? In San Francisco as in Baltimore (3:1 ratio)? These distinct variations exist even at the state level. For example, rates of black homicide in California are triple those in Maryland (Wilbanks 1986). Must whites then be part of the black subculture of violence in California, given that white homicide rates are also more than triple the rates for whites in Maryland? We think not. The sources of violent crime appear to be remarkably invariant across race and rooted instead in the structural differences among communities, cities, and states in economic and family organization.

## The Ecological Concentration of Race and Social Dislocations

Having demonstrated the similarity of black-white variations by ecological context, we turn to the second logical question. To what extent are blacks as a group differentially exposed to criminogenic structural conditions? More than 40 years after Shaw and McKay's assessment of race and urban ecology, we still cannot say that blacks and whites share a similar environment—especially with regard to concentrated urban poverty. Consider the following. Although approximately 70 percent of all poor non-Hispanic whites lived in non-poverty areas in the ten largest U.S. central cities (as determined by

the 1970 census) in 1980, only 16 percent of poor blacks did. Moreover, whereas less than 7 percent of poor whites lived in extreme poverty or ghetto areas, 38 percent of poor blacks lived in such areas (W. J. Wilson et al. 1988, 130). In the nation's largest city, New York, 70 percent of poor blacks live in poverty neighborhoods; by contrast, 70 percent of poor whites live in non-poverty neighborhoods (Sullivan 1989, 230). Potentially even more important, the majority of poor blacks live in communities characterized by high rates of family disruption. Poor whites, even those from "broken homes," live in areas of relative family stability (Sampson 1987; Sullivan 1989).

The combination of urban poverty and family disruption concentrated by race is particularly severe. As an example, we examined race-specific census data on the 171 largest cities in the United States as of 1980. To get some idea of concentrated social dislocations by race, we selected cities where the proportion of blacks living in poverty was equal to or less than the proportion of whites, and where the proportion of black families with children headed by a single parent was equal to or less than that for white families. Although we knew that the average national rate of family disruption and poverty among blacks was two to four times higher than among whites, the number of distinct ecological contexts in which blacks achieve equality to whites is striking. In not one city over 100,000 in the United States do blacks live in ecological equality with whites when it comes to these basic features of economic and family organization. Accordingly, racial differences in poverty and family disruption are so strong that the "worst" urban contexts in which whites reside are considerably better than the average context of black communities (Sampson 1987, 354).

Taken as a whole, these patterns underscore what W. J. Wilson (1987) has labeled "concentration effects," that is, the effects of living in a neighborhood that is overwhelmingly impoverished. These concentration effects, reflected in a range of outcomes from degree of labor force attachment to social deviance, are created by the constraints and opportunities that the residents of inner-city neighborhoods face in terms of access to jobs and job networks, involvement in quality schools, availability of marriageable partners, and exposure to conventional role models.

The social transformation of the inner city in recent decades has resulted in an increased concentration of the most disadvantaged segments of the urban black population—especially poor, female-headed families with children. Whereas one of every five poor blacks resided in ghetto or extreme poverty areas in 1970, by 1980 nearly two out of every five did so (W. J. Wilson et al. 1988, 131). This change has been fueled by several macrostructural forces. In particular, urban minorities have been vulnerable to structural economic changes related to the deindustrialization of central cities (e.g., the shift from goods-producing to service-producing industries; increasing polarization of the labor market into low-wage and high-wage sectors; and relocation of manufacturing out of the inner city). The exodus of middle-and upper-income black families from the inner city has also removed an important social buffer that could potentially deflect the full impact of prolonged joblessness and industrial transformation. This thesis is based on the assumption that the basic institutions of an area (churches, schools, stores, recreational facilities, etc.) are more likely to remain viable if the core of their support comes from more economically stable families in inner-city neighborhoods (W. J. Wilson 1987, 56). The social milieu of increasing stratification among blacks differs significantly from the environment that existed in inner cities in previous decades (see also Hagedorn 1988).

Black inner-city neighborhoods have also disproportionately suffered severe population and housing loss of the sort identified by Shaw and McKay (1942) as disrupting the social and institutional order. Skogan (1986, 206) has noted how urban renewal and forced migration contributed to the wholesale uprooting of many urban black communities, especially the extent to which freeway networks driven through the hearts of many cities in the 1950s destroyed viable, low-income communities. For example, in Atlanta one in six residents was dislocated by urban renewal; the great majority of those dislocated were poor blacks (Logan and Molotch 1987, 114). Nationwide, fully 20 percent of all central-city housing units occupied by blacks were lost in the period 1960–70 alone. As Logan and Molotch (1987, 114) observe, this displacement does not even include that brought about by more routine market forces (evictions, rent increases, commercial development).

Of course, no discussion of concentration effects is complete without recognizing the negative consequences of deliberate policy decisions to concentrate minorities and the poor in public housing. Opposition from organized community groups to the building of public housing in their neighborhoods, de facto federal policy to tolerate extensive segregation against blacks in urban housing markets, and the decision by local governments to neglect the rehabilitation of existing residential units (many of them single-family homes), have led to massive, segregated housing projects that have become ghettos for the minorities and disadvantaged (see also Sampson 1990). The cumulative result is that, even given the same objective socioeconomic status, blacks and whites face vastly different environments in which to live, work, and raise their children. As Bickford and Massey (1991, 1035) have argued, public housing is a federally funded, physically permanent institution for the isolation of black families by race and class and must therefore be considered an important structural constraint on ecological area of residence.

In short, the foregoing discussion suggests that macrostructural factors—both historic and contemporary—have combined to concentrate urban black poverty and family disruption in the inner city. These factors include but are not limited to racial segregation, structural economic transformation and black male joblessness, class-linked outmigration from the inner city, and housing discrimination. It is important to emphasize that when segregation and concentrated poverty represent structural constraints embodied in public policy and historical patterns of racial subjugation, notions that individual differences (or self-selection) explain community-level effects on violence are considerably weakened (see Sampson and Lauritsen 1994).

## Implications

The consequences of these differential ecological distributions by race raise the substantively plausible hypothesis that correlations of race and crime may be systematically confounded with important differences in community contexts. As Testa has argued with respect to escape from poverty:

> Simple comparisons between poor whites and poor blacks would be confounded with the fact that poor whites reside in areas which are ecologically and economically very different from poor blacks. Any observed relationships involving race would reflect, to some unknown degree, the relatively superior ecological niche many poor whites occupy with respect to jobs, marriage opportunities, and exposure to conventional role models (quoted in W. J. Wilson 1987: 58–60).

Regardless of a black's individual-level family or economic situation, the average community of residence thus differs dramatically from that of a similarly situated white (Sampson 1987). For example, regardless of whether a black juvenile is raised in an intact or single-parent family, or a rich or poor home, he or she will not likely grow up in a community context similar to that of whites with regard to family structure and income. Reductionist interpretations of race and social class camouflage this key point.

In fact, a community conceptualization exposes the "individualistic fallacy"—the often-invoked assumption that individual-level causal relations necessarily generate individual-level correlations. Research conducted at the individual level rarely questions whether obtained results might be spurious and confounded with community-level processes. In the present case, it is commonplace to search for individual-level (e.g., constitutional) or group-level (e.g., social class) explanations for the link between race and violence. In our opinion these efforts have largely failed, and so we highlight contextual sources of the race-violence link among individuals. More specifically, we posit that the most important determinant of the relationship between race and crime is the differential distribution of blacks in communities characterized by (1) *structural social disorganization* and (2) *cultural social isolation*, both of which stem from the concentration of poverty, family disruption, and residential instability.

Before explicating the theoretical dimensions of social disorganization, we must also expose what may be termed the "materialist fallacy"—that economic (or materialist) causes necessarily produce economic motivations. Owing largely to Merton's (1938) famous dictum about social structure and anomie, criminologists have assumed that if economic structural factors (e.g., poverty) are causally relevant it must be through the motivation to commit acquisitive crimes. Indeed, "strain" theory was so named to capture the hypothesized pressure on members of the lower classes to commit crime in their pursuit of the American dream. But as is well known, strain or materialist theories have not fared well empirically (Kornhauser 1978). The image of the offender stealing to survive flourishes only as a straw man, knocked down most recently by Jack Katz, who argues that materialist theory is nothing more than "twentieth-century sentimentality about crime" (1988, 314). Assuming, however, that those who posit the relevance of economic structure for crime rely on motivational pressure as an explanatory concept, is itself a fallacy. The theory of social disorganization does see relevance in the ecological concentration of poverty, but not for the materialist reasons Katz (1988) presupposes. Rather, the conceptualization we now explicate rests on the fundamental properties of structural and cultural organization.

## THE STRUCTURE OF SOCIAL (DIS)ORGANIZATION

In their original formulation Shaw and McKay held that low economic status, ethnic heterogeneity, and residential mobility led to the disruption of community social organization, which in turn accounted for variations in crime and delinquency rates (1942; 1969). As recently extended by Kornhauser (1978), Bursik (1988), and Sampson and Groves (1989), the concept of social disorganization may be seen as the inability of a community structure to realize the common values of its residents and maintain effective social controls. The *structural* dimensions of community social disorganization refer to the prevalence and interdependence of social networks in a community—both informal (e.g., the density of acquaintanceship; intergenerational kinship ties; level of anonymity) and formal (e.g., organizational participation; institutional stability)—and in the span of collective supervision that the community directs toward local problems.

This social-disorganization approach is grounded in what Kasarda and Janowitz (1974, 329) call the "systemic" model, where the local community is viewed as a complex system of friendship and kinship networks, and formal and informal associational ties are rooted in family life and ongoing socialization processes (see also Sampson 1991). From this view social organization and social disorganization are seen as different ends of the same continuum of systemic networks of community social control. As Bursik (1988) notes, when formulated in this way, social disorganization is clearly separable not only from the processes that may lead to it (e.g., poverty, residential mobility), but also from the degree of criminal behavior that may be a result. This conceptualization also goes beyond the traditional account of community as a strictly geographical or spatial phenomenon by focusing on the social and organizational networks of local residents (see Leighton 1988).

Evidence favoring social-disorganization theory is available with respect both to its structural antecedents and to mediating processes. In a recent paper, Sampson and Lauritsen (1994) reviewed in depth the empirical literature on individual, situational, and community-level sources of interpersonal violence (i.e., assault, homicide, robbery, and rape). This assessment revealed that community-level research conducted in the past twenty years has largely supported the original Shaw and McKay model in terms of the exogenous correlates of poverty, residential mobility, and heterogeneity. What appears to be especially salient is the *interaction* of poverty and mobility. As anticipated by Shaw and McKay (1942) and Kornhauser (1978), several studies indicate that the effect of poverty is most pronounced in neighborhoods of high residential instability (see Sampson and Lauritsen 1994).

In addition, recent research has established that crime rates are positively linked to community-level variations in urbanization (e.g., population and housing density), family disruption (e.g., percentage of single-parent households), opportunity structures for predatory crime (e.g., density of convenience stores), and rates of community change and population turnover (see also Bursik 1988; Byrne and Sampson 1986; Reiss 1986). As hypothesized by Sampson and Groves (1989), family disruption, urbanization, and the anonymity accompanying rapid population change all undercut the capacity of a community to exercise informal social control, especially of teenage peer groups in public spaces.

Land et al. (1990) have also shown the relevance of *resource deprivation, family dissolution,* and *urbanization* (density, population size) for explaining homicide rates across cities, metropolitan areas, and states from 1960 to 1980. In particular, their factor of resource deprivation/affluence included three income variables—median income, the percentage of families below the poverty line, and the Gini index of income inequality—in addition to the percentage of population that is black and the percentage of children not living with both parents. This coalescence of structural conditions with race supports the concept of concentration effects (W. J. Wilson 1987) and is consistent with Taylor and Covington's finding (1988) that increasing entrenchment of ghetto poverty was associated with large increases in violence. In these two studies the correlation among structural indices was not seen merely as a statistical nuisance (i.e., as multicolinearity), but as a predictable substantive outcome. Moreover, the Land et al. (1990) results support Wilson's argument that concentration effects grew more severe from 1970 to 1980 in large cities. Urban disadvantage thus appears to be increasing in ecological concentration.

It is much more difficult to study the intervening mechanisms of social disorganization directly, but at least two recent studies provide empirical support for the theory's structural dimensions. First, Taylor et al. (1984) examined variations in violent crime (e.g., mugging, assault, murder, rape) across sixty-three street blocks in Baltimore in 1978. Based on interviews with 687 household respondents, Taylor et al. (1984, 316) constructed block-level measures of the proportion of respondents who belonged to an organization to which coresidents also belonged, and the proportion of respondents who felt responsible for what happened in the area surrounding their home. Both of these dimensions of informal social control were significantly and negatively related to community-level variations in crime, exclusive of other ecological factors (1984, 320). These results support the social-disorganization hypothesis that levels of organizational participation and informal social control—especially of public activities by neighborhood youth—inhibit community-level rates of violence.

Second, Sampson and Groves's analysis of the British Crime Survey in 1982 and 1984 showed that the prevalence of unsupervised teenage peer groups in a community had the largest effects on rates of robbery and violence by strangers. The density of local friendship networks—measured by the proportion of residents with half or more of their friends living in the neighborhood—also had a significant negative effect on robbery rates. Further, the level of organizational participation by residents had significant inverse effects on both robbery and stranger violence (Sampson and Groves 1989, 789). These results suggest that communities characterized by sparse friendship networks, unsupervised teenage peer groups, and low organizational participation foster increased crime rates (see also Anderson 1990).

Variations in these structural dimensions of community social disorganization also transmitted in large part the effects of community socioeconomic status, residential mobility, ethnic heterogeneity, and family disruption in a theoretically consistent manner. For example, mobility had significant inverse effects on friendship networks, family disruption was the largest predictor of unsupervised peer groups, and socioeconomic status had a significant positive effect on organizational participation in 1982. When combined with the results of research on gang delinquency, which point to the salience of informal and formal community structures in controlling the formation of gangs (Short and Strodtbeck 1965; Sullivan 1989; Thrasher 1963), the empirical data suggest that the structural elements of social disorganization have relevance for explaining macrolevel variations in crime.

## Further Modifications

To be sure, social-disorganization theory as *traditionally conceptualized* is hampered by a restricted view of community that fails to account for the larger political and structural forces shaping communities. As suggested earlier, many community characteristics hypothesized to underlie crime rates, such as residential instability, concentration of poor, female-headed families with children, multiunit housing projects, and disrupted social networks, appear to stem directly from planned governmental policies at local, state, and federal levels. We thus depart from the natural market assumptions of the Chicago School ecologists by incorporating the political economy of place (Logan and Molotch 1987), along with macrostructural transformations and historical forces, into our conceptualization of community-level social organization.

Take, for example, municipal code enforcement and local governmental policies toward neighborhood deterioration. In *Making the Second Ghetto: Race and Housing in Chicago, 1940–1960*, Hirsch (1983) documents in great detail how lax enforcement of city housing codes played a major role in accelerating the deterioration of inner-city Chicago neighborhoods. More recently, Daley and Mieslin (1988) have argued that inadequate city policies on code enforcement

and repair of city properties contributed to the systematic decline of New York City's housing stock, and consequently, entire neighborhoods. When considered with the practices of redlining and disinvestment by banks and "block-busting" by real estate agents (Skogan 1986), local policies toward code enforcement—that on the surface are far removed from crime—have in all likelihood contributed to crime through neighborhood deterioration, forced migration, and instability.

Decisions to withdraw city municipal services for public health and fire safety—presumably made with little if any thought to crime and violence—also appear to have been salient in the social disintegration of poor communities. As Wallace and Wallace (1990) argue based on an analysis of the "planned shrinkage" of New York City fire and health services in recent decades: "The consequences of withdrawing municipal services from poor neighborhoods, the resulting outbreaks of contagious urban decay and forced migration which shred essential social networks and cause social disintegration, have become a highly significant contributor to decline in public health among the poor" (1990, 427). The loss of social integration and networks from planned shrinkage of services may increase behavioral patterns of violence that may themselves become "convoluted with processes of urban decay likely to further disrupt social networks and cause further social disintegration" (1990, 427). This pattern of destabilizing feedback (see Skogan 1986) appears central to an understanding of the role of governmental policies in fostering the downward spiral of high crime areas. As Wacquant has recently argued, federal U.S. policy seems to favor "the institutional desertification of the urban core" (1991, 36).

Decisions by government to provide public housing paint a similar picture. Bursik (1989) has shown that the planned construction of new public housing projects in Chicago in the 1970s was associated with increased rates of population turnover, which in turn were related to increases in crime. More generally, we have already noted how the disruption of urban renewal contributed disproportionately to housing loss among poor blacks.

Boiled down to its essentials, then, our theoretical framework linking social-disorganization theory with research on urban poverty and political economy suggests that macrosocial forces (e.g., segregation, migration, housing discrimination, structural transformation of the economy) interact with local community-level factors (e.g., residential turnover, concentrated poverty, family disruption) to impede social organization. This is a distinctly sociological viewpoint, for it focuses attention on the proximate structural characteristics and mediating processes of community social organization that help explain crime, while also recognizing the larger historical, social, and political forces shaping local communities.

## SOCIAL ISOLATION AND COMMUNITY CULTURE

Although social-disorganization theory is primarily structural in nature, it also focuses on how the ecological segregation of communities gives rise to what Kornhauser (1978, 75) terms *cultural* disorganization—the attenuation of societal cultural values. Poverty, heterogeneity, anonymity, mutual distrust, institutional instability, and other structural features of urban communities are hypothesized to impede communication and obstruct the quest for common values, thereby fostering cultural diversity with respect to nondelinquent values. For example, an important component of Shaw and McKay's theory was that disorganized communities spawned delinquent gangs with their own subcultures and norms perpetuated through cultural transmission.

Despite their relative infrequency, ethnographic studies generally support the notion that structurally disorganized communities are conducive to the emergence of cultural value systems and attitudes that seem to legitimate, or at least provide a basis of tolerance for, crime and deviance. For example, Suttles's (1968) account of the social order of a Chicago neighborhood characterized by poverty and heterogeneity supports Thrasher's (1963) emphasis on age, sex, ethnicity, and territory as markers for the ordered segmentation of slum culture. Suttles found that single-sex, age-graded primary groups of the same ethnicity and territory emerged in response to threats of conflict and community-wide disorder and mistrust. Although the community subcultures Suttles discovered were provincial, tentative, and incomplete (Kornhauser 1978, 18), they nonetheless undermined societal values against delinquency and violence. Similarly, Anderson's (1978) ethnography of a bar in Chicago's South-side black ghetto shows how primary values coexisted alongside residual values associated with deviant subcultures (e.g., hoodlums), such as "toughness," "getting big money," "going for bad," and "having fun" (1978, 129–30; 152–58). In Anderson's analysis, lower-class residents do not so much "stretch" mainstream values as "create their own particular standards of social conduct along variant lines open to them" (1978, 210). In this context the use of violence is not valued as a primary goal but is nonetheless expected and tolerated as a fact of life (1978, 134). Much like Rainwater (1970), Suttles (1968), and Horowitz (1987), Anderson suggests that in certain community contexts the wider cultural values are simply not relevant—they become "unviable."

Whether community subcultures are authentic or merely "shadow cultures" (Liebow 1967) cannot be resolved here (see also Kornhauser 1978). But that seems less important than acknowledging that community contexts seem to shape what can be termed *cognitive landscapes* or ecologically structured norms (e.g., normative ecologies) regarding appropriate standards and expectations of conduct. That is, in structurally disorganized slum communities it appears that a system of values emerges in which crime, disorder, and drug use are less than fervently condemned and hence expected as part of everyday life. These ecologically structured social perceptions and tolerances in turn appear to influence the probability of criminal outcomes and harmful deviant behavior (e.g., drug use by pregnant women). In this regard Kornhauser's attack on subcultural theories misses the point. By attempting to assess whether subcultural values are authentic in some deep, almost quasi-religious sense (1978, 1–20), she loses sight of the processes by which cognitive landscapes rooted in social ecology may influence everyday behavior. Indeed, the idea that dominant values become existentially irrelevant in certain community contexts is a powerful one, albeit one that has not had the research exploitation it deserves (cf. Katz 1988).

A renewed appreciation for the role of cultural adaptations is congruent with the notion of *social isolation*—defined as the lack of contact or of sustained interaction with individuals and institutions that represent mainstream society (W. J. Wilson 1987, 60). According to this line of reasoning, the social isolation fostered by the ecological concentration of urban poverty deprives residents not only of resources and conventional role models, but also of cultural learning from mainstream social networks that facilitate social and economic advancement in modern industrial society (W. J. Wilson 1991). Social isolation is specifically distinguished from the culture of poverty by virtue of its focus on adaptations to constraints and opportunities rather than internalization of norms.

As Ulf Hannerz noted in his seminal work *Soulside*, it is thus possible to recognize the importance of macrostructural constraints—that is, avoid the extreme notions of the culture of poverty or the culture of violence, and yet see the "merits of a more subtle kind of cultural analysis" (1969, 182). One could hypothesize a difference, on the one hand, between a jobless family whose mobility is impeded by the macrostructural constraints in the economy and the larger society but nonetheless lives in an area with a relatively low rate of poverty, and on the other hand, a jobless family that lives in an inner-city ghetto neighborhood that is influenced not only by these same constraints but also by the behavior of other jobless families in the neighborhood (Hannerz 1969, 184; W. J. Wilson 1991). The latter influence is one of culture—the extent to which individuals follow their inclinations as they have been developed by learning or influence from other members of the community (Hannerz 1969).

Ghetto-specific practices such as an overt emphasis on sexuality and macho values, idleness, and public drinking are often denounced by those who reside in inner-city ghetto neighborhoods. But because such practices occur much more frequently there than in middle-class society, largely because of social organizational forces, the transmission of these modes of behavior by precept, as in role modeling, is more easily facilitated (Hannerz 1969). For example, youngsters are more likely to see violence as a way of life in inner-city ghetto neighborhoods. They are more likely to witness violent acts, to be taught to be violent by exhortation, and to have role models who do not adequately control their own violent impulses or restrain their own anger. Accordingly, given the availability of and easy access to firearms, knives, and other weapons, adolescent experiments with macho behavior often have deadly consequences (Prothrow-Stith 1991).

The concept of social isolation captures this process by implying that contact between groups of different class and/or racial backgrounds either is lacking or has become increasingly intermittent, and that the nature of this contact enhances effects of living in a highly concentrated poverty area.

Unlike the concept of the culture of violence, then, social isolation does not mean that ghetto-specific practices become internalized, take on a life of their own, and therefore continue to influence behavior no matter what the contextual environment. Rather, it suggests that reducing structural inequality would not only decrease the frequency of these practices; it would also make their transmission by precept less efficient. So in this sense we advocate a renewed appreciation for the ecology of culture, but not the monolithic and hence noncontextual culture implied by the subculture of poverty and violence.

## DISCUSSION

Rejecting both the "individualistic" and "materialist" fallacies, we have attempted to delineate a theoretical strategy that incorporates both structural and cultural arguments regarding race, crime, and urban inequality in American cities. Drawing on insights from social-disorganization theory and recent research on urban poverty, we believe this strategy provides new ways of thinking about race and crime. First and foremost, our perspective views the link between race and crime through contextual lenses that highlight the very different ecological contexts in which blacks and whites reside—regardless of individual characteristics. Second, we emphasize that crime rates among blacks nonetheless vary by ecological characteristics, just as they do for whites. Taken together, these facts suggest a powerful role for community context in explaining race and crime.

Our community-level explanation also departs from conventional wisdom. Rather than attributing to acts of crime a purely economic motive springing from relative deprivation—an individual-level psychological concept—we focus on the mediating dimensions of community social organization to understand variations in crime across areas. Moreover, we acknowledge and try to specify the macrosocial forces that contribute to the social organization of local communities. Implicit in this attempt is the incorporation of the political economy of place and the role of urban inequality in generating racial differences in community structure. As Wacquant observes, American urban poverty is "preeminently a *racial poverty* ... rooted in the *ghetto* as a historically specific social form and mechanism of racial domination" (1991, 36, emphasis in original). This intersection of race, place, and poverty goes to the heart of our theoretical concerns with societal and community organization.

Furthermore, we incorporate culture into our theory in the form of social isolation and ecological landscapes that shape perceptions and cultural patterns of learning. This culture is not seen as inevitably tied to race, but more to the varying structural contexts produced by residential and macroeconomic change, concentrated poverty, family instability, and intervening patterns of social disorganization. Perhaps controversially, then, we differ from the recent wave of structuralist research on the culture of violence (for a review see Sampson and Lauritsen 1994). In an interesting methodological sleight of hand, scholars have dismissed the relevance of culture based on the analysis of census data that provide no measures of culture whatsoever (see especially Blau and Blau 1982). We believe structural criminologists have too quickly dismissed the role of values, norms, and learning as they interact with concentrated poverty and social isolation. In our view, macrosocial patterns of residential inequality give rise to the social isolation and concentration of the truly disadvantaged, engendering cultural adaptations that undermine social organization.

Finally, our conceptualization suggests that the roots of urban violence among today's 15- to 21-year-old cohort may stem from childhood socialization that took place in the late 1970s and early 1980s. Consider that this cohort was born between

1970 and 1976 and spent its childhood in the context of a rapidly changing urban environment unlike that of any previous point in U.S. history. As documented in detail by W. J. Wilson (1987), the concentration of urban poverty and other social dislocations began increasing sharply in about 1970 and continued unabated through the decade and into the 1980s. As but one example, the proportion of black families headed by women increased by over 50 percent from 1970 to 1984 alone (W. J. Wilson 1987, 26). Large increases were also seen in the ecological concentration of ghetto poverty, racial segregation, population turnover, and joblessness. These social dislocations were, by comparison, relatively stable in earlier decades. Therefore, the logic of our theoretical model suggests that the profound changes in the urban structure of minority communities in the 1970s may hold the key to understanding recent increases in violence.

## CONCLUSION

By recasting traditional race and poverty arguments in a contextual framework that incorporates both structural and cultural concepts, we seek to generate empirical and theoretical ideas that may guide further research. The unique value of a community-level perspective is that it leads away from a simple "kinds of people" analysis to a focus on how social characteristics of collectivities foster violence. On the basis of our theoretical framework, we conclude that community-level factors such as the *ecological concentration of ghetto poverty, racial segregation, residential mobility* and population turnover, *family disruption*, and the dimensions of local *social organization* (e.g., density of friendship/acquaintanceship, social resources, intergenerational links, control of street-corner peer groups, organizational participation) are fruitful areas of future inquiry, especially as they are affected by macrolevel public policies regarding housing, municipal services, and

employment. In other words, our framework suggests the need to take a renewed look at social policies that focus on prevention. We do not need more after-the-fact (reactive) approaches that ignore the structural context of crime and the social organization of inner cities.

## DISCUSSION QUESTIONS

1. What were some of the barriers to the sociological study of race and violent crime, according to Sampson and Wilson? How did Shaw and McKay's "community-level" approach help clear these barriers?
2. Why do the authors focus on geographic and community structures over cultural influences, in studying race and crime?
3. What factors seem to account for the higher violent crime rates among blacks in the inner-city? Why do general economic downturns hit these areas harder than suburban or rural environments?

## REFERENCES

Anderson, E. (1978). *A place in the corner*. Chicago: University of Chicago Press.

Anderson, E. (1990). *Streetwise: Race, class and change in an urban community*. Chicago: University of Chicago Press.

Bickford, A., & Massey, D. (1991). Segregation in the second ghetto: racial and ethnic segregation in American public housing, 1977. *Social Forces, 69*, 1011–1036.

Blau, J. R., & Blau, P. M. (1982). The cost of inequality: Metropolitan structure and violent crime. *American Sociological Review, 47*, 114–129.

Bursik, R. J., Jr. (1988). Social disorganization and theories of crime and delinquency: Conflict and consensus. In S. Messner, M. Krohn, & A. Liska (Eds.), *Theoretical integration in the study of* deviance and crime. Albany, NY: State University of New York Press.

Byrne, J., & Sampson, R. J. (1986). Key issues in the social ecology of crime. In J. Byrne & R. J. Sampson (Eds.), *The social ecology of crime.* New York: Springer-Verlag.

Daley, S., & Mieslin, R. (1988). New York City, the landlord: A decade of housing decay. *New York Times*, February 8.

Fingerhut, L. A., & Kleinman, J. C. (1990). International and interstate comparisons if homicide among young males. *Journal of the American Medical Association, 263*, 3292–3295.

Fingerhut, L. A., Kleinman, J., Godfrey, E., & Rosenberg, H. (1991). Firearms mortality among children, youth, and young adults, 1–34 years of age, trends and current status: United states, 1979–88. *Monthly Vital Statistics Report, 39*, 11, 1–16.

Hagedorn, J. (1988). *People and folks: Gangs, crime and the underclass in a rustbelt city.* Chicago: Lake View Press.

Hannerz, U. (1969). *Soulside: Inquiries into ghetto culture and community.* New York: Columbia University Press.

Hawkins, D. (Ed.). (1986). Homicide among Black Americans. Lanham, MD: University Press of America.

Hindelang, M. J. (1976). *Criminal victimization in eight American cities.* Cambridge, MA: Ballinger.

Hindelang, M. J. (1978). Race and involvement in common law personal crimes. *American Sociological Review, 43*, 93–109.

Hinds, M. (1990). Number of killings soars in big cities across U.S. *New York Times*, July 18, 1.

Hirsch, A. (1983). *Making the second ghetto: Race and housing in Chicago,* 1940–1960. Chicago: University of Chicago Press.

Horowitz, R. (1987). Community tolerance of gang violence. *Social Problems, 34*, 437–450.

James, G. (1991). New York killings set record in 1990. *New York Times*, A14.

Jencks, C. (1991). Is violent crime increasing? *The American Prospect, Winter*, 98–109.

Jonassen, C. (1949). A reevaluation and critique of the logic and some methods of Shaw and McKay. *American Sociological Review, 14*, 608–614.

Kasarda, J., & Janowitz, M. (1974). Community attachment in mass society. *American Sociological Review, 39*, 328–339.

Katz, J. (1988). *Seductions of crime: The sensual and moral attractions of doing evil.* New York: Basic Books.

Kornhauser, R. (1978). *Social sources of delinquency.* Chicago: University of Chicago Press.

Land, K., McCall, P., & Cohen, L. (1990). Structural covariates of homicide rates: Are there any invariances across time and space? *American Journal of Sociology, 95*, 922–963.

Leighton, B. (1988). The community concept in criminology: Toward a social network approach. *Journal of Research in Crime and Delinquency, 25*, 351–374.

Liebow, E. (1967). *Tally's corner.* Boston: Little, Brown.

Logan, J., & Molotch, H. (1987). *Urban fortunes: The political economy of place.* Berkeley: University of California Press.

McCord, M., & Freeman, H. (1990). Excess mortality in Harlem. *New England Journal of Medicine, 322*, 173–175.

Mauer, M. (1990). *Young Black men and the criminal justice system: A growing national problem.* Washington, D.C.: The Sentencing Project.

Merton, R. (1938). Social structure and anomie. *American Sociological Review, 3*, 672–682.

Messner, S., & Sampson, R. (1991). The sex ratio, family disruption, and the rates of violent crime: The paradox of demographic structure. *Social Forces, 69*, 693–714.

Prothrow-Stith, D. (1991). *Deadly consequences.* New York: Harper Collins.

Rainwater, L. (1970). *Behind ghetto walls: Black families in a federal slum*. Chicago: Aldine.

Recktenwald, W., & Morrison, B. (1990). *Guns, gangs, drugs make a deadly combination*. Chicago Tribune, July 1, Section 2, 1.

Reiss, A. J., Jr. (1986). Why are communities important in understanding crime? In A. J. Reiss, Jr., & M. Tonry (Eds.), *Communities and crime*. Chicago: University of Chicago Press.

Sampson, R. J. (1987). Urban Black violence: The effect of male joblessness and family disruption. *American Journal of Sociology, 93*, 348–382.

Sampson, R. J. (1990). The impact of housing policies on community social disorganization and crime. *Bulletin of the New York Academy of Medicine, 66*, 526–533.

Sampson, R. J. (1991). Linking the micro and macrolevel dimensions of community social organization. *Social Forces, 70*, 43–64.

Sampson, R. J., & Groves, W. B. (1989). Community structure and crime: Testing social-disorganization theory. *American Journal of Sociology, 94*, 774–802.

Sampson, R. J., & Lauritsen, J. (1994). Violent victimization and offending: Individual, situational, and community-level risk factors. In A. J. Reiss, Jr., & J. Roth (Eds.), *Understanding and preventing violence: Social Influences, Vol. 3*, Committee on Law and Justice, National Research Council. Washington, D.C.: National Academy Press.

Shaw, C., & McKay, H. (1942). *Juvenile delinquency and urban areas*. Chicago: University of Chicago Press.

Shaw, C., & McKay, H. (1969). *Juvenile delinquency and urban areas (rev. ed.)*. Chicago: University of Chicago Press.

Short, J. F., Jr. (1985). The level of explanation problem in criminology. In R. Meir (Ed.), *Theoretical methods in criminology*. Beverly Hills: Sage Publications.

Short, J. F., Jr., & Strodtbeck, F. L. (1965). *Group process and gang delinquency*. Chicago: University of Chicago Press.

Skogan, W. (1986). Fear of crime and neighborhood change. In A. J. Reiss, Jr., & M. Tonry. (Eds.), *Communities and crime*. Chicago: University of Chicago Press.

Stark, E. (1990). The myth of Black violence. *New York Times*, July 18, A21.

Sullivan, M. (1989). *Getting paid: Youth crime and work in the inner city*. Ithaca, NY: Cornell University Press.

Suttles, G. (1968). *The social order of the slum*. Chicago: University of Chicago Press.

Taylor, R., Gottfredson, S., & Brower, S. (1984). *Black crime and fear: Defensible space, local social ties, and territorial functioning*. Journal of Research and Crime and Delinquency, 21, 303–331.

Taylor, R., & Covington, J. (1988). Neighborhood changes in ecology and violence. *Criminology, 26*, 553–590.

Thrasher, F. (1963). *The gang: A study of 1,313 gangs in Chicago (rev. ed.)*. Chicago: University of Chicago Press.

U.S. Department of Justice. (1985). *The risk of violent crime*. Washington, D.C.: Government Printing Office.

Wacquant, L. (1991). *The specificity of ghetto poverty: A comparative analysis of race, class, and urban exclusion in Chicago's Black belt and the Parisian Red Belt*. Paper presented at the Chicago Urban Poverty and Family Life Conference, University of Chicago.

Wallace, R., & Wallace, D. (1990). *Origins of public health collapse in New York City: The dynamics of planned shrinkage, contagious urban decay and social disintegration*. Bulletin of the New York Academy of Medicine, 66, 391–434.

Wilbanks, W. (1986). Criminal homicide offenders in the U.S. In D. Hawkins (Ed.), *Homicide among*

*Black Americans*. Lanham, MD: University Press of America.

Wilson, W. J. (1987). *The truly disadvantaged: The inner city, the underclass, and public policy*. Chicago: University of Chicago Press.

Wilson, W. J. (1991). Studying inner city social dislocations: The challenge of public agenda research. *American Sociological Review, 56*, 1–14.

Wilson, W. J., & Aponte, R., Kirschenman, J., & Wacquant, L. (1988). The ghetto underclass and the changing structure of American poverty. In F. Harris & R. Wilkins (Eds.), *Quiet riots: Race and poverty in the United States*. New York: Pantheon.

Wolfgang, M., & Ferracuti, F. (1967). *The subculture of violence*. London: Tavistock.

# THE HEALTH CARE SYSTEM

# ROOT AND STRUCTURAL CAUSES OF MINORITY HEALTH AND HEALTH DISPARITIES

*By Keon L. Gilbert and Chikarlo R. Leak*

Research shows that to lower morbidity and mortality rates there must be a focus to ameliorate the fundamental, or root, and structural causes of diseases—those causes that affect access to resources to maintain health and prevent disease (House, Kessler, Herzog, Mero, Kinney, and Breslow, 1990; Link and Phelan, 1995; Navarro, 2002). Two main root or structural causes that affect health are race and socioeconomic status. The relationship between race and socioeconomic status are shaped by the intersection of social-historical time periods, political, economic and social systems. Racial and ethnic differences in morbidity and mortality are found across age, gender, geographical context, and for various causes of disease (Geronimus, Bound, and Waidmann, 1999; House and Williams, 2000; Lillie-Blanton, Gayle, Dievler, 1996; Williams, 1999). Differences in socioeconomic status contribute to the unrelenting differences in racial disparities in health (Antonovsky 1967; House, Lepkowski, Kinney, Mero, Kessler, and Herzog, 1994; Kaplan and Lynch, 1999; Link and Phelan, 1995 ; Navarro, 1989; Sorlie, Rogot, Anderson, Johnson, and Backlund, 1992). This chapter will discuss the significance of race and socioeconomic position as root and structural causes of health disparities in the United States and recommend areas for intervention to address and eliminate these health disparities.

## WHY RACE MATTERS FOR HEALTH

Race is a major determinant of health disparities and the main force for social organization in the United States. According to the Grantmakers in Health, it is more than a qualifier or descriptor; it is an underlying condition that restricts participation in society (Grantmakers in Health, 2001). The systematic process of exclusion through various forms of racial discrimination causes psychological distress which leads to multiple acute and chronic health problems (Feagin and McKinney, 2003). Systematic racism affects multiple generations and has locked people of color into a vicious cycle of cause and effect that has created political, economic, social, and cultural stagnation within communities of color resulting in poor access to quality housing (Sewell, 2010), and quality medical and health care. Racism also limits opportunities for people of color to enjoy residential and recreational facilities that can be used to improve their physical health.

Accordingly, the influence of race in America has become so pervasive that it is embedded in American culture (Smith, 1995).

Consequently then, the relationship between race and health is evidenced through the social, economic, psychological and environmental characteristics related to various health outcomes. Williams (1997) identifies six reasons why race is an important determinant of health outcomes: (1) current racial categories capture an important part of the inequality and injustice in American society; (2) racial categories have historically reflected racism; (3) human populations were categorized into races and became consequential for every aspect of life, thereby making race a fundamental organizing principle of society; (4) current racial categories reflect, in part the legislative mandated attempt to monitor the social and economic progress of population groups that had historically experienced differential treatment based on their race; (5) psychological research suggests that the social processes of in-group favoritism and out-group discrimination may be an inevitable part of social interaction; (6) race is central to the formation of identity in racialized societies.

## RACE AND HEALTH

What health researchers in several disciplines such as African American studies, sociology, public health, and anthropology are concerned with is how to explain disease causation using past and present social inequalities in health (Krieger, 1994). Part of understanding the causes of disease requires a new paradigm that seeks to understand the connection between the biological, psychological and social factors that contribute to disease. These factors are shaped by a particular history within the context of the everyday life of the human population. Examining everyday experiences of racism at work for example are evidenced in acute conditions

such as headaches, chest pains, hyperventilation, and hair problems (Feagin and McKinney, 2003). These acute health conditions can over time result into higher risks for chronic diseases such as cardiovascular disease. Poor health behaviors that lead to poor health status can be understood through the social and psychological factors that influence these behaviors and how these behaviors constitute changes in biological functions over time, thereby placing people of color at greater risk for chronic diseases. Additionally, there is a body of research positing that exposure to racial bias adversely affects physiological and psychological functions in laboratory studies (Anderson, Myers, Pickering, and Jackson, 1989; Armstead, Lawler, Gordon, Cross, and Gibbons, 1989; Jones, Harrell, Morris-Prather, Thomas, and Omowale, 1996; Morris-Prather, Harrell, Collins, Leonard, Boss, and Lee, 1996) and racial bias has an inverse relationship to indicators of physical and mental health in epidemiological studies (Williams, 1997).

## RACIAL AND ETHNIC DIVERSITY AND HEALTH DISPARITIES

The social reality of living in the United States is that not everyone will have the same educational, political, economic, or health opportunities, despite the idealistic "American Dream." Racial and ethnic minorities suffer the greatest of these unequal opportunities. The most disadvantaged of minority groups are relegated to environments that lack the necessary resources to improve their quality of life.

As a nation, the U.S. is becoming more diverse through increases in racial and ethnic minority populations, particularly Hispanics and Asians. African Americans, Native Americans, American Indian, Pacific Islanders, Hispanics and Asians all have higher fertility rates than White Americans (LaVeist, 2005). It is projected that by the middle of the 21st Century, White Americans will make up only 50% of the U.S. population (U.S. Census Bureau, 2004). For that reason, a primary goal of Healthy People 2010 is to eliminate health disparities in the United States.

Health disparities are determined by many attributes. In research, definitions vary as to what constitutes a health disparity. Health disparities will be defined here as "the differences in the incidence, prevalence, mortality, and burden of diseases and other adverse health conditions that exist among specific population groups including socioeconomic status (SES) within the United States" (National Institutes of Health [NIH], 2000). Even after adjusting for age, racial/ethnic minorities have worse mortality, morbidity rates and burden of diseases (NIH 2000), creating an unequivocal strain on the U.S. healthcare systems. Many of these health disparities disproportionately affect other segments of the population such as residents of rural areas, women, children, elderly and those with disabilities.

## DISPARITIES IN LIFE EXPECTANCY

Life expectancy is a central outcome in public health and is typically measured as the average number of years a person born in a given year can expect to live based on a set of age-specific death rates. Life expectancy at birth overall has increased dramatically over the past 100 years from 47.3 years to 77 years of age (U.S. Department of Health and Human Services [USDHHS], 2000). However the increases in life expectancy at birth are not shared equally by all groups. The differences in life expectancy at birth demonstrate a substantial need and opportunity for improvements (USDHHS, 2000). According to a report by the Centers for Disease Control and Prevention National Vital Statistics Report for 2003 (Arias, 2006), life expectancy for males was 74.7 years and 80 years for females. Males increased 0.2 years from 2002 while females

only experienced a 0.1 year increase. This illustrates that gender disparities exist as well.

Yet greater disparities are seen in life expectancy by race. In 1993, the overall life expectancy at birth for Blacks was 69.2 years compared to 76.3 years for Whites, a difference of 7.1 years. However, the life expectancy gap between racial groups is narrowing. In 2003, the overall life expectancy at birth for Blacks was 72.6 years compared to 77.9 years for Whites, a difference of 5.3 years (Arias, 2006).

Conversely, these health disparities increase when racial differences in life expectancy are examined by gender. Black males in 2003 could expect to live 68.9 years compared to 75.3 years for White males, a difference of 6.4 years. In contrast, Black females could expect to live 75.9 years which is higher than White males but lacks in comparison to 80.4 years for White women, a difference of 4.5 years (Arias, 2006). Considering life expectancy is a measure of how long a person can expect to live if current mortality rates persist, it is important to examine disease rates that influence mortality and health disparities.

## DISPARITIES IN RATES OF CHRONIC DISEASE

Minority and populations with lower socioeconomic status (SES) are disproportionately burdened by chronic disease and mortality (National Center for Health Statistics [NCHS], 2006; USDHHS, 2000). African Americans have a higher prevalence and increased incidence of disease when compared to Whites for obesity (having a body mass index greater than 30), cancer, hypertension, and diabetes. In addition, African Americans have a higher prevalence and increased incidence of chronic diseases when compared to the national population averages.

Hispanics are more likely to have diabetes when compared to Whites and national population estimates. In addition, 39.4% of Mexican women are obese in comparison to 30.7% of White women and 33.2% of total population. An even more alarming disparity exists when examining the percent of Black women who are obese. It is estimated that 51.1% of Black women are obese. Due to the limited data on Asian/Pacific Islanders and American Indian/Alaska Natives there are limited estimates for some of these chronic diseases. However, it is documented that American Indian/ Alaska Native have an increased prevalence of diabetes when compared to Whites, and as the nation as a whole (NCHS, 2006).

In the United States, it is estimated that 129.6 million or 64% of people between the ages 20–74 are overweight and 30% meet standards to be considered obese (Morrill and Chinn, 2004). Irrespective of race, obesity is 50% more prevalent among women of low SES than among women of higher SES (Morrill and Chinn, 2004). Obesity is also known to be related to chronic diseases, disability, decreased productivity, quality of life and death (Morrill and Chinn, 2004).

On average, minorities have the poorest health and quality of health care in the U.S. (NCHS, 2006). One explanation may be the percent of minorities who are uninsured or in poverty. Blacks, Hispanics, and American Indians are more likely to be uninsured and in poverty when compared to Whites and the total population. Therefore, lack of access to adequate health care or decreased quality of care may contribute to higher rates of chronic diseases among minorities.

## SOCIOECONOMIC STATUS AND THE CONCENTRATION OF POVERTY

Impoverished communities are formed as a result of racial and ethnic minorities subjectivity to many forms of institutional and structural forms racism that has contributed to generations of poverty (see

Oliver and Shapiro; Sewell 2010 in this anthology). Informal and formal policies have reified the status of minorities and prevented significant economic development. For example, Southern crop lien laws in the Jim Crow South gave authority to arrest young Black men for petty crimes and established the precedence to sentence them to life imprisonment. These young Black men were then leased by prisons to former slave owners, thus becoming free laborers without rights or expectations of health care, good nutrition, education and decent housing. Other examples include historical accounts of Black businesses being burned to the ground and Black business owners being lynched. Black poverty has become endemic to American culture and without a social justice framework to redistribute wealth by providing greater economic and educational opportunities for Blacks, forms of poverty will persist (Conley, 2009; Fairclough 2002; Franklin and Moss, 200; Kelley, 2000).

Poverty perpetuates health disparities: poverty leads to poor health and poor health leads to higher medical expenses. There has been a decline in the overall rate of poverty but an increase in the numbers of Americans who are classified as poor. In 2006, 36.5 million people lived below the poverty line. According to the U. S. Census Bureau, of those living below the poverty-line, 8% are Non-Hispanic Whites, 21% are Hispanic, 24% are Black, and 10% are Asian. There are twice the number of Whites as Blacks who are classified as abjectly poor, but Blacks and Hispanics are disproportionately represented because they comprise 12% and 16%, of the U. S. population.

The debate about the relationship between poverty and health in the United States and globally suggest that poor people's health may be a result of several conditions: "(1) their own innate deficiencies, whether moral, intellectual, or biologic; (2) a causal arrow that runs principally from poor health to economic poverty, with illness interfering with earning (and learning) capacity; or (3) social injustice, requiring redistributive justice" (Krieger, 2007). These explanations highlight both individual and structural causes of poverty that further research using a social justice model. A public health perspective that embodies a social justice framework would suggest that poverty exists as a result of structural barriers that have prevented racial and ethnic minorities from access to education.

Statistics are clear on the health benefits of education: more education contributes to better health outcomes, longer life expectancy, and lower rates of chronic disease (Egerter, Braveman, Sadegh-Nobari, Grossman-Kahn, andDekker, 2009; Cutler and Lleras-Muney, 2006). Persistent racial gaps in education fuel poor health outcomes for racial and ethnic minorities throughout the lifespan, warranting heightened attention to the links between educational inequities and health disparities (Haas, 2006; Maralani, 2008). Education can influence health in many ways, in particular educational attainment can be examined in three ways: health knowledge and behaviors; employment and income; and social and psychological factors, including sense of control, social standing and social support (Egerter et al. 2009; Freudenberg and Ruglis, 2007). Although high school completion has improved over time, high dropout rates are increasingly concentrated among low-income, African American, and Hispanic/Latino students. Additionally, the rate at which students leave school between grades 9 and 10 has tripled (Abrams, 2004; Egerter et al., 2009; Freudenberg and Ruglis, 2007). Health research has strongly suggested a statistical relationship between race and socioeconomic status.

However, these statistics do not fully account for the social reality of low or high economic status. For example, there are racial differences in education, income returns for a given level of education (see Lewis and Pattison 2010 in this anthology), wealth or assets associated with a given level of income (see Oliver and Shapiro 1995 in this anthology), purchasing power of income, the stability of employment and the health risks associated with occupational status (Williams, 1997). Reports have shown that dropouts age 25 or older reported being in worse health than adults who are not dropouts, regardless of income (Pleis and Lethbridge-Çejku, 2006). Some indicators of health status show increases after statistical adjustment for socioeconomic status (Williams, 1997). This suggests that socioeconomic status is not measured the same across races, that the conceptualization of socioeconomic status and race is limited and not characterized well. Finally, these data do not account for non-economic forms of racial discrimination. These realities are at the heart of the continuous struggle for social justice and an improved quality of life. Health, therefore, remains a marker of racial discrimination and differences in socioeconomic status, as measured by economic and non-economic forms.

Socioeconomic status is critical in determining the health of minorities and their access to health care. Socioeconomic differences between races contribute to many of the racial differences observed in health (Grantmakers in Health, 2001). Socioeconomic differences between races are a result of policies that were implemented to create these gaps; this then led to health disparities. African Americans earn 59 cents for every dollar earned by Whites in median family income; and White households are generally 10 times wealthier than African American households, when real estate, stock portfolios, and inherited wealth are considered (see Oliver and Shapiro in this anthology, 1995; Conley, 2009). Exposure to diseases comes in many forms. Understanding how poverty results in various outcomes contributes to epidemiologists' understanding of the development of disease in particular groups or classes. The ability to observe and document how the constraints and possibilities many people face on a daily basis can provide important data about the causes of disease. Without these data, researchers will not be able to identify the etiology of disease for the most disadvantaged of society and solutions will not emerge to solve these issues.

## RESIDENTIAL RACIAL SEGREGATION AND HEALTH CONSEQUENCES

The period of slavery began a clear delineation between Black and White spaces (see Zuberi 2001 in this anthology). Plantation living in the South provided a clearer divide between these spaces. Following the Civil War, Reconstruction failed to secure political and social rights of African-Americans (see Katznelson 2006 in this anthology). When the Hayes-Tilden Compromise of 1877 officially ended Reconstruction efforts, African-Americans became socially, politically and economically disenfranchised by politicians and Northern and Southern capitalists who denied African-Americans suffrage rights, financial compensation, and farmland confiscated during and after the Civil War (Fairclough, 2002; Franklin and Moss, 2000; Hine, Harold, and Hine, 2003). This Compromise resulted in withdrawing Union troops from the South, thus thrusting African-Americans into the hands of former slave owners. The South regained control over local problems including health care. Many of the institutions established to support the poor refused to serve African-Americans in a social, cultural, and intellectual climate that viewed African-Americans as biologically predestined to a lower social hierarchy, thus giving birth to and fueling Black Codes and Jim Crow laws (see Drake 1987 in this anthology). These laws are reinforced by structural barriers such as railroad tracks, which demarcate "White" and "Black" spaces. Health hazards persist in these segregated spaces such as poor air quality found in urban and rural areas close to industrial facilities (Mohai, Lantz, Morenoff, House, and

Mero, 2009; Wing, Horton, Muhammad, Grant, Tajik, and Thu, 2008).

The Modern Civil Rights Era ended these formal and informal practices of discrimination, however the impetus for them, the presumed inferiority of minorities, remains and continues to relegate minority groups to socioeconomically deprived environments (Williams and Collins, 2001). Segregation has led to overcrowded homes, which become breeding grounds for many communicable illnesses that can affect entire households, especially respiratory illnesses such as tuberculosis. Overcrowded neighborhoods can also lead to poor health behaviors, such as a lack of physical activity resulting from poor to no recreational structures for physical activity, which is a primary risk factor for obesity. The Centers for Disease Control suggest creating, improving, and promoting places for physical activity which can result in a 25 percent increase in the percentage of residents who exercise at least three times per week (Centers for Disease Control, Physical Activity Guide). Other research studies have found that adults who live near recreation facilities or have aesthetically pleasing places in which to be active engage in more recreational physical activity (Saelens and Handy, 2008; Sallis and Kerr, 2006).

Residential segregation has many social outcomes. Residential segregation determines housing conditions, educational and employment opportunities, and limits economic mobility, all of which adversely affects health. Many low-skilled, high-paying jobs have moved away from the urban centers where many minorities are concentrated to the suburbs that are dominated by Whites and more economically affluent groups (See Sewell 2010). The jobs in many urban centers require skills and training that many people of color do not have as a direct result of poor to few training and educational opportunities (Williams and Collins, 2001).

Segregation results in disinvestments in the urban infrastructure, the physical environment and contributes to a lower quality of life (Schulz, Williams, Israel, and Lempert, 2002). Other consequences of racially motivated segregation are increased concentration of poverty, increased risk of mortality, decreased access to public and private transportation, and increased exposure to crime. Future research on residential segregation should focus on: (1) developing multilevel research designs to examine the effects of individual, neighborhood, and urban-area factors on health outcomes; (2) examining the health effects of residential segregation among all racial and ethnic minorities; (3) considering racial/ethnic segregation along with income segregation and other urban factors such as poverty concentration and metropolitan governance fragmentation; and (4) developing better conceptual frameworks of the pathways that may link various segregation dimensions to specific health outcomes (Acevedo-Garcia, Lochner, Osypuk, and Subramanian, 2003).

## QUALITY OF HEALTH CARE

Technological advances in medicine have drastically improved life expectancy and potentially have allowed for individuals to live more productive lives. However, the increase in life expectancy and quality of life are not equally shared. Instead, minority populations experience a significantly lower life expectancy (Health United States, 2007).

An Institute of Medicine report described how the social hierarchy that exists in the U.S. plays an important role in explaining differences in the quality of care provided to people of color (Smedley, Stith, and Nelson, 2003). These differences occur in the context of historical and contemporary social inequities; are impacted by a variety of sources, including conscious or unconscious stereotyping; and are not explained by racial and ethnic differences in treatment refusal rates (Smedley et al., 2003). Health care organizations are beholden to societal institutions and forces through funding streams, government mandates, and the practices of individual staff members that reify racist ideologies and practices of exclusion (Trubek and Das, 2003; Byrd and Clayton, 2001; Dreachslin, Weech-Maldonado, and Dansky, 2004). Tashiro (2005) suggests that it is very important for health care provider to critically examine their own assumptions about race and ethnicity, and to determine whether they are based on sound evidence or merely a reflection of prevalent stereotypes. An important step in this process is to maintain a constant awareness of race, its social history, and what race is and is not. Furthermore, an essential starting point for appreciating the complexity of institutional racism in today's health care system is to recognize the existence of inequities in the delivery and quality of health care (Sullivan, 2004).

## CONCLUSION

The emphasis on minority health and health disparities are not unique to the United States, however, the magnitude of the difference in health status may vary across time and place (Berkman, 2009; Mackenbach, Kunst, Cavelaars, Groenhof, Geurts, 1997; Mackenbach, Roskam, Schaap, Menvielle, Leinsalu, Kunst, 2008; Pappas, Queen, Hadden, Fisher, 1993; Singh, 2003), thereby suggesting that a better understanding of disparities in health requires an understanding of the magnitude of the differences among different social, economic and racial/ethnic groups (Berkman, 2009). An examination of the social, historical, political, economic and cultural realities of these groups will show patterns of discrimination, causes of poor health behaviors, social disconnectedness, low-wages, educational disparities, and poor to no access to health care facilities. Understanding the root and structural causes of racial and ethnic disparities will, as Krieger (2000) suggests, provide a more full account of what drives patterns of health, disease, and well-being which can produce useful information to guide policies and actions to reduce these disparities in health and promote social well-being.

## ABOUT THE AUTHORS

Keon L. Gilbert completed his Doctorate of Public Health (Dr.PH) in Behavioral and Community Health Sciences at the Graduate School of Public Health, University of Pittsburgh in 2009. Dr. Gilbert holds a joint Master's degree in African American Studies and Public Affairs from Indiana University (Bloomington, Indiana) and a Bachelor of Arts in Biology from Wabash College (Crawfordsville, IN). Dr. Gilbert's key research interests include the application of quantitative and qualitative methods to eliminate health disparities using community based participatory research (CBPR) as his primary approach to research areas such as: social capital, community development, organizational readiness, and working with populations such as African American men. His research seeks to accomplish the following aims to eliminate health disparities: (1) develop diverse partnerships and build community capacity to sustain health initiatives, (2) understand the effects of racism at individual-and-community-levels, and the various systems that reinforce racist ideologies, (3) understand the cultural relevance to health promotion and disease prevention, and (4) promote the development and enhancement of social networks to improve health behaviors.

Chikarlo Leak is a second year Doctorate of Public Health (Dr.PH) student in Health Services at the Graduate School of Public Health, at the University of California, Los Angeles. Chikarlo has a Masters of Public Health degree from San Diego State University and a Bachelors of Science in Health

Science from Slippery Rock University. His master's thesis examined the association of physical activity related psychosocial variables with race and socioeconomic status. The focus of his previous research experiences have centered on utilizing community based approaches to understand health disparities within chronic diseases or behaviors that influence chronic disease such as physical activity. His primary research interests include examining the social and built environmental factors that contribute to health disparities among ethnic/racial minority populations and seniors, and the potential policy implications.

## REFERENCES

Abrams, L., and Haney, W. (2004). Accountability and the grade 9 to 10 transition: the impact on attrition and retention rates. *In G. Orfield (Ed.), Dropouts in America: confronting the graduation rate crisis* (pp. 181–205). Cambridge: Harvard Education Press.

Acevedo-Garcia, D., Lochner K.A., Osypuk, T.L., and Subramanian, S.V. (2003). Future directions in residential segregation and health research: a multilevel approach. *Am J Public Health.* 93(2):215–21.

Anderson, N.B., Myers, H.F., Pickering, T., and Jackson, J.S. (1989). Hypertension in Blacks: psychosocial and biological perspectives. *J Hypertens.* 7(3):161–72.

Antonovsky, A. (1967). Social Class, Life Expectancy, and Overall Mortality. *Milbank Quarterly* 45:31–73.

Arias, E. (2006). United States life tables, (2003). *National Vital Statistics Reports, 54*(14), 1–40. Hyattsville, MD: National Center for Health Statistics.

Armstead CA, Lawler KA, Gorden G, Cross J, and Gibbons J. (1989) Relationship of racial stressors to blood pressure responses and anger expression in Black college students. *Health Psychol.* 8(5):541–56.

Berkman LF. (2009). Social Epidemiology: Social Determinants of Health in the United States: Are We Losing Ground? *Annu Rev Public Health.* 30 19(1) 19.1–19.15

Byrd, W. M., and Clayton, L. (2000). *An American Health Dilemma: A Medical History of African Americans and the Problem of Race, Beginnings to 1900.* New York: Routledge.

Conley, Dalton (2009). *Being Black, Living in Red: Race, Wealth, and Social Policy in America.* Berkeley and Los Angeles: University of California Press

Cutler, D., and Lleras-Muney, A. (2006). *Education and Health: Evaluating Theories and Evidence.* Bethesda, MD: National Bureau of Economic Research.

Dreachslin, J.L., Weech-Maldonado, R., and Dansky, K.H. (2004). Racial and ethnic diversity and organizational behavior: A focused research agenda for health services management. *Social Science and Medicine. 59,* 961–971.

Egerter, S., Braveman, P., Sadegh-Nobari, T., Grossman-Kahn, R.andDekker, M. (2009). *Education Matters for Health Publisher:* RWJF Commission to Build a Healthier America.

Fairclough, Adam. (2001) *Better Day Coming: Blacks and Equality,* 1890–2000. New York: Viking.

Feagin, J.R., and McKinney, K.D. (2003). The Physical Health Consequences of Racism. *In The Many Costs of White Racism.* pp. 65–93 Oxford: Rowman and Littlefield Publishers.

Freudenberg N, Ruglis J. (2007) Reframing school dropout as a public health issue. *Prev Chronic Dis.* 4(4):A107.

Franklin, J.H., and Moss, A.A. (2000). From Slavery to Freedom: A History of African Americans. New York: McGraw-Hill.

Geronimus AT, Bound J, and Waidmann TA. (1999). Poverty, time, and place: variation in excess mortality across selected US populations, 1980–1990. *J Epidemiol* Community Health. 53(6):325–34.

Grantmakers-In-Health. (2001). *Strategies for Reducing Racial and Ethnic Disparities in Health.* Grantmakers in Health. 5 ed. Washington, D.C.: Grantmakers in Health.

Haas, S. (2006). Health selection and the process of social stratification: the effect of childhood health on socioeconomic attainment. *J Health Soc Behav, 47*(4), 339–354. *Health, United States, 2007.* (2007). Retrieved January 2, 2009, from http://www.cdc.gov/nchs/hus.htm.

Hine, D.C., Harrold, S., and Hine, W.C., (2003). *African Americans: A Concise History, Vol. I: To 1877.* Upper Saddle River: Prentice Hall.

House, J.S., and D.R. Williams. 2000. Understanding and Reducing Socioeconomic and Racial/Ethnic Disparities in Health. In *Promoting Health: Intervention Strategies from Social and Behavioral Research,* 81–124. Washington, D.C.: National Academy Press.

House, J.S., Lepkowski, J.M., Kinney, A.M., Mero, R.P., Kessler, R.C., and Herzog, A.R. (1994). The Social Stratification of Aging and Health. *Journal of Health and Social Behavior* 35:213–34.

House, J.S., Kessler, R.C., Herzog, R., Mero, R.P., Kinney, A.M., and Breslow, B. (1990). Age, Socioeconomic Status and Health. *Milbank Quarterly* 68(3):383–411.

Jones, D.R., Harrell, J.P., Morris-Prather, C.E., Thomas, J., and Omowale, N. (1996) Affective and physiological responses to racism: the roles of afrocentrism and mode of presentation. *Ethn Dis.* 6(1–2):109–22.

Kaplan, G.A., and Lynch, J.W. (1999). Socioeconomic considerations in the primordial prevention of cardiovascular disease. *Prev Med.* 29(6 Pt 2):S30–5.

Kelley, R.D. and Lewis, E. (2000). *To Make Our World Anew: A History of African Americans.* New York: Oxford University Press.

Krieger, N. (1994). Epidemiology and the web of causation: Has anyone seen the spider? *Social Science and Medicine, 39,* 887–903.

Krieger, N. (2000). Refiguring "race": Epidemiology, racialized biology, and biological expressions of race relations. *International Journal of Health Services, 30,* 211–216.

Krieger, N. (2007). Why epidemiologists cannot afford to ignore poverty. *Epidemiology, 18,* 658–663.

LaVeist, T. A. (2005). *Minority populations and health: An introduction to health disparities in the united states.* San Francisco: Jossey-Bass.

Lillie-Blanton, M., Parsons, P.E., Gayle, H., Dievler, A. (1996). Racial differences in health: not just Black and White, but shades of gray. *Annu Rev Public Health.* 17:411–48.

Link, B.G., and Phelan, J. (1995). Social Conditions as Fundamental Causes of Disease. *Journal of Health and Social Behavior* 42(extra issue):80–94.

Mackenbach, J.P., Roskam, A.J.R., Schaap, M.M., Menvielle, G., Leinsalu, M., Kunst, A.E. (2008). Socioeconomic status and health inequalitites in European countries. *N. Engl. J. Med.* 358:1–14.

Mackenbach, J.P., Kunst, A.E., Cavelaars, A.E., Groenhof, F., Geurts, J.J. (1997). Socioeconomic inequalities in morbidity and mortality in western Europe. The EU Working Group on Socioeconomic Inequalities in Health. *Lancet* 349:1655–59.

Maralani, V. (2008). The changing relationship between family size and educational attainment over the course of socioeconomic development: evidence from Indonesia. *Demography, 45*(3), 693–717.

Mohai, P., Lantz, P., Morenoff, J., House, J., and Mero, R. (2009). Racial and socioeconomic disparities in residential proximity to polluting industrial facilities: evidence from the Americans' Changing Lives Study. *Am J Public Health, 99 Suppl 3,* S649–656.

Morrill, A.C., and Chinn, C.D. (2004). The obesity epidemic in the United States. *Journal of Public Health, 25*(3/4), 353–366.

Morris-Prather, C.E., Harrell, J.P., Collins, R., Leonard, K.L., Boss, M., Lee, J.W. (1996) Gender differences in mood and cardiovascular responses to socially stressful stimuli. *Ethn Dis.* 6(1–2):123–31.

National Center for Health Statistics. (2006). *Health, United States, 2006 with chartbook on trends in the health of Americans.* Hyattsville, MD: Author.

National Institutes of Health. (2000, October 6). *U.S. NIH strategic research plan to reduce and ultimately eliminate health disparities.* Retrieved January 2, 2009, from http://www.nih.gov/about/hd/strategicplan.pdf.

Navarro, V. (1989). Race or Class, or Race and Class. *International Journal of Health Services* 19(2):311–4.

Navarro, V. (2002). *The Political Economy of Social Inequalities: Consequences for Health and Quality of Life.* New York: Baywood.

Pappas, G., Queen, S., Hadden, W., Fisher, G. (1993). The increasing disparity in mortality between socioeconomic groups in the United States, 1960 and 1986. *N. Engl. J. Med.* 329:103–9.

Physical Activity Guide to Community Preventive Services Website. Centers for Disease Control and Prevention. http://www.thecommunityguide.org/pa/. Accessed March 09, 2009.

Pleis, J., and Lethbridge-Cejku, M. (2006). Summary health statistics for U.S. adults: National Health Interview Survey, 2005. *Vital Health Stat 10*(232), 1–153.

Rice, M. F., and Jones, W. (1994). *Public policy and the Black hospital: From slavery to segregation to integration.* Westport, CT: Greenwood Press.

Rice, M. F., and Jr., W. J. (1990). *Health of Black Americans from post-reconstruction to integration, 1871–1960: An annotated bibliography of sources.* New York: Greenwood Publishing Group.

Saelens, B., and Handy, S. (2008). Built environment correlates of walking: A review. *Medicine and Science in Sports and Exercise.* 40(7) S550–566.

Sallis, J.F., and Kerr, J. (2006). Physical activity and the built environment. *President's Council on Physical Fitness and Sports Research Digest.* 7(No.4): 1–8.

Schulz, A.J., Williams, D.R., Israel, B.A., and Lempert, L.B. (2002). Racial and spatial relations as fundamental determinants of health in Detroit. *Milbank Quarterly.* 80(4):677–707, iv.

Singh, G.K. (2003). Area deprivation and widening inequalities in US mortality, 1969–1998. *Am. J. Public Health* 93:1137–43

Sorlie, P., Rogot, E., Anderson, R., Johnson, N.J., and Backlund, E. (1992). Black-White mortality differences by family income. *Lancet.* 340(8815):346–50.

Smedley, B.D., Stith, A.Y., and Nelson, A.R. (2003). *Unequal Treatment: Confronting Racial and Ethnic Disparities in Health Care,* Washington, D.C.: National Academies Press.

Smith, S. (1995) Sick and Tired of Being Sick and Tired: Black Women's Health Activism in America, 1890–1950. Philadelphia: University of Pennsylvania Press .

Sullivan, L.W. (2004). *Missing persons: Minorities in the health professions, A report of the Sullivan commission on diversity in the healthcare workforce.* W. K. Kellogg Foundation and Duke University School of Medicine. Washington, D.C.: The Sullivan Commission.

Tashiro, C. (2005). The Meaning of Race in Health Care and Research. *Pediatric Nursing* 31 (3/4): 208–210, 305–308.

Trubek, L., and Das, M. (2003). Achieving equality: healthcare governance in transition. *Am J Law Med, 29*(2–3), 395–421.

U.S. Census Bureau. (2004). Projected population of the United States, by race and Hispanic origin: 2000 to 2050. In *U.S. interim projections by age, sex, race, and Hispanic origin.* Retrieved January 2, 2009, from http://www.census.gov/ipc/www/usinterimproj/natprojtab01a.pdf.

U.S. Department of Health and Human Services. (2000, November). *Healthy People 2010: Understanding and improving health* (2nd ed.). Washington, D.C.: U.S. Government Printing Office.

Williams, D.R., and Collins, C. (2001) Racial residential segregation: a fundamental cause of racial disparities in health. *Public Health Rep.* 116(5):404–16.

Williams, D.R. (1999). Race, socioeconomic status, and health. The added effects of racism and discrimination. *Ann N Y Acad Sci.* 896:173–88.

Williams, D.R. (1997). Race and health: basic questions, emerging directions. *Ann Epidemiol.* 7(5):322–33.

Wing, S., Horton, R.A., Muhammad, N., Grant, G.R., Tajik, M., and Thu, K. (2008). Integrating epidemiology, education, and organizing for environmental justice: Community health effects of industrial hog operations. *American Journal of Public Health, 98,* 1390–1397.

# PART 4

CONFRONTING THE PIPELINE: SOCIAL POLICY ISSUES

# Engaging Social Change by Embracing Diversity

By Rashawn Ray

Individuals frequently say that race and ethnic relations is a depressing topic. Well unfortunately, the United States, like most parts of the world, has a sombering history with race. It is difficult to look at the history of the world and not acknowledge the pain our ugly relationship with race has caused. The important thing to remember is that although you may not discriminate against others or hold prejudice attitudes about certain race/ethnic groups, you still may be privileged, marginalized, or hindered by how race as a social structural force intersects with gender, class, education, crime, or employment to shape social interactions and life chances.

So the question that always remains is: What can we do about race and its consequences? The first thing is to acknowledge that race matters. Acknowledge how race privileges or constrains you. This is the same process that men should go through when acknowledging the privileges of maleness. Next, acknowledge how race infuses our language usage, media consumption, and interactions with others. After acknowledging the role of race in social life, you can then begin to learn more about how race functions on individual- and institutional-levels. Subsequently, you can start to hold others accountable for what they say and how they treat others. While it is difficult, we must hold our family members and friends accountable for what they say and do. Making simple statements such as, "That wasn't nice" or "I would appreciate it if you did not make statements like that around me," go a long way in changing the accepted culture about race and ethnic relations. For younger generations making statements such as, "That was so not cool" or "Stop stereotyping, it's not attractive or funny" work very well. Finally, you can take a more activist approach by getting involved in organizations and coalitions aimed to ameliorate systemic racial inequality.

One of the best ways to proceed on this journey is to engage diversity. As we have seen throughout this book, the racial/ethnic make-up of many countries around the world is changing. With these changes come more contact, group threat, and ethnic conflict. However, it is also a time for more harmonious interactions among individuals of diverse backgrounds. It is a time to learn, share, and practice tolerance by confronting the prejudices and biases that we have been socialized to accept.

Race still plays a profound role in determining who is considered what, who has access to opportunities, who can acquire or obtain desirable skills for upward mobility, and who can pass certain resources on to the next generation. As Cornel West's (1993) title asserts, *Race Matters*. However, things are changing. The election of Barack Obama as the 44th U.S. President is a testament to progress. Although many individuals around the world applauded, most countries have yet to elect racial/ethnic minorities in their own countries to high-ranking political positions. Altogether, race is no longer a Black/White issue. In this context, Du Bois' (1903) prophetic statement—"The problem of the 20th century is the problem of the color line"—may be more profound now than ever before.

This text has aimed to outline the conceptual meaning of race, ethnicity, and racism and discuss the main explanations regarding the socioeconomic divide among racial/ethnic groups. I hope it contributes to providing a baseline for incorporating a much needed positive, beneficial, and constructive discourse on race and ethnic relations in social life. Part IV of the anthology—Confronting the Pipeline: Social Policy Issues—focuses on ways to ameliorate racial-based inequalities through social policies and micro-level forms of social change including mentorship and social activism.

Katznelson's (2006) *When Affirmative Action was White: An Untold History of Racial Inequality in the Twentieth-Century America* provides a chilling historical account of the institutional biases ingrained in New Deal and Fair Deal policies such as Social Security and the GI Bill that privileged Whites while denying many Blacks the same access to resources and opportunities. In this anthology, I include an article highlighting many of the major findings and arguments from his book. Below I discuss some of the lingering consequences of the institutional biases of social policies, the triumphs of progress, and perceptions of these race-based policies.

## RACE-BASED SOCIAL POLICIES: CONSEQUENCES, TRIUMPHS, AND PERCEPTIONS

There are many misconceptions centering on social policies such as affirmative action and welfare. A personal story is fitting here. I have a very close friend who is a firefighter. A few years ago his station hired a Black fire chief. He called me stating that the new chief received the position due to affirmative action and that he did not deserve the promotion. He also remarked that some of his fellow colleagues were extremely disgruntled at his accusations and the accusations of others. I asked my friend what is his definition of affirmative action. He stated that affirmative action is allowing Blacks and other minorities to get positions they did not earn or have the credentials for. After explaining to him the actual definition of affirmative action (which I discuss below), I then asked him if he actually looked at his new chief's credentials and resume. My friend replied no. I asked him to do that. A week or so later my friend called and said he has so much respect for his new chief. He said that his credentials were so exceptional he wonders how the new chief did not get a promotion 10 years ago. We then had a very productive discussion about the persistent pipeline of institutional racism (as discussed in Part III of this anthology).

The reason I tell this story is not necessarily because it had a "happy ending" for affirmative action but to highlight the constructive conversation that my friend and I had as a White person and a Black person engaging in a healthy discussion about a contentious topic such as affirmative action. Unfortunately, most people do not engage in these types of discussions across racial/ethnic groups. Therefore, we make assumptions about what others think and why they think it without ever engaging in a healthy conversation. Asking a simple question can tell you so much.

So ask yourself, what is your personal stance on issues such as affirmative action and welfare? Do you know the actual meaning and stipulations of these policies? Do you know when or why these policies were devised? Since Katznelson (2006) goes into much detail about these policies, I will briefly underscore some key parts of his article.

Affirmative Action is defined as the policies and/or programs that seek to rectify past discrimination through active measures to ensure equal opportunity. According to Katznelson, "Affirmative action performs acts of corrective justice. Public policy is used to compensate members of a deprived group for prior losses and for gains unfairly achieved by others that resulted from prior government action." (2006: 556). Corrective justice "identifies interventions that remedy previously unjust decisions that made existing patterns of distribution even more unfair than they otherwise would have been." (Katznelson 2006: 556). Although we are talking about affirmative action in the context of race, affirmative action policies also extend to include gender, nationality, and mental and physical disabilities. Affirmative action is often reduced down to issues about race when it is much broader than that.

In the United States, affirmative action mostly occurs at life course transitional stages such as enrolling in school or applying for jobs. As has been discussed in this anthology, education (Lewis 2010), employment (Bertrand and Mullainathan 2004; Pager 2004), and mortgage loans (Sewell 2010) have all been susceptible to personal, legal, and institutional discrimination against minority groups. When implemented correctly, affirmative action is put in place to open doors that would normally be closed to minorities. To use Sewell's (2010) analogy, affirmative action allows for everyone to have the opportunity to eat *a la carte* and have similar life option menus. In short, affirmative

action simply allows for qualified individuals to knock on the door and potentially sit at the table.

The 1960s is usually where scholars start the discussion regarding affirmative action. As we know, the early 1960s is when individuals, in and outside of the U.S., realized that Blacks were still experiencing blatant forms of discrimination including public lynchings and beatings. Following Brown v. Board of Education and the Voting Rights Act of 1965, America started aiming to function as if it was a race-neutral society. However, as Katznelson asserts, racial neutrality included historical and current forms of White privilege.

In 1961, President John F. Kennedy used affirmative action for the first time by instructing federal contractors to take "affirmative action to ensure that applicants are treated equally without regard to race, color, religion, sex, or national origin." Following President Kennedy's assassination in 1963, President Lyndon B. Johnson continued Kennedy's executive order by legislating the Civil Rights Act of 1964. The Civil Rights Act of 1964 was the landmark legislation that reversed Jim Crow laws by outlawing segregation in schools and public places. It was implemented to establish precedence that individuals should be treated like normal human beings.

President Johnson's Executive Order is as follows:

> "To enforce the constitutional right to vote, to confer jurisdiction upon the district courts of the United States to provide relief against discrimination in public accommodations, to authorize the Attorney General to institute suits to protect constitutional rights in public facilities and public education, to extend the Commission on Civil Rights, to prevent discrimination in federally assisted programs, to establish a Commission on

Equal Employment Opportunity, and for other purposes."

## WHY WAS AFFIRMATIVE ACTION NEEDED?

As Katznelson argues, President Roosevelt's New Deal helped to create the White middle class we see today. Social Security is arguably the most influential and long-lasting social policy in American history. Likewise, the GI Bill is still one of the largest federal initiatives in U.S. history allocating over $95 billion to military soldiers from the early 1940s to the 1970s. While these legislations did not explicitly give privileges to Whites on the basis of race, they excluded Blacks and other minorities in specific strategic ways. For example, legislation that allocated Social Security, set minimum wages, regulated work hours, and established unions did not include professions that were highly represented by Blacks such as farm and domestic work. As a result, over 60 percent of the Black labor force in the 1930s and nearly 75 percent of the Black workers in the South were excluded from these legislations. Additionally, federal funds for assisting the poor and supporting veterans were controlled by local officials who frequently discriminated against Blacks. Consequently, funds were normally only provided to Whites to obtain well-paying jobs, establish economic security, ensure retirement, and build wealth. Katznelson (2006: 547) contends this created a form of "policy apartheid" that mainly benefited Whites.

Although Aid to Dependent Children (ADC), which is commonly known as welfare, was established for families that generally had one parent or caretaker, funds were still withheld from Black families who qualified (Edin and Lein 1997). In fact, about one-third of the Black children who qualified for ADC went without assistance. In the 1940s, Texas, Kentucky, and Mississippi did not participate at all, so children in these states

did not receive assistance. Regarding assistance to the elderly, Blacks in the South, compared to the North, received only half of the assistance they qualified for. Concerning unemployment, it did not cover domestic and farm workers, left the funds in control of states, and required that individuals already be working to qualify.

The GI Bill (Servicemen's Readjustment Act of 1944) aimed to reintegrate veterans returning from war. The GI Bill impacted eight out of 10 men born during the 1920s; roughly 80 percent of men who were in their 30s with families in the 1950s. From these funds, millions of families were able to purchase homes, start business ventures, and send themselves and their children to college. For Black veterans, it was a different story. The GI Bill was distributed federally but controlled locally. As a result, Black veterans, particularly in the South, were not allocated GI Bill funds in the same way as Whites.

This brings up an interesting aside. Individuals wonder about the creation and sustainability of Historical Black Colleges and Universities (HBCUs). Of the Black veterans who did receive funds, 95 percent of them attended HBCUs because they were prohibited from attending Predominately White Institutions (PWIs). Although Blacks represented about 25 percent of the population in the South, only 15 percent of the schools were available to them. These schools were not large universities or smaller, elite colleges. Instead, these schools were very small with half enrolling less than 250 students and 90 percent enrolling less than 1,000 students. Furthermore, less than 5 percent of HBCUs were accredited and none of the schools offered a Ph.D. program. While some of the more prominent HBCUs such as Morehouse, Spelman, Xavier, Fisk, Hampton, and Howard are surviving, other HBCUs continue to falter. Some HBCUs, however, such as Tennessee State University and South Carolina State University have become state schools. At these universities, Whites qualify for minority scholarships.

## THE EMPLOYMENT OF AFFIRMATIVE ACTION

When President Johnson issued the executive order for job opportunities to be expanded to minorities, most of the favorable forms of affirmative action initiatives at the time included quota and point systems. However, these forms of affirmative action came under serious criticism. Although these forms are in limited use today, most individuals who oppose affirmative action do so because they believe Whites are being discriminated against due to minorities being allocated spots not accessible to Whites. The Grutter v. Bollinger (2003, also known as the University of Michigan Law School case) and the Regents of the University of California v. Bakke (1978) cases have received much publicity and played a profound role in shaping public opinion about affirmative action (see Brown 2004; Wilkenfeld 2004; Pollack 2005; Bankston 2006). While there is much to discuss in regards to the details of these important cases, two key components are noteworthy. First, the Supreme Court ruled that diversity is important and beneficial to the healthy development of individuals, companies, and social institutions such as schools. Second, in both cases (roughly 25 years apart) the majority judges stated that hopefully in twenty-five years discrimination will be a thing of the past and racial preferences will no longer be necessary.

What also should be noted is that discrimination cases based on unjust treatment due to the employment of race-based programs are just as likely to be won by Whites as they are by minorities (Katznelson 2006). It is also important to pay attention to the language used for affirmative action legislation. Although legislation places individuals into categories by race, gender, age, sexual orientation, or

disability, court cases are generally on an individual basis. In turn, policies for the group can be upheld while making allowances for individuals. For example, Bakke was permitted to enter medical school in California although race could still be used as a factor in admission policies. Furthermore, while affirmative action is legislated federally, it is frequently institutionalized and enforced locally. Therefore, it is important to check the rules and bylaws for a specific school or company.

## PERCEPTIONS OF RACE-BASED SOCIAL POLICIES

Whites are normally more opposed to race-based policies than other racial groups (see Bobo 2001 in this anthology). Mazzocco and colleagues (2006) conducted a survey-based experiment with 958 Whites to determine the answer to one central question: "How much should you be paid to continue to live the rest of your life as a Black person?" Most respondents replied less than $10,000. In contrast, study participants stated that they would have to be paid about $1 million to give up T.V. This finding implies one of two propositions: 1) Whites think that being Black is not that big of a deal so why should anyone receive compensation for it; or 2) being Black is not worth much. Furthermore, Mahzarin Banaji, a co-investigator on the project, found that nine out of 10 Whites reject proposals for reparations. Mazzocco and colleagues assert that most Whites are not conscious of the persisting forms of racial discrimination and disparities that exist in America.

To test the propositions noted above, these researchers posed the central research question in a few different ways. First, after being told the income disparities between Blacks and Whites, White participants requested roughly $500,000 to be Black, compared to the less than $10,000 originally requested. Second, the study participants were asked to imagine a fictitious country called Atria where individuals were born either to the "majority" group or the "minority" group. Upon given a list of disadvantages of the minority group in Atria, White study participants requested an average of $1 million. What should be noted is that Atria is actually America. The majority group characteristics are current White characteristics, while the minority group characteristics are current Black characteristics. This survey-based experiment can be administered to students to help individuals objectively view the racial disparities that exist in America.

In regards to welfare, Edin and Lein (1997) conducted interviews with roughly 400 single mothers in four cities including Boston, Chicago, Charleston, and San Antonio. They wanted to know if single mothers fair better on or off welfare. Disproving a majority of the cultural theories about welfare mothers, Edin and Lein actually find that these women are more careful with the money they acquire. Although this study was not directly about race, it has huge racial implications based on the perceptions of welfare mothers as Black and lazy. Edin and Lein find that women of all races employ similar strategies for survival and that Black women are actually more frugal with their money. This means that social policies that allow welfare recipients to generate assets are desired among single mothers, despite perceptions to the contrary.

## SOLUTIONS TO RACIAL INEQUALITY

So, where should solutions for racial inequality go from here? Aligning with President Johnson's and Supreme Court Justice Powell's perspective, Katznelson (2006) states that two conditions should be met to warrant affirmative action enactment. First, there must be a clear and concise connection between the affirmative action remedies and historical inequalities. Second, since a color-blind society is desirable, remedies that do not exclusively include race/ethnicity should be initially sought out. For example, universities such as UCLA are starting to view applicants in a holistic fashion by privileging the pluralism of their experiences and background beyond their G.P.A. and test scores.

Oliver and Shapiro ([1995] 2006) assert that ending familial poverty begins by assisting individuals from the bottom up, and not just those who are perceived as the most upwardly mobile. They assert the government should focus on four essential programs including: 1) asset generation for welfare recipients to move from dependency to self-sufficiency; 2) start-up business grants; 3) nontaxable education asset accounts for four year institutions; and 4) renter and homeowner tax credits. Over the past couple of decades, government programs have focused on these issues.

In addition to these macro-level solutions to racial inequality, it is imperative that a discourse be established in the classroom and in social settings to discuss race and ethnic relations candidly. If we do not, similar to how gender is considered by some as a "women only problem" or sexuality is referred to as a "gay only problem," individuals will continue to view race as a "Black or minority only problem." On a trip to Chicago, I met a doctor who recently moved to an urban area on the East Coast. He remarked that he needed to increase his clientele so he decided to visit churches. Some of his fellow doctors were baffled by the target areas. Because certain markets were perceived to be saturated, this White doctor decided to visit Black churches. He stated that church members were very welcoming and many stated that a White person, nonetheless a physician, had never ventured into their sanctuary. The doctor remarked that he not only increased his clientele but has made several new friends that he has much in common with, engaged in more healthy conversations about race than he did in his previous 35 plus years of life, and had gotten many

Blacks to schedule an appointment who had not been to the doctor in years due to previous forms of mistreatment in medical settings. As Jackman and Crane (1986) contend, the quality and quantity of contact across racial/ethnic groups assist in reducing stereotypes and prejudice attitudes. As Mauro and Robertson's (2010) chapter puts forth, everyone can do something to engage social change and embrace diversity, no matter how small or large. It starts with a simple conversation.

## SUPPLEMENTAL READINGS AND RESOURCES

Bankston, Carl. 2006. "*Grutter v. Bollinger*: Weak Foundations?" *Ohio State Law Journal* 67: 1–13.

Brown, Kevin D. 2004. "After Grutter V. Bollinger—Revisiting the Desegregation Era from the Perspective of the Post-Desegregation Era." Constitutional Commentary 21: 41.

Edin, Kathryn and Laura Lein. 1997. *Making Ends Meet: How Single Mothers Survive Welfare And Low-Wage Work*. New York: Russell Sage Foundation.

Jackman, Mary R. and Marie Crane. 1986. ""Some of My Best Friends Are Black …": Interracial Friendship and Whites' Racial Attitudes." *The Public Opinion Quarterly* 50: 459–486.

Johnson, Jacqueline, Sharon Rush, and Joe Feagin. 2000. "Reducing Inequalities: Doing Anti-Racism: Toward an Egalitarian American Society." *Contemporary Sociology, Special Issue: Utopian Visions: Engaged Sociologies for the 21st Century* 9: 95–110.

Katznelson, Ira. 2006. *When Affirmative Action was White: An Untold History of Racial Inequality in the Twentieth-Century America*. New York. Norton.

Mazzocco, Philip J and et al. 2006. "The Cost of Being Black: White Americans Perceptions and the Question of Reparations." *Du Bois Review* 3: 261–297.

Pollak, Louis H. 2005. "Race, law & history: the Supreme Court from *Dred Scott* to *Grutter v. Bollinger*". *Dædalus* 134: 29–41.

Peffley, Mark, Jon Hurwitz, and Paul M. Sniderman. "Racial Stereotypes and Whites' Political Views of Blacks in the Context of Welfare and Crime." *American Journal of Political Science* 41: 30–60.

Thomas, Susan L. 1997. "Women, Welfare, Reform and the Preservation of a Myth." *The Social Science Journals* 34: 351–368.

Wilkenfeld, Joshua. 2004. "Newly Compelling: Re-examining Judicial Construction of Juries in the Aftermath of *Grutter v. Bollinger*." *Columbia Law Review* 104: 2291–2327.

# WHEN IS AFFIRMATIVE ACTION FAIR?
## ON GRIEVOUS HARMS AND PUBLIC REMEDIES

*By Ira Katznelson*

Speaking at Howard University's June 1965 commencement, President Lyndon Johnson opened a national conversation on race, fairness, and affirmative action. Nearly a year after Congress had passed the landmark Civil Rights Act of 1964, and shortly before his successful campaign on behalf of a Voting Rights Act that brought the era of Jim Crow to a close, the president observed that something more, transcending equal treatment, was needed:

> You do not wipe away the scars of centuries by saying: Now you are free to go where you want, and do as you desire, and choose the leaders as you please. You do not take a person who, for years, has been hobbled by chains and liberate him, bring him up to the starting line of a race and then say, "you are free to compete with all the others," and still justly believe that you have been completely fair. Thus is it not enough just to open the gates of opportunity. All our citizens must have the ability to walk through those gates (cited in Katznelson, 2005:173–181).

Declaring this to be "the next and more profound stage of the battle for civil rights," the president shifted grounds and goals. "We seek not just freedom but opportunity. We seek not just legal equity but human ability, not just equality as a right and a theory but equality as a fact and equality as a result."

This clarion speech, "To Fulfill These Rights," featured two main puzzles. It asked, first, why the gap between blacks and whites actually had grown in the two decades after the end of the Second World War. Johnson's account began by observing that "the great majority of Negro Americans ... still, as we meet here tonight, are another nation. Despite the court orders and the laws, despite legislative victories and speeches, for them the walls are rising and the gulf is widening." Citing information provided by Daniel Patrick Moynihan, one of the speech's authors, Johnson chronicled "the facts of this American failure":

> Thirty-five years ago the rate of unemployment for Negroes and whites was about the same. Tonight, the Negro rate is twice as high.
>
> In 1948 the 8 percent unemployment rate for Negro teenage boys was actually

Ira Katznelson, "When is Affirmative Action Fair? On Grievous Harms and Public Remedies," *Social Research: An International Quarterly of the Social Sciences*, vol. 73, no. 2, pp. 541-568. Copyright © 2006 by Social Research: An International Quarterly. Reprinted with permission.

less than that of whites. By last year, that rate had grown to 23 percent, as against 13 percent for whites employed.

Between 1949 and 1959 the income of Negro men relative to white men declined in every section of this country. From 1952 to 1963 the median income of Negro families compared to white actually dropped from 57 percent to 53 percent …

Since 1947 the number of white families living in poverty has decreased 27 percent while the number of poorer nonwhite families decreased by only 3 percent.

How, Johnson inquired, could white and black income and wealth have grown more, not less, distinct in the postwar golden age? What had accounted for these increasing disparities despite nearly two decades of unbroken and unprecedented abundance? "We are not sure," he confessed, "why this is."

Second, he asked what should be done in light of this record. In a post-civil rights period, with the legal playing field leveled, with color expunged as an officially sanctioned badge of deprivation, how might the unequal powers of race be compensated even after the legislative work of the civil rights revolution had been accomplished?

These questions still haunt. Today, the once contentious color-blind standard of nondiscrimination is broadly accepted. So, too, are efforts at outreach and recruitment aimed at increasing the number of applicants for scarce positions in schools and firms. Where agreement stops, however, is where compensatory discrimination starts. "The controversy over affirmative action," Randall Kennedy rightly noted in mid-1980s, "constitutes the most salient current battlefront in the ongoing struggle over the status of the Negro in American life" (Kennedy,

1986: 1327). Nearly two decades later, as American troops were being dispatched to Iraq, Robert Bartley observed in his *Wall Street Journal* column that "second only to the pending war, 'affirmative action' is the issue of the day" (Bartley, 2003: A15). Four decades after Johnson first broached the possibility of affirmative action to rectify the racial gap, advocates of reparations and defenders of nondiscrimination and equal treatment who often seem blind to the organizing power of race in American life have not found common ground. Broad and often unfocused claims for restoration compete with fundamental antiracist principles that direct us to racial neutrality.

I am unhappy with these choices. By returning to the two main issues President Johnson raised at Howard—understanding the sources of the black-white divide, and discerning appropriate terms for affirmative action—it is possible to move beyond options that downplay racism or reinforce racial divisions.

One of the more remarkable features of the president's eloquent address was the role it assigned to the recent past. As Hugh Davis Graham, a historian of affirmative action, has astutely observed, the President's justification found its "grounding not in the Constitution or statutes or in liberal traditions of equal treatment. Rather the social force that justified the new doctrine of race-conscious affirmative action was *history itself*, in the form of past discrimination" (Graham, 2002: 77).

But which history? The primary shortcoming of Johnson's speech was a surprising neglect of the history of public policy that had acted as a key cause of the distressing outcomes he chronicled. As a result, not only did his historical account remain vague, substituting expressive language for hard-edged analysis, but the repertoire of possible answers Johnson announced was unordered and unspecific, leaving unresolved just how he preferred to remedy the cumulative history of racial disadvantage. But if the president provided only a first draft of adequate answers about what to do next, he did pose just the right questions by directing attention to past causes and future possibilities.

Chronicles of affirmative action ordinarily begin in the early 1960s. They focus on the critical moment between 1963 and 1969 when such policies became the federal government's most important vehicle for dealing with employment discrimination, and extend forward to encompass the four decades when affirmative action was directed primarily at improving the circumstances of African Americans. This chronology, however, obscures how a wide array of significant and far-reaching public policies shaped and administered during the New Deal and Fair Deal era of the 1930s and 1940s were crafted and administered in a deeply discriminatory manner. As Congress regulated labor markets and enhanced the powers of employees, provided welfare and social insurance, built a powerful military, and reintegrated soldiers into postwar America, its southern members introduced features designed to fortify their region's social, economic, and political order. The exclusion of many black Americans from the bounty of public policy, and the manner in which these important, large-scale, national programs were managed, launched new and potent sources of racial inequality. The federal government, though seemingly race neutral, functioned as a commanding instrument of white privilege. Because no bills could be legislated into law without the assent of the members of Congress from that region (a result of the balance of partisanship between Republicans and Democrats, the composition of the Democratic Party, and rules that required filibuster-proof votes in the Senate), public policy had to be tailored to meet their preferences, most notably their desire to protect Jim Crow. Still an era of legal segregation in 17 American states and Washington, D.C., the southern wing of the Democratic Party was in a position to dictate the contours of Social Security, key

labor legislation, the GI Bill, and other landmark laws that helped create a modern white middle class in a manner that also protected what these legislators routinely called "the southern way of life."

I will argue, after a review of key features of these policies crafted to meet southern concerns, that fair and "affirmative" remedies for the deep, even chronic, dispossession that continues to afflict a large percentage of black America should focus not on the immense injuries inflicted by slavery or Jim Crow as general organizing social principles, but on the specific harms that date back to these national programs as they were crafted and administered in the 1930s and 1940s.

## I.

ACROSS A RANGE OF PUBLIC POLICIES, SOUTHERN MEMBERS OF CONGRESS used two principal mechanisms to restrict the scope of New Deal and Fair Deal public policy to ensure the continued existence of their region's racial hierarchy. First, whenever the nature of the legislation permitted, they sought to leave out as many African Americans as they could. They achieved this goal not by inscribing race into law but by writing provisions that, in Robert Lieberman's language, were racially laden. (Lieberman, 1998: 7) The most important instances concerned categories of work in which blacks were heavily overrepresented, most notably farm workers and maids. These groups, constituting more than 60 percent of the black labor force in the 1930s, and nearly 75 percent of those who were employed in the South, were excluded from the legislation that created modern unions, from laws that set minimum wages and regulated the hours of work, and from Social Security until the 1950s.

Second, they successfully insisted that the administration of these and other laws, including assistance to the poor and support for veterans, be placed in the hands of local officials who were deeply hostile to black aspirations. Over and over, the bureaucrats who were handed authority by Congress used their capacity to shield the southern system from challenge and disruption.

As a result, at the very moment a wide array of public policies were providing most white Americans with valuable tools to advance their social welfare, insure their old age, get good jobs, acquire economic security, build assets, and gain middle class status—most black Americans were left behind or left out. The national policies enacted in the pre-civil rights, last-gasp era of Jim Crow constituted a massive transfer of quite specific privileges to white Americans. New programs produced economic and social opportunity for favored constituencies and thus widened the gap between white and black Americans in the aftermath of the Second World War.

Though the scope of such racially laden policies was quite broad, incorporating key features of laws affecting labor markets and trade unions, consider two of the most important examples: the way the Social Security Act came into being and the manner in which post-Second World War benefits for veterans in the GI Bill were organized and distributed.

Before 1935, the United States lacked lasting national laws and structures for social welfare. All this changed with the Social Security Act. In the history of American social policy, no legislative enactment has been more significant, influential, or enduring. Even at the start, when it still was relatively diminutive in scale and started slowly, it quickly made use of significant managerial and economic resources by the standards of the time. The law's encompassing scope had enormous potential for African Americans. It provided security against the economic hazards of old age at a time more than half of black men, compared with one-third of white men, remained in the labor market after the age of 75 (Myrdal, 1944: I, 299). It insured against unemployment when 26 percent of black men and

32 percent of black women were out of work—compared to 18 and 24 percent for whites—and it ameliorated poverty by providing old age assistance to the indigent poor and aid to impoverished and dependent children when blacks were less well off in both categories than other potential recipients.

Precisely because they worked longer into old age, were more prone to job layoffs, and disproportionately located at the bottom of the social structure, African Americans who proved eligible did, in fact, gain a great deal from the Social Security Act. In 1940, the year Social Security payments for the elderly began after a sufficient fund had been received, the Social Security Board identified nearly 2.3 million black workers as eligible for old age insurance (Federal Security Agency, 1938: 215). To be sure, as with earlier patterns of relief, their benefits tended to be on the low end. The scale of social security payments hinged in part on prior wages, which, for blacks, often had been derisory. Still, nothing like this scale of assistance previously had been available to the elderly, white or black. A married couple without children who had earned under $50 a month qualified for a grant of $31.50 each month (Sterner, 1943: 215).

Unfortunately, the great majority of blacks were left out. Most African Americans were farm workers or domestics. People in these categories did not qualify. Across the nation, fully 65 percent of African Americans fell outside the reach of this new program; between 70 and 80 percent in different parts of the South (Sterner, 1943: 214). Of course, this excision also left out many whites; indeed, some 40 percent in a country that still was substantially agrarian. Not until 1954, when Republicans controlled the White House, the Senate, and the House of Representatives, and southern Democrats finally lost their ability to mold legislation, were the occupational exclusions that had kept the large majority of blacks out of the social security system eliminated. And even then, African Americans were not able to catch up, since the program required at least five years of contributions before benefits could be received. Thus, for the first quarter-century of its existence, Social Security was characterized by a form of policy apartheid, something neither Roosevelt nor his study commission had advocated.

Without the occupational disabilities that were inserted in the legislation, the program's inclusive and national structure might have powerfully undermined the racialized, low-wage economy on which the region still depended and on whose shoulders Jim Crow stood. As Congress's gatekeepers in control of the key committees, southern members brought their controlling influence to bear on each of the components of the Social Security Act to ensure that this unsettling outcome would not happen. The bill was mainly considered in the Senate Finance Committee and the House Ways and Means Committee. Of the 33 Democrats serving on these committees, 17 were southerners (9 in the Senate; 8 in the House), including the two chairs, Senator Pat Harrison of Mississippi and Robert "Muley" Doughton of North Carolina. These southerners who dominated committee consideration broadly supported Social Security as a source of badly needed help for their poverty-stricken region, but they even more emphatically did not want the federal government to threaten the South's "way of life." At the hearings in the Senate, Harry Byrd, the leader of Virginia's powerful Democratic machine, cautioned that unless adequate protections were introduced, social security could become an instrument by which the federal government would interfere with the way white southerners dealt with "the Negro question" (Hamilton and Hamilton, 1997: 29). At issue was both who would be included in the provisions of the act, especially for old age and unemployment insurance, and how much discretion would be offered the states as they administered the non-social insurance parts of the bill. Accordingly, as Robert

Lieberman has observed, southern representatives had two choices when confronted with the administration's recommendation for a largely inclusive and nationally oriented bill: "make it either less inclusive or less national" (Lieberman, 1998: 38).

They chose both strategies. By fashioning legislation that kept farm workers and maids out, they made old age insurance, the part of the bill that would be managed by a national bureaucracy, less all-encompassing than what the administration had proposed. In contrast, in the social assistance parts of the bill that created Aid to Dependent Children (ADC) and help for the poor elderly, the primary categorical forms of assistance offered by the Social Security Act, they made the legislation less national. These were federal programs whose costs were to be shared between the federal government and the states, and, even more important, these policies would be decisively shaped and administered by the individual states, which were granted a great deal of discretion in setting benefit levels. Southern members successfully resisted pressures to nationalize responsibility for ADC. Rather, by eliminating federal "decency and health" clauses in committee hearings, and by guarding against more than a minimal federal role on the floor of the House and Senate, they succeeded in keeping its key contours, organization, and supervision in the hands of state governors, legislators, and bureaucrats. Though they failed to get Congress to agree to pick up the whole bill for the poorest states, the bulk of which were southern, they did manage to pass a program of assistance to poor families that left all its key elements in local hands.

ADC offered grants to families with minor children raised in circumstances where one parent, usually the father, was absent from the home. Because families were more likely to be headed by women and need was more extensive among African Americans, ADC was disproportionately black from the start, but not uniformly so. Across the United States, 11 percent of children were black when Social Security was signed into law, but comprised 14 percent of the children in the program. In the South, however, state governments used their discretion, including provisions that an ADC home be "suitable," to tilt in the other direction. In Louisiana, 37 percent of the state's children were black, but only 26 percent of ADC clients were. In North Carolina, the comparable figures were 30 and 22; in South Carolina, 48 and 29; in Alabama, 39 and 24; in Arkansas, 24 and 15. Texas, Kentucky, and Mississippi, in the 1940s, did not choose to participate in ADC, so children in these states did entirely without this source of help (Sterner, 1943: 283).

Further, we should note that ADC overall was less generous than the earlier relief programs they had replaced, which, despite all their shortcomings, had injected more monies into poor black communities. Consider the situation in Georgia. Of the nearly 24,000 white and 23,000 black children eligible for aid in 1935, the state offered funds to only a small fraction. There was a huge disparity by race. Drawing on both a Social Security survey and an account by the State Department of Public Welfare, Richard Sterner found that "14.4 per cent of white eligibles but only 1.5 per cent of the Negro eligibles" were funded. Further, more than half of the black cases, as opposed to just 18 percent of the white, could be found in counties with cities of at least 10,000 people. He thus concluded that "while the situation is slightly better in cities, the fact remains that Negro children in Georgia have scarcely benefited from aid to dependent children and have suffered more than white children from the inadequacies of the existing program" (Sterner, 1943: 282–284).

The other main form of categorical help created by the Social Security Act was assistance to the poor elderly—individuals, as most states defined the need, who earned "insufficient income to provide

reasonable subsistence compatible with decency and health." Because most blacks were not eligible for old age insurance, this aspect of the new law was vital to their well-being. Here, as with ADC, the states, not the federal government, set benefit levels, ascertained eligibility, and administered the program. Here, too, the staff making these decisions in the South were entirely white. The degree of black need and the exclusion of most African Americans from other benefits put significant amount of pressure on this program. In the main, southern states managed to contain it, forcing a finding, albeit toothless, by the Social Security Board in Washington in 1940 that in the prior two years "the number of Negroes to whom aid was granted ... was low in proportion to the number who needed assistance" (Sterner, 1943: 274). In the North, blacks were, in fact, represented in higher proportions than their numbers in the over-65 population, but the rate of acceptance in the South was much lower. So, too, were the monthly benefits. In Massachusetts, New York, Pennsylvania, Indiana, Ohio, Illinois, and California, blacks, who were less well off, received slightly higher grants than whites, ranging from $19 to $34 a month. By contrast, in North Carolina, South Carolina, Texas, West Virginia, Virginia, Oklahoma, Delaware, Louisiana, Florida, Alabama, Mississippi, Tennessee, Kentucky, and Arkansas, white benefits were higher than those paid to blacks. Here, benefits often were very low. In five of these states, benefits to blacks averaged under $8 per month. Five more made payments averaging under $10. And yet, in the face of terrible, extreme need, it was not unreasonable for a contemporary observer to conclude that "the old age assistance program has brought about a very considerable improvement in the economic position of the aged Negro (Sterner, 1943: 275–277).

Unemployment insurance, which composed the third key element of the bill, combined both strategies (Amenta, 1998). Here the administration plan was rather more to the liking of southern members of Congress than the main alternative, a bill advanced by Ernest Lundeen of Minnesota and sent to the floor by the non-southern-dominated House Labor Committee. Whereas that option would have paid all unemployed workers benefits drawn from federal funds, Roosevelt's design was considerably more limited. It offered compensation only to unemployed workers whose employers had already made payments on their behalf into an unemployment insurance fund. As a result, unemployment insurance required access to continual and secure work before getting laid off. Further, once shaped by Ways and Means in the House and Finance in the Senate, the bill excluded domestic and farm workers from its protective reach and located control over eligibility and benefit levels in the hands of the states.

## II.

IN SHORT, EACH OF THE OLD AGE, SOCIAL ASSISTANCE, AND UNEMPLOYMENT provisions advanced by the Social Security Act was shaped to racist contours. Perhaps even more surprisingly, southern power also imposed such results on the most important social policy of the 1940s, the Selective Service Readjustment Act of 1944, more commonly known as the GI Bill of Rights.

No other New Deal initiative had as great an impact on changing the country. Aimed at reintegrating 16 million veterans, it reached eight of ten men born during the 1920s. Even today, this legislation, which quickly came to be called the GI Bill of Rights, qualifies as the most wide-ranging set of social benefits ever offered by the federal government in a single, comprehensive initiative. Between 1944 and 1971, federal spending for former soldiers in this "model welfare system" totaled over $95 billion (Levitan and Cleary, 1973: 27, 3). By 1948, 15 percent of the federal budget was devoted to the GI Bill and the Veterans Administration employed 17 percent of the federal work force.

One by one, family by family, these expenditures transformed the United States by the way it eased the pathway of soldiers—the generation that was marrying and setting forth into adulthood—returning to civilian life. With the help of the GI Bill, millions bought homes, attended college, started business ventures, and found jobs commensurate with their skills. More than 200,000 used the GI Bill's access to capital to acquire farms or start businesses. Veterans Administration mortgages paid for nearly 5 million new houses. Residential ownership became the key foundation for economic security for a burgeoning middle class. Accompanying this revolution in how and where Americans lived was the even more impressive expansion of education benefits. By 1950, the federal government had spent more on schooling for veterans than on expenditures for the Marshall Plan, which had successfully rebuilt Europe's devastated economic life after the war. On the eve of the Second World War, some 160,000 Americans were graduating from college each year. By the end of the decade, this number had tripled to some 500,000. At the conclusion of the policy's educational benefits, 2,250,000 veterans had participated in higher education. Another 5,600,000 veterans enrolled in some 10,000 vocational institutions to study a wide array of trades from carpentry to refrigeration, plumbing to electricity, automobile and airplane repair to business training. For most returning soldiers, the full range of benefits—the entire cost of tuition plus a living stipend—was relatively easy to obtain.

As they prepared to return to civilian life, demobilizing blacks thus seemed positioned to take advantage of the boost their status as veterans offered, but their hopes for these opportunities soon largely were dashed. Despite the assistance that black soldiers received, there was, in fact, no greater instrument for widening an already huge racial gap in postwar America than the GI Bill. As southern black veterans attempted to gain from these new benefits, they encountered many well-established and some new restrictions. This combination of entrenched racism and willful exclusion either refused them entry or shunted them into second-class standing and conditions. With the South in control of the leadership of the relevant committees in both the Senate and House, the bill that passed into law was fashioned in a manner that gave formal access to all. Yet it also administered the program locally, so that Jim Crow rules could be secured by way of locally compliant administrative decentralization.

Consider the provisions for education. It was in the South, primarily in historically black colleges, where 95 percent of black veterans used their higher education benefits at a time the collegiate system remained rigidly segregated. Both in absolute numbers and in proportion to their populations, white students had far more college places than blacks. Within the South, where blacks constituted a quarter of the population, white colleges in 1947 outnumbered black schools by more than five to one. In Mississippi, more than half the state's population was black, but just 7 of the 33 institutions; in Tennessee, 8 of 35; in all the South, 102 of 647 (Jenkins, 1947: 460).

Throughout the country, colleges and universities struggled to keep up with the demand for higher education, but both quantitatively and qualitatively the problem was significantly more acute for black institutions, the poorest educational establishments in the country's most deprived region. During the war their enrollments had decreased severely, which saw their financial condition worsen significantly and their ability to maintain their often inadequate facilities diminish. It was to these places that the vast majority of the most talented and best qualified black soldiers had to turn. Yet the relative absence of support from the southern states left most black colleges unable to take in most of the veterans who qualified. In 1947, some 20,000 eligible black veterans could not find places even under incredibly crowded conditions (Olson, 1974: 74). As many as 50,000 others might have sought admission had there been sufficient places. Though separate, moreover, black colleges hardly were equal. Most were small; half enrolled fewer than 250 students and more than 90 percent taught fewer than 1,000 students. Their budgets were stressed. Their facilities often were less than basic. Libraries were deficient; laboratories rudimentary. Their faculty were understaffed and undertrained. Student–faculty ratios usually exceeded twenty to one. Few, not more than 5 percent, were accredited by the Association of American Universities. There were immense disparities in the range of the liberal arts, and in graduate and professional training. No black college had a doctoral program or a certified engineering program. Only in the field of education was there something like parity across the racial divide, itself a reflection of the pressing need for black teachers in segregated primary and secondary schools.

The gap in educational attainment between blacks and whites widened, rather than closed. Of veterans born between 1923 and 1928, 28 percent of whites but only 12 percent of blacks enrolled in college-level programs. Furthermore, blacks spent fewer months than whites in GI Bill schooling (Bound and Tuner, 2002). Overall, the most careful and sophisticated recent study of the impact of its educational provisions demonstrated no difference in attendance or attainment that set apart southern from non-southern whites. All, on average gained quite a lot. But for blacks, the analysis revealed a marked difference between the small minority in northern colleges and students who attended educational institutions in the South. For the latter group, GI Bill higher education had little effect on their educational attainment or their life prospects

(Collins, 2001); white incomes tended to increase quite a bit more than black earnings as a result of gaining an advanced education (Miller, 1966). As a result, at the collegiate level, the GI Bill widened the educational and economic differences across racial lines. Similar experiences prevailed in the vocational training and job placement programs the GI Bill advanced.

Though the GI Bill offered many eligible African Americans more benefits and more opportunity than they possibly could have imagined in the early 1940s, the manner in which the law and its programs were organized and administered, and its ready accommodation to the larger discriminatory context within which it was embedded, were more racially distinct and arguably more cruel than any other New Deal-era program. The differential treatment it meted out to African Americans sharply curtailed the statute's powerful egalitarian promise and significantly widened the country's large racial gap.

## III.

IMAGINE TWO COUNTRIES, ONE THE RICHEST IN THE WORLD, THE OTHER among its most destitute. Then suppose a global program of foreign aid transferred well over $100 billion—but to the rich nation, not the poor. This, in short, is exactly what happened as a result of the cumulative impact of the most important domestic policies of the 1930s and 1940s. The damage to racial equity was immense. With these policies, the country's Gordian knot binding race to class tightened. By contrast, Lyndon Johnson's sweeping and assertive address at Howard University, in June 1965, proposed to loosen this tie. He depicted policies that would not target the black middle-class audience he was addressing but "the poor, the unemployed, the uprooted, and the dispossessed."

Johnson's assertive brand of affirmative action was never implemented, dashed by a number of events: by a radical transformation in race relations, the escalation of the Vietnam War, new divisions within the Democratic Party, and a Republican resurgence. Instead, affirmative action mostly took a different, though valuable, turn that has made American higher education and business firms a good deal more diverse than they otherwise would have been. We cannot return to June 1965, but we can envisage how affirmative action might be renewed and reinvigorated in a form more in harmony with the objectives Johnson proclaimed at Howard University.

Affirmative action performs acts of corrective justice. Public policy is used to compensate members of a deprived group for prior losses and for gains unfairly achieved by others that resulted from prior government action. Corrective justice, the legal philosopher Jules Coleman has noted, is different from a fair allocation of goods. Rather, it identifies interventions that remedy previously unjust decisions that made existing patterns of distribution even more unfair than they otherwise would have been (Coleman, 1983: 6). When is such justice fair and legitimate? How far can its remedies be extended, and on what basis?

These issues are especially pressing for affirmative action's advocates. The arguments and rhetoric for racial neutrality its opponents deploy have not been countered by equally clear and defensible principles except for broad claims to compensation for the generalized history of slavery, segregation, and other forms of racism in American history. Defenders of affirmative action typically argue with a body of principled reasoning appreciably less developed than that of the opposition. "The theory under which affirmative action is justified is often not articulated," Jack Greenberg, the former director-counsel of the NAACP Legal Defense and Educational Fund, has remarked. To the contrary, "advocates often do not define any supporting theory at all" (Greenberg, 2002: 555). Even the legal disputes about affirmative action that have reached the Supreme Court have been marked by this lopsidedness, with the honed principles of opponents confronting the more narrow and pragmatic stance of supporters. This structure of disagreement was present more a quarter-century ago when the Supreme Court decided in *United Steelworkers v. Weber* to permit voluntary agreements that reserve half of all craft training positions until African American workers in a given plant come to match the percentage of blacks in the local labor force. At issue in that case was whether Title VII of the Civil Rights Acts rules out the voluntary adoption of racial quotas to correct racial one-sidedness, and thus whether a compensatory program to remedy "manifest racial imbalance" is permissible when no proof of intentional wrongdoing or active discrimination has been demonstrated. Writing for the majority, Justice William Brennan reasoned in practical terms. He argued that prohibiting such hard targets in the name of the 1964 Civil Rights Act would be excessively ironic. "A law triggered by a Nation's concern over centuries of racial injustice," he wrote, should not be used as the reason to prohibit "race conscious efforts to abolish traditional patterns of racial segregation and hierarchy." Dissenting, Justice William Rehnquist rejoined in a more principled way, stating there is "no irony in a law that prohibits all voluntary racial discrimination, even discrimination directed against whites in favor of blacks." He reasoned that as "the evil inherent in discrimination against Negroes" is its grounding in an "immutable characteristic, utterly irrelevant to employment decisions," discrimination is "no less evil" if it offers preferential treatment to blacks.

A long line of Supreme Court decisions has navigated among these conflicting types of justification. This has not proved easy. Even within the same short period, as in the mid-1980s, the court reached contrasting conclusions. In 1984, the court ruled in *Firefighters v. Stotts* that senior white firefighters could not be laid off to make way for more junior blacks. Two years later, it ruled in *Wygant v. Jackson Board of Education* that minority employment was an insufficient reason to override the seniority white teachers had achieved. Yet it also upheld a judicially ordered racial quota in *Local 28, Sheet Metal Workers' International Association v. EEOC,* finding that the race-conscious remedy of numerical goals could be deployed to end the sharp under representation of African Americans and Hispanics in Local 28, despite the fact that it did have some black members and the International Union had repealed racial restrictions as long ago as 1946. Other decisions, including the 1987 cases of *United States v. Paradise* and *Johnson v. Transportation Agency,* further endorsed promotion quotas and voluntary plans motivated by the under representation of minorities and women rather than direct and personal experience of discrimination. Tightly contested rulings and assessments have continued to characterize court rulings on the subject ever since.

The language of the justices has paralleled the uneven pattern dividing the types of arguments used by affirmative action's supporters and opponents in wider public and scholarly debates. Those opposing affirmative action have tended to argue that it is wrong as a matter of constitutional doctrine and principled tenets. "Every time the government places citizens on racial registers and makes race relevant to the provision of burdens or benefits, it demeans us all," Justice Clarence Thomas, only the second African American to sit on the Supreme Court, wrote in a stinging dissent in *Grutter v. Bollinger,* the June 2003 decision that upheld racial preferences in admissions at the University of Michigan Law School. Arguing to the contrary for the one-vote majority, Justice Sandra Day O'Connor, the first woman justice, claimed that the compensatory steps offered by affirmative action in higher education fulfill a pressing social good by offering paths to leadership for qualified and talented individuals regardless of their race.

Within the long line of court decisions, the opinion Justice Lewis Powell offered in 1978 in *Regents of the University of California v. Bakke* stands out because it both defended and circumscribed affirmative action on grounds that established clear, indeed principled, standards. Powell's guidelines do more than certify the type of affirmative action that was created in the 1960s; they also can guide a more extensive program closer to President Johnson's original intentions.

The Supreme Court had to consider whether the University of California, Davis, could reserve 16 of its 100 medical school places for minorities. Four justices (Warren Burger, William Rehnquist, John Paul Stevens, and Potter Stewart) found that this admissions process violated civil rights laws banning racial discrimination. To prefer on the basis of race, they argued, is wrong and illegal. Four other justices (Harry Blackmun, William Brennan, Thurgood Marshall, and Byron White) rejected Allan Bakke's challenge. They reasoned that race-blind policies in a race-conscious society can make access by minorities too difficult. Justice Lewis Powell, the court's swing voter, agreed that the constitutional requirement of equal protection had been violated by the quota system at Davis. Thus, by a 5-to-4 vote, Bakke was admitted to the medical school. Crucially, though, Powell also found that race could legitimately be used as a "plus" in making decisions on admission.

In so ruling, he intervened in a debate far older than this case. After the Civil War, in the wake of the ratification of the Constitution's Fourteenth Amendment, Congress passed a series of race-conscious Reconstruction measures, most notably the 1866 Freedmen's Bureau Act, offering special remedial support to African Americans. Then, as later, supporters cited the need to rectify deep racial harms. Color-neutral policies, so soon after slavery, mocked the meaning of equality. Then, as later, opponents remonstrated against bills that specially benefited blacks, arguing that it is wrong to make distinctions based on race. They often cited the amendment itself, which stipulates that "No state shall make or enforce any law which shall abridge the privileges or immunities of citizens of the United States; nor shall any State deprive any person of life, liberty, or property, without due process of law; nor deny to any person within its jurisdiction the equal protection of the laws."

The Fourteenth Amendment's language about equal protection for all citizens has provided the bedrock argument for resistance to the way affirmative action has been conducted since 1965. It is not favored treatment as such that is in question. After all, any public policy, whether about taxes, welfare, or trade, confers advantages on some with costs paid by others. Legislation always sorts people into categories and ranks. Rather, it is preferential treatment for a group based on race. A central issue has been whether this mark of distinction ever can be taken into account legitimately in the public realm, and whether specific members of the disadvantaged racial group themselves have suffered harm as a result of membership in the group. Also in question is how collective racial categories can be squared with individual rights, and whether the costs imposed on whites to correct past harms to blacks are fair.

Powell rightly shared in the skepticism about the use of race in public life. Nevertheless, he authorized affirmative action within the scope of equal protection under demanding stipulations, arguing that modifications to color-blind policies could be undertaken to remedy race-based disadvantages when two conditions are met. Otherwise, they are illegitimate. There must be a clear and tight link connecting affirmative action's remedies to specific historical harms based on race. This tie between past action and present policy has to be strong and precise. More general claims about racism in the country's past are not enough. Nor can the goal to be pursued by affirmative action be vague or only of moderate importance. It must be sufficiently valuable as a social good to justify suspending rules that ordinarily must be blind to race. Further, if there is a nonracial way to pursue a given goal, that course should always be preferred. He insisted on these two principles—that racial injuries be specific and clear; and that a compelling public purpose must be identified when racial remedies are applied—because a color-blind society is desirable and color-coding is inherently susceptible to misuse.

Powell's decision upset affirmative action's enemies. Writing in 1979 still as University of Chicago law professor, Antonin Scalia argued that Powell had been wrong to uphold affirmative action in any form. Restorative justice, he claimed, is inherently not right and not constitutional. "The affirmative action system now in place," he wrote, will produce perverse results that will "prefer the son of a prosperous and well-educated black doctor or lawyer—solely because of his race—to the son of a recent refugee from Eastern Europe who is working as a manual laborer to get his family ahead" because it "is based upon concepts of racial indebtedness and racial entitlement rather than individual worth and individual need; that is to say, because it is racist." This new form of "racial presumption" simply is wrong because it traduces color-blind standards. "From racist principles," he concluded, "flow racist results" (Scalia, 1979: 153–154, 157).

Echoing the response to Reconstruction, affirmative action's challengers offer a rationale stressing that each individual should count as any other. Coding by color "is playing with fire" (Jacoby, 1998: 541). Reverse racial discrimination can result in new kinds of discrimination. On this account, it damages the equality of individuals, undermines merit, and stigmatizes members of the group it advantages. Racial categories are too blunt and inclusive to identify citizens who deserve special help. Individual rights always are threatened by racial counting. The price paid by whites is not just. So goes the argument.

Such high-mindedness is too abstract and too removed from the country's historical record. "It is more than a little ironic," Justice Thurgood Marshall observed, in 1978 in his opinion in *Bakke* case, "that, after several hundred years of class-based discrimination against Negroes, the Court is unwilling to hold that a class-based remedy for that discrimination is permissible." Powell disagreed with Marshall on the particular case but not on his broader view. Color-blind claims in the face of the racial dimensions of American history, he understood, furnish the misleading impression that color-conscious public policies supplanted long-standing and publicly legitimate color-blind practices only after the civil rights revolution and after President Johnson's endorsement at Howard University of the standard calling for an equality of results. Glazer himself later took note of the moral authority of affirmative action in light of the history of black subordination. "The only possible comparison with Europe," he commented, "would be if the Saxons of England or the Gauls of France, had been held in a position of caste subservience for centuries." Further, as he acknowledged in a retraction of his former opposition to affirmative action, it is impossible to "ignore the remarkable and unique separation between blacks and others" that continues in American life (Glazer, 1997: 157, 158).

Blacks and whites have remained isolated from each other to a degree that would be even more pronounced if not for the limited type of affirmative action the country currently enjoys. In the half century since *Brown v. Board of Education*, the depth of racial segregation in most American schools, neighborhoods, and families has persisted. Of course, strict legal segregation has ended for schoolchildren, but, to date, racial integration, both in the North and the South, has not proceeded in the face of the pervasive residential separation of the races in suburbs as well as cities. On virtually every social and economic dimension, blacks and whites are still a nation apart. The constellation of concentrated poverty, poor access to jobs, derisory housing conditions, high rates of incarceration, and challenges to traditional family formation continues to define issues of race and racism in the United States. "Negro poverty is not white poverty," Johnson declared, in seeking to understand these "deep, corrosive, obstinate differences." Now as then, the call for colorblindness implicitly scorns these social realities. At best, it is sightless. At worst, it is a soft version of bigotry.

Many supporters of affirmative action greeted Powell's reasoning with dismay, but for rather different reasons. They were unhappy that he had held on more tightly to the principle of equal protection than the four liberal justices who found against Bakke. They also disapproved of his noticeable reluctance to grant African Americans as a group the same constitutional status as individuals who suffer discrimination. For this reason, Ronald Dworkin disputed Powell's insistence on tight standards and stringent inspection before affirmative action could be upheld. Powell, he argued, had failed to see that there is an important difference between the use of racial classification to inflict harm against the downtrodden and its utilization to correct or remedy these injustices (Dworkin, 1977).

Two distinct lines of reasoning about affirmative action have dominated the arguments made by its supporters. Some submit a morally compelling petition demanding reparations for the great injuries of slavery and segregation. Speaking at Riverside Church in 1969, James Foreman, one of the leaders of the Student Non-Violent Coordinating Committee (SNCC), read "The Black Manifesto" demanding $500 million from the country's churches and synagogues for the country's African Americans as recompense for brutality, murder, and exploitation. Since 1988, the National Coalition of Blacks for Reparations has been lobbying for payments to blacks descended from slaves. Its efforts have been endorsed by Michigan Congressman John Conyers, Jr., a leading figure in the Black Caucus. Jesse Jackson has endorsed such a program of financial compensation following the 1999 UN World Conference against Racism, and has made it a leading priority of Rainbow/PUSH. Two years later, a group of African-American lawyers, including Johnnie Cochran Jr., O. J. Simpson's attorney, readied a class action lawsuit seeking nearly a trillion dollars from the federal government.

In truth, the brutal harms inflicted by slavery and Jim Crow are far too substantial to ever properly remedy. Epic historical crimes, like slavery, unremitting racial bigotry, and segregation, are injuries that cannot be requited. There is no adequate rejoinder to losses on this scale. In such situations, the request for large cash transfers places bravado ahead of substance, flirts with demaguery, and risks political irrelevance. These calls also have practical problems. They suffer from slack precision and all-inclusive, grand dimensions. Who would qualify? Only blacks descended from slaves or more recent African immigrants? What scale could cash transfers achieve? How could they ever be more than inadequate tokens? Whatever the abstract merits of such claims, this Utopian politics seems entirely symbolic, not really serious.

Standing on lower ground, other supporters make more modest, pragmatic claims. Business firms defend affirmative action because it insulates them from antidiscrimination lawsuits. Universities appreciate diversity because it promotes intellectual pluralism. Various authorities argue that affirmative action helps secure racial peace and prevent turmoil. Other advocates, convinced that alternative routes to better life changes for minorities are not available, promote affirmative action as the best available tool with which to achieve practical goals in employment and education.

Such utilitarian arguments tend to be shallow. Their ambitions are too small. They fail to make the case for corrective justice except on prudential or practical grounds. Rather than argue forthrightly that the purpose of affirmative action is to put a definitive end to the caste status of blacks in American life and thus also put an end to white privilege, or another such lofty goal, they identify aims that arguably could be attained by other means. Moreover, a pragmatic calculus, once offered, has to be considered in full. After all, it must be conceded, under some circumstances affirmative action can increase racial animosities, reduce standards in hiring and admissions, and damage the self-respect of its beneficiaries. To argue for affirmative action simply in pragmatic terms thus opens its various programs to cost-benefit calculations. Without a larger context of principles and priorities, it usually proves impossible to sort out when a system of preferences is compelling and when it is not.

In contrast to both sets of critics, I think Powell's fine-grained assessment of affirmative action was just right. It would be callous to ignore the tremendous and devastating impact of racism in American life. In light of the particular harms inflicted on blacks in multiple institutional spheres, it has to be possible to override the understanding that equal protection ordinarily applies to individuals, not racial groups. But such exceptions must be narrowly tailored. They must serve a sufficient public purpose to overcome a nonracial constitutional and moral presumption, and they must be conditional on the character and strength of the ties that connect specific past harms to present remedies. Every violation of color-blind norms, in short, must be justified with the goal of a just color-blind society in mind. Impartiality should be the dominant norm. Wherever possible, race should not count for or against any given person. Not every injustice should be answered with preferential policies. When such corrective justice is undertaken by the federal government, it must plausibly indicate the relationship between the victims of the given wrong and the recipients, some time later, of public benefits; and it has to show why a particular remedy is a good choice to compensate for wrongs committed in the past.

## IV.

BUILDING ON POWELL'S PRINCIPLES HAS SIGNIFICANT ADVANTAGES. First, his demand for strict scrutiny appropriately sets the bar high, but not beyond reach. It balances a widely shared desire to make color neutrality the dominant norm with the cheerless recognition that this goal cannot be achieved if the role race has played in American life is downplayed or, worse, ignored. As such, this jurisprudence can appeal to the broad middle of the political spectrum. Properly explained and elaborated, it can widen the spectrum of support for affirmative action. Within the public at large, this approach offers the best chance to make it possible to win backing for what inevitably is a difficult set of policies to persuade nonbeneficiaries to approve.

As settled law, Powell's deeply historical approach has been applied to the type of affirmative action developed during the Johnson and Nixon administrations, but it also can shape and motivate a considerably broader effort that might target affirmative action at those who are less well-off. Affirmative action is constitutional, on his view, when the discrimination being remedied is specific, identifiable, and broadly institutional. Generalized racism or specific acts of individual prejudice or discrimination do not qualify for this kind of governmental response.

These distinctions place the onus of proof on the character of the historical evidence that is deployed to justify rectification. A focus on the policies about welfare and work, as well as war and postwar, which the southern wing of the Democratic Party successfully imposed during the New Deal and Fair Deal, is consistent with this requirement. They provide the content Powell requires to justify acts of official rectification.

The *Bakke* decision, as we have seen, focused on higher education. In that context, Powell argued that affirmative action to achieve educational diversity was permissible because it addressed the specific situation created by the historical pattern of nearly all-white higher education. Considered in the policy context of the Roosevelt and Truman administrations, however, the harms inflicted on blacks by exclusion from national public policies invite a radical shift in focus and justification for affirmative action. Because such policies in the last-gasp era of Jim Crow constituted a massive transfer of privileges to white Americans, affirmative action can be redirected to this imbalance. The history of advantages offered to most whites and denied to many blacks in New Deal and Fair Deal policies is a particular story of targeted official institutional bias and great consequence. By understanding how the playing field fashioned by such fundamental public policies as Social Security, the Wagner Act, military segregation, and the GI Bill was racially skewed by design, and how their powerful negative effects have compounded in the past two generations, the type of affirmative action Lyndon Johnson envisioned can be advanced.

This history has been missing from public debate. This historical amnesia has weakened the case for affirmative action. The usual sole focus on present imbalances produces claims for racial rectification without offering enough historical justification to bring its benefits to most African Americans. Since all the major tools the federal government deployed during the New Deal and Fair Deal created a powerful, if unstated, program of affirmative action for white Americans, the case for even more extensive affirmative action is more compelling than current lines of argument favoring such policies. Even today's proponents of affirmative action pay almost no heed to this recent record of profound and pervasive racial bias. This omission produces more than defective history. It also limits the scope of public debate about affirmative action.

With hindsight, we can see that Justice Powell did more than turn a situational defeat into a strategic constitutional victory for affirmative action. The rules he designed to assess when the "plus" of race and affirmative action should be allowed to come into play can provide a framework to address affirmative action today. When this largely forgotten history is revealed and openly discussed, paths can emerge that could return us to the goals set forth by Lyndon Johnson at Howard.

Retrospectively, we can also see how Johnson's graduation speech anticipated Powell's standards. The president's analysis of how the racial gap had widened, though deficient, sought to clarify the facts regarding the present status of blacks in American society. He provided a model of justification for affirmative action by summarizing the racial gap, arguing about causes, and spelling out why the divide distinguishing racial groups constitutes a major public concern. By taking these steps, he fulfilled Justice Powell's second stipulation. He also sought to connect his remedies to the causes he had identified. In this approach, he followed Justice Powell's first requirement.

Combining Powell's principles and Johnson's ambition propels us back to the moment when key national policies advantaged whites. They also push us forward to a framework for public policies that can respond to the injuries inflicted by officially sanctioned racism. Though motivated by a desire to protect Jim Crow, many of the methods and instruments those programs used were adopted on a nonracial basis. A renewed and extended program of affirmative action could offer a reciprocal possibility. Responding to nonracial racism, affirmative action could be established in ways that at least partially transcend race, even while primarily rectifying racial injustice.

## NOTES

This work draws from and summarizes evidence and arguments elaborated more fully in Katznelson (2005).

## REFERENCES

Amenta, Edward. *Bold Relief: Institutional Politics and the Origins of Modern American Social Policy.* Princeton: Princeton University Press, 1998.

Bartley, Robert. "'Affirmative Action': Devil in the Details." *Wall Street Journal,* 10 Feb. 2003.

Bound, John, and Sarah Turner. "Going to War and Going to College: Did World War II and the G.I. Bill Increase Educational Attainment for Returning Veterans?" *Journal of Labor Economics* 20 (October 2002).

Coleman, Jules. "Moral Theories of Torts: Their Scope and Limits. Part II." *Law and Philosophy* 2:3 (1983).

Collins, William J. "Race, Roosevelt, and Wartime Production: Fair Employment in World War II Labor Markets." *American Economic Review* 91 (March 2001).

Dworkin, Ronald. "Bakke's Case: Are Quotas Unfair?" *New York Review of Books.* 10 Nov 1977.

Federal Security Agency. Social Security Board. *Old-Age and Survivors' Insurance Statistics: Employment and Wages of Covered Workers: 1938.* Washington, D.C.: US Government Printing Office, 1940.

Glazer, Nathan. *We Are All Multiculturalists Now.* Cambridge: Harvard University Press, 1997.

Graham, Hugh Davis. *Collision Course: The Strange Convergence of Affirmative Action and Immigration Policy.* New York: Oxford University Press, 2002.

Greenberg, Jack. "Affirmative Action in Higher Education: Confronting the Condition and the Theory." *Boston College Law Review* 43:3 (2002).

Hamilton, Dona Cooper, and Charles V. Hamilton. *The Dual Agenda.* New York: Columbia University Press, 1997.

Jacoby, Tamar. *Someone Else's House: America's Unfinished Struggle for Integration.* New York: The Free Press, 1998.

Jenkins, Martin D. "The Availability of Higher Education for Negroes in the Southern States." *Journal of Negro Education* 16 (Summer 1947).

Katznelson, Ira. *When Affirmative Action Was White: An Untold History of Racial Inequality in Twentieth-Century America.* New York: Norton, 2005.

Kennedy, Randall. "Persuasion and Distrust: A Comment on the Affirmative Action Debate." *Harvard Law Review* 99 (1986).

Levitan, Sar A., and Karen A. Cleary. *Old Wars Remain Unfinished: The Veterans Benefits System.* Baltimore: Johns Hopkins University Press, 1973.

Lieberman, Robert C. *Shifting the Color Line: Race and the American Welfare State.* Cambridge: Harvard University Press, 1998.

Miller, Herman Phillip. *Income Distribution in the United States.* Washington, D.C.: US Government Printing Office. 1966.

Myrdal, Gunnar. *An American Dilemma.* Vol. 1. New York: Harper and Brothers, 1944.

Olsen, Keith W. *The G.I. Bill, The Veterans, and The Colleges.* Lexington: University of Kentucky Press, 1974.

Scalia, Antonin. "The Disease as Cure: 'In Order to Get Beyond Racism, We Must First Take Account of Race.'" *Washington University Law Quarterly* 147:1 (1979).

Sterner, Richard. *The Negro's Share: A Study of Income, Consumption, Housing, and Public Assistance.* New York: Harper and Brothers. 1943.

# ENGAGING FUTURE LEADERS

## PEER EDUCATION AT WORK IN COLLEGES AND UNIVERSITIES

*By Alta Mauro and Jason Robertson*

College-aged students live and make meaning in intense social networks, where their peers have tremendous influence. Knowing the power of peer influence, many institutions have employed peer education as an effective means of disseminating information and teaching. When they are armed with accurate and developmentally-appropriate information, students can expose their peers to a myriad of information, engage them in meaningful dialogue and conversation, and ultimately, teach them. This social interaction results in support from one student to the other, modeling of productive thought processes and positive behaviors, and empowerment toward higher level thinking (Bandura, 1994).

Various forms of peer education programs have been in existence for many years. Many were started to support those in drug or alcohol treatment programs, but they have since been used to address other social concerns, namely sexual health and safety, and teenage pregnancy. Colleges and universities employ peer education as a means of empowering students as change agents, affecting their peers in meaningful ways. In this chapter, the authors will introduce peer education as a method

of teaching college students about human difference and diversity, or the state of being different or diverse. This can be achieved statistically, regardless of the *marker* of difference (race, ethnicity, nationality, gender, gender expression, sexual orientation, religious affiliation, physical ability, etc.). Multiculturalism means the preservation of different cultures and cultural identities within a unified society, state, or nation. Different than diversity, multiculturalism is not statistical, but a condition of intentional inclusion of cultural difference.

The authors also outline methods of using peer education to teach social justice and justification for using this form of education. *Social justice* is most often described as the equal distribution of advantages and disadvantages within a given society (Adams, 1997). Adams, Bell and Griffin define the goal of social justice as "full and equal participation of all groups in a society that is mutually shaped to meet their needs" with the primary goals of social justice education being increasing personal awareness, expanding knowledge, and encouraging action (Adams, 1997). The chapter begins with theories and models of social justice education, followed by information on institutional barriers to employing social justice education programs at the university level, guidelines for strategic planning, curriculum development, training and evaluation of peer educators.

## WHY SOCIAL JUSTICE EDUCATION?

Acquiring cultural competence skills allows us to move from discussion to dialogue. Discussions usually entail one or more parties defending or "selling" their ideas to others. Dialogue entails presenting many ideas and alternatives so that all parties may establish meaning that is organic to the group. The goal of the former is to narrow options and decide on a solution; the goal of the latter is to achieve new learning and to gain greater insight (Senge, 1990). In short, those who are culturally competent are able to move beyond gathering or sharing facts that build a case, per se; they exchange ideas couched in cultural contexts, and determine meaning with the others with whom they interact. Thus, cultural competence skills are vital for those seeking success in any endeavor.

Honing cultural competence skills will ensure one's ability to navigate our diverse society successfully. It will also allow an individual to shift from a position of self-advocacy to one of community concern, and increased action for the benefit of their own cultural or affinity group. Individual and self-serving needs will remain, but the desire to establish or strengthen commitments to one's own community become increasingly important. A person who purposefully learns about him or herself as a cultural being, the experiences of others who are culturally different, and allows this knowledge to influence both their worldview and behaviors is one prone to explore how their actions affect others, and how our interconnectedness affects and is affected by our identity. As this person becomes increasingly socially conscious, they are drawn to personal reflection, purposeful education on our collective history and subsequent social challenges, and action toward achieving social justice goals.

People endeavoring to learn more about themselves as cultural beings often explore the arts and music, travel extensively and engage in foreign cultural activities, and seek ways to demonstrate their learning with others. They develop connections to new and different communities. During the college years, this translates into learning a new language and studying abroad, joining a religious or faith-based organization, affiliating with race or ethnicity-specific affinity groups, etc. Others become active as peer educators, hoping to teach their fellow students cultural competence skills and how to establish connections with others.

## PEER EDUCATION AS A METHOD OF SOCIAL JUSTICE EDUCATION

Serving as a peer educator is one way that students can establish or strengthen a commitment to their community. Peer educators can serve in many capacities on their campuses. They are trained as teachers or program leaders, but they ultimately serve as role models to others within their campus community (Sloane & Zimmer, 1993). Peer educators can be utilized to facilitate a complex, interrelated model of individuals who see their identity connected to the identity of their community (Villarruel, Jemmott, Howard, Taylor & Bush, 1998). Likewise, by serving as a peer educator, students can shift from focusing on their individual selves to adopting a community-based approach to addressing community issues (Fabiano, 1994).

Recent research bears that peer education takes place on college campuses whether through formal programming or informal student-to-student conversation (Brack, Millard, Shah, 2008). Those peer education programs which are formal are established on set curricula. Others are less formal, and occur through informal interactions staged in residence halls, dining halls, or other student-centered spaces where conversations occur naturally. Developmentally, college-aged students are naturally curious. Moreover, they expect to explore cultural difference during their tenure in college (Harper & Hurtado, 2007). Thus, conversations about culture and cultural identity are often sparked in places outside the classroom. Ideally, students who are educated on issues of social justice and trained to facilitate conversations with their peers would be in place to dispense accurate information; however, we know that many more conversations regarding issues of difference happen in the moment than do in formal educational settings (Smith, 2002; 2009). One significant benefit of having peer educators in place is that they are able to make use of their existing social networks to relay accurate information that results in a more organized and influential support of their peers (Brack, Millard, Shah, 2008).

The methods applied to utilizing peer education are as varied as there are peer education programs and advisors. Some programs are similar to formal tutoring or other forms of one-on-one work; others include group presentations and campus outreach. Either form includes some form of training. The methods that are adopted should depend on the desired outcomes of the program (i.e. pure information or awareness-raising, behavioral change, skill development, etc.) (Turner & Shepherd, 1999). This distinction is key in the development of a structured evaluation plan, which is necessary to determine the success of the overall program.

Additionally, it is expected and assumed that the peer educators will also be affected as a result of their peer education experience. Researchers conducting one study reported that peer educators regarded the opportunity to help others and contribute to society as a benefit for participation in a peer education program (Bandura, Millard, Peluso, & Ortman, 2000)). It is expected that this opportunity to affect change would be attractive to most peer educators, and especially to those who desire to address intercultural and social justice issues.

## THEORY UNDERLYING PEER EDUCATION

Two theories that support the concept of peer education are social learning theory and social identity theory, both of which describe key aspects of the role that peer educators play. Social Learning Theory, developed by Bandura and colleagues in 1977, states that learning occurs within a social context and that people learn from one another through observation, imitation and modeling (Bandura, 1977; Drug Info, 2006). Bandura (1977) states:

"Learning would be exceedingly laborious, not to mention hazardous, if people had to rely solely on the effects of their own actions to inform them what to do. Fortunately, most human behavior is learned observationally through modeling: from observing others one forms an idea of how new behaviors are performed, and on later occasions this coded information serves as a guide for action." (p 22).

Modeling is the key component to this theory. Students view their peers exhibit a behavior and the consequences of that behavior, and go on to adopt a behavior that is similar. Similar to young children, young adults need to experiment with multiple behaviors and understand the consequences before committing to one type of behavior. In order to establish this particular behavior as a *practice*, students need the opportunity to try on the behavior and determine the effect the behavior will have on them.

Positive reinforcement is particularly important in this instance (Bandura, 1977). Students need to be encouraged in their pursuit of new sets of behaviors, both from their peers and other people with influence in their lives. Students are most likely to learn from peers who are both knowledgeable and popular; thus role model credibility is an important attribute when considering peer educators in order to support the development of desired behavior change within a population. Turner and Shepherd report that the degree to which we are influenced by modeled behavior depends on the characteristics of the models, the attributes of the observers (i.e. whether or not the learner is developmentally ready to adopt the new behavior set), and the perceived consequences of adopting the behavior" (Turner & Shepherd, 1999, p. 237).

The heart of the peer education approach draws upon the credibility that peers tend to have with their social networks. According to Sloane and Zimmer (1993), people are more likely to listen to someone who is a member of their social group or who is similar to them and faces similar issues and concerns. Many students value their social groups and seek information in these realms on a regular basis. According to the Spring 2008 National College Health Assessment, 61.1% of the students surveyed sought information from their friends on a regular basis. This highlights the important role that peer educators can play in helping to reach educate students. Since students are already engaging in information gathering and sharing among these networks of friends, harnessing the power of these networks and training students is a logical step to combating problem behavior and either underscoring or challenging societal norms (Turner & Shepherd, 1999).

In addition to a peer educators' ability to demonstrate and teach specific, socially-acceptable behaviors, they are often expected to serve as role models for other members of their campus community. Klepp, Harper, and Perry (1986) state that peer educators should serve as positive role models for their peers and as such, help relay social

information, rather than just provide content-specific facts. This expectation may be more difficult to attain for those peer educators whose role is to affect change regarding social justice and diversity than for others. This often requires them to go against societal norms and pressures and take a stand on issues that many of their peers have not addressed. Professionals who create these programs must be sure to provide opportunities for peer educators to process potential feelings of loneliness or alienation from their friends (and sometimes, family members), many of whom have not fully explored social justice issues intellectually, or been affected by them emotionally. It is critical that peer educators understand that they are not alone in caring about these issues, even if they are seemingly alone in their commitment to eradicating social ills in their community.

Social learning theory also states that peers reinforce socially-learned behaviors (Turner & Shepherd, 1999). Peer educators have numerous opportunities to exercise influence; this influence is increased as the rate and intensity of interactions are increased. The peer education model is most effective when students are broadly engaged in conversation about social justice frequently and publicly, and when the goal of the dialogue is the creation of new knowledge (Nonaka, 1994). Thus peer education programs designed to address social justice concerns must engage the whole community, and initiatives should not include continual dialogue rather than individual, disjointed attempts to discuss particular issues.

Another tenet of social learning theory that has particular application for peer education is self-efficacy. Self-efficacy:

> relates to a person's confidence in performing a particular behavior and their expectations of success. It is more likely for a person to put into practice socially

learned behavior if they think it will be effective. Therefore, it is no use providing peers merely with the appropriate information if in social and interactive situations they cannot [utilize the information] (Turner & Shepherd, 1999, p. 239).

In short, peer educators need to feel empowered to act in their role, not merely educated on the issues. The likelihood that peer educators will be able to utilize information to educate others in a "real life" situation is low, unless they have been encouraged to be bold in their work with their peers. This not only has implications for students working with their peers, but also for those designing training programs. In order to position peer educators to utilize the concepts they learn in the training process, the information must be presented in such a manner that students are able to understand it, practice it, and integrate the new knowledge into their personality and have it be reflected in their daily activities.

Another theory that underscored the effectiveness of peer education is social identity theory, which states that an individual has multiple social identities all of which are derived from their perceived membership in various social groups (Hogg & Vaughan, 2002). The basic premise is that when a person is a member of a group, they derive a sense of belonging or identity from the group, and are more likely to assert influence over their peers in that group. In this regard, peer educators who possess characteristics similar to other group members have credibility, and are able to address issues or concerns more readily than those who do not.

## MENTAL MODELS, CHANGE, ASSUMPTIONS AND DIALOGUE: IMPORTANT AREAS TO EXPLORE WITH PEER EDUCATORS

We all view our world through lenses influenced by our experiences, thoughts, and beliefs (Senge, 1990, p. 175). Previous experiences help to inform our current thoughts, beliefs, and ways of interacting with the world around us. These concepts, called mental models, are internal images of how the world works that impacts our actions because they influence how we see the world around us (Senge, 1990, p. 175; Klein, 1998, p. 45). Mental models provide the context in which we view and interpret new material, and determine how stored information is relevant in new situations (Klein, 1998, p. 45). In short, we are often unable to make sense of new ideas because we lack the foundational knowledge that would enable us to connect the new concept with one we had mastered previously. It is no wonder then, that many efforts to affect social change fail; people often lack a baseline understanding of human interconnectedness, and are thus unable to adopt the feelings of obligation to others which are necessary to provoke them to advocacy and action on another's behalf.

A firm understanding of terms such as social justice, diversity, multiculturalism, equality, equity, and inclusion is necessary in order to engage in true intercultural engagement, through which, individuals—regardless of their identity markers can understand and be understood. The goal of intercultural engagement is increased interaction and the exchange of ideas between cultural brokers which leads to pluralism. This helps peer educators to work through their own mental models and understand the lens through which they see things. It requires that the students move beyond cataloguing basic concepts about foreigners and "Others," and that we truly understand what drives cultural behaviors and patterns of communication indicative of different cultural groups. This way, we may respect others and their ways of sharing, share communication spaces, and learn to move among various cultural groups without shaming or disrespecting others, or without endangering or ostracizing ourselves. These competencies empower us to interact with others and to engage in meaningful dialogue with those who are different from ourselves, regardless of the nature of the difference. This *cultural literacy*, or the ability to acquire, interpret, and apply knowledge about other cultures, is an invaluable skill for those seeking to live, learn, travel, do business, or compete in an increasingly-global society.

People who are uncomfortable with the idea of change will go to great lengths to resist it (McCain and Jukes, 2001, p. 3). McCain and Jukes (2001) refer to this phenomenon as paradigm paralysis (p. 13). A paradigm is a model, perspective, value system, frame of reference, filter, or worldview that guides one's actions (McCain and Jukes, 2001). In trying to maintain the safety of their status quo, a person either rejects information that would cause them to adjust their purview or refuses to accept that the new information has implications on their behavior. The lenses that one uses to view pending change(s) are tinted by past experiences and impede many change processes. It takes substantial effort to consider multiple perspectives once someone has constructed their worldview and intentionally inhibited their ability to empathize or agree with others (McCain and Jukes, 2001).

The paralysis that often grips those confronted with change is referred to as "the big assumption" or dynamic equilibrium (Kegan and Lahey, 2001). These assumptions bind us in our current ways of thinking, some existing below our level of consciousness (Senge, 1990). Likewise, dynamic equilibrium works to ensure that change does not occur (Kegan and Lahey, 2001). Given this tendency, the most attractive progressive ideas can be overwhelmed or submerged by deeply entrenched mental models

(Senge, 1990). This can lead to closedmindedness and resistance to ideas that present as different from our own. Harnessing the power of peer influence, the peer educator can help people to divorce themselves from such entrenched models.

Many people seek methods of interacting with *others* that are not emotionally-taxing. Some decide to disregard cultural differences and interact with others based on unifying characteristics. People are comforted by the idea of a common humanity, and choose to treat all people with equal respect that they feel should be given to any human. Others adopt *The Golden Rule* as a guide for interacting with others. Altruistic in nature, this makes people feel good, as if they are doing the proverbial *right thing*. The problem with this approach is that it encourages an individual to overestimate the *sameness* and to disregard important differences that may exist between themselves and others. It denies the other of their identity, markers of which might be highly salient (Monahan, 2006). This common practice of *color-blindness* is ineffective for these reasons. We all have cultural baggage which should be honored and accommodated in order for us to feel validated and respected. It is insensitive to deny the significance of another person's cultural influence; this disregard often blocks authentic communication and the exchange of ideas. A more appropriate approach to interacting with others is *The Platinum Rule*: "Do unto others as they would have you do unto them" (Polk, H. 2007). This allows the *doer* to respect the other, but to treat them in a way that is validating, respectful of their culture and cultural traditions, and honors the interdependence of both individuals.

In their book, *Seven Languages for Transformation*, Kegan and Lahey (2001) outline an exercise designed to help individuals understand their immunity to change and create enough cognitive and emotional trust that one can (at least temporarily) win some distance from their own dynamic equilibrium (Kegan and Lahey, 2001). The objective of the exercise is to help people examine the way in which the words that they use everyday affect their ability to change. Often people espouse one commitment, but are actually working counter to that commitment. The vocabulary that we have available to us regulates the forms of thinking, feeling, and meaning-making to which we have access. This, then, determines how we view and move through the world. (Kegan and Lahey, 2001).

A related example is the interchanging of the words *diversity, interculturalism, social justice,* or other terms that are commonly associated with difference. It is critical to delineate between these terms so that all stakeholders understand collective goals. For example, university officials must be clear as to whether the institution's goals are to achieve greater diversity (i.e. to increase the number of women and/or ethnic minorities), encourage interculturalism (increasing the rate at which students have meaningful interactions and dialogue with *others),* or to establish social justice education (giving voice to silenced groups on campus and beyond, and empowering students toward advocacy). Although all of these are desirable goals with potentially parallel processes, they are best achieved incrementally and require careful planning as opposed to more broad approaches. Without achieving this clarity, members of the campus community may engage in disparate work, often times at the expense of other university goals.

## INSTITUTIONAL BARRIERS

There are significant institutional barriers to the promotion of social justice on college campuses. It is not foreign for a college or university's mission or vision to lack mention of diversity, culture or multiculturalism, or social justice. Further, many institutions fail to include issues of diversity or inclusion in their official strategic plans. As has been discussed, diversity can be reflected numerically, but inclusion and validation for members of a diverse community requires the purposeful engagement of all members of that community (Robinson, 2003). It is imperative that a university's strategic plan include specific, measurable goals, achievable directives for members of the community, and clear indications of accountability. For example, Virginia Tech's University Diversity Plan is composed of Five Strategic Goals, each of which includes tasks, measures, assignments and timelines, ensuring constant action toward their ideal community. Institutions that do not take these or similar steps toward achieving inclusion often find that members of their community are frustrated, lack confidence in administration's promises of action, and disenchanted with seemingly disconnected diversity efforts.

Other institutions that endeavor to achieve inclusive campus environments define diversity, ensuring that members of the community are employing a common language and are, thus, positioned to work toward a common goal; explains the university's rationale for pursuing greater diversity; outlines prerequisites for success, or those factors that must exist in order for diversity efforts to thrive; outlines university vision and mission statements; details the processes of achieving diversity; states measures to be used in assessing success; and makes clear those measures of accountability that are in place. The existence of the plan itself does not ensure success, but the fact that it is in place (and is a public document) ensures that members of the community—from senior administration to individual faculty members to student leaders can be held accountable.

## CULTURE OF THE INSTITUTION

Transforming the culture of a university requires understanding its core values, assumptions that guide or preclude interaction across varying levels of influence, and beliefs about what it means to belong to that community (Hrabowski & Maton, 2009). It is imperative that this attention to campus culture be reflected in any plans to affect institutional change, particularly when that change is in relation to issues of identity. Often, senior administrators and staff members are eager to work toward inclusion, but others fear that attempting to achieve such goals will mean a break from tradition, particularly those traditions which alumni recall as most meaningful in binding them to the institution.

Each institution has its own traditions designed to unify members of the campus community. Students of color often report that these events are unwelcoming and that they serve to reinforce messages of their not belonging. These events and subsequent messages are different than the *microaggressions* that students of color often report; they are characteristically exclusive events or spaces on campus that are designed by whatever students are in the majority, for their own enjoyment, most likely without regard to other students and what might appeal to them (Feagin Hernan, Vera & Imani, 1996). For example, students of color at predominately White institutions (PWIs) often report feeling that they do not belong at mainstream campus events like Homecoming, tailgates, or others that are communicated as being open to the campus. Strange and Banning found that campus environments not only influences certain behaviors, but also communicates important nonverbal or symbolic messages, which may contradict those messages given verbally or in university publications (Strange & Banning, 2001). Students report that these messages may be more truthful than written messages as well, so they begin to distrust or disregard university messages altogether. Acknowledging that students (and even faculty and staff) will share these sentiments in regards to university spaces, events, and often,

long-standing traditions is fundamental in validating the experience of ethnic minorities or other traditionally marginalized groups, and thus, critical for establishing a foundation of communication upon which to establish inclusive practices.

Many institutions will acknowledge and validate the feelings of its members and seek to achieve social justice goals, but will, in fact, merely promote surface dialogue, encouraging members of the campus community to participate in low-risk activities dealing with elementary information (Kay & Stringer, 2005). These activities often take the form of truncated diversity or sensitivity trainings, or guest lecturers who speak on relevant issues but are not positioned to engage the audience in meaningful ways. These are all good starts, but are insufficient in achieving true campus inclusion. Further examples of institutional promotion of surface dialogue involve faculty members who will attempt to infuse intercultural themes in their curricula but may choose texts that only address surface issues and do not incite deep, personal reflection on behalf of their students. Other faculty members are well-intentioned, and seek to promote tolerance by avoiding controversial topics in the classroom, hoping to keep students from saying or writing something that will offend others; still others develop and enforce various ground rules for classroom discussion.

An institutional commitment to sustained dialogue about social justice issues can result in improved relations across issues of difference and can have a positive impact on the campus climate (Parker, 2006). Different than lecture series or hosted speakers, the sustained dialogue process calls for a commitment by members of the group to convene at regular intervals, or at least to remain engaged in relevant conversations, so that the community creates and sustains meaning over time. Additionally, the goal of sustained dialogue is to do more than scratch the surface, but to create spaces for the meaningful exchange of ideas. Several universities employ these formal programs that demonstrate their institutional commitment to bringing members of the campus community together to open lines of communication (and keep them open).

## STRATEGIC PLANNING

It is insufficient (and often, a waste of resources) for key administrators to make a *top-down* commitment to diversity when other members of the community are uninformed, ill-advised, understaffed or otherwise at a loss for resources, or just plain disinterested in the administration's agenda. It is equally wasteful for members of the campus community to attempt to increase diversity or achieve inclusion if they lack power to enact policies or direct funds. It is critical that upper administration understand the need to achieve structural diversity (yet maintain the institution's reputation, academic index, and other markers or distinction), influence others in the spirit of multiculturalism, and empower individuals to share their experiences and frustrations with one another, toward the end goal of achieving a culture of inclusion. Connecting and engaging with participants is essential (Morijikan & Bellack, 2005).

The student voice is a loud one, and the power of a collective student body should not be underestimated. However, the power of the Board of Trustees must not be discounted, even in the face of student demand. There are several examples of student protest that have not yielded the results students imagined it would, because appropriate attention was not paid to those values that the institution is wedded to, and which serve as guiding principles for those operating in and around campus. In communicating why strategic planning around diversity and cultural competence is so critical to the University of Pennsylvania School of Nursing, Assistant Dean Mary Lou de Leon Siantz stated:

> The importance of clear communication in transforming academic environments cannot be overlooked. Engaging an audience, framing a clear message, and communicating effectively across a broad spectrum of stakeholders are essential. Persuading, enlisting support, and motivating to act are at the core of implementing a strategic vision (de Leon Siantz, 2008).

## ENGAGING THE INSTITUTION IN DIALOGUE AROUND SOCIAL JUSTICE

As previously mentioned, acquiring cultural competence skills allows one to move from discussion to dialogue. Discussions usually entail defending or "selling" ideas to others. Dialogue entails presenting many ideas and alternatives so that all parties may establish meaning that is organic to the group. Dialogue allows individuals to explore the underlying causes of the processes that interfere with communication between individuals and even organizational divisions (Bohm, Factor, Garrett, 1991; Bohm, 2004; Simmons, 1999). Often, one's inability to discuss issues that matter leads to division. When used correctly, dialogue can serve as a tool to extend one individuals' understanding of a topic and establish collective meaning with others (The Dialogue Group, n.d.).

## FUNDING PEER EDUCATION PROGRAMS

Peer education programs are more cost effective than other methods of delivering outreach programs and services (Jones, 1992; HEA, 1993; Peers, Ledwith, & Johnston, 1993). Though this may be the case, peer education programs still need to be funded through stable budgets if they are to remain in place long enough to truly affect cultural climate change. Securing funding is especially difficult in a time when colleges and universities are eliminating human and financial resources across functional areas.

Grant funding is often a way to fund peer education programs. Peer education programs are usually a component of the overall work that is funded by these grants (at least at the federal or state level). It may be possible to secure seed money to support the development of these peer education programs. The problem with this form of funding is that it usually expires within a short period of time (one to three years on average).

Another means of funding a peer education program is through departmental budgets. If the program supports the departmental mission and responsibilities for its execution are included in a staff member's job description, costs associated with program materials, training, and other needs can be covered in standard operating budgets. Peer education programs can also become recognized student organizations at the college or university, further integrating them into campus life. This allows them to be included on rosters of official campus groups and makes them eligible to receive student government funds to address training or programming needs.

## DEVELOPING GOALS AND OBJECTIVES FOR SOCIAL JUSTICE PEER EDUCATION PROGRAMS

An assessment of campus climate, culture, and needs must be considered and incorporated into the development of peer education programs. This serves to embed the program in the overall mission of the institution. Below are a few examples of objectives that were developed for a social justice peer education program at one institution.

Administrators and faculty members intended for the social justice education program to:

- plant seeds of understanding and genuine respect across cultures;
- promote cultural diversity;
- create an open environment where members of the campus community can discuss sensitive social justice topics; and
- Approach and overcome barriers and boundaries to authentic communication.

Clearly articulated goals for the peer education program are key. Potential program goals are:

For Peer Educators:

- To afford peer educators opportunities to clarify individual identities;
- To provide an intellectual space for students who value social justice to unite;
- To enhance leadership skills and multicultural competence of peer educators;
- To inspire peer educators to incorporate social justice ideals into their lives after college.

For Undergraduate Participants

- To offer opportunities for fun, interactive and informative programs related to social justice topics;
- To create safe spaces for students to have honest conversation in the absence of others perceived to be in positions of power;
- To challenge students to think critically about their world view; and
- To meet students where they are, literally—within residence hall communities, Greek enclaves, club meetings, etc.—and figuratively, in order to maximize their satisfaction with the educational experience.

## HOW PEER EDUCATION CURRICULA ARE DEVELOPED

Peer education curricula are developed with careful attention to detail. As such, planning is an important component to curriculum development. Necessary considerations include 1) defining the purpose of the program; 2) defining goals, objectives and measures of success of the program; 3) connecting program goals to overall university mission and, where applicable, strategic plans; 4) identifying the target audience for the program; 5) assessing the needs of the target audience; 6) determining the gap between available and necessary funds and resources; 7) developing work plans, timelines, and marketing campaigns; 8) developing assessment and evaluation procedures; and 9) identifying evaluation timelines and reporting structures. This careful planning can set the stage for a successful peer education program.

The purpose of the peer education program might be intuitive, but should be clarified at the onset of planning. The purpose should be explored in light of the institution's mission and vision, so that administrators and key faculty members may understand how and why they should invest energy and resources toward the program's success.

As important as the individual needs of the specific institution is the incorporation of best practices and theory relevant in the field. Methods of training students on issues of racism and ethnocentrism, homophobia, the history of gender inequality, and other forms of oppression can be benchmarked against the standards set forth by various professional organizations in higher education. Coupled with relevant data gathered from institutional climate or perception surveys or other means of assessment ensure that program content is salient, developmentally appropriate and palatable, and viable for those students being trained and the campus community at large.

Once the target population has been identified, program organizers must determine their educational and developmental needs related to social justice. It is particularly important to understand attitudes and beliefs of students towards *others,* particularly on and around campus. This understanding of what issues need to be addressed should influence the curriculum and provide direction for peer educators and other facilitators.

Once the purpose, goals, objectives, and target audience needs have been identified, it is important to determine the human and financial resources available to address the concerns as they currently exist. This can include staffing, interested and capable students, funding, and other needs. The availability of resources will also guide how the curriculum can be developed and to what degree it can be implemented and evaluated. It may occur that campus needs *and* interest are high, but resources will not allow for both the full implementation of a robust curriculum and proper assessment; in this case, a simpler version of the original program plan should be implemented so that resources can be allocated for evaluation and reporting. Lastly, a comprehensive work plan positions organizers to delineate tasks and feasible timelines.

## RECRUITMENT OF PEER EDUCATORS

Klein, Sondag, and Drolet (1994) noted in a study of peer educators that many people who choose to become peer educators believed strongly in their ability to be effective in social situations. This points to a high degree of self-efficacy and the belief that they can integrate new knowledge for the sake of helping others. A method of identifying these students is to solicit recommendations from faculty colleagues who would have access to them through classes which focus on related issues. Faculty recommendations may encourage more

**Table 1: Components of a Peer Education Program Orientation & Content Preparation**

| Program Component | Content to be included |
|---|---|
| Orientation | • Mission of the group<br>• Goals and objectives<br>• Issues and concerns the group will address and their importance to the target audience<br>• Relationship of the program to its host organization<br>• Underlying philosophy of peer education |
| Content Preparation | • Setting ground rules with participants and creating buy-in;<br>• Presentation skills;<br>• Program planning and execution;<br>• Self-care;<br>• Content knowledge in the areas of diversity and social justice (or other topic if the program's focus is not social justice);<br>• Program curriculum;<br>• Conceptual framework of the philosophical foundation of the program and relationship to the program functionality;<br>• Tools that peer educators can utilize (i.e. games, props, educational videos and other publications);<br>• Opportunities for peer educators to explore and develop their skills (in a safe environment and receive feedback prior to actual events, programs i.e. role plays, serving as discussion leaders in mock programs) and feedback from others in the program; and<br>• Mentorship from peer educators who have been in the program. |

student involvement, instilling a sense of pride and recognition of potential in would-be peer educators.

Personal credibility of peer educators is also important in modeling appropriate behaviors. It is critical that peer educators be perceived as authentic and believable, knowledgeable, and compassionate. Program organizers should strive to create diverse groups of peer educators that represent various academic majors, socioeconomic statuses, ethnicities and races, and cultural backgrounds, as well as leaders of other, pre-existing clubs and organizations. This way, students can look to the group of peer educators and perceive a semblance of kinship, or at least that someone in the group may share similar perceptions or hesitations, and thus, can empathize and validate them (Brack, Millard, &

Shah, 2008). Diversity in the group will ensure greater reach and influence with campus audiences. An application and interview process to will ensure that potential peer educators are screened properly.

## TRAINING PEER EDUCATORS

Although much of a peer educator's experience will be gained through their work on the job, training helps to set the basic framework for success. A poorly structured training can result in a program failing to meet its goals and earning a mediocre reputation on campus and beyond. The foundation of any peer education program should be the orientation to the program. The remainder of the training time should be spent preparing the peer educators to be as successful as possible in their role. Table 1 outlines the components of a typical peer education program orientation and content preparation, both of which are necessary to ensure participant success.

Addressing these topics up front allows the students to understand organizer expectations, and the role of their advisors and/or coordinators. A thorough orientation will also serve to weed out any students who are hesitant about serving in the role. One program that may be used to explore the exploration of a peer education curriculum is the Certified Peer Educator Training from The BACCHUS Network (www.bacchusgamma.org). Although related to alcohol, sexual health, and mental health concerns directly, the premise of the training program is transferrable to other content-based peer education programs.

## EVALUATION

Determining the impact of a social justice peer education program on the overall campus is a tiered process. First, goals and objectives must be both actionable and measurable. It is critical to determine how organizers and outside observers will know if—and when—the program has met stated objectives. This will drive what type of data will need to be collected. There are two basic types of evaluations that can be performed for peer education groups. (In order to capture the most valuable information, program organizers must conduct both outcome evaluations, the results of which can be used to improve the program in the future.)

Process evaluations use simple measures to gather information on program implementation and operation (Advocates for Youth, n.d.). A process evaluation that focuses on the peer education program members can be thought of as a checklist of things that are done to prepare the members from a training perspective (i.e. content review, signing confidentiality statements, reviewing a code of ethics, etc.). There are numerous psychosocial inventories that measure cultural competence or cultural sensitivity which would be effective in assessing a peer educator's mastery of the program content; the Intercultural Development Inventory is an example of a potential pre- and post-test to measure student learning. Videotaping a student's final presentation and critiquing it is a way to assess their mastery of presentation skills.

When initiating a process evaluation for the campus in relation to the peer education program, organizers should chronicle all that was done to execute the actual program, what content material was addressed and through what medium, and what learning outcomes were in place. Organizers should also indicate the target audience and what measures were used to attract them to the program. By recording this information, the advisor or program coordinator is able to review programmatic efforts and determine if objectives were achieved. Additionally, the organizers are able to quantify their efforts.

An outcome evaluation measures the overall effect of the program on the target audience

(Advocates for Youth, n.d.). In this case, there are two target audiences, the peer educators and student attendees (Bandura, Millard, Peluso, & Ortman, 2000). When conducting an outcomes evaluation with the peer educators themselves, organizers should focus on the training and actual experience of serving in this role and its impact on the student's ability to interact with and educate others. Again, psychosocial batteries can quantify the peer educators' knowledge, attitudes, and beliefs about program content and cultural teachings prior to and after training is complete. Additionally, each peer educator could be required to keep a journal where they could record feelings and new content-related knowledge. The progression of their journals entries will indicate a heightened sense of consciousness and an increased ability to think critically about issues of social justice.

An outcome evaluation of the campus community will help to determine the impact the peer education program has had on the climate. This evaluation may include focus groups with student participants who have attended peer-facilitated sessions, in order to determine the extent to which students understand the content, retain, and integrate their learnings into their daily lives. A campus climate survey that assesses feelings of belonging, safety, inclusion and other markers of cross-cultural engagement may be implemented prior to the initiation of the peer education program; comparing this data with climate survey data after the peer education program has been in place for a set period of time will also indicate the program's effectiveness. This survey could include a question or questions that indicate how students receive social justice information on their campus, and the level of believability for each source. This would indicate whether or not students are accustomed to receiving this type of information outside the classroom, and if they would be receptive to learning from their peers. Additionally, students should be survey

or otherwise queried to determine their intent to use the peer education program and/or the office in which it is housed as a resource with regards to social justice.

The final step of any evaluation is analyzing the data. Although the analysis may be difficult and tenuous, the final report must be easily understood by the peer educators, faculty with whom the program organizers might partner, university staff, and other stakeholders. It is important to note the areas in which the program excels and where there are growth opportunities, but do so in a common language that is accessible to all end users. Program findings should be disseminated widely, as to champion successes and create greater buy in from potential campus partners. Data is also a way to demonstrate to peer educators that their work has an impact on their community, and to identify areas for growth. Once data is analyzed and shared with stakeholders, organizers should create an action plan that both outlines the steps which will improve the program and methods for addressing weaknesses, including timelines, additional measures, and persons responsible.

## CONCLUSION

A thorough understanding of terms related to diversity, multiculturalism, and social justice will position students, faculty, and staff to work together in creating a community of engagement and inclusion. Colleges and universities are obligated to provide opportunities for students to acquire significant cultural competence skills if they are going to serve as leaders ready to meet the global challenges of the upcoming decades. Social justice peer education is a cost effective, rewarding program that allows students to educate their peers, engaging them in meaningful dialogue about issues affecting our collective society. By committing to peer education, college and universities position students to move forward as change agents, serving as leaders in a complex, diverse world.

Well-trained, committed peer educators can act as change agents, helping to empower themselves and others to step out and up for broad societal issues. These students initiate social justice dialogue, making the invisible visible and giving voice to the silent. They serve as gatekeepers, advancing the university's commitment to achieving an institutional culture marked by equity and engagement. As Margaret Mead stated, "[a] small group of thoughtful people could change the world. Indeed, it's the only thing that ever has."

## ABOUT THE AUTHORS

**Alta Mauro** is a native Hoosier, earning both a Bachelor's degree in English Education and a Master's degree in Higher Education/Student Affairs from Indiana University. Her student affairs experience includes residence life and judicial affairs, student organization advisorship and fraternity/sorority engagement, pre-college transition programming, and multicultural affairs. Alta's professional interests include: cultural competence and intercultural communication, social justice education, curricular reform, peer education, strategic planning, and campus engagement. She has been integral in establishing peer education programs related to diversity and social justice at several institutions. Alta currently serves as the Director of the Office of Multicultural Affairs at Wake Forest University.

**Jason Robertson** has worked as a health educator in the college setting for the past eight years. He is currently the Wellness Coordinator at The University of North Carolina at Greensboro where he coordinates the peer education and the tobacco cessation and prevention programs. His main areas of interest include: peer education, social justice and health, men's health, GLBT health, sexual health issues, tobacco use prevention, and health promotion among fraternity and sorority members. He is also the Director of Outreach and Training on the new suicide prevention grant from the Substance Abuse and Mental Health Services Administration.

Jason received his bachelor's degree in Biomedical Science from Averett University in Danville, Virginia, a Master's of Public Health degree in Public Health Education from the University of North Carolina at Greensboro, and an Education Specialist degree in Higher Education Administration from Appalachian State University. He is currently pursuing a Doctor of Health Science (DHSc) degree from Nova Southeastern University. Jason is a Certified Health Education Specialist (CHES) through the National Commission for Health Education Credentialing, a Registered Health Educator (RHEd) with the North Carolina Board of Registry for Health Education, and a Certified Tobacco Cessation Treatment Specialist (CTCTS).

## REFERENCES

Adams, M., Bell, L. A., & Griffin, P. (Eds.) (1997). *Teaching for diversity and social justice: a sourcebook.*. New York: Routledge.

Advocates for Youth (n.d.). Evaluating the peer education program. Retrieved October 1, 2009 from www.advocatesforyouth.org/storage/advfy/documents/TAP7.pdf .

Bandura, A. (1994). Self-efficacy. In V. S. Ramachaudran (Ed.), *Encyclopedia of human behavior* (Vol. 4, pp. 71–81). New York: Academic Press. (Reprinted in H. Friedman [Ed.], *Encyclopedia of mental health*. San Diego: Academic Press, 1998).

Bandura, A. (1977) Social learning theory. Prentice-Hall, Englewood Cliffs, NJ.

Bandura, A.S., Millard, M., Peluso, E.A., & Ortman, N. (2000). Effects of peer education training on peer educators: leadership, self-esteem, health knowledge, and health behaviors. Journal of College Student Development, 41 (5), pp. 471–478.

Bohm, D. (2004). On Dialogue. London: Routledge. Bohm, D., Factor, D. Garrett, P. (1991).

Brack, A.B., Millard, M. & Shah, K. (2008). Are peer educators really peers? Journal of American College Health, 56, 566–568.

Drug Info Clearinghouse (2006). Prevention research quarterly: Peer education. Retrieved October 1, 2009 from www.druginfo.adf.org.au.

Harper, S. R. & Hurtado, S. (2007). Nine themes in campus racial climates and implications for institutional transformation.

Hayes-Bautista, E., David, Hsu, P., Perez, A., Gamboa, C. (2002). The 'browning' of the graying of America: Diversity in the elderly population and policy implications. *Generations,* 26: 15–24.

HEA (1993) Peers in Partnership: HIV/AIDS Education with Young People in the Community. Health Education Authority, London.

Hogg, M.A. & Vaughan, G.M. (2002). *Social Psychology (3rd ed. )* London: Prentice Hall.

Klein, D.A. (1998). The link between individual and organizational learning. In The strategic management of intellectual capital. Boston: Butterworth-Heinemann.

Klepp, K. I., Halper, A. and Perry, C. L. (1986) The efficacy of peer leaders in drug abuse prevention. *Journal of School Health*, 56, 407–411.

Kegan, R. & Lahey, L.L. (2001). Seven Languages For Transformation: How the Way We Talk Can Change the Way We Work. San Francisco: Jossey-Bass.

Jones, M. (1992). It pays to use peer leaders. Education and Health, 10(4), 49–54.

McCain, T. & Jukes, I. (2001). Windows on the future: Education in the age of technology. Thousand Oaks, CA: Corwin Press, Inc.

Monahan, M. (2006). Race, Colorblindness, and Continental Philosophy. Philosophy Compass 1(6), 547–563.

Nonaka, I. (1994). A Dynamic Theory of Organizational Knowledge Creation. *Organization Science,* 5(1), 14–37.

Peers, I. S., Ledwith, F. and Johnston, M. (1993) Community youth project HIV/AIDS. University of Manchester School of Education Report to the Health Education Authority.

Robinson, M., Pfeiffer, C., & Buccigrossi, J. (2003). Business Case for Inclusion and Engagement. wetWare, Inc. Rochester, NY.

Turner, G & Shepherd, J (1999). A method in search of a theory: peer education and health promotion. Health Education Research, 14(2), 235–247.

Senge, P. (1990). Mental Models. In The fifth discipline: The art and practice of the learning organization. New York: Doubleday, pp.174–204.

Senge, P., Ross, R ., Smith, B., Roberts, C., & Kleiner, A. (1994). The ladder of inference. In The fifth discipline fieldbook. New York: Doubleday, pp.242–246.

Simmons, A. (1999). A safe place for dangerous truths: using dialogue to overcome fear and distrust at work. New York: Amacom American Management Association.

Sloane, B., & Zimmer, C. (1993). The power of peer health education. Journal of American College Health, 41, 241–245.

Smith, M. K. (2002; 2009) Informal Education in schools and colleges, *The Encyclopaedia of Informal Education.* Taken from http://www.infed.org/schooling/inf-sch.htm.

Strange, C. C. & Banning, J.H. (2001) *Educating by Design: Creating Campus Learning Environments That Work.* San Francisco: Jossey-Bass.

The Dialogue Group (n.d.). What is dialogue? pp.1–7. Retrieved March 9, 2008 from http://www.thedialoguegrouponline.com.

Villarruel, A.M., Jemmott, L.S., Howard, M., Talyor, L, & Bush, E. (1998). Practice what we preach: Knowledge, beliefs, and behaviors of adolescents and adolescent peer educators. Jorunal of the Association of Nurses in AIDS Care, 9(5), 61–72.

# WHAT DO WE THINK ABOUT RACE?

*By Lawrence D. Bobo*

## I. INTRODUCTION

My task, in a sense, is to answer the question of whether America is moving toward becoming a genuinely "color-blind" society or remains a society deeply polarized by race. I approach this task as a social scientist who has long studied the social psychology of race in America. Studies of racial attitudes in the U.S. present a difficult puzzle. On the one hand, several recent studies emphasize the steadily improving racial attitudes of white Americans, especially in terms of their attitudes toward African Americans. These attitudinal trends are reinforced by many more tangible indicators, most notably the size, relative security, and potentially growing influence of the black middle class. On the other hand, there is evidence of persistent negative stereotyping of racial minorities, evidence of widely divergent views of the extent and importance of racial discrimination to modern race relations, and evidence of deepening feelings of alienation among black Americans. These more pessimistic attitudinal trends are reinforced by such tangible indicators as the persistent problem of racial segregation of neighborhoods and schools, discrimination in access to housing and employment, innumerable everyday acts of racial bias and numerous signs of the gulf in perception that often separates black and white Americans

My remarks today will touch on five aspects of the research on racial attitudes: (1) the predominant and important trend toward positive change concerning the goals of integration and equal treatment; (2) the evident difficulty of moving from these goals to concrete support for change in social policy and individual living conditions; (3) the problem of persistent stereotyping; (4) the differing views of racial discrimination; and (5) the possible deepening of black alienation. Wherever possible I emphasize trends. It is essential to have a sense of whether and how much things have changed if we are to make sense of where we stand today or might head in the future. Although my remarks will emphasize what we know about the views of white Americans toward African Americans, I will cast a multiracial scope at several important points.

By way of foreshadowing what is to come let me say that we now have a deeply rooted national consensus on the ideals of racial equality and integration. These high ideals founder on racial differences in preferred levels of integration; they founder on sharp racial differences in beliefs about racial discrimination; they founder on the persistence of negative racial stereotypes; and they result in policy stagnation and mutual misunderstanding. Although America has turned away from Jim Crow racism, it heads into an uncertain future.

## II. NEW PRINCIPLES OF EQUALITY AND INTEGRATION

The single clearest trend in studies of racial attitudes has involved a steady and sweeping movement toward endorsing the principles of racial equality and integration. When major national assessments of racial attitudes were first conducted in the 1940s, clear majorities of white Americans advocated that we be a society that segregated its schools, neighborhoods, and public transportation, that practiced job discrimination against African Americans, and that drew a sharp line against the possibility of mixed or interracial marriages. Thus, in the early 1940s, 68% of white Americans expressed the view that black and white school children should go to separate schools, 54% felt that public transportation should be segregated, and 54% felt that whites should receive preference over blacks in access to jobs. By the early 1960s each of these attitudes had declined substantially. So much so that the questions on public transportation and access to jobs were dropped from national surveys in the early 1970s: virtually all white Americans endorsed the idea that transportation should be integrated and that access to jobs should be equal without regard to race. The issue of integrated schools remained more divided. However, the trend here has been equally steady. Thus, by 1995 fully 96% of white Americans expressed the view that white and black school children should go to the same schools.

Three points about this transformation of basic principles or norms that should guide race relations bear noting. First, there is some variation across domains of life in the degree of endorsement of the principle of racial equality and integration. In general, the more public and impersonal the arena, the greater the evidence of the movement toward endorsing ideals of integration and equality. Thus, support for unconstrained access to housing for blacks has also undergone tremendous positive change, but still lags behind the case of schools or jobs. More telling, willingness to allow racially mixed marriages still encounters some resistance, with 1 in 5 whites as recently as 1990 supporting laws that would ban such marriages. And an even higher fraction, as the figure shows, personally disapproves of such marriages.

Second, African Americans have long rejected segregation. Although the available pool of data for tracing long-term trends in the views of African Americans is much more limited than that for whites, it is clear that the black population has overwhelming favored integrated schools and neighborhoods and desired equal access to employment opportunity.

Third, the positive trend on these principles across the domains of schools, public transportation, jobs, housing, politics, and even intermarriage is steady and unabated. Despite intense discussion of a possible "racial backlash" in the 1960s in response to black protests, or in the 1970s in response to school busing efforts and the implementation of affirmative action, or even more recently in the wake of events such as the riots in Los Angeles in 1992, the support for principles of racial equality and integration has been sweeping and robust. So much so, that it is reasonable to describe it as a change in fundamental norms with regard to race.

## III. THE COMPLEXITY OF CHANGING HOW WE LIVE AND WHAT WE WANT GOVERNMENT TO DO

Unfortunately, it is not possible to infer from the tremendous positive change on principles of equality and integration that either public policy or the texture of day-to-day life for most Americans would quickly come to mirror this apparent consensus. Consider first the issue of integrating neighborhoods and schools. It is clear that numbers matter, as the figure shows. When surveys ask whites about their willingness to live in integrated areas or to send their children to integrated schools, as the proportion of blacks rises the willingness to enter a situations falls. Surveys have documented a steady increase in the openness to both residential and school integration. So much so, that almost no whites object to having a black neighbor or to sending their own children to an integrated school. But objections rise considerably as the number of black students grows.

The meaning of integration also differs for Blacks and Whites. It is clear that most whites prefer to live in overwhelmingly white neighborhoods even though open to having a small number of blacks in their neighborhood. Blacks prefer to be present in substantial numbers, numbers large enough to be uncomfortable in the eyes of most whites and impractical on a large scale basis: it is not possible, given differences in population size, for all blacks to live in a neighborhood that is at least half black.

With respect to public policy issues, we are all aware that there have been longstanding debates over equal opportunity policies and affirmative action. The trend data suggest that there is a significant *substantive* division in opinion. Programs that are *compensatory* in nature—that aim to equip minorities to be more effective competitors or that engage in special outreach and recruitment efforts—are reasonably popular. Policies that call for explicit racial *preferences* have long been unpopular,

with the use of quotas rejected by Whites and Blacks alike.

There is, however, a sharp divergence of opinion about affirmative action type policies by race as well. As the next two figures, drawing on data from surveys conducted in Los Angeles, illustrate. Blacks but also Latinos tend to support affirmative action type policies whether aimed at improving training and competitive resources of minority group members or calling for "special preferences" in hiring and promotion. But a majority of whites support the more compensatory policies while resisting strongly "preferential" policies.

## IV. PERSISTENT NEGATIVE STEREOTYPING

A major piece of the puzzle behind the limits to integration and to social policy with respect to race lies in the problem of anti-minority, especially anti-Black stereotypes. There is evidence that negative racial stereotypes of minority groups, especially of blacks and Latinos, remain common among whites. There is also evidence that minority groups may also stereotype one another, though the story here is a good deal more complicated. In a major national survey conducted in 1990, well over 50% of whites rated Blacks and Latinos as less intelligent. Similar proportions rated Blacks and Latinos as prone to violence. Well over two-thirds rated Blacks and Latinos as actually *preferring* to live off of welfare.

One example of such patterns is shown in the figure. Substantial fractions of whites rated Blacks and Latinos as less intelligent, as preferring to live off of welfare, and as hard to get along with socially. Research suggests that these stereotypes differ in several important ways from stereotypes that were prevalent in the past. First, they are much more likely to be understood as the product of environmental and group cultural traditions than was true in the past. In the past, they were unequivocally taken as the product of natural endowment. Second, there is growing evidence that many whites are aware of traditional negative stereotypes of Blacks, anyone immersed in American culture would be, but personally reject the negative stereotype and its implications. The problem is that in many face-to-face interactions, the old cultural stereotype controls perception and behavior. The end result is bias and discrimination against minorities.

## V. DISAGREEMENT ON THE PREVALENCE OF RACIAL DISCRIMINATION

In many ways, the centerpiece of the modern racial divide comes in the evidence of sharply divergent beliefs about the current level, effect, and very nature of discrimination. Blacks and Latinos, and many Asian Americans as well, feel it and perceive it in most domains of life. Many Whites acknowledge that some discrimination remains, yet they tend to down play its contemporary importance. The figure gives an example of these perceptions.

However, minorities not only perceive more discrimination, they see it as more "institutional" in character. Many Whites tend to think of discrimination as either mainly an historical legacy of the past or as the idiosyncratic behavior of the isolated bigot. In short, to White America, the officers who beat Abner Louima constitute a few bad apples. To African Americans, they are the tip of the iceberg. White America regards the Texaco tapes as shocking. To Black America the tapes merely reflect the ones who got caught.

But the difference in perception cuts deeper than this. For African Americans and Latinos (and to a lesser extent among Asians) modern racial bias and discrimination are central factors in the problem of minority disadvantage. While many Whites recognize that discrimination plays some part in higher rates of unemployment, poverty, and a range of hardships in life that minorities often face, the central cause is usually understood to be the level of effort and cultural patterns of the minority groups themselves. For minorities, especially African Americans, if race remains a problem it is because of something about how our institutions operate. For whites, it is mainly something about minorities themselves.

It is difficult to overestimate the importance of the sharp divide over the understanding and experience of racial discrimination to the present day racial impasse in America.

## VI. DEEPENING PESSIMISM AND ALIENATION

In many corners there is a feeling of pessimism about the state of race relations. A 1997 survey conducted by the Joint Center for Political and Economic research found that only 2 in 5 blacks rated relations in their community as "excellent" or "good" and that more than 1 in 5 rated race relations as "poor." In contrast, 59% of whites rated local race relations as "excellent" or "good" though better than 1 in ten rated them as "poor." The results of a recent Gallup survey are, in respects, more pessimistic. There, roughly a third of blacks and whites described race relations as having gotten worse in the past year. What is more, 58% of blacks and 54% whites expressed the view that "relations between blacks and whites will always be a problem for the United States."

This problem takes the form of particularly acute cynicism and alienation among black Americans, though there are some signs of frustrations among Latinos and some Asians as well. Among blacks, University of Chicago political scientist Michael Dawson's National Black Politics Survey, conducted in 1993, found that 86% of African Americans agreed with the statement that "American society just hasn't dealt fairly with black people." Fifty-seven percent of African Americans rejected the idea that "American society has provided black people a fair opportunity to get ahead in life." And 81% agreed with the idea that "American society owes black people a better chance in life than we currently have."

A major survey of Los Angeles county residents that I conducted in 1992 shows that while blacks expressed the highest and most consistently alienated views, an important fraction of the Latino and Asian population do so as well. Thus, for example, 64% of Latinos in L.A. County and 42% of Asians agreed with the idea that their groups were owed a better chance in life. This places these two groups in between the high sense of deprivation observed among African Americans and the essentially nonexistent feeling of deprivation observed among whites.

The concern over black cynicism, however, is acute for two reasons. First, there are signs that the feelings of alienation and deprivation are greatest in an unexpected place: among the black middle class, especially so among well-educated and high-earning African Americans. Second, there is a concern that these feelings of alienation and deprivation may be contributing to a weakening commitment to the goal of racial integration. Among the potentially discouraging signs in this regard are a recent significant rise in the number of African Americans who think it is time to form a separate national political party. The 1993 National Black Politics Survey showed that this figure was at 50%, up substantially from about 30% in 1984. In addition, African Americans continue to feel a strong connection between the fate of the group as a whole and that of the individual African American. Thus, the 1993 National Black Politics Study shows a slow but steady rise in the proportion of African Americans who expressed the view that there was a strong connection between their fate as individuals and the fate of the group as a whole. This tendency is especially pronounced among highly educated African Americans.

## VII. CONCLUSIONS AND IMPLICATIONS

The glass is half full or half empty, depending upon what one chooses to emphasize. If one compares the racial attitudes prevalent in the 1940s with those commonly observed today, it is easy to be optimistic. A nation once comfortable as a deliberately segregationist and racially discriminatory society has not only abandoned that view, but positively endorses the goal of racial integration and equal treatment. There is no sign whatsoever of retreat from this ideal despite many events that many thought would call it into question. The magnitude, steadiness, and breadth of this change should be lost on no one.

The death of Jim Crow Racism has left us in an uncomfortable place, however, a place that I sometimes call a state of Laissez Faire racism. We have high ideals, but openness to very limited amounts of integration at the personal level remains; there is political stagnation over some types of affirmative action, quite negative stereotypes of racial minorities persist, and a wide gulf in perceptions regarding the importance of racial discrimination remains. The level of misunderstanding and miscommunication is thus easy to comprehend.

The positive patterns in attitude and belief have important parallels in more concrete social trends. Two examples. Matching the broad shift in attitudes on the principle of residential integration and openness to at least small amounts of real racial mixing in neighborhoods is borne out in demographic data showing modest declines in racial residential segregation in most metropolitan areas and in the growing suburbanization of Blacks, Latinos and Asians. In addition, the greater tolerance for interracial marriages, including Black-white marriages, is mirrored in the significant rise in the number of such unions. (Though we should always bear in mind that attitudes are but one important input to behavior. Most centrally, situational constraints, such as equal opportunity mandates and anti-discrimination laws or the expectations of significant others in our lives, affect whether or not and when there is a correspondence between individual attitude and behavior. And, of course, racial segregation remains a severe problem, and Black-White intermarriages are the least common form of racial intermarriage for Whites.)

Is it possible to change attitudes? The record of change that I have reviewed makes it plain that attitudes can change and in important ways. Education and information can help. The better educated, especially those who have gone onto college, are typically found to express more positive racial attitudes. It is also clear that many Americans hold inaccurate beliefs about the size of racial minority groups and about such social conditions as group differences in the level of welfare dependency. However, education and informational campaigns are unlikely to do the job that remains ahead of us if we are to genuinely become one society in the next century. Attitudes are most likely to change when the broad social conditions that create and reinforce certain types of outlooks change and when the push to make such change comes from a united national leadership that speaks with moral conviction of purpose. That is, it is essential to speak to joblessness and poverty in the inner city, to failing schools, and to myriad forms of racial bias and discrimination that people of color often experience, but have not yet effectively communicated to their fellow White Americans.

To pose the question directly: Are we moving toward a color-blind society or toward deepening racial polarization? America is not a color-blind society. We stand uncomfortably at a point of defeating Jim Crow racism, but unsure whether to, on the one hand, through benign neglect, allow the current inequalities and polarizations to take deeper root, or, on the other hand, to face directly and pro-actively the challenges of bias, miscommunication and racism that remain.

As a people, we feel quite powerfully the tug, the exhortation of Dr. King's dream to become a nation that embodies the ideals of racial equality and integration. We appear to be at a point of un-certainty, misunderstanding and re-assessment. It is important to seize upon the steady commitment to ideals of racial equality and integration. The risk of failing to do so, is that a new, free-market ideology of racism—laissez faire racism—may take hold, po-tentially worsening an already serious racial divide.